PROCEDURAL ELEMENTS FOR COMPUTER GRAPHICS

PROCEDURAL ELEMENTS FOR COMPUTER GRAPHICS

David F. Rogers

Professor of Aerospace Engineering
and
Director, Computer Aided Design
and Interactive Graphics
United States Naval Academy, Annapolis, Md.

McGraw-Hill Book Company

New York   St. Louis   San Francisco   Auckland   Bogotá   Hamburg
Johannesburg   London   Madrid   Mexico   Montreal   New Delhi
Panama   Paris   São Paulo   Singapore   Sydney   Tokyo   Toronto

This book was computer phototypeset in Times Roman, by TYX Corporation.
The editors were Kiran Verma and David A. Damstra;
the production supervisor was Joe Campanella;
project supervision was by the author.
The cover was designed by Fern Logan and the author.
R. R. Donnelley & Sons Company was printer and binder.

PROCEDURAL ELEMENTS FOR COMPUTER GRAPHICS

2 3 4 5 6 7 8 9 0 D O C D O C 8 9 8 7 6 5

ISBN 0-07-053534-5

Cover illustration credits:

Front cover: A dimetric view of three blocks rendered by John O. Jenkins at the Johns Hopkins University Applied Physics Laboratory using a Watkins algorithm developed as part of a class project.

Back cover: Orthographic and isometric views of three blocks rendered by John O. Jenkins at The Johns Hopkins University Applied Physics Laboratory using a Watkins algorithm developed as part of a class project.

Library of Congress Cataloging in Publication Data

Rogers, David F., date
    Procedural elements for computer graphics.

    Includes bibliographical references and index.
    1. Computer graphics. I. Title.
T385.R63   1985   001.64'43   83-24403
ISBN 0-07-053534-5

To my mother Gladys Marion (Zoller) Rogers (1906–)
and my father Lewis Freeman Rogers (1906–1981)
who provided such a fine start in life.

CONTENTS

Preface   xi

Chapter 1   Introduction to Computer Graphics   1

   1-1   Overview of Computer Graphics   1
   1-2   Types of Graphics Devices   3
   1-3   Storage Tube Graphics Displays   3
   1-4   Calligraphic Refresh Graphics Displays   5
   1-5   Raster Refresh Graphics Displays   8
   1-6   Cathode Ray Tube Basics   15
   1-7   Color CRT Raster Scan Basics   16
   1-8   Video Basics   17
   1-9   Interactive Devices   20
   1-10   Summary   28
   1-11   References   28

Chapter 2   Raster Scan Graphics   29

   2-1   Line Drawing Algorithms   29
   2-2   Digital Differential Analyzer   30
   2-3   Bresenham's Algorithm   34
   2-4   Integer Bresenham's Algorithm   38
   2-5   General Bresenham's Algorithm   40
   2-6   Circle Generation — Bresenham's Algorithm   42
   2-7   Scan Conversion — Generation of the Display   51
   2-8   Real-Time Scan Conversion   52
   2-9   Run-Length Encoding   56
   2-10   Cell Encoding   60

2-11	Frame Buffers	62
2-12	Addressing the Raster	64
2-13	Line Display	66
2-14	Character Display	67
2-15	Solid Area Scan Conversion	69
2-16	Polygon Filling	69
2-17	Scan-Converting Polygons	70
2-18	A Simple Ordered Edge List Algorithm	73
2-19	A More Efficient Ordered Edge List Algorithm	74
2-20	The Edge Fill Algorithm	79
2-21	The Edge Flag Algorithm	81
2-22	Seed Fill Algorithms	83
2-23	A Simple Seed Fill Algorithm	85
2-24	A Scan Line Seed Fill Algorithm	88
2-25	Fundamentals of Antialiasing	92
2-26	Simple Area Antialiasing	95
2-27	The Convolution Integral and Antialiasing	98
2-28	Halftoning	102
2-29	References	108

Chapter 3 Clipping **111**

3-1	Two-Dimensional Clipping	111
3-2	Sutherland-Cohen Subdivision Line Clipping Algorithm	121
3-3	Midpoint Subdivision Algorithm	125
3-4	Generalized Two Dimensional Line Clipping for Convex Boundaries	131
3-5	Cyrus-Beck Algorithm	135
3-6	Interior and Exterior Clipping	146
3-7	Identifying Convex Polygons and Determining the Inward Normal	146
3-8	Splitting Concave Polygons	151
3-9	Three-Dimensional Clipping	152
3-10	Three-Dimensional Midpoint Subdivision Algorithm	155
3-11	Three-Dimensional Cyrus-Beck Algorithm	157
3-12	Clipping in Homogeneous Coordinates	162
3-13	Determining the Inward Normal and Three-Dimensional Convex Sets	164
3-14	Splitting Concave Volumes	166
3-15	Polygon Clipping	168
3-16	Reentrant Polygon Clipping — Sutherland-Hodgman Algorithm	169
3-17	Concave Clipping Regions — Weiler-Atherton Algorithm	179
3-18	Character Clipping	185
3-19	References	187

Chapter 4 Hidden Lines and Hidden Surfaces **189**

4-1	Introduction	189
4-2	Floating Horizon Algorithm	191
4-3	Roberts Algorithm	205
4-4	Warnock Algorithm	240
4-5	Weiler-Atherton Algorithm	259

4-6   A Subdivision Algorithm for Curved Surfaces   264
4-7   z-Buffer Algorithm   265
4-8   List Priority Algorithms   272
4-9   Scan Line Algorithms   279
4-10 Scan Line z-Buffer Algorithm   280
4-11 A Spanning Scan Line Algorithm   284
4-12 Scan Line Algorithms for Curved Surfaces   292
4-13 A Visible Surface Ray Tracing Algorithm   296
4-14 Summary   305
4-15 References   306

Chapter 5 Rendering   309

5-1   Introduction   309
5-2   A Simple Illumination Model   311
5-3   Determining the Surface Normal   317
5-4   Determining the Reflection Vector   320
5-5   Gouraud Shading   323
5-6   Phong Shading   325
5-7   A Simple Illumination Model with Special Effects   330
5-8   A More Complete Illumination Model   332
5-9   Transparency   340
5-10 Shadows   345
5-11 Texture   354
5-12 A Global Illumination Model Using Ray Tracing   363
5-13 A More Complete Global Illumination Model Using Ray
      Tracing   379
5-14 Recent Advances in Rendering   381
5-15 Color   383
5-16 References   408

      Appendixes   411

      Appendix A Pseudocode   411
      Appendix B Projects   417

      Index   423

PREFACE

Computer graphics is now a mature discipline. Both hardware and software are available that facilitate the production of graphical images as diverse as line drawings and realistic renderings of natural objects. A decade ago the hardware and software to generate these graphical images cost hundreds of thousands of dollars. Today, excellent facilities are available for expenditures in the tens of thousands of dollars and lower performance, but in many cases adequate facilities are available for tens of hundreds of dollars. The use of computer graphics to enhance information transfer and understanding is endemic in almost all scientific and engineering disciplines. Today, no scientist or engineer should be without a basic understanding of the underlying principles of computer graphics. Computer graphics is also making deep inroads into the business, medical, advertising, and entertainment industries. The presence in the boardroom of presentation slides prepared using computer graphics facilities as well as more commonplace business applications is considered the norm. Three-dimensional reconstructions using data obtained from CAT scans is becoming commonplace in medical applications. Television as well as other advertising media are now making frequent use of computer graphics and computer animation. The entertainment industry has embraced computer graphics with applications as diverse as video games and full-length feature films. Even art is not immune, as evidenced by some of the photos included in this book.

It is almost a decade now since the appearance of the companion volume to this book, **Mathematical Elements for Computer Graphics**. During that time significant strides in raster scan graphics have been made. The present volume concentrates on these aspects of computer graphics. The book starts with an introduction to computer graphics hardware with an emphasis on the conceptual understanding of cathode ray tube displays and of interactive devices. The following chapters look at raster scan graphics including line and circle drawing, polygon filling, and antialiasing algorithms; two- and three-dimensional clipping including clipping to arbitrary convex volumes; hidden-line and hidden-surface algorithms including ray tracing; and finally, rendering, the "art" of making realistic pictures, including local and global illumination models, texture, shadows, transparency, and color effects. The book continues the presentation technique of its predecessor. Each thorough topic discussion is followed by presentation of a detailed algorithm or a worked example, and where appropriate both.

The material in the book can be used in its entirety for a semester-long first formal course in computer graphics at either the senior undergraduate or graduate level with an emphasis on raster scan graphics. If a first course in computer graphics based on the material in the companion volume **Mathematical Elements for Computer Graphics** is presented, then the material in this book is ideal for a second course. This is the way it is used by the author. If broader material coverage in a single-semester course is desired, then the two volumes can be used together. Suggested topic coverage is: Chapter 1 of both volumes, followed by Chapters 2 and 3 with selected topics from Chapter 4 of **Mathematical Elements for Computer Graphics**, then selected topics from Chapter 2 (e.g., 2-1 to 2-5, 2-7, 2-15 to 2-19, 2-22, 2-23, 2-28), Chapter 3 (e.g., 3-1, 3-2, 3-4 to 3-6, 3-9, 3-11, 3-15, 3-16), Chapter 4 (e.g., 4-1, part of 4-2 for backplane culling, 4-3, 4-4, 4-7, 4-9, 4-11, 4-13), and Chapter 5 (e.g., 5-1 to 5-3, 5-5, 5-6, 5-14) of the present volume. The book is also designed to be useful to professional programmers, engineers, and scientists. Further, the detailed algorithms and worked examples make it particularly suitable for self-study at any level. Sufficient background is provided by college level mathematics and a knowledge of a higher-level programming language. Some knowledge of data structures is useful but not necessary.

There are two types of algorithms presented in the book. The first is a detailed procedural description of the algorithm, presented in narrative style. The second is more formal and uses an algorithmic 'language' for presentation. Because of the wide appeal of computer graphics, the choice of an algorithmic presentation language was especially difficult. A number of colleagues were questioned as to their preference. No consensus developed. Computer science faculty generally preferred PASCAL but with a strong sprinkling of C. Industrial colleagues generally preferred FORTRAN for compatibility with existing software. The author personally prefers BASIC because of its ease of use. Consequently, detailed algorithms are presented in pseudocode. The pseudocode used is based on extensive experience teaching computer graphics to classes that do not enjoy knowledge of a common programming language. The pseudocode is easily converted to any of the common computer languages. An appendix discusses the pseudocode used. The pseudocode algorithms presented in the book have all been either directly implemented from the pseudocode or the pseudocode has been derived from an operating program in one or more of the common programming languages. Implementations range from BASIC on an Apple IIe to PL1 on an IBM 4300 with a number of variations in between. A suit of demonstration programs in available from the author.

A word about the production of the book may be of interest. The book was computer typeset using the TEX typesetting system at TYX Corporation of Reston, Virginia. The manuscript was coded directly from handwritten copy. Galleys and two sets of page proofs were produced on a laser printer for editing and page makeup. Final reproduction copy ready for art insertion was produced on a phototypesetter. The patience and assistance of Jim Gauthier and Mark Hoffman at TYX while the limits of the system were explored and solutions to all the myriad small problems found is gratefully acknowledged. The outstanding job done by Louise Bohrer and Beth Lessels in coding the handwritten manuscript is gratefully acknowledged. The usually fine McGraw-Hill copyediting was supervised by David Damstra and Sylvia Warren.

No book is ever written without the assistance of many individuals. The book is based on material prepared for use in a graduate level course given at the Johns Hopkins University Applied Physics Laboratory Center beginning in 1978. Thanks are due the many students in this and other courses from whom I have learned so much. Thanks are due Turner Whitted who read the original outline and made valuable suggestions. Thanks are expressed to my colleagues Pete Atherton, Brian Barsky, Ed Catmull, Rob Cook, John Dill, Steve Hansen, Bob Lewand, Gary Meyer, Alvy Ray Smith, Dave Warn, and Kevin Weiler, all of whom read one or more chapters or sections, usually in handwritten manuscript form, red pencil in hand. Their many suggestions and comments served to make this a better book. Thanks are extended to my colleagues Linda Rybak and Linda Adlum who read the entire manuscript and checked the examples. Thanks are due three of my students: Bill Meier who implemented the Roberts algorithm, Gary Boughan who originally suggested the test for convexity discussed in Sec. 3-7, and Norman Schmidt who originally suggested the polygon splitting technique discussed in Sec. 3-8. Thanks are due Mark Meyerson who implemented the splitting algorithms and assured that the technique was mathematically well founded. The work of Lee Billow and John Metcalf who prepared all the line drawings is especially appreciated.

Special thanks are due Steve Satterfield who read and commented on all 800 handwritten manuscript pages. Need more be said!

Special thanks are also due my eldest son Stephen who implemented all of the hidden surface algorithms in Chapter 4 as well as a number of other algorithms throughout the book. Our many vigorous discussions served to clarify a number of key points.

Finally, a very special note of appreciation is extended to my wife Nancy and to my other two children, Karen and Ransom, who watched their husband and father disappear into his office almost every weeknight and every weekend for a year and a half with never a protest. That is support! Thanks.

David F. Rogers

CHAPTER ONE

INTRODUCTION TO COMPUTER GRAPHICS

Computer graphics is now a maturing technology. The underlying elements of manipulative transformations and curve and surface descriptions are well understood and documented (see Refs. 1-1 to 1-3). Raster scan technology, clipping, hidden lines and hidden surfaces, color, shading, texture, and transparency effects are also understood but still developing. It is these latter topics which are of present interest.

1-1 OVERVIEW OF COMPUTER GRAPHICS

Computer graphics is a complex and diversified technology. To begin to understand the technology it is necessary to subdivide it into manageable parts. This can be accomplished by considering that the end product of computer graphics is a picture. The picture may, of course, be used for a large variety of purposes; e.g., it may be an engineering drawing, an exploded parts illustration for a service manual, a business graph, an architectural rendering for a proposed construction or design project, an advertising illustration, or a single frame from an animated movie. The picture is the fundamental cohesive concept in computer graphics. We must therefore consider how

Pictures are represented in computer graphics
Pictures are prepared for presentation
Previously prepared pictures are presented
Interaction with the picture is accomplished

Although many algorithms accept picture data as polygons or edges, each polygon or edge can in turn be represented by vertex points. Points, then, are the fundamental building blocks of picture representation. Of equal fundamental importance is the algorithm which explains how to organize the points. To

1

illustrate this consider a unit square in the first quadrant. The unit square can be represented by its four corner points (see Fig. 1-1)

$$P_1(0, 0), \quad P_2(1, 0), \quad P_3(1, 1), \quad P_4(0, 1)$$

An associated algorithmic description might be

Connect $P_1 P_2 P_3 P_4 P_1$ in sequence

The unit square can also be described by four edges

$$E_1 \equiv P_1P_2, \quad E_2 \equiv P_2P_3, \quad E_3 \equiv P_3P_4, \quad E_4 \equiv P_4P_1$$

Here the algorithmic description is

Display $E_1 E_2 E_3 E_4$ in sequence

Finally, either the points or edges can be used to describe the unit square as a single polygon, e.g.,

$$S_1 = P_1 P_2 P_3 P_4 P_1 \qquad \text{or} \qquad P_1 P_4 P_3 P_2 P_1$$

or

$$S_1 = E_1 E_2 E_3 E_4$$

The fundamental building blocks, i.e. points, can be represented as either pairs or triplets of numbers depending on whether the data are two- or three-dimensional. Thus, (x_1, y_1) or (x_1, y_1, z_1) would represent a point in either two- or three-dimensional space. Two points would represent a line or edge, and a collection of three or more points a polygon. These points, edges, or polygons are collected or stored in a data base. The data used to prepare the picture for presentation is rarely the same as that used to present the picture. The data used to present the picture is frequently called a display file. The display file will represent some portion, view, or scene of the picture represented by the total data base. The displayed picture is usually formed by rotating, translating, scaling, and performing various projections on the data. These basic orientation or viewing preparations are generally performed using a 4×4 transformation matrix operating on the data represented in homogeneous

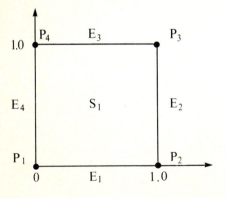

Figure 1-1 Picture data descriptions.

coordinates (see Ref. 1-1). Frequently these operations are implemented in hardware. Hidden line or hidden surface removal, shading, transparency, texture, or color effects may be added before final presentation. If the picture represented by the entire data base is not to be presented, the appropriate portion must be selected. This is a process called clipping. Clipping may be two- or three-dimensional as appropriate. In some cases the clipping window or volume may have holes in it or may be irregularly shaped. Clipping to standard two- and three-dimensional regions is frequently implemented in hardware.

Almost all pictures involve the presentation of textual material. Characters can be generated in either hardware or software. If generated in software, they can be manipulated and treated like any other portion of the picture. If generated in hardware, they are maintained as character codes until just prior to display. Usually only limited manipulative capabilities are provided; e.g., only limited rotations and sizes are available. Clipping of hardware-generated characters is generally not possible. Either the entire character is displayed or none of it is displayed.

1-2   TYPES OF GRAPHICS DEVICES

The display medium for computer graphics-generated pictures has become widely diversified. Typical examples are pen-and-ink plotters, dot matrix, electrostatic or laser printer plotters, film, storage tube, calligraphic refresh, and raster scan cathode ray tube (CRT) displays. Because the large majority of computer graphics systems utilize some type of CRT display and because most of the fundamental display concepts are embodied in CRT display technology, we will limit our discussion to CRT displays. Other display technologies are discussed in Refs. 1-1 to 1-3.

The three most common types of CRT display technologies are direct-view storage tube (line drawing), calligraphic (line drawing) refresh, and raster scan (point plotting) refresh displays. With recent advances, an individual display may incorporate more than one technology. In discussing the various displays we take a user's, or conceptual, point of view; i.e., we are generally concerned with functional capabilities and not with the details of the electronics.

1-3   STORAGE TUBE GRAPHICS DISPLAYS

The direct-view storage tube is conceptually the simplest of the CRT displays. The storage tube display, also called a bistable storage tube, can be considered a CRT with a long-persistence phosphor. A line or character will remain visible (up to an hour) until erased. A typical display is shown in Fig. 1-2. To draw a line on the display the intensity of the electron beam is increased sufficiently to cause the phosphor to assume its permanent bright "storage" state. The display is erased by flooding the entire tube with a specific voltage which causes the

Figure 1-2 Storage tube graphics display.

phosphor to assume its dark state. Erasure takes about 1/2 second. Because the entire tube is flooded, all lines and characters are erased. Thus, individual lines and characters cannot be erased, and the display of dynamic motion or animation is not possible. An intermediate state (write-through mode) is sometimes used to provide limited refresh capability (see below). Here, the electron beam is intensified to a point that is just below the threshold that will cause permanent storage but is still sufficient to brighten the phosphor. Because the image in this mode does not store, it must be redrawn or repainted continuously in order for it to be visible.

A storage tube display is flicker-free (see below) and capable of displaying an "unlimited" number of vectors. Resolution is typically 1024 × 1024 addressable points (10 bits) on an 8 × 8 inch square (11-inch-diagonal CRT) or 4096 × 4096 (12 bits) on either a 14 × 14 inch square (19-inch-diagonal CRT) or an 18 × 18 inch square (25-inch-diagonal CRT). Typically only 78 percent of the addressable area is viewable in the vertical direction.

A storage tube display is a line drawing or random scan display. This means that a line (vector) can be drawn directly from any addressable point to any other addressable point. Hard copy is relatively easy, fast, and inexpensive to obtain. Conceptually, a storage tube display is somewhat easier to program than a calligraphic or raster scan refresh display. Storage tube CRT displays can be combined with microcomputers into stand-alone computer graphics systems or incorporated into graphics terminals. When incorporated into terminals, alphanumeric and graphic information are passed to the terminal by a host computer over an interface. Although parallel interfaces are available, typically a serial interface which passes information 1 bit at a time is used. Because of the typically low interface speed and the erasure characteristics, the level of interactivity with a storage tube display is lower than with either a refresh or raster scan display.

1-4   CALLIGRAPHIC REFRESH GRAPHICS DISPLAYS

In contrast to the storage tube display, a calligraphic (line drawing or vector) refresh CRT display uses a very short-persistence phosphor. These displays are frequently called random scan displays (see below). Because of the short persistence of the phosphor, the picture painted on the CRT must be repainted or refreshed many times each second. The minimum refresh rate is at least 30 times each second, with a recommended rate of 40 to 50 times each second. Refresh rates much lower than 30 times each second result in a flickering image. The effect is similar to that observed when a movie film is run too slowly. The resulting picture is difficult to use and disagreeable to look at.

The basic calligraphic refresh display requires two elements in addition to the CRT. These are the display buffer and the display controller. The display buffer is contiguous memory containing all the information required to draw the picture on the CRT. The display controller's function is to repeatedly cycle through this information at the refresh rate. Two factors which limit the complexity (number of vectors displayed) of the picture are the size of the display buffer and the speed of the display controller. A further limitation is the speed at which picture information can be processed, i.e. transformed and clipped, and textual information generated.

Figure 1-3 shows two block diagrams of two high-performance calligraphic refresh displays. In both cases it is assumed that picture transformations such as rotation, translation, scaling, perspective, and clipping are implemented in hardware in the picture processor. In the first case (Fig. 1-3a) the picture processor is slower than the refresh rate for useful pictures (4000 to 5000 vectors). Thus, the picture data sent by the host central processing unit (CPU) to the graphics display is processed before being stored in the display buffer. Here the display buffer contains only those precise instructions which are required by the vector/character generator to draw the picture. Vectors are generally held in screen coordinates. The display controller reads information from the display buffer and sends it to the vector/character generator. When the display controller reaches the end of the display buffer, it returns to the beginning and cycles through the buffer again.

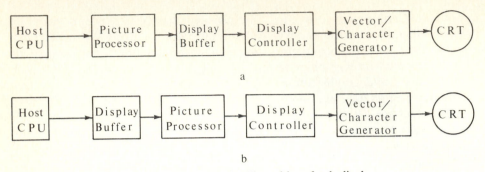

a

b

Figure 1-3 Conceptual block diagrams of calligraphic refresh displays.

This first configuration also gives rise to the concepts of double buffering and separate update and refresh rates. Since in this configuration the picture processor is too slow to generate a complex new or updated picture within one refresh cycle, the display buffer is divided into two parts. While an updated picture is being processed and written into one half of the buffer, the display controller is refreshing the CRT from the other half of the buffer. When the updated picture is complete, the buffers are swapped and the process is repeated. Thus, a new or updated picture may be generated every second, third, fourth, etc., refresh cycle. Double buffering prevents part of the old picture being displayed along with part of the new updated picture during one or more refresh cycles.

In the second configuration (see Fig. 1-3b) the picture processor is faster than the refresh rate for complex pictures. Here, the original picture data base sent from the host CPU is held directly in the display buffer. Vectors are generally held in user (world) coordinates as floating point numbers. The display controller reads information from the display buffer, passes it through the picture processor, and sends it to the vector generator in one refresh cycle. This implies that picture transformations are performed "on the fly" within one refresh cycle.

In either configuration, each vector, character, and picture drawing instruction exists in the display buffer. Hence, any individual element may be changed independent of any other element. This feature, in combination with the short persistence of the CRT phosphor, allows the display of dynamic motion. Figure 1-4 illustrates this concept. Figure 1-4 shows the picture displayed during four successive refresh cycles. The visible solid line is the displayed line for the current refresh cycle, and the invisible dotted line is for the previous refresh cycle. Between refresh cycles the location of the end of the line, B, is changed. The line will appear to rotate about the point A.

In many pictures only portions of the picture are dynamic. In fact, in many applications the majority of the picture is static. This leads to the concept of segmentation of the display buffer. Figure 1-5 illustrates this idea. Here, the baseline, the cross-hatching, and the letter A used to show the support for the line AB are static; i.e., they do not change from refresh cycle to refresh cycle.

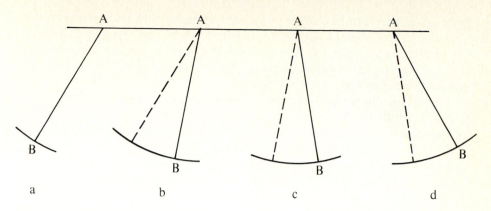

Figure 1-4 Dynamic motion.

In contrast, the location of the end of the line *AB* and the letter *B* change from refresh cycle to refresh cycle to show dynamic motion. These separate portions of the picture data base are placed in separate segments of the display buffer. Since the static segment of the display buffer does not change, it can be ignored by the picture processor for the configuration shown in Fig. 1-3a. This significantly reduces the work load on the picture processor when updating a picture. In this case, only the picture in the dynamic segment need be updated. Further, it reduces the amount of data that need be transmitted from the host CPU to the picture processor during each picture update.

For the configuration shown in Fig. 1-3b a different type of segmentation is possible. Recall that for this configuration the picture data base is stored in the display buffer in world (user) coordinates and picture processing occurs on the fly once each refresh cycle. For the picture in Fig. 1-5 two segments are created in the display buffer, a static and a dynamic segment. However, picture processing occurs on the fly. Dynamic update of the information in the

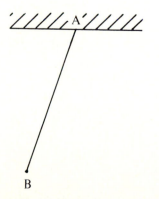

Figure 1-5 Display buffer segmentation.

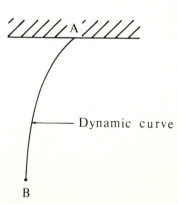

Figure 1-6 Intelligent display buffer segmentation.

dynamic segment can be accomplished using functions available in the picture processor. Thus, picture update can occur locally within the graphics device, and communication with the host CPU is unnecessary. For the particular case shown in Fig. 1-5 the only picture processor function required for local dynamic update is rotation about the point A.

Figure 1-6 illustrates a picture for which dynamic update requires communication with the host CPU, i.e., intelligent update of the picture. Again two segments are created, a static segment comprised of the baseline, cross-hatching, and the letter A, and a dynamic segment comprised of the curve AB and the letter B. Assume that the shape of the curve AB will change from refresh cycle to refresh cycle depending upon physical factors. Thus, the shape must be computed by an application program running in the host CPU. In order to update the dynamic picture segment new data, e.g. curve shape, must be sent to and stored in the display buffer.

Although the concept of picture segmentation has been introduced through dynamic motion examples, it is not limited to dynamic motion or animation. Any picture can be segmented. Picture segmentation is particularly useful for interactive graphics programs. The concept is similar to modular programming. The choice of modular picture segments, their size, and their complexity depends on the particular application. Individual picture elements can be as simple as single points or as complex as complete object descriptions. Reference 1-3 provides additional discussion.

To illustrate the importance of the communication speed, or bandwidth, between the host CPU and the graphics device consider the requirements for intelligently updating a curved line with 250 segments or points describing it. Each point is described by three coordinates. If we assume that a floating point representation with six significant figures (characters) is used, and that a single 8-bit byte is used to represent a character, then for a refresh rate of 30 frames per second and an update every refresh cycle the required communication bandwidth is

$$30[(no.\ points)(no.\ coor./point)(no.\ of\ sig.\ figs./point)(no.\ bits/char.)]$$

or $$30(250)(3)(6)(8) = 1,080,000\ bits/s$$

Thus, the required bandwidth can easily exceed 1 megabit per second. For complicated three-dimensional sculptured surfaces, the required bandwidth can easily exceed 10 times this, i.e., 10 megabits per second. In most cases this dictates a parallel or direct memory access (DMA) interface between the host CPU and the graphics device to support real-time intelligent dynamic graphics. A typical calligraphic refresh display is shown in Fig. 1-7.

1-5 RASTER REFRESH GRAPHICS DISPLAYS

Both the storage tube CRT display and the random scan refresh display are line drawing devices. That is, a straight line can be drawn directly from any addressable point to any other addressable point. In contrast is the raster CRT

Figure 1-7 Calligraphic refresh display. (*Courtesy of Evans & Sutherland Computer Corp.*)

graphics device. A raster CRT graphics device can be considered a matrix of discrete cells each of which can be made bright. Thus, it is a point plotting device. It is not possible except in special cases to directly draw a straight line from one addressable point, or pixel, in the matrix to another addressable point or pixel. The line can only be approximated by a series of dots (pixels) close to the path of the line. Figure 1-8 illustrates the basic concept. Only in the special cases of completely horizontal, vertical, or 45° lines will a straight line of dots or pixels result. This is shown in Fig. 1-8. All other lines will appear

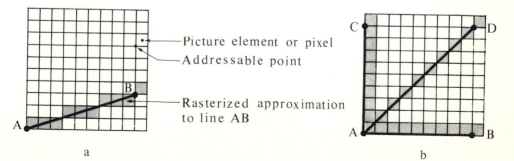

Figure 1-8 Rasterization of a line.

as a series of stair steps. This is called aliasing or the "jaggies." Antialiasing is addressed in Chap. 2.

The most common method of implementing a raster CRT graphics device utilizes a frame buffer. A frame buffer is a large, contiguous piece of computer memory. As a minimum there is one memory bit for each location or pixel (picture element) in the raster. This amount of memory is called a bit plane. A 512×512 element square raster requires 2^{18} ($2^9 = 512$; $2^{18} = 512 \times 512$) or 262,144 memory bits in a single bit plane. The picture is built up in the frame buffer 1 bit at a time. Since a memory bit has only two states (binary 0 or 1), a single bit plane yields a black-and-white display. Since the bit plane is a digital device, while the raster CRT is an analog device which requires an electrical voltage, conversion from a digital representation to an analog signal must take place when information is read from the frame buffer and displayed on the raster CRT graphics device. This is accomplished by a digital-to-analog converter (DAC). Each pixel in the frame buffer must be accessed and converted before it is visible on the raster CRT. A schematic diagram of a single-bit-plane black-and-white frame buffer raster CRT graphics device is shown in Fig. 1-9.

Color or gray levels can be incorporated into a frame buffer raster graphics device by using additional bit planes. Figure 1-10 schematically shows an N-bit-plane gray level frame buffer. The intensity of each pixel on the CRT is controlled by a corresponding pixel location in each of the N bit planes. The binary value (0 or 1) from each of the N bit planes is loaded into corresponding positions in a register. The resulting binary number is interpreted as an intensity level between 0 and $2^N - 1$. This is converted into a voltage between 0 (dark) and $2^N - 1$ (full intensity) by the DAC. A total of 2^N intensity levels can be achieved. Figure 1-10 illustrates a system with three bit planes for a total of 8 (2^3) intensity levels. Each bit plane requires the full complement of memory for a given raster resolution; e.g., a three-bit-plane frame buffer for a 512×512 raster requires 786,432 ($3 \times 512 \times 512$) memory bits.

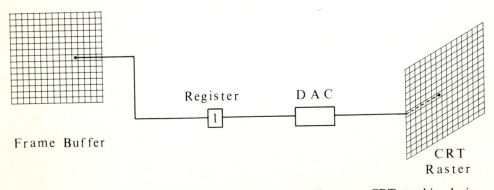

Frame Buffer Register DAC CRT Raster

Figure 1-9 A single-bit-plane black-and-white frame buffer raster CRT graphics device.

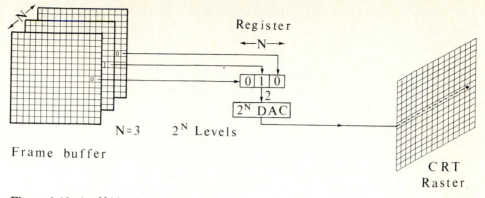

Figure 1-10 An *N*-bit-plane black-and-white gray level frame buffer.

An increase in the number of available intensity levels can be achieved for a modest increase in required memory by using a look-up table. This is shown schematically in Fig. 1-11. Upon reading the bit planes in the frame buffer, the resulting number is used as an entry index into the look-up table. The look-up table must contain 2^N entries. Each entry in the look-up table can contain W bits. W may be greater than N. When this occurs, 2^W intensities are available; but only 2^N different intensities are available at one time. To get additional intensities the look-up table must be changed (reloaded).

Since there are three primary colors, a simple color frame buffer can be implemented with three bit planes, one for each primary color. Each bit plane drives an individual color gun for each of the three primary colors used in color video. These three colors are combined at the CRT to yield eight colors. The

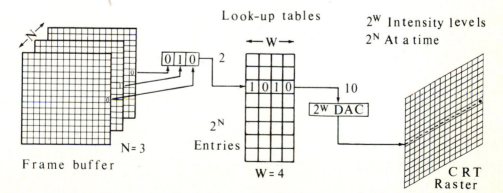

Figure 1-11 An *N*-bit-plane black-and-white gray level frame buffer with a *W*-bit-wide look-up table.

eight obtainable colors and appropriate binary codes are shown in Table 1-1. A simple color raster frame buffer is shown schematically in Fig. 1-12.

Additional bit planes can be used for each of the three color guns. Figure 1-13 shows a schematic of a multiple-bit-plane color frame buffer with 8 bit planes per color, i.e., a 24-bit-plane frame buffer. Each group of bit planes drives an 8-bit DAC. Each group can generate 256 (2^8) shades or intensities of red, green, or blue. These can be combined into 16,777,216 [$(2^8)^3 = 2^{24}$)] possible colors. This is a "full" color frame buffer.

The full color frame buffer can be further expanded by using the groups of bit planes as indices to color look-up tables. This is shown schematically in Fig. 1-14. For N bit planes per color with W-bit-wide color look-up tables $(2^3)^N$ colors from a palette of $(2^3)^W$ possible colors can be shown at any one time. For example, for a 24-bit-plane ($N = 8$) frame buffer with three 10-bit-wide ($W = 10$) color look-up tables, 16,777,216 (2^{24}) colors from a palette of 1,073,741,824 (2^{30}) colors, i.e., about 17 million colors from a palette of a little more than 1 billion, can be obtained.

Because of the large number of pixels in a raster scan graphics device, achieving real-time performance and acceptable refresh or frame rates can be

Table 1-1 Simple 3-Bit Plane Frame Buffer Color Combinations

	Red	Green	Blue
Black	0	0	0
Red	1	0	0
Green	0	1	0
Blue	0	0	1
Yellow	1	1	0
Cyan	0	1	1
Magenta	1	0	1
White	1	1	1

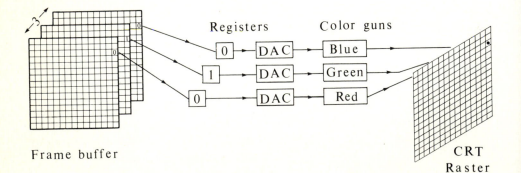

Figure 1-12 Simple color frame buffer.

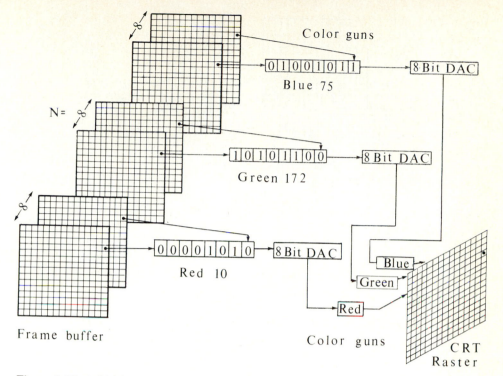

Figure 1-13 A 24-bit-plane color frame buffer.

difficult. For example, if pixels are accessed individually with an average access time of 200 nanoseconds (200×10^{-9} second), then it requires 0.0524 second to access each of the pixels in a 512×512 frame buffer. This is equivalent to a refresh rate of 19 frames (pictures) per second, well below the required minimum refresh rate of 30 frames per second. A 1024×1024 frame buffer contains slightly more than 1 million bits (1 megabit) and at 200 nanoseconds average access time requires 0.21 second to access each of the pixels. This is 5 frames per second. A 4096×4096 frame buffer contains 16.78 million bits per memory plane! At a 200-nanosecond access time per pixel it requires 0.3 second to access each of the pixels. To achieve a refresh rate of 30 frames per second a 4096×4096 raster requires an average effective access rate of 2 nanoseconds per pixel.

Real-time performance with raster scan graphics devices is achieved by accessing pixels in groups of 16, 32, or 64 or more simultaneously. In the case of color frame buffers each pixel may contain up to 32 bits; i.e., all bit planes for an individual pixel are accessed together. With an average access time of 1600 nanoseconds for each group of pixels, real-time performance for 512×512 and 1024×1024 frame buffers is possible.

Although real-time performance with acceptable refresh rates is more difficult to achieve with a raster CRT device than with a calligraphic or line draw-

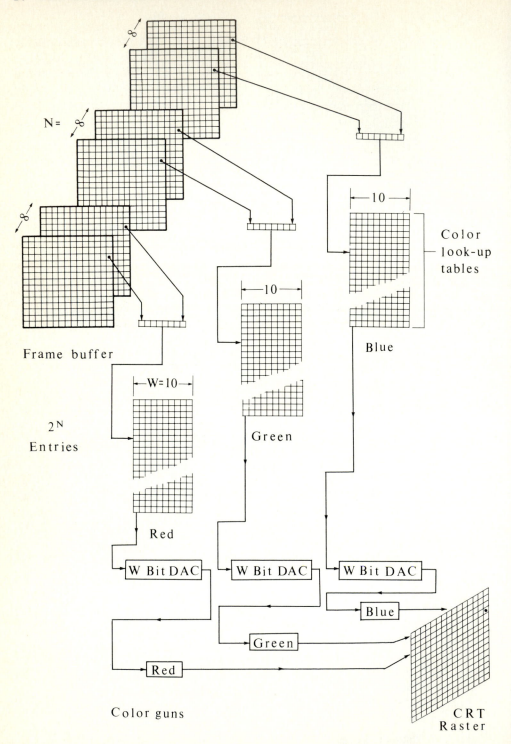

Figure 1-14 A 24-bit-plane color frame buffer with 10-bit-wide look-up tables.

ing refresh display, solid figure representations in delicate shades of color are easier. Solid "polygonal" figure representation with a raster is conceptually simple. This is shown in Fig. 1-15. Here a representation of the solid figure bounded by the lines L_1, L_2, L_3, L_4 is achieved by setting all the pixels within the bounding polygon to the appropriate code in the frame buffer. This is solid area "scan conversion," algorithms for which are discussed in Chap. 2.

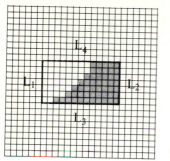

Figure 1-15 Solid figures with a raster graphics device.

1-6   CATHODE RAY TUBE BASICS

A frame buffer as described above is not itself a display device. It is simply used to assemble the picture. The most common display device used with a frame buffer is a video (TV) monitor. An understanding of raster displays, and to some extent line drawing refresh displays, requires a basic understanding of CRTs and video display techniques.

The CRT used in video monitors is shown schematically in Fig. 1-16. A cathode (negatively charged) is heated until electrons "boil" off in a diverging cloud (electrons repel each other because they have the same charge). These electrons are attracted to a highly charged positive anode. This is the phosphor coating on the inside of the face of the large end of the CRT. If allowed to continue uninterrupted, the electrons would simply flood the entire face of the

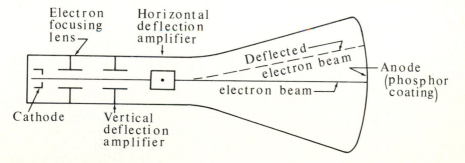

Figure 1-16 Cathode ray tube.

CRT with a bright glow. However, the cloud of electrons is focused into a narrow, precisely collimated beam with an electron lens. At this point the focused electron beam produces a single bright spot at the center of the CRT. The electron beam is deflected or positioned to the left or right of the center and/or above or below the center by means of horizontal and vertical deflection amplifiers.

It is at this point that line drawing displays, both storage and refresh, and raster scan displays differ. In a line drawing display the electron beam may be deflected directly from any arbitrary position to any other arbitrary position on the face of the CRT (anode). Since the phosphor coating on the CRT face is continuous, a perfectly straight line will result. In contrast, in a raster scan display the beam is deflected in a set, rigidly controlled pattern. This pattern comprises the video picture. The phosphor on the face of the raster CRT is not continuous but rather composed of a myriad of small spots in a fixed pattern.

1-7 COLOR CRT RASTER SCAN BASICS

A color raster scan CRT is similar to the standard black-and-white CRT described in the previous section. In the color raster scan CRT there are three electron guns, one for each of the three primary colors, red, green, and blue. The electron guns are frequently arranged in a triangular pattern corresponding to a similar triangular pattern of red, green, and blue phosphor dots on the face of the CRT (see Fig. 1-17). To ensure that the individual electron guns excite the correct phosphor dots (e.g., the red gun excites only the red phosphor dot), a perforated metal grid is placed between the electron guns and the face of the CRT. This is the shadow mask of the standard shadow mask color CRT. The perforations in the shadow mask are arranged in the same triangular pattern as the phosphor dots. The distance between perforations is called the pitch. The color guns are arranged so that the individual beams converge and intersect at the shadow mask (see Fig. 1-18). Upon passing through the hole in the shadow mask the red beam, for example, is prevented

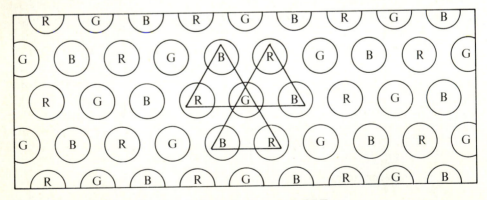

Figure 1-17 Phosphor dot pattern for a shadow mask CRT.

or masked from intersecting either the green or blue phosphor dot. It can only intersect the red phosphor dot. By varying the strength of the electron beam for each individual primary color, different shades can be obtained. These primary color shades can be combined into a large number of colors for each pixel. For a high-resolution display there are usually two to three color triads for each pixel.

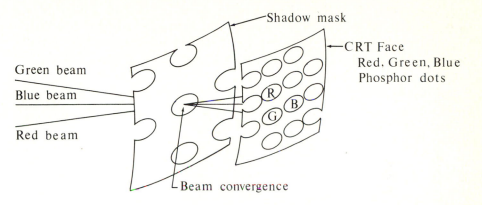

Figure 1-18 Color CRT electron gun and shadow mask arrangement.

1-8   VIDEO BASICS

The process of converting the rasterized picture stored in a frame buffer to the rigid display pattern of video is called scan conversion. The scanning pattern and the frequency of repetition are based on both visual perception and electronic principles. The human visual perception system requires a finite amount of time to examine the elements of a picture. However, this time should be short enough that the persistence of vision will overcome flicker to give the impression of a continuous presentation. A number of factors affect flicker, including image brightness and the particular CRT screen phosphor used. Experience indicates that a practical minimum picture presentation or update rate is 25 frames per second provided the minimum refresh or repetition rate is twice this, i.e., 50 frames per second. This is actually what is done with movie film. With movie film 24 frames per second are presented, but the presentation of each frame is interrupted so that it is presented twice for an effective repetition rate of 48 frames per second. Thus, for film the update rate is 24 and the refresh rate is 48. The same effect is achieved in video with a technique called interlacing.

Video is a raster scan technique. The American standard video system uses a total of 525 horizontal lines with a frame or viewing aspect ratio of 4:3; i.e., the viewing area is three-quarters as high as it is wide. The repetition or frame rate is 30 frames per second. However, each frame is divided into two fields, each containing one half of the picture. The two fields are interlaced or interwoven. The fields are presented alternatively every other 1/60 second. One field contains all the odd-numbered lines (1, 3, 5, ...), and the other the even-numbered lines (2, 4, 6, ...). The scanning pattern begins at the upper left corner of the screen with the odd field. Each line in the field is scanned or presented from the left to the right. As the electron beam moves across the screen from left to right it also moves vertically downward but at a much slower rate. Thus, the "horizontal" scan line is in fact slightly slanted. When the beam reaches the right edge of the screen, it is made invisible and rapidly returned to the left edge. This is the horizontal retrace which usually requires approximately 17 percent of the time allowed for one scan line. The process is then repeated with the next odd scan line. Since half of 525 is 262 1/2 lines, the beam will be at the bottom center of the screen when the odd scan line field is complete (see Figs. 1-19 and 1-20). The beam is then quickly returned to the top center of the screen. This is the odd field vertical retrace. The time required for the vertical retrace is equivalent to that for 21 lines. The even scan line field is then presented. The even scan line field ends in the lower right hand corner. The even field vertical retrace returns the beam to the upper left hand corner, and the entire sequence is repeated. Thus, two fields are presented for each frame, i.e., 60 fields per second. Since the eye perceives the field repetition rate, this technique significantly reduces flicker.

Although the American standard video system calls for 525 lines, only 483 lines are actually visible because a time equivalent to 21 lines is required to accomplish the vertical retrace for each field.[†] During this time the electron

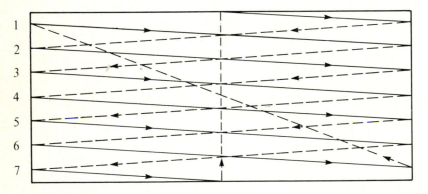

Figure 1-19 Schematic of a seven-line interlaced scan line pattern. The odd field begins with line 1. The horizontal retrace is shown dashed. The odd field vertical retrace starts at the bottom center. The even field vertical retrace starts at the bottom right.

[†] Many raster scan graphics devices use this time for processing other information.

beam is invisible or blanked. The time available for each scan line is easily calculated for a frame repetition rate of 30 as

$$\frac{1}{30} \frac{second}{frame} \times \frac{1}{525} \frac{frame}{scan\ line} = 63.5 \frac{microseconds}{scan\ line}$$

Since approximately 10 1/2 microseconds is required for horizontal retrace, the visible portion of each scan line must be completed in 53 microseconds. With a normal video aspect ratio of 4:3 there are 644 pixels on each scan line. The time available to access and display a pixel is thus

$$53 \frac{microseconds}{scan\ line} \times \frac{1}{644} \frac{scan\ line}{pixels} = 82\ nanoseconds$$

Many frame buffer-based raster scan displays sample the picture at a resolution of 512 pixels per scan line. At this resolution approximately 103 nanoseconds is available to access and display a pixel. Equivalent results are obtained for the 625-line 25-frame repetition rate used in most of Europe and Great Britian.

The interlace technique described above is not required when presenting a video picture. However, this noninterlaced picture will not be compatible with a standard television set. When such a noninterlaced picture is presented, the frame repetition rate must be increased to 60 frames per second to avoid flicker. This, of course, reduces the available pixel access and display time by a factor of 2. Higher line and pixel-per-line resolutions also decrease the available pixel access and display time; e.g., a 1024 × 1024 resolution requires a pixel access and display time a quarter of that required by a 512 × 512 resolution— approximately 25 nanoseconds! Thus, a very fast frame buffer memory and an equally fast DAC are required.

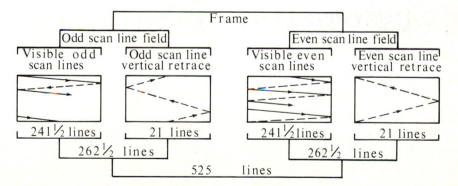

Figure 1-20 A 525-line standard frame schematic.

1-9   INTERACTIVE DEVICES

Once the picture has been presented, interaction with or modification of the picture is required. To meet this requirement a number of interactive devices have been developed. Among these devices are tablets, light pens, joysticks, mice, control dials, function switches or buttons, and of course the common alphanumeric keyboard. Before discussing these physical devices it is appropriate to discuss the functional capabilities of interactive graphics devices. The functional capabilities are generally considered to be of four or five types (see Refs. 1-3 to 1-6). The logical interaction devices are a locator, a valuator, a pick, and a button. A fifth functional capability called keyboard is frequently included because of the general availability of the alphanumeric keyboard. In fact, a keyboard can conceptually and functionally be considered a collection of buttons.

The locator function provides coordinate information in either two or three dimensions. Generally the coordinate numbers returned are in the conceptual or device space and may be either relative or absolute. The valuator function provides a single value. Generally this value is a real number between zero and some real maximum. The button function is used to select and activate events or procedures which control the interactive flow. It generally provides only binary (on or off) digital information. The pick function identifies or selects objects or subpictures within the displayed picture. The logical keyboard processes textual information. A typical keyboard is shown in Fig. 1-21.

The tablet is the most common locator device. A typical tablet is shown in Fig. 1-22. Tablets may be used either in conjunction with a CRT graphics display or stand alone. In the latter case they are frequently referred to as digitizers. The tablet itself consists of a flat surface and a penlike stylus which

Figure 1-21 An alphanumeric keyboard. (*Courtesy of Evans & Sutherland Computer Corp.*)

is used to indicate a location on the tablet surface. Usually the proximity of the stylus to the tablet surface can also be sensed. When used in conjunction with a CRT display, feedback from the CRT face is provided by means of a small tracking symbol which follows the movement of the stylus on the tablet surface. When used as a stand-alone digitizer, feedback is provided by digital readouts.

Tablets provide either two- or three-dimensional coordinate information. A three-dimensional tablet is shown in Fig. 1-23. The values returned are in tablet coordinates. Software converts the tablet coordinates to user coordinates. Typical resolution and accuracy is 0.01 to 0.001 inch. When used in conjunction with a CRT display, the resolution of the tablet should equal or exceed that of the display.

A number of different principles have been used to implement tablets. The original RAND tablet (see Ref. 1-7) uses an orthogonal matrix of individual wires beneath the tablet surface. Each wire is individually coded such that the stylus acting as a receiver picks up a unique digital code at each intersection. Decoding yields the x, y coordinates of the stylus. The obvious limitations on the resolution of such a matrix-encoded tablet are the density of the wires and the receiver's ability to resolve a unique code. The accuracy is limited by the linearity of the individual wires as well as the parallelism of the wires in the two orthogonal directions.

An interesting implementation for a tablet utilizes sound waves. The stylus is used to create a spark which generates a sound wave. The sound wave moves outward from the stylus on the surface of the tablet in a circular wave front. Two sensitive ribbon microphones are mounted at right angles on the sides of the tablet. By accurately measuring the time that it takes the sound

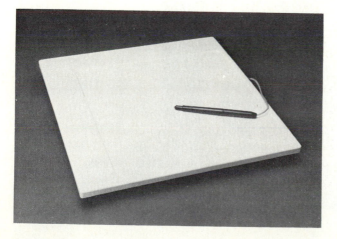

Figure 1-22 A typical tablet. (*Courtesy of Adage, Inc.*)

wave to travel from the stylus to the microphones, the coordinate distances can be determined. This technique may be extended to three dimensions (see Fig. 1-23).

The most popular tablet implementation is based on an electromagnetic principle. In this tablet implementation electric pulses travel through a sheet of magnetostrictive material used as the tablet surface. The stylus and appropriate counters are used to determine the time it takes for alternate pulses parallel to the x- and y-coordinate axes to travel from the edge of the tablet to the stylus. These times are readily converted into x, y coordinates.

A locator device similar to a tablet is the touch panel. In a typical touch panel light emitters are mounted in two adjacent edges with companion light detectors mounted in the opposite adjacent edges. Anything, e.g. a finger, interrupting the two orthogonal light beams yields an x, y coordinate pair. Because of its poor resolution, the touch panel is most useful for gross pointing operations. In this capacity it is frequently mounted in front of a CRT screen.

Locator devices such as the joystick, track ball, and mouse are frequently implemented using sensitive variable resistors or potentiometers as part of a voltage divider. Control dials which are valuators are similarly implemented. The accuracy is dependent on the quality of the potentiometer, typically 0.1 to 10 percent of full throw. Although resolution of the potentiometer is basically infinite, use in a digital system requires analog-to-digital (A/D) conversion. Typically the resolution of the A/D converter ranges from 8 to 14 bits, i.e., from 1 part in 2^8 (256) to 1 part in 2^{14} (16384). Valuators are also implemented

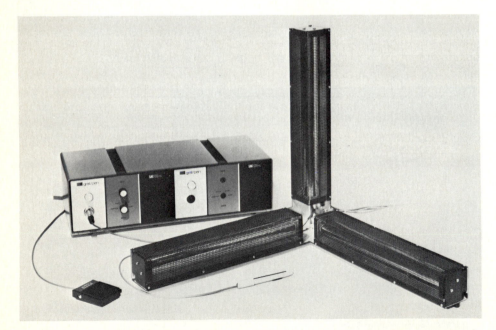

Figure 1-23 A three-dimensional sonic tablet. (*Courtesy of Science Accessories Corp.*)

with digital shaft encoders which, of course, provide a direct digital output for each incremental rotation of the shaft. Typical resolutions are 1 part in 2^8 (256) to 1 part in 2^{10} (1024) for each incremental rotation of the shaft.

A typical valuator is the joystick. A joystick is shown in Fig. 1-24. A movable joystick is generally implemented with two valuators, either potentiometers or shaft encoders, mounted in the base. The valuators provide results proportional to the movement of the shaft. A third dimension can readily be incorporated into a joystick, e.g., by using a third valuator to sense rotation of the shaft. A tracking symbol is normally used for feedback.

The track ball is similar to the joystick. It is most often seen in radar installations, e.g., in air traffic control. Here, a spherical ball is mounted in a base with only a portion projecting above the surface. The ball is free to rotate in any direction. Two valuators, either potentiometers or shaft encoders, mounted in the base sense the rotation of the ball and provide results proportional to its relative position. In addition to feedback from the normal tracking symbol, users obtain tactile feedback from the rotation rate or angular momentum of the ball.

The joystick and track ball both have a fixed location with a fixed origin. The mouse (Ref. 1-8) on the other hand has only a relative origin. A typical mouse consists of two rubber-rimmed wheels mounted at right angles in a small, lightweight box. As the mouse is moved across a surface the wheels drive the shafts of two valuators, either potentiometers or shaft encoders. The cumulative movement of the shafts provides x, y coordinates. A typical mouse is shown in Fig. 1-25. The mouse can be picked up, moved, and set back

Figure 1-24 Joystick. (*Courtesy of Measurement Systems, Inc.*)

Figure 1-25 Mouse. (*Courtesy of Apple Computer, Inc.*)

down in a different orientation. In this case the coordinate system in which data is generated, i.e. the mouse, is changed, but not the data coordinate system itself. Under these circumstances the tracking symbol used for feedback does not move when the mouse is not in contact with the surface. The mouse suffers from inaccuracies due to wheel slippage, especially during diagonal movements. Recently mice that work on both optical and magnetic principles have become available. Both eliminate the inaccuracies due to wheel slippage.

Perhaps the simplest of the valuators is the control dial. Control dials, shown in Fig. 1-26, are essentially sensitive rotating potentiometers or accurate digital shaft encoders. They generally are used in groups and are particularly useful for activating rotation, translation, scaling, or zoom functions.

Buttons or function switches, shown in Fig. 1-27, are either toggle or push-button switches. They may be either continuously closed, continuously open, or momentary-contact switches. The most convenient type of function switch incorporates both capabilities. Software-controlled lights indicating which switches or buttons are active are usually provided. Buttons and switches are frequently incorporated into other devices. For example, the stylus of a tablet usually has a switch in the tip activated by pushing down on the stylus. A mouse also incorporates one or more buttons.

The light pen is the only true pick device. The pen, shown schematically in Fig. 1-28, contains a sensitive photoelectric cell and associated circuitry. Since the basic information provided by the light pen is timing, it depends on the picture being repeatedly produced in a predictable manner. This precludes its use with a storage tube CRT display. The use of a light pen is limited to refresh displays, either line drawing or raster scan.

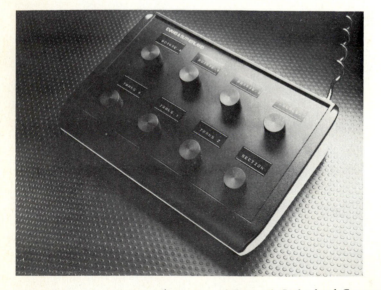

Figure 1-26 Control dials. (*Courtesy of Evans & Sutherland Computer Corp.*)

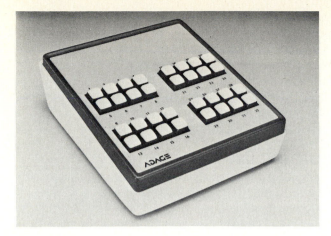

Figure 1-27 Function switches. (*Courtesy of Adage, Inc.*)

When the light pen is activated and placed over an intensified area of the CRT on a line drawing refresh display, a signal is sent to the display controller This signal allows the particular instruction in the display buffer being executed at that time to be determined. Tracing back through the display controller allows determination of the particular line segment, object, or subpicture that

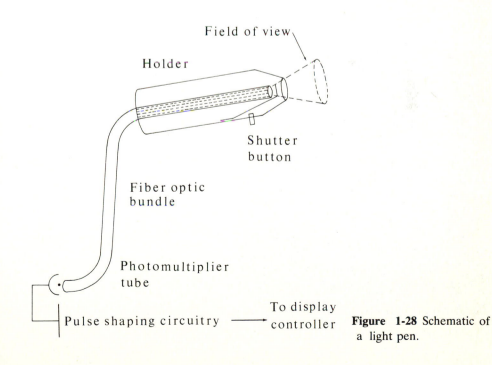

Figure 1-28 Schematic of a light pen.

was picked. A light pen can also be used as a locator on a line drawing refresh device by using a tracking symbol.

Since in a raster scan display the picture is generated in a fixed sequence, the light pen is used to determine the horizontal scan line (y coordinate) and the position on the scan line (x coordinate). Again, by tracing back through the controller, the particular line segment, object, or subpicture can be determined. This is somewhat complicated by the interlace scheme. The above description also indicates that, on a raster scan device, a light pen can be used as a locator rather than as a pick device.

Although physical devices are available to implement all the logical interactive devices, an individual graphics device may not have the appropriate physical devices available. Thus, simulation of the logical interactive devices is required. An example is shown in Fig. 1-29, where a light pen is being used to simulate a logical button function by picking light buttons from a menu.

The tablet is one of the most versatile of the physical devices. It can be used as a digitizer to provide x, y coordinate information. In addition, it can readily be used to simulate all the logical interactive functions. This is shown in Fig. 1-30. The tablet itself is a locator (a in Fig. 1-30). The button function can be implemented by using a tracking symbol. The tracking symbol is positioned

Figure 1-29 A light pen used to simulate a logical button function via menu picking. (*Courtesy of Adage, Inc.*)

at or near menu buttons using the tablet stylus. The tablet coordinates are compared with the known x, y coordinates of the menu buttons. If a match is obtained, then that button is activated (b in Fig. 1-30). A keyboard can be implemented in a similar manner (c in Fig. 1-30).

A single valuator is usually implemented in combination with a button. The particular function for evaluation is selected by a button, usually in a menu. The valuator may then be simulated by a "number line" (d in Fig. 1-30). Moving the tracking symbol along the line generates x and y coordinates one of which is interpreted as a percentage of the valuator's range.

The pick function can be implemented using a locator by defining the relative x and y coordinates of a small "hit window." The hit window is then made the tracking symbol, and the stylus used to position it. The x, y coordinates of each of the line segments, objects, or subpictures of interest are then compared with those of the current location of the hit window. If a match is obtained, then that entity is picked. Implemented in software this can be slow for complex pictures. Implemented in hardware yields no noticeable delay. Although a light pen cannot be used as a digitizer, it, like the tablet, can also be used to simulate all the logical interactive functions.

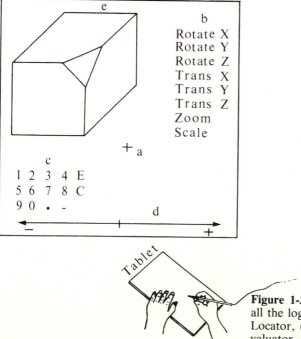

Figure 1-30 A tablet used to simulate all the logical interactive functions. (a) Locator, (b) button, (c) keyboard, (d) valuator, (e) pick.

1-10 SUMMARY

This chapter has attempted to provide a basic conceptual overview of computer graphics and computer graphics hardware. A more detailed and practical view can only be obtained by comparing actual hardware and software with these concepts.

1-11 REFERENCES

1-1 Rogers, David F., and Adams, J. Alan, *Mathematical Elements for Computer Graphics,* McGraw-Hill Book Company, New York, 1976.

1-2 Newman, William M., and Sproull, Robert F., *Principles of Interactive Computer Graphics* 2d ed., McGraw-Hill Book Company, New York, 1979.

1-3 Foley, J. D., and Van Dam, A., *Fundamentals of Interactive Computer Graphics,* Addison-Wesley Publishing Company, Reading, Mass., 1982.

1-4 Foley, J. D., and Wallace, V. L., "The Art of Natural Man-Machine Conversation," *Proc. IEEE,* Vol. 62, pp. 462–471, 1974.

1-5 Wallace, V. L., "The Semantics of Graphic Input Devices," *Computer Graphics,* Vol. 10, pp. 61–65, 1976.

1-6 Ohlson, Mark, "System Design Considerations for Graphics Input Devices," *Computer,* pp. 9–18, Nov. 1978.

1-7 Bergeron, R. D., Bono, P. R., and Foley, J. D., "Graphics Programming Using the Core System," *Computing Surveys*, Vol. 10, pp. 389–443, 1978.

1-8 Davis, M. R., and Ellis, T. O., "The RAND Tablet: A Man-Machine Graphical Communication Device," AFIPS Conf. Proc., Vol. 26, Part I, 1964 FJCC, pp. 325–332, 1964.

CHAPTER TWO

RASTER SCAN GRAPHICS

Raster scan graphics devices require special procedures to generate the display, to draw straight lines or curves, and to fill polygons to give the impression of solid areas. This chapter examines these procedures.

2-1 LINE DRAWING ALGORITHMS

Since a cathode ray tube (CRT) raster display can be considered a matrix of discrete cells (pixels) each of which can be made bright, it is not possible to directly draw a straight line from one point to another. The process of determining which pixels will provide the best approximation to the desired line is properly known as rasterization. Combined with the process of rendering the picture in scan line order it is known as scan conversion. For horizontal, vertical, and 45° lines the choice of raster elements is obvious. For any other orientation the choice is more difficult. This is shown in Fig. 2-1.

Before discussing specific line drawing algorithms it is useful to consider the general requirements for such algorithms, i.e., what are the desirable characteristics for these lines. Certainly straight lines should appear as straight lines, and they should start and end accurately. Further, displayed lines should

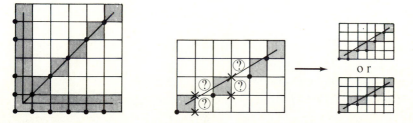

Figure 2-1 Rasterization of straight lines.

have constant brightness along their length independent of the line length and orientation. Finally the lines should be drawn rapidly. As with most design criteria not all can be completely satisfied. The very nature of a raster scan display precludes the generation of a completely straight line except for special cases. Nor is it possible for a line to precisely begin and end at specified locations. However, with reasonable display resolution, acceptable approximations are possible.

Only for horizontal, vertical, and 45° lines will the brightness be constant along the length. For all other orientations the rasterization will yield uneven brightness. This is shown in Fig. 2-1. Even for the special cases, the brightness is orientation dependent; e.g., note that the effective spacing between pixels for the 45° line is greater than for the vertical and horizontal lines. This will make the vertical and horizontal lines appear brighter than the 45° line. Providing equal brightness along lines of varying length and orientation requires the calculation of a square root. This will slow down the calculation. The compromise generally made is to calculate only an approximate line length, reduce the calculations to a minimum preferably using integer arithmetic, and implement the result in hardware or firmware.

Most line drawing algorithms use incremental methods to simplify the calculations. An algorithmic example of an incremental method is

    a simple incremental algorithm

        position = start
        step = increment
  1 **if** position − end < accuracy **then** 4
      if position > end **then** 2
      if position < end **then** 3
  2 position = position − step
      go to 1
  3 position = positon + step
      go to 1
  4 **finish**

The simple line rasterizing algorithm given in the next section illustrates the application of incremental methods.

2-2 DIGITAL DIFFERENTIAL ANALYZER

One technique for obtaining a rasterized straight line is to solve the governing differential equation. For a straight line

$$\frac{dy}{dx} = \text{constant} \qquad \text{or} \qquad \frac{\Delta y}{\Delta x} = \frac{y_2 - y_1}{x_2 - x_1}$$

The solution is

$$y_{i+1} = y_i + \Delta y$$

$$y_{i+1} = y_i + \frac{y_2 - y_1}{x_2 - x_1} \Delta x \tag{2-1}$$

where x_1, y_1 and x_2, y_2 are the end points of the required straight line and y_i is the initial value for any given step along the line. In fact, Eq. (2-1) represents a recursion relation for successive values of y along the required line. Used to rasterize a line, it is called a digital differential analyzer (DDA). For a simple DDA either Δx or Δy, whichever is larger, is chosen as one raster unit. A simple algorithm which will work in all quadrants is

digital differential analyzer *(DDA) routine for rasterizing a line*

the line end points are (x_1, y_1) *and* (x_2, y_2) *assumed not equal*
Integer *is the integer function. Note: Many Integer functions are floor functions; i.e., Integer$(-8.5) = -9$ rather than -8. The algorithm assumes this is the case.*
Sign *returns* $-1, 0, 1$ *as its argument is* $<0, = 0, >0$

    approximate the line length
    if abs$(x_2 - x_1) \geq$ abs$(y_2 - y_1)$ **then**
        Length $=$ abs$(x_2 - x_1)$
    else
        Length $=$ abs$(y_2 - y_1)$
    end if
    select the larger of Δx *or* Δy *to be one raster unit*
    $\Delta x = (x_2 - x_1)/$Length
    $\Delta y = (y_2 - y_1)/$Length
    round the values rather than truncate
    using the sign function makes the algorithm work in all quadrants
    $x = x_1 + 0.5*$**Sign**(Δx)
    $y = y_1 + 0.5*$**Sign**(Δy)
    begin main loop
    $i = 1$
    while $(i \leq$ Length$)$
        Plot(Integer(x), **Integer**$(y))$
        $x = x + \Delta x$
        $y = y + \Delta y$
        $i = i + 1$
    end while
    finish

An example illustrates the algorithm.

Example 2-1   Simple DDA First Quadrant

Consider the line from (0, 0) to (5, 5). Use the simple DDA to rasterize this line. Evaluating the steps in the algorithm yields

initial calculation

$x_1 = 0$
$y_1 = 0$
$x_2 = 5$
$y_2 = 5$
Length = 5
$\Delta x = 1$
$\Delta y = 1$
x = 0.5
y = 0.5

incrementing through the main loop yields

i	Plot	x	y
		0.5	0.5
1	(0, 0)		
		1.5	1.5
2	(1, 1)		
		2.5	2.5
3	(2, 2)		
		3.5	3.5
4	(3, 3)		
		4.5	4.5
5	(4, 4)		
		5.5	5.5

The results are shown plotted in Fig. 2-2. Note that the end points are both apparently exact and that the selected pixels are equally spaced along the line. The appearance of the line is quite acceptable. However, if i is initialized to zero instead of to one as shown, the pixel at location (5, 5) is activated. This can lead to undesirable results. If the address of a pixel is given by the integer coordinates of the lower left corner, then activating the pixel location (5, 5) will yield an apparently incorrect end point for the line (see Fig. 2-2). In addition, if a series of successive line segments is drawn, then the pixel at location (5, 5) will be activated twice; once at the end of a line segment and again at the beginning of the successive line segment. This may be seen as either a brighter pixel or perhaps a pixel of a different or odd color. The next example illustrates results in the third quadrant.

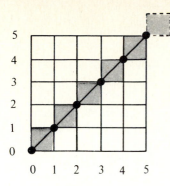

Figure 2-2 Results for a simple DDA in the first quadrant.

Example 2-2 Simple DDA Third Quadrant

Consider the line from $(0, 0)$ to $(-8, -4)$ in the third quadrant. Evaluating the algorithm yields

initial calculations

$x_1 = 0$
$y_1 = 0$
$x_2 = -8$
$y_2 = -4$
Length = 8
$\Delta x = -1$
$\Delta y = -0.5$
$x = -0.5$
$y = -0.5$

incrementing through the main loop
assuming a floor integer function yields

i	Plot	x	y
		-0.5	-0.5
1	$(-1, -1)$		
		-1.5	-1.0
2	$(-2, -1)$		
		-2.5	-1.5
3	$(-3, -2)$		
		-3.5	-2.0
4	$(-4, -2)$		
		-4.5	-2.5
5	$(-5, -3)$		
		-5.5	-3.0
6	$(-6, -3)$		
		-6.5	-3.5

7	$(-7, -4)$		
		-7.5	-4.0
8	$(-8, -4)$		
		-8.5	-4.5

The results are shown in Fig. 2-3.

Although the results shown in Fig. 2-3 appear quite acceptable, considering the lines from $(0, 0)$ to $(-8, 4)$ and $(8, -4)$ will show that the rasterized line lies to one side of the actual line and that an extra point occurs at one end of the line; i.e., the algorithm is orientation dependent. Hence, the end point accuracy deteriorates. Further, if a true integer function rather than the assumed floor function is used, the results are again different. Thus, either a more complicated algorithm which will run slower must be used, or line end point and position accuracy must be compromised. In addition, the algorithm suffers from the fact that it must be performed using floating point arithmetic. A more suitable algorithm is given in the next section.

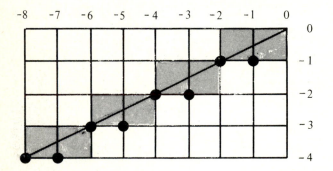

Figure 2-3 Results for a simple DDA in the third quadrant.

2-3 BRESENHAM'S ALGORITHM

Although originally developed for digital plotters, Bresenham's algorithm (Ref. 2-1) is equally suited for use with CRT raster devices. The algorithm seeks to select the optimum raster locations to represent a straight line. To accomplish this the algorithm always increments by one unit in either x or y depending on the slope of the line. The increment in the other variable, either zero or one, is determined by examining the distance between the actual line location and the nearest grid locations. This distance is called the error.

The algorithm is cleverly constructed so that only the sign of this error term need be examined. This is illustrated in Fig. 2-4 for a line in the first octant, i.e., for a line with a slope between zero and one. From Fig. 2-4 note

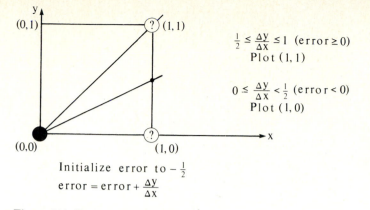

$$\frac{1}{2} \leq \frac{\Delta y}{\Delta x} \leq 1 \quad (\text{error} \geq 0)$$
Plot (1, 1)

$$0 \leq \frac{\Delta y}{\Delta x} < \frac{1}{2} \quad (\text{error} < 0)$$
Plot (1, 0)

Initialize error to $-\frac{1}{2}$

$$\text{error} = \text{error} + \frac{\Delta y}{\Delta x}$$

Figure 2-4 Basis of Bresenham's algorithm.

that, if the slope of the required line through (0, 0) is greater than 1/2, then its intercept with the line $x = 1$ will be closer to the line $y = 1$ than to the line $y = 0$. Hence, the raster point at (1, 1) better represents the path of the line than that at (1, 0). If the slope is less than 1/2, then the opposite is true. For a slope of precisely 1/2 there is no clear choice. Here the algorithm chooses (1, 1).

Not all lines pass precisely through a raster point. This is illustrated in Fig. 2-5 where a line of slope 3/8 initially passes through the raster point at (0, 0) and subsequently crosses three pixels. Also illustrated is the calculation of the error in representing the line by discrete pixels. Since it is desirable to check only the sign of the error term, it is initialized to $-1/2$. Thus, if the slope

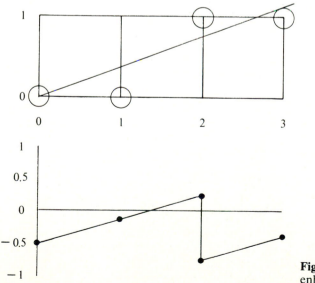

Figure 2-5 Error term in Bresenham's algorithm.

of the line is greater than or equal to 1/2, its value at the next raster point one unit away (1, 0) can be determined by adding the slope of the line to the error term, i.e.,

$$e = e + m$$

where m is the slope. In this case, with e initialized to $-1/2$,

$$e = -1/2 + 3/8 = -1/8$$

Since e is negative, the line will pass below the middle of the pixel. Hence, the pixel at the same horizontal level better approximates the location of the line so y is not incremented. Again, incrementing the error term by the slope yields

$$e = -1/8 + 3/8 + 1/4$$

at the next raster point (2, 0). Here, e is positive which shows that the line passes above the midpoint. The raster element at the next higher vertical location (2, 1) better approximates the position of the line. Hence, y is incremented by one unit. Before considering the next pixel, it is necessary to reinitialize the error term. This is accomplished by subtracting one from it. Thus,

$$e = 1/4 - 1 = -3/4$$

Notice that the intercept of the vertical line at $x = 2$ and the desired line is $-1/4$ with respect to the line $y = 1$. Reinitializing to $-1/2$ relative to zero for the error term yields, as above, $-3/4$. Continuing to the next raster unit yields

$$e = -3/4 + 3/8 = -3/8$$

Since e is negative, the y value is not incremented. This discussion illustrates that the error term is a measure of the y intercept of the desired line at each raster element referenced to $-1/2$.

Bresenham's algorithm for the first octant, i.e., for $0 \leq \Delta y \leq \Delta x$ is given below.

Bresenham's line rasterization algorithm for the first octant

the line end points are (x_1, y_1) *and* (x_2, y_2) *assumed not equal*
Integer *is the integer function*
x, y, Δx, Δy *are assumed integer;* e *is real*

    initialize variables
    x = x₁
    y = y₁
    Δx = x₂ − x₁
    Δy = y₂ − y₁
    initialize e *to compensate for a nonzero intercept*

$$e = \Delta y/\Delta x - 1/2$$
begin the main loop
for i = 1 **to** Δx
    Plot(x, y)
    while (e $\geq$ 0)
        y = y + 1
        e = e $-$ 1
    end while
    x = x + 1
    e = e + $\Delta y/\Delta x$
next i
finish

A flowchart is given in Fig. 2-6. An example is given below.

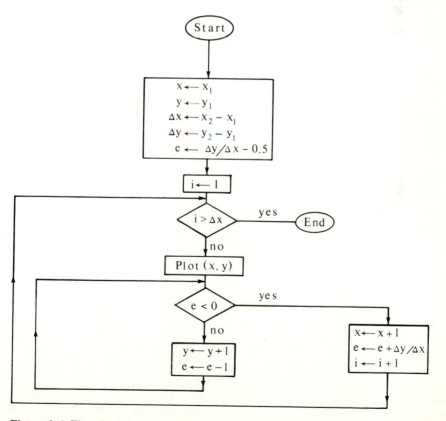

Figure 2-6 Flowchart for Bresenham's algorithm.

Example 2-3   Bresenham's Algorithm

Consider the line from (0, 0) to (5, 5). Rasterizing the line with the Bresenham algorithm yields

initial calculations

$$x = 0$$
$$y = 0$$
$$\Delta x = 5$$
$$\Delta y = 5$$
$$e = 1 - 1/2 = 1/2$$

incrementing through the main loop yields

i	Plot	e	x	y
		1/2	0	0
1	(0, 0)			
		−1/2	0	1
		1/2	1	1
2	(1, 1)			
		−1/2	1	2
		1/2	2	2
3	(2, 2)			
		−1/2	2	3
		1/2	3	3
4	(3, 3)			
		−1/2	3	4
		1/2	4	4
5	(4, 4)			
		−1/2	4	5
		1/2	5	5

The results are shown in Fig. 2-7 and are as expected. Note that the raster unit at (5, 5) is not activated. This raster unit may be activated by changing the **for-next** loop to 0 **to** Δx. The first raster unit at (0, 0) may be eliminated by moving the **Plot** statement to just before **next** i.

2-4   INTEGER BRESENHAM'S ALGORITHM

Bresenham's algorithm as presented above requires the use of floating point arithmetic and division to calculate the slope of the line and to evaluate the error term. The speed of the algorithm can be increased by using integer arithmetic and eliminating the division. Since only the sign of the error term is important, the simple transformation

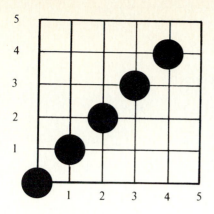

Figure 2-7 Results for Bresenham algorithm in the first octant.

$$\bar{e} = 2e\Delta x$$

of the error term in the previous algorithm yields an integer algorithm. This allows the algorithm to be efficiently implemented in hardware or firmware. The modified integer arithmetic algorithm for the first octant, i.e., for $0 \leq \Delta y \leq \Delta x$, is

> **Bresenham's integer algorithm** *for the first octant*
>
> *the line end points are* (x_1, y_1) *and* (x_2, y_2) *assumed not equal*
> *all variables are assumed integer*
>
> $x = x_1$
> $y = y_1$
> $\Delta x = x_2 - x_1$
> $\Delta y = y_2 - y_1$
>   *initialize* $\bar{e}$ *to compensate for a nonzero intercept*
> $\bar{e} = 2*\Delta y - \Delta x$
>   *begin the main loop*
>   **for** $i = 1$ to Δx
>   **Plot**(x, y)
>   **while** $(\bar{e} \geq 0)$
> $y = y + 1$
> $\bar{e} = \bar{e} - 2*\Delta x$
>   **end while**
> $x = x + 1$
> $\bar{e} = \bar{e} + 2*\Delta y$
>   **next** i
>   **finish**

The flowchart in Fig. 2-6 is applicable with appropriate changes in the calculation of the error term.

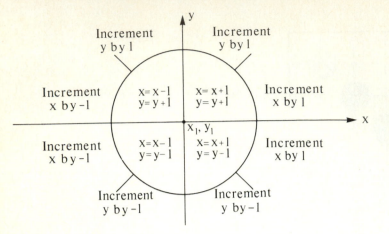

Figure 2-8 Conditions for general Bresenham's algorithm.

2-5 GENERAL BRESENHAM'S ALGORITHM

A full implementation of Bresenham's algorithm requires modification for lines lying in the other octants. These can easily be developed by considering the quadrant in which the line lies and its slope. When the absolute magnitude of the slope of the line is greater than 1, y is incremented by one and Bresenham's error criterion is used to determine when to increment x. Whether x or y is incremented by ± 1 depends on the quadrant. This is illustrated in Fig. 2-8. The general algorithm can be stated as

>*generalized integer Bresenham's algorithm for all quadrants*
>
>*the line end points are (x_1, y_1) and (x_2, y_2) assumed not equal*
>*all variables are assumed integer*
>*the **Sign** function returns $-1, 0, 1$ as its argument is $< 0, = 0,$ or > 0*
>
>>*initialize variables*
>>$x = x_1$
>>$y = y_1$
>>$\Delta x = abs(x_2 - x_1)$
>>$\Delta y = abs(y_2 - y_1)$
>>$s_1 = \textbf{Sign}(x_2 - x_1)$
>>$s_2 = \textbf{Sign}(y_2 - y_1)$
>>*interchange Δx and Δy depending on the slope of the line*
>>**if $\Delta y > \Delta x$ then**
>>>Temp $= \Delta x$
>>>$\Delta x = \Delta y$
>>>$\Delta y = $ Temp

```
            Interchange = 1
    else
            Interchange = 0
    end if
    initialize the error term to compensate for a nonzero intercept
    ē = 2*Δy − Δx
    main loop
    for i = 1 to Δx
        Plot(x, y)
        while (ē ≥ 0)
            if Interchange = 1 then
                x = x + s₁
            else
                y = y + s₂
            end if
            ē = ē − 2*Δx
        end while
        if Interchange = 1 then
            y = y + s₂
        else
            x = x + s₁
        end if
        ē = ē + 2*Δy
    next i
    finish
```

$$\bar{e} = 2*\Delta y - \Delta x$$

for $i = 1$ to Δx

while $(\bar{e} \geq 0)$

if Interchange $= 1$ then

$x = x + s_1$

else

$y = y + s_2$

end if

$\bar{e} = \bar{e} - 2*\Delta x$

end while

if Interchange $= 1$ then

$y = y + s_2$

else

$x = x + s_1$

end if

$\bar{e} = \bar{e} + 2*\Delta y$

Example 2-4   Generalized Bresenham's algorithm

To illustrate the general Bresenham algorithm consider the line from (0, 0) to (−8, −4). This line was previously considered in Example 2-2 using a simple DDA algorithm

initial calculations

$x = 0$
$y = 0$
$\Delta x = 8$
$\Delta y = 4$
$s_1 = -1$
$s_2 = -1$
Interchange $= 0$
$e = 0$

incrementing through the main loop

i	Plot	e	x	y
		0	0	0
1	(0, 0)			
		− 16	0	− 1
		− 8	− 1	− 1
2	(− 1, − 1)			
		0	− 2	− 1
3	(− 2, − 1)			
		− 16	− 2	− 2
		− 8	− 3	− 2
4	(− 3, − 2)			
		0	− 4	− 2
5	(− 4, − 2)			
		− 16	− 4	− 3
		− 8	− 5	− 3
6	(− 5, − 3)			
		0	− 6	− 3
7	(− 6, − 3)			
		− 16	− 6	− 4
		− 8	− 7	− 4
8	(− 7, − 4)			
		0	− 8	− 4

The results are shown in Fig. 2-9. Comparison with Fig. 2-3 shows that the results are different.

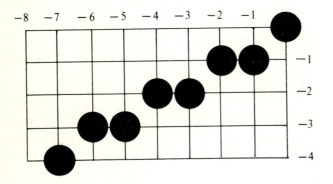

Figure 2-9 Results for Bresenham's general algorithm in the third quadrant.

2-6   CIRCLE GENERATION—BRESENHAM'S ALGORITHM

In addition to rasterizing straight lines it is necessary to rasterize other more complicated functions. Considerable attention has been given to conic sections, i.e., circles, ellipses, parabolas, hyperbolas (see Refs. 2-2 to 2-5). The circle

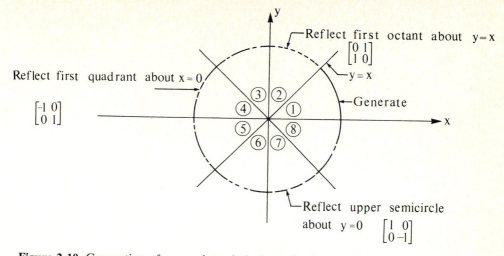

Figure 2-10 Generation of a complete circle from the first octant.

has of course received the greatest attention. (See also Refs. 2-6 to 2-9.) One of the most efficient and easiest to derive of the circle algorithms is due to Bresenham (Ref. 2-10). To begin, note that only one octant of the circle need be generated. The other parts can be obtained by successive reflections. This is illustrated in Fig. 2-10. If the first octant (0 to 45° ccw) is generated, the second octant can be obtained by reflection through the line $y = x$ to yield the first quadrant. The results in the first quadrant are reflected through the line $x = 0$ to obtain those in the second quadrant. The combined results in the upper semicircle are reflected through the line $y = 0$ to complete the circle. Figure 2-10 gives the appropriate two-dimensional reflection matrices.

To derive Bresenham's circle generation algorithm consider the first quadrant of an origin-centered circle. Notice that, if the algorithm begins at $x = 0$, $y = R$, then for clockwise generation of the circle y is a monotonically decreasing function of x in the first quadrant (see Fig. 2-11). Similarly, if the algorithm

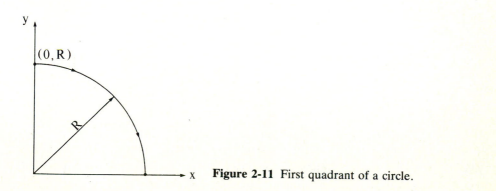

Figure 2-11 First quadrant of a circle.

begins at $y = 0$, $x = R$, then for counterclockwise generation of the circle x is a monotonically decreasing function of y. Here, clockwise generation starting at $x = 0$, $y = R$ is chosen. The center of the circle and the starting point are both assumed to be located precisely at pixel elements.

For any given point on the circle, then, for clockwise generation of the circle there are only three possible selections for the next pixel which best represents the circle: horizontally to the right, diagonally downward to the right, and vertically downward. These are labeled m_H, m_D, m_V, respectively, in Fig. 2-12. The algorithm chooses the pixel which minimizes the square of the distance between one of these pixels and the true circle, i.e. the minimum of

$$m_H = |(x_i + 1)^2 + (y_i)^2 - R^2|$$
$$m_D = |(x_i + 1)^2 + (y_i - 1)^2 - R^2|$$
$$m_V = |(x_i)^2 + (y_i - 1)^2 - R^2|$$

The calculations can be simplified by noting that there are only five possible types of intersections of the circle and the raster grid in the vicinity of the point (x_i, y_i). These are shown in Fig. 2-13.

The difference between the square of the distance from the center of the circle to the diagonal pixel at $(x_i + 1, y_i - 1)$ and the distance to a point on the circle R^2 is

$$\Delta_i = (x_i + 1)^2 + (y_i - 1)^2 - R^2$$

As with the Bresenham line rasterizing algorithm, it is desirable to use only the sign of an error term, rather than the magnitude, to select the appropriate pixel which best represents the actual circle.

If $\Delta_i < 0$, then the diagonal point $(x_i + 1, y_i - 1)$ is inside the actual circle, i.e. case 1 or 2 in Fig. 2-13. It is clear that either the pixel at $(x_i + 1, y_i)$, i.e. m_H, or that at $(x_i + 1, y_i - 1)$, i.e. m_D, must be chosen. To decide which, first consider case 1 by examining the difference between the squares of the distance

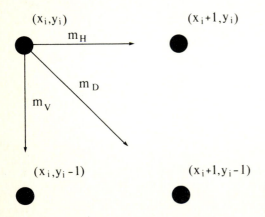

Figure 2-12 First quadrant pixel selections.

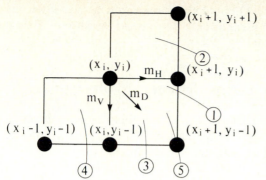

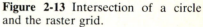

Figure 2-13 Intersection of a circle and the raster grid.

from the actual circle to the pixel at m_H and the distance from the actual circle to the pixel at m_D, i.e.

$$\delta = |(x_i + 1)^2 + (y_i)^2 - R^2| - |(x_i + 1)^2 + (y_i - 1)^2 - R^2|$$

If $\delta < 0$, then the distance from the actual circle to the diagonal pixel (m_D) is greater than that to the horizontal pixel (m_H). Conversely, if $\delta > 0$, then the distance to the horizontal pixel (m_H) is greater. Thus, if

$$\delta \leq 0 \quad \text{choose } m_H \text{ at } (x_i + 1, y_i)$$
$$\delta > 0 \quad \text{choose } m_D \text{ at } (x_i + 1, y_i - 1)$$

The horizontal move has been selected when $\delta = 0$, i.e., when the distances are equal.

The work involved in evaluating δ can be reduced by noting that for case 1

$$(x_i + 1)^2 + (y_i)^2 - R^2 \geq 0$$
$$(x_i + 1)^2 + (y_i - 1)^2 - R^2 < 0$$

because the diagonal pixel at $(x_i + 1, y_i - 1)$ is always inside the circle and the horizontal pixel at $(x_i + 1, y_i)$ is always outside the circle. Thus, δ may be evaluated as

$$\delta = (x_i + 1)^2 + (y_i)^2 - R^2 + (x_i + 1)^2 + (y_i - 1)^2 - R^2$$

Completing the square for the $(y_i)^2$ term by adding and subtracting $-2y_i + 1$ yields

$$\delta = 2\left[(x_i + 1)^2 + (y_i - 1)^2 - R^2\right] + 2y_i - 1$$

Using the definition for Δ_i gives

$$\delta = 2(\Delta_i + y_i) - 1$$

which is considerably simpler.

In considering case 2 of Fig. 2-13, note that, since y is a monotonically decreasing function, the horizontal pixel at $(x_i + 1, y_i)$ must be chosen. Examining the components of δ shows that

$$(x_i + 1) + (y_i)^2 - R^2 < 0$$
$$(x_i + 1) + (y_i - 1)^2 - R^2 < 0$$

since both the horizontal pixel at $(x_i + 1, y_i)$ and the diagonal pixel at $(x_i + 1, y_i - 1)$ lie inside the actual circle for case 2. Hence, $\delta < 0$ and the correct pixel at $(x_i + 1, y_i)$ is selected using the same criteria as in case 1.

If $\Delta_i > 0$, then the diagonal point $(x_i + 1, y_i - 1)$ is outside the actual circle, i.e. case 3 or 4 in Fig. 2-13. Here, it is clear that either the pixel at $(x_i + 1, y_i - 1)$, i.e. m_D, or that at $(x_i, y_i - 1)$, i.e. m_V, must be chosen. Again the decision criteria can be obtained by first considering case 3 and examining the difference between the squares of the distance from the actual circle to the diagonal pixel at m_D and the distance from the actual circle to the pixel at m_V, i.e.

$$\delta' = |(x_i + 1)^2 + (y_i - 1)^2 - R^2| - |(x_i)^2 + (y_i - 1)^2 - R^2|$$

If $\delta' < 0$, then the distance from the actual circle to the vertical pixel at $(x_i, y_i - 1)$ is greater and the diagonal move m_D to the pixel at $(x_i + 1, y_i - 1)$ should be chosen. Conversely, if $\delta' > 0$, then the distance from the actual circle to the diagonal pixel is greater and the vertical move to the pixel at $(x_i, y_i - 1)$ should be chosen, Thus, if

$$\delta' \leq 0 \quad \text{choose } m_D \text{ at } (x_i + 1, y_i - 1)$$
$$\delta' > 0 \quad \text{choose } m_V \text{ at } (x_i, y_i - 1)$$

Here the diagonal move has been selected when $\delta' = 0$, i.e., when the distances are equal.

Again examination of the components of δ' shows that

$$(x_i + 1)^2 + (y_i - 1)^2 - R^2 \geq 0$$
$$(x_i)^2 + (y_i - 1)^2 - R^2 < 0$$

since the diagonal pixel at $(x_i + 1, y_i - 1)$ is outside the actual circle while the vertical pixel at $(x_i, y_i - 1)$ is inside the actual circle for case 3. This allows δ' to be written as

$$\delta' = (x_i + 1)^2 + (y_i - 1)^2 - R^2 + (x_i)^2 + (y_i - 1)^2 - R^2$$

Completing the square for the $(x_i)^2$ term by adding and subtracting $2x_i + 1$ yields

$$\delta' = 2\left[(x_i + 1)^2 + (y_i - 1)^2 - R^2\right] - 2x_i - 1$$

Using the definition of Δ_i then gives

$$\delta' = 2(\Delta_i - x_i) - 1$$

Now, considering case 4, again note that, since y is a monotonically decreasing function as x monotonically increases, the vertical pixel at $(x_i, y_i - 1)$ must be selected. Examining the components of δ' for case 4 shows that

$$(x_i + 1)^2 + (y_i - 1)^2 - R^2 > 0$$
$$(x_i)^2 + (y_i - 1)^2 - R^2 > 0$$

since both the vertical and diagonal pixels are outside the actual circle. Hence, $\delta' > 0$ and the correct choice of m_V is selected using the same criteria developed for case 3.

It remains only to examine case 5 of Fig. 2-13, which occurs when the diagonal pixel at $(x_i + 1, y_i - 1)$ lies on the actual circle, i.e., for $\Delta_i = 0$. Examining the components of δ shows that

$$(x_i + 1)^2 + (y_i)^2 - R^2 > 0$$
$$(x_i + 1)^2 + (y_i - 1)^2 - R^2 = 0$$

Hence, $\delta > 0$ and the diagonal pixel at $(x_i + 1, y_i - 1)$ is selected. Similarly the components of δ' are

$$(x_i + 1)^2 + (y_i - 1)^2 - R^2 = 0$$
$$(x_i)^2 + (y_i - 1)^2 - R^2 < 0$$

and $\delta' < 0$ which is the condition for selecting the correct diagonal move to $(x_i + 1, y_i - 1)$. Thus, the case of $\Delta_i = 0$ is satisfied by the same criteria as for $\Delta_i < 0$ or for $\Delta_i > 0$.

Summarizing the results above yields

$\Delta_i < 0$		
$\delta \leq 0$	choose the pixel at $(x_i + 1, y_i)$ →	m_H
$\delta > 0$	choose the pixel at $(x_i + 1, y_i - 1)$ →	m_D
$\Delta_i > 0$		
$\delta' > 0$	choose the pixel at $(x_i + 1, y_i - 1)$ →	m_D
$\delta' > 0$	choose the pixel at $(x_i, y_i - 1)$ →	m_V
$\Delta_i = 0$	choose the pixel at $(x_i + 1, y_i - 1)$ →	m_D

Simple recursion relationships which yield an incremental implementation of the algorithm are easily developed. First, consider the horizontal movement m_H to the pixel at $(x_i + 1, y_i)$. Call this next pixel location $(i+1)$. The coordinates of the new pixel and the value of Δ_i are then

$$x_{i+1} = x_i + 1$$
$$y_{i+1} = y_i$$
$$\Delta_{i+1} = (x_{i+1} + 1)^2 + (y_{i+1} - 1)^2 - R^2$$

$$= (x_{i+1})^2 + 2x_{i+1} + 1 + (y_i - 1)^2 - R^2$$
$$= (x_i + 1)^2 + (y_i - 1)^2 - R^2 + 2x_{i+1} + 1$$
$$= \Delta_i + 2x_{i+1} + 1$$

Similarly the coordinates of the new pixel and the value of Δ_i for the move m_D to $(x_i + 1, y_i - 1)$ are

$$x_{i+1} = x_i + 1$$
$$y_{i+1} = y_i - 1$$
$$\Delta_{i+1} = \Delta_i + 2x_{i+1} - 2y_{i+1} + 2$$

Those for the move m_V to $(x_i, y_i - 1)$ are

$$x_{i+1} = x_i$$
$$y_{i+1} = y_i - 1$$
$$\Delta_{i+1} = \Delta_i - 2y_{i+1} + 1$$

A pseudo implementation of the Bresenham circle algorithm is given below.

Bresenham's incremental circle algorithm *for the first quadrant*

all variables are assumed integer

```
        initialize the variables
        xi = 0
        yi = R
        Δi = 2(1 − R)
        Limit = 0
1       Plot(xi, yi)
        if yi ≤ Limit then 4
        determine the case 1 or 2, 4 or 5, or 3
        if Δi < 0 then 2
        if Δi > 0 then 3
        if Δi = 0 then 20
        determine whether case 1 or 2
2       δ = 2Δi + 2yi − 1
        if δ ≤ 0 then 10
        if δ > 0 then 20
        determine whether case 4 or 5
3       δ' = 2Δi − 2xi − 1
        if δ' ≤ 0 then 20
        if δ' > 0 then 30
        perform the moves
        move mH
10      xi = xi + 1
        Δi = Δi + 2xi + 1
```

go to 1

move m_D

20    $x_i = x_i + 1$

     $y_i = y_i - 1$

     $\Delta_i = \Delta_i + 2x_i - 2y_i + 2$

go to 1

move m_V

30    $y_i = y_i - 1$

     $\Delta_i = \Delta_i - 2y_i + 1$

go to 1

4   **finish**

The limit variable is set to zero to terminate the algorithm at the horizontal axis. This yields the circle in the first quadrant. If only a single octant is desired, then setting Limit = Integer $(R/\sqrt{2})$ will yield the second octant (see Fig. 2-10). Reflection about $y = x$ will then yield the first quadrant. A flowchart is given in Fig. 2-14.

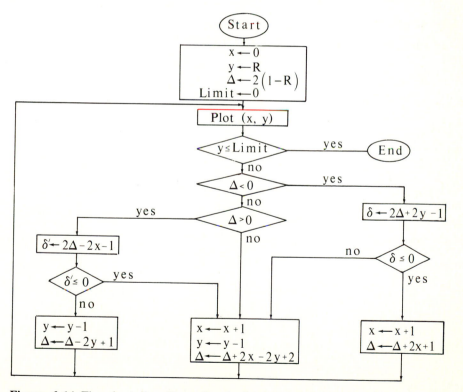

Figure 2-14 Flowchart for Bresenham's incremental circle algorithm in the first quadrant.

Example 2-5 Bresenham's Circle Algorithm

To illustrate the circle generation algorithm, consider the origin-centered circle of radius 8. Only the first quadrant is generated.

initial calculations

$$x = 0$$
$$y = 8$$
$$\Delta_i = 2(1 - 8) = -14$$
$$\text{Limit} = 0$$

incrementing through the main loop

    1   **Plot**(0, 8)
       $y_i >$ Limit   continue
       $\Delta_i < 0$ **go to 2**
    2   $\delta = 2(-14) + 2(8) - 1 = -13 < 0$ **go to 10**
  10 $x = 0 + 1 = 1$
       $\Delta_i = -14 + 2 + 1 = -11$
       go to 1
    1   **Plot**(1, 8)
       $y_i >$ Limit   continue
       $\Delta_i < 0$ **go to 2**
    2   $\delta = 2(-11) + 2(8) - 1 = -7 < 0$ **go to 10**
  10 $x = 1 + 1 = 2$
       $\Delta_i = -11 + 2(2) + 1 = -6$
       go to 1
    1   **Plot**(2, 8)

        .

        .

        .

       continue

The details of each successive pass through the algorithm are summarized in the table below. The list of pixels selected by the algorithm is (0, 8), (1, 8), (2, 8), (3, 7), (4, 7), (5, 6), (6, 5), (7, 4), (7, 3), (8, 2), (8, 1), (8, 0)

Plot	Δ_i	δ	δ'	x	y
	-14			0	8
(0, 8)					
	-11	-13		1	8
(1, 8)					
	-6	-7		2	8
(2, 8)					
	-12	3		3	7
(3, 7)					
	-3	-11		4	7
(4, 7)					
	-3	7		5	6

(5, 6)				
	1	5	6	5
(6, 5)				
	9	−11	7	4
(7, 4)				
	4	3	7	3
(7, 3)				
	18	−7	8	2
(8, 2)				
	17	19	8	1
(8, 1)				
	18	17	8	0
(8, 0)				
	complete			

The results are shown in Fig. 2-15 along with the actual circle. The algorithm is easily generalized for other quadrants or for circular arcs.

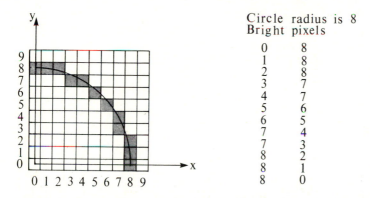

Figure 2-15 Results for Bresenham's incremental circle generation algorithm.

2-7 SCAN CONVERSION—GENERATION OF THE DISPLAY

In order to display the rasterized image using video technology it is necessary to organize the picture into the precise pattern required by the video display (see Sec. 1-8). This is the process called scan conversion. In contrast to the display list for a random scan or line drawing display (see Sec. 1-4) which contains only information about lines or characters, here the display list must contain information about every pixel on the screen. Further, it is necessary that this information be organized and presented at video rates in scan line order, that is, from the top to the bottom and from left to right. Four ways of accomplishing this are real-time scan conversion, run-length encoding, cell organization, and frame buffer memory.

2-8   REAL-TIME SCAN CONVERSION

In real-time or on-the-fly scan conversion the picture is randomly represented in terms of visual attributes and geometric properties. Typical visual attributes are color, shade, and intensity, while x, y coordinates, slopes, and text are typical geometric properties. These geometric properties are ordered in y. The processor scans through this information and calculates the intensity of every pixel on the screen during the presentation of each frame. With real-time scan conversion large amounts of memory are unnecessary. Memory requirements are usually limited to that necessary to hold the display list plus one scan line. Further, since picture information is held in a randomly organized display list, it is easy to add or delete information from the list. This greatly facilitates dynamic presentations. However, the complexity of the display is limited by the speed of the display processor. This usually means that the number of lines or polygons in the picture, the number of intersections on a scan line, or the number of gray scales or colors is limited.

The simplest implementation for real-time scan conversion processes the entire display list to obtain the intersections (if any) of each line in the display list with a particular scan line each time a scan line is displayed. At video refresh rates only 63.5 microseconds is available to process the entire display list each time a scan line is displayed. This short time precludes using this technique for more than the simplest line drawing display. Since, in general, not every line in a picture will intersect every scan line, the amount of work required can be reduced by maintaining an active edge list. The active edge list contains those lines in the picture which intersect the scan line.

The active edge list can be developed and maintained using a number of techniques. The lines in the picture are first sorted by the largest value of y. A particularly simple technique uses two floating pointers into this sorted list. A begin pointer is used to indicate the beginning of the active edge list, and an end pointer to indicate the end of the active edge list. A single line drawing along with three typical scan lines is shown in Fig. 2-16a. Figure 2-16b shows a typical sorted list of the lines in the figure. The begin pointer is initially set at the beginning of the list, i.e. at *BC*. The end pointer is set at the last line in the list that begins *above* the scan line under consideration, i.e. at *BD*. As the scan moves down the picture the end pointer is moved down to include those new lines which now start on or above the current scan line. At the same time the begin pointer is moved down to eliminate lines which end above the current scan line. This is illustrated in Fig. 2-16b for the scan lines labeled 2 and 3 in Fig. 2-16a. Figures 2-16c and d illustrate a problem with this simple algorithm. The sort order of the lines which begin at the same y value influences the size of the active edge list. For example, in Fig. 2-16d the line *BC* never drops off the active edge list. Thus, more information than necessary may be processed.

These and similar problems may be eliminated at the expense of additional data structure. Further, the calculation of the intersection of each line in the

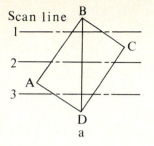

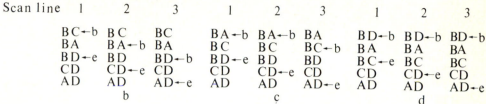

Figure 2-16 A simple active edge list.

picture with individual scan lines may be simplified. First, a y-bucket sort of all the lines in the picture is performed. A y-bucket sort,[†] illustrated in Fig. 2-17b, simply creates a storage location or bucket for each scan line. If, for example, there are 512 scan lines, then 512 buckets are used. As the lines in the display list are examined, information about each line is placed in the bucket corresponding to the largest y value of the line. For simple black-and-white line drawings only the x intercept on the bucket scan line, Δx the change in the x intercept from scan line to scan line, and Δy the number of scan lines crossed by the line need be recorded. For simple pictures most of the y buckets will be empty.

The active edge list for the current scan line is formed by adding information from the y bucket corresponding to that scan line. The x intercepts are sorted into scan line order, and the active edge list scan-converted. After the active edge list is scan-converted, Δy for each line on the active edge list is decremented by one. If $\Delta y < 0$, the line is dropped from the active edge list. Finally, the x intercepts for the new scan line are obtained by adding Δx to the previous values for each line on the active edge list. The process is repeated for all scan lines. The active edge list for scan lines 3, 5, and 7 for the simple line drawing of Fig. 2-17a is given in Fig. 2-17c.

If a fixed y-bucket size is used, a fixed amount of storage is available for intersections on each scan line. Thus, the maximum number of intersections on any given scan line is predetermined. Hence, the complexity of the picture is limited. One technique for avoiding this limit is to use a sequential indexed list

---

[†]A bucket sort is a form of radix sort with the radix equal to the number of buckets (scan lines). See Knuth, Ref. 2-11.

Scan line

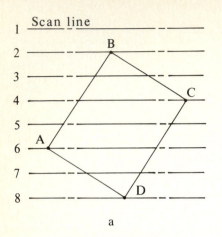

a

y-bucket

1	null
2	$x_{BA}, \Delta x_{BA}, \Delta y_{BA},$
	$x_{BC}, \Delta x_{BC}, \Delta y_{BC}$
3	null
4	$x_{CD}, \Delta x_{CD}, \Delta y_{CD}$
5	null
6	$x_{AD}, \Delta x_{AD}, \Delta y_{AD}$
7	null
8	null

b

Active Edge List

Scan line 3: $x_{BA} + \Delta x_{BA}, \Delta x_{BA},$
$\Delta y_{BA} - 1, x_{BC} + \Delta x_{BC},$
$\Delta x_{BC}, \Delta y_{BC} - 1$

Scan line 5: $x_{BA} + 3\Delta x_{BA}, \Delta x_{BA},$
$\Delta y_{BA} - 3, x_{CD} + \Delta x_{CD},$
$\Delta x_{CD}, \Delta y_{CD} - 1$

Scan line 7: $x_{CD} + 3\Delta x_{CD}, \Delta x_{CD},$
$\Delta y_{CD} - 3, x_{AD} + \Delta x_{AD},$
$\Delta x_{AD}, \Delta y_{AD} - 1$

c

		=	Completion or null. End of scan line.

y-bucket

1		
2	1	
3		
4	8	
5		
6	12	
7		
8		

Indexed List

1	x_{BA}
2	Δx_{BA}
3	Δy_{BA}
4	x_{BC}
5	Δx_{BC}
6	Δy_{BC}
7	
8	x_{CD}
9	Δx_{CD}
10	Δy_{CD}
11	
12	x_{AD}
13	Δx_{AD}
14	Δy_{AD}
15	

d

Figure 2-17 A y-bucket sort, active edge list, and sequential indexed data structure.

for the data structure. In this case, each y bucket contains only a pointer to the location in the data structure of the information for the first line originating on that scan line. The sequential indexed list and the data structure for Fig. 2-17a are shown in Fig. 2-17d. For the particular data structure shown, it is assumed that data for a given scan line are accessed in groups of three until a null or completion is indicated.

The technique for determining line intersections with individual scan lines yields acceptable results for vertical and near vertical lines. However, for nearly horizontal lines very few intersection points will be calculated. This will yield an unacceptable line representation. A simple solution is to determine the intersections on two successive scan lines and activate all the pixels between the intersections. This is shown in Fig. 2-18. For horizontal line segments the end points are used.

Since the entire picture is processed for each video frame, real-time scan conversion lends itself to highly interactive graphics. When a y-bucket sort is used, lines can be added to or deleted from the display list by simply adding or deleting them from the appropriate y bucket and the associated data structure. This is easiest for fixed-length y buckets as shown above in Fig. 2-17b. In order to conveniently add and delete lines to the display, a linked list data structure is used. This is shown in Fig. 2-19. Note that in the linked list shown in Fig. 2-19b the end of each data group and the location of the next data group on that scan line, e.g. item 4, as well as the completion of the link, are required. If the line BD is now added to the figure, the linked list is modified as shown in Fig. 2-19d. The information about the line BD is added at the end of the data list. The display processor is directed to this location by the modified link instruction at location 8. If the line BC is now deleted from the figure, the linked list is modified as shown in Fig. 2-19f. Here, notice that the link instruction at location 4 has been modified to jump around the locations containing information about the line BC.

This simple example illustrates the basic concepts for modifying a linked list for interactive graphics applications. However, it does not illustrate all the

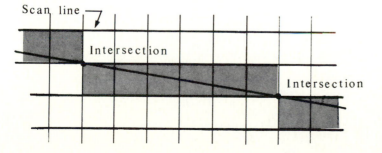

Figure 2-18 A simple scan conversion technique for nearly horizontal lines.

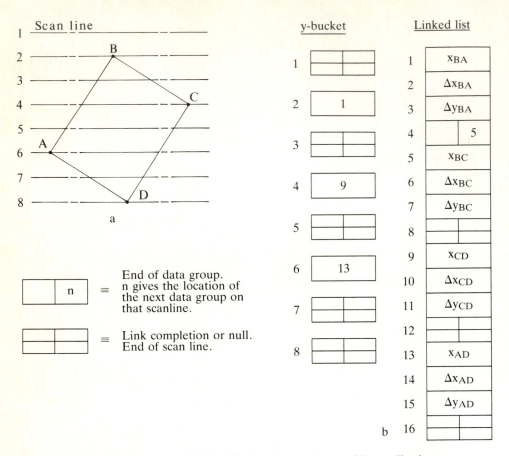

Figure 2-19 A *y*-bucket sort and linked list for interactive graphics applications.

required features. For example, it should be obvious that as illustrated the length of the list will continuously grow unless the "lost" locations (5 to 8 in Fig. 2-19f) are reused or the list is compressed. For further discussion of linked lists and data structures see, for example, Ref. 2-12.

Because of the difficulty of accomplishing the above algorithm in software in the short time available for one video frame, successful software implementations have been used principally for aircraft flight, ship navigation, and similar simulation systems.

2-9 RUN-LENGTH ENCODING

Run-length encoding seeks to take advantage of the fact that large areas of the picture have the same intensity or color. In its simplest form run-length encoding specifies only an intensity and the number of successive pixels on a

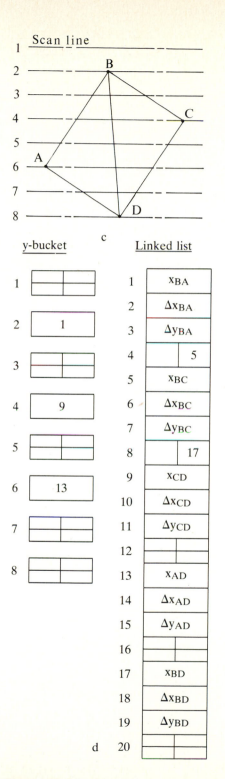

c

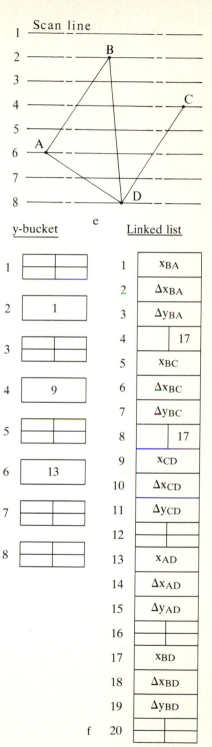

e

Figure 2-19 (Continued.)

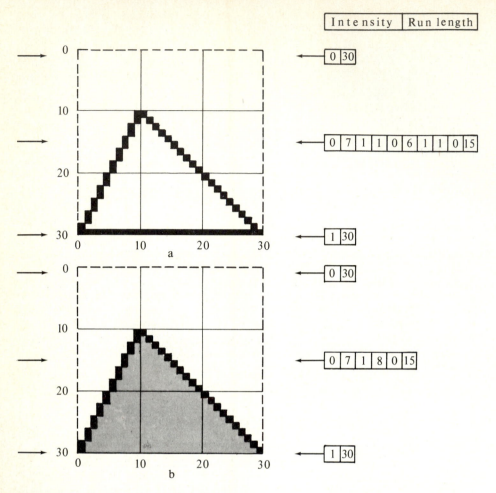

Figure 2-20 Run-length-encoded pictures.

given scan line with that intensity. Figure 2-20a shows a simple black-and-white line drawing on a 30 × 30 raster and the associated encoding for scan lines 1, 15, and 30. The encoded data is to be considered in groups of two. The first number is the intensity, and the second is the number of successive pixels on that scan line with that intensity

Intensity	Run Length

Thus, in Fig. 2-20a scan line 1 has 30 pixels of zero intensity, i.e., black or the background intensity. The complete picture can be encoded with 208 numbers. Pixel-by-pixel storage, i.e., one piece of information for each pixel (a bit map), would require 900 intensity values for the 30 × 30 raster of Fig. 2-20a. The data compression using run-length encoding in this case is 4.33:1.

Solid figures are easily handled with run-length encoding. This is shown in Fig. 2-20b along with the encoding for scan lines 1, 15 and 30. Of particular interest is scan line 15. For Fig. 2-20b the entire picture can be encoded using 136 numbers for a data compression of 6.62:1. Pictures with solid figures encode with fewer pieces of information than line or wire frame drawings because two edges are covered with one pair of intensity-length values.

This simple run-length encoding scheme can easily be extended to include color. For color, the intensity of each of the red, green, and blue color guns is given followed by the number of successive pixels for that color on that scan line, e.g.

Red Intensity	Green Intensity	Blue Intensity	Run Length

For a simple color display in which each individual color gun is either completely off (0) or fully on (1), the encoding for scan line 15 of Fig. 2-20b with a yellow triangle on a blue background is (see Table 1-1)

0	0	1	7	1	1	0	8	0	0	1	15

Data compression for run-length-encoded pictures can approach 10:1. This is significant not only because it saves memory but also because it saves storage space for computer-generated animated sequences or film. It also saves transmission time for wire photos and facsimile where run-length encoding is extensively used. For example, consider the storage requirements for a $512 \times 512 \times 8$ resolution picture for a 30-second animated film sequence at video rates (30 frames per second). The storage requirement is

$$(512 \times 512 \times 8 \times 30 \times 30)/(8 \text{ bits/byte}) = 236 \text{ megabytes}$$

This will fit only on the largest disk units. However, even a modest run-length encoding data compression of 4:1 will allow storage on a single small to medium-sized disk.

Run-length encoding has disadvantages. Since the run lengths are stored sequentially, adding or deleting lines or text from the picture is difficult and time-consuming. There is overhead involved with both encoding and decoding the picture. Finally the storage requirement can approach twice that for pixel-by-pixel storage for short runs. This is illustrated in Fig. 2-21 where the picture consists of alternate black and white vertical lines one pixel wide. Here the run-length encoding is

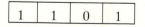

1	1	0	1

repeated 15 times. Thus, a total of 1800 values must be stored for the run-length-encoded picture in contrast to 900 for pixel-by-pixel storage. This is a data compression of 1/2.

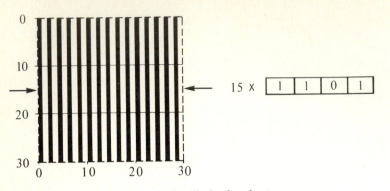

Figure 2-21 Run-length encoding limits for short runs.

Laws (Ref. 2-13) and Hartke, Sterling, and Shemer (Ref. 2-14) discuss efficient implementation of run-length encoding schemes.

2-10 CELL ENCODING

Run-length encoding considers the picture linearly or one-dimensionally. Cell encoding seeks to represent areas of the picture, i.e. cells, with a minimum of information. The simplest alphanumeric CRT terminal uses cell encoding to allow real-time operation. In such a terminal the screen area is divided into cells or areas large enough to contain one character. For example, the screen may be divided into areas containing 8 × 8 pixels. This yields 64 × 64 cells for a 512 × 512 display or 60 × 80 cells for a 480 × 640 video compatible display with a standard 4:3 aspect ratio. A cell of 8 × 8 pixels is usually used for a 5 × 7 dot matrix character display. The extra pixels are used for spacing between characters and for lower case characters with descenders. An example is shown in Fig. 2-22. Since every other row of cells is left blank for readability, the

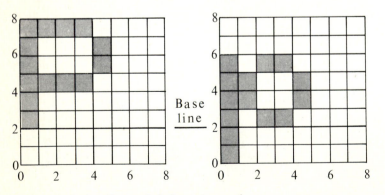

Figure 2-22 A cell-encoded character mask.

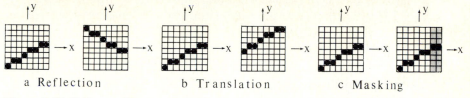

a Reflection   b Translation   c Masking

Figure 2-23 Cell encoding.

latter configuration yields the 30 lines of 80 characters each typical of many alphanumeric displays. Other cell sizes are also used. For example, a cell containing 8×10 pixels, typically used for 7×9 dot matrix characters, yields an alphanumeric display with 24 lines of 80 characters each. The pixel patterns for each character are stored in read-only memory.

The cell encoding technique can be extended to include line drawings by also storing line segment patterns in read-only memory. Combinations of these segments in adjacent cells can then be used to construct complete lines. For any $n \times n$ cell there are 2^{n^2} possible pixel patterns. For any reasonable value of n this is far too many patterns to store; e.g., if $n = 8$, then $2^{n^2} = 1.8 \times 10^{19}$. However, not all patterns represent possible line segments. For example, Bresenham's algorithm discussed above shows that for lines with slope between 0 and 1 there are at most $2^n - 1$ patterns which represent line segments. Finally, Jordan and Barrett (Ref. 2-15) have shown that by using translation, reflection, and masking techniques only 108 line segment patterns are required for an 8×8 cell.

Figure 2-23 illustrates a line segment starting at the lower left hand corner of an 8×8 cell. The line was rasterized using Bresenham's algorithm. The line has a positive slope. Reflection about the x axis (Fig. 2-23a) yields a line of negative slope starting at the upper left hand corner. Translation vertically in y yields a line starting above the base of the cell (Fig. 2-23b). Translating both in x and y yields a line starting in the interior of the cell. Masking off a portion of a line as shown in Fig. 2-23c provides for the short segments at the end of a line. In order to allow intersecting lines within a cell, provision is made for combining cell patterns using a logical OR operator. Successive application of this operation allows an infinite variety of intersection patterns. This is shown in Fig. 2-24.

Interacting with a cell-encoded display is discussed by Barrett and Jordan (Ref. 2-16). Interaction is most efficient when a linked list is used to maintain the top-to-bottom, left-to-right ordering of the display file. However, the level of interaction possible is not high.

Figure 2-24 Logical OR combinations of cell-encoded line segments.

Cell encoding has been extended to color displays and to solid image representations (Ref. 2-17). However, data compression rates are not as great as for black-and-white (bilevel) displays.

2-11 FRAME BUFFERS

In introducing raster refresh graphic displays in Chap. 1 the tacit assumption was made that the raster display was implemented as a frame buffer. It was further assumed that the frame buffer consisted of random access semiconductor memory. Although this is the most common method of implementing a frame buffer, rotating memory, either disk or drum, can also be used (see Refs. 2-18 and 2-19).

Frame buffers have also been implemented using shift registers (see Ref. 2-20). A shift register can conceptually be considered as a first in, first out (FIFO) stack. If the stack is full, then as new data bits are added to the top of the stack the first data bits are pushed out the bottom. The data pushed out of the stack can be interpreted as the intensity of a pixel on a scan line. Shift register frame buffers can be implemented using one shift register per pixel on a scan line with each shift register as long as the number of scan lines. In this case each shift register contributes one pixel on a horizontal scan line. Alternately, they can be implemented as a single large shift register of length equal to the number of pixels on a scan line times the number of scan lines.

Figure 2-25 shows a simple six-line display with eight pixels per scan line. A shift register frame buffer is also shown. The frame buffer is implemented with eight shift registers each 6 bits long. The bit pattern for the display is shown in the frame buffer. The pattern for the scan line labeled 3 in the display is shown about to be pushed out of the bottom of the shift registers. The sequencing of

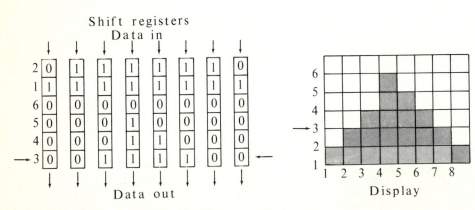

Figure 2-25 Shift register frame buffer.

Host CPU	Update process	Frame buffer	Refresh process	Display controller		Video monitor

Figure 2-26 Frame buffer graphics system.

the output of the shift registers must be carefully controlled to correspond to the video scan rate.

Both rotating memory and shift register frame buffer implementations exhibit low levels of interactivity. For rotating memory implementations this is because of disk access time. For shift register implementations reduced interactivity occurs because changes can only be made as bits are being added to the register.

Conceptually the configuration of a frame buffer graphics system is similar to that for a line drawing refresh display as shown in Fig. 2-26. An application program running in the host computer updates the frame buffer as needed. The display controller cycles through the frame buffer in scan line order and passes the required information to the video monitor to refresh the display. The frame buffer can be implemented either as part of the host computer memory or as a separate memory. These configurations are shown in Fig. 2-27 imple-

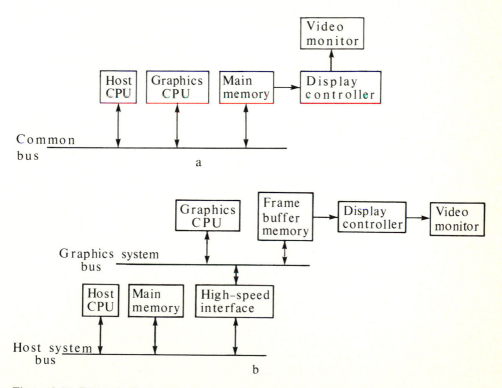

Figure 2-27 Frame buffer architecture.

mented with a common bus structure. Although implementing the frame buffer in the main memory (see Fig. 2-27a) makes it possible to manipulate the buffer with the host processor, it is generally more efficient to add a special-purpose graphics processor to the system. The graphics processor handles the detailed manipulation of the frame buffer upon receipt of commands from the main processor. With a single memory and two processors on a common bus, bus contention can occur. This reduces the overall system performance. Thus, for high-performance systems the architecture shown in Fig. 2-27b is generally preferred. Here, the frame buffer memory is separate from the main memory, which eliminates bus contention. Further, the graphics subsystem can be optimized to meet the update requirements of the frame buffer and hence increase system performance.

2-12   ADDRESSING THE RASTER

It is conceptually easiest to consider a pixel in a raster or frame buffer to have two-dimensional coordinates x, y as shown in Fig. 2-28. Digital memory is, however, arranged as a single linear list of addresses. Thus, it is necessary to convert from the two-dimensional x, y representation to the linear list. Assuming that the starting address in memory is not zero then the conversion is given by

$$\text{Address} = (x_{\max} - x_{\min})(y - y_{\min}) + (x - x_{\min}) + \text{base address}$$

The first term counts the number of rows. The second term adds the location in the row, and the final term adds the starting address. The pixel is identified by its lower left hand corner coordinates.

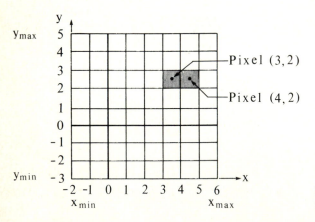

Figure 2-28 Raster coordinate system.

Example 2-6 Addressing the Raster

Consider the pixel at location (3, 2) in the small raster shown in Fig. 2-28. Here, $x_{max} = 6$, $x_{min} = -2$, $y_{max} = 5$, and $y_{min} = -3$, with the first pixel in the lower left hand corner stored in the first memory location; the base or starting address is 1. Hence, the memory address is

$$\begin{aligned}
\text{Address} &= [6 - (-2)][2 - (-3)] + [3 - (-2)] + 1 \\
&= (8)(5) + 5 + 1 \\
&= 40 + 6 \\
&= 46
\end{aligned}$$

This can be checked by counting the squares.

The scheme also works for x positive to the right and y positive downward provided the pixel is addressed by the coordinates of its upper left hand corner.

For a given frame buffer x_{max}, x_{min}, y_{min} and the base address are normally constant. The equation can thus be rewritten as

$$\text{Address} = K_1 + K_2 y + x$$

where

$$K_1 = \text{base address} - K_2 y_{min} - x_{min}$$
$$K_2 = x_{max} - x_{min}$$

Hence, calculating the pixel address in frame buffer memory requires only two adds and a multiply. When pixels are addressed successively, incremental calculations can be used to further reduce the work involved in determining the pixel address. In particular,

$$\begin{aligned}
\text{Address}(x \pm 1, y) &= K_1 + K_2 y + x \pm 1 \\
&= \text{Address}(x, y) \pm 1 \\
\text{Address}(x, y \pm 1) &= K_1 + K_2(y \pm 1) + x \\
&= \text{Address}(x, y) \pm K_2 \\
\text{Address}(x \pm 1, y \pm 1) &= K_1 + K_2(y \pm 1) + x \pm 1 \\
&= \text{Address}(x, y) \pm K_2 \pm 1
\end{aligned}$$

Here, only a single add or subtract is needed for either horizontal or vertical increments in the raster, and only two adds or subtracts for diagonal increments. The multiply is eliminated.

Example 2-7 Incrementally Addressing the Raster

Consider the pixel located at (4, 2) in the raster shown in Fig. 2-28. Here

$$K_2 = 6 - (-2) = 8$$
$$K_1 = 1 - (8)(-3) - (-2) = 27$$

and

$$\text{Address} = 27 + (8)(2) + 4 = 47$$

Recalling the result for the pixel at (3, 2) from the previous example and using the incremental calculation yields

$$\text{Address}(x + 1, \ y) = \text{Address}(x, y) + 1$$
$$\text{Address}(4, 2) \qquad = 46 + 1 = 47$$

2-13   LINE DISPLAY

Addressing the frame buffer in this way allows it to conceptually be treated similar to a storage tube graphics display. The frame buffer is first cleared or set to the background intensity or color. Instead of writing vectors directly to the display screen, either the Bresenham or the DDA algorithm is used to rasterize the line and the appropriate pixels are written to the frame buffer. When the picture or frame is complete, the display controller reads the frame buffer in scan line order and presents the result to the video monitor.

Selective erase of lines can be implemented by again using the rasterizing algorithm to write the appropriate pixels to the frame buffer in the background intensity or color. This eliminates the line. However, Fig. 2-29 illustrates a problem with this technique. If the erased line crosses another line, then a hole will be left in that line. Figure 2-29a shows two intersecting lines. If the

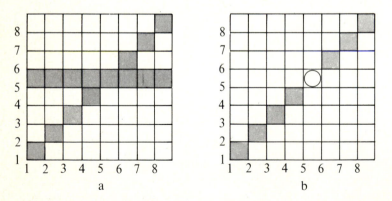

Figure 2-29 Selective erase of lines in a frame buffer.

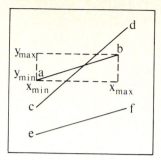

Figure 2-30 Boxing or minimax tests.

horizontal line at $y = 5$ is erased by writing the background intensity or color to the frame buffer, then a hole in the remaining line at pixel (5, 5) results. It is not difficult to detect these holes and fill them. It is only necessary to determine the intersection of the deleted line with all other lines in the picture. For a complex picture this can be time-consuming.

Boxing or minimax tests can be used to reduce the work required. This technique is shown in Fig. 2-30. Only lines which pass through the dotted box formed from the minimum and maximum values of x and y for the line segment ab can possibly intersect ab. The tests for each line segment are then

minimax or boxing test

    if (Xlinemax < Xboxmin) **or**
       (Xlinemin > Xboxmax) **or**
       (Ylinemax < Yboxmin) **or**
       (Ylinemin > Yboxmax)
    then
       no intersection
    else
       calculate intersection
    finish

2-14 CHARACTER DISPLAY

Alphanumeric characters are written to the frame buffer using a mask. A character mask is a small raster which contains the relative locations of the pixels used to represent the character (see Fig. 2-22). Special symbols unique to a particular application, e.g., resistors, capacitors, or mathematical symbols, can also be represented with a character mask. The mask itself simply contains binary values indicating whether or not a particular pixel in the mask is used to represent the character or symbol shape. For simple black-and-white displays a 1 normally indicates that a pixel is used in the representation, and a 0 that it is not. For color displays additional bits are used to provide multiple color shades directly or as indices to a color look-up table.

The character may be inserted into the frame buffer by indicating the location in the frame buffer (x_0, y_0) of the origin of the mask. Then each pixel in the mask is displaced by the amount x_0, y_0. A simple algorithm to accomplish this for a binary mask is

Mask insertion *into the frame buffer*

$\text{Xmin}, \text{Xmax}, \text{Ymin}, \text{Ymax}$ *are the limits of the mask*
x_0, y_0 *is the location in the frame buffer*

> **for** j = Ymin **to** Ymax $- 1$
>> **for** i = Xmin **to** Xmax $- 1$
>>> **if** Mask$(i, j) <> 0$ **then**
>>>> write Mask(i, j) to the frame buffer at $(x_0 + i, y_0 + j)$
>>> **else**
>>> **end if**
>> **next** i
> **next** j
> **finish**

A character in the frame buffer can be erased by rewriting it to the frame buffer using the background intensity or color.

The character mask can be modified as it is written to the frame buffer to produce alternate character styles or orientations. Some simple modifications are shown in Fig. 2-31. Figure 2-31a shows the original character mask. By writing the mask to two successive frame buffer locations x_0 and $x_0 + 1$ a bold-faced character is obtained. This is shown in Fig. 2-31b. The character can be rotated as shown in Fig. 2-31c or skewed to give the appearance of italics as shown in Fig. 2-31d.

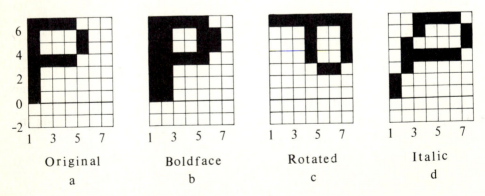

Original   Boldface   Rotated   Italic
a   b   c   d

Figure 2-31 Transformed character masks.

2-15   SOLID AREA SCAN CONVERSION

So far the discussion has been concerned with the presentation of lines on a raster scan device. However, one of the unique characteristics of a raster scan device is the ability to present solid areas. The generation of solid areas from simple edge or vertex descriptions is called solid area scan conversion, polygon filling, or contour filling. Several techniques can be used to fill a contour. They generally divide into two broad categories: scan conversion and seed fill.

Scan conversion techniques attempt to determine, in scan line order, whether or not a point is inside a polygon or contour. These algorithms generally proceed from the "top" of the polygon or contour to the "bottom." The scan conversion techniques are equally applicable to line drawing displays. With line drawing displays they are used for cross-hatching or shading of contours as shown in Fig. 2-32.

Seed fill techniques assume that some point inside the closed contour is known. The algorithms then proceed to search for points adjacent to the seed point that are inside the contour. If the adjacent point is not inside the contour, then a boundary of the contour has been found. If the adjacent point is inside the contour, then it becomes a new seed point and the search continues recursively. Seed fill algorithms are only applicable to raster devices.

Figure 2-32 Contour cross-hatching or shading.

2-16   POLYGON FILLING

Many closed contours are simple polygons. If the contour is composed of curved lines, it can be approximated by a suitable polygon or polygons. The simplest method of filling a polygon is to examine every pixel in the raster to see if it is inside the polygon. Since most pixels will not be inside the polygon, this technique is wasteful. The amount of work can be reduced by computing the bounding box for the polygon. The bounding box is the smallest rectangle that contains the polygon. Only those points inside the bounding box are examined. This is shown in Fig. 2-33. Using a bounding box for the polygon shown in Fig. 2-33a significantly reduces the number of pixels examined. However, for the polygon shown in Fig. 2-33b, the reduction is considerably smaller.

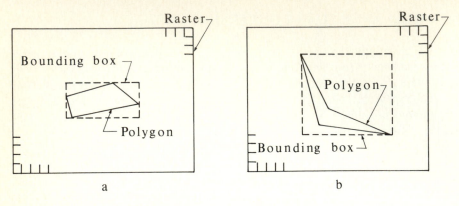

Figure 2-33 Polygon bounding box.

2-17 SCAN-CONVERTING POLYGONS

A more efficient technique than the inside test can be developed by taking advantage of the fact that, except at boundary edges, adjacent pixels are likely to have the same characteristics. This property is referred to as spatial coherence. For a raster scan graphics device adjacent pixels on a scan line are likely to have the same characteristics. This is scan line coherence.

The characteristics of pixels on a given scan line change only where a polygon edge intersects the scan line. These intersections divide the scan line into regions.

For the simple polygon shown in Fig. 2-34 the scan line labeled 2 intersects the polygon at $x = 1$ and $x = 8$. These intersections divide the scan line into three regions

$x < 1$	outside the polygon
$1 \leq x \leq 8$	inside the polygon
$x > 8$	outside the polygon

Similarly the scan line labeled 4 is divided into five regions

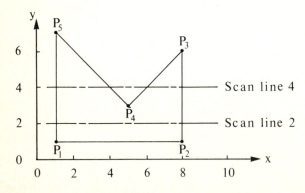

Figure 2-34 Solid area scan conversion.

$x < 1$	outside the polygon
$1 \le x \le 4$	inside the polygon
$4 < x < 6$	outside the polygon
$6 \le x \le 8$	inside the polygon
$x > 8$	outside the polygon

The intersections for scan line 4 are not necessarily determined in left-to-right order. For example, if the polygon is specified by the vertex list $P_1P_2P_3P_4P_5$ and the edge list by successive pairs of vertices, P_1P_2, P_2P_3, P_3P_4, P_4P_5, P_5P_1, then the intersections of the edges with scan line 4 will be determined as 8, 6, 4, 1. They must then be sorted into ascending order in x, i.e. 1, 4, 6, 8.

In determining the intensity, color, or shade of the pixels on a scan line the sorted intersections are considered in pairs. For each interval formed by a pair of intersections, the intensity or color is that of the polygon. For intervals between pairs of intersections, the intensity or color is that of the background. Of course, from the beginning of the scan line until the first intersection, and from the last intersection to the end of the scan line the intensity or color is that specified for the background. For the polygon in Fig. 2-34 the pixels from 0 to 1, 4 to 6, and 8 to 10 on scan line 4 are set at the background color, while those from 1 to 4 and 6 to 8 are set at the polygon intensity or color.

Determining exactly which pixels are to be activated requires some care. Consider the simple rectangular polygon shown in Fig. 2-35. The coordinates of the rectangle are (1, 1), (5, 1), (5, 4), (1, 4). The scan lines 1 to 4 have intersections with the polygon edges at $x = 1$ and 5. Recalling that a pixel is addressed by its lower left hand corner coordinates, then for each of the scan lines, the pixels with x coordinates of 1, 2, 3, 4, and 5 would be activated. The result is shown in Fig. 2-35a. Note that the area covered by the activated pixels is 20 units, while the true area of the rectangle is 12 units.

Modification of the scan line coordinate system and the activation test corrects this problem. This is shown in Fig. 2-35b. The scan lines are considered to pass through the center of the row of pixels, i.e., at the half interval as shown in Fig. 2-35b. The test for activation is modified to consider whether the center

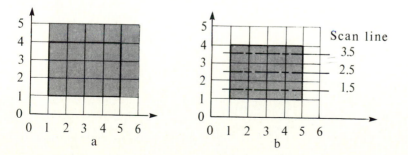

Figure 2-35 Scan line coordinate systems.

of the pixel to the right of the intersection is within the interval. However, the pixels are still addressed by the coordinates of the lower left hand corner. This technique yields the correct result as shown in Fig. 2-35b.

Horizontal edges cannot intersect a scan line and are thus ignored. This does not mean that horizontal edges are not formed. They are formed by the bottom and top edges of the rows of pixels. This is also illustrated in Fig. 2-35. Figure 2-35b illustrates that the modified scan line coordinate system yields the correct top and bottom edge for the polygon.

An additional difficulty occurs when a scan line intersects the polygon precisely at a vertex. Figure 2-36 illustrates this problem. Using the half scan line convention, the scan line at $y = 3.5$ intersects the polygon at 2, 2 and 8. This is an odd number of intersections. Hence, extracting the pixels in pairs will yield an incorrect result; i.e., the pixels at (0, 3), and (1, 3) will be set at the background color, the pixel at (2, 3) at the polygon color, those from (3, 3) to (7, 3) at the background color, and those at (8, 3) and (9, 3) at the polygon color. Observation suggests that at a scan line-polygon vertex intersection only one intersection should be counted. For the scan line at $y = 3.5$, this would give the correct result. However, examining the scan line at $y = 1.5$, which has two intersections at (5, 5), shows that this technique is incorrect. For this scan line extracting the pixels in pairs will yield the correct result; i.e., only the pixel at (5, 1) is set to the polygon color. If only one intersection is counted at the vertex, then the pixels from (0, 1) to (4, 1) are set at the background color and those from (5, 1) to (9, 1) at the polygon color.

The correct result is obtained by counting two intersections when the scan line-polygon vertex intersections occur at local maxima or minima of the polygon and only one if not. Whether the vertex under consideration is a local polygon maximum or minimum can be determined by examining the end points of the two edges meeting at the vertex. If the y values of these edges are both greater than the vertex being considered, then the vertex is a local minimum. If both are less than the vertex being considered, then the vertex is a local maximum. If one is greater and one less, then the vertex is neither a local minimum nor

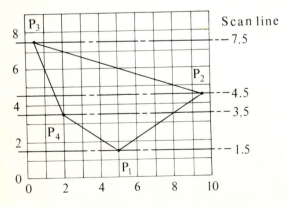

Figure 2-36 Scan line intersection singularities.

a local maximum. In Fig. 2-36, P_1 is a local minimum, P_3 a local maximum, and P_2 and P_4 are neither local maxima nor minima. Hence, two scan line intersections are counted at P_1 and P_3 and only one at P_2 and P_4.

2-18 A SIMPLE ORDERED EDGE LIST ALGORITHM

Using the techniques discussed above, efficient algorithms for scan-converting solid area polygons can be developed. These are called ordered edge list algorithms. They depend upon sorting the polygon edge-scan line intersections into scan line order. The efficiency of the algorithms depend on the efficiency of the sorting. A particularly simple algorithm is

A simple ordered edge list algorithm

To prepare the data:

Determine for each polygon edge the intersections with the half interval scan lines. A Bresenham or DDA algorithm can be used for this. Horizontal edges are ignored. Store each intersection $(x, y + 1/2)$ in a list.

Sort the list by scan line and increasing x on the scan line; i.e., (x_1, y_1) precedes (x_2, y_2) if $y_1 > y_2$ or $y_1 = y_2$ and $x_1 \leq x_2$.

To scan-convert the data:

Extract pairs of elements from the sorted list (x_1, y_1) and (x_2, y_2). The structure of the list ensures that $y = y_1 = y_2$ and $x_1 \leq x_2$. Activate pixels on the scan line y for integer values of x such that $x_1 \leq x + 1/2 \leq x_2$.

Example 2-8 Simple Ordered Edge List

Consider the polygon shown in Fig. 2-34. The polygon vertices are $P_1(1, 1)$, $P_2(8, 1), P_3(8, 6), P_4(5, 3)$, and $P_5(1, 7)$. Intersections with the half interval scan lines are

scan line 1.5:	(8, 1.5), (1, 1.5)
scan line 2.5:	(8, 2.5), (1, 2.5)
scan line 3.5:	(8, 3.5), (5.5, 3.5), (4.5, 3.5), (1, 3.5)
scan line 4.5:	(8, 4.5), (6.5, 4.5), (3.5, 4.5), (1, 4.5)
scan line 5.5:	(8, 5.5), (7.5, 5.5), (2.5, 5.5), (1, 5.5)
scan line 6.5:	(1.5, 6.5), (1, 6.5)
scan line 7.5:	none

The complete list sorted in scan line order from the top to the bottom and then from left to right is

(1, 6.5), (1.5, 6.5), (1, 5.5), (2.5, 5.5), (7.5, 5.5), (8, 5.5), (1, 4.5), (3.5, 4.5), (6.5, 4.5), (8, 4.5), (1, 3.5), (4.5, 3.5), (5.5, 3.5), (8, 3.5), (1, 2.5), (8, 2.5), (1, 1.5), (8, 1.5)

Extracting pairs of intersections from the list and applying the algorithm given above yields the pixel activation list

(1, 6)
(1, 5), (2, 5), (7, 5)
(1, 4), (2, 4), (3, 4), (6, 4), (7, 4)
(1, 3), (2, 3), (3, 3), (4, 3), (5, 3), (6, 3), (7, 3)
(1, 2), (2, 2), (3, 2), (4, 2), (5, 2), (6, 2), (7, 2)
(1, 1), (2, 1), (3, 1), (4, 1), (5, 1), (6, 1), (7, 1)

The result is shown in Fig. 2-37. Notice that both vertical edges and the bottom edge are given correctly.

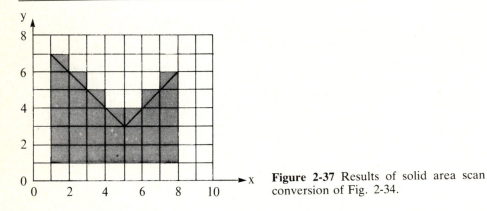

Figure 2-37 Results of solid area scan conversion of Fig. 2-34.

2-19   MORE EFFICIENT ORDERED EDGE LIST ALGORITHMS

The simple algorithm given in the previous section generates a large list which must be completely sorted. Making the sort more efficient will improve the algorithm. This can be accomplished by separating the vertical scan line sort in y from the horizontal scan line sort in x using a y-bucket sort as previously discussed in Sec. 2-8. In particular the algorithm is now

A more efficient ordered edge list algorithm

To prepare the data:

Determine for each polygon edge the intersections with the half interval scan lines, i.e., at $y + 1/2$. A Bresenham or DDA algorithm can be used for this. Ignore horizontal edges. Place the x coordinate of the intersection in the bucket corresponding to y.

As each scan line is addressed, i.e. for each y bucket, sort the list of x intersections into increasing order; i.e., x_1 precedes x_2 if $x_1 \leq x_2$.

To scan-convert the data:

> For each scan line extract pairs of intersections from the x-sorted list. Activate pixels on the scan line y corresponding to that bucket for integer values of x such that $x_1 \le x + 1/2 \le x_2$.

The above algorithm first sorts into scan line order with the y-bucket sort and then into order on the scan line. Thus, scan conversion begins prior to completion of the full sorting process. Further, with this algorithm it is somewhat easier to add or delete information from the display list. Here, it is only necessary to add or delete information from the appropriate y buckets. Hence, only the individual scan lines affected by the change need be resorted. An example further illustrates the algorithm.

Example 2-9   A More Efficient Ordered Edge List

Reconsider the polygon shown in Fig. 2-34 and discussed in Example 2-8. First, y buckets for scan lines 0 to 8 are established as shown in Fig. 2-38. The intersections obtained by considering each edge in turn counterclockwise from P_1 are also shown in the buckets in Fig. 2-38a unsorted in x. The intersections were calculated using the half scan line technique. For illustrative purposes they are also shown sorted in Fig. 2-38b. In practice a small scan line buffer as shown in Fig. 2-38c may be used to contain the x-sorted intersection values. This allows more efficient additions to or deletions from the intersection list. They can simply be added to the end of each y-bucket list since the x sort does not take place until an individual scan line is moved to the scan line buffer. Hence, a completely sorted y-bucket list does not need to be maintained.

Extracting pairs of intersections from the x-sorted list and applying the algorithm above yields the pixel activation list for each scan line. The result is the same as in Example 2-8. It is shown in Fig. 2-37.

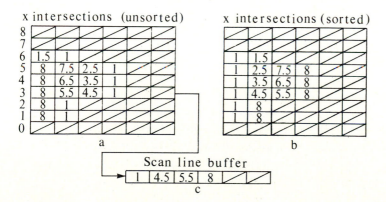

Figure 2-38 y buckets for the scan lines for the polygon of Fig. 2-34.

Although this second algorithm simplifies the sorting task, it either limits the number of intersections on a given scan line or requires the allocation of large amounts of storage, much of which may not be used. By using a linked list this problem can be overcome at the expense of additional data structure. The precalculation of the intersection of each scan line with each polygon edge is time-consuming. It also requires the storage of considerable data. By introducing an active edge list as previously discussed for real-time scan conversion (see Sec. 2-8), data storage is further reduced and scan line intersections can be calculated incrementally. The resulting algorithm is

An ordered edge list algorithm using an active edge list

To prepare the data:

Determine for each polygon edge, using the half interval scan lines, i.e. at $y + 1/2$, the highest scan lines intersected by the edge.

Place the polygon edge in the y bucket corresponding to this scan line.

Store the initial x intersection value, the number of scan lines crossed by the polygon edge, Δy, and the x increment Δx from scan line to scan line in a linked list.

To scan-convert the data:

For each scan line examine the corresponding y bucket for any new edges. Add any new edges to the active edge list.

Sort the x intercepts from the active edge list into increasing order; i.e., x_1 precedes x_2 if $x_1 \leq x_2$.

Extract pairs of intersections from the sorted x list. Activate pixels on the scan line y for integer values of x such that $x_1 \leq x + 1/2 \leq x_2$. For each edge on the active edge list decrement Δy by 1. If $\Delta y < 0$, drop the edge from the active edge list. Calculate the new x intercept $x_{new} = x_{old} + \Delta x$.

Advance to the next scan line.

This algorithm assumes that all data has been previously converted to a polygonal representation. Whitted (Ref. 2-21) gives a more general algorithm which removes this restriction.

Example 2-10   Ordered Edge List with an Active Edge List

Again consider the simple polygon shown in Fig. 2-34. Examining the list of polygon edges shows that scan line 5 is the highest intersected by edges P_2P_3 and P_3P_4, and scan line 6 the highest intersected by edges P_4P_5 and P_5P_1. The structure of the linked list containing data for the nine y buckets corresponding to the nine scan lines (0 to 8) of Fig. 2-34 is shown conceptually in Fig. 2-39a.

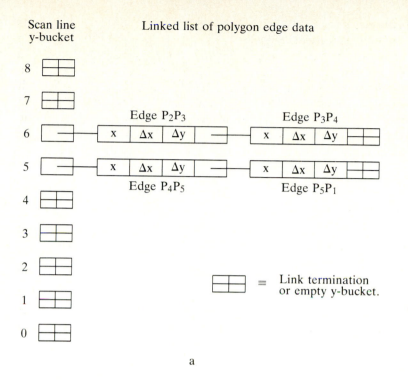

a

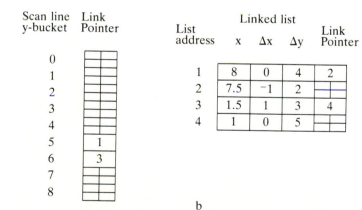

b

Figure 2-39 Conceptual linked list for the polygon of Fig. 2-34.

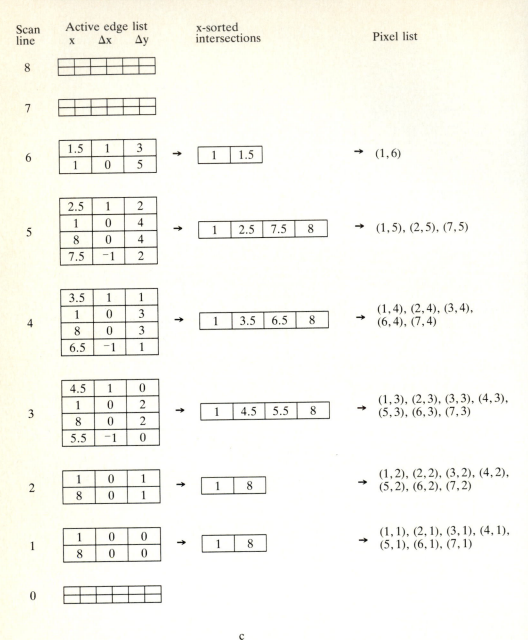

Scan line	Active edge list x	Δx	Δy	x-sorted intersections				Pixel list

8

7

| 1.5 | 1 | 3 |
| 1 | 0 | 5 |
→ | 1 | 1.5 | → (1,6)

2.5	1	2
1	0	4
8	0	4
7.5	−1	2
→ | 1 | 2.5 | 7.5 | 8 | → (1,5), (2,5), (7,5)

3.5	1	1
1	0	3
8	0	3
6.5	−1	1
→ | 1 | 3.5 | 6.5 | 8 | → (1,4), (2,4), (3,4), (6,4), (7,4)

4.5	1	0
1	0	2
8	0	2
5.5	−1	0
→ | 1 | 4.5 | 5.5 | 8 | → (1,3), (2,3), (3,3), (4,3), (5,3), (6,3), (7,3)

| 1 | 0 | 1 |
| 8 | 0 | 1 |
→ | 1 | 8 | → (1,2), (2,2), (3,2), (4,2), (5,2), (6,2), (7,2)

| 1 | 0 | 0 |
| 8 | 0 | 0 |
→ | 1 | 8 | → (1,1), (2,1), (3,1), (4,1), (5,1), (6,1), (7,1)

0

c

Figure 2-39 (Continued.)

Notice that most of the buckets are empty. A practical implementation is shown in Fig. 2-39b. Here, the y-bucket list is a one-dimensional array, one element for each scan line. The array element corresponding to each scan line bucket contains only a simple pointer into the data array used for the linked list which is also shown in Fig. 2-39b.

The linked list is implemented as an $n \times 4$ array. For each array index n the four elements contain the x intersection for a polygon edge with the highest scan line crossed by that edge, the x increment from scan line to scan line for that polygon edge, the number of scan lines crossed by the polygon edge, and the link pointer to the list address for data for the next polygon edge beginning on that scan line. This is shown in Fig. 2-39b. Note that the y bucket for scan line 5 contains the link pointer 1 corresponding to the first address in the linked data list. The first three columns in the linked data list contain data about the edge P_2P_3. The number in the fourth column is the link pointer to the next data address.

The active edge is implemented as an $n \times 3$ stack array. The contents of the active edge list are shown for all nine scan lines in Fig. 2-39c. The scan lines (y buckets) are examined sequentially from the top of the picture starting with scan line 8. Since the y buckets for scan lines 8 and 7 are empty, the active edge list is also empty. Scan line 6 adds two elements to the active edge list, and scan line 5 two more. At scan line 2, Δy for edges P_3P_4 and P_4P_5 become less than zero. Hence, they are dropped from the active edge list. Similarly, edges P_2P_3 and P_5P_1 are dropped at scan line 0. Finally, note that at scan line 0 the y bucket is empty, that the active edge list is empty, and there are no further y buckets. Hence, the algorithm is complete.

For each scan line the x intersections of the active edges for that scan line are extracted from the active edge list, sorted into increasing x order, and placed in a span buffer implemented as a $1 \times n$ array. From the span buffer the intersections are extracted in pairs. The active pixel list is then determined using the above algorithm. The combined pixel list for all the scan lines is the same as in the previous examples. The result is again shown in Fig. 2-37.

2-20 THE EDGE FILL ALGORITHM

The ordered edge list algorithm is very powerful. Each pixel in the display is visited only once. Hence, the input/output requirements are minimized. The end points of each group or span of active pixels are calculated before output. This allows the use of a shading algorithm along the span to obtain fully shaded pictures. Since the algorithm is independent of the input/output details, it can be made device independent. The algorithm's main disadvantage is the expense associated with maintaining and sorting the various lists. An alternate solid area scan conversion technique eliminates most of these lists. This alternate technique is the edge fill algorithm (Ref. 2-22).

The edge fill algorithm described below is very simple.

Edge fill algorithm

> For each scan line intersecting a polygon edge at (x_1, y_1) complement all pixels whose midpoints lie to the right of (x_1, y_1) i.e., for (x, y_1), $x + 1/2 > x_1$.

The half scan line convention is used to calculate the scan line-edge intersections. The algorithm is applied to each polygon edge individually. The order in which the polygon edges are considered is unimportant. Figure 2-40 shows the various stages in scan-converting the solid area of the example polygon of Fig. 2-34. Notice that the activated pixels are not the same as for the ordered edge list. In particular the edge fill algorithm does not activate pixels at (5, 3), (6, 4), (7, 5); i.e., the edge P_3P_4 is rasterized differently. The difference is in the way pixels that are exactly half inside and half outside the polygon are handled. The ordered edge list algorithm always activates these pixels. The edge fill algorithm activates them only if the inside of the polygon lies to the left of the center of the pixel.

The algorithm is most conveniently used with a frame buffer. This allows the polygon edges to be considered in completely arbitrary order. As each edge is considered, the appropriate pixels in the frame buffer corresponding to an edge-scan line intersection are addressed. When all edges have been considered, the frame buffer is read to the display device in scan line order. Figure 2-40 illustrates the main disadvantages of the algorithm; i.e., for complex pictures each individual pixel may be addressed many times. Hence, the algorithm is limited by input/output considerations.

The number of pixels addressed by the edge fill algorithm can be reduced by introducing a fence (Ref. 2-23). This is the fence fill algorithm. The basic

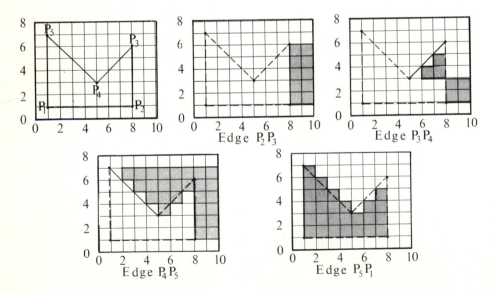

Figure 2-40 Edge fill algorithm.

idea is illustrated in Fig. 2-41 again for the example polygon of Fig. 2-34. In particular, the fence fill algorithm is

The fence fill algorithm

For each scan line intersecting a polygon edge:

If the intersection is to the left of the fence, complement all pixels whose midpoint lies to the right of the intersection of the scan line and the edge and to the left of the fence.

If the intersection is to the right of the fence, complement all pixels whose midpoint lies to the left of or on the intersection of the scan line and the edge and to the right of the fence.

The half scan line conversion is used. A convenient fence location is usually one of the polygon vertices. Again, the algorithm is most conveniently used with a frame buffer. The disadvantage of both the edge fill and fence fill algorithms is the number of pixels addressed more than once. This can be eliminated by a modification called the edge flag algorithm (Ref. 2-24). The edge fill, fence fill, and edge flag algorithms are not limited to simple polygons.

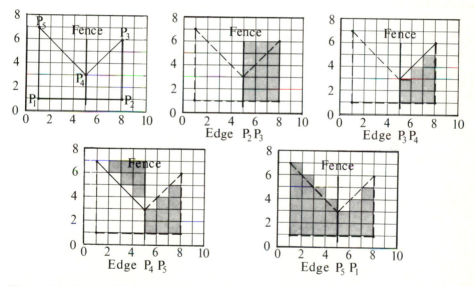

Figure 2-41 Fence fill algorithm.

2-21   THE EDGE FLAG ALGORITHM

The edge flag algorithm (Ref. 2-24) is a two-step process. The first step is to outline the contour. This establishes pairs of span bounding pixels on each scan line. The second step is to fill between these bounding pixels. The algorithm may be more explicitly stated as follows:

The edge flag algorithm

Contour outline:

Using the half scan line convention for each edge intersecting the polygon, set the leftmost pixel whose midpoint lies to the right of the intersection; i.e., for $x + 1/2 > x_{intersection}$, to the boundary value.

Fill:

For each scan line intersecting the polygon
Inside = FALSE
for x = 0 (left) to x = x_{max} (right)
if the pixel at x is set to the boundary value **then** negate Inside
if Inside = TRUE **then**
set the pixel at x to the polygon value
else
reset the pixel at x to the background value
end if
next x

Example 2-11   Edge Flag Algorithm

Consider the application of the edge flag algorithm to the example polygon of Fig. 2-34. First the contour is outlined. The result is shown in Fig. 2-42a. Pixels at (1, 1), (1, 2), (1, 3), (1, 4), (1, 5), (1, 6), (2, 6), (3, 5), (4, 4), (5, 3), (6, 3), (7, 4), (8, 5), (8, 4), (8, 3), (8, 2), (8, 1) are activated.

The polygon is then filled. To illustrate this the scan line at 3 is extracted and shown in Fig. 2-42b. Pixels at $x = 1, 5, 6,$ and 8 on this scan line have been activated to outline the contour. Applying the fill algorithm yields

Initially
Inside = FALSE

For $x = 0$ — The pixel is not set to the boundary value and Inside = FALSE. Thus, no action is taken.

For $x = 1$ — The pixel is set to the boundary value, Inside is negated to TRUE. Inside = TRUE so the pixel is set to the polygon value.

For $x = 2, 3, 4$ — The pixel is not set to the boundary value. Inside = TRUE so the pixel is set to the polygon value.

For $x = 5$ — The pixel is set to the boundary value, Inside is negated to FALSE. Inside = FALSE so the pixel is set to the background value.

For $x = 6$ — The pixel is set to the boundary value, Inside is negated to TRUE. Inside = TRUE so the pixel is set to the polygon value.

For $x = 7$ — The pixel is not set to the boundary value. Inside = True so the pixel is set to the polygon value.

For $x = 8$ — The pixel is set to the boundary value, Inside is negated to FALSE. Inside = FALSE so the pixel is set to the background.

The result is shown in Fig. 2-42c. The final result for the complete polygon is the same as for the edge fill algorithm as shown in Fig. 2-40.

The edge flag algorithm visits each pixel only once. Hence, the input/output requirements are considerably less than for the edge fill or fence fill algorithms. When used with a frame buffer, none of these algorithms requires building, maintaining, and sorting edge lists. Implemented in software, the ordered edge list and the edge flag algorithms execute at about the same speed (Ref. 2-21). However, the edge flag algorithm is suitable for hardware or firmware implementation where it executes one to two orders of magnitude faster than the ordered edge list algorithm (Ref. 2-24). For simple pictures real-time animation is possible.

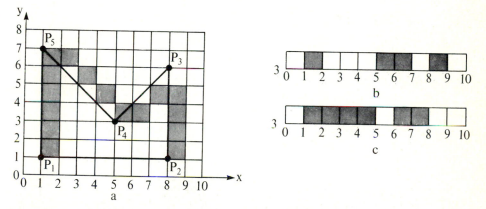

Figure 2-42 Edge flag algorithm.

2-22   SEED FILL ALGORITHMS

The algorithms discussed above fill the polygon in scan line order. A different approach is used in the seed fill algorithms. The seed fill algorithms assume that at least one pixel interior to a polygon or region is known. The algorithm then attempts to find and color or fill all other pixels interior to the region. Regions may be either interior- or boundary-defined. If a region is interior-defined, then all the pixels in the interior of the region have one color or value and all the pixels exterior to the region have another as shown in Fig. 2-43. If a region is boundary-defined, then all the pixels on the region boundary have a unique

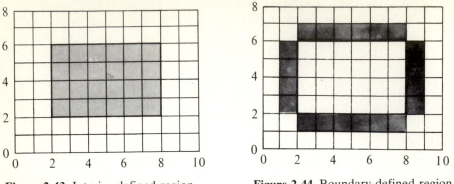

Figure 2-43 Interior-defined region.

Figure 2-44 Boundary-defined region.

value or color as shown in Fig. 2-44. None of the pixels interior to the region can have this unique value. However, pixels exterior to the boundary may also have the boundary value. Algorithms that fill interior-defined regions are referred to as flood fill algorithms, and those that fill boundary-defined regions as boundary fill algorithms. The discussion below concentrates on boundary fill algorithms. However, the companion flood fill algorithms can be developed in an analogous manner.

Interior- or boundary-defined regions may be either 4-connected or 8-connected. If a region is 4-connected, then every pixel in the region may be reached by a combination of moves in only four directions: left, right, up, down. For an 8-connected region every pixel in the region may be reached by a combination of moves in the two horizontal, two vertical, and four diagonal directions. An 8-connected algorithm will fill a 4-connected region, but a 4-connected algorithm will not fill an 8-connected region. Simple examples of 4-, and 8-connected interior-defined regions are shown in Fig. 2-45. Although each of the subregions of the 8-connected region shown in Fig. 2-45b is 4-connected, passage from one subregion to the other requires an 8-connected algorithm. However, if each of the subregions is a separate 4-connected region, each to be filled with a separate color or value, then use of an 8-connected algorithm causes both regions to be incorrectly filled with a single color or value.

Figure 2-46 shows the 8-connected region of Fig. 2-45 redefined as a boundary-defined region. Figure 2-46 illustrates that where a region is 8-connected,

4-Connected
a

8-Connected
b

Figure 2-45 Four- and 8-connected interior-defined regions.

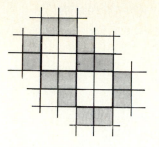

Figure 2-46 Four- and 8-connected boundary-defined regions.

i.e., where the two subregions touch at the corners, the boundary is 4-connected. It also illustrates that, for 4-connected regions, the boundary is 8-connected. The discussion below concentrates on 4-connected algorithms. The equivalent 8-connected algorithms can easily be obtained by attempting to fill in eight rather than four directions.

2-23   A SIMPLE SEED FILL ALGORITHM

A simple seed fill algorithm for a boundary-defined region can be developed using a stack. A stack is simply an array or other storage space into which values may be sequentially placed or from which they may be sequentially removed. As new values are added to or pushed onto the stack, all previously stored values are pushed down one level. As values are removed or popped from the stack, previously stored values float or pop up one level. Such a stack is referred to as a first in, last out (FILO) or push-down stack. A simple seed fill algorithm is then

Simple seed fill algorithm using a stack

Push the seed pixel onto the stack.

While the stack is not empty

Pop a pixel from the stack.

Set the pixel to the required value.

For each of the 4-connected pixels adjacent to the current pixel, check if it is a boundary pixel or if it has already been set to the required value. In either case ignore it. Otherwise, push it onto the stack.

The algorithm can be modified for 8-connected regions by looking at the 8-connected pixels rather than only the 4-connected pixels. A more formal statement of the algorithm assuming the existence of a seed pixel and a boundary-defined region is

simple seed fill algorithm for 4-connected boundary-defined regions

Seed(x, y) *is the seed pixel*
Push *is a function for placing a pixel on the stack*
Pop *is a function for removing a pixel from the stack*

 Pixel(x, y) = Seed(x, y)
 initialize stack
 Push Pixel(x, y)
 while (stack not empty)
  get a pixel from the stack
  Pop Pixel(x, y)
  if Pixel(x, y) <> New value **then**
   Pixel(x, y) = New value
  else
   examine the surrounding pixels to see if they should be placed
   onto the stack
   if (Pixel(x + 1, y) <> New value **and**
    Pixel(x + 1, y) <> Boundary value) **then**
    Push Pixel(x + 1, y)
   if (Pixel(x, y + 1) <> New value **and**
    Pixel(x, y + 1) <> Boundary value) **then**
    Push Pixel(x, y + 1)
   if (Pixel(x − 1, y) <> New value **and**
    Pixel(x − 1, y) <> Boundary value) **then**
    Push Pixel(x − 1, y)
   if (Pixel(x, y − 1) <> New value **and**
    Pixel(x, y − 1) <> Boundary value) **then**
    Push Pixel(x, y − 1)
  end if
 end while

The algorithm examines the 4-connected pixels and pushes them onto the stack counterclockwise beginning with the pixel to the right of the current pixel.

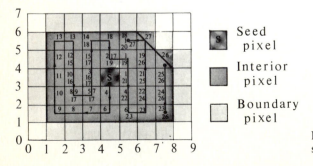

Seed pixel

Interior pixel

Boundary pixel

Figure 2-47 Seed fill using a simple stack algorithm.

Example 2-12 Simple Seed Fill Algorithm

As an example of the application of the algorithm consider the boundary-defined polygonal region defined by the vertices (1, 1), (8, 1) (8, 4), (6, 6), and (1, 6) as shown in Fig. 2-47. The seed pixel is at (4, 3). The algorithm proceeds to fill the polygon pixel by pixel as shown by the line in Fig. 2-47 with the arrows. The numbers in each pixel give the stack location of the pixel as the algorithm proceeds. Notice that some pixels contain more than one number. This indicates that the pixel has been pushed onto the stack more than once. When the algorithm reaches pixel (5, 5) the stack is 23 levels deep and contains the pixels (7, 4), (7, 3), (7, 2), (7, 1), (6, 2), (6, 3), (5, 6), (6, 4), (5, 5), (4, 4), (3, 4), (3, 5), (2, 4), (2, 3), (2, 2), (3, 2), (5, 1), (3, 2), (5, 2), (3, 3), (4, 4), (5, 3).

Since all the pixels surrounding that at (5, 5) contain either boundary values or new values, none are pushed onto the stack. Hence, pixel (7, 4) is popped off of the stack and the algorithm proceeds to fill the column (7, 4), (7, 3), (7, 2), (7, 1). When pixel (7, 1) is reached, again the surrounding pixels either already contain the new value or are boundary pixels. Since the polygon is completely filled at this point, popping pixels from the stack until it is empty causes no additional pixels to be filled. When the stack is empty, the algorithm is complete.

The polygon in Example 2-12 is a simple open region. The algorithm will also properly fill regions containing holes. This is illustrated in the next example.

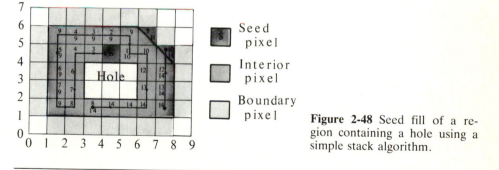

Seed pixel

Interior pixel

Boundary pixel

Figure 2-48 Seed fill of a region containing a hole using a simple stack algorithm.

Example 2-13 Simple Seed Fill Algorithm for Polygon with a Hole

As an example of the application of the algorithm to a polygonal boundary-defined region containing a hole consider Fig. 2-48. Here, the polygon vertices are the same as in the previous example, i.e., (1, 1), (8, 1), (8, 4), (6, 6), and (1, 6). The interior hole is defined by (3, 2), (6, 2), (6, 4), (3, 4). The seed pixel is at (4, 4). Because of the interior hole the algorithm fills the polygon along a quite different path than in Example 2-12. This new path is shown by the arrowed line in Fig. 2-48. Again, the numbers in each pixel give the stack location as the algorithm proceeds. When the algorithm reaches pixel (3, 1) all the 4-connected surrounding pixels either contain the new value or are boundary pixels. Hence, no pixels are pushed onto the stack. At this point the stack is 14 levels deep. It contains the pixels (7, 1), (7, 2), (7, 3), (6, 5), (7, 4), (6, 5), (3, 1), (1, 2), (1, 3), (1, 4), (2, 5), (3, 5), (4, 5), (5, 4).

After popping the pixel (7, 1) from the stack, the algorithm fills the column (7, 1), (7, 2), (7, 3), (7, 4) without pushing any additional pixels onto the stack. At pixel (7, 4) again all 4-connected surrounding pixels contain either the new value or are boundary pixels. Returning to the stack, the algorithm finds no new pixels until that at (6, 5). Filling the pixel at (6, 5) completes the polygon fill. The algorithm completes processing of the stack without further filling. When the stack is empty, the algorithm is complete.

2-24   A SCAN LINE SEED FILL ALGORITHM

Both of the above examples show that the stack can become quite large. Further, they show that the stack frequently contains duplicate or unnecessary information. An algorithm which minimizes stack size attempts to seed only one pixel in any uninterrupted scan line span (Ref. 2-25). This is called a scan line seed fill algorithm. An uninterrupted span is a group of contiguous pixels on a single scan line. Here, a heuristic approach is used to develop the algorithm. A more theoretical approach, based on graph theory, is also possible (Ref. 2-26).

The scan line seed fill algorithm is applicable to boundary-defined regions. The 4-connected boundary-defined region may be either convex or concave and may contain one or more holes. The region exterior to and adjacent to the boundary-defined region may not contain pixels with a value or color corresponding to the one used to fill the region or polygon. Conceptually, the algorithm works in four steps.

Scan line seed fill algorithm

A seed pixel on a span is popped from a stack containing the seed pixel.

The span containing the seed pixel is filled to the right and left of the seed pixel along a scan line until a boundary is found.

The algorithm remembers the extreme left and the extreme right pixels in the span as *Xleft* and *Xright*.

In the range of *Xleft* $\leq x \leq$ *Xright* the scan lines immediately above and immediately below the current scan line are examined to see if they completely contain either boundary pixels or previously filled pixels. If these scan lines do not contain either boundary or previously filled pixels, then in the range *Xleft* $\leq x \leq$ *Xright* the extreme right pixel in each span is marked as a seed pixel and pushed onto the stack.

The algorithm is initialized by pushing a single seed pixel onto the stack and is complete when the stack is empty. The algorithm jumps holes and indentations in the region boundary as shown in Fig. 2-49 and in the example

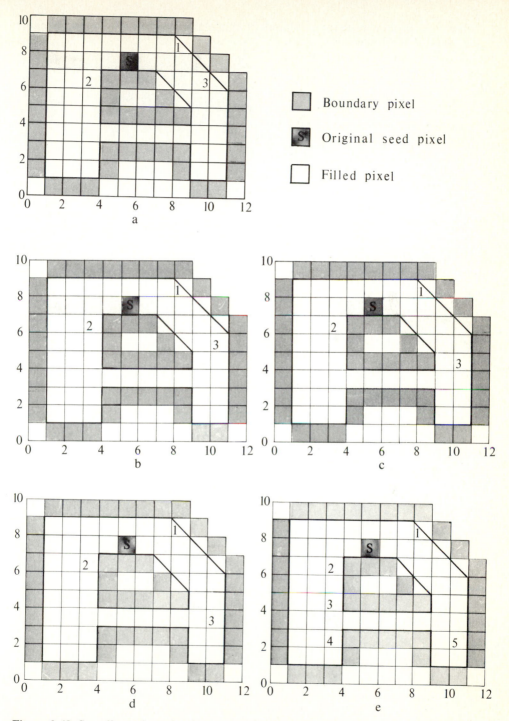

Figure 2-49 Scan-line-oriented polygon seed fill algorithm.

below. A more complete statement of the algorithm is given in the pseudo implementation below.

scan line seed fill algorithm

Seed(x, y) *is the seed pixel*
Pop *is a function for removing a pixel from the stack*
Push *is a function for placing a pixel onto the stack*
    initialize stack
  Push Seed(x, y)
  while (stack not empty)
    get the seed pixel and set it to the new value
    Pop Pixel(x, y)
    Pixel(x, y) = Fill value
    save the x *coordinate of the seed pixel*
    Savex = x
    fill the span to the right of the seed pixel
    x = x + 1
    while Pixel(x, y) <> Boundary value
      Pixel(x, y) = Fill value
      x = x + 1
    end while
    save the extreme right pixel
    Xright = x − 1
    reset the x *coordinate to the value for the seed pixel*
    x = Savex
    fill the span to the left of the seed pixel
    x = x − 1
    while Pixel(x, y) <> Boundary value
      Pixel(x, y) = Fill value
      x = x − 1
    end while
    save the extreme left pixel
    Xleft = x + 1
    reset the x *coordinate to the value for the seed pixel*
    x = Savex
    check that the scan line above is neither a polygon boundary nor has been previously completely filled; if not, seed the scan line
    start at the left edge of the scan line subspan
    x = Xleft
    y = y + 1
    while x <= Xright
      seed the scan line above
      Pflag = 0
      while (Pixel(x, y) <> Boundary value **and**
        Pixel(x, y) <> Fill value **and** x < Xright)

```
            if Pflag = 0 then Pflag = 1
            x = x + 1
        end while
    push the extreme right pixel onto the stack
    if Pflag = 1 then
            if (x = Xright and Pixel(x, y) <> Boundary value
              and Pixel(x, y) <> Fill value) then
                Push Pixel(x, y)
            else
                Push Pixel(x − 1, y)
            end if
            Pflag = 0
    end if
    continue checking in case the span is interrupted
    Xenter = x
    while ((Pixel(x, y) = Boundary value or Pixel(x, y)
      = Fill value) and x < Xright)
        x = x + 1
    end while
    make sure that the pixel coordinate is incremented
        if x = Xenter then x = x + 1
end while
```

Check that the scan line below is not a polygon boundary nor has been previously completely filled

this algorithm is exactly the same as that for checking the scan line above except that $y = y − 1$ is subsituted for $y = y + 1$

```
end while
finish
```

Here the function **Pop** gets the x, y coordinates of a pixel from the stack and the function **Push** places them onto the stack.

Example 2-14 Scan Line Seed Fill

Consider the application of the above algorithm to the boundary-defined polygonal region shown in Fig. 2-49. The algorithm is initialized by pushing the polygon seed pixel, labeled Seed $(5, 7)$ in Fig. 2-49a, onto the stack. This pixel is initially popped from the stack as the span seed. The span containing the seed is then filled to the right and to the left. The span limits are found to be *Xright* = 9 and *Xleft* = 1. The scan line above is then examined. It is neither a boundary nor has it been previously filled. The extreme right hand pixel in the range $1 \leq x \leq 9$ is $(8, 8)$. This pixel, labeled 1 in Fig. 2-49a, is pushed onto the stack. The scan line below is examined and determined to be neither a boundary nor previously filled. Within the range *Xleft* $\leq x \leq$ *Xright* there are two subspans. The left subspan is seeded with the pixel $(3, 6)$, labeled 2 in Fig. 2-49a, which is pushed onto the stack. The right subspan is seeded with the pixel (9, 6), which is also pushed onto the stack. Notice that this pixel (9, 6) is not the extreme right pixel in the span. However, it is the extreme right pixel in the range $Xleft \leq x \leq Xright$, i.e., in the range $1 \leq x \leq 9$. One pass through the algorithm is now complete.

The algorithm continues by popping the top pixel from the stack. Here, it fills spans on the right side of the polygon on successively lower scan lines. The results are shown in Figs. 2-49b to d. The seed for scan line 3 shown in Fig. 2-49d is pixel (10, 3). Filling the span to the right and left yields $Xleft = 1$ and $Xright = 10$. Examining the scan line above yields the seed pixel (3, 4) in the left subspan which is pushed onto the stack. The right subspan is already filled. Examining the scan line below yields the seed pixel (3, 2) for the left subspan and (10, 2) for the right subspan. These pixels are also pushed onto the stack. The maximum stack depth occurs at this scan line.

From here, the algorithm continues to completion with only one additional point of interest. After filling the 4-connected polygonal subregions seeded with the pixels labeled 5, 4 and 3 in Fig. 2-49e, the pixel labeled 2 is popped from the stack. Here, the algorithm finds that all pixels on the seed scan line, on the scan line above, and on the scan line below have already been filled. Thus, no additional pixels are pushed onto the stack. The algorithm then pops the pixel labeled 1 as the seed pixel and fills the scan line. Again, no additional pixels are pushed onto the stack. The stack is now empty, the polygon filled, and the algorithm complete.

In comparison with the seed fill algorithm of Sec. 2-23 the maximum stack depth in the above example is five. Other techniques for polygon or region seed fill are discussed in Ref. 2-27.

2-25   FUNDAMENTALS OF ANTIALIASING

To provide effective antialiasing it is necessary to understand the causes of aliasing itself. Fundamentally, the appearance of aliasing effects is due to the fact that lines, polygon edges, color boundaries, etc., are continuous, whereas a raster device is discrete. To present the line, polygon edge, etc., on the raster display device it must be sampled at discrete locations. This can have surprising results. For example, consider a signal such as an edge, as shown in Fig. 2-50a. A second signal of lower frequency is given in Fig. 2-50c. If both signals are sampled or rasterized at the same rate, as shown by the small crosses, then the reconstructed signals are identical, as illustrated in Figs. 2-50b and d. Figure 2-50d is called an alias of the sample in Fig. 2-50b and hence of the signal in Fig. 2-50a. The high-frequency signal (Fig. 2-50a) has been undersampled. In order to prevent aliasing, a signal must be sampled at a rate at least twice the highest frequency in the signal. Undersampling causes highly periodic images to be rendered incorrectly. For example, a picket fence or venetian blind might appear as a few broad stripes rather than many individual smaller stripes.

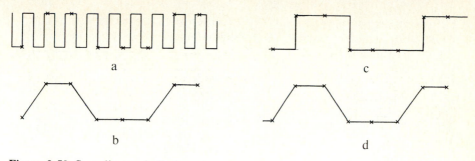

Figure 2-50 Sampling and aliasing.

The previous sections and the above discussion illustrate two of three general manifestations of aliasing in computer-generated images: jagged edges and incorrectly rendered fine detail or texture. The third occurs for very small objects. If an object is smaller than the size of a pixel or does not cover the point within a pixel at which the pixel attributes are evaluated, it will not be included in the resulting picture. Alternately, if the small object covers the point at which the pixel attributes are calculated, it may overly influence those attributes. The left hand pixel in Fig. 2-51 shows this. If the center of the pixel is used to determine the attributes, then the entire pixel would exhibit those of the small object. The right hand pixels in Fig. 2-51 illustrate objects that would be ignored or lost. Notice that long, thin objects can also be ignored. These effects are particularly noticeable in animation sequences. Figure 2-52 shows a small triangle in three frames of an animation sequence. If pixel attributes are determined at the pixel center, then in the first frame the object is not visible, in the second it is, and in the third it is again invisible. In the animation sequence the small object would flash on and off.

Fundamentally, there are two methods of antialiasing. The first is to increase the sample rate. This is accomplished by increasing the resolution of the raster. Finer detail is thus included. However, there is a limit to the ability of CRT raster scan devices to display very fine rasters. Presently the practical limit is about 2000 pixels per scan line. This limit suggests that the raster be calculated at higher resolution and displayed at lower resolution using some type of averaging to obtain the pixel attributes at the lower resolution (see Ref. 2-28).

Two types of averaging are shown in Fig. 2-53. Figure 2-53a shows a uniform average of the surrounding pixels for resolution reductions of 2 and 4.

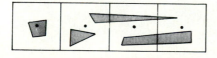

Figure 2-51 Aliasing effects on small objects.

Figure 2-52 Aliasing effects in animation.

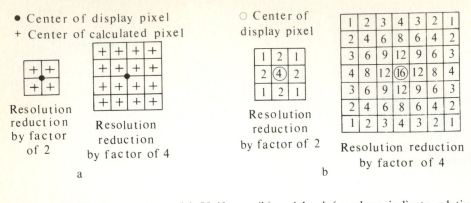

Figure 2-53 Pixel averaging. (a) Uniform, (b) weighted (numbers indicate relative weights).

Each display pixel is divided into subpixels to form the higher resolution raster. Pixel attributes are determined at the center of each subpixel and averaged to obtain the attributes for the display pixel. Somewhat better results can be obtained by considering more subpixels and weighting their influence when calculating the display pixel attributes. Figure 2-53b shows weighted averages suggested by Crow (Ref. 2-28) for resolution reductions of 2 and 4. For these weighted averages, resolution reduction by a factor of 2 considers nine subpixels, and reduction by a factor of 4 forty-nine subpixels.

Figure 2-54 shows a complex scene displayed at a resolution of 256 × 256 pixels. Figure 2-54a was calculated at a resolution of 512 × 512 and Fig. 2-54b at 1024 × 1024. Uniform averaging was used to obtain the displayed resolution of 256 × 256 pixels. Figures 2-55a and b show the same scene calculated at resolutions of 512 × 512 and 1024 × 1024, respectively, and displayed at 256 × 256 using the weighted averages of Fig. 2-53b.

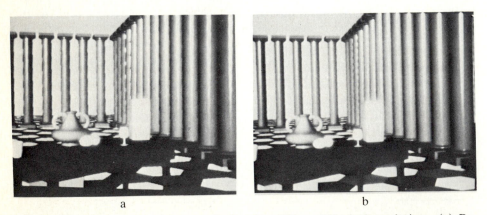

Figure 2-54 High-resolution images displayed at 256 × 256 pixel resolution. (a) Reduced from 512 × 512, (b) reduced from 1024 × 1024 using uniform averaging. (*Courtesy of F. Crow.*)

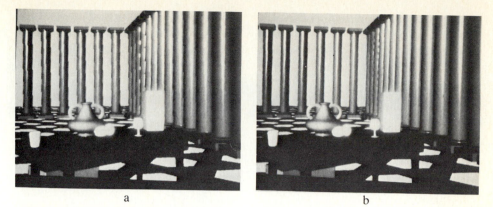

a   b

Figure 2-55 High-resolution images displayed at 256 × 256 pixel resolution. (a) Reduced from 512 × 512, (b) reduced from 1024 × 1024 using weighted averaging. (*Courtesy of F. Crow.*)

The second method of antialiasing is to treat a pixel as a finite area rather than as a point. A heuristic technique is given in the next section. The mathematical foundation is given in Sec. 2-27. Treating a pixel as a finite area is equivalent to prefiltering the image.

2-26   SIMPLE AREA ANTIALIASING

In the line rasterization and polygon fill algorithms discussed above the intensity or color of a pixel was determined by the intensity or color of a single point within the pixel area. These techniques assume that the pixel is a mathematical point rather than a finite area. For example, recalling Fig. 2-4 and the Bresenham algorithm, the intensity of pixels was determined by the location of the single point of intersection of the line and the pixel boundary. In the polygon solid area scan conversion techniques discussed above, the determination of whether or not a pixel was inside or outside the polygon was based on the location of the center of the pixel. If inside, the entire pixel area was activated. If outside, the entire pixel area was ignored. For simple bilevel displays, i.e., black or white, polygon color or background color, this technique is necessary. The result is the characteristic stair step or jagged polygon edge or line. Fundamentally the stair step effect is due to undersampling the line or polygon edge to make it conform to the discrete pixels of the display as discussed in the previous section.

For multiple intensities, i.e., gray scales or multiple color shades the appearance of the edge or line can be improved by blurring. A simple heuristic approach is to let the intensity of a pixel along a polygon edge be proportional

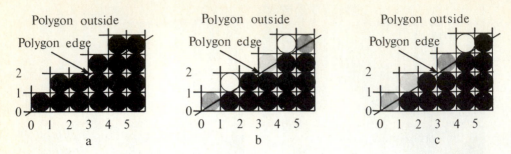

Figure 2-56 Simple antialiased polygon edge. (a) No antialiasing, (b) intensity proportional to area inside polygon, (c) modified Bresenham.

to the area of the pixel inside the polygon. Figure 2-56 illustrates this simple form of antialiasing. A single polygon edge with slope 5/8 is shown. The inside of the polygon is to the right. In Fig. 2-56a the polygon edge is rasterized using a standard Bresenham algorithm with only two intensity levels. The edge exhibits the characteristic jagged or stair step pattern. In Fig. 2-56b the area of the pixel inside the polygon is used to select one of eight (0 to 7) intensity levels. Notice that some pixels that are totally black in Fig. 2-56a are white in Fig. 2-56b because less than one-eighth of the pixel area is inside the polygon.

A simple modification of Bresenham's algorithm yields an approximation to the pixel area inside the polygon (Ref. 2-29). This approximation can be used to modulate the intensity. When a line of slope m ($0 \leq m \leq 1$) crosses a pixel, either one or two pixels may be involved, as shown in Fig. 2-57. If only one pixel is crossed (Fig. 2-57a), then the area to the right and below the line is $y_i + m/2$. If two pixels must be considered (Fig. 2-57b), the area for the lower pixel is $1 - (1 - y_i)^2/2m$ and for the upper $(y_i - 1 + m)^2/2m$. For a line in the first octant with slope $0 \leq m \leq 1$, the area of the upper pixel may be sufficiently small that it will be ignored by the simple heuristic approach described above, e.g., pixel (1, 1) in Fig. 2-56b. However, combining this area with that of the

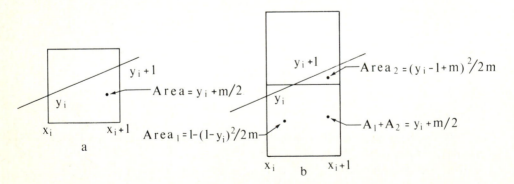

Figure 2-57 Bresenham's algorithm with area antialiasing.

lower pixel more realistically represents the polygon edge. The combined area for the two pixels is given by $y_i + m/2$.

If the quantity $w = 1 - m$ is added to the error term in Bresenham's original algorithm, i.e., introduce the transformation $\bar{e} = e + w$, then $0 \le \bar{e} \le 1$. Now the error term $\bar{e}$ is a measure of the area of the pixel inside the polygon, i.e., of $y_i + m/2$. With these modifications the initial value of the error term is 1/2. With this addition the algorithm given in Fig. 2-6 will always yield an intensity of one-half the maximum for the first pixel. By relocating the plot or output statement, a more realistic value is obtained for this first pixel. Further, the intensity can be obtained directly rather than as a decimal fraction of the maximum by multiplying the slope (m), the weighting factor (w), and the error term $\bar{e}$ by the maximum number of available intensity levels I. The modified algorithm is then

modified Bresenham algorithm with antialiasing
the line is from (x_1, y_1) to (x_2, y_2)
I is the number of available intensity levels
all variables are assumed integer

> *initialize the variables*
> $x = x_1$
> $y = y_1$
> $\Delta x = x_2 - x_1$
> $\Delta y = y_2 - y_1$
> $m = I*(\Delta y/\Delta x)$
> $w = I - m$
> $\bar{e} = 1/2$
> **Plot**$(x, y, m/2)$
> **while** $(x < \Delta x)$
>> **if** $\bar{e} < w$ **then**
>>> $x = x + 1$
>>> $\bar{e} = \bar{e} + m$
>> **else**
>>> $x = x + 1$
>>> $y = y + 1$
>>> $\bar{e} = \bar{e} - w$
>> **end if**
> **Plot**$(x, y, \bar{e})$
> **end while**
> **finish**

The intensity for the first pixel assumes that the line starts at a pixel address. A flowchart is given in Fig. 2-58. Figure 2-56c illustrates the results for a line with slope $m = 5/8$ and eight intensity levels. The algorithm can be extended to the other octants in a manner similar to that for the fundamental Bresenham algorithm (see Sec. 2-5).

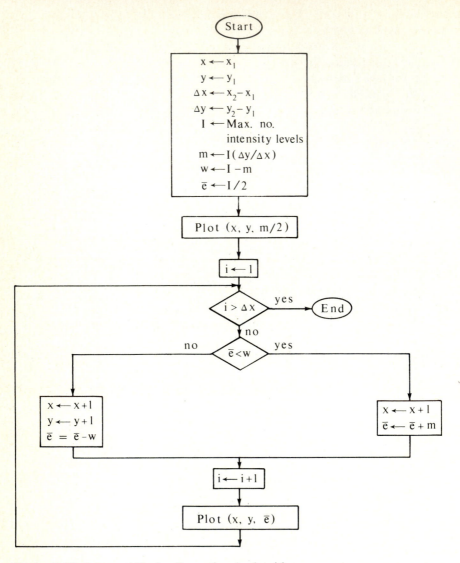

Figure 2-58 Area antialiasing Bresenham's algorithm.

2-27 THE CONVOLUTION INTEGRAL AND ANTIALIASING

Extension of the simple antialiasing methods discussed in the previous section requires use of a mathematical technique called the convolution integral. For antialiasing, the signal, i.e., the picture, is convolved with a convolution kernel. The result is used to determine the pixel attributes. The convolution integral is given by

$$c(\xi) = \int_{-\infty}^{\infty} h(\xi - x)y(x) \; dx$$

where

$h(\xi - x)$ is the convolution kernel or function

$y(x)$ is the function being convolved

$c(\xi)$ is the convolution of $h(\xi - x)$ and $y(x)$

It is extremely difficult to visualize the physical meaning of the convolution integral from the mathematical definition. However, a simple graphical analysis makes it clear (see Ref. 2-30).

Consider the convolution of the function $y(x) = x$, $0 \le x \le 1$ with a simple box or square convolution kernel $h(x) = 1$, $0 \le x \le 1$. The graphical representation of the convolution kernel is shown in Fig. 2-59a. The convolution kernel is reflected about the ordinate to yield $h(-x)$ as shown in Fig. 2-59b. The reflected kernel is then translated to the right by an amount ξ to form $h(\xi - x)$, see Fig. 2-59c. This reflected, translated function is then multipled together with the function being convolved $y(x)$ (see Fig. 2-59d) for various values of ξ as shown in Fig. 2-59e. The area under the combined curves (functions) is the value of the convolution integral $c(\xi)$ which is also shown in Fig. 2-59e. Notice that for this case the convolution integral is nonzero only in the range $0 \le x \le 2$. Thus, determining the convolution integral is equivalent to reflecting the con-

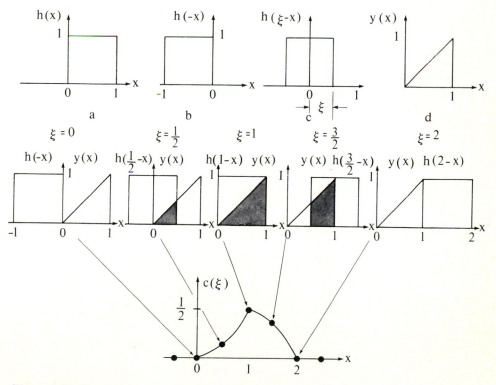

Figure 2-59 Convolution.

volution kernel, sliding it past the function, multiplying the two functions together, and determining the area under the combined curves.

Mathematically the convolution kernel is

$$h(x) = 1 \qquad 0 \le x \le 1$$

Reflecting yields

$$h(-x) = 1 \qquad -1 \le x \le 0$$

Translating by ξ gives

$$h(\xi - x) = 1 \qquad \xi - 1 \le x \le \xi$$

Since both the convolution kernel and the function $y(x)$ being convolved are nonzero for finite ranges, the limits on the convolution integral are also finite. How are those limits determined? Figure 2-59 clearly illustrates that the lower limit is the maximum of the minimum values for which both functions are nonzero and the upper limit is the minimum of the maximum values for which both functions are nonzero. Thus,

$$c(\xi) = \int_{-\infty}^{\infty} h(\xi - x)y(x)\ dx = \int_{0}^{\xi} h(\xi - x)y(x)\ dx \qquad 0 \le \xi \le 1$$

$$= \int_{\xi-1}^{1} h(\xi - x)y(x)\ dx \qquad 1 \le \xi \le 2$$

Substituting for $h(\xi - x)$ and $y(x)$ yields

$$c(\xi) = \int_{0}^{\xi} (1)(x)\ dx = \frac{x^2}{2}\Big]_{0}^{\xi} = \frac{\xi^2}{2} \qquad 0 \le \xi \le 1$$

$$= \int_{\xi-1}^{1} (1)(x)\ dx = \frac{x^2}{2}\Big]_{\xi-1}^{1} = \frac{\xi}{2}(2 - \xi) \qquad 1 \le \xi \le 2$$

which are both parabolic functions as shown in Fig. 2-59e. If the slope of the line is m rather than 1, then the results generalize to $m\xi^2/2$ and $(m\xi/2)(2 - \xi)$.

   To see how this technique relates to antialiasing recall the heuristic intensity modulation technique using the area of the pixel inside the polygon to determine the pixel intensity. Examining the convolution function $c(\xi)$ given above shows that for $m \le 1$ the value of the convolution function at the right hand edge of the pixel, i.e., at $x = \xi = 1$, is the area of the pixel inside the polygon, i.e. $m/2$, (see Fig. 2-50a with $y_i = 0$). For $m > 1$ the value of the convolution integral gives the summation of the areas inside the polygon for the two pixels crossed (see Fig. 2-50b with $y_i = 0$). The result is easily generalized for $y_i \ne 0$. Thus, the two previous algorithms (the heuristic area modulation algorithm and the modified Bresenham algorithm) are equivalent to the convolution of the edge functions, i.e., the straight line $y = mx + b$, with a box function or convolution kernel evaluated at the right hand edge of the pixel.

Figure 2-60 Prefiltered antialiased image at a resolution of 256 × 256 pixels. (*Courtesy of F. Crow.*)

The convolution operation is frequently called filtering, where the convolution kernel is the filter function. The simple area technique discussed above prefilters the image. Prefiltering adjusts the pixel attributes of the computed resolution before displaying the image. The technique of computing the image at a resolution higher than the display resolution and averaging the attributes of several pixels to obtain those at a lower display resolution may be considered a postfiltering operation (see Figs. 2-54 and 2-55).

Although the simple box filter or convolution kernel yields acceptable results, triangular and Gaussian filters yield better results (see Ref. 2-30). Two-dimensional filters are also used. Simple box, pyramidal, conical, and two-dimensional Gaussian convolution kernels or filter functions have been investigated (see Refs. 2-30 to 2-34). Figure 2-60 shows the same scene as Figs. 2-54 and 2-55 computed at a resolution of 256 × 256 pixels, prefiltered with a simple box filter and displayed at a resolution of 256 × 256.

Simple convolution filters are not always effective for small polygons of area less than a pixel or for long, thin polygons. However, antialiasing can be implemented using clipping (see Chap. 3 and Ref. 2-28). The edges of the pixel area form the clipping window. Each individual polygon is clipped against the edges of the window. The remaining polygonal area compared to the pixel area is used to modulate the pixel intensity. If multiple small polygons are present within a pixel, then the average, either uniform or weighted, of their attributes is used to modulate the pixel attributes. An example is shown in Fig. 2-61.

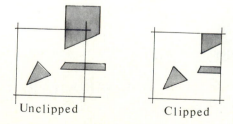

Unclipped   Clipped   **Figure 2-61** Antialiasing using clipping.

2-28 HALFTONING

Antialiasing is a technique using multiple intensity levels to obtain increased visual resolution. Halftoning, on the other hand, is a technique for using a minimum number of intensity levels, generally black and white, to obtain increased visual resolution, i.e., gray scaling or multiple intensity levels. The halftoning technique is quite old. It was originally used in the weaving of silk pictures and other textiles. Modern halftone printing was invented by Stephen Hargon in 1880. With this technique a wide range of photographic gray scales is available using a strictly bilevel display medium: black ink on white paper. Halftone printing is a screen or cellular process (see Ref. 2-35). The size of the cell varies depending on the fineness of the screen and length of exposure. Because of the low paper quality, screens with 50 to 90 dots per inch are used for newspaper photographs. The higher quality paper used in books and magazines allows the use of screens with 100 to 300 dots per inch. The success of the halftone process depends on the human visual system being an integrator; i.e., it blends or smooths discrete information.

The visual resolution of computer-generated images can be increased using a technique called patterning. In contrast to halftone printing, which uses variable cell sizes, patterning generally uses fixed cell sizes. For a display of fixed resolution, several pixels are combined to yield a pattern cell. Thus, patterning trades spatial resolution for improved visual resolution. Fig. 2-62a illustrates one possible group of patterns for a bilevel black-and-white display. Four pixels are used for each cell. This arrangement yields five possible intensity or gray levels (0 to 4). In general, for a bilevel display, the number of possible intensities is one more than the number of pixels in a cell. Care must be taken in selecting the patterns, otherwise unwanted small-scale structure is introduced. For example, neither of the patterns shown in Figs. 2-62b or c should be used. For a large constant-intensity area Fig. 2-62b will result in unwanted horizontal lines and Fig. 2-62c in unwanted vertical lines appearing in the image. The

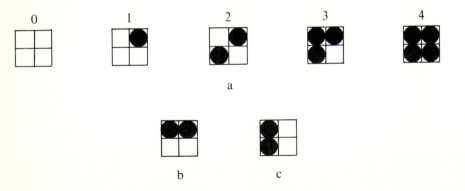

Figure 2-62 2 × 2 bilevel pattern cells.

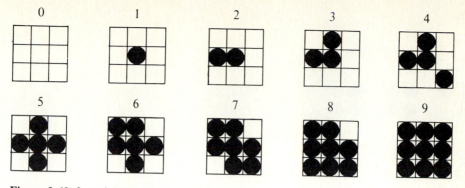

Figure 2-63 3 × 3 bilevel pattern cells.

number of intensity levels available can be increased by increasing the cell size. Patterns for a 3 × 3 pixel cell are shown in Fig. 2-63. These patterns yield ten (0 to 9) intensity levels. Pattern cells need not be square. A 3 × 2 pixel cell yielding seven (0 to 6) intensity levels is shown in Fig. 2-64.

If multiple dot sizes are available, additional intensity levels can be obtained. Figure 2-65 shows patterns for a 2 × 2 pixel cell with two dot sizes. This yields 9 intensity levels. A similar 3 × 3 pixel cell with two dot sizes would yield 27 intensity levels. If more than 1 bit per pixel is available, additional intensity levels are also possible. For a 2 × 2 pixel pattern cell 2 bits per pixel will yield 13 intensity levels as shown in Fig. 2-66. More bits per pixel or larger cell patterns will yield corresponding increases in available intensity levels (Ref. 2-36).

Patterning results in the loss of spatial resolution. This is acceptable if the image is of lower resolution than the display. Techniques for improving visual resolution while maintaining spatial resolution have also been developed (see Ref. 2-37). The simplest is to use a fixed threshold for each pixel. If the image intensity exceeds some threshold value the pixel is white, otherwise it is black.

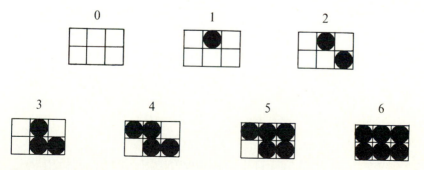

Figure 2-64 3 × 2 bilevel pattern cells.

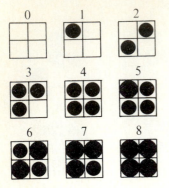

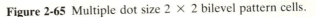

Figure 2-65 Multiple dot size 2 × 2 bilevel pattern cells.

if $I(x, y) > T$ **then** White **else** Black

where $I(x, y)$ is the intensity of the image at pixel (x, y), White corresponds to the maximum display intensity, and Black corresponds to the minimum display intensity. The threshold is usually set at approximately half the maximum display intensity. Figure 2-67b shows results for the photograph of Fig. 2-67a with $T = 150$. For each pixel location, the intensity of the original photograph was quantized in the range 0 to 255, i.e. 8 bits. Figure 2-67b illustrates that a simple thresholding technique results in the loss of considerable fine detail. This is particularly noticeable in the hair and facial features. The fine detail is lost because of the relative large errors in displayed intensity for each pixel.

A technique developed by Floyd and Steinberg (Ref. 2-38) distributes this error to surrounding pixels. Further, the algorithm is cleverly constructed such that the error is always distributed downward and to the right. Hence, if the image is computed in scan line order, no backtracking is necessary. In particular, the Floyd-Steinberg algorithm distributes the error three-eighths to the right, three-eighths downward, one-fourth diagonally. This is shown in

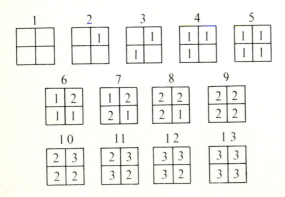

Figure 2-66 Two bits per pixel 2 × 2 pattern cells.

(a)

(b)

(c)

Figure 2-67 Bilevel display techniques. (a) Original photograph, (b) simple thresholding, (c) ordered dither with 8×8 dither matrix. (*Courtesy of J. F. Jarvis, Bell Laboratories.*)

Fig. 2-68. With the threshold midway between the maximum and minimum display intensities, $T = $ (Black + White)/2, the algorithm is

Floyd Steinberg error distribution algorithm

Xmin, Xmax, Ymin, Ymax *are the raster limits for each scan line–top to bottom*

$\quad$ T = (Black + White)/2

$\quad$ **for** y = Ymax **to** Ymin **step** $-$ 1

$\qquad$ *for each pixel on a scan line–left to right*

$\qquad$ **for** x = Xmin **to** Xmax

$\qquad\quad$ *determine pixel display value for threshold* T *and calculate error*

$\qquad\quad$ **if** $I(x, y) < T$ **then**

$\qquad\qquad$ Pixel(x, y) = Black

$\qquad\qquad$ Error = $I(x, y) -$ Black

$\qquad\quad$ **else**

$\qquad\qquad$ Pixel(x, y) = White

$\qquad\qquad$ Error = $I(x, y) -$ White

$\qquad\quad$ **end if**

$\qquad\quad$ *display pixel*

$\qquad\quad$ **Display** Pixel(x, y)

$\qquad\quad$ *distribute error to neighboring pixels*

$\qquad\quad$ $I(x+1, y) = I(x+1, y) + 3{*}\text{Error}/8$

$\qquad\quad$ $I(x, y-1) = I(x, y-1) + 3{*}\text{Error}/8$

$\qquad\quad$ $I(x+1, y-1) = I(x+1, y-1) + \text{Error}/4$

$\qquad$ **next** x

$\quad$ **next** y

$\quad$ **finish**

$\quad$ Distributing the error to neighboring pixels improves the detail in the image because it preserves the information inherent in the image.

$\quad$ Another technique for bilevel displays which increases the visual resolution without reducing the spatial resolution is dither. The technique attempts to introduce a random error into the image. This error is added to the image

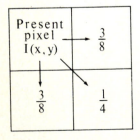

Figure 2-68 Error distribution for Floyd-Steinberg algorithm.

intensity of each pixel before comparison with the selected threshold value. Adding a completely random error does not yield an optimum result. However, an optimum additive error pattern which minimizes pattern texture effects does exist (see Ref. 2-39). The error pattern is added to the image in a repeating checkerboard pattern. This technique is called ordered dither. The smallest ordered dither pattern or matrix is 2×2. An optimum 2×2 matrix, orignally given by Limb (Ref. 2-40), is

$$[D_2] = \begin{bmatrix} 0 & 2 \\ 3 & 1 \end{bmatrix}$$

Larger dither patterns, 4×4, 8×8, etc., are obtained using the recursion relation (see Ref. 2-37)

$$[D_n] = \begin{bmatrix} 4D_{n/2} & 4D_{n/2} + 2U_{n/2} \\ 4D_{n/2} + 3U_{n/2} & 4D_{n/2} + U_{n/2} \end{bmatrix} \quad n \geq 4$$

where n is the matrix size and

$$[U_n] = \begin{bmatrix} 1 & 1 & \ldots & 1 \\ 1 & 1 & & \\ \vdots & & & \\ 1 & & & \end{bmatrix}$$

For example, the 4×4 dither matrix is

$$[D_4] = \begin{bmatrix} 0 & 8 & 2 & 10 \\ 12 & 4 & 14 & 6 \\ 3 & 11 & 1 & 9 \\ 15 & 7 & 13 & 5 \end{bmatrix}$$

As these two examples show n^2 intensities can be reproduced from a dither matrix D_n. Further, the image does not lose spatial resolution as n is increased. The ordered dither algorithm is

Ordered dither algorithm

Xmin, Xmax, Ymin, Ymax *are the raster limits for each scan line–top to bottom*
Mod *is a function that returns the modulo value of its arguments*
    for y = Ymax **to** Ymin **step** -1
        for each pixel on a scan line–left to right
        for x = Xmin **to** Xmax
            determine position in dither matrix
            i = (x **Mod** n) + 1
            j = (y **Mod** n) + 1

> *determine pixel display value*
> **if** $I(x, y) < D(i, j)$ **then**
> $Pixel(x, y) = Black$
> **else**
> $Pixel(x, y) = White$
> **end if**
> *display pixel*
> **Display** $Pixel(x, y)$
>   **next** x
> **next** y
> **finish**

Figure 2-67c shows the image in the original photograph of Fig. 2-67a processed with an 8 × 8 ordered dither matrix. The 8 × 8 dither matrix effectively introduces 64 intensity levels. Figure 2-67c shows that considerable fine detail is restored. The Floyd-Steinberg algorithm and ordered dither can be applied to color images (Ref. 2-41). Patterning techniques can also be used with color (Ref. 2-42).

2-29 REFERENCES

2-1 Bresenham, J.E., "Algorithm for Computer Control of a Digital Plotter," *IBM System Journal,* Vol. 4, pp. 25–30, 1965.

2-2 Pitteway, M.L.V., "Algorithm for Drawing Ellipses or Hyperbolas with a Digital Plotter," *Computer Journal*, Vol. 10, pp. 282–289, 1967.

2-3 Jordon, B.W., Jr., Lennon, W.J., and Holm, B.D., "An Improved Algorithm for the Generation of Nonparametric Curves," *IEEE Trans. Comput.*, Vol. C-22, pp. 1052–1060, 1973.

2-4 Belser, K., Comment on "An Improved Algorithm for the Generation of Nonparametric Curves," *IEEE Trans. Comput.*, Vol. C-25, p. 103, 1976.

2-5 Ramot, J., "Nonparametric Curves," *IEEE Trans. Comput.*, Vol. C-25, pp. 103–104, 1976.

2-6 Horn, B.K.P., "Circle Generators for Display Devices," *Computer Graphics and Image Processing,* Vol. 5, pp. 280–288, 1976.

2-7 Badler, N.I., "Disk Generator for a Raster Display Device," *Computer Graphics and Image Processing,* Vol. 6., pp. 589–593, 1977.

2-8 Doros, M., "Algorithms for Generation of Discrete Circles, Rings, and Disks," *Computer Graphics and Image Processing,* Vol. 10, pp. 366–371, 1979.

2-9 Suenaga, Y., Kamae, T., and Kobayashi, T., "A High-speed Algorithm for the Generation of Straight Lines and Circular Arcs," *IEEE Trans. Comput.*, Vol. C-28, pp. 728–736, 1979.

2-10 Bresenham, J., "A Linear Algorithm for Incremental Digital Display of Circular Arcs," *CACM,* Vol. 20, pp. 100–106, 1977.

2-11 Standish, Thomas A., *Data Structures Techniques,* Addison-Wesley Publishing Company, Reading, Mass., 1980.

2-12 Knuth, Donald, E., *The Art of Computer Programming,* Vol. 3, *Sorting and Searching,* Addison-Wesley Publishing Company, Reading, Mass. 1973.

2-13 Laws, B.A., "A Gray-Scale Graphic Processor Using Run-Length Encoding," *Proc. IEEE Conf. Comput. Graphics, Pattern Recognition, Data Struct.*, pp. 7–10, May 1975.

2-14 Hartke, David H., Sterling, Warren M., and Shemer, Jack E., "Design of a Raster Display Processor for Office Applications," *IEEE Trans. Comput.*, Vol. C-27, pp. 337–348, 1978.

2-15 Jordan, B.W., and Barrett, R.C., "A Cell Organized Raster Display for Line Drawings, *CACM*," Vol. 17, pp. 70–77, 1974.

2-16 Barrett, R.C., and Jordan, B.W., "Scan Conversion Algorithms for a Cell Organized Raster Display," *CACM*, Vol. 17, pp. 157–163, 1974.

2-17 Willett, Ken, "The 4027—Adding a Color Dimension to Graphics," *Tekscope*, Vol. 10, pp. 3–6.

2-18 Negroponte, N., "Raster Scan Approaches to Computer Graphics," *Computers & Graphics*, Vol. 2, pp. 179–193, 1977.

2-19 Baecker, Ronald, "Digital Video Display Systems and Dynamic Graphics," *Computer Graphics*, Vol. 13, pp. 48–56, 1979 (*Proc. SIGGRAPH* 79).

2-20 McCracken, T.E., Sherman, B.W., and Dwyer, S.J., III, "An Economical Tonal Display for Interactive Graphics and Image Analysis Data," *Computers & Graphics*, Vol. 1, pp. 79–94, 1975.

2-21 Whitted, Turner, "A Software Test-Bed for the Development of 3-D Raster Graphics Systems," *Computer Graphics*, Vol. 15, pp. 271–277, 1981 (*Proc. SIGGRAPH* 81).

2-22 Ackland, Bryan, and Weste, Neil, "Real Time Animation on a Frame Store Display System," *Computer Graphics*, Vol. 14, pp. 182–188, 1980 (*Proc. SIGGRAPH* 80).

2-23 Dunlavey, Michael R., "Efficient Polygon-Filling Algorithms for Raster Displays," *Trans. on Graphics*, Vol. 2, pp. 264–273, 1983.

2-24 Ackland, Bryan, and Weste, Neil, "The Edge Flag Algorithm—A Fill Method for Raster Scan Displays," *IEEE Trans. Comput.*, Vol. C-30, pp. 41–48, 1981.

2-25 Smith, Alvy Ray, "Tint Fill," *Computer Graphics*, Vol. 13, pp. 276–283, 1979 (*Proc. SIGGRAPH* 79).

2-26 Shani, Uri, "Filling Regions in Binary Raster Images: A Graph-Theoretic Approach," *Computer Graphics*, Vol. 14, pp. 321–327, 1980 (*Proc. SIGGRAPH* 80).

2-27 Pavlidis, Theo, "*Algorithms for Graphics and Image Processing*," Computer Science Press, Rockville, Md. 1982.

2-28 Crow, Franklin C., "A Comparism of Antialiasing Techinques," *IEEE CG & A*, Vol. 1, pp. 40–47, 1981.

2-29 Pitteway, M.L.V., and Watkinson, D.J., "Bresenham's Algorithm with Gray Scale," *CACM*, Vol. 23, pp. 625–626, 1980.

2-30 Brigham, E. Oran, *The Fast Fourier Transform*, Prentice-Hall, Englewood Cliffs, 1974.

2-31 Crow, Franklin C., "The Aliasing Problem in Computer-Generated Shaded Images," *CACM*, Vol. 20, pp. 799–805, 1977.

2-32 Feibush, Eliot A., Levoy, Marc, and Cook, Robert L., "Synthetic Texturing Using Digital Filters," *Computer Graphics*, Vol. 14, pp. 294–301, 1980 (*Proc. SIGGRAPH* 80).

2-33 Warnock, John, "The Display of Characters Using Gray Level Sample Arrays," *Computer Graphics*, Vol. 14, pp. 302–307, 1980 (*Proc. SIGGRAPH* 80).

2-34 Gupta, Satish, and Sproull, Robert F., "Filtering Edges for Gray-Scale Displays," *Computer Graphics*, Vol. 15, pp. 1–6, 1981 (*Proc. SIGGRAPH* 81).

2-35 *Halftone Methods for the Graphic Arts* (Q3), 3d ed., Eastman Kodak, Rochester, N.Y. 1982.

2-36 Pirsch, P. and Netravali, A.N., "Transmission of Gray Level Images by Multilevel Dither Techniques," *Computers & Graphics*, Vol. 7, pp. 31–44, 1983.

2-37 Jarvis, J.F., Judice, C.N., and Ninke, W.H., "A Survey of Techniques for the Display of Continuous Tone Pictures on Bilevel Displays," *Computer Graphics and Image Processing*, Vol. 5, pp. 13–40, 1976.

2-38 Floyd, R., and Steinberg, L., "An Adaptive Algorithm for Spatial Gray Scale, SID 1975," *Int. Symp. Dig. Tech., Pap.*, pp. 36–37, 1975.

2-39 Bayer, B.E., "An Optimum Method For Two-Level Rendition of Continuous-Tone Pictures," *Int. Conf. Commun., Conf. Rec.*, pp. (26-11)–(26-15), 1973.

2-40 Limb, J.O., "Design of Dither Waveforms for Quantized Visual Signals," *Bell System Technical Journal*, Vol. 48, pp. 2555–2582, 1969.

2-41 Heckbert, Paul, "Color Image Quantization For Frame Buffer Display," *Computer Graphics*, Vol. 16, pp. 297–307, 1982, (*Proc. SIGGRAPH* 82).

2-42 Kubo, Sachio, "Continuous Color Presentation Using a Low-Cost Ink Jet Printer," *Proc. Comput. Graphics Tokyo 84*, 24–27 April, 1984, Tokyo, Japan.

THREE
CLIPPING

Clipping, the process of extracting a portion of a data base, is fundamental to several aspects of computer graphics. In addition to its more typical use in selecting only the specific information required to display a particular scene or view from a larger environment, Chap. 2 has shown that it is useful for antialiasing. Succeeding chapters will show that clipping is useful in hidden line, hidden surface, shadow, and texture algorithms as well. Although beyond the scope of this text, the algorithms and concepts discussed here can be used to implement advanced clipping algorithms that clip polygonal volumes against polygonal volumes. Such algorithms can be used to perform the boolean operations required for simple solid modelers, e.g. the intersection and union of simple cubical and quadric volumes. These approximate solutions are adequate for many applications.

Clipping algorithms are two- or three-dimensional and are for regular or irregular regions or volumes. Clipping algorithms can be implemented in hardware or software. When implemented in software, clipping algorithms are often slower than required for real-time applications. For this reason both two- and three-dimensional clipping algorithms have been implemented in hardware or firmware. These implementations are usually confined to regular clipping regions or volumes. However, very-large-scale integrated (VLSI) circuits offer the possibility of more general implementations which operate at real-time speeds (Ref. 3-1) for both regular and irregular clipping regions or volumes.

3-1 TWO-DIMENSIONAL CLIPPING

Figure 3-1 shows a two-dimensional scene and a regular clipping window. It is defined by left (L), right (R), top (T), and bottom (B) two-dimensional edges. A regular clipping window is rectangular, with its edges aligned with those of the object space or display device. The purpose of a clipping algorithm is

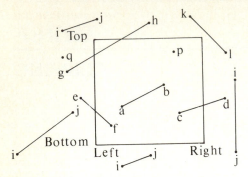

Figure 3-1 Two-dimensional clipping window.

to determine which points, lines, or portions of lines lie within the clipping window. These points, lines, or portions of lines are retained for display. All others are discarded.

Since large numbers of lines or points must be clipped for a typical scene or picture, the efficiency of clipping algorithms is of particular interest. In many cases the large majority of points or lines are either interior to or exterior to the clipping window. Therefore, it is important to be able to quickly accept a line like *ab* or a point like *p* or reject a line like *ij* or a point like *q* in Fig. 3-1.

Points are interior to the clipping window provided that

$$x_L \le x \le x_R \qquad \text{and} \qquad y_B \le y \le y_T$$

The equal sign indicates that points on the window boundary are included within the window.

Lines are interior to the clipping window and hence visible if both end points are interior to the window, e.g., line *ab* in Fig. 3-1. However, if both end points of a line are exterior to the window, the line is not necessarily completely exterior to the window, e.g., line *gh* in Fig. 3-1. If both end points of a line are completely to the right of, completely to the left of, completely above, or completely below the window, then the line is completely exterior to the window and hence invisible. This test will eliminate all the lines labeled *ij* in Fig. 3-1. It will not eliminate either line *gh*, which is partially visible, or line *kl*, which is totally invisible.

If *a* and *b* are the end points of a line, then an algorithm for identifying completely visible and most invisible lines might be:

simple visibility algorithm

a *and* b *are the end points of the line with components* x *and* y

> *for each line*
> *check if the line is totally visible*

if any coordinate of either end point is outside the window, then the line is not totally visible
if $x_a < x_L$ **or** $x_a > x_R$ **then** 1
if $x_b < x_L$ **or** $x_b > x_R$ **then** 1
if $y_a < y_B$ **or** $y_a > y_T$ **then** 1
if $y_b < y_B$ **or** $y_b > y_T$ **then** 1
line is totally visible
Draw line
go to 3
check for totally invisible lines
if both end points are left, right, above, or below the window, the line is trivially invisible

1   **if** $x_a < x_L$ **and** $x_b < x_L$ **then** 2
     if $x_a > x_R$ **and** $x_b > x_R$ **then** 2
     if $y_a > y_T$ **and** $y_b > y_T$ **then** 2
     if $y_a < y_B$ **and** $y_b < y_B$ **then** 2
     the line is partially visible or diagonally crosses the corner invisibly
     determine the intersections
2   *line is invisible*
3   *next line*

Here x_L, x_R, y_T, y_B are the x and y coordinates, respectively, of the left, right, top, and bottom of the window edges. The order in which the tests for visibility or invisibility are performed is immaterial. Some lines will require all four tests before being accepted as totally visible or trivially rejected as totally invisible. Other lines will require only one test. It is also immaterial whether the test for totally visible or totally invisible lines is performed first. However, the line–window edge intersection calculation is computationally expensive and should be performed last.

The tests for totally visible lines and the region tests given above for totally invisible lines can be formalized using a technique due to Dan Cohen and Ivan Sutherland. The technique uses a four-digit (bit) code to indicate which of nine regions contain the end point of a line. The four-bit codes are shown in Fig. 3-2. The rightmost bit is the first bit. The bits are set to 1 based on the following scheme:

First-bit set   — if the end point is to the left of the window
Second-bit set — if the end point is to the right of the window
Third-bit set   — if the end point is below the window
Fourth-bit set — if the end point is above the window

Otherwise, the bit is set to zero. From this it is obvious that, if both end point codes are zero, then both ends of the line lie inside the window and the line is visible.

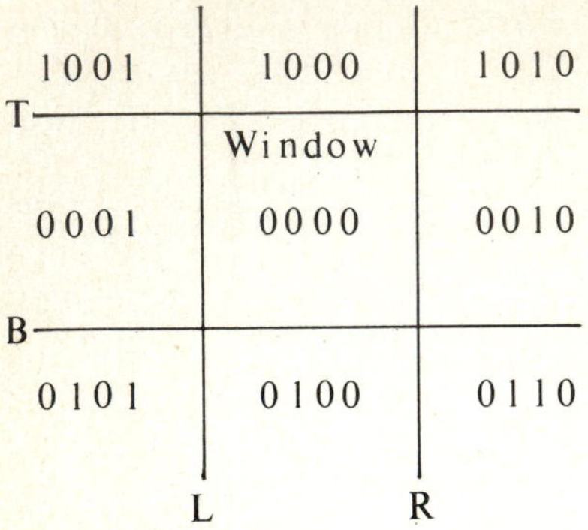

```
1001        1000        1010
T
            Window
0001        0000        0010

B
0101        0100        0110

      L           R
```

Figure 3-2 Codes for line end point regions.

The end point codes can also be used to trivially reject totally invisible lines. Consider the truth table:

True and False	→	False		1 and 0	→	0
False and True	→	False	False = 0	0 and 1	→	0
False and False	→	False	→	0 and 0	→	0
True and True	→	True	True = 1	1 and 1	→	1

which is equivalent to the logical **and** operator. If the bit-by-bit logical intersection of the two end point codes is *not zero*, then the line is totally invisible and may be trivially rejected. The several examples shown in Table 3-1 will help to clarify these statements. Notice in Table 3-1 that, when the logical intersection is not zero, the line is in fact totally invisible. However, when the

Table 3-1 End Point Codes

Line (see Fig. 3-1)	End point codes (see Fig. 3-2)		Logical intersection	Comments
ab	0000	0000	0000	Totally visible
ij	0010	0110	0010	Totally invisible
ij	1001	1000	1000	Totally invisible
ij	0101	0001	0001	Totally invisible
ij	0100	0100	0100	Totally invisible
cd	0000	0010	0000	Partially visible
ef	0001	0000	0000	Partially visible
gh	0001	1000	0000	Partially visible
kl	1000	0010	0000	Totally invisible

logical intersection is zero, the line may be totally or partially visible, or in fact totally invisible. It is for this reason that it is necessary to check both end point codes separately to determine total visibility.

End point code checking can easily be implemented when bit manipulation routines are available. One possible software implementation that does not use bit manipulation routines is shown in the algorithms given below.

If totally visible and trivially invisible lines are determined first, then only potentially partially visible lines, for which the logical intersection of the end point codes is zero, are passed to the line intersection routine. This routine must also, of course, properly identify totally invisible lines that are passed to it.

The intersection between two lines can be determined either parametrically or nonparametrically. Explicitly the equation of the infinite line through $P_1(x_1, y_1)$ and $P_2(x_2, y_2)$ is

$$y = m(x - x_1) + y_1 \qquad \text{or} \qquad y = m(x - x_2) + y_2$$

where

$$m = \frac{y_2 - y_1}{x_2 - x_1}$$

is the slope of the line. The intersections with the window edges are given by

Left:	$x_L, y = m(x_L - x_1) + y_1$	$m \neq \infty$
Right:	$x_R, y = m(x_R - x_1) + y_1$	$m \neq \infty$
Top:	$y_T, x = x_1 + (1/m)(y_T - y_1)$	$m \neq 0$
Bottom:	$y_B, x = x_1 + (1/m)(y_B - y_1)$	$m \neq 0$

Example 3-1 shows that the explicit method permits rejection of improper intersections by simply comparing the intersection values with the window edges.

Example 3-1   Explicit Two-Dimensional Clipping

Consider the clipping window and the lines shown in Fig. 3-3. For the line from $P_1(-3/2, 1/6)$ to $P_2(1/2, 3/2)$ the slope is

$$m = \frac{y_2 - y_1}{x_2 - x_1} = \frac{3/2 - 1/6}{1/2 - (-3/2)} = \frac{2}{3}$$

and the intersections with the window edge are

Left:	$x = -1$	$y = (2/3)[-1 - (-3/2)] + 1/6$
		$= 1/2$
Right:	$x = 1$	$y = (2/3)[1 - (-3/2)] + 1/6$
		$= 11/6$

which is greater than y_T and thus rejected.

Top:	$y = 1$	$x = -3/2 + (3/2)[1 - 1/6]$
		$= -1/4$
Bottom:	$y = -1$	$x = -3/2 + (3/2)[-1 - (1/6)]$
		$= -13/4$

which is less than x_L and thus rejected.

Similarly for the line from $P_3(-3/2, -1)$ to $P_4(3/2, 2)$

$$m = \frac{y_2 - y_1}{x_2 - x_1} = \frac{2 - (-1)}{3/2 - (-3/2)} = 1$$

and

Left: $\quad x = -1 \quad y = (1)[-1 - (-3/2)] + (-1)$
$\qquad\qquad\qquad\quad = -1/2$

Right: $\quad x = 1 \quad y = (1)[1 - (-3/2)] + (-1)$
$\qquad\qquad\qquad\quad = 3/2$

which is greater than y_T and thus rejected.

Top: $\quad\quad y = 1 \quad\quad x = -3/2 + (1)[1 - (-1)]$
$\qquad\qquad\qquad\qquad\quad = 1/2$

Bottom: $\quad y = -1 \quad x = -3/2 + (1)[-1 - (-1)]$
$\qquad\qquad\qquad\qquad\quad = -3/2$

which is less than x_L and thus rejected.

In developing the structure of an efficient clipping algorithm some special cases must be considered. Recalling the discussion above, if the slope of the line is infinite, it is parallel to the left and right edges, and only the top and bottom edges need be checked for intersections. Similarly, if the slope is zero, the line is parallel to the top and bottom edges, and only the left and right edges need be checked for intersections. Finally, if either end point code is zero, one end point is interior to the window, and only one intersection can occur. Figure 3-4 gives a flowchart for an algorithm based on these considerations. A pseudo implementation is given below.

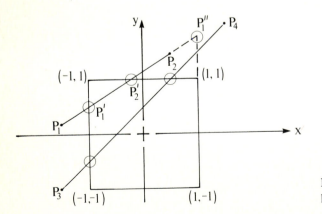

Figure 3-3 Two-dimensional parametric clipping.

Explicit two-dimensional clipping algorithm

P_1 and P_2 are the end points of the line
x_L, x_R, y_T, y_B are the left, right, top, and bottom window coordinates
Iflag is the visibility indicator, -1 invisible, 0 visible

> calculate the end point codes
> put the codes for each end into 1 × 4 arrays called P1code and P2code
> first end point: P_1
> **if** $x_1 < x_L$ **then** P1code(4) = 1 **else** P1code(4) = 0
> **if** $x_1 > x_R$ **then** P1code(3) = 1 **else** P1code(3) = 0
> **if** $y_1 < y_B$ **then** P1code(2) = 1 **else** P1code(2) = 0
> **if** $y_1 > y_T$ **then** P1code(1) = 1 **else** P1code(1) = 0
> second end point: P_2
> **if** $x_2 < x_L$ **then** P2code(4) = 1 **else** P2code(4) = 0
> **if** $x_2 > x_R$ **then** P2code(3) = 1 **else** P2code(3) = 0
> **if** $y_2 < y_B$ **then** P2code(2) = 1 **else** P2code(2) = 0
> **if** $y_2 > y_T$ **then** P2code(1) = 1 **else** P2code(1) = 0
> initialize the visibility flag, the drawing points P_1' and P_2', and the
> counter
> Icount = 0
> Iflag = 0
> $P_1' = P_1$
> $P_2' = P_2$
> check for totally visible line
> Sum1 = 0
> Sum2 = 0
> **for** i = 1 **to** 4
>   Sum1 = Sum1 + P1code(i)
>   Sum2 = Sum2 + P2code(i)
> **next** i
> **if** Sum1 = 0 **and** Sum2 = 0 **then** 7
> line is not totally visible
> check for trivial invisible case
> calculate the logical intersection of the end point codes
> Inter = 0
> **for** i = 1 **to** 4
>   Inter = Inter + Integer((P1code(i) + P2code(i))/2)
>   **if** Inter < > 0 **then**
>   Iflag = -1
>   **go to** 7
>   **end if**
> **next** i
> line may be partially visible
> check for first point inside window
> **if** Sum1 = 0 **then**

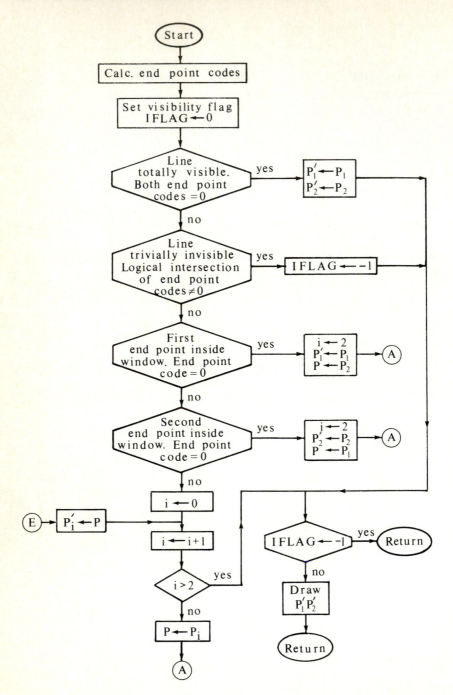

Figure 3-4 Flowchart for explicit two-dimensional clipping.

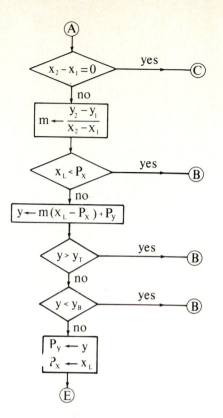

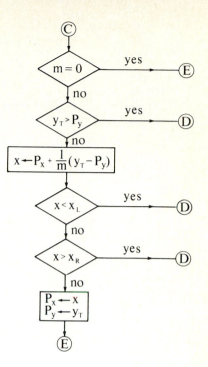

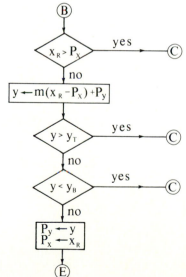

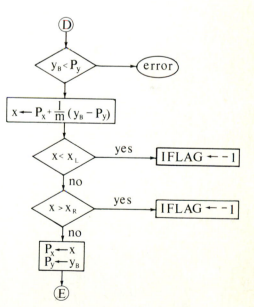

Figure 3-4 (Continued.)

Icount = 2
$P_1' = P_1$
$P = P_2$
go to 2
end if
check for second point inside window
if Sum2 = 0 **then**
    Icount = 2
    $P_2' = P_2$
    $P = P_1$
    go to 2
end if
neither end point inside window

1   Icount = Icount + 1
    if Icount $\geq$ 2 **then** 7
    $P = P_{Icount}$
    initialize m *to a very large number to represent an infinite slope*
    m = Large
    check the left-side intercept
    check for vertical line

2   **if** $(x_2 - x_1) = 0$ **then** 4
    $m = (y_2 - y_1)/(x_2 - x_1)$
    if $x_L < P_x$ **then** 3
    $y = m*(x_L - P_x) + P_y$
    if $y > y_T$ **then** 3
    if $y < y_B$ **then** 3
    a proper intercept has been found
    $P_y = y$
    $P_x = x_L$
    go to 1
    check the right-side intercept

3   **if** $x_R > P_x$ **then** 4
    $y = m*(x_R - P_x) + P_y$
    if $y > y_T$ **then** 4
    if $y < y_B$ **then** 4
    a proper intercept has been found
    $P_y = y$
    $P_x = x_R$
    go to 1
    check the top edge intercept
    check for horizontal line

4   **if** m = 0 **then** 1
    if $y > P_y$ **then** 5
    $x = (1/m)*(y_T - P_y) + P_x$

if $x < x_L$ **then** 5
if $x > x_R$ **then** 5
a proper intercept has been found
$P_x = x$
$P_y = y_T$
go to 1
check the bottom intercept
5     $x = (1/m)*(y_B - P_y) + P_x$
if $x < x_L$ **then** 6
if $x > x_R$ **then** 6
a proper intercept has been found
$P_x = x$
$P_y = y_B$
go to 1
the line is really invisible
6   Iflag $= -1$
completion and drawing routine
7   **if** Iflag $= -1$ **then** 8
Draw $P_1'P_2'$
process next line
8   **finish**

3-2 SUTHERLAND-COHEN SUBDIVISION LINE-CLIPPING ALGORITHM

The algorithm in the previous section is similar to one developed by Dan Cohen and Ivan Sutherland. The previous algorithm clips the line successively against each of the window edges and examines the resulting intersection point to see if it is within the window, i.e., is a proper intercept. This is done first for the line P_1P_2 to yield $P_1'P_2$ and then for the line P_2P_1' to yield $P_2'P_1'$, the clipped line.

The Sutherland-Cohen algorithm also divides the line at a window edge. In contrast it does not check to see if the intersection point is within the window but rather attempts to accept or reject the two resulting segments using the line end point codes for the segments. Recalling line P_1P_2 of Fig. 3-3 immediately reveals a difficulty with this simple technique. If P_1P_2 is clipped against the left edge of the window, the two new segments are P_1P_1' and $P_1'P_2$. The end point codes for both these segments indicate that they both may be partially visible. Hence, neither can be rejected as invisible or accepted as visible. The key to the Sutherland-Cohen algorithm is always knowing that one of the end points is outside the window. Thus, the segment from this end point to the intersection point can always be rejected as invisible. The algorithm then proceeds with the remainder of the line. In effect this replaces the original end point with the intersection point. Simply stated, the Sutherland-Cohen algorithm is

For each window edge:

For the line P_1P_2, determine if the line is totally visible or can be trivially rejected as invisible.

If P_1 is outside the window continue; otherwise, swap P_1 and P_2.

Replace P_1 with the intersection of P_1P_2 and the window edge.

Example 3-2 further illustrates the algorithm.

Example 3-2   Sutherland-Cohen Clipping

Again consider the line P_1P_2 clipped against the window shown in Fig. 3-3. The end point codes for $P_1(-3/2, 1/6)$ and $P_2(1/2, 3/2)$ are (0001) and (1000), respectively. The line is neither totally visible nor trivially invisible. P_1 is outside the window.

The intersection with the left edge ($x = -1$) of the window is $P_1'(-1, 1/2)$. Replace P_1 with P_1' to yield the new line $P_1(-1, 1/2)$ to $P_2(1/2, 3/2)$.

The end point codes for P_1 and P_2 are now (0000) and (1000), respectively. The line is neither totally visible nor trivially invisible.

P_1 is inside the window. Swap P_1 and P_2 to yield the new line $P_1(1/2, 3/2)$ to $P_2(-1, 1/2)$. Also swap the end point codes.

The intersection with the right edge ($x = 1$) of the window is $P_1''(1, 11/6)$. Replace P_1 with P_1'' to yield the new line $P_1(1, 11/6)$ to $P_2(-1, 1/2)$.

The end point codes for P_1 and P_2 are now (1000) and (0000), respectively. The line is neither totally visible nor trivially invisible.

P_1 is outside the window.

The intersection with the top edge ($y = 1$) of the window is $P_2'(-1/4, 1)$. Replace P_1 with P_2' to yield the new line $P_1(-1/4, 1)$ to $P_2(-1, 1/2)$.

The end point codes for P_1 and P_2 are (0000) and (0000), respectively. The line is totally visible.

The procedure is complete.

Draw the line.

A pseudo implementation of the algorithm is given below. Because the same concept is repeatedly applied, subroutine modules are used to determine the visibility of a line segment, the end point codes, and the logical intersection of the end point codes.

Sutherland-Cohen two-dimensional clipping algorithm

Window *is a 1 × 4 array containing the left, right, bottom, and top edges* (x_L, x_R, y_B, y_T) *of the rectangular clipping window*
P_1 *and* P_2 *are the end points of the line with* x *and* y *component* $P_1x, P_1y,$

and P_2x, P_2y

Iflag *is used to indicate a vertical slope;* -1 *vertical, 0 nonvertical*

    initialize Iflag

    Iflag $= 0$

    check for vertical line

    if $P_2x - P_1x = 0$ **then**

        Iflag $= -1$

    else

        calculate slope

        Slope $= (P_2y - P_1y)/(P_2x - P_1x)$

    end if

    for each window edge

    for $i = 1$ **to** 4

        call Cohen(P_1, P_2, Window; Visible)

        if Visible $=$ yes **then** 2

        if Visible $=$ no **then** 3

        check for a vertical line

        if Iflag $= -1$ and $i \leq 2$ **then** 1

        select the appropriate intersection routine

        if $i \leq 2$ **then**

            Intery $=$ Slope*(Window$_i$ $- P_1x$) $+ P_1y$

            $P_1x =$ Window$_i$

            $P_1y =$ Intery

        else

            if Iflag $= -1$ **then**

                $P_1y =$ Window$_i$

            else

                Interx $= (1/\text{Slope})*($Window$_i$ $- P_1y$) $+ P_1x$

                $P_1x =$ Interx

                $P_1y =$ Window$_i$

            end if

        end if

1   **next** i

    draw the visible line

2   Draw P_1P_2

3   **finish**

subroutine module to determine the visibility of a line segment

subroutine Cohen(P_1, P_2, Window; Visible)

P_1 *and* P_2 *are the end points of the line segment* *with* x *and* y *components* P_1x, P_1y *and* P_2x, P_2y

Window *is a* 1×4 *array containing the left, right, bottom, and top edges* (x_L, x_R, y_B, y_T) *of the retangular clipping window*

Visible *is a flag, no, partial, yes as the line segment is totally invisible, partially visible, or totally visible*

    calculate the end point codes

```
    call Endpoint(P₁, Window; P1code, Sum1)
    call Endpoint(P₂, Window; P2code, Sum2)
    check if the line is totally visible
    if Sum1 = 0 and Sum2 = 0 then Visible = yes
    check if the line is trivially invisible
    call Logical(P1code, P2code; Inter)
    if Inter < > 0 then Visible = no
    the line may be partially visible
    Visible = partial
    check that P₁ is outside
    if Sum1 = 0 then 1
    swap the end points
    Temp = P₁
    P₁ = P₂
    P₂ = Temp
1   return
```

subroutine module to calculate the end point codes

subroutine Endpoint(P, Window; Pcode, Sum)

P_x, P_y *are the* x *and* y *components of the point* P
Window *is a 1 × 4 array containing the left, right, bottom, and top edges*
(x_L, x_R, y_B, y_T) *of the rectangular clipping window*
Pcode *is a 1 × 4 array containing the end point code*
Sum *is the element-by-element sum of* Pcode

```
    determine the end point codes
    if Pₓ < xL then Pcode(4) = 1 else Pcode(4) = 0
    if Pₓ > xR then Pcode(3) = 1 else Pcode(3) = 0
    if Py < yB then Pcode(2) = 1 else Pcode(2) = 0
    if Py > yT then Pcode(1) = 1 else Pcode(1) = 0
    calculate the sum
    Sum = 0
    for i = 1 to 4
        Sum = Sum + Pcode(i)
    next i
    return
```

subroutine module to find logical intersection

subroutine Logical(P1code, P2code; Inter)

P1code *is a 1 × 4 array containing end point codes*
P2code *is a 1 × 4 array containing end point codes*
Inter *is the sum of the bits for the logical intersection*

```
    Inter = 0
    for i = 1 to 4
        Inter = Inter + Integer((P1code(i) + P2code(i))/2)
    next i
    return
```

3-3   MIDPOINT SUBDIVISION ALGORITHM

The previous algorithm requires the calculation of the intersection of the line with the window edge. This direct calculation can be avoided by performing a binary search for the intersection by always dividing the line at its midpoint. The algorithm, which is a special case of the Sutherland-Cohen algorithm, was proposed by Sproull and Sutherland (Ref. 3-2) for implementation in hardware. Implemented in software the algorithm is slower than using direct calculation of the intersection of the line with the window edge as discussed above. Implementation in hardware is fast and efficient because a parallel architecture can be used and hardware addition and division by 2 are very fast. In hardware, division by 2 can be accomplished by shifting each bit to the right. For example, the 4-bit binary representation of decimal 6 is 0110. Shifting each bit to the right by one yields 0011 which is decimal 3 = 6/2.

The algorithm uses the line end point codes and associated tests to immediately identify totally visible lines, e.g., line a in Fig. 3-5, and trivially invisible lines, e.g., line b in Fig. 3-5. Lines which cannot be immediately identified using these tests, e.g., lines c to g in Fig. 3-5, are subdivided into two equal parts. The tests are then applied to each half until the intersection with the window edge is found or the length of the divided segments is infinitesimal, i.e. a point, e.g. line f in Fig. 3-5. The visibility of the point is then determined. The result is to perform a logarithmic search for the intersection point. The maximum number of subdivisions is equal to the precision of the representation of the end points of the line.

To illustrate the technique consider lines c and f of Fig. 3-5. Although line f is not visible, it crosses the corner and cannot be trivially rejected. Subdivision at the midpoint P_{m_1} allows the half $P_{m_1}P_2$ to be trivially rejected. The half $P_{m_1}P_1$ again crosses the corner and cannot be trivially rejected. Further, subdivision at P_{m_2} allows rejection of $P_{m_2}P_1$ as invisible. Subdivision of the remaining portion $P_{m_1}P_{m_2}$ continues until the intersection of the line with the extension of the right-hand window edge is found within some specified accuracy. This point is then examined and found to be invisible. Hence, the entire line is invisible.

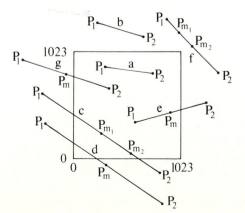

Figure 3-5 Midpoint subdivision.

From the end point codes line c of Fig. 3-5 is also neither totally visible, nor can it be trivially rejected as invisible. Subdivision at the midpoint P_{m_1} yields the same result for both halves. Setting aside the segment $P_{m_1}P_1$ for later consideration, the segment $P_{m_1}P_2$ is further subdivided at P_{m_2}. The segment $P_{m_1}P_{m_2}$ is now totally visible, and the segment $P_{m_2}P_2$ partially visible. The segment $P_{m_1}P_{m_2}$ could now be drawn. However, this would result in the visible portion of the line being inefficiently drawn as a series of short segments. Instead the point P_{m_2} is remembered as the current farthest visible point from P_1. Subdivision of the segment $P_{m_2}P_2$ continues. Each time a visible midpoint is found it is declared the current farthest visible point from P_1, until the intersection with the bottom edge of the window is determined to some specified accuracy. This intersection is then declared the farthest visible point from P_1. The segment $P_{m_1}P_1$ is then examined in the same way. For line c of Fig. 3-5 the farthest visible point from P_2 is the intersection with the left hand window edge. The visible portion of the line P_1P_2 is then drawn between the two intersections.

For lines like c and d of Fig. 3-5 the midpoint subdivision algorithm performs two logarithmic searches for the two farthest visible points from the ends of the line. These are the intersections with the window edges. Each midpoint subdivision is a crude guess at these points. For lines like e and g which have one end point visible, one of these searches is trivial. In a software implementation the two searches are performed sequentially. In a hardware implementation they are performed in parallel. The algorithm can be formalized in three steps (Ref. 3-3).

For each end point:

If the end point is visible, then it is the farthest visible point. The process is complete. If not, continue.

If the line is trivially determined to be invisible, no output is generated. The process is complete. If not, continue.

Guess at the farthest visible point by dividing the line P_1P_2 at its midpoint P_m. Apply the tests above to the two segments P_1P_m and P_mP_2. If P_mP_2 is trivially rejected as invisible, the midpoint is an overestimation of the farthest visible point. Continue with P_1P_m. Otherwise, the midpoint is an underestimation of the farthest visible point. Continue with P_2P_m. If the segment becomes so short that the midpoint corresponds to the accuracy of the machine or, as specified, to the end points, evaluate the visibility of the point and the process is complete.

A specific example better illustrates the algorithm.

Example 3-3   Midpoint Subdivision

Consider the window in the screen coordinates shown in Fig. 3-5 to have left, right, bottom, and top edges of 0, 1023, 0, 1023, respectively. The line c has end points $P_1(-307, 631)$ and $P_2(820, -136)$ in screen coordinates. The end point code for P_1 is (0001), and that for P_2 is (0100). Both end point codes are not zero, so the line is not totally visible. The logical intersection of the end point codes is (0000). The line may not be trivially rejected as invisible. Look for the intersections.

The midpoint is

$$x_m = \frac{x_2 + x_1}{2} = \frac{820 - 307}{2} = 256.5 = 256$$

$$y_m = \frac{y_2 + y_1}{2} = \frac{-136 + 631}{2} = 247.5 = 247$$

using integer arithmetic. The end point code for the midpoint is (0000). Neither segment P_1P_m nor P_2P_m is either totally visible or trivially invisible. Putting aside the segment P_2P_m and continuing with P_1P_m the subdivision process continues as shown in Table 3-2.

Table 3-2

P_1	P_2	P_m	Comment
−307, 631	820, −136	256, 247	Save P_mP_2, continue P_1P_m
−307, 631	256, 247	−26, 439	Continue P_mP_2
−26, 439	256, 247	115, 343	Continue P_1P_m
−26, 439	115, 343	44, 391	Continue P_1P_m
−26, 439	44, 391	9, 415	Continue P_1P_m
−26, 439	9, 415	−9, 427	Continue P_mP_2
−9, 427	9, 415	0, 421	Success
256, 247	820, −136	538, 55	Recall saved P_mP_2, continue P_mP_2
538, 55	820, −136	679, −41	Continue P_1P_m
538, 55	679, −41	608, 7	Continue P_mP_2
608, 7	679, −41	643, −17	Continue P_1P_m
608, 7	643, −17	625, −5	Continue P_1P_m
608, 7	625, −5	616, 1	Continue P_mP_2
616, 1	625, −5	620, −2	Continue P_1P_m
616, 1	620, −2	618, −1	Continue P_1P_m
616, 1	618, −1	617, 0	Success

The actual equation of the line P_1P_2 yields intersection points at (0, 422) and (620, 0). The differences are due to integer arithmetic truncation.

A flowchart of the algorithm is shown in Fig. 3-6. A pseudo implementation of the algorithm is shown below.

midpoint subdivision two-dimensional clipping algorithm

Window *is a 1 × 4 array containing the left, right, bottom, and top edges*
(x_L, x_R, y_B, y_T) *of the rectangular clipping window*
P_1 *and* P_2 *are the end points of the line*
  calculate the end point codes
  put the codes for each end into 1 × 4 arrays called P1code *and* P2code
  first end point: P_1
  call Endpoint(P_1, Window; P1code, Sum1)
  second end point: P_2
  call Endpoint(P_2, Window; P2code, Sum2)
  check if the line is totally visible
  if Sum1 $= 0$ **and** Sum2 $= 0$ **then** 5
  the line is not totally visible

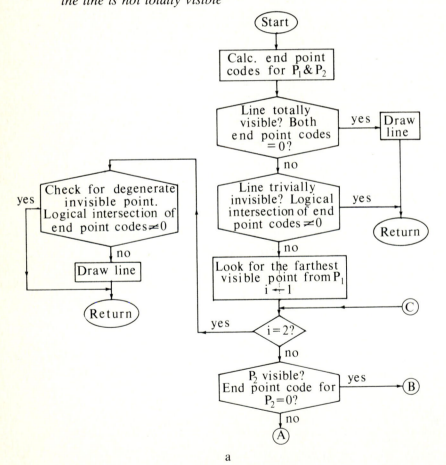

a

Figure 3-6 Flowchart for midpoint subdivision algorithm.

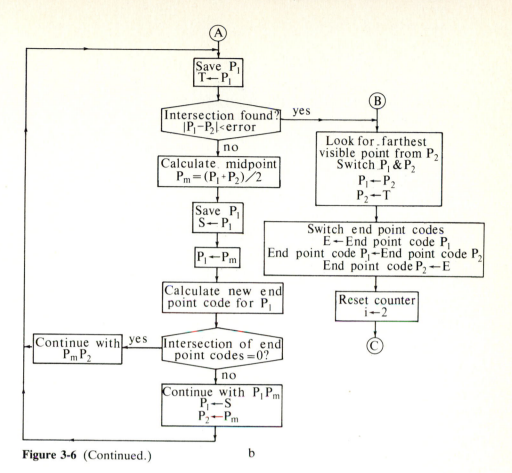

Figure 3-6 (Continued.)   b

check for trivially invisible case
call Logical(P1code, P2code; Inter)
if Inter $<>0$ **then** 6
line may be partially visible
look for farthest visible point from P_1
$i = 1$
process complete

1   **if** $i = 2$ **then** 4
is P_2 *the farthest visible point from* P_1?
if Sum2 $= 0$ **then** 3
save original P_1

2   Temp $= P_1$
has intersection been found?
if $|P_1 - P_2| <$ Error **then** 3
calculate the midpoint
$P_m = (P_1 + P_2)/2$

save current P_1
Save = P_1
replace P_1 *with the midpoint*
$P_1 = P_m$
calculate the new end point code for P_1
call Endpoint(P_1, Window; P1code, Sum1)
check if the segment $P_m P_2$ *is trivially invisible*
call Logical(P1code, P2code; Inter)
if Inter = 0 **then** 2
$P_m P_2$ *invisible, continue with* $P_1 P_m$
P_1 = Save
$P_2 = P_m$
go to 2
the farthest visible point from P_1 *has been found*
look for the farthest visible point from P_2
switch P_1 *and* P_2

3     $P_1 = P_2$
P_2 = Temp
switch the end point codes
Endcode = P1code
P1code = P2code
P2code = Endcode
reset counter
i = 2
go to 1
both intersections have now been found
check for degenerate invisible point

4   **call** Logical(P1code, P2code; Inter)
if Inter < > **then** 6

5   Drawline

6   **finish**

subroutine module to calculate the end point codes

subroutine Endpoint(P1, Window; Pcode, Sum)

P_x, P_y *are the* x *and* y *components of the point* P
Window *is a 1 × 4 array containing the left, right, bottom, and top edges*
(x_L, x_R, y_B, y_T) *of the rectangular clipping window*
Pcode *is a 1 × 4 array containing the end point code*
Sum *is the element by element sum of* Pcode
    determine the end point codes
    if $P_x < x_L$ **then** Pcode(4) = 1 **else** Pcode(4) = 0
    if $P_x > x_R$ **then** Pcode(3) = 1 **else** Pcode(3) = 0
    if $P_y < y_B$ **then** Pcode(2) = 1 **else** Pcode(2) = 0
    if $P_y > y_T$ **then** Pcode(1) = 1 **else** Pcode(1) = 0
    calculate the sum
    Sum = 0

```
    for i = 1 to 4
        Sum = Sum + Pcode(i)
    next i
    return
```

subroutine module to find logical intersection

subroutine Logical(P1code, P2code; Inter)
P1code *is a 1 × 4 array containing end point codes*
P2code *is a 1 × 4 array containing end point codes*
Inter *is the sum of the bits for the intersection*

```
    Inter = 0
    for i = 1 to 4
        Inter = Inter + Integer((P1code(i) + P2code(i))/2)
    next i
    return
```

The previous explicit clipping algorithm determined the end point codes and their logical intersection within the body of the algorithm. Here subroutine modules are used because new end point codes and logical intersections are repeatedly required.

3-4 GENERALIZED TWO-DIMENSIONAL LINE CLIPPING FOR CONVEX BOUNDARIES

The algorithms presented above assume that the clipping window is a regular rectangular polygonal boundary. For many purposes the clipping window is not a regular rectangular polygon. For example, suppose that the rectangular clipping window is rotated with respect to the coordinate system as shown in Fig. 3-7. Then neither of the algorithms discussed above is applicable. Cyrus and Beck have developed an algorithm for clipping to arbitrary convex regions (Ref. 3-4).

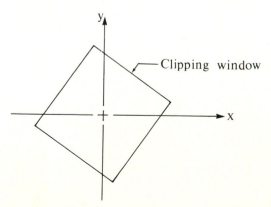

Figure 3-7 Rotated clipping window.

Before specifically developing the Cyrus-Beck algorithm in the next section, consider clipping a parametrically defined line to a window. The parametric equation of a line segment from P_1 to P_2 is

$$P(t) = P_1 + (P_2 - P_1)t \qquad 0 \le t \le 1 \tag{3-1}$$

where t is the parameter. Restricting the range of t to $0 \le t \le 1$ makes it a line segment rather than an infinite line. The parametric description of a line is independent of any coordinate system. This attribute makes the parametric form particularly useful for determining the intersection between a line and the edge of an arbitrary convex polygon. The technique is first illustrated with a regular rectangular window.

For a two-dimensional Cartesian coordinate system, Eq. (3-1) yields a pair of parametric equations, one for each coordinate, i.e.,

$$x(t) = x_1 + (x_2 - x_1)t \qquad 0 \le t \le 1 \tag{3-2a}$$

$$y(t) = y_1 + (y_2 - y_1)t \qquad 0 \le t \le 1 \tag{3-2b}$$

For a rectangular clipping window one of the coordinates of the intersection with each edge is known. Only the other need be calculated. From Eq. (3-1) the value of the parameter t for any point on the line segment is

$$t = \frac{P(t) - P_1}{P_2 - P_1}$$

From Eq. (3-2) the specific value of t corresponding to the intersection with the window edge is

For the left edge: $\qquad t = \dfrac{x_L - x_1}{x_2 - x_1} \qquad 0 \le t \le 1$

For the right edge: $\qquad t = \dfrac{x_R - x_1}{x_2 - x_1} \qquad 0 \le t \le 1$

For the top edge: $\qquad t = \dfrac{y_T - y_1}{y_2 - y_1} \qquad 0 \le t \le 1$

For the bottom edge: $\qquad t = \dfrac{y_B - y_1}{y_2 - y_1} \qquad 0 \le t \le 1$

where x_L, x_R, y_B, y_T are the coordinates of the left, right, bottom, and top window edges. If solutions of these equations yield values of t outside the range $0 \le t \le 1$, then those solutions are discarded since they represent points beyond the end of the line segment.

Example 3-4   Simple Partially Visible Line

Consider the partially visible line from $P_1(-3/2, -3/4)$ to $P_2(3/2, 1/2)$ clipped to the window $(-1, 1, -1, 1)$, i.e., x_L, x_R, y_B, y_T as shown in Fig. 3-8.
For the left edge:

$$t = \frac{x_L - x_1}{x_2 - x_1} = \frac{-1 - (-3/2)}{3/2 - (-3/2)} = \frac{1/2}{3} = \frac{1}{6}$$

For the right edge:

$$t = \frac{x_R - x_1}{x_2 - x_1} = \frac{1 - (-3/2)}{3/2 - (-3/2)} = \frac{5/2}{3} = \frac{5}{6}$$

For the bottom edge:

$$t = \frac{y_B - y_1}{y_2 - y_1} = \frac{-1 - (-3/4)}{1/2 - (-3/4)} = \frac{-1/4}{5/4} = \frac{-1}{5}$$

which is less than zero and is thus rejected. For the top edge:

$$t = \frac{y_T - y_1}{y_2 - y_1} = \frac{1 - (-3/4)}{1/2 - (-3/4)} = \frac{7/4}{5/4} = \frac{7}{5}$$

which is greater than one and is also rejected. The visible portion of the line is then from $1/6 \le t \le 5/6$.

The x and y coordinates of the intersection points are obtained from the parametric equations. In particular, for $t = 1/6$ Eq. (3-2) yields

$$x(1/6) = -3/2 + [3/2 - (-3/2)](1/6) = -1$$

which of course is already known since $x = -1$ represents the intersection with the left edge of the window. The y coordinate is

$$y(1/6) = -3/4 + [1/2 - (-3/4)](1/6) = -13/24$$

Similarly for $t = 5/6$

$$[x(5/6) \quad y(5/6)] = [-3/2 \quad -3/4] + [3/2 - (-3/2) \quad 1/2 - (-3/4)] (5/6)$$
$$= [1 \quad 7/24]$$

where the separate calculations for the x and y coordinates have been combined into one. Again, since the line intersects the right hand edge the x coordinate for the parameter value of 5/6 is already known.

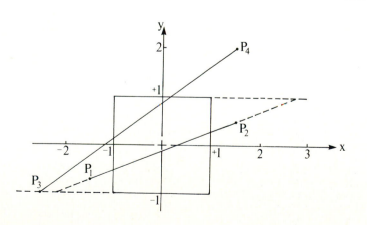

Figure 3-8 Parametric clipping of partially visible lines.

From the above example the technique appears to be simple and straightforward. However, there are some difficulties which are best illustrated by further examples.

Example 3-5   Partially Visible Line

Consider the line from $P_3(-5/2, -1)$ to $P_4(3/2, 2)$ also shown in Fig. 3-8 and again clipped to the window $(-1, 1, -1, 1)$. Here, the intersection points are given by the parametric values

$$t_L = 3/8 \qquad t_R = 7/8 \qquad t_B = 0 \qquad t_T = 2/3$$

and all four values of t fall in the range $0 \le t \le 1$.

It is well known that, if a straight line segment intersects a convex polygon, it can do so in at most two points. Hence, only two of the four parameter values found in the above example are required. Rearranging the four parameter values into a numerically increasing sequence yields t_B, t_L, t_T, t_R. Inspection of Fig. 3-8 shows that the required values are $t_L = 3/8$ and $t_T = 2/3$ which yield intersection points at $(-1, 1/8)$ and $(1/6, 1)$, respectively. These parameter values are the maximum minimum value and the minimum maximum value of the t parameters. Formally determining these values is a simple classical problem in linear programming. An algorithm for this is given in the next section.

As in any clipping algorithm, the ability to quickly identify and separate totally visible and totally invisible lines is important. The next two examples illustrate some further difficulties.

Example 3-6   Totally Visible Lines

Consider the entirely visible line $P_1(-1/2, 1/2)$ to $P_2(1/2, -1/2)$, again clipped to the window $(-1, 1, -1, 1)$ as shown in Fig. 3-9. The parameter values for the window edge intersections are

$$t_L = -1/2 \qquad t_R = 3/2 \qquad t_B = 3/2 \qquad t_T = -1/2$$

All these values are outside the range $0 \le t \le 1$.

From Example 3-6 it appears that a technique for identifying totally visible lines has been found. However, the next example illustrates that this is not the case.

Example 3-7   Totally Invisible Lines

Consider the totally invisible line $P_3(3/2, -1/2)$ to $P_4(2, 1/2)$ also shown in Fig. 3-9. The clipping window is again $(-1, 1, -1, 1)$. Here the parametric values for the window edge intersections are

$$t_L = -5 \qquad t_R = -1 \qquad t_B = -1/2 \qquad t_T = 3/2$$

Again, all these values are outside the range $0 \le t \le 1$.

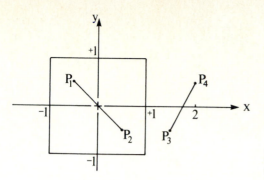

Figure 3-9 Parametric clipping of visible and invisible lines.

The result given in Example 3-7 is the same condition previously identified with a totally visible line. But in contrast to the line P_1P_2 of Example 3-6, the line P_3P_4 is invisible. From these two examples, it is evident that for parametric lines no simple, unique method for distinguishing totally visible or totally invisible lines is available. It is also evident that a more formal approach to the problem is required.

3-5   CYRUS-BECK ALGORITHM

To develop a reliable clipping algorithm it is necessary to find a reliable technique for determining whether a point on a line is inside, on, or outside a window. The Cyrus-Beck algorithm (Ref. 3-4) uses the normal vector to accomplish this.

Consider a convex clipping region R. Although R is not limited to a two-dimensional region, the examples used for the present discussion will assume one. Thus, R may be any convex planar polygon. It may *not* be a concave polygon. An inward normal vector for any point a on the boundary of R is given by the vector dot product

$$\mathbf{n} \cdot (\mathbf{b} - \mathbf{a}) \geq 0$$

where b is any other point on the boundary of R. To see this, recall that the dot product of two vectors $\mathbf{V}_1$ and $\mathbf{V}_2$ is given by

$$\mathbf{V}_1 \cdot \mathbf{V}_2 = |\mathbf{V}_1||\mathbf{V}_2| \cos \theta$$

where θ is the smaller of the angles formed by $\mathbf{V}_1$ and $\mathbf{V}_2$. Note that if $\theta = \pi/2$ then $\cos \theta = 0$ and $\mathbf{V}_1 \cdot \mathbf{V}_2 = 0$; i.e., when the dot product of two vectors is zero, the two vectors are perpendicular. Figure 3-10 shows a convex region R, i.e. a clipping window. At the point a on the boundary both the inner normal $\mathbf{n}_i$ and the outer normal $\mathbf{n}_o$ are shown along with several vectors to other points on the region boundary. The angle between $\mathbf{n}_i$ and any of the vectors is always in the range $-\pi/2 \leq \theta \leq \pi/2$. In this range the cosine is always positive. Hence, the dot product is always positive, as stated above. However, the angle between the outer normal and any of these vectors is always $\pi - \theta$ and $\cos (\pi - \theta) = -\cos \theta$ is always negative. To further illustrate this, consider the following example.

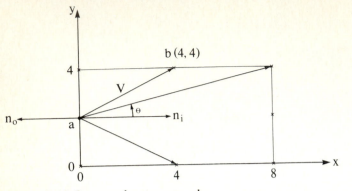

Figure 3-10 Inner and outer normals.

Example 3-8 Inner and Outer Normals

Consider the rectangular region in Fig. 3-10. Here the inner and outer normals at a are $\mathbf{n}_i = \mathbf{i}$ and $\mathbf{n}_o = -\mathbf{i}$, respectively, where $\mathbf{i}$ is the unit vector in the x direction. Table 3-3 shows the values of the dot product of the inner and outer normals and vectors from a to various points b on the region boundary. As a specific example note that the inner normal at a is

$$\mathbf{n}_i = \mathbf{i}$$

The vector from $a\,(0, 2)$ to $b\,(4, 4)$ is

$$\mathbf{b} - \mathbf{a} = 4\mathbf{i} + 2\mathbf{j}$$

The dot product is

$$\mathbf{n}_i \cdot (\mathbf{b} - \mathbf{a}) = \mathbf{i} \cdot (4\mathbf{i} + 2\mathbf{j}) = 4$$

Table 3-3

a	b	$\mathbf{n}_i \cdot (\mathbf{b} - a)$	$\mathbf{n}_o \cdot (\mathbf{b} - a)$
(0, 2)	(0, 4)	0	0
	(4, 4)	4	-4
	(8, 4)	8	-8
	(8, 2)	8	-8
	(8, 0)	8	-8
	(4, 0)	4	-4
	(0, 0)	0	0

The zero values in Table 3-3 indicate that the vector and the inner and outer normals are perpendicular.

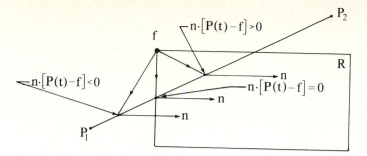

Figure 3-11 Vector directions.

Returning to the determination of the intersection of a line and a window edge, again consider the parametric representation of the line from P_1 to P_2:

$$P(t) = P_1 + (P_2 - P_1)t \qquad 0 \le t \le 1$$

If f is a boundary point of the convex region R and $\mathbf{n}$ is an inner normal for one of its boundaries, then for any particular value of t, i.e., any particular point on the line P_1P_2,

$$\mathbf{n} \cdot [\mathbf{P(t)} - \mathbf{f}] < 0$$

implies that the vector $\mathbf{P(t)} - \mathbf{f}$ is pointed away from the interior of R.

$$\mathbf{n} \cdot [\mathbf{P(t)} - \mathbf{f}] = 0$$

implies that $\mathbf{P(t)} - \mathbf{f}$ is pointed parallel to the plane containing f and perpendicular to the normal.

$$\mathbf{n} \cdot [\mathbf{P(t)} - \mathbf{f}] > 0$$

implies that $\mathbf{P(t)} - \mathbf{f}$ is pointed toward the interior of R as illustrated in Fig. 3-11. Together these conditions show that, if the convex region R is closed, i.e., for the two-dimensional case a closed convex polygon, an infinite line which intersects the region does so at precisely two points. Further, these two points do not lie on the same boundary plane or edge. Thus,

$$\mathbf{n} \cdot [\mathbf{P}(t) - \mathbf{f}] = 0$$

has only one solution. If the point f lies in the boundary plane or edge for which $\mathbf{n}$ is the inner normal, then that point t on the line $P(t)$ which satisfies this condition is the intersection of the line and the boundary plane.

Example 3-9 Cyrus-Beck Clipping—Partially Visible Lines

Consider the line from $P_1(-1, 1)$ to $P_2(9, 3)$ clipped to the rectangular region shown in Fig. 3-12. The equation of the line P_1P_2 is $y = 0.2(x + 6)$ which intersects the window at $(0, 1.2)$ and $(8, 2.8)$. The parametric representation of the line P_1P_2 is

$$P(t) = P_1 + (P_2 - P_1)t = [-1 \ \ 1] + [10 \ \ 2]t$$
$$= (10t - 1)\mathbf{i} + (2t + 1)\mathbf{j} \qquad 0 \le t \le 1$$

where $\mathbf{i}$, $\mathbf{j}$ are the unit vectors in the x and y directions respectively. The four inner normals are

Left: $\mathbf{n}_L = \mathbf{i}$
Right: $\mathbf{n}_R = -\mathbf{i}$
Bottom: $\mathbf{n}_B = \mathbf{j}$
Top: $\mathbf{n}_T = -\mathbf{j}$

Choosing $f(0, 0)$ for the left edge yields

$$\mathbf{P(t)} - \mathbf{f} = (10t - 1)\mathbf{i} + (2t + 1)\mathbf{j}$$

and

$$\mathbf{n}_L \cdot [\mathbf{P(t)} - \mathbf{f}] = 10t - 1 = 0$$

or

$$t = 1/10$$

is the intersection of the line and the left edge of the clipping window. Hence,

$$P(1/10) = [-1 \quad 1] + [10 \quad 2](1/10) = [0 \quad 1.2]$$

which is the same as that explicitly calculated.
Choosing $f(8, 4)$ for the right edge yields

$$\mathbf{P(t)} - \mathbf{f} = (10t - 9)\mathbf{i} + (2t - 3)\mathbf{j}$$

and

$$\mathbf{n}_R \cdot [(\mathbf{P(t)} - \mathbf{f}] = -(10t - 9) = 0$$

or

$$t = 9/10$$

as the intersection point of the line and the right edge. Specifically

$$P(9/10) = [-1 \quad 1] + [10 \quad 2](9/10) = [8 \quad 2.8]$$

which is also the same as the explicit calculation.
Using $f(0, 0)$ for the bottom edge yields

$$\mathbf{n}_B \cdot [\mathbf{P(t)} - \mathbf{f}] = (2t + 1) = 0$$

or

$$t = -1/2$$

which is outside the range $0 \le t \le 1$ and is thus rejected.
Using $f(8, 4)$ for the top edge yields

$$\mathbf{n}_T \cdot [\mathbf{P(t)} - \mathbf{f}] = -(2t - 3) = 0$$

or

$$t = 3/2$$

which is also outside the range $0 \le t \le 1$ and is also rejected. The visible range for the line P_1P_2 clipped to the rectangular region of Fig. 3-12 is $1/10 \le t \le 9/10$ or from $(0, 1.2)$ to $(8, 2.8)$.

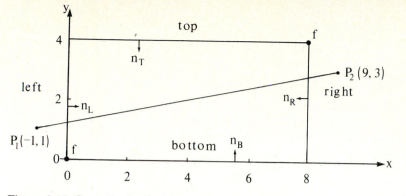

Figure 3-12 Cyrus-Beck clipping—partially visible line.

This example shows that the intersection points can easily be found. Identifying totally visible and totally invisible lines is illustrated by three further examples.

Example 3-10   Cyrus-Beck—Totally Visible Lines

Consider the line $P_1(1, 1)$ to $P_2(7, 3)$ clipped to the rectangular window shown in Fig. 3-13. The parametric representation of the line P_1P_2 is

$$P(t) = [1 \quad 1] + [6 \quad 2]t$$

The results, using the inner normals and boundary points of Example 3-9, are given in Table 3-4.

Table 3-4

Edge	n	f	P(t)−f	n · [P(t)−f]	t
Left	$\mathbf{i}$	(0, 0)	$(\ 1 + 6t)\,\mathbf{i} + (\ 1 + 2t)\,\mathbf{j}$	$1 + 6t$	$-1/6$
Right	$-\mathbf{i}$	(8, 4)	$(-7 + 6t)\,\mathbf{i} + (-3 + 2t)\,\mathbf{j}$	$7 - 6t$	$7/6$
Bottom	$\mathbf{j}$	(0, 0)	$(\ 1 + 6t)\,\mathbf{i} + (\ 1 + 2t)\,\mathbf{j}$	$1 + 2t$	$-1/2$
Top	$-\mathbf{j}$	(8, 4)	$(-7 + 6t)\,\mathbf{i} + (-3 + 2t)\,\mathbf{j}$	$3 - 2t$	$3/2$

All the intersection values for t are outside the range $0 \le t \le 1$. The entire line is visible.

The next two examples consider two types of invisible lines. One line is totally to the left of the window and could be declared invisible using the end point codes discussed above. The second crosses the window corner outside the window itself. It cannot be declared invisible using the end point codes.

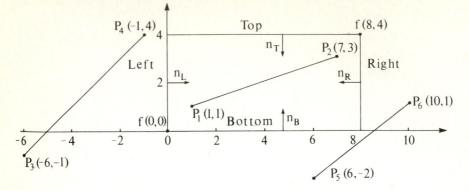

Figure 3-13 Cyrus-Beck clipping—visible and invisible lines.

Example 3-11   Cyrus-Beck—Trivially Invisible Line

Consider the line $P_3(-6, -1)$ to $P_4(-1, 4)$ clipped to the rectangular window shown in Fig. 3-13. The line is invisible. The parametric representation is

$$P(t) = [-6 \quad -1] + [5 \quad 5]t$$

The results using the inner normals and boundary points of the previous examples are given in Table 3-5.

Table 3-5

Edge	n	f	$P(t) - f$	$n \cdot [P(t) - f]$	t
Left	i	(0, 0)	$(-6 + 5t)\,i + (-1 + 5t)\,j$	$-6 + 5t$	$t = 6/5$
Right	$-i$	(8, 4)	$(-14 + 5t)\,i + (-5 + 5t)\,j$	$-(-14 + 5t)$	$t = 14/5$
Bottom	j	(0, 0)	$(-6 + 5t)\,i + (-1 + 5t)\,j$	$-1 + 5t$	$t = 1/5$
Top	$-j$	(8, 4)	$(-14 + 5t)\,i + (-5 + 5t)\,j$	$-(-5 + 5t)$	$t = 1$

Examination of the results in Table 3-5 shows that the intersection values for the left and right edges are both outside the range $0 \le t \le 1$, but those for the top and bottom are both within the range $0 \le t \le 1$. Based on this the line might initially be assumed visible in the range $1/5 \le t \le 1$. However, further consideration of the intersections for the left and right edges shows that both intersection values of the parameter are greater than one. This shows that the window is completely to the right of the line. Hence the line is invisible.

If in the above example P_3 and P_4 were interchanged, then the results would show that the window was completely to the left of the line. The direction of the line is important in arriving at the decision about the invisibility of the line. The next example further explores this question.

Example 3-12   Cyrus-Beck—Nontrivially Invisible Line

Here the line from $P_5(6, -2)$ to $P_6(10, 1)$ again clipped to the rectangular window of Fig. 3-13, is considered. The parametric representation is

$$P(t) = [6 \quad -2] + [4 \quad 3]t$$

Using the inner normals and boundary points of the previous examples yields the results given in Table 3-6.

Table 3-6

Edge	n	f	$P(t)-f$	$n \cdot [P(t)-f]$	t
Left	i	(0, 0)	$(\ 6 + 4t)\,i + (-2 + 3t)\,j$	$6 + 4t$	$t = -3/2$
Right	$-i$	(8, 4)	$(-2 + 4t)\,i + (-6 + 3t)\,j$	$-(-2 + 4t)$	$t = \ \ 1/2$
Bottom	j	(0, 0)	$(\ 6 + 4t)\,i + (-2 + 3t)\,j$	$-2 + 3t$	$t = \ \ 2/3$
Top	$-j$	(8, 4)	$(-2 + 4t)\,i + (-6 + 3t)\,j$	$-(-6 + 3t)$	$t = \ \ 2$

The results show that the intersections for the left and the top edges fall outside the required range. However, the intersections for the right and bottom edges are within the proper range. But, considering the direction of the line to be from P_5 to P_6, it is not possible for the line to intersect the right edge at $t = 1/2$ before it intersects the bottom edge at $t = 2/3$ and still pierce the region R, i.e. the window. Thus, the line is invisible.

From these examples it is clear that apparently visible lines can be correctly identified by also considering the direction of the line. This observation is exploited in the formal statement of the Cyrus-Beck algorithm given below.

To formalize the algorithm, again recall that the parametric representation of a line is

$$P(t) = P_1 + (P_2 - P_1)t \qquad 0 \le t \le 1 \qquad (3\text{-}3)$$

and that the dot product of an inner normal and the vector from any point on the parametric line to any other point on the boundary, i.e.,

$$n_i \cdot [P(t) - f_i] \qquad i = 1, 2, 3, \ldots \qquad (3\text{-}4)$$

is positive, zero, or negative for a point on the parametric line interior to the region, on the region boundary, or exterior to the region. This relation is applied for each boundary plane or edge i of the region. Combining Eqs. (3-3) and (3-4) yields

$$n_i \cdot [P_1 + (P_2 - P_1)t - f_i] = 0 \qquad (3\text{-}5)$$

as the condition for a point on the parametric line which lies on the boundary of the region, i.e. the intersection point. Alternately, Eq. (3-5) becomes

$$n_i \cdot [P_1 - f_i] + n_i \cdot [P_2 - P_1]t = 0 \qquad (3\text{-}6)$$

Noting that the vector $P_2 - P_1$ defines the direction of the line and that the vector $P_1 - f_i$ is proportional to the distance from the end point of the line to the boundary point, let

$$\mathbf{D} = \mathbf{P}_2 - \mathbf{P}_1$$

the directorix or direction of the line and

$$\mathbf{w}_i = \mathbf{P}_1 - \mathbf{f}_i$$

a weighting factor. Equation (3-6) then becomes

$$t(\mathbf{n}_i \cdot \mathbf{D}) + \mathbf{w}_i \cdot \mathbf{n}_i = 0 \qquad (3\text{-}7)$$

Solving for t yields

$$t = -\frac{\mathbf{w}_i \cdot \mathbf{n}_i}{\mathbf{D} \cdot \mathbf{n}_i} \qquad \mathbf{D} \neq 0 \qquad i = 1, 2, 3, \dots \qquad (3\text{-}8)$$

$\mathbf{D} \cdot \mathbf{n}_i$ can be zero only if $\mathbf{D} = 0$, which implies that $P_2 = P_1$, i.e. a point. If

$$\mathbf{w}_i \cdot \mathbf{n}_i \quad \begin{aligned} &< 0, \text{ the point is outside} \\ &= 0, \text{ on the boundary of} \\ &> 0, \text{ inside} \end{aligned}$$

the region or window.

Equation (3-8) is used to obtain the value of t for the intersection of the line with each edge of the window. If t is outside the range $0 \le t \le 1$, then it can be ignored. Although it is known that the line can intersect the convex window in at most two points, i.e., at two values of t, Eq. (3-8) may yield several values of t in the range $0 \le t \le 1$. These will separate into two groups, a lower limit group near the beginning of the line and an upper limit group near the end of the line. What is required is to find the largest lower limit and the smallest upper limit. If $\mathbf{D}_i \cdot \mathbf{n}_i > 0$, then the calculated value of t is near the beginning of the line and the lower limit value of t is sought. If $\mathbf{D}_i \cdot \mathbf{n}_i < 0$, then the value of t is near the end of the line and the upper limit value of t is sought. Figure 3-14 gives a flowchart of an algorithm which uses these conditions to solve the resulting linear programming problem. A pseudo implementation of the algorithm is given below.

Cyrus-Beck two-dimensional clipping algorithm

P_1 and P_2 *are the end points of the line*
the number of edges for the clipping region is k
the $\mathbf{n}_i$ *are the* k *normal vectors*
the f_i *are the* k *boundary points, one in each edge*
D_i *is the directorix of the line,* $P_2 - P_1$
w_i *is the weighting function,* $P_1 - f_i$
t_L, t_U *are the lower and upper parameter limits*

> *initialize the parameter limits assuming the entire line is visible*
> $t_L = 0$
> $t_U = 1$
> *calculate the directorix* D
> $D = P_2 - P_1$
> *start the main loop*
> **for** i = 1 **to** k
> > *calculate* w_i, $\mathbf{D} \cdot \mathbf{n}_i$ *and* $w_i \cdot \mathbf{n}_i$ *for this value of* i

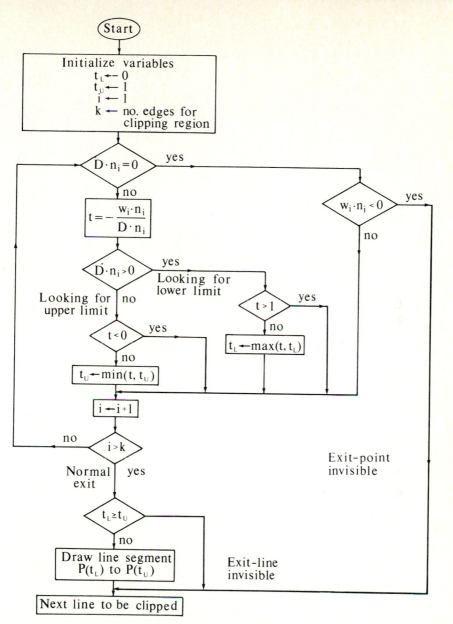

Figure 3-14 Flowchart for the Cyrus-Beck clipping algorithm.

$w_i = P_1 - f_i$
call Dotproduct(D, n_i; Ddotn)
call Dotproduct(w_i, n_i; wdotn)
is the line a point?
if Ddotn $= 0$ **then** 2

the line is not a point, calculate t
t = − Wdotn/Ddotn
looking for the upper or the lower limit
if Ddotn > 0 **then** 1
looking for the upper limit
is t *within the range 0 to 1?*
if t < 0 **then** 3
t_U = **Min**(t, t_U)
go to 3
looking for the lower limit

1   **if** t > 1 **then** 3
t_L = **Max**(t, t_L)
go to 3
the line is a point

2   **if** Wdotn < 0 **then** 4
the point is visible with respect to the current edge

3   **next** i
a normal exit from the loop has occurred
check if the line is in fact invisible
if $t_L \geq t_U$ **then** 4
Draw line segment $P(t_L)$ to $P(t_U)$

4   Process next line

subroutine module to calculate the dot product

subroutine Dotproduct(Vector1, Vector2; Dproduct)

Vector1 *is the first vector with components* x *and* y
Vector2 *is the second vector with components* x *and* y
Dproduct *is the dot or inner product*
Dproduct = Vector1x∗Vector2x + Vector1y∗Vector2y
return

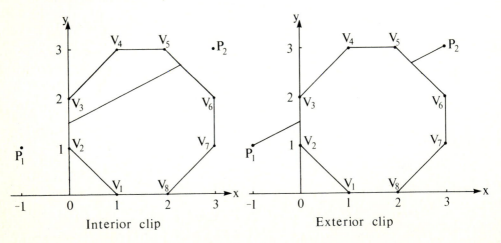

Interior clip   Exterior clip

Figure 3-15 Cyrus-Beck interior and exterior clipping of a many-sided polygon.

To illustrate that the algorithm is not limited to rectangular windows consider the following example.

Example 3-13   Cyrus-Beck—Irregular Window

Figure 3-15 shows an eight-sided polygonal clipping window. The line $P_1(-1, 1)$ to $P_2(3, 3)$ is to be clipped to this window. Table 3-7 illustrates the complete results of the Cyrus-Beck algorithm. As a specific example consider the edge from V_5 to V_6. The algorithm yields

$$D = P_2 - P_1 = [3 \quad 3] - [-1 \quad 1] = [4 \quad 2]$$

For the boundary point $f(2, 3)$

$$w = P_1 - f = [-1 \quad 1] - [2 \quad 3] = [-3 \quad -2]$$

For the edge $V_5 V_6$ the inner normal is

$$n = [-1 \quad -1]$$

Hence

$$D \cdot n = -6 < 0$$

and the upper limit is being sought.

$$w \cdot n = 5$$

and

$$t_U = -\frac{5}{-6} = \frac{5}{6}$$

Table 3-7

Edge	n		f	w		$w \cdot n$	$D \cdot n$†	t_L	t_U
$V_1 V_2$	[1	1]	(1, 0)	[2	1]	-1	6	1/6	
$V_2 V_3$	[1	0]	(0, 2)	[-1	-1]	-1	4	1/4	
$V_3 V_4$	[1	-1]	(0, 2)	[-1	-1]	0	2	0	
$V_4 V_5$	[0	-1]	(2, 3)	[-3	-2]	2	-2		1
$V_5 V_6$	[-1	-1]	(2, 3)	[-3	-2]	5	-6		5/6
$V_6 V_7$	[-1	0]	(3, 1)	[-4	0]	4	-4		1
$V_7 V_8$	[-1	1]	(3, 1)	[-4	0]	4	-2		2
$V_8 V_1$	[0	1]	(1, 0)	[-2	1]	1	2	-1/2	

†$D \cdot n < 0$ upper limit (t_U), $D \cdot n > 0$ lower limit (t_L).

Examining Table 3-7 shows that the maximum lower limit is $t_L = 1/4$ and the minimum upper limit is $t_U = 5/6$. As shown in Fig. 3-15 the line is visible from $1/4 \leq t \leq 5/6$ or from $(0, 3/2)$ to $(7/3, 8/3)$.

3-6 INTERIOR AND EXTERIOR CLIPPING

The emphasis of the discussions in the previous section was on clipping a line to the interior of a region or polygon. However, it is also possible to clip a line to the exterior of a region or polygon, i.e., to determine what portion or portions of a line lie outside a region and to draw those exterior portions. For example, the visible portions of the line P_1P_2 of Fig. 3-15 exterior to the window are $0 \le t < 1/6$ and $5/6 < t \le 1$, or from $(-1, 1)$ to $(0, 3/2)$ and $(7/3, 8/3)$ to $(3, 3)$. The results of both an interior and an exterior clip of the line are shown in Fig. 3-15.

Exterior clipping is important in a multiwindow display environment as shown in Fig. 3-16. In Fig. 3-16 windows 1 to 3 have priority over the display window, and windows 1 and 3 have priority over window 2. Consequently data in the display window is clipped to the interior of the display window itself and to the exterior of windows 1 to 3. Data in window 2 is clipped to the interior of the window itself and to the exterior of windows 1 and 3. Data in windows 1 and 3 only need be clipped to the interior of the individual windows.

Exterior clipping can also be used to clip a line to a concave polygonal window. Figure 3-17 shows a concave polygon described by the vertices $V_1V_2V_3V_4V_5V_6V_1$. A convex polygon can be formed from this concave polygon by connecting the vertices V_3 and V_5, as shown by the dashed line in Fig. 3-17. Using the Cyrus-Beck algorithm, the line P_1P_2 is clipped to the interior of this polygon. An exterior clip to the polygon $V_3V_5V_4V_3$ of the resulting line $P_1'P_2'$ then yields the required result, i.e. $P_1'P_2''$.

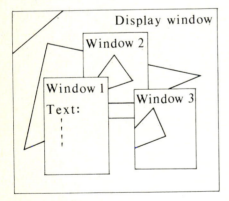

Figure 3-16 Clipping in a multiwindow environment.

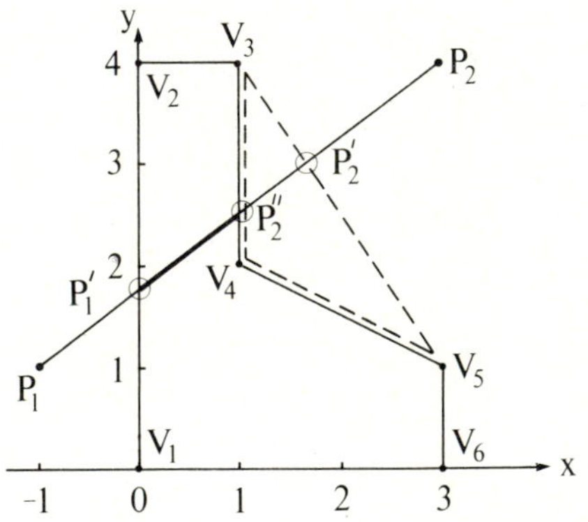

Figure 3-17 Clipping a line to a concave polygon.

3-7 IDENTIFYING CONVEX POLYGONS AND DETERMINING THE INWARD NORMAL

To use the Cyrus-Beck clipping algorithm it is necessary to first ensure that the clipping region is convex and then to determine the inner normals for each edge. Two-dimensional polygonal windows can be determined to be either concave or convex by calculating the vector cross products of adjacent edges. The conclusions to be drawn from the signs of the vector cross products are

All zero	— the polygon is collinear
Some positive and some negative	— concave polygon
All positive or zero	— convex polygon and the inner normal points to the left looking along the direction of the edge
All negative or zero	— convex polygon and the inner normal points to the right looking along the direction of the edge

This is illustrated in Fig. 3-18.

Alternately, one of the polygon vertices can be selected as a base and the vector cross products calculated for the vectors from this base to successive pairs of polygon vertices. The interpretation of the results is unchanged.

The vector cross product is normal to the plane of the polygon. For two planar vectors V_1 and V_2 the cross product is $(V_{x_1}V_{y_2} - V_{y_1}V_{x_2})\mathbf{k}$, where $\mathbf{k}$ is the unit vector perpendicular to the plane of the vectors.

The normal vector for a polygon edge can be determined by recalling that the dot product of two perpendicular vectors is zero. If n_x and n_y are the unknown components of the normal and V_{e_x} and V_{e_y} are the components of a known edge vector, then

$$\mathbf{n} \cdot \mathbf{V}_e = (n_x\mathbf{i} + n_y\mathbf{j}) \cdot (V_{e_x}\mathbf{i} + V_{e_x}\mathbf{j}) = n_xV_{e_x} + n_yV_{e_y} = 0$$

or

$$n_xV_{e_x} = -n_yV_{e_y}$$

Since only the direction of the normal is required, n_y is assumed equal to 1 without loss of generality. Hence, the normal vector is

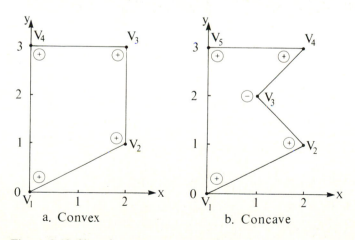

a. Convex   b. Concave

Figure 3-18 Signs for vector cross products.

$$\mathbf{n} = -\frac{V_{e_y}}{V_{e_x}}\mathbf{i} + \mathbf{j}$$

If the edge vector is formed from two polygon vertices V_{i-1} and V_i, and if the dot product of the vector from V_{i-1} to V_{i+1} and the normal is positive, $\mathbf{n}$ is the inner normal. Otherwise, $\mathbf{n}$ is the outer normal. In this case, the inner normal is obtained by reversing the signs of the x and y components. A simple example illustrates the technique.

Example 3-14   Vector Cross Products

Figure 3-18a shows a simple convex polygon and Fig. 3-18b a concave polygon. Tables 3-8 and 3-9 give complete results. As a specific example, the vector cross product at V_2 and the inner normal for the edge V_1V_2 for the polygon of Fig. 3-18a are determined.

For the adjacent edges at V_2

$$\mathbf{V_1V_2} = 2\mathbf{i} + \mathbf{j} \qquad \mathbf{V_2V_3} = 2\mathbf{j}$$

The vector cross product is

$$\mathbf{V_1V_2} \otimes \mathbf{V_2V_3} = 4\mathbf{k}$$

where $\mathbf{k}$ is the unit normal perpendicular to the plane of the vectors. The cross product is positive. Table 3-8 shows that the cross products for all the vertices are positive. The polygon is thus convex. Table 3-9 shows that for the polygon of Fig. 3-18b the cross product at V_3 is negative, whereas all the others are positive. Hence, this polygon is concave.

The normal for the edge vector $\mathbf{V_1V_2}$ is

$$\mathbf{n} = -\frac{1}{2}\mathbf{i} + \mathbf{j}$$

or alternately

$$\mathbf{n} = -\mathbf{i} + 2\mathbf{j}$$

The vector $\mathbf{V_1V_3}$ is

$$\mathbf{V_1V_3} = 2\mathbf{i} + 3\mathbf{j}$$

Hence

$$\mathbf{n} \cdot \mathbf{V_1V_3} = (-\mathbf{i} + 2\mathbf{j}) \cdot (2\mathbf{i} + 3\mathbf{j}) = 4 > 0$$

and this is an inner normal

Table 3-8

Vertex	Vectors	Cross product				
V_1	$\mathbf{V_4V_1} \otimes \mathbf{V_1V_2}$	[0	-3] $\otimes$ [2	1]	=	$+6$
V_2	$\mathbf{V_1V_2} \otimes \mathbf{V_2V_3}$	[2	1] $\otimes$ [0	2]	=	$+4$
V_3	$\mathbf{V_2V_3} \otimes \mathbf{V_3V_4}$	[0	2] $\otimes$ [-2	0]	=	$+4$
V_4	$\mathbf{V_3V_4} \otimes \mathbf{V_4V_1}$	[-2	0] $\otimes$ [0	-3]	=	$+6$

Table 3-9

Vertex	Vectors	Cross product						
V_1	$\mathbf{V_5V_1} \otimes \mathbf{V_1V_2}$	[0	-3] $\otimes$ [2	1]	=	$+6$
V_2	$\mathbf{V_1V_2} \otimes \mathbf{V_2V_3}$	[2	1] $\otimes$ [-1	1]	=	$+3$
V_3	$\mathbf{V_2V_3} \otimes \mathbf{V_3V_4}$	[-1	1] $\otimes$ [1	1]	=	-2
V_4	$\mathbf{V_3V_4} \otimes \mathbf{V_4V_5}$	[1	1] $\otimes$ [-2	0]	=	$+2$
V_5	$\mathbf{V_4V_5} \otimes \mathbf{V_5V_1}$	[-2	0] $\otimes$ [0	-3]	=	$+6$

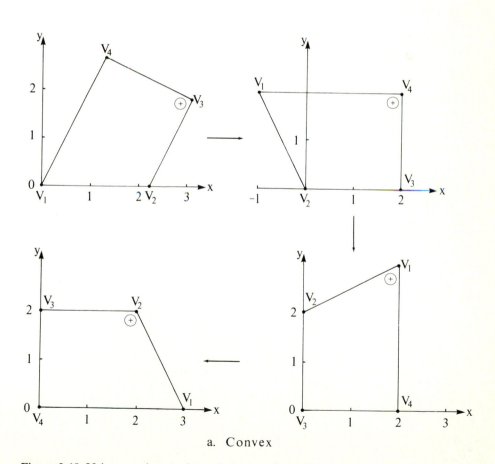

a. Convex

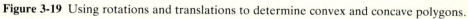

Figure 3-19 Using rotations and translations to determine convex and concave polygons.

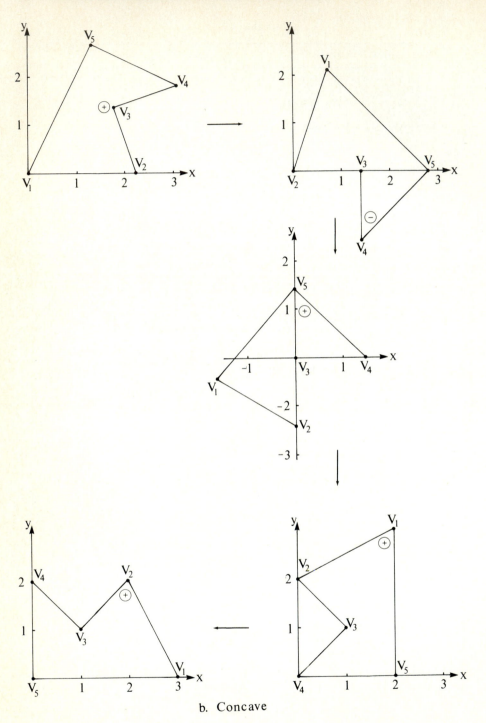

b. Concave

Figure 3-19 (Continued.)

Alternately, a procedure involving translation and rotation of the polygonal window can be used to determine both the convexity of the window and the inner normal for each edge. The procedure is

For each vertex of the polygonal window, translate the polygon such that the ith vertex is at the origin.

Rotate the polygonal window about the origin such that the $(i + 1)$th vertex is on the positive x axis.

Examine the sign of the y component of the $(i + 2)$th vertex.

If all the $(i + 2)$th vertices have the same sign for the y component, the polygonal window is convex; if not, it is concave.

If the $(i+2)$th vertex has a zero y component, then the ith, $(i+1)$th, $(i+2)$th vertices are collinear.

If all the $(i + 2)$th vertices have zero y components, the polygonal window is degenerate, i.e., a line.

For each edge of a convex polygon, the inner normal has components in the rotated coordinate system of zero and the sign of the $(i+2)$th y component.

In determining the original direction of the inner normal, only the inverse rotations are applied.

Figure 3-19 illustrates the various stages in the procedure for both the convex and concave polygons of Fig. 3-18. The appropriate rotation and translation algorithms are given in Ref. 1-1.

3-8   SPLITTING CONCAVE POLYGONS

Many algorithms require that polygonal clipping regions be convex. The Cyrus-Beck clipping algorithm presented above is an example. Additional examples are presented in subsequent sections. A simple extension of the translation and rotation technique for determining whether a polygon is convex or concave allows splitting or dividing simple concave polygons into multiple convex polygons. The procedure can be incorporated into the previous algorithm. If the polygon vertices are specified counterclockwise, the procedure is

For each vertex of the polygon, translate such that the ith vertex is at the origin.

Rotate the polygon clockwise about the origin such that the $(i + 1)$th vertex is on the positive x axis.

Examine the sign of the y component of the $(i + 2)$th vertex. If the sign is positive or zero, the polygon is convex with respect to this edge. If the sign is negative, the polygon is concave. Split the polygon.

The polygon is split along the positive x axis; i.e., the intersection of each polygon edge that crosses the coordinate axis is found. Two new polygons are formed, one from the vertices above the axis and the closest intersection with $x > x_{i+1}$, and the second from the vertices below the axis and the same intersection point.

The algorithm is reentered with the split-off polygons until they are all declared convex

The algorithm does not yield an optimum split in the sense of the minimum number of convex polygons. Also, the algorithm will not properly split polygons whose edges intersect.

An example will further illustrate the procedure.

Example 3-15 Splitting Concave Polygons

Consider the concave polygon shown in Fig. 3-19b. With the vertex V_2 at the origin and V_3 on the positive x axis, the sign of the y component of V_4 is negative. Hence, the polygon is concave. Splitting the polygon along the coordinate axis yields $V_3V_4V_5$ as the split off polygon below the axis and $V_1V_2V_3V_5$ as the split off polygon above the axis. Reentering the algorithm with $V_3V_4V_5$ and $V_1V_2V_3V_5$ shows that they are both convex. Hence, the algorithm is complete.

3-9 THREE-DIMENSIONAL CLIPPING

Before extending the methods discussed above to three dimensions, it is necessary to discuss the shape of the clipping volume. The two common three-dimensional clipping volumes are a rectangular parallelepiped, i.e. a box, used for parallel or axonometric projections, and a truncated pyramidal volume, frequently called a frustum of vision, used for perspective projections. These volumes, shown in Fig. 3-20, are six-sided; left, right, top, bottom, hither (near), and yon (far). There is also the necessity of clipping to unusual volumes.

As in two-dimensional clipping, lines that are totally visible or trivially invisible can be identified using an extension of the Cohen-Sutherland end point codes. For three-dimensional clipping, a 6-bit end point code is used. Again, the first bit is the rightmost bit. The bits are set to 1 using an extension of the two-dimensional scheme. Specifically,

First bit set   — if the end point is to the left of the volume
Second bit set — if the end point is to the right of the volume
Third bit set   — if the end point is below the volume
Fourth bit set — if the end point is above the volume
Fifth bit set   — if the end point is in front of the volume
Sixth bit set   — if the end point is behind the volume

Otherwise, the bit is set to zero. Again, if both end point codes are *zero*, then both ends of the line are visible; and the line is visible. Also, if the bit-by-bit logical intersection of the two end point codes is *not zero*, then the line is totally invisible. If the logical intersection is zero, the line may be partially visible or totally invisible. In this case it is necessary to determine the intersection of the line and the clipping volume.

Determining the end point codes for a rectangular parallelepiped clipping volume is a straight forward extension of the two-dimensional algorithm. However, the perspective clipping volume shown in Fig. 3-20b requires additional consideration. One technique (see Ref. 1-3) is to transform the clipping volume into a canonical volume with $x_{right} = 1, x_{left} = -1, y_{top} = 1, y_{bottom} = -1$, at $z_{yon} = 1$. If $z_{hither} = a$, where $0 < a \leq 1$ and the center of projection is at the origin, in a left-handed coordinate system, then the end point code conditions are considerably simplified.

A more straightforward technique, which requires less distortion of the clipping volume, makes the line connecting the center of projection and the center of the perspective clipping volume coincident with the z axis in a right-handed coordinate system as shown in Fig. 3-20b.

A top view of the perspective clipping volume is shown in Fig. 3-21. The equation of the line which represents the right hand plane in this view is

$$x = \frac{z - z_{CP}}{z_Y - z_{CP}} x_R = z\alpha_1 + \alpha_2$$

where

$$\alpha_1 = \frac{x_R}{z_Y - z_{CP}} \quad \text{and} \quad \alpha_2 = -\alpha_1 z_{CP}$$

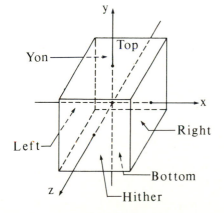

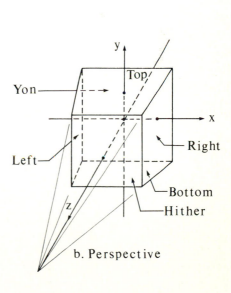

a. Parallel   b. Perspective

Figure 3-20 Three-dimensional clipping.

The equation of this plane can be used to determine whether a point is to the right, on, or to the left of the plane, i.e., outside the volume, on the right hand plane, or inside the volume. Substituting the x and z coordinates of a point P into $x - z\alpha_1 - \alpha_2$ yields the following results

$$
\begin{aligned}
f_R = x - z\alpha_1 - \alpha_2 \ &> 0 && \text{if } P \text{ is to the right of the plane} \\
&= 0 && \text{if } P \text{ is on the plane} \\
&< 0 && \text{if } P \text{ is to the left of the plane}
\end{aligned}
$$

Test functions for the left, top, and bottom planes are:

$$
\begin{aligned}
f_L = x - z\beta_1 - \beta_2 \ &< 0 && \text{if } P \text{ is to the left of the plane} \\
&= 0 && \text{if } P \text{ is on the plane} \\
&> 0 && \text{if } P \text{ is to the right of the plane}
\end{aligned}
$$

where

$$
\beta_1 = \frac{x_L}{z_Y - z_{CP}} \qquad \text{and} \qquad \beta_2 = -\beta_1 z_{CP}
$$

and

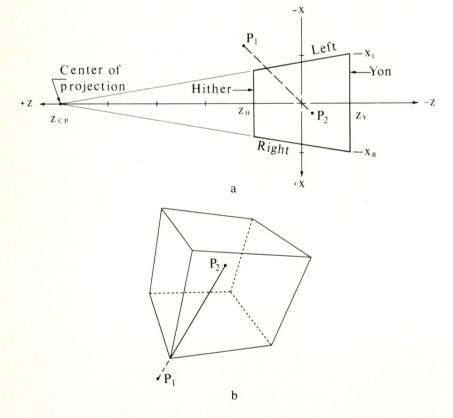

Figure 3-21 Views of perspective clipping volume.

$$f_T = y - z\gamma_1 - \gamma_2 > 0 \quad \text{if } P \text{ is above the plane}$$
$$= 0 \quad \text{if } P \text{ is on the plane}$$
$$< 0 \quad \text{if } P \text{ is below the plane}$$

where

$$\gamma_1 = \frac{y_T}{z_Y - z_{CP}} \quad \text{and} \quad \gamma_2 = -\gamma_1 z_{CP}$$

and

$$f_B = y - z\delta_1 - \delta_2 < 0 \quad \text{if } P \text{ is below the plane}$$
$$= 0 \quad \text{if } P \text{ is on the plane}$$
$$> 0 \quad \text{if } P \text{ is above the plane}$$

where

$$\delta_1 = z_{CP} \quad \text{and} \quad \delta_2 = -\delta_1 z_{CP}$$

Finally the test functions for the hither and yon planes are

$$f_H = z - z_H > 0 \quad \text{if } P \text{ is in front of the plane}$$
$$= 0 \quad \text{if } P \text{ is on the plane}$$
$$< 0 \quad \text{if } P \text{ is behind the plane}$$

and

$$f_Y = z - z_Y < 0 \quad \text{if } P \text{ is behind the plane}$$
$$= 0 \quad \text{if } P \text{ is on the plane}$$
$$> 0 \quad \text{if } P \text{ is in front of the plane}$$

As z_{CP} approaches infinity, the clipping volume approaches a rectangular parallelepiped. The test functions also approach those for a rectangular parallelepiped.

As pointed out by Liang and Barsky (Ref. 3-5) this approach may not yield the correct codes if the end points lie behind the center of projection. This is because the left and right and the top and bottom planes of the perspective clipping volume intersect at the center of projection. Thus a point can be right of right and left of left simultaneously. Liang and Barsky suggest a technique for correcting this. In principle it is only necessary to reverse the left-right, top-bottom code bits if $z < z_{CP}$. See also Sec. 3-12.

3-10 THREE-DIMENSIONAL MIDPOINT SUBDIVISION ALGORITHM

The midpoint subdivision algorithm given above (see Sec. 3-3) extends directly to three dimensions. For the pseudo code implementation, the array dimensions for the Pcodes and Window arrays must be changed and the Endpoint and Logical subroutines rewritten for three dimensions. A pseudo code implementation for the three-dimensional end point code subroutine is

subroutine module for calculating three-dimensional perspective volume end point codes

subroutine Endpoint(P, Window; Pcode, Sum)

P_x, P_y, P_z *are the x and y components of the point* P
Window *is a 1 × 7 array containing the left, right, bottom, top, hither, yon edges and the center of projection* $(x_L, x_R, y_B, y_T, z_H, z_Y, z_{CP})$
Pcode *is a 1 × 6 array containing the end point code*
Sum *is the element-by-element sum of* Pcode
   calculate $\alpha_1, \alpha_2, \beta_2, \gamma_1, \gamma_2, \delta_1, \delta_2$
   $\alpha_1 = x_R/(z_Y - z_{CP})$
   $\alpha_2 = -\alpha_1 z_{CP}$
   $\beta_1 = x_L/(z_Y - z_{CP})$
   $\beta_2 = -\beta_1 z_{CP}$
   $\gamma_1 = y_T/(z_Y - z_{CP})$
   $\gamma_2 = -\gamma_1 z_{CP}$
   $\delta_1 = y_B/(z_Y - z_{CP})$
   $\delta_2 = -\delta_1 z_{CP}$
   determine the end point codes
   if $P_x - P_z\beta_1 - \beta_2 < 0$ **then** Pcode(6) = 1 **else** Pcode(6) = 0
   if $P_x - P_z\alpha_1 - \alpha_2 > 0$ **then** Pcode(5) = 1 **else** Pcode(5) = 0
   if $P_y - P_z\delta_1 - \delta_2 < 0$ **then** Pcode(4) = 1 **else** Pcode(4) = 0
   if $P_y - P_z\gamma_1 - \gamma_2 > 0$ **then** Pcode(3) = 1 **else** Pcode(3) = 0
   if $P_z - z_H > 0$ **then** Pcode(2) = 1 **else** Pcode(2) = 0
   if $P_z - z_Y < 0$ **then** Pcode(1) = 1 **else** Pcode(1) = 0
   calculate the sum
   Sum = 0
   for i = 1 **to** 6
        Sum = Sum + Pcode(i)
   next i
   return

An example for the three-dimensional midpoint clipping algorithm is given below.

Example 3-16   Three-Dimensional Midpoint Subdivision

Consider a line from $P_1(-600, -600, 600)$ to $P_2(100, 100, -100)$ in screen units clipped to the perspective volume with $x_R = y_T = 500$, $x_L = y_B = -500$ at the yon clipping plane. The hither and yon clipping planes are $z_H = 357.14$, $z_Y = -500$. The center of projection is $z_{CP} = 2500$. A top view is shown in Fig. 3-21a and a perspective view in 3-21b. The clipping volume test functions are

Right:	$f_R =$	$6x + z - 2500$
Left:	$f_L =$	$6x - z + 2500$
Top:	$f_T =$	$6y + z - 2500$
Bottom:	$f_B =$	$6y - z + 2500$
Hither:	$f_H =$	$z - 357.14$
Yon:	$f_Y =$	$z + 2500$

The end point code for P_1 is (010101), and that for P_2 is (000000). Since both end point codes are not zero, the line is not totally visible. The logical intersection of the end point codes is (00000). The line is not trivially invisible. Since the end point code for P_2 is (000000), P_2 is inside the volume. Hence, it is the farthest visible point from P_1. Thus, only one intersection with the volume occurs. The midpoint is

$$x_m = \frac{x_2 + x_1}{2} = \frac{100 + (-600)}{2} = -250$$

$$y_m = \frac{y_2 + y_1}{2} = \frac{100 + (-600)}{2} = -250$$

$$z = \frac{z_2 + z_1}{2} = \frac{-100 + 600}{2} = 250$$

using integer arithmetic. The end point code for the midpoint is (000000). The segment $P_m P_2$ is totally visible. The segment $P_1 P_m$ is partially visible. Continue with $P_1 P_m$. The subdivision continues in Table 3-10.

Table 3-10

P_1	P_2	P_m	Comment
$-600, -600, 600$	$100, 100, -100$	$-250, -250, 250$	Continue $P_1 P_m$
$-600, -600, 600$	$-250, -250, 250$	$-425, -425, 425$	Continue $P_m P_2$
$-425, -425, 425$	$-250, -250, 250$	$-338, -338, 337$	Continue $P_1 P_m$
$-425, -425, 425$	$-338, -338, 337$	$-382, -382, 381$	Continue $P_m P_2$
$-382, -382, 381$	$-338, -338, 337$	$-360, -360, 359$	Continue $P_m P_2$
$-360, -360, 359$	$-338, -338, 337$	$-349, -349, 348$	Continue $P_1 P_m$
$-360, -360, 359$	$-349, -349, 348$	$-355, -355, 353$	Continue $P_1 P_m$
$-360, -360, 359$	$-355, -355, 353$	$-358, -358, 356$	Continue $P_m P_2$
$-358, -358, 356$	$-355, -355, 353$	$-357, -357, 354$	Continue $P_1 P_m$
$-358, -358, 356$	$-357, -357, 354$	$-358, -358, 355$	Continue $P_m P_2$
$-358, -358, 355$	$-357, -357, 354$	$\boxed{-358, -358, 354}$	Success

The actual intersection point is $(-357.14, -357.14, 357.14)$. The difference is due to the use of integer arithmetic in the algorithm.

3-11   THREE-DIMENSIONAL CYRUS-BECK ALGORITHM

In developing the Cyrus-Beck algorithm (Ref. 3-4) for two-dimensional clipping, no restriction was placed on the shape of the clipping region except that it be convex. The clipping region can therefore be a three-dimensional convex volume. The algorithm developed previously is directly applicable. Instead of k being the number of edges, it is now the number of planes (see Fig. 3-14).

All vectors now have three components; x, y, z. The extension of the Dot-product subroutine module to three-dimensional vectors is straightforward. To more fully illustrate the algorithm, consider the following examples. The first considers clipping to a rectangular parallelepiped, i.e., to a box.

Example 3-17 Three-Dimensional Cyrus-Beck Algorithm

A line from $P_1(-2, -1, 1/2)$ to $P_2(3/2, 3/2, -1/2)$ is to be clipped to the volume $(x_L, x_R, y_B, y_T, z_H, z_Y) = (-1, 1, -1, 1, 1, -1)$ as shown in Fig. 3-22. By inspection the six inner normals are

Top:	$\mathbf{n}_T =$	$-\mathbf{j} = [\ 0 \quad -1 \quad 0]$
Bottom:	$\mathbf{n}_B =$	$\mathbf{j} = [\ 0 \quad 1 \quad 0]$
Right:	$\mathbf{n}_R =$	$-\mathbf{i} = [-1 \quad 0 \quad 0]$
Left:	$\mathbf{n}_L =$	$\mathbf{i} = [\ 1 \quad 0 \quad 0]$
Hither:	$\mathbf{n}_H =$	$-\mathbf{k} = [\ 0 \quad 0 \quad -1]$
Yon:	$\mathbf{n}_Y =$	$\mathbf{k} = [\ 0 \quad 0 \quad 1]$

The points in each clipping plane may also be selected by inspection. By choosing points at the end of a diagonal between opposite corners of the clipping volume, two are sufficient. Thus,

$$f_T = f_R = f_H(1, 1, 1)$$

and

$$f_B = f_L = f_Y(-1, -1, -1)$$

Alternately the center or a corner point of each clipping plane could be used. The directorix for the line P_1P_2 is

$$\mathbf{D} = \mathbf{P}_2 - \mathbf{P}_1 = [3/2 \quad 3/2 \quad -1/2] - [-2 \quad -1 \quad 1/2]$$
$$= [7/2 \quad 5/2 \quad -1]$$

For the boundary point $f_L(-1, -1, -1)$

$$\mathbf{w} = \mathbf{P}_1 - \mathbf{f} = [-2 \quad -1 \quad 1/2] - [-1 \quad -1 \quad -1]$$
$$= [-1 \quad 0 \quad 3/2]$$

and for the left hand clipping plane the inner normal is

$$\mathbf{n}_L = [1 \quad 0 \quad 0]$$

Hence

$$\mathbf{D} \cdot \mathbf{n}_L = [7/2 \quad 5/2 \quad -1] \cdot [1 \quad 0 \quad 0] = 7/2 > 0$$

and the lower limit is being sought

$$\mathbf{w} \cdot \mathbf{n}_L = [-1 \quad 0 \quad 3/2] \cdot [1 \quad 0 \quad 0] = -1$$

and

$$t_L = -\frac{-1}{7/2} = 2/7$$

Table 3-11 gives the complete results.

Table 3-11

Plane	**n**	f	**w**	**w · n**	**D · n**†	t_L	t_U
Top	[0 −1 0]	(1, 1, 1)	[−3 −2 −1/2]	2	−5/2		4/5
Bottom	[0 1 0]	(−1, −1, −1)	[−1 0 3/2]	0	5/2	0	
Right	[−1 0 0]	(1, 1, 1)	[−3 −2 −1/2]	3	−7/2		6/7
Left	[1 0 0]	(−1, −1, −1)	[−1 0 3/2]	−1	7/2	2/7	
Hither	[0 0 −1]	(1, 1, 1)	[−3 −2 −1/2]	1/2	1	−1/2	
Yon	[0 0 1]	(−1, −1, −1)	[−1 0 3/2]	3/2	−1		3/2

†$\mathbf{D \cdot n} < 0$ upper limit (t_U), $\mathbf{D \cdot n} > 0$ lower limit (t_L).

Examining Table 3-11 shows that the maximum lower limit is $t_L = 2/7$ and the minimum upper limit is $t_U = 4/5$. The parametric equation of the line P_1P_2 is

$$P(t) = [-2 \quad -1 \quad 1/2] + [7/2 \quad 5/2 \quad -1]t$$

Substituting t_L and t_U yields

$$\begin{aligned} P(2/7) &= [-2 \quad -1 \quad 1/2] + [7/2 \quad 5/2 \quad -1](2/7) \\ &= [-1 \quad -2/7 \quad 3/14] \end{aligned}$$

as the intersection point with the left clipping plane and

$$\begin{aligned} P(4/5) &= [-2 \quad -1 \quad 1/2] + [7/2 \quad 5/2 \quad -1](4/5) \\ &= [4/5 \quad 1 \quad -3/10] \end{aligned}$$

as the intersection with the top clipping plane.

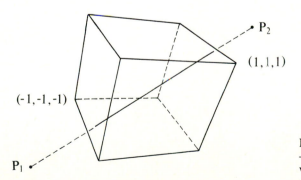

P_2

$(1,1,1)$

$(-1,-1,-1)$

P_1

Figure 3-22 Cyrus-Beck clipping —three-dimensional rectangular volume.

Clipping to a standard perspective volume is only slightly more complex. Here, the inner normals must be determined formally rather than by inspection.

Example 3-18   Clipping to a Perspective Volume

Consider the same line as in Example 3-17, i.e., $P_1(-2, -1, 1/2)$ to $P_2(3/2, 3/2, -1/2)$, clipped to the perspective volume with $(x_L, x_R, y_B, y_T, z_H, z_Y) = (-1, 1, -1, 1, 1, -1)$, with a center of projection at $z_{CP} = 5$. See Fig. 3-20b.

The inner normals for the hither and yon clipping planes may be obtained by inspection. Those for the remaining four clipping planes may be calculated from the cross products of vectors from the center of projection to the corners at $z = 0$, the plane of projection. These vectors are

$$\mathbf{V}_1 = [\ 1 \quad 1 \ -5]$$
$$\mathbf{V}_2 = [-1 \quad 1 \ -5]$$
$$\mathbf{V}_3 = [-1 \ -1 \ -5]$$
$$\mathbf{V}_4 = [\ 1 \ -1 \ -5]$$

The inner normals are then

$$\mathbf{n}_T = \mathbf{V}_1 \otimes \mathbf{V}_2 = [\quad 0 \ -10 \ -2]$$
$$\mathbf{n}_L = \mathbf{V}_2 \otimes \mathbf{V}_3 = [\ 10 \quad 0 \ -2]$$
$$\mathbf{n}_B = \mathbf{V}_3 \otimes \mathbf{V}_4 = [\quad 0 \quad 10 \ -2]$$
$$\mathbf{n}_R = \mathbf{V}_4 \otimes \mathbf{V}_1 = [-10 \quad 0 \ -2]$$
$$\mathbf{n}_H = [0 \ 0 \ -1]$$
$$\mathbf{n}_Y = [0 \ 0 \quad 1]$$

Since the center of projection is in four of the six planes, it is convenient to take

$$f_T = f_L = f_B = f_R(0, 0, 5)$$

and the center of the hither and yon planes

$$f_H(0, 0, 1) \quad \text{and} \quad f_Y(0, 0, -1)$$

as the boundary points.

The directorix for P_1P_2 is again

$$\mathbf{D} = \mathbf{P}_2 - \mathbf{P}_1 = [7/2 \ 5/2 \ -1]$$

For the boundary point in the left hand clipping plane

$$\mathbf{w} = \mathbf{P}_1 - \mathbf{f}_L = [-2 \ -1 \ 1/2] - [0 \ 0 \ 5]$$
$$= [-2 \ -1 \ -9/2]$$

Noting that

$$\mathbf{D} \cdot \mathbf{n}_L = [7/2 \ 5/2 \ -1] \cdot [10 \ 0 \ -2] = 37 > 0$$

and the lower limit is being sought. Then for

$$\mathbf{w} \cdot \mathbf{n}_L = [-2 \ -1 \ -9/2] \cdot [10 \ 0 \ -2] = -11$$

and

$$t_L = -\frac{-11}{37} = \frac{11}{37} = 0.297$$

Table 3-12 gives the complete results.

Table 3-12

Plane	n	f	w	w · n	D · n†	t_L	t_U
Top	[0 −10 −2]	(0, 0, 5)	[−2 −1 −9/2]	19	−23		0.826
Bottom	[0 10 −2]	(0, 0, 5)	[−2 −1 −9/2]	−1	27	0.037	
Right	[−10 0 −2]	(0, 0, 5)	[−2 −1 −9/2]	29	−33		0.879
Left	[10 0 −2]	(0, 0, 5)	[−2 −1 −9/2]	−11	37	0.297	
Hither	[0 0 −1]	(0, 0, 1)	[−2 −1 −1/2]	1/2	1	−0.5	
Yon	[0 0 1]	(0, 0, −1)	[−2 −1 3/2]	3/2	−1		1.5

†$\mathbf{D} \cdot \mathbf{n} < 0$ upper limit (t_U), $\mathbf{D} \cdot \mathbf{n} > 0$ lower limit (t_L).

Table 3-12 shows that the maximum lower limit is $t_L = 0.297$ and the minimum upper limit is $t_U = 0.826$. From the parametric equation the intersection values are

$$P(0.297) = [-0.961 \quad -0.258 \quad 0.203]$$

and

$$P(0.826) = [0.891 \quad 1.065 \quad -0.323]$$

for the left and top clipping planes.

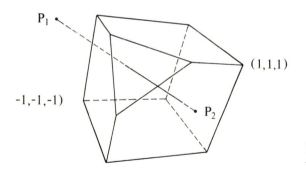

Figure 3-23 Cyrus-Beck clipping —odd three-dimensional volume.

As a final example a nonstandard clipping volume with seven clipping planes is considered.

Example 3-19 Clipping to an Arbitrary Volume

The clipping volume is shown in Fig. 3-23. It is a cube with one corner removed. The polygons describing each face have vertices.

Right: (1, −1, 1), (1, −1, −1), (1, 1, −1), (1, 1, 1)
Left: (−1, −1, 1), (−1, −1, −1), (−1, 1, −1), (−1, 1, 0), (−1, 0, 1)
Bottom: (1, −1, 1), (1, −1, −1), (−1, −1, −1), (1, −1, −1)
Top: (1, 1, 1), (1, 1, −1), (−1, 1, −1), (−1, 1, 0), (0, 1, 1)

Hither: $(1, -1, 1), (1, 1, 1), (0, 1, 1), (-1, 0, 1), (-1, -1, 1)$
Yon: $(-1, -1, -1), (1, -1, -1), (1, 1, -1), (-1, 1, -1)$
Skew: $(-1, 0, 1), (0, 1, 1), (-1, 1, 0)$

Table 3-13 gives the complete results for the line $P_1(-2, 3/2, 1)$ to $P_2(3/2, -1, -1/2)$ clipped to this volume.

Table 3-13

Plane	n			f			w			w · n	D · n†	t_L	t_U
Top	[0	−1	0]	(1,	1,	1)	[−3	1/2	0]	−1/2	5/2	1/5	
Bottom	[0	1	0]	(−1,	−1,	−1)	[−1	5/2	2]	5/2	−5/2		1
Right	[−1	0	0]	(1,	1,	1)	[−3	1/2	0]	3	−7/2		6/7
Left	[1	0	0]	(−1,	−1,	−1)	[−1	5/2	2]	−1	7/2	2/7	
Hither	[0	0	−1]	(1,	1,	1)	[−3	1/2	0]	0	3/2	0	
Yon	[0	0	1]	(−1,	−1,	−1)	[−1	5/2	2]	2	−3/2		4/3
Skew	[1	−1	−1]	(−1,	0,	1)	[−1	3/2	0]	−5/2	15/2	1/3	

†$D · n < 0$ upper limit (t_U), $D · n > 0$ lower limit (t_L).

From the table the maximum lower limit is $t_L = 1/3$, and the minimum upper limit is $t_U = 6/7$. The intersection points are thus

$$P(1/3) = [−5/6 \quad 2/3 \quad 1/2]$$

in the skew plane and

$$P(6/7) = [1 \quad −9/14 \quad −2/7]$$

in the right hand plane.

Note that the computational expense of the Cyrus-Beck algorithm grows linearly with the number of edges or planes to be clipped.

3-12   CLIPPING IN HOMOGENEOUS COORDINATES

If clipping is to be performed in homogeneous coordinates (see Ref. 1-1) considerable care must be taken if a perspective transformation is also used. The fundamental reason is that a single plane does not necessarily divide a line into two parts: one inside the clipping region and one outside the clipping region. The line may "wrap around" through infinity such that two segments are visible inside the region. Blinn (Ref. 3-6) shows that clipping all line segments *before* completing the perspective transformation by dividing by the homogeneous coordinate eliminates the segments that "return from infinity." Liang and Barsky (Ref. 3-5) have developed a line clipping algorithm that includes homogeneous coordinates. They obtain the correct result by modifying the limits of the viewing volume which is assumed to be a frustum of vision.

The Cyrus-Beck algorithm correctly clips a line to the perspective frustum of vision provided that the line exists entirely in front of the eye point or center of projection (see Example 3-18). However, if the line passes behind the center of projection, the algorithm rejects the line even if partially visible. In practice, the correct result is obtained by first clipping the line to the physical volume described in ordinary coordinate space and then applying the perspective transformation to the results. Note that any affine transformations (e.g. rotations, translations, etc.) may be applied to both the clipping volume and the line before the perspective transformation is applied. A further example illustrates these points.

Example 3-20   Cyrus-Beck With Line Passing Behind the Center of Projection

Consider the line $P_1(0, 1, 6)$ to $P_2(0, -1, -6)$ clipped to the physical volume $(x_L, x_R, y_B, y_T, z_H, z_Y) = (-1, 1, -1, 1, -1, 1)$ from a center of projection at $z = 5$. The line P_1P_2 passes through the clipping volume but originates behind the center of projection.

After applying the perspective transformation (see Ref. 1-1) the end points of the line in homogeneous coordinates are

$$P_1[0 \quad 1 \quad 6 \quad -1/5] \quad \text{and} \quad P_2[0 \quad -1 \quad -6 \quad 11/5]$$

Dividing through by the homogeneous coordinate yields the ordinary coordinates

$$P_1(0, -5, -30) \quad \text{and} \quad P_2(0, -5/11, -30/11)$$

Notice that P_1, which was originally in front of the clipping volume but behind the center of projection, has now wrapped around through infinity to a location behind the clipping volume. Since both end points are now outside the clipping volume, the Cyrus-Beck algorithm will reject the line as invisible.

Recalling the inner normals and the points in each clipping plane from Example 3-17, the line is first clipped to the physical volume $(-1, 1, -1, 1, -1, 1)$. Here, the directorix for P_1P_2 is

$$\mathbf{D} = \mathbf{P_2} - \mathbf{P_1} = [0 \quad -1 \quad -6] - [0 \quad 1 \quad 6] = [0 \quad -2 \quad -12]$$

The results are given in Table 3-14.

Table 3-14

Plane	n	f	w	w · n	D · n†	t_L	t_U
Top	[0 −1 0]	(1, 1, 1)	[−1 0 5]	0	2	0	
Bottom	[0 1 0]	(−1, −1, −1)	[1 2 7]	2	−2		1
Right	[−1 0 0]	(1, 1, 1)	[−1 0 5]	1	0		
Left	[1 0 0]	(−1, −1, −1)	[1 2 7]	1	0		
Hither	[0 0 −1]	(1, 1, 1)	[−1 0 5]	−5	12	5/12	
Yon	[0 0 1]	(−1, −1, −1)	[1 2 7]	7	−12		7/12

†$\mathbf{D \cdot n} < 0$ upper limit (t_U), $\mathbf{D \cdot n} > 0$ lower limit (t_L).

Examining Table 3-14 shows that the line is visible from $5/12 \le t \le 7/12$. The end points of the clipped line in physical space are

$$P(5/12) = [0 \quad 1 \quad 6] + [0 \quad -2 \quad -12](5/12) = [0 \quad 1/6 \quad 1]$$

$$P(7/12) = [0 \quad 1 \quad 6] + [0 \quad -2 \quad -12](7/12) = [0 \quad -1/6 \quad -1]$$

Transforming these end points to perspective space using homogeneous coordinates (see Ref. 1-1) yields

$$
\begin{bmatrix}
0 & 1/6 & 1 & 1 \\
0 & -1/6 & -1 & 1
\end{bmatrix}
\begin{bmatrix}
1 & 0 & 0 & 0 \\
0 & 1 & 0 & 0 \\
0 & 0 & 1 & -1/5 \\
0 & 0 & 0 & 1
\end{bmatrix}
=
\begin{bmatrix}
0 & 5/24 & 5/4 & 1 \\
0 & -5/36 & -5/6 & 1
\end{bmatrix}
$$

as the visible portion of the line. This is the correct result

---

3-13 DETERMINING THE INWARD NORMAL AND THREE-DIMENSIONAL CONVEX SETS

The two-dimensional technique using rotations and translations previously used to identify convex polygons and to determine the inward normal may be extended to three-dimensional plane volumes. The three-dimensional procedure is

For each polygonal face plane of the volume:

Translate the volume such that one of the vertices of the polygon face is at the origin.

Rotate about the origin such that one of the two adjacent polygon edges is coincident with one of the coordinate axes, e.g. the x axis.

Rotate about this coordinate axis until the polygonal face lies in the coordinate plane, e.g. the $z = 0$ plane.

Examine the sign of the coordinate component perpendicular to this plane for all other vertices of the volume, e.g. the z component.

If all the vertices have the same sign or are zero, then the volume is convex with respect to this plane. If the volume is convex for all its face planes, then it is convex; if not, it is concave.

If for each face the value of the coordinate component perpendicular to this plane is zero, then the volume is degenerate; i.e., it is a plane.

For each convex plane, the inner normal has components in the rotated coordinate system of zero and the sign of the coordinate components perpendicular to the plane in which the face plane lies.

In determining the original direction of the inner normal, only the inverse rotations need be applied.

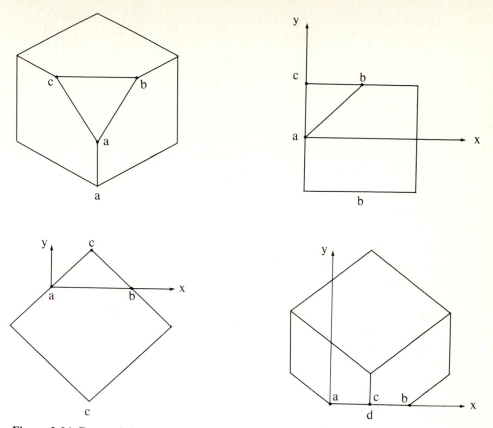

Figure 3-24 Determining a convex volume and the inner normal.

Example 3-21   Determining the Convexity of a Volume

As a specific example, again consider the cube with one corner removed previously described in Example 3-19. The cube is shown in Fig. 3-24a. The convexity of the clipping volume with respect to the face labeled *abc* in Fig. 3-24a is to be determined using the above algorithm. The volume is first translated such that point *a* is at the origin. The 4 × 4 homogeneous coordinate transformation matrix is (see Ref. 1-1)

$$[T] = \begin{bmatrix} 1 & 0 & 0 & 0 \\ 0 & 1 & 0 & 0 \\ 0 & 0 & 1 & 0 \\ 1 & 0 & -1 & 1 \end{bmatrix}$$

The result is shown, projected onto the $z = 0$ plane, in Fig. 3-24b. Rotation about the z axis by $\theta = -45°$ makes the edge *ab* coincident with with the x axis. The homogeneous coordinate transformation matrix is (see Ref. 1-1)

$$[R_z] = \begin{bmatrix} \cos\theta & \sin\theta & 0 & 0 \\ -\sin\theta & \cos\theta & 0 & 0 \\ 0 & 0 & 1 & 0 \\ 0 & 0 & 0 & 1 \end{bmatrix}$$

The result is shown in Fig. 3-24c again projected onto the $z = 0$ plane. It remains to rotate about the x axis to make the plane abc coincident with the coordinate plane $y = 0$. The coordinates of the point c in Fig. 3-24c are $(0.565685, 0.565685, -0.8)$. The rotation angle about x is given by

$$\alpha = \tan^{-1}\left(\frac{y}{z}\right) = \tan^{-1}\left(\frac{0.565685}{-0.8}\right) = -35.2644°$$

Rotation by this angle will place the volume below the coordinate plane $y = 0$. Rotation by $(180 - \alpha)$ degrees will place the volume above the plane. The latter result is shown in Fig. 3-24d projected onto the $z = 0$ plane. The rotation matrix is

$$[R_x] = \begin{bmatrix} 1 & 0 & 0 & 0 \\ \cos\alpha & \sin\alpha & 0 & 0 \\ -\sin\alpha & \cos\alpha & 1 & 0 \\ 0 & 0 & 0 & 1 \end{bmatrix}$$

The y coordinates of all the other points in the volume are positive. Hence, the volume is convex with respect to the plane abc.

The inner normal for the plane abc in this orientation is

$$\mathbf{n}' = [0 \quad \text{Sign}(y) \quad 0] = [0 \quad 1 \quad 0]$$

Applying the inverse rotations yields

$$\mathbf{n} = [0.5774 \quad -0.5774 \quad -0.5774]$$

or

$$\mathbf{n} = [1 \quad -1 \quad -1]$$

as expected. To prove the volume convex this operation must be performed for each face plane.

3-14 SPLITTING CONCAVE VOLUMES

The three-dimensional Cyrus-Beck clipping algorithm requires a convex volume. However, the ability to clip to concave volumes is desirable. This can be accomplished by internal and external clipping to appropriate convex volumes which constitute the concave volume. This is similar to the technique previously discussed for clipping to concave polygons (Sec. 3-6). The task of splitting simple concave volumes into constituent convex volumes can be accomplished by an extension of the translation and rotation technique presented in the previous section. The algorithm assumes that the volume is polyhedral. The procedure is

For each polygonal face plane of the volume:

Translate such that one of the vertices of the polygon face is at the origin.

Rotate about the origin such that one of the adjacent polygon edges is coincident with one of the coordinate axes, e.g. the x axis.

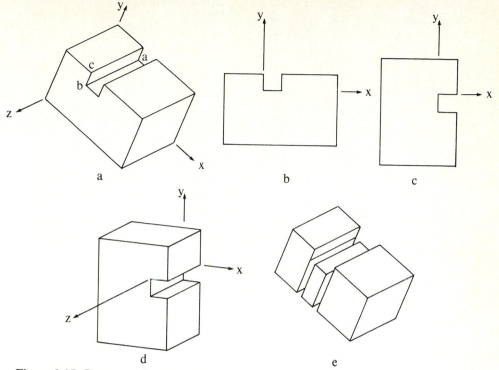

Figure 3-25 Concave volume splitting.

Rotate about this coordinate axis until the polygon face lies in the coordinate plane, e.g. the $z = 0$ plane.

Examine the sign of the coordinate component perpendicular to this plane for all other vertices of the volume, e.g. the z component.

If all the vertices have the same sign or are zero, then the volume is convex with respect to this plane. If not, it is concave. Split the volume along the coordinate plane in which the face polygon lies.

Reenter the algorithm with each of the split-off volumes. Continue until each is shown to be convex.

Example 3-22 Splitting Concave Volumes

Consider the concave volume shown in Fig. 3-25a. The polygons describing each face are

Back:	$P_1(3, 0, 0)$, $P_2(0, 0, 0)$, $P_3(0, 2, 0)$, $P_4(1, 2, 0)$
	$P_5(1, 3/2, 0)$, $P_6(3/2, 3/2, 0)$, $P_7(3/2, 2, 0)$, $P_8(3, 2, 0)$
Front:	$P_9(3, 0, 2)$, $P_{10}(0, 0, 2)$, $P_{11}(0, 2, 2)$, $P_{12}(1, 2, 2)$
	$P_{13}(1, 3/2, 2)$, $P_{14}(3/2, 3/2, 2)$, $P_{15}(3/2, 2, 2)$, $P_{16}(3, 2, 2)$
Left:	$P_2(0, 0, 0)$, $P_{10}(0, 0, 2)$, $P_{11}(0, 2, 2)$, $P_3(0, 2, 0)$

Right:	$P_1(3, 0, 0)$, $P_8(3, 2, 0)$, $P_{16}(3, 2, 2)$, $P_9(3, 0, 2)$
Bottom:	$P_1(3, 0, 0)$, $P_2(0, 0, 0)$, $P_{10}(0, 0, 2)$, $P_9(3, 0, 2)$
Top left:	$P_{10}(0, 0, 2)$, $P_4(1, 2, 0)$, $P_3(0, 2, 0)$, $P_{11}(0, 2, 2)$
Left notch:	$P_{13}(1, 3/2, 2)$, $P_5(1, 3/2, 0)$, $P_4(1, 2, 0)$, $P_{12}(1, 2, 2)$
Bottom notch:	$P_{13}(1, 3/2, 2)$, $P_{14}(3/2, 3/2, 2)$, $P_6(3/2, 3/2, 0)$, $P_5(1, 3/2, 0)$
Right notch:	$P_6(3/2, 3/2, 0)$, $P_7(3/2, 2, 0)$, $P_{15}(3/2, 2, 2)$, $P_{14}(3/2, 3/2, 2)$
Top right:	$P_{16}(3, 2, 2)$, $P_8(3, 2, 0)$, $P_7(3/2, 2, 0)$, $P_{15}(3/2, 2, 2)$

Using the above algorithm, the convexity of the volume with respect to the face called the left notch and labeled abc in Fig. 3-25a is examined. The volume is first translated such that the point P_5, labeled a in Fig. 3-25a, is at the origin. This also places P_{13}, labeled b in Fig. 3-25a, on the positive z axis. The translation factors are -1, $-3/2$, 0 in the x, y, z directions, respectively. The result is shown projected onto the $z = 0$ plane in Fig. 3-25b. Rotation about the z axis by $-90°$ makes the plane abc coincident with the $y = 0$ coordinate plane. The result is shown in Figs. 3-25c and d projected onto the $z = 0$ plane.

Examination of the y coordinates shows that the volume is concave. It is split into two volumes, V_1 and V_2, along the plane $y = 0$. V_1 is above the plane $y = 0$, and V_2 below, The face planes in the original orientation are

V_1:

Left:	$P_2(0, 0, 0)$, $P_{10}(0, 0, 2)$, $P_{11}(0, 2, 2)$, $P_3(0, 2, 0)$
Right lower:	$P'_{10}(1, 0, 2)$, $P'_5(1, 0, 0)$, $P_5(1, 3/2, 0)$, $P_{13}(1, 3/2, 2)$
Right upper:	$P_{13}(1, 3/2, 2)$, $P_5(1, 3/2, 0)$, $P_4(1, 2, 0)$, $P_{12}(1, 2, 2)$
Top:	$P_{10}(0, 0, 2)$, $P_4(1, 2, 0)$, $P_3(0, 2, 0)$, $P_{11}(0, 2, 2)$
Bottom:	$P_2(0, 0, 0)$, $P'_5(1, 0, 0)$, $P'_{10}(1, 0, 2)$, $P_{10}(0, 0, 2)$
Front:	$P_{10}(0, 0, 2)$, $P'_{10}(1, 0, 2)$, $P_{13}(1, 3/2, 2)$, $P_{12}(1, 2, 2)$, $P_{11}(0, 2, 2)$
Back:	$P'_5(1, 0, 0)$, $P_2(0, 0, 0)$, $P_3(0, 2, 0)$, $P_4(1, 2, 0)$, $P_5(1, 3/2, 0)$

V_2:

Left:	$P'_5(1, 0, 0)$, $P'_{10}(1, 0, 2)$, $P_{13}(1, 3/2, 2)$, $P_5(1, 3/2, 0)$
Right:	$P_1(3, 0, 0)$, $P_8(3, 2, 0)$, $P_{16}(3, 2, 2)$, $P_9(3, 0, 2)$
Right notch:	$P_6(3/2, 3/2, 0)$, $P_7(3/2, 2, 0)$, $P_{15}(3/2, 2, 2)$, $P_{14}(3/2, 3/2, 2)$
Bottom notch:	$P_{13}(1, 3/2, 2)$, $P_{14}(3/2, 3/2, 2)$, $P_6(3/2, 3/2, 0)$, $P_5(1, 3/2, 0)$
Top right:	$P_{16}(3, 2, 2)$, $P_8(3, 2, 0)$, $P_7(3/2, 2, 0)$, $P_{15}(3/2, 2, 2)$
Bottom:	$P'_5(1, 0, 0)$, $P_1(3, 0, 0)$, $P_9(3, 0, 2)$, $P'_{10}(1, 0, 2)$

When the two volumes are passed through the algorithm a second time, V_1 is declared convex and V_2 is split into two volumes which are subsequently found to be convex. The result is shown in Fig. 3-25e in an exploded view.

3-15   POLYGON CLIPPING

The previous discussion has concentrated on clipping lines. Polygons can of course be considered as collections of lines. For line drawing applications it is not too important if polygons are subdivided into lines before clipping. When a closed polygon is clipped as a collection of lines, the original closed polygon becomes one or more open polygons or discrete lines as shown in Fig. 3-26.

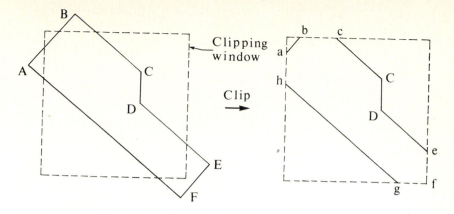

Figure 3-26 Polygon clipping—open polygons.

However, when polygons are considered as solid areas, it is necessary that closed polygons remain closed. In Fig. 3-26 this requires that the lines *bc*, *ef* *fg*, and *ha* be added to the polygon description. Adding *ef* and *fg* is particularly difficult. Considerable difficulty also occurs when clipping a polygon results in several disjoint smaller polygons as shown in Fig. 3-27. For example, the lines *ab* and *cd* shown in Fig. 3-27 are frequently included in the clipped polygon description. If, for example, the original polygon is declared red on a blue background, the lines *ab* and *cd* will also appear red on a blue background. This is contrary to expectation.

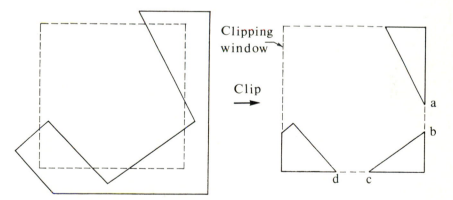

Figure 3-27 Polygon clipping—disjoint polygons.

3-16 REENTRANT POLYGON CLIPPING—SUTHERLAND-HODGMAN ALGORITHM

The fundamental idea behind the Sutherland-Hodgman algorithm (Ref. 3-7) is that it is easy to clip a polygon against a single edge or clipping plane. The procedure is to clip the original polygon and each resulting intermediate polygon

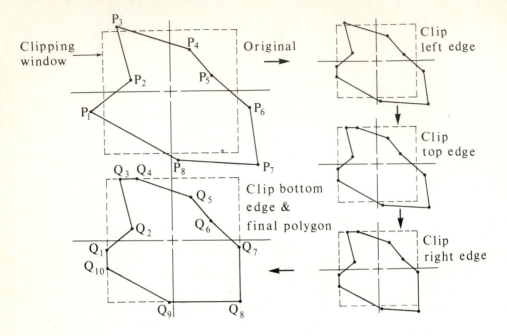

Figure 3-28 Reentrant polygon clipping.

against a single edge, each edge in succession. Figure 3-28 illustrates the procedure for a rectangular window. The polygon is originally defined by a list of vertices $P_1, \ldots, P_n$ which imply a list of edges $P_1 P_2,\ P_2 P_3, \ldots, P_{n-1} P_n,\ P_n P_1$. In Fig. 3-28 these edges are first clipped against the left edge of the window to yield the intermediate polygon shown. The clipping algorithm is then reentered with the intermediate polygon to be clipped against the top edge. This yields a second intermediate polygon. The process is repeated until the polygon is clipped against all the window edges. The steps are shown in Fig. 3-28. Notice that the addition of the corner point labeled Q_8 in the final clipped polygon is now trivial. The algorithm will clip any polygon, convex or concave, planar or nonplanar, against any convex polygonal clipping window. The order in which the polygon is clipped against the various window edges is immaterial.

The output of the algorithm is a list of polygon vertices all of which are on the visible side of a clipping plane. Since each edge of the polygon is individually compared with the clipping plane, only the relationship between a single edge and a single clipping plane need be considered. If each point P, except the first, in the polygon vertex list is considered as the terminal vertex of an edge, and if the starting vertex S of that edge is the vertex just previous to P in the list, then there are only four possible relationships between the edge and the clipping plane. These are shown in Fig. 3-29.

The result of each polygon edge-clipping plane comparison is the output to the clipped polygon list of no, one, or two vertices. If the edge is entirely visible, then P is output. It is not necessary to output S, the starting vertex,

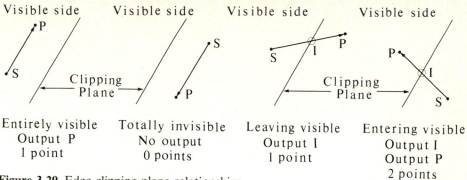

Figure 3-29 Edge-clipping plane relationships.

since, if each vertex is considered sequentially, S was the terminating vertex of the previous edge and has already been output. If the edge is entirely invisible, no output is required.

If the edge is partially visible, then it is either entering or leaving the visible side of the clipping plane. If the edge is leaving the visible region, the intersections of the polygon edge and the clipping plane must be calculated and output. If the edge is entering the visible region, the intersection with the clipping plane must again be calculated and output. Since P, the terminating vertex, is now visible, it must also be output.

For the first point of the polygon it is only necessary to determine if it is visible. If it is visible, then it is output and saved as S. If it is not visible, no output occurs but it is still saved as S the starting point.

The final edge P_nP_1 must be considered separately. This is done by saving the first point as F. Then the final edge becomes P_nF and may now be considered exactly as any other edge.

Before presenting the complete algorithm, there are two additional considerations: determining the visibility of a point and determining the intersection of the polygon edge and the clipping plane. Determining the visibility of a point is equivalent to determining on which side of the clipping plane the point lies. If successive edges of the clipping polygon are considered in a clockwise direction, the inside of the polygon is always to the right. If counterclockwise, the inside is to the left. Previously two methods of determining the location (visibility) of a point with respect to a line or plane have been considered: examining the sign of the dot product of the normal vector and a vector from a point in the line or plane to the point under consideration (see Sec. 3-5) and substitution of the point coordinates into the equation of the line or plane (see Sec. 3-9). This latter technique is a variation of that proposed by Sutherland and Hodgman in Ref. 3-7.

Another technique is to examine the sign of the z component of the cross product of two vectors which lie in a plane. If two points in the clipping plane are P_1 and P_2, and the point under consideration is P_3, then these three points define a plane. Two vectors which lie in that plane are $\mathbf{P_1P_2}$ and $\mathbf{P_1P_3}$. If this plane is considered the xy plane, then the vector cross product $\mathbf{P_1P_3} \otimes \mathbf{P_1P_2}$ has

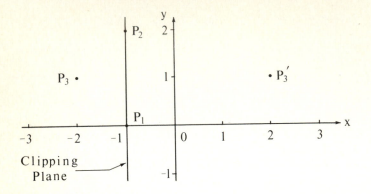

Figure 3-30 Visibility tests.

only a z component given by $(x_3 - x_1)(y_2 - y_1) - (x_3 - y_1)(x_2 - x_1)$. If the sign of the z component is positive, zero, or negative, then P_3 is to the right, on, or to the left of the line $P_1 P_2$.

All these techniques are particularly simple for rectangular clipping windows parallel to the coordinate axes.

Example 3-23 Relation of a Point to a Plane

Consider a clipping plane at $x = w = -1$ perpendicular to the x axis as shown in Fig. 3-30. The locations of two points $P_3(-2, 1)$ and $P_3'(2, 1)$ are to be determined with respect to the clipping plane.

Using the cross-product technique with $P_1(-1, 0)$ and $P_2(-1, 2)$ yields for P_3

$$(y_3 - y_1)(x_3 - x_2) = (1 - 0)[-2 - (-1)] = -1 < 0$$

which indicates P_3 is to the left of $\mathbf{P}_1\mathbf{P}_2$, and for P_3'

$$(y_3' - y_1)(x_3' - x_2) = (1 - 0)[2 - (-1)] = 3 > 0$$

which indicates P_3' is to the right of $\mathbf{P}_1\mathbf{P}_2$

The substitution technique is particularly simple. Here the test function is $x - w$. For P_3

$$x_3 - w = -2 - (-1) = -1 < 0$$

and for P_3'

$$x_3' - w = 2 - (-1) = 3 > 0$$

which indicates that P_3 and P_3' are to the left and right of $\mathbf{P}_1\mathbf{P}_2$, respectively.

Choosing the inner normal as $\mathbf{n} = [1 \;\; 0]$ and the point in the clipping plane as $f(-1, 0)$ and taking the dot product of the vectors yields for P_3

$$\mathbf{n} \cdot [\mathbf{P}_3 - \mathbf{f}] = [1 \;\; 0] \cdot [-1 \;\; 1] = -1 < 0$$

and for P_3'

$$\mathbf{n} \cdot [\mathbf{P}_3' - \mathbf{f}] = [1 \quad 0] \cdot [3 \quad 1] = 3 > 0$$

which again indicates that P_3 is to the left and P_3' is to the right of the clipping plane.

Using these visibility tests, a polygon edge is totally visible or totally invisible if both end points are totally visible or totally invisible. If one end point is visible and the other invisible, then the polygon edge intersects the clipping plane and its intersection point must be calculated. Any of the line intersection (clipping) techniques discussed above may be used, e.g., Cyrus-Beck (see Sec. 3-5), explicit or parametric (see Secs. 3-1 and 3-4), or the midpoint subdivision (see Sec. 3-3). Again, as has been illustrated above, these techniques are particularly simple for rectangular clipping windows parallel to the coordinate axis. The Cyrus-Beck and midpoint subdivision techniques are of course completely general. However, the intersection of two general parametric lines in the two-dimensional plane requires further discussion.

Two line segments with end points P_1, P_2 and P_3, P_4, respectively, can be parametrically represented as

$$P(s) = P_1 + (P_2 - P_1)s \qquad 0 \le s \le 1$$

and

$$P(t) = P_3 + (P_4 - P_3)t \qquad 0 \le t \le 1$$

At the intersection point $P(s) = P(t)$. Recalling that $P(s)$ and $P(t)$ are vector valued functions, i.e., $P(s) = [x(s) \quad y(s)]$ and $P(t) = [x(t) \quad y(t)]$ yields two equations in the two unknown parameter values s and t at the intersection; i.e., $x(s) = x(t)$, $y(s) = y(t)$ at the intersection point. If there is no solution, then the lines are parallel. If either s or t is outside the required range, the segments do not intersect. A matrix formulation is particularly convenient.

Example 3-24   Intersection of Parametric Lines

Consider the two line segments $P_1[0 \quad 0]$ to $P_2[3 \quad 2]$ and $P_3[3 \quad 0]$ to $P_4[0 \quad 2]$ as shown in Fig. 3-31. Then

$$P(s) = [0 \quad 0] + [\ 3 \quad 2]s$$
$$P(t) = [3 \quad 0] + [-3 \quad 2]t$$

Equating the x and y components yields

$$3s = 3 - 3t$$
$$2s = 2t$$

Solving yields

$$s = t = 1/2$$

The intersection point is then

$$P_i(s) = [0 \quad 0] + [3 \quad 2](1/2)$$
$$= [3/2 \quad 1]$$

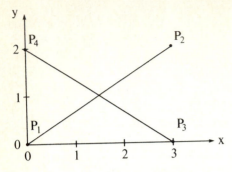

Figure 3-31 Intersection of parametric lines.

Sutherland and Hodgman (Ref. 3-7) suggest an alternate approach to generating successive intermediate polygons as discussed here. In developing the Sutherland-Hodgman algorithm, recall that each polygon edge is considered successively. Hence, with minor changes the same code can be used for each edge. The last vertex is handled specially. Figure 3-32, adapted from Ref. 3-7, gives a flowchart of the algorithm. Figure 3-32a is applied to every vertex, while Fig. 3-32b is used only for the last vertex. A pseudo implementation which generates and stores intermediate polygons is given below.

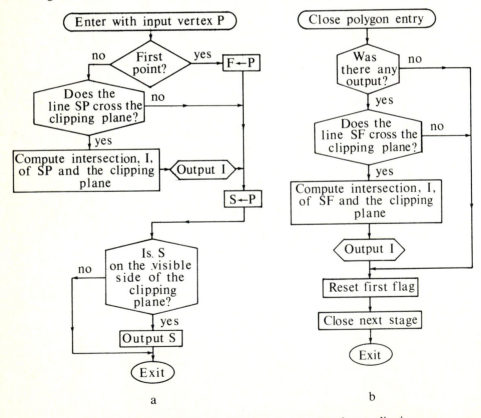

Figure 3-32 Flowchart for Sutherland-Hodgman reentrant polygon clipping.

Sutherland and Hodgman show how the generation and storage of intermediate polygon vertices can be avoided. Specifically, instead of clipping each edge (vertex) of the polygon against a single window plane, each polygon edge (vertex) is clipped successively against all the window planes. As soon as a polygon edge (vertex) is clipped against a window plane the algorithm calls itself recursively to clip the result against the next window plane. This makes the algorithm more suitable for hardware implementation.

Sutherland-Hodgman polygon clipping algorithm

P *is the input polygon array*
Q *is the output polygon array*
W *is the clipping window array. The first vertex is repeated as the last vertex*
Nin *is the number of input polygon vertices*
Nout *is the number of output polygon vertices*
Nw *is the number of clipping polygon vertices plus one*
all polygon vertices are given in clockwise order

    for each window edge
   for $i = 1$ **to** Nw $- 1$
       set the output counter and zero the output array
       Nout $= 0$
       Q $= 0$
       clip each polygon edge against this window edge
       for $j = 1$ **to** Nin
          treat the first point specially
          if $j <> 1$ **then** 1
          save first point
          F $= P_j$
          go to 2
          check if this polygon edge crosses the window edge
   1   **call** Cross(S, P_j, W_i, W_{i+1}; Spcross)
          if Spcross $=$ no **then** 2
          if the polygon edge crosses the window edge calculate the intersection point
          call Intersect(S, P_j, W_i, W_{i+1}; Pintersect)
          output the intersection point
          call Output (Pintersect, Nout,Q)
          replace the first point
   2   S $= P_j$
          check if the second point on the polygon edge (now S) is visible
          call Visible(S, W_i, W_{i+1}; Svisible)
          if Svisible < 0 **then** 3
          if the point is visible output it
          call Output(S, Nout, Q)
  3   **next** j
       closure—treat the edge P_nP_1
       if there has been no output skip to the next window edge

> **if** Nout = 0 **then** 5
> *check if the last polygon edge crosses the window edge*
> **call** Cross(S, F, W_i, W_{i+1}; Spcross)
> **if** Spcross = no **then** 4
> *if the polygon edge crosses the window edge calculate the intersection*
> **call** Intersect(S, F, W_i, W_{i+1}; Pintersect)
> *output the intersection*
> **call** Output(Pintersect, Nout, Q)
> *The polygon is now clipped against the edge W_i to W_{i+1}*
> *the algorithm is now reentered with the clipped polygon*
> 4   P = Q
>   Nin = Nout
> 5   **next** i
>   **finish**

subroutine module to determine if the polygon edge and the window edge intersect

subroutine Cross(Start, Point, W1, W2; Spcross)

> *determine the visibility of the starting point of the polygon edge*
> **call** Visible(Start, W1, W2; Pvisible)
> Pvisible1 = Pvisible
> *determine the visibility of the end point of the polygon edge*
> **call** Visible(Point, W1, W2; Pvisible)
> Pvisible2 = Pvisible
> *a polygon edge which begins or ends on a window edge is considered not to cross the edge. This point will have previously been output*
> **if** Pvisible1 < 0 **and** Pvisible2 > 0 **or**
> Pvisible1 > 0 **and** Pvisible2 < 0 **then**
>   Spcross = yes
> **else**
>   Spcross = no
> **end if**
> **return**

subroutine module to determine visibility

subroutine Visible(Point, P1, P2; Pvisible)

the visibility of Point is to be determined with respect to the edge P_1P_2
Pvisible < 0 Point *is invisible*
        = 0 Point *is on the edge* P_1P_2
        > 0 Point *is visible*
the routine uses the cross-product technique
the Sign function returns − 1, 0, 1 as the argument is negative, zero, or positive
Temp1 = (Pointx − P1x)*(P2y − P1y)
Temp2 = (Pointy − P1y)*(P2x − P1x)
Temp3 = Temp1 − Temp2

Pvisible = Sign(Temp3)
return

subroutine module to calculate intersection of two lines

subroutine Intersect(P1, P2, W1, W2; Pintersect)
the routine uses a parametric line formulation
the lines P_1P_2 and W_1W_2 are assumed two-dimensional
the matrix for the parameter values is obtained by equating the x and y
components of the two parametric lines
Coeff *is a 4 × 4 matrix containing the parameter coefficients*
Parameter *is a 2 × 1 matrix containing the parameters*
Right *is a 2 × 1 matrix for the right hand sides of the equations*
Invert *is the matrix inversion function*
Parameter(1, 1) *is the polygon edge intersection value*
Multiply *is the matrix multiply function*

> *fill the coefficient matrix*
> Coeff(1, 1) = P2x − P1x
> Coeff(1, 2) = W1x − W2x
> Coeff(2, 1) = P2y − P1y
> Coeff(2, 2) = W1y − W2y
> *fill the right hand side matrix*
> Right(1, 1) = W1x − P1x
> Right(2, 1) = W1y − P1y
> *invert the coefficient matrix*
> *it is not necessary to check for a singular matrix because intersection is*
> *ensured*
> Coeff = Invert(Coeff)
> *solve for the parameter matrix*
> Parameter = (Coeff) Multiply (Right)
> *calculate the intersection points*
> Pintersect = P1 + (P2 − P1)*Parameter(1, 1)
> **return**

subroutine module for polygon output

subroutine Output(Vertex,Nout,Q)

Vertex contains the output point
> *increment the number of output vertices and add to Q*
> Nout = Nout + 1
> Q(Nout) = Vertex
> **return**

Example 3-25 below further illustrates the Sutherland-Hodgman algorithm. It also illustrates a particular characteristic of the algorithm, i.e., degenerate boundaries. The existence of these degenerate boundaries is not important in many applications, e.g., solid area scan conversion. However, some applications, e.g., some hidden surface algorithms, necessitate their elimination. This can be accomplished by sorting the vertices as suggested in Ref. 3-7.

Example 3-25   Sutherland-Hodgman Polygon Clipping

Consider the polygon with vertices given in Table 3-15 below and shown in Fig. 3-33 clipped to the square window with planes $x_{left} = -1$, $x_{right} = 1$, $y_{bottom} = -1$, $y_{top} = 1$. As a specific example consider the edge from P_1 to P_2 clipped to the left hand window plane. Considering the window planes to be given in clockwise order the inside or visible side is to the right. With the use of the substitution method described above (see Example 3-23), the test function $x - w$ is

$$x - w = x - (-1) = x + 1$$

For $P_1(1/2, -3/2)$

$$x_1 + 1 = 1/2 + 1 > 0$$

Thus, P_1 is to the right of the clipping plane and visible.
      For $P_2(-2, -3/2)$

$$x_2 + 1 = -2 + 1 < 0$$

Thus, P_2 is invisible. The edge P_1P_2 crosses the clipping plane. Hence, the intersection must be calculated. Using the parametric line solution (see Example 3-24) yields $x = -1$, $y = -3/2$.

Table 3-15

	Original polygon	Clipped against left edge	Clipped against top edge	Clipped against right edge	Final polygon
P_1	(1/2, −3/2)	(1/2, −3/2)	(1/2, −3/2)	(1/2, −3/2)	(−1, −1)
P_2	(−2, −3/2)	(−1, −3/2)	(−1, −3/2)	(−1, −3/2)	(−1, 1)
P_3	(−2, 2)	(−1, 2)	(−1, 1)	(−1, 1)	(1, 1)
P_4	(3/2, 2)	(3/2, 2)	(3/2, 1)	(1, 1)	(1, 0)
P_5	(3/2, 0)	(3/2, 0)	(3/2, 0)	(1, 0)	(1/2, 0)
P_6	(1/2, 0)	(1/2, 0)	(1/2, 0)	(1/2, 0)	(1/2, 1)
P_7	(1/2, 3/2)	(1/2, 3/2)	(1/2, 1)	(1/2, 1)	(−1, 1)
P_8	(−3/2, 3/2)	(−1, 3/2)	(−1, 1)	(−1, 1)	(−1, 0)
P_9	(−3/2, 1/2)	(−1, 0)	(−1, 0)	(−1, 0)	(0, −1)

The results are shown in Fig. 3-33. Of particular interest is the last clipping stage, i.e., against the bottom window plane. Up until this stage P_1 has survived. Hence, the intermediate polygon vertex lists have remained in the same order as the original vertex list. However, P_1 is eliminated by the clip against the bottom window plane. The vertex list now starts at the intermediate vertex corresponding to P_2. The last vertex in the final clipped polygon list represents the intersection of the polygon edge P_9P_1 with the bottom window plane.

      Note the four degenerate edges or boundaries in the upper left corner of the clipping window as shown in Fig. 3-33 for the final polygon.

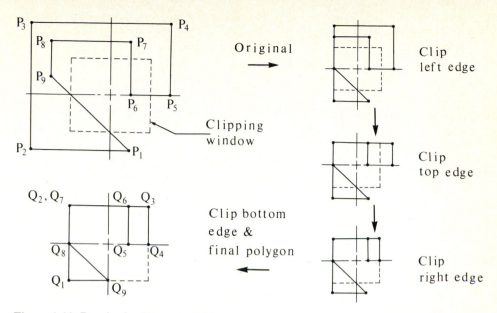

Figure 3-33 Results for Example 3-24.

The Sutherland-Hodgman algorithm as presented above concentrated on clipping to a two-dimensional window. In fact, the algorithm is more general. Any planar or nonplanar polygon can be clipped to a convex clipping volume by calculating the intersection with a three-dimensional clipping plane using the Cyrus-Beck algorithm. The Sutherland-Hodgman clipping algorithm can also be used to split concave polygons (see Sec. 3-8 and Ref. 3-7).

Liang and Barsky (Ref. 3-8) have developed a new algorithm for polygon clipping. As presented the algorithm is optimized for rectangular clipping windows but is extendable to arbitrary convex windows. The algorithm is based on concepts from their two- and three-dimensional line clipping algorithm (Ref. 3-5). Tests indicate that for rectangular windows the optimized algorithm is twice as fast as the Sutherland-Hodgman algorithm.

3-17 CONCAVE CLIPPING REGIONS—WEILER-ATHERTON ALGORITHM

The clipping algorithms previously discussed require a convex clipping region. In the context of many applications, e.g., hidden surface removal, the ability to clip to concave regions is required. A powerful but somewhat more complex clipping algorithm developed by Weiler and Atherton (Ref. 3-9) meets this requirement. The Weiler-Atherton algorithm is capable of clipping a concave polygon with interior holes to the boundaries of another concave polygon, also with interior holes. The polygon to be clipped is the subject polygon. The clipping region is the clip polygon. The new boundaries created by clipping the subject polygon against the clip polygon are identical to portions of the clip polygon. No new edges are created. Hence, the number of resulting polygons is minimized.

The algorithm describes both the subject and the clip polygon by a circular list of vertices. The exterior boundaries of the polygons are described clockwise, and the interior boundaries or holes counterclockwise. When traversing the vertex list, this convention ensures that the inside of the polygon is always to the right. The boundaries of the subject polygon and the clip polygon may or may not intersect. If they intersect, then the intersections occur in pairs. One of the intersections occurs when a subject polygon edge enters the inside of the clip polygon and one when it leaves. Fundamentally, the algorithm starts at an entering intersection and follows the exterior boundary of the subject polygon clockwise until an intersection with the clip polygon is found. At the intersection a right turn is made, and the exterior boundary of the clip polygon is followed clockwise until an intersection with the subject polygon is found. Again, at the intersection, a right turn is made, with the subject polygon now being followed. The process is continued until the starting point is reached. Interior boundaries of the subject polygon are followed counterclockwise. See Fig. 3-34.

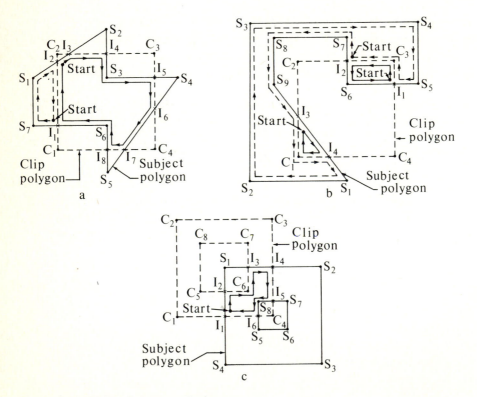

Figure 3-34 Weiler-Atherton clipping.

A more formal statement of the algorithm is:

Determine the intersections of the subject and clip polygons.

> Add each intersection to the subject and clip polygon vertex lists. Tag each intersection vertex and establish a bidirectional link between the subject and clip polygon lists for each intersection vertex.

Process nonintersecting polygon borders.

> Establish two holding lists: one for boundaries which lie inside the clip polygon and one for boundaries which lie outside. Ignore clip polygon boundaries which are outside the subject polygon. Clip polygon boundaries inside the subject polygon form holes in the subject polygon. Consequently a copy of the clip polygon boundary goes on both the inside and the outside holding list. Place the boundaries on the appropriate holding list.

Create two intersection vertex lists.

> One, the entering list, contains only the intersections for the subject polygon edge entering the inside of the clip polygon. The other, the leaving list, contains only the intersections for the subject polygon edge leaving the inside of the clip polygon. The intersection type will alternate along the boundary. Thus, only one determination is required for each pair of intersections.

Perform the actual clipping.

> Polygons inside the clipping polygon are found using the following procedure.

> > Remove an intersection vertex from the entering list. If the list is empty, the process is complete.

> > Follow the subject polygon vertex list until an intersection is found. Copy the subject polygon list up to this point to the inside holding list.

> > Using the link, jump to the clip polygon vertex list.

> > Follow the clip polygon vertex list until an intersection is found. Copy the clip polygon vertex list up to this point to the inside holding list.

> > Jump back to the subject polygon vertex list.

> > Repeat until the starting point is again reached. At this point the new inside polygon has been closed.

> Polygons outside the clipping polygon are found using the same procedure, except that the initial intersection vertex is obtained from the

leaving list and the clip polygon vertex list is followed in the *reverse* direction. The polygon lists are copied to the outside holding list.

Attach any holes, i.e. interior boundaries, to their associated exterior boundaries. Since exterior boundaries are specified clockwise and interior boundaries counterclockwise, this is most conveniently accomplished by testing the directionality of the boundaries. The process is complete.

Several examples will serve to more fully illustrate the algorithm.

Example 3-26 Weiler-Atherton Polygon Clipping—Simple Polygon

Consider the subject polygon shown in Fig. 3-34a clipped to the square clipping polygon shown in Fig. 3-34a. The intersection points between the two polygons are also shown and labeled I_i. The subject polygon and the clip polygon vertex lists are shown below. The intersection vertices $I_2, I_4, I_6,$ and I_8 are placed on the entering list and the vertices I_1, I_3, I_5, I_7 on the leaving list.

Subject polygon list	Clip polygon list	Subject polygon list	Clip polygon list
S_1	C_1	S_1	C_1
Start I_2	I_1	I_2	I_1 Finish
I_3	I_2 Finish	I_3	I_2
S_2	C_2	S_2	C_2
I_4	I_3	I_4	I_3
S_3	I_4	S_3	I_4
I_5	C_3	I_5	C_3
S_4	I_5	S_4	I_5
I_6	I_6	I_6	I_6
I_7	C_4	I_7	C_4
S_5	I_7	S_5	I_7
I_8	I_8	I_8	I_8
S_6	C_1	S_6	C_1
I_1		I_1 Start	
S_7		S_7	
S_1		S_1	

| Inside polygon | | Outside polygon | |

To form the inside polygon, the first intersection on the entering list, I_2, is removed. The procedure described above yields the results shown by the solid line with the arrows in Fig. 3-34a and in the subject and clip polygon lists shown above. The resulting inside polygon is

$$I_2 I_3 I_4 S_3 I_5 I_6 I_7 I_8 S_6 I_1 I_2$$

The other intersection vertices on the entering list, i.e. $I_4, I_6,$ and I_8, yield the same clipped polygon.

To form the outside polygons, the first intersection on the leaving list, I_1, is removed. The procedure described above yields the results shown by the dashed line with the arrows in Fig. 3-34a and in the subject and clip polygon lists also shown above. Notice that the clip polygon list is traversed in the reverse direction from I_2 to I_1. The resulting outside polygon is

$$I_1 S_7 S_1 I_2 I_1$$

Similarly removing I_3, I_5, and I_7 from the leaving list yields the outside polygons

$$I_3 S_2 I_4 I_3 \quad \text{and} \quad I_5 S_4 I_6 I_5 \quad \text{and} \quad I_7 S_5 I_8 I_7$$

respectively.

A somewhat more complex subject polygon which partially surrounds the clip polygon is shown in the next example.

Example 3-27   Weiler-Atherton Polygon Clipping—Surrounding Polygon

The subject and clip polygons and their intersections are shown in Fig. 3-34b. The intersection vertices I_1 and I_3 are placed on the entering list and I_2 and I_4 on the leaving list. The subject and clip polygon lists are then

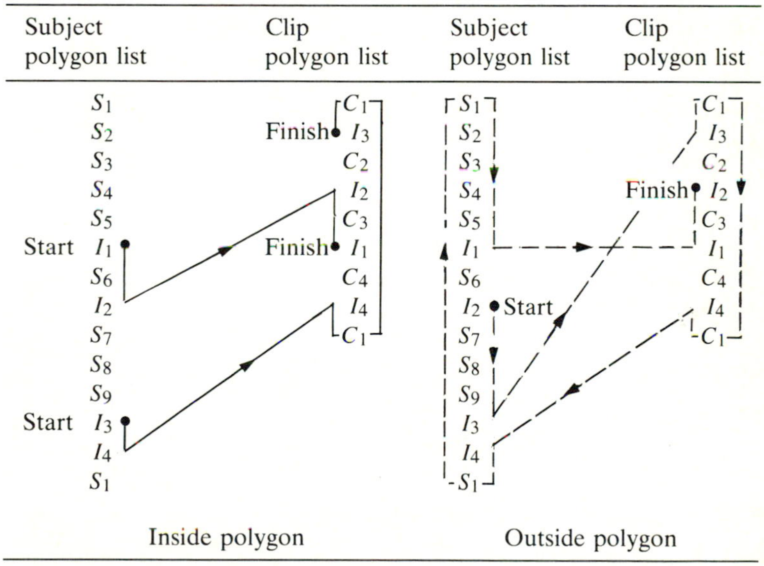

Subject polygon list	Clip polygon list	Subject polygon list	Clip polygon list
Inside polygon		Outside polygon	

To form the inside polygons, remove first I_1 and then I_3 from the entering list. The results are shown by the solid line with the arrows in Fig. 3-34b and in the subject and clip polygon lists above. The resulting clipped inside polygons are

$$I_1 S_6 I_2 C_3 I_1 \quad \text{and} \quad I_3 I_4 C_1 I_3$$

respectively. Notice that two clipped inside polygons result.

Removing I_2 from the leaving polygon list yields

$$I_2 S_7 S_8 S_9 I_3 C_1 I_4 S_1 S_2 S_3 S_4 S_5 I_1 C_3 I_2$$

for the outside polygon. I_4 yields the same polygon. The results are indicated by the dashed line in Fig. 3-34b and in the polygon lists above. Again, notice that the clip polygon list is traversed in the reverse direction for the outside polygon.

The final example shows a concave polygon with a hole clipped to a concave window also having a hole.

Example 3-28 Weiler-Atherton Clipping—Boundaries With Holes

The subject and clip polygons and their intersections are shown in Fig. 3-34c. The intersection vertices I_1, I_3, and I_5 are placed on the entering list, and I_2, I_4, and I_6 on the leaving list. The subject and clip polygon lists are

Subject polygon list	Clip polygon list		Subject polygon list	Clip polygon list
S_1	C_1		S_1	C_1
I_3	C_2		I_3	C_2
I_4	C_3	Outer	I_4	C_3
S_2	I_4	border	S_2	I_4
S_3	I_5		S_3	I_5
S_4	C_4		S_4	C_4
Start I_1	I_6		I_1	I_6
I_2	I_1 Finish		I_2 Start	I_1
S_1	C_1		S_1	C_1
S_5	C_5		S_5	C_5
S_6	I_2		S_6	I_2 Finish
S_7	C_6	Hole	S_7	C_6
I_5	I_3	border	I_5	I_3
S_8	C_7		S_8	C_7
I_6	C_8		I_6	C_8
S_5	C_5		S_5	C_5
Inside polygon			Outside polygon	

Notice that the interior boundaries, i.e. the hole, vertices are listed in counterclockwise order. The interior and exterior boundary lists are individually circular.

When I_1 is removed from the entering list, the algorithm yields

$$I_1 I_2 C_6 I_3 I_4 I_5 S_8 I_6 I_1$$

for the inside polygon as shown by the solid lines with arrows in Fig. 3-34c and the subject and clip polygon lists above. I_3 and I_5 from the entering list yield the same polygon.

Removing I_2 from the leaving list yields the outside polygon

$$I_2S_1I_3C_6I_2$$

Note that the subject polygon list contains two separate boundaries, an inner boundary and an outer boundary, each of which is individually circular. Therefore, the transfer from S_1 at the bottom of the outer boundary list is to S_1 at the top of the outer boundary list rather than to S_5 on the hole boundary list. Transfer from an exterior to an interior boundary always occurs by a jump from the subject to the clip polygon list or vice versa, as shown by the dashed line in the subject and clip polygon lists above. Similarly, I_4 and I_6 from the leaving list both yield the outside polygon

$$I_4S_2S_3S_4I_1I_6S_5S_6S_7I_5I_4$$

In order for the Weiler-Atherton algorithm to work correctly, care must be taken with the identification and placement of intersections. Grazing conditions, i.e., when a subject polygon vertex or edge lies on or is coincident with a clip polygon edge, are not considered intersections. Examples of these conditions are shown in Fig. 3-35a. Similarly, clip and subject polygon intersections such as those shown in Fig. 3-35b must be placed correctly to avoid degenerate polygon edges. Specifically, the points marked with an x in Fig. 3-35b are considered intersections, whereas those marked with a dot are not. Additional implementation details are given in Refs. 3-10 and 3-11.

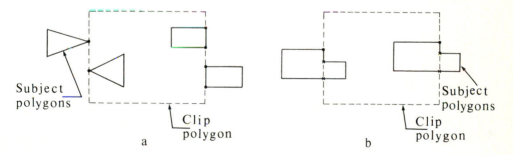

Figure 3-35 Intersection details for the Weiler-Atherton algorithm.

3-18 CHARACTER CLIPPING

Characters or text are generated in software, firmware, or hardware. Characters may be formed from individual lines or strokes or from dot matrix representations. Stroke characters generated in software may be treated as any other line; i.e., they may be rotated, translated, scaled, and clipped to arbitrary windows in arbitrary orientations using the algorithms discussed above. Figure 3-36 shows a typical example.

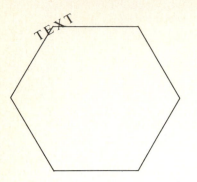

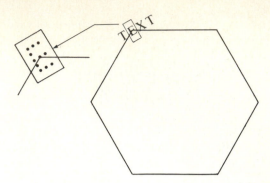

Figure 3-36 Clipping of software stroke-generated characters.

Figure 3-37 Clipping of software dot matrix-generated characters.

Dot matrix character representations generated in software may be treated in a similar fashion. The process is, however, somewhat more tedious. In particular, if the character box surrounding the character is clipped to any arbitrary window, then each pixel of the character mask is compared with the clipped box to determine if it is inside or outside. If inside, it is activated. If outside, no action is taken. Figure 3-37 illustrates this.

Clipping of hardware-generated characters is more limited. Generally any character which is not totally visible is eliminated. This can by accomplished by clipping the character box against the window. If the entire box is inside the window, the character is displayed; otherwise, it is not. When the rectangular character box is aligned with a rectangular window, only one diagonal of the character box need be compared with the window. See Fig. 3-37. For odd-shaped windows or when the rectangular character box is not aligned with the window, both diagonals must be compared with the window as shown in Fig. 3-38.

When characters are generated in firmware, character clipping facilities may be very limited or very extensive. The extent depends on the clipping algorithm also implemented in firmware.

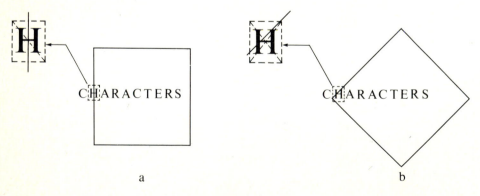

a   b

Figure 3-38. Clipping of hardware-generated characters.

3-19 REFERENCES

3-1 Clark, James, H., "The Geometry Engine: A VLSI Geometry System for Graphics," *Computer Graphics,* Vol. 16, pp. 127–133, 1982 (Proc. SIGGRAPH 82).

3-2 Sproull, Robert, F., and Sutherland, Ivan, E., "A Clipping Divider," 1968 Fall Joint Computer Conference, Thompson Books, Washington, D.C., pp. 765–775, 1968.

3-3 Newman, William, M., and Sproull, Robert, F., *Principles of Interactive Computer Graphics*, 2d ed., McGraw-Hill Book Company, New York, 1979.

3-4 Cyrus, M., and Beck, J., "Generalized Two- and Three-Dimensional Clipping," *Computers & Graphics,* Vol. 3, pp. 23–28, 1978.

3-5 Liang, You-Dong and Barsky, Brian, "A New Concept and Method for Line Clipping," ACM *Transactions on Graphics*, to appear.

3-6 Blinn, J.F., and Newell, M. E., "Clipping Using Homogeneous Coordinates," *Computer Graphics*, Vol. 12, pp. 245–251, 1978 (Proc. SIGGRAPH 78).

3-7 Sutherland, Ivan, E., and Hodgman Gary, W., "Reentrant Polygon Clipping," *CACM,* Vol. 17, pp. 32–42, 1974.

3-8 Liang, You-Dong, and Barsky, Brian, "An Analysis and Algorithm for Polygon Clipping," *CACM*, Vol. 26, pp. 868–877,1983.

3-9 Weiler, Kevin, and Atherton, Peter, "Hidden Surface Removal Using Polygon Area Sorting," *Computer Graphics,* Vol. 11, pp. 214–222, 1977 (Proc. SIGGRAPH 77).

3-10 Weiler, Kevin, "Hidden Surface Removal Using Polygon Area Sorting," Masters Thesis, Program of Computer Graphics, Cornell University, January 1978.

3-11 Weiler, Kevin, "Polygon Comparison Using a Graph Representation," *Computer Graphics,* Vol. 14, pp. 10–18, 1980 (Proc. SIGGRAPH 80).

CHAPTER FOUR

HIDDEN LINES AND HIDDEN SURFACES

The hidden line/hidden surface problem is one of the more difficult in computer graphics. Hidden line/hidden surface algorithms attempt to determine the lines, edges, surfaces, or volumes that are visible or invisible to an observer located at a specific point in space.

4-1 INTRODUCTION

The need for eliminating hidden lines, edges, surfaces, or volumes is illustrated in Fig. 4-1. Figure 4-1a shows a typical wire frame drawing of a cube. A wire frame drawing represents a three-dimensional object as a line drawing of its edges. Figure 4-1a can be interpreted either as a view of the cube from above and to the left or from below and to the right. The alternate views can be seen by blinking and refocusing the eyes. This ambiguity can be eliminated by removing the lines or surfaces that are invisible from the two alternate viewpoints. The results are shown in Fig. 4-1b and c.

The complexity of the hidden line/hidden surface problem has resulted in a large number of diverse solutions. Many of these are for specialized applications. There is no best solution to the hidden line/hidden surface problem. Fast algorithms that can provide solutions at video frame rates (30 frames per second) are required for real-time simulations, e.g. in aircraft simulation. Algorithms that can provide detailed realistic solutions including shadows,

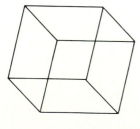 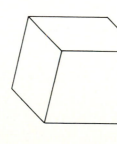 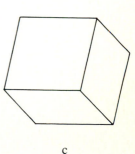

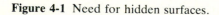

a   b   c

Figure 4-1 Need for hidden surfaces.

transparency, and texture effects, with reflections and refractions in a multitude of subtle shades of color, are also required, e.g. in computer animation. These algorithms are slower, often requiring several minutes or even hours of computation. Technically, transparency, texture, reflection, etc., are not part of the hidden line/hidden surface problem. They are more appropriately part of the rendering of the picture. Rendering is the process of interpreting or presenting a picture or scene realistically. These effects are discussed in detail in Chap. 5. However, many of these effects are incorporated into hidden surface algorithms and consequently are touched on in the present discussion. There is a tradeoff between speed and detail. No single algorithm can provide both. As faster algorithms are developed, more rendering detail can be incorporated. However, inevitably more detail will be required.

All hidden line/hidden surface algorithms involve sorting (Ref. 4-1). The order in which sorting of the geometric coordinates occurs is generally immaterial to the efficiency of the algorithms. The principal sort is based on the geometric distance of a volume, surface, edge, or point from the viewpoint. The fundamental assumption made in this distance sort is that, the farther an object is from the viewpoint, the more likely the object is to be totally or partially obscured by one closer to the viewpoint. After establishing the distance or depth priority, it remains to sort laterally and vertically to determine whether in fact an object is obscured by those closer to the viewpoint. The efficiency of a hidden line/hidden surface algorithm depends significantly on the efficiency of the sorting process. Coherence, i.e., the tendency for the characteristics of a scene to be locally constant, is used to increase the efficiency of the sort. For raster scan hidden surface algorithms, the use of coherence to improve sorting results in algorithms that bear a strong resemblance to the scan-conversion algorithms discussed previously in Chap. 2.

Hidden line/hidden surface algorithms can be classified based on the coordinate system or space in which they are implemented (Ref. 4-1). Object space algorithms are implemented in the physical coordinate system in which the objects are described. Very precise results, generally to the precision of the machine, are available. These results can be satisfactorily enlarged many times. Object space algorithms are particularly useful in precise engineering applications. Image space algorithms are implemented in the screen coordinate system in which the objects are viewed. Calculations are performed only to the precision of the screen representation. This is generally quite crude, typically 512×512 integer points. Scenes calculated in image space and significantly enlarged do not give acceptable results. For example, the end points of lines may not match. List priority algorithms are partially implemented in both coordinate systems.

Theoretically, the computational work for an object space algorithm that compares every object in a scene with every other object in the scene grows as the number of objects squared (n^2). Similarly, the work for an image space algorithm which compares every object in the scene with every pixel location in screen coordinates theoretically grows as nN. Here, n is the number of objects (volumes, planes, or edges) in the scene, and N is the number of pixels. Theoretically, object space algorithms require less work than image space algorithms for $n < N$. Since N is typically $(512)^2$, most algorithms should theoretically be implemented in object space. In practice, this is not the case, image space algorithms are more efficient because it is easier to take advantage of coherence in a raster scan implementation of an image space algorithm.

The following sections examine several object and image space algorithms in detail. Each algorithm illustrates one or more fundamental ideas in the implementation of hidden line/hidden surface algorithms.

4-2 FLOATING HORIZON ALGORITHM

The floating horizon algorithm is most frequently used to remove hidden lines from three-dimensional representations of surface functions of the form

$$F(x, y, z) = 0$$

Functions of this form arise from diverse applications in mathematics, engineering, and science, as well as other disciplines.

A number of algorithms using this technique have been developed (Refs. 4-2 to 4-6). Since the representation of the function is of principal interest, the algorithm is usually implemented in image space. The fundamental idea behind the technique is to convert the three-dimensional problem to two dimensions by intersecting the surface with a series of parallel cutting planes at constant values of x, y, or z. This is shown in Fig. 4-2, where constant values of z define the parallel planes. The function $F(x, y, z) = 0$ is reduced to a curve in each of these parallel planes, i.e. to

$$y = f(x, z) \qquad \text{or} \qquad x = g(y, z)$$

where z is constant for each of the parallel planes.

Thus, the surface is built up of a series of curves in each of these planes, as shown in Fig. 4-3. Here, it is assumed that the resulting curves are single-

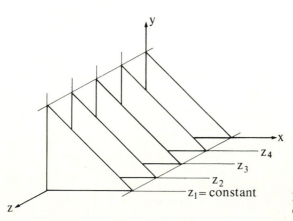

Figure 4-2 Constant-coordinate cutting planes.

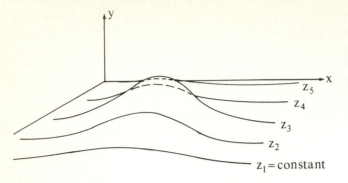

Figure 4-3 Curves in constant-coordinate cutting planes.

valued functions of the independent variables. If the result is projected onto the $z = 0$ plane as shown in Fig. 4-4, an algorithm for removing the hidden portions of the surface is immediately recognized. The algorithm first sorts the $z =$ constant planes by increasing distance from the viewpoint. Beginning with the $z =$ constant plane closest to the viewpoint, the curve in each plane is generated; i.e., for each x coordinate in image space the appropriate y value is determined. The hidden line algorithm is then

> If at any given value of x the y value of the curve in the current plane is larger than the y value for any previous curve at that x value, then the curve is visible. Otherwise, it is hidden.

This is shown by the dashed lines in Fig. 4-4. Implementation of the algorithm is quite simple. An array of size equal to the resolution of image space in the x direction is used to contain the largest value of y at each x location. The values in this array represent the current "horizon." Thus, the horizon "floats up" as each succeeding curve is drawn. Effectively, this is a one-line hidden line algorithm.

The algorithm works fine unless some of the succeeding curves dip below the first curve, as shown in Fig. 4-5a. These curves are normally visible as the bottom of the surface, however, the above algorithm will treat them as invisible. The lower side of the surface is made visible by modifying the algorithm to accommodate a lower horizon that floats down as the algorithm progresses. This is implemented by using a second array of size equal to the resolution of the image space in the x direction containing the smallest value of y at each x location. The algorithm is now

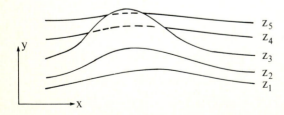

Figure 4-4 Projection of curves onto the $z = 0$ plane.

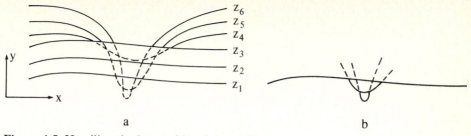

Figure 4-5 Handling the lower side of the surface.

If at any given value of x the y value of the curve in the current plane is larger than the maximum y value or smaller than the minimum y value for any previous curve at that x value, then the curve is visible. Otherwise it is hidden.

The result is shown in Fig. 4-5b.

The above algorithms assume that the value of the function, i.e. y, is available at each x location in image space. If, however, y is not available (calculated) at each x location, then the upper and lower floating horizon arrays cannot be maintained. In this case linear interpolation between the known locations is used to fill the upper and lower floating horizon arrays as shown in Fig. 4-6. If the visibility of the line changes, this simple interpolation technique will not yield the correct result. The effect is shown in Fig. 4-7a. Assuming that the fill operation occurs after the visibility check, then when the current line goes from visible to invisible (segment AB in Fig. 4-7a), the point at x_{n+k}, y_{n+k} is declared invisible, the line from x_n, y_n to x_{n+k}, y_{n+k} is not drawn, and the fill operation is not performed. A gap is left between the current line and the previous line. When a segment of the current line goes from invisible to visible (segment CD in Fig. 4-7a), the point at x_{m+k}, y_{m+k} is declared visible, the line from x_m, y_m to x_{m+k}, y_{m+k}, is drawn, and the fill operation is performed. Thus, an invisible portion of the segment is drawn. Further, the floating horizon arrays will not contain the proper values. This can lead to additional adverse

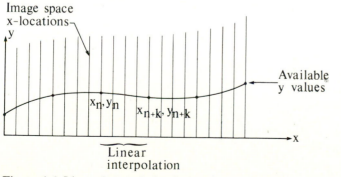

Figure 4-6 Linear interpolation between data points.

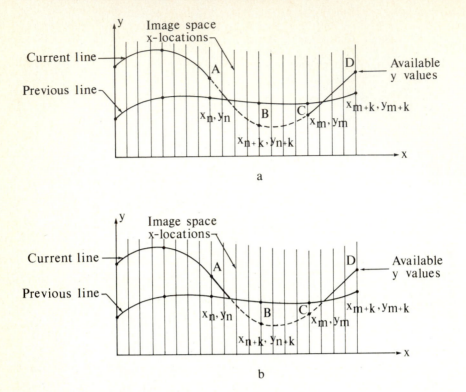

Figure 4-7 The effect of intersecting lines.

effects for subsequent lines. Hence, it is necessary to solve for the intersection of the segments of the current and previous lines.

There are several techniques for obtaining the intersection of the lines. On a raster scan display, x can be incremented by 1 beginning at x_n or x_m (see Fig. 4-7a). The y value at this image space x coordinate is obtained by adding the slope of the line to the y value at the previous x coordinate. The visibility of the new point at $x + 1$ and $y + \Delta y$ is determined. If the point is visible, its associated pixel is activated. If not, the pixel is not activated and x is incremented. The process is repeated until x_{n+k} or x_{m+k} is reached. This technique provides a sufficiently accurate intersection for raster scan displays. A similar but somewhat more elegant method is to perform a binary search for the intersection (Ref. 4-6).

An accurate intersection of the two interpolated straight lines between x_n, y_n and x_{n+k}, y_{n+k} (see Fig. 4-7) on the current and previous lines is given by

$$x = x_n + \frac{\Delta x(y_{np} - y_{nc})}{(\Delta y_p - \Delta y_c)}$$

and

$$y = m(x - x_n) + y_n$$

where

$$\Delta x = x_{n+k} - x_n$$
$$\Delta y_p = (y_{n+k})_p - (y_n)_p$$
$$\Delta y_c = (y_{n+k})_c - (y_n)_c$$
$$m = [(y_{n+k}) - (y_n)]/\Delta x$$

and the subscripts c and p refer to the current and previous lines, respectively. The result is shown in Fig. 4-7b. The algorithm is now

If at any given value of x the y value of the curve in the current plane is larger than the maximum y value or smaller than the minimum y value for any previous curve at that x value, then the curve is visible. Otherwise it is hidden.

If the line from the previous x value (x_n) to the current x value (x_{n+k}) is becoming visible or invisible, calculate the intersection (x_i).

Draw the line from x_n to x_{n+k} if the segment is totally visible, from x_n to x_i if the segment becomes invisible, or from x_i to x_{n+k} if the segment becomes visible.

Fill the upper and lower floating horizons.

The above algorithm exhibits an anomaly when the curve in one of the planes further from the viewpoint extends beyond the "edge" of the curves in the planes closer to the viewpoint. The effect is shown in Fig. 4-8, where planes $n-1$ and n are closer to the viewpoint and have already been processed. The result shows the effect when the current plane $n + 1$ is processed. After processing the lines $n-1$ and n, the upper horizon contains the initial value for x locations 0 and 1, the value for the line n for x locations 2 to 17 and the value for the line $n-1$ for x locations 18 to 20. The lower horizon contains the initial value for x locations 0 and 1, values for the line n at x locations 2 to 4, and values for the line $n-1$ for x locations 5 to 20. In processing the current line ($n + 1$), the algorithm declares it to be visible at $x = 4$. This is shown by the solid line in Fig. 4-8. A similar effect occurs at the right hand edge at $x = 18$. The effect gives the appearance of a ragged edge. The solution to this ragged

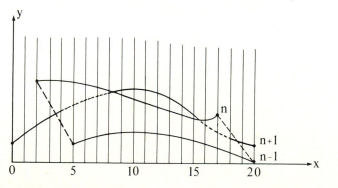

Figure 4-8 The ragged edge effect.

edge problem is to insert values into the upper and lower horizon arrays corresponding to the dashed lines in Fig. 4-8. Effectively this creates a false edge. An algorithm for accomplishing this for both edges is

Left side fill:

If P_n is the first point on the first line, save P_n as P_{n-1} and continue. Otherwise create the edge from P_{n-1} to P_n.

Fill in the upper and lower horizons from this edge and save P_n as P_{n-1}.

Right side fill:

If P_n is the last point on the first line, save P_n as P_{n-1} and continue. Otherwise create the edge from P_{n-1} to P_n.

Fill in the upper and lower horizons from this edge and save P_n as P_{n-1}.

The complete algorithm is now

For each $z = $ constant plane.

Fill in the left edge.

For each point on the curve in a $z = $ constant plane.

If at any given value of x the y value of the curve in the current plane is larger than the maximum y value or smaller than the minimum y value for any previous curve at that x value, then the curve is visible. Otherwise it is hidden.

If the line from the previous x value (x_n) to the current x value (x_{n+k}) is becoming visible or invisible, calculate the intersection.

Draw the line from x_n to x_{n+k} if the segment is totally visible, from x_n to x_i if the segment becomes invisible, or from x_i to x_{n+k} if the segment becomes visible.

Fill the upper and lower floating horizons.

Fill in the right edge.

If the function contains very narrow regions (spikes), then the algorithm may yield incorrect results. Figure 4-9 illustrates the effect. Here, the lowest line ($z = 1$) contains a spike. At $x = 8$, the next line ($z = 2$) is declared visible. At $x = 12$, the line ($z = 2$) is declared invisible, the intersection is determined, and the line ($z = 2$) is drawn visibly from $x = 8$ to the intersection. From $x = 12$ to $x = 16$ the line ($z = 2$) again becomes visible, the intersection is determined, and the line is drawn visibly from the intersection to $x = 16$. On the next line ($z = 3$) at $x = 8$, the line is visible; and it is also declared visible at $x = 12$. Hence, the line is drawn visibly from $x = 8$ to $x = 12$, even though it passes behind the spike. This effect is caused by computing the function and evaluating the visibility at less than the image space resolution; i.e., the function is undersampled (see Sec. 2-25). When narrow regions occur, the function must

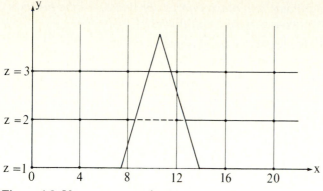

Figure 4-9 Very narrow regions.

be computed at more points. In Fig. 4-9, if the function is computed at 0, 2, 4, . . . , 18, 20 rather than at 0, 4, . . . , 16, 20, the algorithm will correctly draw the line $z = 3$.

Figure 4-10 shows a typical floating horizon result. A pseudo implementation of the algorithm is given below.

floating horizon algorithm
Hscreen *is the resolution of the screen in the horizontal direction*
Vscreen *is the resolution of the screen in the vertical direction*
Upper *is the array containing the upper horizon values*
Lower *is the array containing the lower horizon values*
Y *is the current value of the function* $y = f(x, z)$ *for* $z = constant$
Cflag *is the visibility flag for the current point*
Pflag *is the visibility flag for the previous point*
    0 = *invisible*
    1 = *visible above upper horizon*
  −1 = *visible below lower horizon*
Draw *is a graphics command that draws a visible line between the specified coordinates*
Xmin, Xmax *are the minimum and maximum x coordinates for the function*
Xinc *is the increment between x values*

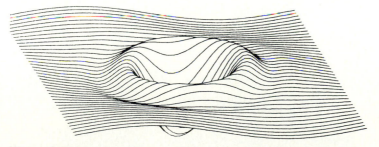

Figure 4-10 The function $y = (1/5) \sin x \cos z - (3/2) \cos (7a/4) \exp (-a)$, $a = (x - \pi)^2$ $+ (z - \pi)^2$ displayed for 0 to 2π using a floating horizon algorithm.

Zmin, Zmax *are the minimum and maximum z coordinates for the function*
Zinc *is the increment between z = constant planes*

Dimension Upper(Hscreen), Lower(Hscreen)
initialize variables
Xleft = − 1
Yleft = − 1
Xright = − 1
Yright = − 1
initialize the horizon arrays
Upper = 0
Lower = Vscreen
evaluate the function for each constant z plane
start with the closest plane, Zmax
for z = Zmax **to** Zmin **step** − Zinc
    initialize the previous x and y values, Xprev, Yprev
    Xprev = Xmin
    Yprev = f(Xmin, z)
    if a viewing transformation is used it should be applied to Xprev,
    Yprev, *and z at this point*
    fill the left side
    call Efill(x, y, Xleft, Yleft; Upper, Lower)
    call Visibility(x, y, Upper, Lower; Pflag)
    for each point on the curve in the constant z plane
    for x = Xmin **to** Xmax **step** Xinc
        y = f(x, z)
        if a viewing transformation is used it should be applied at this point
        check the visibility of the current point and fill the horizon as appropr
        call Visibility(x, y, Upper, Lower; Cflag)
        if Cflag = Pflag **then**
            if Cflag = 1 **or** Cflag = − 1 **then**
                Draw(Xprev, Yprev, x, y)
                call Horizon(Xprev, Yprev, x, y; Upper, Lower)
            else
            end if
        if the visibility has changed calculate the intersection and fill the horizo
        else
            if Cflag = 0 **then**
                if Pflag = 1 **then**
                    call Intersect(Xprev, Yprev, x, y, Upper; Xi, Yi)
                else
                    call Intersect(Xprev, Yprev, x, y, Lower; Xi, Yi)
                end if
            Draw(Xprev, Yprev, Xi, Yi)
            call Horizon(Xprev, Yprev, Xi, Yi; Upper, Lower)

```
                else
                  if Cflag = 1 then
                    if Pflag = 0 then
                      call Intersect(Xprev, Yprev, x, y, Lower; Xi, Yi)
                      Draw(Xi, Yi, x, y)
                      call Horizon(Xi, Yi, x, y; Upper, Lower)
                    else
                      call Intersect(Xprev, Yprev, x, y, Lower; Xi, Yi)
                      Draw(Xprev, Yprev, Xi, Yi)
                      call Horizon(Xprev, Yprev, Xi, Yi; Upper, Lower)
                      call Intersect(Xprev Yprev, x, y, Upper; Xi, Yi)
                      Draw(Xi, Yi, x, y)
                      call Horizon(Xi, Yi, x, y; Upper, Lower)
                    end if
                  else
                    if Pflag = 0 then
                      call Intersect(Xprev, Yprev, x, y, Lower; Xi, Yi)
                      Draw(Xi, Yi, x, y)
                      call Horizon(Xi, Yi, x, y; Upper, Lower)
                    else
                      call Intersect(Xprev, Yprev, x, y, Upper; Xi, Yi)
                      Draw(Xprev, Yprev, Xi, Yi)
                      call Horizon(Xprev, Yprev, Xi, Yi; Upper, Lower)
                      call Intersect(Xprev, Yprev, x, y, Lower; Xi, Yi)
                      Draw(Xi, Yi, x, y)
                      call Horizon(Xi, Yi, x, y; Upper, Lower)
                    end if
                  end if
                end if
              end if
              reinitialize Pflag, Xprev, Yprev
              Pflag = Cflag
              Xprev = x
              Yprev = y
          next x
          fill the right side
          call Efill(x, y, Xright, Yright; Upper, Lower)
        next z
        finish
    subroutine module to fill the edge
    subroutine Efill(x, y, Xedge, Yedge; Upper, Lower)
        if Xedge is −1 then this is the first curve and the edge is not created
        if Xedge = − 1 then 1
        call Horizon(Xedge, Yedge, x, y; Upper, Lower)
1       Xedge = x
```

```
        Yedge = y
        return
```

subroutine module to determine the visibility of a point

subroutine Visibility(x, y, Upper, Lower; Cflag)

the visibility of the point is to be determined with respect to the upper and lower floating horizons. If the point is on the horizon it is declared visible.
Cflag = 0 *invisible*
        = 1 *visible above the upper horizon*
        = − 1 *visible below the lower horizon*
x *is assumed integer*

```
        if y < Upper(x) and y > Lower(x) then
            Cflag = 0
        else
            if y ≥ Upper(x) then
                Cflag = 1
            else
                Cflag = − 1
            end if
        end if
        return
```

subroutine module to fill the floating horizon arrays

subroutine Horizon(X1, Y1, X2, Y2; Upper, Lower)

the algorithm uses linear interpolation to fill the horizon arrays between X1 *and* X2.
Max(a, b) *yields the larger of a and b*
Min(a, b) *yields the smaller of a and b*
Sign *returns* − 1, 0, 1 *if the sign of its argument is* < 0, =0, > 0
Xinc *is used to determine the direction of the fill*

```
        Xinc = Sign (X2 − X1)
        check for vertical slope
        if Xinc = 0 then
            Upper(X2) = Max(Upper(X2), Y2)
            Lower(X2) = Min(Lower(X2), Y2)
        else
            Slope = (Y2 − Y1)/(X2 − X1)
            for x = X1 to X2 step Xinc
                y = Slope*(x − X1) + Y1
                Upper(x) = Max(Upper(x), y)
                Lower(x) = Min (Lower(x), y)
            next x
        end if
        return
```

subroutine module to calculate the intersection of the current line with the horizon

subroutine Intersect(X1, Y1, X2, Y2, Array; Xi, Yi)
the routine calculates the intersection between two straight lines
Array *contains the appropriate horizon*
    Xinc = **Sign**(X2 − X1)
    check for an infinite slope
    if Xinc = 0 **then**
        Xi = X2
        Yi = Array(X2)
    else
        calculate the intersection
        Slope = (Y2 − Y1)/(X2 − X1)
        Ysign = **Sign**(Y1 − Array(X1 + Xinc))
        Yi = Y1
        while (**Sign**(Yi − Array(Xi + Xinc)) = Ysign)
            for Xi = X1 **to** X2 **step** Xinc
                Yi = Yi + Slope
            next Xi
        end while
        Xi = Xi + Xinc
    end if
    return

An example further illustrates the technique.

Example 4-1   Floating Horizon

Consider the geometric functions described in Table 4-1. The functions are given in the $z = 0$, 30, and 60 planes. Two curves are given in each plane. The first is a straight line, and the second describes a sawtooth wave above and below the plane in which the straight line lies. Two lines at the same constant z values are easily processed by the floating horizon algorithm. However, the order in which they are processed affects the final appearance. Here, the straight line is considered first.

Table 4-1

Curve number	Point number	x	y	z	Comment
1	1	0	0	0	Sawtooth
	2	2	4	0	wave
	3	6	−4	0	
	4	8	0	0	
2	5	0	0	0	Straight
	6	8	0	0	line
3	7	0	0	3	Sawtooth
	8	2	4	3	wave
	9	6	−4	3	
	10	8	0	3	

Table 4-1 (Cont.)

Curve number	Point number	x	y	z	Comment
4	11	0	0	3	Straight line
	12	8	0	3	
5	13	0	0	6	Sawtooth
	14	2	4	6	wave
	15	6	−4	6	
	16	8	0	6	
6	17	0	0	6	Straight
	18	8	0	6	line

Before displaying the surface described in Table 4-1, it is necessary to apply a viewing transformation. First, the surface is rotated 30° about the y axis, followed by a 15° rotation about the x axis. The result is projected onto the $z = 0$ plane from a point of projection at infinity on the $+z$ axis (see Ref. 1-1). The resulting 4×4 homogeneous coordinate transformation matrix is

$$\begin{bmatrix} 0.866 & 0.129 & 0 & 0 \\ 0 & 0.966 & 0 & 0 \\ 0.5 & -0.224 & 0 & 0 \\ 0 & 0 & 0 & 1 \end{bmatrix}$$

Applying the transformation yields the results given in Table 4-2. These results have been scaled to an integer grid with $0 \le x \le 100$ and $-50 \le y \le 50$, i.e. to image space coordinates.

Table 4-2

Curve number	Point number	x	y
1	1	0	0
	2	17	41
	3	52	−31
	4	69	10
2	5	0	0
	6	69	10
3	7	15	−7
	8	32	35
	9	67	−38
	10	84	36
4	11	15	−7
	12	84	36

Table 4-2 (Cont.)

Curve number	Point number	x	y
5	13	30	−13
	14	47	28
	15	82	−44
	16	99	−3
6	17	30	−13
	18	99	−3

Sorting the curves into z priority order and recalling that the straight line in each constant z plane is to be processed first shows that the curves are to be processed in the reverse order given in Table 4-2, namely, 6, 5, 4, 3, 2, 1.

The upper and lower horizons are initialized to −50 and 50 respectively, as shown in Table 4-3 for selected horizontal screen locations. Also shown in Table 4-3 and Figs. 4-11a to f are the values (to the nearest integer) as the algorithm processes each line. The dashed lines are the false edges created by the left and right edge fill.

Table 4-3

x		0	10	20	30	40	50	60	70	80	90	100
Initially	U	−50	−50	−50	−50	−50	−50	−50	−50	−50	−50	−50
	L	50	50	50	50	50	50	50	50	50	50	50
Fig. 4-11a	U	−50	−50	−50	−13	−12	−10	−9	−7	−6	−4	−50
curve 6	L	50	50	50	−13	−12	−10	−9	−7	−6	−4	50
Fig. 4-11b	U	−50	−50	−50	−13	10	22	1	−7	−6	−4	−50
curve 5	L	50	50	50	−13	−12	−10	−9	−19	−40	−25	50
Fig. 4-11c	U	−50	−50	−6	−4	10	22	1	1	3	1	−50
curve 4	L	50	50	−9	−13	−12	−10	−9	−19	−40	−25	50
Fig. 4-11d	U	−50	−50	5	29	19	22	1	1	3	1	−50
curve 3	L	50	50	−9	−13	−12	−10	−23	−30	−40	−25	50
Fig. 4-11e	U	0	1	5	29	19	22	9	10	5	1	−50
curve 2	L	0	−4	−9	−13	−12	−10	−23	−30	−40	−25	50
Fig. 4-11f	U	0	24	36	29	19	22	9	10	5	1	−50
curve 1	L	0	−4	−9	−13	−12	−28	−23	−30	−40	−25	50

The above algorithm and example consider the function $y = F(x, z)$ for constant z only. Frequently it is convenient to plot curves of both constant z and x. When this is done, a cross-hatching effect is obtained. Initially it might seem that cross-hatching could be accomplished by superimposing two results, one with z = constant planes and one with x = constant planes. Figure 4-12

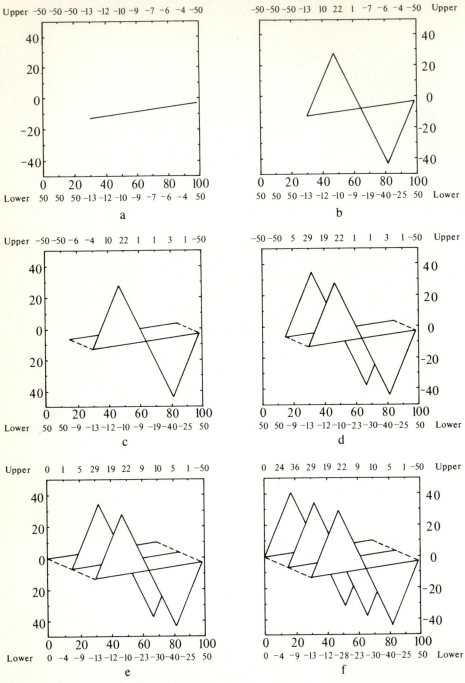

Upper −50 −50 −50 −13 −12 −10 −9 −7 −6 −4 −50

Lower 50 50 50 −13 −12 −10 −9 −7 −6 −4 50

a

−50 −50 −50 −13 10 22 1 −7 −6 −4 −50 Upper

50 50 50 −13 −12 −10 −9 −19 −40 −25 50 Lower

b

Upper −50 −50 −6 −4 10 22 1   1   3   1 −50

Lower 50 50 −9 −13 −12 −10 −9 −19 −40 −25 50

c

−50 −50 5 29 19 22 1   1   3   1 −50 Upper

50 50 −9 −13 −12 −10 −23 −30 −40 −25 50 Lower

d

Upper 0   1   5 29 19 22 9 10   5   1 −50

Lower 0 −4 −9 −13 −12 −10 −23 −30 −40 −25 50

e

0 24 36 29 19 22 9 10   5   1 −50 Upper

0 −4 −9 −13 −12 −28 −23 −30 −40 −25 50 Lower

f

Figure 4-11 Results for Example 4-1.

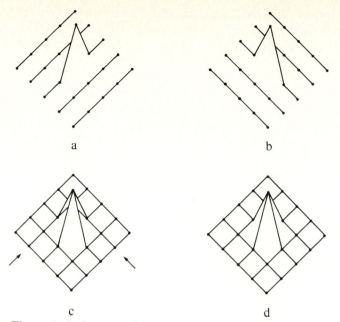

a   b

c   d

Figure 4-12 Cross-hatching. (a) Lines of constant z, (b) lines of constant x, (c) superposition of (a) and (b), (d) correct result.

shows that this is not the case (see Ref. 4-3). Notice in particular Fig. 4-12c, where the arrows indicate the incorrect result. The correct result, shown in Fig. 4-12d, is obtained by processing the curves in either the z or x = constant planes, whichever are most nearly horizontal in the usual order. However, after each nearly horizontal curve is processed, the parts of the curves in the orthogonal constant planes between this curve and the next curve must be processed. Of course, the same upper and lower floating horizon arrays must be used for both sets of curves. In particular, if for the function $y = F(x, y)$, z = constant curves are most nearly horizontal, then after processing the curve for z_1, the curves for x = constant between z_1 and z_2 are processed before the curve for z_2 is processed. If cross-hatching is used, left and right edge fills should not be used.

4-3 ROBERTS ALGORITHM

The Roberts algorithm represents the first known solution to the hidden line problem (Refs. 4-7 and 4-8). It is a mathematically elegant solution which operates in object space. The algorithm first eliminates the edges or planes from each volume that are hidden by the volume itself. Subsequently, each remaining edge of each volume is compared to each of the remaining volumes to determine what portion or portions, if any, are hidden by these volumes. Thus, computational requirements for the Roberts algorithm theoretically increase as the number of objects squared. This, in combination with increased interest in raster scan displays that operate in image space has led to a lack of interest in the Roberts algorithm. However, the mathematical techniques used in the algorithm are simple, powerful, and accurate. Further, the algorithm may be used to illustrate several important concepts. Finally, more recent implementations using a preliminary z priority sort and simple boxing or minimax tests exhibit a near linear growth with the number of objects.

The Roberts algorithm requires that all volumes or objects in a picture be convex. Concave volumes must be subdivided into component convex volumes (see Sec. 3-13). The algorithm considers a convex planar polygonal volume to be represented by a collection of intersecting planes. The equation of a plane in 3-space is

$$ax + by + cz + d = 0 \tag{4-1}$$

In matrix notation the result is

$$[x \ \ y \ \ z \ \ 1] \begin{bmatrix} a \\ b \\ c \\ d \end{bmatrix} = 0$$

or

$$[x \ \ y \ \ z \ \ 1] [P]^T = 0$$

where $[P]^T = [a \ \ b \ \ c \ \ d]$ represents the plane. A convex solid can thus be represented by a volume matrix of plane equation coefficients, e.g.

$$[V] = \begin{bmatrix} a_1 & a_2 & \cdots & a_n \\ b_1 & b_2 & & b_n \\ c_1 & c_2 & & c_n \\ d_1 & d_2 & & d_n \end{bmatrix}$$

where each column represents the coefficients of a single plane.

Recall that a general point in space is represented in homogeneous coordinates by the position vector (see Ref. 1-1):

$$[S] = [x \ \ y \ \ z \ \ 1]$$

Further, recall that, if $[S]$ is on the plane, then $[S] \cdot [P] = 0$ (see Sec. 3-5). If $[S]$ is not on the plane, the sign of the dot product indicates which side it is on. The Roberts algorithm uses the convention that points on the side of a plane corresponding to the inside of a volume yield positive dot products. To illustrate these ideas, consider the following example.

Example 4-2   Volume Matrix

The six planes describing an origin-centered unit cube are $x_1 = 1/2$, $x_2 = -1/2$, $y_3 = 1/2$, $y_4 = -1/2$, $z_5 = 1/2$, and $z_6 = -1/2$ as shown in Fig. 4-13. The equation of the right hand plane is

$$x_1 + 0y_1 + 0z_1 - (1/2) = 0$$

or

$$2x_1 - 1 = 0$$

The complete volume matrix is

$$[V] = \begin{bmatrix} \overset{①}{1} & \overset{②}{1} & \overset{③}{0} & \overset{④}{0} & \overset{⑤}{0} & \overset{⑥}{0} \\ 0 & 0 & 1 & 1 & 0 & 0 \\ 0 & 0 & 0 & 0 & 1 & 1 \\ -1/2 & 1/2 & -1/2 & 1/2 & -1/2 & 1/2 \end{bmatrix} = \begin{bmatrix} \overset{①}{2} & \overset{②}{2} & \overset{③}{0} & \overset{④}{0} & \overset{⑤}{0} & \overset{⑥}{0} \\ 0 & 0 & 2 & 2 & 0 & 0 \\ 0 & 0 & 0 & 0 & 2 & 2 \\ -1 & 1 & -1 & 1 & -1 & 1 \end{bmatrix}$$

This volume matrix must be tested against a point known to be inside the volume to ensure that the signs of each plane equation are correct. If the sign of the dot product for any plane is not greater than zero, then the plane equation must be multiplied by -1. A point inside the cube at $x = 1/4$, $y = 1/4$, $z = 1/4$ has the homogeneous coordinate position vector

$$[S] = [1/4 \quad 1/4 \quad 1/4 \quad 1] = [1 \quad 1 \quad 1 \quad 4]$$

Taking the dot product with the volume matrix yields

$$[S] \cdot [V] = [1 \quad 1 \quad 1 \quad 4] \begin{bmatrix} \overset{①}{2} & \overset{②}{2} & \overset{③}{0} & \overset{④}{0} & \overset{⑤}{0} & \overset{⑥}{0} \\ 0 & 0 & 2 & 2 & 0 & 0 \\ 0 & 0 & 0 & 0 & 2 & 2 \\ -1 & 1 & -1 & 1 & -1 & 1 \end{bmatrix}$$

$$= [\overset{①}{-2} \quad \overset{②}{6} \quad \overset{③}{-2} \quad \overset{④}{6} \quad \overset{⑤}{-2} \quad \overset{⑥}{6}]$$

Here, the results for the first, third, and fifth plane equations (columns) are negative and hence are constituted incorrectly. Multiplying these equations (columns) by -1 yields the correct volume matrix for the cube:

$$[V] = \begin{bmatrix} \overset{①}{-2} & \overset{②}{2} & \overset{③}{0} & \overset{④}{0} & \overset{⑤}{0} & \overset{⑥}{0} \\ 0 & 0 & -2 & 2 & 0 & 0 \\ 0 & 0 & 0 & 0 & -2 & 2 \\ 1 & 1 & 1 & 1 & 1 & 1 \end{bmatrix}$$

In the above example, the plane equations were determined by inspection. Of course, this is not always possible. There are several useful techniques for the more general case. Although the equation of a plane, Eq. (4-1), contains four unknown coefficients, the equation can always be normalized so that $d = 1$. Hence, only three noncollinear points are required to determine the coefficients. Applying the normalized form of Eq. (4-1) to three noncollinear points $(x_1, y_1, z_1), (x_2, y_2, z_2), (x_3, y_3, z_3)$ yields

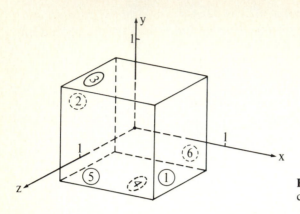

Figure 4-13 Origin-centered unit cube.

$$ax_1 + by_1 + cz_1 = -1$$
$$ax_2 + by_2 + cz_2 = -1$$
$$ax_3 + by_3 + cz_3 = -1$$

In matrix form this is

$$
\begin{bmatrix} x_1 & y_1 & z_1 \\ x_2 & y_2 & z_2 \\ x_3 & y_3 & z_3 \end{bmatrix}
\begin{bmatrix} a \\ b \\ c \end{bmatrix} =
\begin{bmatrix} -1 \\ -1 \\ -1 \end{bmatrix}
$$

or

$$[X][C] = [D] \tag{4-2}$$

Solving for the coefficients of the plane yields

$$[C] = [X]^{-1}[D]$$

Alternately, if the normal vector to the plane is known, e.g.

$$\mathbf{n} = a\mathbf{i} + b\mathbf{j} + c\mathbf{k}$$

where $\mathbf{i}$, $\mathbf{j}$, and $\mathbf{k}$ are the unit vectors in the x, y, z directions, respectively, then the plane equation is

$$ax + by + cz + d = 0 \tag{4-3}$$

The value of d is obtained from any point in the plane. In particular, if the components of a point in the plane are (x_1, y_1, z_1) then

$$d = -(ax_1 + by_1 + cz_1) \tag{4-4}$$

Because the computational work involved in hidden line/hidden surface algorithms increases with the number of polygons, it is advantageous to use polygons with more than three sides to describe surfaces. These polygons may be both concave and nonplanar. A technique due to Martin Newell (Ref. 4-1) gives both an exact solution for the plane equation for planar polygons and a "best" approximation for almost planar polygons. The technique is equivalent to determining the normal at each polygon vertex by taking the cross-product of the adjacent edges and averaging the results. If a, b, c, d are the coefficients of the plane equation, then

$$a = \sum_{i=1}^{n} (y_i - y_j)(z_i + z_j)$$

$$b = \sum_{i=1}^{n} (z_i - z_j)(x_i + x_j) \tag{4-5}$$

$$c = \sum_{i=1}^{n} (x_i - x_j)(y_i + y_j)$$

where

if $i = n$ **then** $j = 1$ **else** $j = i + 1$

and d is obtained using any point in the plane. Example 4-3 illustrates these techniques.

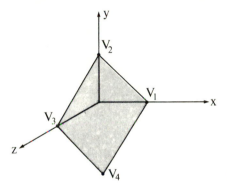

Figure 4-14 Plane in 3-space.

Example 4-3 Plane Equations

Consider the quadrilateral planar polygon described by the four vertices $V_1(1, 0, 0)$, $V_2(0, 1, 0)$, $V_3(0, 0, 1)$, and $V_4(1, -1, 1)$. See Fig. 4-14. Using the vertices V_1, V_2, V_4 and Eq. (4-2) yields

$$\begin{bmatrix} 1 & 0 & 0 \\ 0 & 1 & 0 \\ 1 & -1 & 1 \end{bmatrix} \begin{bmatrix} a \\ b \\ c \end{bmatrix} = \begin{bmatrix} -1 \\ -1 \\ -1 \end{bmatrix}$$

or solving for the coefficients of the plane equation

$$\begin{bmatrix} a \\ b \\ c \end{bmatrix} = \begin{bmatrix} 1 & 0 & 0 \\ 0 & 1 & 0 \\ -1 & 1 & 1 \end{bmatrix} \begin{bmatrix} -1 \\ -1 \\ -1 \end{bmatrix} = \begin{bmatrix} -1 \\ -1 \\ -1 \end{bmatrix}$$

The plane equation is then

$$-x - y - z + 1 = 0$$

or

$$x + y + z - 1 = 0$$

Alternately, the normal to the plane can be obtained by finding the cross-product of two adjacent vectors at one of the vertices, e.g. V_1

$$\mathbf{n} = \mathbf{V_1V_2} \otimes \mathbf{V_1V_3} = \begin{vmatrix} \mathbf{i} & \mathbf{j} & \mathbf{k} \\ (x_2 - x_1) & (y_2 - y_1) & (z_2 - z_1) \\ (x_3 - x_1) & (y_3 - y_1) & (z_3 - z_1) \end{vmatrix}$$

or

$$\mathbf{n} = \begin{vmatrix} \mathbf{i} & \mathbf{j} & \mathbf{k} \\ -1 & 1 & 0 \\ -1 & 0 & 1 \end{vmatrix} = \mathbf{i} + \mathbf{j} + \mathbf{k}$$

where $\mathbf{i}$, $\mathbf{j}$, $\mathbf{k}$ are the unit vectors in the x, y, z directions, respectively. Using Eq. (4-4) and V_4, the constant term in the plane equation is

$$d = -1(1 - 1 + 1) = -1$$

Hence, the plane equation is again

$$x + y + z - 1 = 0$$

Turning now to Newell's technique for $n = 4$, Eq. (4-5) yields

$$a = (y_1 - y_2)(z_1 + z_2) + (y_2 - y_3)(z_2 + z_3) + (y_3 - y_4)(z_3 + z_4) \\ + (y_4 - y_1)(z_4 + z_1) \\ = (-1)(0) + (1)(1) + (1)(2) + (-1)(1) = 2$$

$$b = (z_1 - z_2)(x_1 + x_2) + (z_2 - z_3)(x_2 + x_3) + (z_3 - z_4)(x_3 + x_4) \\ + (z_4 - z_1)(x_4 + x_1) \\ = (0)(1) + (-1)(0) + (0)(1) + (1)(2) = 2$$

$$c = (x_1 - x_2)(y_1 + y_2) + (x_2 - x_3)(y_2 + y_3) + (x_3 - x_4)(y_3 + y_4) \\ + (x_4 - x_1)(y_4 + y_1) \\ = (1)(1) + (0)(1) + (-1)(-1) + (0)(-1) = 2$$

and using V_4 the constant term is

$$d = -(2 - 2 + 2) = -2$$

After dividing by 2 the plane equation is again

$$x + y + z - 1 = 0$$

Example 4-4 further illustrates Newell's technique for almost planar polygons.

Example 4-4 Nonplanar Polygons

Consider the almost planar polygon described by the four vertices $V_1(1, 0, 0)$, $V_2(0, 1, 0)$, $V_3(0, 0, 1)$, and $V_4(1.1, -1, 1)$. Calculating the normal at each vertex by taking the cross-product of the two adjacent edges yields

$$n_1 = V_1V_2 \otimes V_1V_4 = i + j + 0.9k$$
$$n_2 = V_2V_3 \otimes V_2V_1 = i + j + k$$
$$n_3 = V_3V_4 \otimes V_3V_2 = i + 1.1j + 1.1k$$
$$n_4 = V_4V_1 \otimes V_4V_3 = i + 1.1j + k$$

Averaging the normals yields

$$n = i + 1.05j + k$$

Solving for the constant term in the plane equation using one of the vertices, e.g. V_1, yields $d = -1$. Hence the approximate plane equation is

$$x + 1.05y + z - 1 = 0$$

Newell's method gives the same result. In particular,

$$a = (-1)(0) + (1)(1) + (1)(2) + (-1)(1) = 2$$
$$b = (0)(1) + (-1)(0) + (0)(1.1) + (1)(2.1) = 2.1$$
$$c = (1)(1) + (0)(1) + (-1.1)(-1) + (0.1)(-1) = 2$$

Solving for d using V_1 and dividing by 2 yields the same approximate plane equation. The approximate plane passes through the line $x = z$ and contains the vertices V_1 and V_3. However, V_2 and V_4 are slightly displaced on either side of the plane.

Before applying a hidden line/hidden surface algorithm a three-dimensional viewing transformation is frequently used to obtain the desired view of the scene. The volume matrices for the objects in the transformed scene can be obtained by either transforming the original volume matrices or calculating new volume matrices from the transformed vertices or points.

If $[B]$ is the homogeneous coordinate matrix representing the original vertices of a volume and $[T]$ is a 4×4 viewing transformation, then the transformed vertices are (see Ref. 1-1)

$$[BT] = [B][T] \tag{4-6}$$

where $[BT]$ is the transformed vertex matrix. Recalling Eq. (4-2) yields the original plane equations for the volume

$$[B][V] = [D] \tag{4-7}$$

where $[V]$ is the volume matrix and $[D]$ is the right hand matrix of zeros. Similarly, the transformed plane equations are given by

$$[BT][VT] = [D] \tag{4-8}$$

where $[VT]$ is the transformed volume matrix. Equating Eq. (4-7) and (4-8) yields

$$[BT][VT] = [B][V]$$

Substituting Eq. (4-6), eliminating $[B]$, and premultiplying by $[T]^{-1}$ gives

$$[VT] = [T]^{-1}[V]$$

Thus, the transformed volume matrix is obtained by premultiplying the original volume matrix by the inverse of the viewing transformation. An example illustrates this.

Example 4-5 Volume Manipulation

Consider translating the unit cube centered at the origin three units to the right in the positive x direction. The appropriate 4×4 transformation matrix (see Ref. 1-1) is

$$[T] = \begin{bmatrix} 1 & 0 & 0 & 0 \\ 0 & 1 & 0 & 0 \\ 0 & 0 & 1 & 0 \\ 3 & 0 & 0 & 1 \end{bmatrix}$$

and its inverse, which can be obtained formally or by inspection, is

$$[T]^{-1} = \begin{bmatrix} 1 & 0 & 0 & 0 \\ 0 & 1 & 0 & 0 \\ 0 & 0 & 1 & 0 \\ -3 & 0 & 0 & 1 \end{bmatrix}$$

Premultiplying the volume matrix for the unit cube obtained in Example 4-2 by $[T]^{-1}$ yields the volume matrix for the translated cube:

$$[VT] = [T]^{-1}[V] = \begin{bmatrix} 1 & 0 & 0 & 0 \\ 0 & 1 & 0 & 0 \\ 0 & 0 & 1 & 0 \\ -3 & 0 & 0 & 1 \end{bmatrix} \overset{\textstyle \substack{①\;\;②\;\;③\;\;④\;\;⑤\;\;⑥}}{\begin{bmatrix} -2 & 2 & 0 & 0 & 0 & 0 \\ 0 & 0 & -2 & 2 & 0 & 0 \\ 0 & 0 & 0 & 0 & -2 & 2 \\ 1 & 1 & 1 & 1 & 1 & 1 \end{bmatrix}}$$

$$= \overset{\textstyle \substack{①\;\;②\;\;③\;\;④\;\;⑤\;\;⑥}}{\begin{bmatrix} -2 & 2 & 0 & 0 & 0 & 0 \\ 0 & 0 & -2 & 2 & 0 & 0 \\ 0 & 0 & 0 & 0 & -2 & 2 \\ 7 & -5 & 1 & 1 & 1 & 1 \end{bmatrix}}$$

Translating an origin-centered unit cube three units to the right places the left hand face at $x = 2\,1/2$ and the right hand face at $x = 3\,1/2$. The first column of the transformed volume matrix yields the plane equation for the right hand face:

$$-2x + 7 = 0 \qquad \text{or} \qquad x = 3\ 1/2$$

as required. Similarly the second column yields

$$2x - 5 = 0 \qquad \text{or} \qquad x = 2\ 1/2$$

for the left hand face as expected.

Recall from Example 4-2 that the point

$$[S] = [1/4 \quad 1/4 \quad 1/4 \quad 1] = [1 \quad 1 \quad 1 \quad 4]$$

was inside the untransformed volume. Hence $[S] \cdot [V] \geq 0$. However, the point $[S]$ is outside the translated volume. Examining the dot product of $[S]$ and the transformed volume matrix:

$$[S] \cdot [VT] = [1 \quad 1 \quad 1 \quad 4] \cdot [VT] = [26 \quad -18 \quad 2 \quad 6 \quad 2 \quad 6]$$

where the columns are numbered ① ② ③ ④ ⑤ ⑥

yields a negative element in the second column corresponding to the left hand face of the cube. This shows that the point is outside the volume. In fact, it is to the left of the left hand face, i.e., on the wrong side of the left hand face, as shown by the negative sign.

If the point matrix $[S]$ is transformed by postmultiplying by the transformation matrix, then

$$[ST] = [S][T] = [1 \quad 1 \quad 1 \quad 4][T] = [13 \quad 1 \quad 1 \quad 4] = [3\ 1/4 \quad 1/4 \quad 1/4 \quad 1]$$

Testing the transformed point at $x = 3\ 1/4$ against the transformed volume matrix yields

$$[ST] \cdot [VT] = [2 \quad 6 \quad 2 \quad 6 \quad 2 \quad 6]$$

where the columns are numbered ① ② ③ ④ ⑤ ⑥

which shows that it is inside the transformed volume.

Recalling that planes are of infinite extent, and that the dot product of a point and the volume matrix is negative when the point is outside the volume, suggests a method for using the volume matrix to identify planes which are hidden by the volume itself. Example 4-5 shows that only the specific plane (column) in the volume matrix for which a point is declared outside yields a negative dot product. In Example 4-5, this is the left hand plane (second column) for the transformed volume $[VT]$ and the untransformed point $[S]$. The concept is illustrated in Fig. 4-15.

If the view or eyepoint is at infinity on the positive z axis looking toward the origin, then the view direction is toward negative infinity on the z axis. In homogeneous coordinates this vector is represented by (see Ref. 1-1)

$$[E] = [0 \quad 0 \quad -1 \quad 0]$$

$[E]$ also represents the point at infinity on the negative z axis. In fact $[E]$ represents any point on the plane at $z = -\infty$, i.e. any point $(x, y, -\infty)$. Thus, if the dot product of $[E]$ and the plane in the volume matrix is negative, then

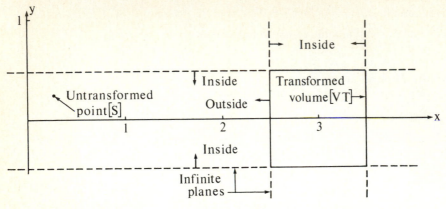

Figure 4-15 A point outside a volume.

$[E]$ is outside these planes. Consequently, these planes are hidden with respect to a viewpoint anywhere on the plane at $z = \infty$, and the test point at $z = -\infty$ is hidden by the volume itself, as illustrated in Fig. 4-16. These planes are called self-hidden planes or backfaces. Hence,

$$[E] \cdot [V] < 0$$

identifies self-hidden planes or backfaces. Note that for axonometric projections (eyepoint at infinity) this is equivalent to looking for positive values in the third row of the volume matrix.

This technique is the simplest hidden surface algorithm for single convex polygonal volumes. It is also used to eliminate the self-hidden or backplanes from a scene before applying most of the hidden surface algorithms subsequently discussed in this chapter. When used this way it is frequently called back-plane culling. For convex polygonal volumes the number of polygonal faces is reduced by approximately half. The technique is equivalent to calculating the surface normal for each individual polygon. A negative surface normal

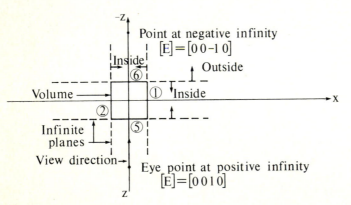

Figure 4-16 Self-hidden planes.

indicates that the normal points away from the viewer and hence the polygon is hidden. The technique can also be used for simple shading (see Chap. 5). The intensity or shade of the polygon is made proportional to the magnitude of the surface normal. An example further illustrates the concept.

Example 4-6 Self-hidden Planes

Again consider the origin-centered unit cube as shown in Fig. 4-16. The eye-point is on the positive z axis at $[0\ 0\ 1\ 0]$ looking toward the origin. Thus, the test point, or direction of view, is given by $[E] = [0\ 0\ -1\ 0]$. Taking the dot product with the volume matrix yields

$$[E] \cdot [V] = [0\ 0\ -1\ 0] \begin{array}{c} \text{①} \quad \text{②} \quad \text{③} \quad \text{④} \quad \text{⑤} \quad \text{⑥} \\ \begin{bmatrix} -2 & 2 & 0 & 0 & 0 & 0 \\ 0 & 0 & -2 & 2 & 0 & 0 \\ 0 & 0 & 0 & 0 & -2 & 2 \\ 1 & 1 & 1 & 1 & 1 & 1 \end{bmatrix} \end{array} = \begin{array}{c} \text{①} \quad \text{②} \quad \text{③} \quad \text{④} \quad \text{⑤} \quad \text{⑥} \\ [0 \quad 0 \quad 0 \quad 0 \quad 2\ -2\ ] \end{array}$$

and the negative sign in the sixth column indicates that this face is self-hidden. Inspection of Fig. 4-16 confirms this. The zero results indicate planes that are parallel to the direction of view.

This technique for identifying self-hidden planes in effect performs an axonometric projection onto a plane at infinity from any point in 3-space. Viewing transformations including perspective are applied prior to identifying the self-hidden planes. When the viewing transformation includes perspective, the full perspective transformation from one 3-space to another must be used and not a perspective projection onto some two-dimensional plane (see Ref. 1-1). The full perspective transformation yields a distorted three-dimensional volume which in effect is then projected onto a plane at infinity when the self-hidden planes are identified. The effect is equivalent to a perspective projection from some point of projection onto a finite plane of projection.

The viewing transformation can be applied to the volume with the eyepoint remaining fixed. Alternately, the volume remains fixed. The equivalent eye-point and view direction are obtained by postmultiplying by the inverse of the viewing transformation. The next example illustrates these techniques.

Example 4-7 Self-hidden Plane with Viewing Transformation

Consider the origin-centered unit cube rotated about the y axis by $45°$. The viewing transformation is (see Ref. 1-1)

$$[R_y] = \begin{bmatrix} \cos\phi & 0 & -\sin\phi & 0 \\ 0 & 1 & 0 & 0 \\ \sin\phi & 0 & \cos\phi & 0 \\ 0 & 0 & 0 & 1 \end{bmatrix}_{\phi = 45°} = \begin{bmatrix} 1/\sqrt{2} & 0 & -1/\sqrt{2} & 0 \\ 0 & 1 & 0 & 0 \\ 1/\sqrt{2} & 0 & 1/\sqrt{2} & 0 \\ 0 & 0 & 0 & 1 \end{bmatrix}$$

The transformed volume matrix is obtained by premultiplying by the inverse of the viewing transformation. For a pure rotation, the inverse of the viewing transformation is its transpose. Thus

$$[R_y]^{-1} = [R_y]^T = \begin{bmatrix} \cos\phi & 0 & \sin\phi & 0 \\ 0 & 1 & 0 & 0 \\ -\sin\phi & 0 & \cos\phi & 0 \\ 0 & 0 & 0 & 1 \end{bmatrix} = \begin{bmatrix} 1/\sqrt{2} & 0 & 1/\sqrt{2} & 0 \\ 0 & 1 & 0 & 0 \\ -1/\sqrt{2} & 0 & 1/\sqrt{2} & 0 \\ 0 & 0 & 0 & 1 \end{bmatrix}$$
$$\phi = 45°$$

The transformed volume matrix is

$$[VT] = [R_y]^{-1}[V] = \begin{bmatrix} \overset{①}{-2/\sqrt{2}} & \overset{②}{2/\sqrt{2}} & \overset{③}{0} & \overset{④}{0} & \overset{⑤}{-2/\sqrt{2}} & \overset{⑥}{2/\sqrt{2}} \\ 0 & 0 & -2 & 2 & 0 & 0 \\ 2/\sqrt{2} & -2/\sqrt{2} & 0 & 0 & -2/\sqrt{2} & 2/\sqrt{2} \\ 1 & 1 & 1 & 1 & 1 & 1 \end{bmatrix}$$

From an eyepoint on the positive z axis [0 0 1 0] looking toward the origin, the view direction or test point is given by

$$[E] = [0 \;\; 0 \;\; -1 \;\; 0]$$

Taking the dot product of $[E]$ and the transformed volume matrix yields

$$[E] \cdot [VT] = [\overset{①}{-2/\sqrt{2}} \quad \overset{②}{2/\sqrt{2}} \quad \overset{③}{0} \quad \overset{④}{0} \quad \overset{⑤}{2/\sqrt{2}} \quad \overset{⑥}{-2/\sqrt{2}}]$$

Hence, the first and sixth planes which correspond to the left and rear planes in the original orientation are self-hidden. Figure 4-17a confirms this. Notice also that, when the volume is transformed and the view direction fixed, taking the dot product of the test point and the transformed volume matrix and looking for negative signs is equivalent to looking for positive terms in the third row of the transformed volume matrix.

The equivalent eyepoint for the untransformed volume corresponding to the rotation about the y axis is

$$[0 \;\; 0 \;\; 1 \;\; 0][R_y]^{-1} = [-1/\sqrt{2} \;\; 0 \;\; 1/\sqrt{2} \;\; 0] = [-1 \;\; 0 \;\; 1 \;\; 0]$$

i.e., a point at positive infinity on the line $-x = z$ as shown in Fig. 4-17b. Similarly the equivalent view direction and test point are

$$[ET] = [E][R_y]^{-1} = [0 \;\; 0 \;\; -1 \;\; 0][R_y]^{-1} = (1/\sqrt{2})[1 \;\; 0 \;\; -1 \;\; 0]$$

This is a point at negative infinity on the line $-x = z$. Taking the dot product of the equivalent view direction and the untransformed volume matrix yields

$$[ET] \cdot [V] = (1\sqrt{2}) [\overset{①}{-2} \quad \overset{②}{2} \quad \overset{③}{0} \quad \overset{④}{0} \quad \overset{⑤}{2} \quad \overset{⑥}{-2}]$$

which again indicates that the first and sixth planes are self-hidden. Figure 4-17b confirms this.

Having identified the self-hidden planes, it remains to identify the self-hidden lines. A self-hidden line is formed by the intersection of two self-hidden

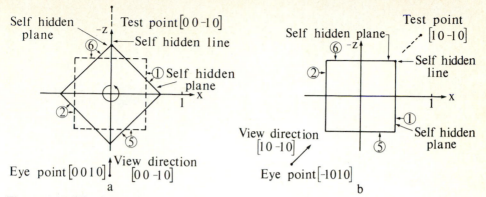

Figure 4-17 Viewing transformation and self-hidden planes.

planes. Although in Example 4-6 plane ⑥ is self-hidden, no lines are self-hidden because only one plane is self-hidden. However, in Example 4-7, the edge formed by the intersection of planes ① and ⑥ is self-hidden.

After first eliminating the self-hidden lines, it is necessary to consider whether an individual line is hidden by any other volume in the picture or scene. In order to accomplish this, every remaining line or edge must be compared with all the other volumes in the scene or picture. Here, using a priority sort (z sort) and simple minimax or bounding box tests allows the elimination of entire groups or clusters of lines and volumes. For example, if all volumes in the scene are sorted into a priority list using the z value of the nearest vertex to represent the distance from the eye, then no volume on the list for which the nearest vertex is farther from the eye than the farthest end point of a line can obscure that line. Further, of the remaining volumes, no volume whose bounding box is completely to the right, to the left, above, or below that for the line can obscure the line. Using these techniques significantly reduces the number of volumes with which an individual line or edge must be compared.

To compare a single line P_1P_2 with a single volume, it is convenient to use a parametric representation of the line:

$$P(t) = P_1 + (P_2 - P_1)t \qquad 0 \leq t \leq 1$$

or

$$\mathbf{v} = \mathbf{s} + \mathbf{d}t$$

where $\mathbf{v}$ is the position vector of the line, $\mathbf{s}$ is the starting point, and $\mathbf{d}$ is the direction of the line. The objective is to determine whether the line is hidden. If it is hidden, then the objective is to determine the values of t for which it is hidden. To accomplish this, another parametric line from any point on $P(t)$ to the eyepoint at $\mathbf{g}$ is formed:

$$\mathbf{Q}(\alpha, t) = \mathbf{u} = \mathbf{v} + \mathbf{g}\alpha = \mathbf{s} + \mathbf{d}t + \mathbf{g}\alpha \qquad 0 \leq t \leq 1,\, \alpha \geq 0$$

Here α and t perform similar functions. A given value of t yields a point on the line $P(t)$, and α yields a point on the line from this point to the eyepoint.

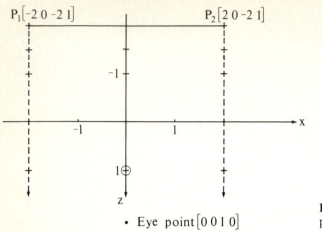

• Eye point $[0\ 0\ 1\ 0]$

Figure 4-18 The parametric plane.

In fact, $Q(\alpha, t)$ represents a plane in 3-space. Specifying both α and t locates a point on this plane. The value of α is positive because only the part of the plane between the line $P(t)$ and the eyepoint can contain volumes which obscure the line.

Example 4-8   Parametric Plane

Consider the line from $P_1(-2, 0, -2)$ to $P_2(2, 0, -2)$ viewed from a position at positive infinity in the z direction (see Fig. 4-18). In homogeneous coordinates P_1 and P_2 are

$$P_1 = [-2\ \ 0\ \ -2\ \ 1]$$
$$P_2 = [\ \ 2\ \ 0\ \ -2\ \ 1]$$

Hence

$$P(t) = \mathbf{v} = \mathbf{s} + \mathbf{d}t = [-2\ \ 0\ \ -2\ \ 1] + [4\ \ 0\ \ 0\ \ 0]t$$

The eyepoint vector is

$$\mathbf{g} = [0\ \ 0\ \ 1\ \ 0]$$

and

$$Q(\alpha, t) = \mathbf{s} + \mathbf{d}t + \mathbf{g}\alpha = [-2\ \ 0\ \ -2\ \ 1] + [4\ \ 0\ \ 0\ \ 0]t + [0\ \ 0\ \ 1\ \ 0]\alpha$$

Figure 4-18 and Table 4-4 show the effect of varying t and α. As a specific example, assume $t = 0.5$ and $\alpha = 3$. Then

$$P(0.5) = \mathbf{v} = [-2\ \ 0\ \ -2\ \ 1] + [4\ \ 0\ \ 0\ \ 0](0.5)$$
$$= [\ \ 0\ \ 0\ \ -2\ \ 1]$$

which is the point on the line P_1P_2 where it crosses the z axis at $z = -2$. For $\alpha = 3$

$$Q(3, 0.5) = \mathbf{v} + \mathbf{g}\alpha = [0\ \ 0\ \ -2\ \ 1] + [0\ \ 0\ \ 1\ \ 0](3)$$
$$= [0\ \ 0\ \ \ \ 1\ \ 1]$$

which is the point on the z axis at $z = 1$. This point is shown by the dot in Fig. 4-18. Each of the points given in Table 4-4 is indicated by crosses in Fig. 4-18. Notice that each of the lines is parallel to the z axis.

Table 4-4

t	α	$\mathbf{v}(t)$	$Q(\alpha, t)$
0	0	[−2 0 −2 1]	[−2 0 −2 1]
	1/2		[−2 0 −3/2 1]
	1		[−2 0 −1 1]
	2		[−2 0 0 1]
	3		[−2 0 1 0]
1/2	0	[0 0 −2 1]	[0 0 −2 1]
	1/2		[0 0 −3/2 1]
	1		[0 0 −1 1]
	2		[0 0 0 1]
	3		[0 0 1 0]
1	0	[2 0 −2 1]	[2 0 −2 1]
	1/2		[2 0 −3/2 1]
	1		[2 0 −1 1]
	2		[2 0 0 1]
	3		[2 0 1 0]

Recall that for a point inside a volume, the dot product of the point and the volume matrix is positive. If the point is inside the volume, it is hidden. Therefore, to determine the part of a line hidden by a volume it is only necessary to find the values of α and t for which the dot product of $Q(\alpha, t)$ and the volume is positive. Taking the dot product of $Q(\alpha, t) = \mathbf{u}$ and the transformed volume yields

$$h = \mathbf{u} \cdot [VT] = \mathbf{s} \cdot [VT] + t\mathbf{d} \cdot [VT] + \alpha \mathbf{g} \cdot [VT] > 0 \qquad 0 \le t \le 1,\ \alpha \ge 0$$

If each component of h is nonnegative for some t and α, the line is hidden by the volume for those values of t. Defining

$$p = \mathbf{s} \cdot [VT]$$
$$q = \mathbf{d} \cdot [VT]$$
$$w = \mathbf{g} \cdot [VT]$$

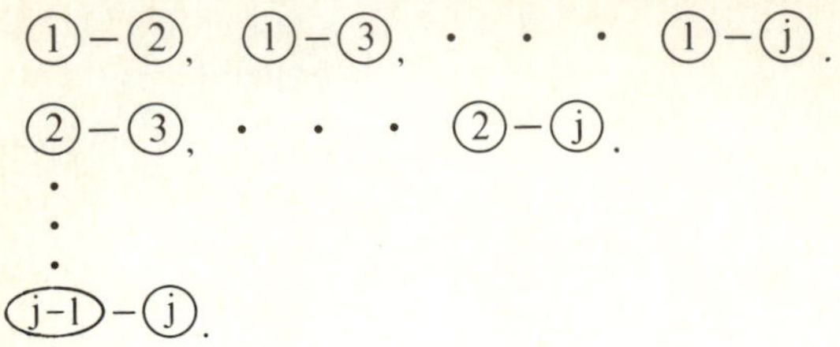

$\text{①} - \text{②}, \quad \text{①} - \text{③}, \quad \cdot \quad \cdot \quad \cdot \quad \text{①} - \text{ⓙ}.$

$\text{②} - \text{③}, \quad \cdot \quad \cdot \quad \cdot \quad \text{②} - \text{ⓙ}.$

$\vdots$

$\boxed{\text{ⓙ-1}} - \text{ⓙ}.$

Total number of solutions for j equations $= \dfrac{(j-1)(j)}{2}.$

Figure 4-19 Solution technique for α, t.

the condition

$$h_j = p_j + tq_j + aw_j > 0 \qquad 0 \le t \le 1, \, a \ge 0$$

where j counts the columns in the volume matrix, must hold for all values of j; i.e., for all the planes describing a volume. The dividing case for visibility or invisibility is when $h_j = 0$. For $h_j = 0$ the point lies on the plane. Setting $h_j = 0$ for each of the planes yields a series of equations in α, t all of which must be satisfied. This can be accomplished by solving each of the equations with each of the others in pairs, to find all possible values of α and t for which the line is marginally visible. This is shown in Fig. 4-19. The number of possible solutions for j equations (planes) is $(j)(j - 1)/2$. Each of the solutions in the range $0 \le t \le 1, \, a \ge 0$ is tested against all the other equations to ensure that the condition $h_j \ge 0$ is satisfied. A search of the valid solutions is performed to yield the minimum maximum value (t_{minmax}) and the maximum minimum value (t_{maxmin}) of the parameter t. The line is hidden from $t_{maxmin} < t < t_{minmax}$. This latter requirement is a simple classical linear programming problem. An algorithm, similar to that previously given for the Cyrus-Beck clipping algorithm (see Sec. 3-5), for this solution is given below. First some examples will help clarify the discussion.

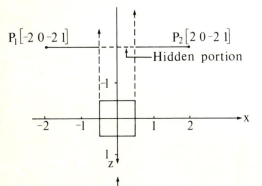

$P_1 [-2\ 0\ -2\ 1]$ $P_2 [2\ 0\ -2\ 1]$

Hidden portion

View direction → Eye point $[0\ 0\ 1\ 0]$

Figure 4-20 Testing a line against a volume.

Example 4-9 Testing Lines Against Volumes

Again consider the origin-centered unit cube. The line from $P_1[-2 \ 0 \ -2 \ 1]$ to $P_2[2 \ 0 \ -2 \ 1]$ passes behind the cube and is partially hidden by the cube as shown in Fig. 4-20. Again

$$P(t) = \mathbf{v} = [-2 \ 0 \ -2 \ 1] + [4 \ 0 \ 0 \ 0]t$$

and

$$\mathbf{s} = [-2 \ 0 \ -2 \ 1]$$
$$\mathbf{d} = [\ 4 \ 0 \ \ 0 \ 0]$$

For an eyepoint at infinity on the positive z axis

$$\mathbf{g} = [0 \ 0 \ 1 \ 0]$$

Here the untransformed cube is considered. Hence,

$$[VT] = [V] = \begin{bmatrix} -2 & 2 & 0 & 0 & 0 & 0 \\ 0 & 0 & -2 & 2 & 0 & 0 \\ 0 & 0 & 0 & 0 & -2 & 2 \\ 1 & 1 & 1 & 1 & 1 & 1 \end{bmatrix}$$

Forming p, q, and w by taking the dot product of $\mathbf{s}$, $\mathbf{d}$, and $\mathbf{g}$ with $[VT]$ yields

$$p = \mathbf{s} \cdot [VT] = [\ 5 \ -3 \ 1 \ 1 \ \ 5 \ -3]$$
$$q = \mathbf{d} \cdot [VT] = [-8 \ \ 8 \ 0 \ 0 \ \ 0 \ \ 0]$$
$$w = \mathbf{g} \cdot [VT] = [\ 0 \ \ 0 \ 0 \ 0 \ -2 \ \ 2]$$

From these results six equations corresponding to the condition

$$h_j = p_j + tq_j + \alpha w_j > 0$$

are formed, one for each of the six planes representing the faces of the cube. Specifically,

① $5 - 8t$ > 0

② $-3 + 8t$ > 0

③ 1 > 0

④ 1 > 0

⑤ 5 $- 2\alpha > 0$

⑥ -3 $+ 2\alpha > 0$

The third and fourth of these equations simply state that the condition is always satisfied. They correspond to the physical condition that the line is always "inside" the infinitely extended top and bottom surfaces of the cube. Setting the other four equations to zero yields $t = 5/8$, $t = 3/8$, $\alpha = 5/2$, and $\alpha = 3/2$. Of course, this is a particularly simple example. The equations can essentially be solved by inspection, however, in general this is not the case.

Each of these equations represents a straight line in α, t space. It is instructive to consider a graphical solution, as shown in Fig. 4-21. The cross-hatching indicates the side of the line on which possible solutions exist. Clearly, all the conditions $h_j > 0$ are satisfied only within the bounded region indicated. Thus

$$t_{\text{maxmin}} = 3/8 \quad \text{and} \quad t_{\text{minmax}} = 5/8$$

The line is hidden for $3/8 < t < 5/8$ and visible for $0 \leq t \leq 3/8$ and $5/8 \leq t \leq 1$.

Using the parametric equation of the line

$$P(3/8) = [-2 \ \ 0 \ \ -2 \ \ 1] + [4 \ \ 0 \ \ 0 \ \ 1](3/8) = [-1/2 \ \ 0 \ \ -2 \ \ 1]$$

and

$$P(5/8) = [-2 \ \ 0 \ \ -2 \ \ 1] + [4 \ \ 0 \ \ 0 \ \ 1](5/8) = [1/2 \ \ 0 \ \ -2 \ \ 1]$$

as shown in Fig. 4-20.

The above example yields two values of t. Hence it is possible to assign a t_{maxmin} and a t_{minmax}. What if solution of the equations yields only one value of t? The next examples illustrate this problem and its solution.

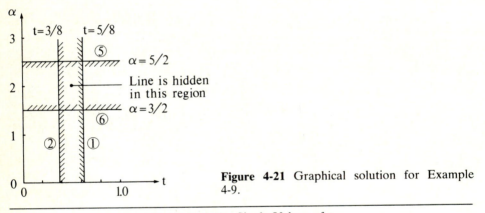

Figure 4-21 Graphical solution for Example 4-9.

Example 4-10 Single Values of t

Continuing to use the origin-centered cube, consider the line $P_1[1 \ \ 0 \ \ -1 \ \ 1]$ to $P_2[0 \ \ 0 \ \ -1 \ \ 1]$ as shown in Fig. 4-22. Here

$$P(t) = \mathbf{v} = [1 \ \ 0 \ \ -1 \ \ 1] + [-1 \ \ 0 \ \ 0 \ \ 0]t$$

and

$$\mathbf{s} = [\ 1 \ \ 0 \ \ -1 \ \ 1]$$
$$\mathbf{d} = [-1 \ \ 0 \ \ \ 0 \ \ 0]$$

with

$$\mathbf{g} = [0 \ \ 0 \ \ 1 \ \ 0]$$

for the untransformed cube, i.e. $[VT] = [V]$, p, q, and w become

$$p = \mathbf{s} \cdot [VT] = [-1 \ \ \ \ 3 \ \ 1 \ \ 1 \ \ \ \ 3 \ \ -1]$$
$$q = \mathbf{d} \cdot [VT] = [\ 2 \ \ -2 \ \ 0 \ \ 0 \ \ \ \ 0 \ \ \ \ 0]$$
$$w = \mathbf{g} \cdot [VT] = [\ 0 \ \ \ \ 0 \ \ 0 \ \ 0 \ \ -2 \ \ \ \ 2]$$

Forming the equations for the $h_j > 0$ condition yields

    ① $\ -1 + 2t \quad\quad > 0$

    ② $\ \ \ 3 - 2t \quad\quad > 0$

$$\begin{array}{ccc}
③ & 1 & >0 \\
④ & 1 & >0 \\
⑤ & 3 & -2\alpha >0 \\
⑥ & -1 & +2\alpha >0
\end{array}$$

Solution of these equations for $h_j = 0$ yields $t = 1/2$, $t = 3/2$, $\alpha = 3/2$, $\alpha = 1/2$. The solution for $t = 3/2$ is rejected because it is outside the permissible range $0 \le t \le 1$. Hence only one value of t is found. The graphical solution is shown in Fig. 4-23a. Again, the cross-hatching indicates the side of the line on which possible solutions exist. Clearly no bounded region is formed. However, the stated solution technique has not considered the boundary conditions represented by the lines $t = 0$ and $t = 1$. As shown in Fig. 4-23b, adding these lines to the solution clearly forms the required bounded region. Thus,

$$t_{maxmin} = 1/2 \quad \text{and} \quad t_{minmax} = 1$$

Further, the conditions $h_j > 0$ are all satisfied by both these values of t. Hence the line is visible for $0 \le t \le 1/2$, i.e. for

$$P(0) = [1 \quad 0 \quad -1 \quad 1] + [-1 \quad 0 \quad 0 \quad 0](0) = [1 \quad 0 \quad -1 \quad 1]$$

to

$$P(1/2) = [1 \quad 0 \quad -1 \quad 1] + [-1 \quad 0 \quad 0 \quad 0](1/2) = [1/2 \quad 0 \quad -1 \quad 1]$$

Reversing the direction of the line, i.e. interchanging P_1 and P_2, places the solution region between $t = 0$ and $t = 1/2$.

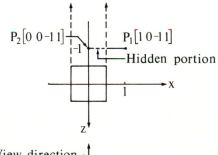

View direction→ Eye point $[0 \ 0 1 \ 0]$

Figure 4-22 Testing a line with a hidden end point against a volume.

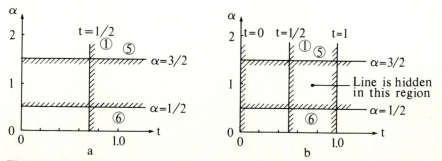

Figure 4-23 Graphical solution for Example 4-10.

A further example illustrates that the $\alpha = 0$ boundary must also be considered.

Example 4-11   Alpha Boundary

Consider the untransformed cube and the line $P_1[1\ \ 0\ \ 2\ \ 1]$ to $P_2[-1\ \ 0\ \ -2\ \ 1]$ as shown in Fig. 4-24. The line P_1P_2 penetrates the volume. Here

$$P(t) = \mathbf{v} = [1\ \ 0\ \ 2\ \ 1] + [-2\ \ 0\ \ -4\ \ 0]t$$

and

$$\mathbf{s} = [\ 1\ \ 0\ \ \ \ 2\ \ 1]$$
$$\mathbf{d} = [-2\ \ 0\ \ -4\ \ 0]$$

Again the eyepoint is at infinity and

$$\mathbf{g} = [0\ \ 0\ \ 1\ \ 0]$$

For the untransformed cube, i.e. $[VT] = [V]$

$$p = \mathbf{s} \cdot [VT] = [-1\ \ \ \ 3\ \ 1\ \ 1\ \ -3\ \ \ \ 5]$$
$$q = \mathbf{d} \cdot [VT] = [\ \ 4\ \ -4\ \ 0\ \ 0\ \ \ \ 8\ \ -8]$$
$$w = \mathbf{g} \cdot [VT] = [\ \ 0\ \ \ \ 0\ \ 0\ \ 0\ \ -2\ \ \ \ 2]$$

The resulting equations for $h_j > 0$ are

    ① $-1 + 4t$ > 0

    ② $3 - 4t$ > 0

    ③ 1 > 0

    ④ 1 > 0

    ⑤ $-3 + 8t - 2\alpha > 0$

    ⑥ $5 - 8t + 2\alpha > 0$

Solution of these equations for $h_j = 0$ yields a single valid result, $t = 1/4$. The solution is shown graphically in Fig. 4-25a. Again cross-hatching indicates the side of the line on which possible solutions exist. No valid bounded region exists. Adding the boundaries at $t = 0$ and $t = 1$ as shown in Fig. 4-25b yields a bounded region between $t = 3/4$ and $t = 1$. However, as shown by the cross-hatching, this region is not valid since, for $t > 3/4$, $h_j > 0$ is not satisfied for $j = 2$. Adding the boundary at $\alpha = 0$ also yields a valid bounded region with solutions at $t = 3/8$ and $t = 3/4$. It is this region that yields $t_{maxmin} = 3/8$ and $t_{minmax} = 3/4$. Hence the line is visible for

$$0 \leq t \leq 3/8 \qquad \text{and} \qquad 3/4 \leq t \leq 1$$

or for

$$P(0) = [1\ \ 0\ \ 2\ \ 1] \quad \text{to} \quad P(3/8) = [1/4\ \ 0\ \ 1/2\ \ 1]$$

and

$$P(3/4) = [-1/2\ \ 0\ \ -1\ \ 1] \qquad \text{to} \qquad P(1) = [-1\ \ 0\ \ -2\ \ 1]$$

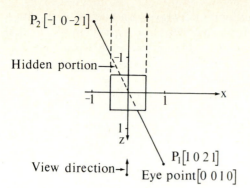

$P_2 [-1\ 0 -2\ 1]$

Hidden portion—

-1

-1 1 X

1

z

View direction→

$P_1 [1\ 0\ 2\ 1]$

Eye point $[0\ 0\ 1\ 0]$

Figure 4-24 Testing a penetrating line against a volume.

The $\alpha = 0$ boundary solutions occur for penetrating (objects).

One technique for adding the lines at these penetrating junctures to the scene is to save all the penetrating points. Lines are formed by connecting each penetrating point in a pair of penetrating volumes to every other penetrating point in that pair of volumes. These lines are then tested against all remaining volumes. The visible lines are the juncture lines.

These examples show that solutions satisfying $h_j > 0$ also exist for the boundaries of the region described by $0 \le t \le 1$ and $\alpha \ge 0$. Thus the three equations corresponding to these boundaries, i.e., $t = 0$, $t - 1 = 0$, and $\alpha = 0$, must be added to the solution set $h_j = 0$. The number of solutions is now $(j+2)$ $(j + 3)/2$, where j is the number of planes describing a convex volume.

As previously mentioned, selecting the maximum minimum and the minimum maximum values of t from the possible valid solutions is a simple linear programming problem. Its solution is equivalent to identifying the valid bounded region for the graphical solutions shown in Figs. 4-21, 4-23, and 4-25. The flowchart in Fig. 4-26 provides a solution algorithm for the minimax problem. It is assumed that the algorithm is used only for lines that are known to be partially or totally hidden. All self-hidden lines and all totally visible lines are identified and eliminated before the algorithm is used. The algorithm is entered with t and α from the solution of the pair of linear equations numbered e_1 and

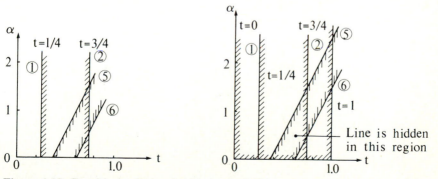

Figure 4-25 Graphical solution for Example 4-11.

and e_2, t_{min} and t_{max} (the current minimum and maximum values of t), and n (the number of equations in the solution set). The first part of the algorithm ensures that the condition $h_j > 0$ is satisfied. If this condition is satisfied, the second part looks for t_{min} and t_{max}. The result is t_{maxmin} and t_{minmax}.

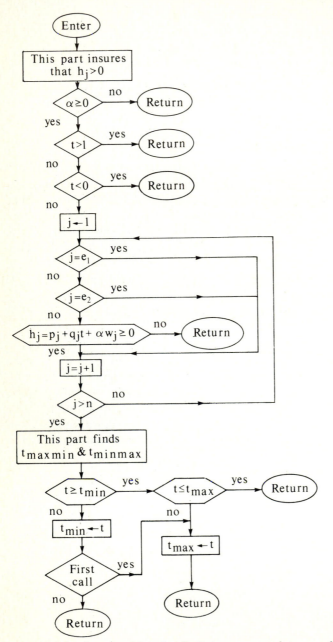

Figure 4-26 An algorithm for finding t_{maxmin} and t_{minmax} for the Roberts hidden line technique.

The solution technique discussed above is computationally expensive. Hence, it is efficient to look for ways to quickly identify totally visible lines. The basic idea is to determine if both end points of a line lie between the eyepoint and a visible plane. Recall that

$$\mathbf{u} = \mathbf{s} + t\mathbf{d} + \alpha\mathbf{g}$$

For $\alpha = 0$, $\mathbf{u}$ represents the line itself. Further, if $\alpha = 0$, then $t = 0$ and $t = 1$ yield the end points of the line. Also recall that

$$h_j = \mathbf{u} \cdot [VT] = p_j + q_j t + w_j \alpha$$

and note that, for $t = 0$, p_j is the dot product of the end point of the line and the jth plane of the volume. Similarly, $p_j + q_j$ is the dot product of the other end point of the line and the jth plane of the volume. Finally, recall that the jth plane of a volume is visible if $w_j \leq 0$. Thus, if $w_j \leq 0$ and $p_j \leq 0$, then one end point of the line is either on the visible plane or between the visible plane and the eyepoint. If $p_j + q_j \leq 0$, then the other end point is also either on the visible plane or between the plane and the eyepoint. Hence, the line is totally visible if for any j

$$w_j \leq 0 \quad \text{and} \quad p_j \leq 0 \quad \text{and} \quad p_j + q_j \leq 0$$

These conditions ensure that $h_j \leq 0$ cannot be satisfied for any $\alpha \leq 0$ and $0 \leq t \leq 1$. Thus, no part of the line can be hidden, and it is totally visible.

Example 4-12   Totally Visible Lines

For the origin-centered cube, consider the line from $P_1[-2 \ 0 \ 2 \ 1]$ to $P_2[2 \ 0 \ 2 \ 1]$ which, as shown in Fig. 4-27, passes in front of the cube. Here,

$$\mathbf{v} = \mathbf{s} + \mathbf{d}t = [-2 \ 0 \ 2 \ 1] + [4 \ 0 \ 0 \ 0]t$$

and with the eyepoint at infinity in the z direction

$$\mathbf{s} = [-2 \ 0 \ 2 \ 1]$$
$$\mathbf{d} = [\ 4 \ 0 \ 0 \ 0]$$
$$\mathbf{g} = [\ 0 \ 0 \ 1 \ 0]$$

For the untransformed cube $[VT] = [V]$ and

$$
\begin{array}{ccccccc}
 & ① & ② & ③ & ④ & ⑤ & ⑥ \\
p = \mathbf{s} \cdot [VT] = [& 5 & -3 & 1 & 1 & -3 & 5] \\
q = \mathbf{d} \cdot [VT] = [& -8 & 8 & 0 & 0 & 0 & 0] \\
w = \mathbf{g} \cdot [VT] = [& 0 & 0 & 0 & 0 & -2 & 2]
\end{array}
$$

Note that

$$w_5 < 0 \quad \text{and} \quad p_5 < 0 \quad \text{and} \quad p_5 + q_5 < 0$$

Thus, the line is totally visible.

As an additional example, consider the line from $P_3[-1 \ 1 \ 1 \ 1]$ to $P_4[1 \ 1 \ -1 \ 1]$, which passes diagonally above the cube. This line is also shown in Fig. 4-27. Here,

$$s = [-1 \quad 1 \quad 1 \quad 1]$$
$$d = [\; 2 \quad 0 \quad -2 \quad 0]$$
$$g = [\; 0 \quad 0 \quad 1 \quad 0]$$

and

$$
\begin{array}{cccccc}
& \text{①} & \text{②} & \text{③} & \text{④} & \text{⑤} & \text{⑥} \\
p = s \cdot [VT] = [& 3 & -1 & -1 & 3 & -1 & 3] \\
q = d \cdot [VT] = [& -4 & 4 & 0 & 0 & 4 & -4] \\
w = g \cdot [VT] = [& 0 & 0 & 0 & 0 & -2 & 2]
\end{array}
$$

Note that

$$w_5 < 0 \qquad \text{and} \qquad p_5 < 0 \qquad \text{but} \qquad p_5 + q_5 > 0$$

However,

$$w_3 = 0 \qquad \text{and} \qquad p_3 < 0 \qquad \text{and} \qquad p_3 + q_3 < 0$$

Again the line is totally visible.

Although the top plane (plane ③) is "edge-on" to an eye-point at infinity on the z axis, mathematically the line P_3P_4 of the above example is between the eye and the visible plane. A similar condition occurs for the bottom and the two side planes.

Unfortunately, there is no easy test for totally invisible lines. It is, of course, possible to determine that the end points of a line are both behind a hidden plane. However, because the plane is of infinite extent, it is not possible to determine if the ends of the line extend beyond the volume (see Fig. 4-22). Totally invisible lines must be found using the general solution technique. In this case, the hidden portion is from $t = 0$ to $t = 1$.

An efficient implementation of the Roberts algorithm is given below. The algorithm is divided into three parts. The first part analyzes each volume separately to eliminate the self-hidden planes. The second part compares the remaining edges of each volume against all the others to find the line segments hidden by the others. The third part constructs the junction lines for penetrating

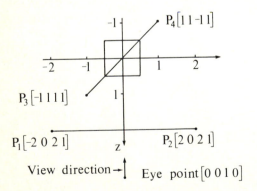

View direction → | Eye point $[0\,0\,1\,0]$ **Figure 4-27** Totally visible lines.

volumes. The algorithm assumes that a volume consists of polygonal planar faces, the faces consist of edges, and the edges consist of individual vertices. All vertices, edges, and faces are associated with a specific volume.

Eliminate the the self-hidden planes.

For each volume in the scene.

Form face polygons and edges from the volume vertex list.

Calculate the plane equation for each face polygon of the volume.

Check the sign of the plane equation.

Calculate a point inside the volume as the average of the vertices.

Calculate the dot product of the plane equation and the point inside the volume.

If the dot product is < 0, change the sign of the plane equation.

Form the volume matrix.

Premultiply by the inverse of the viewing transformation including perspective.

Calculate and save the bounding box values x_{max}, x_{min}, y_{max}, y_{min}, z_{max}, z_{min} for the transformed volume.

Identify the self-hidden planes.

Take the dot product of the test point at infinity and the transformed volume matrix.

If the dot product is < 0, then the plane is hidden.

Eliminate the entire polygon forming the plane. This eliminates the necessity for separately identifying hidden lines as the intersection of two hidden planes.

Eliminate the line segments for each volume hidden by all other volumes in the scene.

If there is only one volume, the algorithm is complete.

Form a priority list of the volumes.

Perform a z sort. Sort on the maximum z coordinate of the vertices of the transformed volumes. The first and highest priority volume on the sorted list is the one with minimum maximum z. In the right handed coordinate system used, this is the farthest volume from an eyepoint at z infinity.

For each volume on the priority list.

Test the non-self-hidden edges against all other volumes in the scene. The volume whose edges are being tested is the test object. The volume against which it is currently being tested is the test volume. A test object normally need be tested only against lower priority test volumes.

Perform bounding box tests for the test object and the test volume.

If x_{min}(test volume) $> x_{max}$(test object) **or**
x_{max}(test volume) $< x_{min}$(test object) **or**
y_{min}(test volume) $> y_{max}$(test object) **or**
y_{max}(test volume) $< y_{min}$(test object)

then the test volumes cannot hide any edges of the test object. Continue to the next test volume. Otherwise,

Perform preliminary penetration tests to see if the test object penetrates the test volume and possibly obscures part of it.

Test the maximum z value of the test object against the minimum z value of the test volume.

If z_{max}(test object) $< z_{min}$(test volume), then penetration is not possible. Continue with the next volume. Otherwise,

Test for visible penetration.

If z_{max}(test object) $> z_{max}$(test volume), then the test object may penetrate the front face of the test volume.

Set the visible penetration flag for later use. Place the penetrating volume on the penetration list.

If x_{max}(test object) $> x_{min}$(test volume) **or**
x_{min} (test object) $< x_{max}$(test volume)
then the test object may penetrate the side of the volume.

Set the visible penetration flag for later use. Place the penetrating volume on the penetration list.

If y_{max}(test object) $> y_{max}$(test volume) **or**
y_{min}(test object) $< y_{min}$(test volume)
then the test object may penetrate the top or bottom of the test volume.

Set the visible penetration flag for later use. Place the penetrating volume on the penetration list.

If the penetration list is empty, set the no penetration flag.

Perform edge tests.

Calculate **s** and **d** for the edge.

Calculate p, q, w for each plane of the test volume.

Test for total visibility. If the edge is totally visible, skip to the next edge.

Form the $h_j = 0$ equations and solve simultaneously in pairs, including the $t = 0$ and $t = 1$ boundaries. If the visible penetration flag is set, then include the $\alpha = 0$ boundary. Save the penetrating points. Otherwise ignore the $\alpha = 0$ boundary.

> For each t, α solution check $0 \leq t \leq 1$, $\alpha \geq 0$, and $h_j > 0$ for all other planes. If these conditions are satisfied, find t_{maxmin} and t_{minmax}.

Calculate the visible line segments and save for testing against lower priority volumes.

Determine visible junction lines for penetrating volumes.

If the visible penetration flag is not set, skip to the display routine.

If no penetrating points have been recorded, skip to the display routine.

Form possible junction edges by connecting all penetrating points for the two penetrating volumes.

Test all junction edges against both penetrating volumes for visibility.

Test the surviving visible junction edges against all volumes in the scene for visibility. Save the visible segments.

Display remaining visible edge segments.

Note that the algorithm can also be implemented with a reverse priority list. The above algorithm was used to produce the dimetric view of the three objects shown in Fig. 4-28.

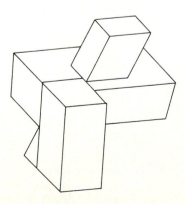

Figure 4-28 Hidden lines removed from a dimetric view of penetrating objects.

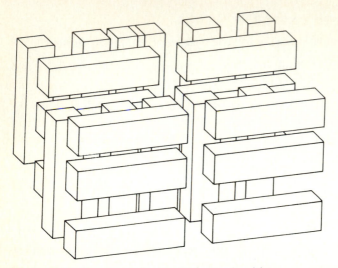

Figure 4-29 Test scene for the Roberts algorithm.

Timing results for scenes similar to that shown in Fig. 4-29, with up to 1152 blocks, indicate a very nearly linear growth in computational expense with the number of blocks (Ref. 4-9). Petty and Mach (Ref. 4-8) note a similar result for a Roberts algorithm implemented using Warnock-style area subdivision (see Sec. 4-3). The principal disadvantage of the Roberts algorithm is the requirement for convex volumes. A detailed illustrative example is given below.

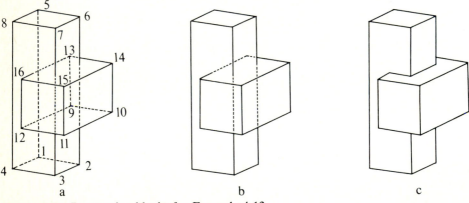

Figure 4-30 Penetrating blocks for Example 4-13.

Example 4-13   Complete Roberts Algorithm

Consider the two intersecting blocks shown in Fig. 4-30. The blocks are described by the following vertex point data bases.

Block 1				Block 2			
Vertex number	x	y	z	Vertex number	x	y	z
1	0	0	1	9	1	2	0
2	2	0	1	10	3	2	0
3	2	0	3	11	3	2	4
4	0	0	3	12	1	2	4
5	0	6	1	13	1	4	0
6	2	6	1	14	3	4	0
7	2	6	3	15	3	4	4
8	0	6	3	16	1	4	4

The vertex numbers are shown in Fig. 4-30a. The edge lists are

Block 1		Block 2	
Edge	Joins vertices	Edge	Joins vertices
1	1–2	13	9–10
2	2–3	14	10–11
3	3–4	15	11–12
4	4–1	16	12– 9
5	5–6	17	13–14
6	6–7	18	14–15
7	7–8	19	15–16
8	8–5	20	16–13
9	1–5	21	9–13
10	2–6	22	10–14
11	3–7	23	11–15
12	4–8	24	12–16

These edges are formed into face polygons for two blocks.

Block 1		Block 2	
Polygon number	Edges	Polygon number	Edges
1	2, 11, 6, 10	7	14, 23, 18, 22
2	4, 12, 8, 9	8	21, 20, 24, 16
3	5, 6, 7, 8	9	17, 18, 19, 20
4	1, 2, 3, 4	10	13, 14, 15, 16
5	3, 12, 7, 11	11	15, 24, 19, 23
6	1, 10, 5, 9	12	13, 22, 17, 21

The volume matrices for the blocks in the given orientation can be developed at this point, checked for correct sign by taking a point inside, and then transformed by premultiplying by the inverse of the viewing transformation. However, in this example the alternate approach of first transforming the volume vertex matrices by postmultiplying by the viewing transformation and then determining the transformed plane equations and hence the transformed volume matrices is used.

Here, a viewing transformation, comprised of a $-30°$ rotation about the y axis ($\phi = 30°$), followed by a $+15°$ rotation about the x axis ($\theta = 15°$), is used. The combined transformation is (see Ref. 1-1)

$$[T] = [R_x][R_y] = \begin{bmatrix} \cos\phi & \sin\phi\,\sin\theta & -\sin\phi\,\cos\theta & 0 \\ 0 & \cos\theta & \sin\theta & 0 \\ \sin\phi & -\cos\phi\,\sin\theta & \cos\phi\,\cos\theta & 0 \\ 0 & 0 & 0 & 1 \end{bmatrix}$$

$$= \begin{bmatrix} 0.866 & -0.129 & 0.483 & 0 \\ 0.0 & 0.966 & 0.259 & 0 \\ -0.5 & -0.224 & 0.837 & 0 \\ 0.0 & 0.0 & 0.0 & 1 \end{bmatrix}$$

Transforming, the point data bases become

$$[PT_1] = [P_1][T] = \begin{bmatrix} -0.5 & -0.224 & 0.837 & 1 \\ 1.232 & -0.483 & 1.802 & 1 \\ 0.232 & -0.933 & 3.475 & 1 \\ -1.5 & -0.672 & 2.510 & 1 \\ -0.5 & 5.571 & 2.389 & 1 \\ 1.232 & 5.313 & 3.355 & 1 \\ 0.232 & 4.864 & 5.028 & 1 \\ -1.5 & 5.123 & 4.062 & 1 \end{bmatrix} \begin{matrix} 1 \\ 2 \\ 3 \\ 4 \\ 5 \\ 6 \\ 7 \\ 8 \end{matrix}$$

and

$$[PT_2] = [P_2][T] = \begin{bmatrix} 0.866 & 1.802 & 1.001 & 1 \\ 2.598 & 1.544 & 1.967 & 1 \\ 0.598 & 0.647 & 5.313 & 1 \\ -1.134 & 0.906 & 4.347 & 1 \\ 0.866 & 3.734 & 1.518 & 1 \\ 2.598 & 3.475 & 2.484 & 1 \\ 0.598 & 2.579 & 5.830 & 1 \\ -1.134 & 2.838 & 4.864 & 1 \end{bmatrix} \begin{matrix} 9 \\ 10 \\ 11 \\ 12 \\ 13 \\ 14 \\ 15 \\ 16 \end{matrix}$$

The plane equations for each of the faces of the two blocks in this orientation can be obtained by Newell's technique as discussed above. For example, the face described by polygon 1 uses the four vertices labeled 2, 3, 7, 6 in Fig. 4-30a. Newell's technique (see Example 4-3) using the transformed points yields the plane equation

$$-20.791x + 3.106y - 11.593z + 48.001 = 0$$

Rewriting this result to correspond to that obtained by transforming the volume matrix from the original orientation yields

$$-0.866x + 0.129y - 0.483z + 2 = 0$$

The transformed volume matrix in this form is then

$$[VT_1] = \begin{array}{cccccc} \text{①} & \text{②} & \text{③} & \text{④} & \text{⑤} & \text{⑥} \\ \begin{bmatrix} -0.866 & 0.866 & 0 & 0 & 0.5 & -0.5 \\ 0.129 & -0.129 & -0.966 & 0.966 & 0.224 & -0.224 \\ -0.483 & 0.483 & -0.259 & 0.259 & -0.837 & 0.837 \\ 2 & 0 & 6 & 0 & 3 & -1 \end{bmatrix} \end{array}$$

and similarly

$$[VT_2] = \begin{array}{cccccc} \textcircled{7} & \textcircled{8} & \textcircled{9} & \textcircled{10} & \textcircled{11} & \textcircled{12} \end{array}$$

$$[VT_2] = \begin{bmatrix} -0.866 & 0.866 & 0 & 0 & 0.5 & -0.5 \\ 0.129 & -0.129 & -0.966 & 0.966 & 0.224 & -0.224 \\ -0.483 & 0.483 & -0.259 & 0.259 & -0.837 & 0.837 \\ 3 & -1 & 4 & -2 & 4 & 0 \end{bmatrix}$$

With the eyepoint at $[0 \ 0 \ 1 \ 0]$ the test point is

$$[E] = [0 \ 0 \ -1 \ 0]$$

Looking for the self-hidden planes in volume 1 yields

$$\begin{array}{cccccc} \textcircled{1} & \textcircled{2} & \textcircled{3} & \textcircled{4} & \textcircled{5} & \textcircled{6} \end{array}$$
$$[E] \cdot [VT_1] = [0.483 \ -0.483 \ 0.259 \ -0.259 \ 0.837 \ -0.837]$$

Similarly for volume 2

$$\begin{array}{cccccc} \textcircled{7} & \textcircled{8} & \textcircled{9} & \textcircled{10} & \textcircled{11} & \textcircled{12} \end{array}$$
$$[E] \cdot [VT_2] = [0.483 \ -0.483 \ 0.259 \ -0.259 \ 0.837 \ -0.837]$$

The negative signs show that planes (polygons) 2, 4, and 6 in volume 1 and 8, 10, 12 in volume 2 are self-hidden. Intersections of these polygons represent invisible edges. In particular, the edges 1, 4, and 9 in the first volume and 13, 16, and 21 in the second volume represent the intersection of two self-hidden planes and are thus hidden. The result is shown in Fig. 4-30b.

The remaining lines in each volume are checked to see if they are hidden by the other volume. First check if the volumes interpenetrate. Testing volume 1 against volume 2 using the transformed point vertices shows that

$$(z_{max})_{vol.1} = 5.028 > (z_{min})_{vol.2} = 1.001$$

Hence, penetration is possible. Further,

$$(x_{max})_{vol.1} = 1.232 > (x_{min})_{vol.2} = -1.134$$

and penetration occurs. Thus, the $\alpha = 0$ boundary must be included in the solution set.

The remaining edges of volume 1 are tested against volume 2. As a specific example, consider edge 2 between vertices 2 and 3. Here,

$$\mathbf{v} = \mathbf{s} + \mathbf{d}t = [1.232 \ -0.483 \ 1.802 \ 1] + [-1 \ -0.45 \ 1.673 \ 0]t$$

Taking the dot product of $\mathbf{s}$ and $\mathbf{d}$ with $[VT_2]$ yields

$$\begin{array}{cccccc} \textcircled{1} & \textcircled{2} & \textcircled{3} & \textcircled{4} & \textcircled{5} & \textcircled{6} \end{array}$$
$$p = \mathbf{s} \cdot [VT_2] = [1 \ \ 1 \ \ 4 \ -2 \ \ 3 \ \ 1]$$

$$\begin{array}{cccccc} \textcircled{1} & \textcircled{2} & \textcircled{3} & \textcircled{4} & \textcircled{5} & \textcircled{6} \end{array}$$
$$q = \mathbf{d} \cdot [VT_2] = [0 \ \ 0 \ \ 0 \ \ 0 \ -2 \ \ 3]$$

For an eyepoint at positive infinity in the z direction

$$\mathbf{g} = [0 \ 0 \ 1 \ 0]$$

and

$$w = \mathbf{g} \cdot [VT_2] = \begin{array}{cccccc} ① & ② & ③ & ④ & ⑤ & ⑥ \\ [-0.483 & 0.483 & -0.259 & 0.259 & -0.837 & 0.837] \end{array}$$

Checking to see if the line is totally visible shows that the conditions

$$w_j \leq 0 \quad \text{and} \quad p_j \leq 0 \quad \text{and} \quad p_j + q_j \leq 0$$

are not satisfied for any plane. This is because the infinite plane containing the bottom (plane ④) of volume 2 could hide the edge. Forming the hidden edge conditions h_j yields

$$
\begin{array}{lll}
① & 1 & -0.483a \geq 0 \\
② & 1 & +0.483a \geq 0 \\
③ & 4 & -0.259a \geq 0 \\
④ & -2 & +0.259a \geq 0 \\
⑤ & 3 \ -2t & -0.837a \geq 0 \\
⑥ & 1 + 2t & +0.837a \geq 0
\end{array}
$$

Solving these equations successively in pairs shows that the condition $h_j \geq 0$ for all j cannot be met. Hence, no portion of the edge is hidden, and it is totally visible. The details of the remaining solutions for the edges of volume 1 hidden by volume 2 are given in Tables 4-5 and 4-6. Note that $\mathbf{g}$ and w are constant.

The solution diagrams for edges 10 and 11 are shown in Figs. 4-31a and b. Both edges penetrate volume 2. Edge 10 is hidden for $0.244 < t < 0.667$. This corresponds to the line from the point $(1.232, 0.815, 2.150)$ to the point $(1.232, 3.381, 2.837)$. Edge 11 is hidden for $0.282 < t < 0.667$, which corresponds to the line from $(0.232, 0.703, 3.913)$ to $(0.232, 2.933, 4.510)$.

The $a = 0$ boundary yields penetrating points at $t = 0.333$ and 0.667 for both edges. These values of t correspond to the points $(1.232, 1.449, 2.320)$ and

Table 4-5

Edge	Joins vertices	s				d			
2	2–3	[1.232	−0.483	1.802	1]	[−1.0	−0.45	1.673	0]
3	3–4	[0.232	−0.931	3.46	1]	[−1.732	0.259	−0.966	0]
5	5–6	[−0.5	5.571	2.389	1]	[1.732	−0.259	0.966	0]
6	6–7	[1.232	5.313	3.355	1]	[−1.0	−0.448	1.673	0]
7	7–8	[0.232	4.864	5.028	1]	[−1.732	0.259	−0.966	0]
8	8–5	[−1.5	5.123	4.062	1]	[1.0	0.448	−1.673	0]
10	2–6	[1.232	−0.483	1.802	1]	[0.0	5.796	1.553	0]
11	3–7	[0.232	−0.931	3.475	1]	[0.0	5.796	1.553	0]
12	4–8	[−1.5	−0.672	2.510	1]	[0.0	5.796	1.553	0]

Table 4-6

Edge	Joins vertices	p	q	Comment
2	2–3	[1 1 4 −2 3 1]	[1 0 0 0 −2 2]	Totally visible; full solution
3	3–4	[1 1 4 −2 1 3]	[2 −2 0 0 0 0]	Totally visible; full solution
5	5–6	[3 −1 −2 4 3 1]	[−2 2 0 0 0 0]	Totally visible; $w_3 < 0$, $p_3 < 0$, $p_3 + q_3 < 0$
6	6–7	[1 1 −2 4 3 1]	[1 0 0 0 −2 2]	Totally visible; $w_3 < 0$, $p_3 < 0$, $p_3 + q_3 < 0$
7	7–8	[1 1 −2 4 1 3]	[2 −2 0 0 0 0]	Totally visible; $w_3 < 0$, $p_3 < 0$, $p_3 + q_3 < 0$
8	8–5	[3 −1 −2 4 1 3]	[1 0 0 0 2 −2]	Totally visible; $w_3 < 0$, $p_3 < 0$, $p_3 + q_3 < 0$
10	2–6	[1 1 4 −2 3 1]	[1 0 0 −6 6 0]	Penetrating; hidden $0.244 < t < 0.667$; see Fig. 4-31a
11	3–7	[1 1 4 −2 1 3]	[1 0 0 −6 6 0]	Penetrating; hidden $0.282 < t < 0.667$; see Fig. 4-31b
12	4–8	[3 −1 4 −2 1 3]	[1 0 0 −6 6 0]	Totally visible; full solution

(1.232, 3.381, 2.837) for edge 10 and to (0.232, 1.001, 3.993) and (0.232, 2.933, 4.510) for edge 11. These four points are saved as penetration points.

Comparing the non-self-hidden edges of volume 2 against volume 1 yields the results shown in Tables 4-7 and 4-8. Edge 17 is partially hidden by volume 1.

Table 4-7

Edge	Joins vertices	s				d			
14	10−11	[2.598	1.544	1.967	1]	[−2.0	−0.897	3.346	0]
15	11−12	[0.598	0.647	5.313	1]	[−1.732	0.259	−0.966	0]
17	13−14	[0.866	3.734	1.518	1]	[1.732	−0.259	0.966	0]
18	14−15	[2.598	3.475	2.484	1]	[−2.0	−0.897	3.346	0]
19	15−16	[0.598	2.579	5.830	1]	[−1.732	0.259	−0.966	0]
20	16−13	[−1.134	2.838	4.864	1]	[2.0	0.897	−3.346	0]
22	10−14	[2.60	1.544	1.967	1]	[0	1.932	0.518	0]
23	11−15	[0.598	0.647	5.313	1]	[0	1.932	0.518	0]
24	12−16	[−1.134	0.906	4.347	1]	[0	1.932	0.518	0]

Specifically, as shown in Fig. 4-31c, edge 17 is hidden from $0 \le t < 0.211$, which corresponds to the line from (0.866, 3.734, 1.518) to (1.232, 3.679, 1.722). Edge 20 penetrates the front face (plane 5) of volume 1 at $t = 0.25$. Hence, it is hidden from $0.25 < t \le 1.0$ which corresponds to the line from (−0.634, 3.062, 4.28) to (0.866, 3.734, 1.518). The solution region is shown in Fig. 4-31d. The point (−0.634, 3.062, 4.028) is saved as a penetrating point. The solution region also shows that the point for $t = 0.75, \alpha = 0$ is a penetrating point. This value of t corresponds to the point (0.366, 3.511, 2.355).

There are six penetrating points:

$$[PP] = \begin{bmatrix} 1.232 & 1.449 & 2.320 & 1 \\ 1.232 & 3.381 & 2.837 & 1 \\ 0.232 & 1.001 & 3.993 & 1 \\ 0.232 & 2.933 & 4.510 & 1 \\ -0.634 & 3.062 & 4.028 & 1 \\ 0.366 & 3.511 & 2.355 & 1 \end{bmatrix} \begin{matrix} ⑰ \\ ⑱ \\ ⑲ \\ ⑳ \\ ㉑ \\ ㉒ \end{matrix}$$

Connecting each of these lines to each of the others in turn yields 30 possible junction lines. Each of these lines must be tested against each of the volumes. The large majority are invisible. By inspection, only the lines connecting points 18 and 20, and 20 and 21 are of interest. These lines are totally visible. In fact, they are the junction lines. The details of the complete solution are left as an exercise. The complete result is shown in Fig. 4-30c.

Table 4-8

Edge	Joins vertices	p	q	Comment
14	10–11	[−1 3 4 2 3 −1]	[0 0 0 0 −4 4]	Totally visible; $w_1 < 0$, $p_1 < 0$, $p_1 + q_1 < 0$
15	11–12	[−1 3 4 2 −1 3]	[2 −2 0 0 0 0]	Totally visible; $w_5 < 0$, $p_5 < 0$, $p_5 + q_5 < 0$
17	13–14	[1 1 2 4 3 −1]	[−2 2 0 0 0 0]	Partially hidden; $0 \leq t < 0.211$
18	14–15	[−1 3 2 4 3 −1]	[0 0 0 0 −4 4]	Totally visible; $w_1 < 0$, $p_1 < 0$, $p_1 + q_1 < 0$
19	15–16	[−1 3 2 4 −1 3]	[2 −2 0 0 0 0]	Totally visible; $w_5 < 0$, $p_5 < 0$, $p_5 + q_5 < 0$
20	16–13	[1 1 2 4 −1 3]	[0 0 0 0 4 −4]	Penetrating; hidden $0.25 < t \leq 1.0$
22	10–14	[−1 3 4 2 3 −1]	[0 0 −2 2 0 0]	Totally visible; $w_1 < 0$, $p_1 < 0$, $p_1 + q_1 < 0$
23	11–15	[−1 3 4 2 −1 3]	[0 0 −2 2 0 0]	Totally visible; $w_1 < 0$, $p_1 < 0$, $p_1 + q_1 < 0$
24	12–16	[1 1 4 2 −1 3]	[0 0 −2 2 0 0]	Totally visible; $w_5 < 0$, $p_5 < 0$, $p_5 + q_5 < 0$

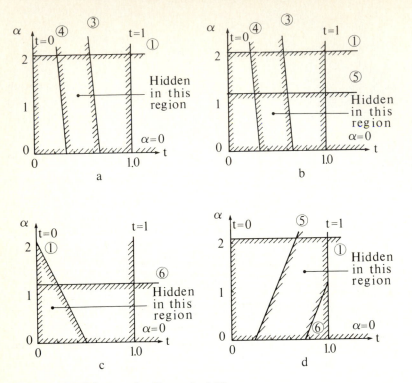

Figure 4-31 Solutions for Example 4-13.

4-4 WARNOCK ALGORITHM

The basic ideas behind the Warnock algorithm are very general. They are, by analogy, based on an hypothesis of how the human eye-brain combination processes information contained in a scene. The hypothesis is that very little time or effort is expended on areas that contain little information. The majority of the time and effort is spent on areas of high information content. As an example, consider an otherwise empty table top with a bowl of fruit on it. The color, texture, etc., of the entire table top require minimal time to perceive. Attention is focused on the fruit bowl. Where on the table is it located? How large is it? What kind of bowl: wooden, ceramic, plastic, glass, metal? What color bowl: red, blue, silver, dull, glossy, etc.? What kind of fruit does it contain: peaches, grapes, pears, bananas, apples? What color apples: red, yellow, green? Does the apple have a stem? In each case the area of interest narrows, and the level of detail sought increases. Further, if, at a particular level a specific question cannot be answered immediately, it is temporarily put aside for later consideration. The Warnock algorithm and its derivatives attempt to take advantage of the fact that large areas of a display are similar, e.g., the table in the above discussion. This characteristic is known as area coherence; i.e., adjacent areas (pixels) in both the x and y directions tend to be similar.

Since the Warnock algorithm is concerned with what is displayed, it works in image space. It considers a window in image space and seeks to determine if the window is empty or if the contents of the window are simple enough to display. If not, the window is subdivided until either the contents of a subwindow are simple enough to display or the subwindow size is at the limit of desired resolution. In the latter case, the remaining information in the window is evaluated and the result displayed at a single intensity or color. Antialiasing can be incorporated by carrying the subdivision process to less than display pixel resolution and averaging the subpixel attributes to determine the display pixel attributes (see Sec. 2-25).

Specific implementations of the Warnock algorithm vary in the method of subdividing the window and in the details of the criteria used to decide whether the contents are simple enough to display directly. In Warnock's original presentation of the algorithm (Refs. 4-10 and 4-11) each window is subdivided into four equal subwindows. This implementation of the algorithm and a common variation allowing for subdivision of the window at polygon boundaries are discussed in the present section. Another variation that subdivides the window into polygonal windows developed by Weiler and Atherton (Ref. 4-12) is discussed in the next section. Catmull (Refs. 4-13 and 4-14) has also applied the basic subdivision concept to the display of curved surfaces. This technique is discussed in Sec. 4-6.

Figure 4-32 illustrates the progress of the simplest implementation of the Warnock algorithm. Here, a window that is too complicated to display is subdivided into four equal windows. Further, a window that contains anything is always subdivided until the resolution of the display is reached. Figure 4-32a shows a scene composed of two simple polygons. Figure 4-32b shows the result with the hidden lines removed. Notice that the horizontal rectangle is partially hidden by the vertical rectangle. Figures 4-32c and d show the process of subdivision for a display resolution of 256×256. Since $2^8 = 256$, a maximum of eight subdivisions are required to reach the resolution of the display. If the subwindows are considered in the order lower left, lower right, upper left, upper right, then the subwindows of level 1a labeled 2a, 4a, 4b, 4c, 5a, 5b are declared empty and displayed at the background intensity during the course of the subdivision.

Here, the number indicates the subdivision level, and the letter the quadrant. The first subwindow examined at the pixel level that contains a feature of interest is the one labeled 8a. At this point it is necessary to decide whether a hidden line or a hidden surface algorithm is desired. If a hidden line algorithm is desired, then the pixel corresponding to subwindow 8a is activated because a visible edge passes through it. The result is to display the visible edges of the polygons as a series of pixel-sized dots, as shown in Fig. 4-32e.

Subsequent consideration of the window labeled 8d in Fig. 4-32d best illustrates the difference between implementation as a hidden line and as a hidden surface algorithm. For a hidden line algorithm, the pixel-sized window 8d does not contain any polygon edges. Therefore, it is declared empty and displayed at the background intensity or color. For a hidden surface algorithm, the pixel-sized window 8d is examined to see if it is surrounded by any of the polygons in the scene. If it is, all the polygons surrounding the pixel are tested to see which one is closer to the eyepoint at this pixel location. The test is performed

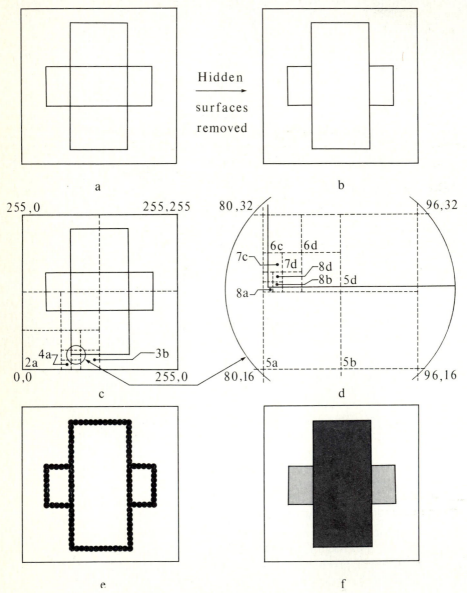

Figure 4-32 Warnock algorithm subdivision.

at the pixel center. The pixel is then displayed at the intensity or color of the closest polygon. If no surrounding polygons are found, the pixel-sized window is empty. Thus, it is displayed at the background color or intensity. The pixel-sized window labeled 8d is surrounded by the vertical rectangle. Thus, it is displayed at the color or intensity for that rectangle. The result is shown in Fig. 4-32f.

The addition of antialiasing to the hidden surface algorithm is illustrated by reconsidering window 8a in Fig. 4-32d. Subdividing this window yields four subpixel-sized windows. Only one of these windows, the upper right hand one, is surrounded by the polygon. The other three are empty. Averaging the results for the four subpixels (see Sec. 2-25) shows that the pixel-sized window 8a should be displayed at one-quarter the intensity of the rectangle. Similarly, the pixel labeled 8b would be displayed at half the intensity of the rectangle. The pixel-sized windows can, of course, be subdivided more than once to allow for weighted averaging of the subpixel characteristics, as discussed in Sec. 2-25.

The subdivision process yields a tree structure for the subwindows as shown in Fig. 4-33.[†] The root of the tree is the display window. Each node represented by the box contains the coordinates of the lower left hand corner and the length of the side of the subwindow. Assuming that subdivided windows are processed in the order *abcd*, i.e., from left to right at a particular subdivision level in the tree, then Fig. 4-33 shows the active path through the tree structure to the pixel-sized window labeled 8a. The active node at each level is indicated by the heavy line. Examination of Figs. 4-32 and 4-33 shows that, at a particular level, all windows to the left of the active node are empty. Thus, they have been previously displayed at the background color or intensity. All windows to the right of the active node at a particular level remain to be processed, i.e., declared empty or subdivided, as the tree is traversed in the reverse direction.

The above algorithm is sufficient to solve either the hidden line or hidden surface problem. However, both the simplicity of the subdivision criteria and the rigidity of the subdivision algorithm maximize the number of subdivisions. The algorithm can be made more efficient by using both more complex subdivision algorithms and more complex subdivision criteria. Figure 4-34a illustrates one common alternate subdivision algorithm and compares it to the previous fixed subdivision algorithm, as shown in Fig. 4-34b.

The subdivisions shown in Fig. 4-34a are obtained by using the bounding box of the polygon. Note that the subwindows need not be square. The algorithm can be recursively applied to any polygon wholly contained within a window or subwindow. If only a single polygon exists within a window, and if it is wholly contained within the window, then it is easy to display, that polygon without further subdivision. A subdivision algorithm such as this is particularly useful in minimizing the number of subdivisions for simple scenes (see Fig. 4-34). However, as scene complexity increases, its advantage decreases.

[†]The Warnock algorithm is the first known implementation of a quadtree data structure.

In considering more complex subdivision criteria, it is convenient to define the relationship of several types of polygons to a window. In particular, a polygon is

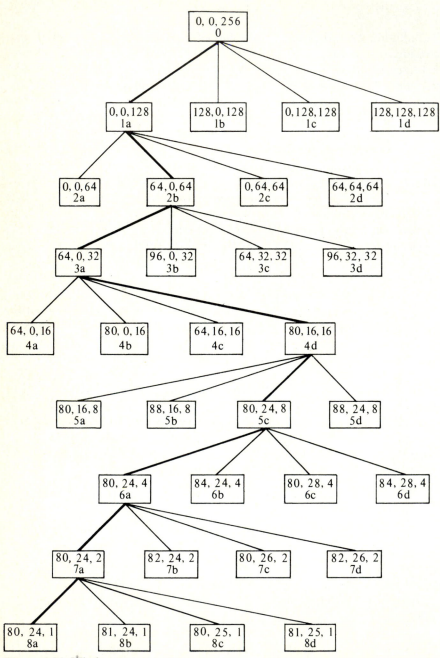

Figure 4-33 Window tree structure.

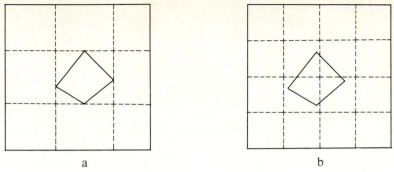

a   b

Figure 4-34 Comparison of subdivision algorithms.

disjoint if it is totally outside the window
contained if it is totally inside the window
intersecting if it intersects the window
surrounding if it completely contains the window

An example of each of these polygon types is shown in Fig. 4-35. Using these definitions, the following decision criteria can be applied to a window. Assembled into an algorithm they yield

For each window:

If all the polygons in the scene are disjoint from the window, then the window is empty. It is displayed at the background intensity or color without further subdivision.

If only a single polygon is contained within the window, the area of the window outside the polygon is filled with the background intensity or color; and the polygon is filled with the appropriate intensity or color.

If a single polygon intersects the window, the area of the window outside the polygon is filled with the background intensity or color; and the portion of the intersecting polygon within the window is filled with the appropriate intensity or color.

If the window is surrounded by a single polygon, and if there are no other polygons in the window, then the window is filled with the intensity or color appropriate for the surrounding polygon.

Disjoint   Contained   Intersecting   Surrounding

Figure 4-35 Polygon types.

If at least one surrounding polygon is found, and if it is the polygon closest to the eye, then the window is filled with the intensity or color appropriate for the surrounding polygon.

Otherwise, subdivide the window.

The first four of these criteria deal with the relationship of single polygons to the window. They are used to reduce the number of subdivisions. The last criterion is the key to the hidden surface problem. It attempts to find a single surrounding polygon that is closer to the eye then any other polygon in the window. Obviously, this surrounding polygon will obscure or hide all the other polygons in the window. Thus, it represents the visible feature in the scene for this window.

Implementing these decision criteria requires techniques for determining whether a polygon is disjoint from, contained within, intersects, or surrounds a window. For rectangular windows, bounding box or minimax tests can be used to determine whether a polygon is disjoint from a window (see Secs. 2-13 and 3-1). In particular, if x_L, x_R, y_B, y_T define the four edges of a window and $x_{min}, x_{max}, y_{min}, y_{max}$ the bounding box surrounding a polygon, then the polygon is disjoint from the window if any of the following conditions is satisfied

$$x_{min} > x_R$$
$$x_{max} < x_L$$
$$y_{min} > y_T$$
$$y_{max} < y_B$$

as shown in Fig. 4-36a. Further, the polygon is contained within the window if the bounding box is contained within the window i.e., if

$$x_{min} \geq x_L \quad \text{and} \quad x_{max} \leq x_R \quad \text{and} \quad y_{min} \geq y_B \quad \text{and} \quad y_{max} \leq y_T$$

as shown in Fig. 4-36b.

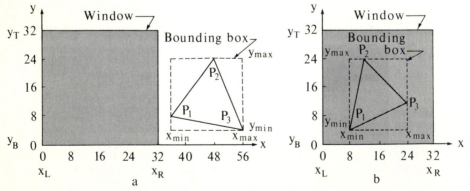

Figure 4-36 Boxing tests for disjoint and contained polygons.

Example 4-14 Disjoint and Contained Polygons

Consider a square window with edges x_L, x_R, y_B, y_T equal to 0, 32, 0, 32. Two polygons, the first with vertices $P_1(36, 8), P_2(48, 24)$, and $P_3(56, 4)$, and the second with vertices $P_1(8, 4)$, $P_2(12, 24)$, and $P_3(24, 12)$, as shown in Fig. 4-36a, are to be tested against this window.

The bounding box for the first polygon, $x_{min}, x_{max}, y_{min}, y_{max}$, is 36, 56, 4, 24. Since

$$(x_{min} = 36) > (x_R = 32)$$

the polygon is disjoint from the window.

Similarly the bounding box for the second polygon, $x_{min}, x_{max}, y_{min}, y_{max}$ is 8, 24, 4, 24 as shown in Fig. 4-36b. Here the condition

$$(x_{min} = 8) > (x_L = 0) \quad \text{and} \quad (x_{max} = 24) < (x_R = 32) \quad \text{and}$$
$$(y_{min} = 4) > (y_B = 0) \quad \text{and} \quad (y_{max} = 24) < (y_T = 32)$$

is satisfied. Hence, the polygon is contained within the window.

A simple substitution test can be used to determine if a polygon intersects a window. The coordinates of the window vertices are substituted into a test function formed from the equation of the line defining a polygon edge (see Sec. 3-16 and Example 3-23). If the sign of the test function is the same for each window vertex, then all the vertices lie on the same side of the line; and there is no intersection. If the signs are different, then the polygon intersects the window. If none of the polygon edges intersects the window, the polygon is either disjoint or surrounds the window. If the equation of the line through two polygon vertices $P_1(x_1, y_1)$ and $P_2(x_2, y_2)$ is $y = mx + b$, then the test function is

$$T.F. = y - mx - b$$

where

$$m = \frac{y_2 - y_1}{x_2 - x_1} \qquad x_2 - x_1 \neq 0$$

$$b = y_1 - mx_1$$

and

$$T.F. = x - x_1 \qquad x_2 - x_1 = 0$$

An example illustrates the technique.

Example 4-15 Intersecting Polygons

Consider the square window with x_L, x_R, y_B, y_T equal to 8, 32, 8, 32 and the two polygons with vertices $P_1(8, 4)$, $P_2(12, 24)$, and $P_3(40, 12)$ and with vertices $P_1(4, 4)$, $P_2(4, 36)$, $P_3(40, 36)$, and $P_4(32, 4)$, as shown in Fig. 4-37. The test function for the polygon edge P_1P_2 in Fig. 4-37a is obtained from

$$m = \frac{y_2 - y_1}{x_2 - x_1} = \frac{24 - 4}{12 - 8} = \frac{20}{4} = 5$$

$$b = y_1 - mx_1 = 4 - 5(8) = -36$$

$$T.F. = y - mx - b = y - 5x + 36$$

Substituting the coordinate of each window corner into the test function yields

$$T.F.(8, 8) = 8 - 5(8) + 36 = 4$$

$$T.F.(8, 32) = 32 - 5(8) + 36 = 28$$

$$T.F.(32, 32) = 32 - 5(32) + 36 = -92$$

$$T.F.(32, 8) = 8 - 5(32) + 36 = -116$$

Since the test function changes sign, the polygon edge intersects the window edge as shown in Fig. 4-37a. Hence, the polygon is an intersector. There is no need to check the other polygon edges.

The results for the polygon shown in Fig. 4-37b are given in Table 4-9. None of the polygon edges intersects the window. Hence, the polygon is either disjoint or a surrounder. Figure 4-37b shows that it is a surrounder.

Table 4-9

Polygon edge	Test function	Window coordinates	Test function result	Comment
P_1P_2	$x - 4$	(8, 8)	4	Nonintersecting
		(8, 32)	4	
		(32, 32)	28	
		(32, 8)	28	
P_2P_3	$y - 36$	(8, 8)	−28	Nonintersecting
		(8, 32)	−4	
		(32, 32)	−4	
		(32, 8)	−28	
P_3P_4	$y - 4x + 124$	(8, 8)	100	Nonintersecting
		(8, 32)	124	
		(32, 32)	28	
		(32, 8)	4	
P_4P_1	$y - 4$	(8, 8)	4	Nonintersecting
		(8, 32)	28	
		(32, 32)	28	
		(32, 8)	4	

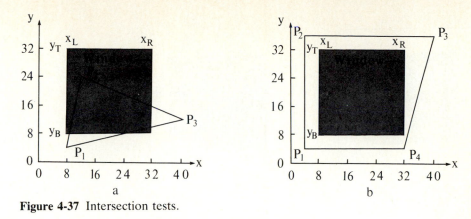

Figure 4-37 Intersection tests.

The simple bounding box test discussed above will not identify all disjoint polygons, e.g., a polygon that encloses a corner of the window as shown in Fig. 4-38a. More complex tests are required. Two are of particular interest, the infinite line test and the angle counting test. Both assume that intersecting and contained polygons have been previously identified. Both can be used to identify disjoint and surrounding polygons.

For the infinite line test, a line is drawn from any part of the window, e.g. a corner, to infinity. The number of intersections of the line and the polygon of interest are counted. If the number is even (or zero), the polygon is disjoint; if odd, the polygon surrounds the window as shown in Fig. 4-38a. If the line passes through a vertex of the polygon as shown in Fig. 4-38b, uncertainty results. This uncertainty is resolved by counting two intersections at a concave vertex (P_2 in Fig. 4-38b) and only one at a convex vertex (P_4 in Fig. 4-38b) (see also Sec. 2-15). Changing the slope of the line also eliminates the uncertainty.

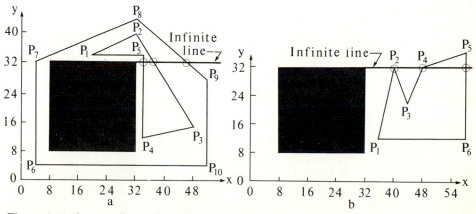

Figure 4-38 Surrounding polygon test.

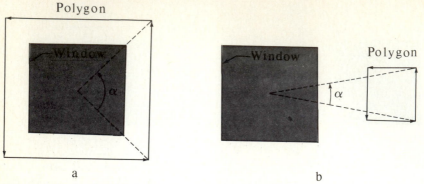

Figure 4-39 Angle counting test.

The angle counting test is illustrated in Fig. 4-39. Proceeding either clockwise or counterclockwise around the polygon, the angles formed between lines from any point in the window to the initial and final vertices of a polygon edge are summed. As shown in Fig. 4-39, the center of the window is a convenient point. The sum of these angles is interpreted as follows:

Sum = 0   the polygon is disjoint from the window.

Sum = ±360n   the polygon surrounds the window n times.

The actual determination of the sum is considerably simplified by realizing that the precision of the individual angle calculations need not be high. In fact, sufficient precision is obtained by counting only the whole octants (45° increments) subtended by the individual angles as shown in Fig. 4-40. The implementation is similar to that for the line end point codes used for clipping (see Sec. 3-1). Here, the octant regions are numbered 0 to 7 counterclockwise. The number of whole octants subtended is obtained by taking the difference between the region numbers of the polygon edge end points and applying the following algorithm:

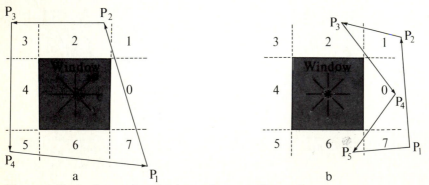

Figure 4-40 Angle test for disjoint and surrounding polygons.

$\Delta\alpha$ = (second end point region number) − (first end point region number):

if $\Delta\alpha > 4$ **then** $\Delta\alpha = \Delta\alpha - 8$
if $\Delta\alpha < -4$ **then** $\Delta\alpha = \Delta\alpha + 8$
if $\Delta\alpha = 0$ **then** the polygon edge is split at a window edge and the process repeated with the two segments.

Summing the individual polygon edge contributions yields

$\sum\Delta\alpha = 0$ the polygon is disjoint from the window.

       $= \pm 8n$ the polygon surrounds the window.

Example 4-16   Angle Test for Surrounding and Disjoint Polygons

Consider the window and the polygons shown in Fig. 4-40. For the polygon shown in Fig. 4-40a, the number of octants subtended by the edge P_1P_2 is

$$\Delta\alpha_{12} = 2 - 7 = -5 < -4$$
$$= -5 + 8 = 3$$

Similarly, for the remaining polygon edges

$$\Delta\alpha_{23} = 3 - 2 = 1$$
$$\Delta\alpha_{34} = 5 - 3 = 2$$
$$\Delta\alpha_{41} = 7 - 5 = 2$$

The sum of the angles subtended by all the polygon edges is

$$\sum\Delta\alpha = 3 + 1 + 2 + 2 = 8$$

Thus, the polygon surrounds the window.

For the polygon shown in Fig. 4-40b

$$\Delta\alpha_{12} = 1 - 7 = -6 < -4$$
$$= -6 + 8 = 2$$
$$\Delta\alpha_{23} = 2 - 1 = 1$$
$$\Delta\alpha_{34} = 0 - 2 = -2$$
$$\Delta\alpha_{45} = 6 - 0 = 6 > 4$$
$$= 6 - 8 = -2$$
$$\Delta\alpha_{51} = 7 - 6 = 1$$

and

$$\sum\Delta\alpha = 2 + 1 - 2 - 2 + 1 = 0$$

Thus, the polygon is disjoint from the window.

A hierarchical application of these techniques based on the computational work involved is advantageous. If only the simplest Warnock algorithm is implemented, then it is not necessary to identify either contained or intersecting polygons. Subdivision will eventually make contained or intersecting polygons either disjoint or surrounding polygons. Any remaining conflicts are resolved at the pixel level. For this simple algorithm, only the bounding box test need be used to identify empty windows. If this simple test fails, the algorithm subdivides the window until the pixel level is reached. Since even at the pixel level a disjoint polygon of the form shown in Fig. 4-40b can exist, it is necessary to apply a more rigorous algorithm to determine if the window is empty or surrounded by one or more polygons.

The more complex algorithm discussed above attempts to identify contained, intersector, more complex disjoint polygons, and surrounding polygons for larger windows in order to avoid subdivision. These tests require more work. Hence, there is a tradeoff between the work associated with subdivision and the work associated with early identification of displayable windows. A more complex algorithm might implement the tests at each window in the following order.

> The simple bounding box test for identifying most empty windows and windows with a single contained polygon. These windows are immediately displayed.

> The simple intersector test for identifying windows with a single intersecting polygon. The polygon is clipped and displayed. For example, the polygon in Fig. 4-34b would be displayed after one subdivision.

> The more complex disjoint and surrounder tests for identifying additional empty windows and windows with a single surrounding polygon. These windows are immediately displayed.

At this point either subdivision occurs or an attempt is made to find a single surrounding polygon that is closer to the eyepoint than any other polygon. If subdivision occurs, this question is delayed until the pixel level. In either case, a depth calculation is required.

The depth calculation is performed by comparing the depth (z coordinate) of the planes of the polygons at the window corners. If the depth of a surrounding polygon is greater than the depth of all other polygons at the corners of the window, then the surrounding polygon hides all the other polygons in the window. Hence, the window can be displayed at the intensity or color of the surrounding polygon. Note that this is a sufficient but not a necessary condition for a surrounding polygon to hide all other polygons in the window. Figure 4-41 illustrates that extending the plane of a polygon to intersect the window corners may result in failure to identify a surrounding polygon that hides all others in the window.

In particular, if an extended polygon is hidden by a surrounding polygon at the window corners, then the polygon itself is hidden by the surrounding polygon (as in Fig. 4-41). If an extended polygon is not hidden by the surrounding polygon, it is not obvious whether the polygon itself is hidden or not (b in Fig. 4-41). The conflict is resolved by subdividing the window.

The depth of an extended polygon at the window corners can be obtained from the plane equations for the polygons (see Sec. 4-3 and Example 4-3). For example, if the plane equation is

$$ax + by + cz + d = 0$$

and the window corner coordinates are x_w, y_w, then

$$z = -(d + ax_w + by_w)/c \qquad c \neq 0$$

yields the depth of the extended polygon at the window corner.

All of the above discussion assumes that every polygon is compared to every window. For complex scenes this is very inefficient. The efficiency can be improved by performing a depth priority sort (z sort). The sort order of the polygons is based on the z coordinate of the polygon vertex nearest the eyepoint. In a right handed coordinate system, the polygon with the maximum z-coordinate value for its nearest vertex is closest to the eyepoint. This polygon appears first on the sorted polygon list.

When processing each window, the algorithm looks for surrounding polygons. When a surrounding polygon is found, its vertex farthest from the eye is remembered as z_{smin}. As each successive polygon on the list is considered, the z-coordinate value of its nearest vertex z_{pmax} is compared to z_{smin}. If $z_{pmax} < z_{smin}$, then clearly this polygon is hidden by the surrounding polygon and need not be considered further. Figure 4-41 illustrates that this is a sufficient but not a necessary condition; e.g., the polygons labeled a in Fig. 4-41 need not be considered further, but the polygon labeled b must.

The size of the list of polygons processed for each window is reduced by taking advantage of information about the polygon obtained earlier in the algorithm. In particular, if a polygon surrounds a window, then clearly it surrounds all subwindows of that window and need not be processed further. In addition, if a polygon is disjoint from a window, then it is disjoint from all subwindows of that window and need not be considered when processing those subwindows. Only intersector and contained polygons from the previous window need be processed further.

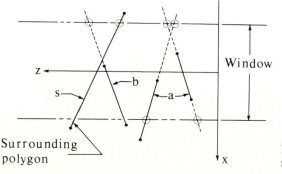

Surrounding polygon

Figure 4-41 Depth comparisons for surrounding polygons.

To take advantage of this information, three lists are used; one for surrounding polygons, one for disjoint polygons, and one for intersecting and contained polygons (see Ref. 4-11). As the subdivision progresses, polygons are added or removed from the appropriate list. The level at which a polygon is first added to a particular list is also retained. This information is used when the tree in Fig. 4-33 is traversed in the reverse direction. At each subdivision level, the surrounding polygon list is processed first to find the closest surrounding polygon. The intersector/contained polygon list is then processed to see if the surrounding polygon hides all the intersector and contained polygons. The disjoint polygon list is ignored.

The underlying concept and a number of possible enhancements of the Warnock algorithm have been discussed. It should be clear that no single Warnock algorithm exists. The implementation details vary from algorithm to algorithm. A pseudo code implementation of the most basic algorithm is given below. If the window size is greater than the display resolution and contains any feature of interest, the algorithm always subdivides the window. For windows greater than pixel size, a simple bounding box test is used to identify disjoint polygons. For pixel-sized windows a more sophisticated test is used that determines the visible polygon by examining the z coordinate of each polygon at the center of the pixel. No depth priority sort is used, nor is advantage taken of prior information about window-polygon relationships. The algorithm is implemented using a pushdown stack. The maximum stack length is

$$3(\text{screen resolution in bits } - 1) + 5$$

This simple algorithm is sufficient to demonstrate the principle without becoming submerged in data structures. For convex polygonal volumes a back-plane cull (see Sec. 4-2) is performed before passing polygons to the algorithm. A flowchart is shown in Fig. 4-42.

a simple implementation of the Warnock algorithm

a square display window is assumed
if there is anything in a window the algorithm always subdivides
the window is subdivided into four equal-sized square windows
every polygon is compared with every window
all data is assumed transformed to display window (image space) coordinates
an initial back-plane cull of self-hidden planes is assumed prior to entering the algorithm
Vertex *is an m × 3 array containing the x, y, z coordinates of each polygon* vertex.
m is the total number of polygon vertices in the scene. The vertices are assumed specified in clockwise order
N *is the number of polygons in the scene*
Polygon *is an N × 11 array containing information about individual polygons*
Polygon(, 1) *is a pointer to the location of the first polygon vertex in the* Vertex array

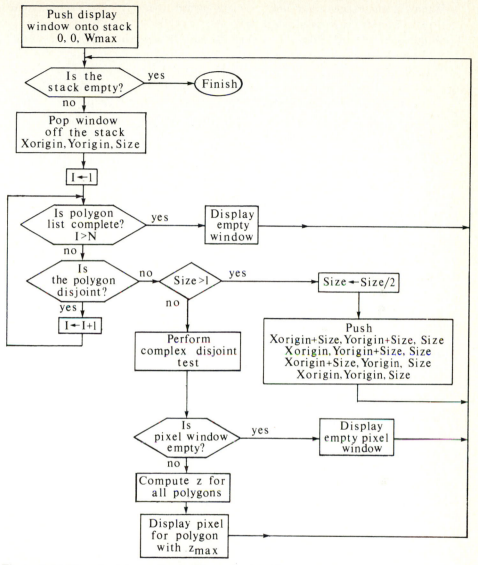

Figure 4-42 Flowchart for a simple Warnock algorithm.

Polygon(, 2) *is the number of vertices for the polygon*

Polygon(, 3) *is the intensity or color associated with the polygon*

Polygon(, 4–7) *contain the coefficients of the plane equation, a, b, c, d, for the polygon*

Polygon(, 8–11) *contain the bounding box values,* x_{min}, x_{max}, y_{min}, y_{max}, *for the polygon*

Push *is a function that places windows on a pushdown stack*

Pop *is a function that removes windows from a pushdown stack*

Wmax *is the maximum x and y extent of the window. The origin of the display window is assumed at 0, 0.*

Window *is a 1 × 3 array containing the current window origin and size as* Window(Xorigin, Yorigin, Size)

Disjoint *is a flag,*

    = 0 for empty windows

    ≥ 1 for nonempty windows

    initialize the background color for black

    Background = 0

    push the display window onto the stack

    Push Window(0, 0, Wmax)

    while (stack not empty)

        get a window from the stack

        Pop Window(Xorigin, Yorigin, Size)

        initialize polygon counter

        i = 1

        Disjoint = 0

        for each polygon perform a bounding box test to find disjoint polygons

        while (i ≤ N **and** Disjoint = 0)

            call Box(i, Polygon, Window; Disjoint)

            i = i + 1

        end while

        if at least one polygon is not disjoint, subdivide or display pixel

        if Disjoint > 0 **then**

            if window is not pixel size, subdivide

            if Size > 1 **then**

                Size = Size/2

                Push Window(Xorigin + Size, Yorigin + Size, Size)

                Push Window(Xorigin, Yorigin + Size, Size)

                Push Window(Xorigin + Size, Yorigin, Size)

                Push Window(Xorigin, Yorigin, Size)

            else

                if window is pixel-sized, calculate attributes

                call Cover(Vertex, N, Polygon, Window; Pnumber)

                if Pnumber > 0 **then**

                    call Display(Window, Polygon(Pnumber, 3))

                else

                  display the empty window

                  call Display(Window, Background)

                end if

            end if

        else

            call Display(Window, Background)

        end if

    end while
    finish

subroutine to perform a simple bounding box test
subroutine Box(i, Polygon, Window; Disjoint)
    calculate Xleft, Xright, Ybottom, Ytop
    Xleft = Window(1, 1)
    Xright = Window(1, 1) + Window(1, 3) − 1
    Ybottom = Window(1, 2)
    Ytop = Window(1, 2) + Window(1, 3) − 1
    perform bounding box tests
    Disjoint = 1
    if Polygon (i, 8) > Xright **then** Disjoint = 0
    if Polygon (i, 9) < Xleft **then** Disjoint = 0
    if Polygon (i, 10) > Ytop **then** Disjoint = 0
    if Polygon (i, 11) < Ybottom **then** Disjoint = 0
    return

subroutine to display a window
subroutine Display(Window, Intensity)
Setpixel(x, y, I) *is a function to set a pixel at coordinates x, y to the intensity I*
    for j = Window(1, 2) **to** Window(1, 2) + Window(1, 3) − 1
        for i = Window(1, 1) **to** Window(1, 1) + Window(1, 3) − 1
            Setpixel(i, j, Intensity)
        next i
    next j
    return

subroutine to check if a polygon covers the center of a window
subroutine Cover(Vertex, N, Polygon, Window; Pnumber)

a polygon covers a pixel-sized window if the center of the window is inside the polygon
if the polygon vertices are specified in clockwise order, then the inside is always to the right
the algorithm uses the Visibility subroutine presented in Sec. 3-16
if no covering polygon is found, Pnumber = 0
if at least one covering polygon is found, then Pnumber is set to the visible polygon
    initialize Zmax to zero. This assumes that all polygons are in the positive half space, Z ≥ 0
    Zmax = 0
    initially assume there are no covering polygons
    Pnumber = 0
    set up window center

```
Pointx = Window(1, 1) + Window(1, 3)/2
Pointy = Window(1, 2) + Window(1, 3)/2
for each polygon
for i = 1 to N
    Index = Polygon(i, 1)
    for each polygon edge
    for j = 1 to Polygon (i, 2) − 1
        P1x = Vertex(Index, 1)
        P1y = Vertex(Index, 2)
        P2x = Vertex(Index + 1, 1)
        P2y = Vertex(Index + 1, 2)
        note that Point, P1, P2 are shorthand for Pointx, Pointy, etc.
        call Visible(Point, P1, P2; Pvisible)
        if Pvisible < 0 then 1
        Index = Index + 1
    next j
    take care of last edge
    P1x = Vertex(Index, 1)
    P1y = Vertex(Index, 2)
    P2x = Vertex(Polygon(i, 1), 1)
    P2y = Vertex(Polygon(i, 1), 2)
    call Visible(Point, P1, P2; Pvisible)
    if Pvisible ≥ 0 then
        call Compute(Vertex, i, Polygon, Window; z)
        if z > Zmax then
            Zmax = z
            Pnumber = i
        end if
    end if
1   next i
    return
```

subroutine to calculate the pixel intensity

subroutine Compute(Vertex, N, Polygon, Window; z)

the equation of the polygon plane is used to calculate the polygon nearest the eyepoint for this pixel
Max is the maximum function

```
    calculate the x and y coordinates of the pixel center
    Xcenter = Window(1, 1) + Window(1, 3)/2
    Ycenter = Window(1, 2) + Window(1, 3)/2
    determine z at the pixel center
    check for an edge on the polygon through the pixel center
    note that a polygon of this nature may be totally missed or appear as a
```

disconnected series of dots—an example of aliasing
if Polygon(i, 6) = 0 **then**
    for j = 2 **to** Polygon(i, 2)
        z = Max(Vertex(j, 3), Vertex(j − 1, 3))
    next j
else
    calculate z from the plane equation
    A = Polygon(i, 4)
    B = Polygon(i, 5)
    C = Polygon(i, 6)
    D = Polygon(i, 7)
    z = − (A∗Xcenter + B∗Ycenter + D)/C
end if
return

An example serves to illustrate the algorithm.

Example 4-17   Warnock Algorithm

Consider the three polygons

  1:   (10, 3, 20), (20, 28, 20), (22, 28, 20), (22, 3, 20)
  2:   (5, 12, 10), (5, 20, 10), (27, 20, 10), (27, 12, 20)
  3:   (15, 15, 25), (25, 25, 5), (30, 10, 5)

to be displayed at a resolution of 32 × 32 pixels using the simple Warnock algorithm described above. The first two polygons are rectangles perpendicular to the z axis at $z = 20$ and $z = 10$, respectively. The third is a triangle that penetrates both rectangles as shown in Fig. 4-43a. Figure 4-43b shows a hidden line view from a point at infinity on the positive z axis. Figure 4-43c shows the contents of the frame buffer upon completion of the algorithm. The numbers in the boxes correspond to the polygon descriptions given above. The algorithm proceeds from the lower left corner to the right and upward. The box outlines indicate the size of the window subdivisions processed at each step in the algorithm. For example, notice the large (8 × 8) empty window in the lower left corner. This window is displayed without further subdivision. The figures show that the triangle is partially obscured by the second rectangle, penetrates the rectangle, is partially visible, is then obscured by the first rectangle, and then penetrates the first rectangle with the apex visible.

4-5   WEILER-ATHERTON ALGORITHM

Weiler and Atherton (Ref. 4-12) attempt to minimize the number of subdivisions in a Warnock-style algorithm by subdividing along polygon boundaries. The basis of the algorithm is the Weiler-Atherton polygon clipper previously

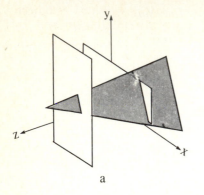

a

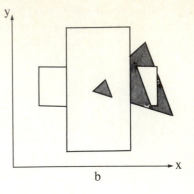

b

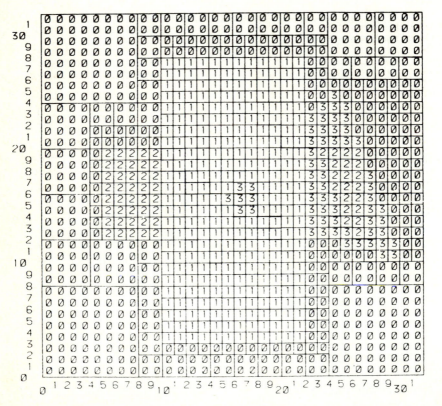

c

Figure 4-43 Polygon example for the simple Warnock algorithm.

discussed in Sec. 3-17. The output of the algorithm, which operates in object space to an arbitrary accuracy, is polygons. Since the output consists of complete polygons, the algorithm can easily be used for hidden line as well as hidden surface elimination. The hidden surface algorithm involves four steps:

A preliminary depth sort.

A clip or polygon area sort based on the polygon nearest the eyepoint.

Removal of the polygons behind that nearest the eyepoint.

Recursive subdivision, if required, and a final depth sort to remove any ambiguities.

A preliminary depth sort is used to establish an approximate depth priority list. Assuming that the eyepoint is located at infinity on the positive z axis, the polygon closest to the eyepoint and the first polygon on the list is the one with the vertex having the largest z coordinate.

A copy of the first polygon on the preliminary depth-sorted list is used as the clip polygon. The remaining polygons on the list, including the first polygon, are subject polygons. Two lists are established: an inside list and an outside list. Using the Weiler-Atherton clipping algorithm, each of the subject polygons is clipped against the clip polygon. This is a two-dimensional clip of the projections of the clip and the subject polygons. The portion of each subject polygon inside the clip polygon, if any, is placed on the inside list. The portion outside the clip polygon, if any, is placed on the outside list. This part of the algorithm is an xy or area sort. An example is shown in Fig. 4-44. Figure 4-45 illustrates the inside and outside polygon lists for the scene in Fig. 4-44. The depth of each polygon on the inside list is now compared to that of the clip polygon. Using the x, y coordinates of the vertices of the subject polygons on the inside list and their plane equations, the depth (z coordinate) of each vertex

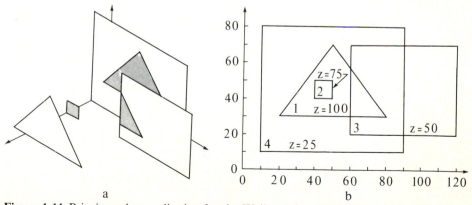

a
b

Figure 4-44 Priority polygon clipping for the Weiler-Atherton hidden surface algorithm.

Inside polygon list   Outside polygon list

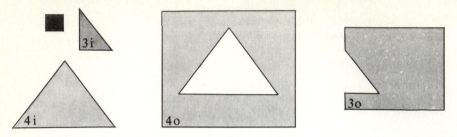

Figure 4-45 Inside and outside polygon lists.

is calculated and compared with the minimum z-coordinate value (z_{cmin}) for the clip polygon. If none of the z-coordinate values of the subject polygons on the inside list is larger than z_{cmin}, then all the subject polygons on the inside list are hidden by the clip polygon (see Fig. 4-44). These polygons are eliminated, and the inside polygon list displayed. Note that here the only remaining polygon on the inside list is the clip polygon. The algorithm continues with the outside list.

If the z coordinate for any polygon on the inside list is greater than z_{cmin}, then the subject polygon on the inside list lies at least partially in front of the clip polygon. Figure 4-46 illustrates how this can occur. In this case the original preliminary depth sort is in error. The algorithm recursively subdivides the area, using the offending polygon as the new clip polygon. The inside list is used as the subject polygon list. The original clip polygon is now clipped against the new clip polygon. Note that the new clip polygon is a copy of the complete original polygon, not the remainder after the original clip. Using a copy of the complete polygon for the new clip polygon minimizes the number of subdivisions.

A simple example more fully illustrates the algorithm.

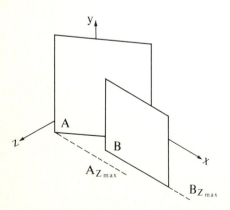

Figure 4-46 Condition for an error in the initial z sort.

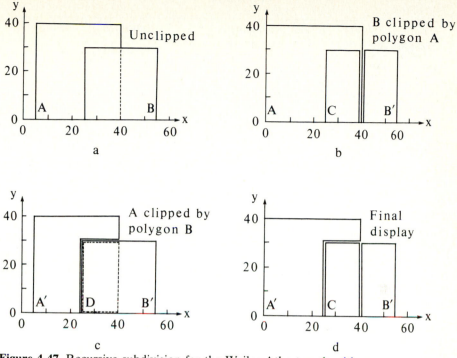

Figure 4-47 Recursive subdivision for the Weiler-Atherton algorithm.

Example 4-18   Weiler-Atherton Hidden Surface Algorithm

Consider the two rectangular polygons shown in Fig. 4-46. Polygon A has vertices (5, 0, 25), (40, 0, 5), (40, 40, 5), and (5, 40, 25). Polygon B has vertices (25, 0, 20), (55, 0, 20) (55, 30, 20), and (25, 30, 20). Figure 4-47a shows the unclipped scene from an eyepoint at infinity on the positive z axis. Although polygon B obscures part of polygon A, the preliminary depth sort places A before B on the sorted list. A copy of polygon A is used as the initial clip polygon. The initial subject polygon list contains both A and B, as shown in Table 4-10. Table 4-10 and Fig. 4-47b show the result of clipping the subject polygon list against polygon A. The inside list now contains polygons A and C, and the outside list polygon B'. Comparing the depths of polygons A and C to the clip polygon shows that C is in front of the clip polygon. The algorithm recursively subdivides the area by using polygon B, of which C is a part, as the clip polygon and the inside list as the subject polygon list. The result is shown in Fig. 4-47c and Table 4-10. The portion labeled A' is clipped away and placed on the outside list. The portion labeled D is placed on the inside list. Comparing the polygons C and D on the inside list with the clip polygon B shows that D is obscured. Hence it is eliminated. C is coincident with B, the clip polygon. It remains on the inside list. Recursion is not necessary. Polygon C is displayed. The algorithm continues to completion by extracting polygons B' and A' from the outside list. The details are given in Table 4-10. The final result is shown in Fig. 4-47d.

Table 4-10

Clip polygon	Subject polygons	Inside list	Beginning outside list	Final outside list	Display	Comment
A	A B	A C		B'		Recursion
B	A C	C D	B'	A'	C	Continue with outside list
				B'		
A'	A'	A'	B'	B'	A'	
B'	B'	B'	B'		B'	

One additional detail of the algorithm is of interest. When a single polygon cyclically overlaps the clip polygon, i.e., lies both in front of and behind the clip polygon (see Fig. 4-48a), no recursive subdivision is required. Here, all material behind the cyclical polygon has already been removed by the previous clip. It is only necessary to clip the original polygon against the cyclical polygon and display the result. The unnecessary recursive subdivision can be prevented by maintaining a list of polygons previously used as clipping polygons. If during recursive subdivision the current clipping polygon appears on this list, then a cyclical overlapping polygon has been found. No additional recursion is necessary. Note that the algorithm directly handles cases of cyclical overlap among several polygons, as shown in Fig. 4-48b.

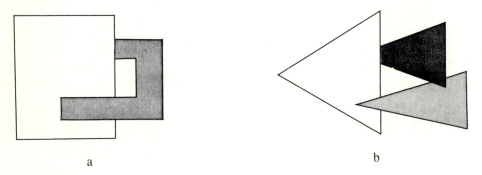

a   b

Figure 4-48 Cyclically overlapping polygons.

4-6 A SUBDIVISION ALGORITHM FOR CURVED SURFACES

Both the basic Warnock and the Weiler-Atherton subdivision algorithms assume that the scene is represented by a collection of planar polygons. However, many objects are represented by curved surfaces, e.g., aircraft, ships, automobiles, and chinaware etc. Polygonal approximations to these curved surfaces do not always yield adequate representations; e.g., silhouette edges appear as short, connected, straight line segments rather than as continuous curves. Catmull (Refs. 4-13 and 4-14) has developed a Warnock-style subdivision algorithm for curved surface display. Although Catmull applied the algorithm to bicubic surface patches, it is general enough to be applied to any curved surface. In contrast to the Warnock algorithm that recursively divides image space, the Catmull algorithm recursively subdivides the surface. Simply stated, the algorithm is

Recursively subdivide the surface into subpatches until a subpatch, transformed into image space, covers at most one pixel center.

Compute the attributes of the surface at this pixel and display the pixel.

Figure 4-49a shows a surface patch and its subdivision into pixel-sized subpatches. Unless the surface is highly curved, it is usually sufficient to use a polygonal approximation to the curved subpatch to decide whether it covers just one pixel center (see Fig. 4-49b). The subdivision process results in subpatches that do not cover any pixel center. The attributes of these patches are assigned to the nearest pixel center. Subpatches that are outside the viewing window are, of course, discarded. Subpatches that intersect the viewing window edge are further subdivided until a clear inside or outside decision is possible.

The efficiency of the algorithm depends on the efficiency of the curved surface subdivision technique. Catmull has suggested one technique for bicubic surface patches. Cohen, Lyche, and Riesenfeld (Ref. 4-15) suggest a more general technique for B-spline surfaces.

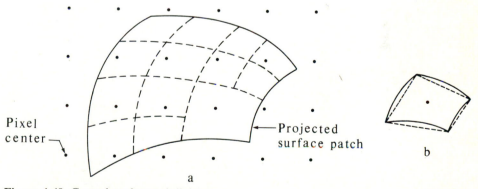

Figure 4-49 Curved surface subdivision.

4-7   z-BUFFER ALGORITHM

The z buffer is one of the simplest of the hidden surface algorithms. The technique was originally proposed by Catmull (Ref. 4-14) and is an image space algorithm. The z buffer is a simple extension of the frame buffer idea. A frame buffer is used to store the attributes (intensity) of each pixel in image space. The z buffer is a separate depth buffer used to store the z coordinate or depth of every visible pixel in image space. In use, the depth or z value of a new pixel to be written to the frame buffer is compared to the depth of that pixel stored in the z buffer. If the comparison indicates that the new pixel is in front of the pixel stored in the frame buffer, then the new pixel is written to the frame buffer and the z buffer updated with the new z value. If not, no action is taken. Conceptually, the algorithm is a search over x, y for the largest value of $z(x, y)$.

The simplicity of the algorithm is its greatest advantage. In addition, it handles the hidden surface problem and the display of complex surface intersections trivially. Scenes can be of any complexity. Since image space is of fixed size, the increase in computational work with the complexity of the scene is at most linear. Since elements of a scene or picture can be written to the frame or z buffer in arbitrary order, they need not be sorted into depth priority order. Hence, the computation time associated with a depth sort is eliminated.

The amount of storage required is the principal disadvantage of the algorithm. If the scene is transformed and clipped to a fixed range of z coordinates, then a z buffer of fixed precision can be used. Depth information must be maintained to a higher precision than lateral x, y information; 20 bits is usually sufficient. A $512 \times 512 \times 24$ bit-plane frame buffer, in combination with a $512 \times 512 \times 20$ bit z buffer, requires almost *1.5 megabytes* of storage. However, decreasing memory costs are making dedicated z-buffer memory and associated hardware practical.

An alternative to dedicated z-buffer memory is to use either main memory or mass storage for the z buffer. Smaller amounts of storage result from subdividing the image space into 4, 16, or more subsquares or bands. In the limit, a single-scan-line z buffer can be used. In the latter case an interesting scan line algorithm results (see Sec. 4-9). Because each scene element is processed multiple times, segmenting the z buffer generally increases the time required to process a scene. However, area sorting so that all polygons are not processed for each subsquare or band can significantly reduce the increase.

A further disadvantage of the z buffer is the difficulty and expense of implementing antialiasing, transparency, and translucency effects. Because the algorithm writes pixels to the frame buffer in arbitrary order, the necessary information for prefiltering antialiasing techniques (see Sec. 2-27) is not easily available. For transparency and translucency effects (see Sec. 5-9), pixels may be written to the frame buffer in incorrect order, leading to local errors.

Although prefiltering antialiasing techniques are possible (see Ref. 4-13), they are difficult to apply. However, postfiltering (subpixel averaging) techniques (see Sec. 2-26) are relatively easy to apply. Recalling that postfiltering antialiasing techniques compute the scene at an image space resolution greater than the display resolution; two approaches to postfiltering antialising are possible. The first uses a larger than display space resolution image space frame buffer and a display space resolution z buffer. The depth of the image is computed only at the center of the group of subpixels to be averaged. If intensity scaling is used to indicate distance from the observer, this technique may not be adequate.

The second technique maintains both increased image space resolution frame and z buffers. Upon displaying the image, both the pixel and the depth information are averaged. This technique requires very large amounts of storage. For example, a $512 \times 512 \times 24$ bit-plane image with 20 bits of z buffer computed at a factor of 2 increase in both x and y resolution and antialiased using uniform averaging (see Fig. 2-53a) requires almost 6 *megabytes* of storage. More formally stated, the z-buffer algorithm is

Set the frame buffer to the background intensity or color.

Set the z buffer to the minimum z value.

Scan-convert each polygon in arbitrary order.

For each Pixel(x, y) in the polygon, calculate the depth $z(x, y)$ at that pixel.

Compare the depth $z(x, y)$ with the value stored in the z buffer at that location, Zbuffer(x, y).

If $z(x, y) >$ Zbuffer(x, y), then write the polygon attributes (intensity, color, etc.) to the frame buffer and replace Zbuffer(x,y) with $z(x,y)$.

Otherwise, no action is taken.

A back-face cull (see Sec. 4-2), where appropriate, is applied as a preliminary step.

If the plane equation for each polygon is available, calculation of the depth at each pixel on a scan line can be done incrementally. Recall the plane equation

$$ax + by + cz + d = 0$$

and

$$z = -(ax + by + d)/c \neq 0$$

On a scan line $y =$ constant. Thus, the depth of the pixel at $x_1 = x + \Delta x$ along the scan line is

$$z_1 - z = -(ax_1 + d)/c + (ax + d)/c = a(x - x_1)/c$$

or

$$z_1 = z - (a/c)\Delta x$$

But $\Delta x = 1$, so

$$z_1 = z - (a/c)$$

An example serves to further illustrate the algorithm.

Example 4-19   z-Buffer Algorithm

Consider the rectangle with corner coordinates $P_1(10, 5, 10)$, $P_2(10, 25, 10)$, $P_3(25, 25, 10)$, $P_4(25, 5, 10)$ and the triangle with vertices $P_5(15, 15, 15)$, $P_6(25, 25, 5)$, $P_7(30, 10, 5)$. The triangle penetrates the rectangle from behind, as shown in Fig. 4-50. The polygons are to be displayed at an image resolution of 32×32, using a simple 2-bit-plane frame buffer. In the frame buffer the background is represented by 0, the rectangle by 1, and the triangle by 2. The z buffer is $32 \times 32 \times 4$ bit planes. The z-buffer range is thus from 0 to 16. The viewpoint is at infinity on the positive z axis, as shown in Fig. 4-50b.

Initially both the frame buffer and the z buffer are set to zero. After scan-converting the rectangle, the frame buffer contents are

```
0 0 0 0 0 0 0 0 0 0 0 0 0 0 0 0 0 0 0 0 0 0 0 0 0 0 0 0 0 0 0 0
0 0 0 0 0 0 0 0 0 0 0 0 0 0 0 0 0 0 0 0 0 0 0 0 0 0 0 0 0 0 0 0
0 0 0 0 0 0 0 0 0 0 0 0 0 0 0 0 0 0 0 0 0 0 0 0 0 0 0 0 0 0 0 0
0 0 0 0 0 0 0 0 0 0 0 0 0 0 0 0 0 0 0 0 0 0 0 0 0 0 0 0 0 0 0 0
0 0 0 0 0 0 0 0 0 0 0 0 0 0 0 0 0 0 0 0 0 0 0 0 0 0 0 0 0 0 0 0
0 0 0 0 0 0 0 0 0 0 0 0 0 0 0 0 0 0 0 0 0 0 0 0 0 0 0 0 0 0 0 0
0 0 0 0 0 0 0 0 0 0 0 0 0 0 0 0 0 0 0 0 0 0 0 0 0 0 0 0 0 0 0 0
0 0 0 0 0 0 0 0 0 0 1 1 1 1 1 1 1 1 1 1 1 1 1 1 1 1 0 0 0 0 0 0
0 0 0 0 0 0 0 0 0 0 1 1 1 1 1 1 1 1 1 1 1 1 1 1 1 1 0 0 0 0 0 0
0 0 0 0 0 0 0 0 0 0 1 1 1 1 1 1 1 1 1 1 1 1 1 1 1 1 0 0 0 0 0 0
0 0 0 0 0 0 0 0 0 0 1 1 1 1 1 1 1 1 1 1 1 1 1 1 1 1 0 0 0 0 0 0
0 0 0 0 0 0 0 0 0 0 1 1 1 1 1 1 1 1 1 1 1 1 1 1 1 1 0 0 0 0 0 0
0 0 0 0 0 0 0 0 0 0 1 1 1 1 1 1 1 1 1 1 1 1 1 1 1 1 0 0 0 0 0 0
0 0 0 0 0 0 0 0 0 0 1 1 1 1 1 1 1 1 1 1 1 1 1 1 1 1 0 0 0 0 0 0
0 0 0 0 0 0 0 0 0 0 1 1 1 1 1 1 1 1 1 1 1 1 1 1 1 1 0 0 0 0 0 0
0 0 0 0 0 0 0 0 0 0 1 1 1 1 1 1 1 1 1 1 1 1 1 1 1 1 0 0 0 0 0 0
0 0 0 0 0 0 0 0 0 0 1 1 1 1 1 1 1 1 1 1 1 1 1 1 1 1 0 0 0 0 0 0
0 0 0 0 0 0 0 0 0 0 1 1 1 1 1 1 1 1 1 1 1 1 1 1 1 1 0 0 0 0 0 0
0 0 0 0 0 0 0 0 0 0 1 1 1 1 1 1 1 1 1 1 1 1 1 1 1 1 0 0 0 0 0 0
0 0 0 0 0 0 0 0 0 0 1 1 1 1 1 1 1 1 1 1 1 1 1 1 1 1 0 0 0 0 0 0
0 0 0 0 0 0 0 0 0 0 1 1 1 1 1 1 1 1 1 1 1 1 1 1 1 1 0 0 0 0 0 0
0 0 0 0 0 0 0 0 0 0 1 1 1 1 1 1 1 1 1 1 1 1 1 1 1 1 0 0 0 0 0 0
0 0 0 0 0 0 0 0 0 0 1 1 1 1 1 1 1 1 1 1 1 1 1 1 1 1 0 0 0 0 0 0
0 0 0 0 0 0 0 0 0 0 1 1 1 1 1 1 1 1 1 1 1 1 1 1 1 1 0 0 0 0 0 0
0 0 0 0 0 0 0 0 0 0 1 1 1 1 1 1 1 1 1 1 1 1 1 1 1 1 0 0 0 0 0 0
0 0 0 0 0 0 0 0 0 0 1 1 1 1 1 1 1 1 1 1 1 1 1 1 1 1 0 0 0 0 0 0
0 0 0 0 0 0 0 0 0 0 1 1 1 1 1 1 1 1 1 1 1 1 1 1 1 1 0 0 0 0 0 0
0 0 0 0 0 0 0 0 0 0 0 0 0 0 0 0 0 0 0 0 0 0 0 0 0 0 0 0 0 0 0 0
0 0 0 0 0 0 0 0 0 0 0 0 0 0 0 0 0 0 0 0 0 0 0 0 0 0 0 0 0 0 0 0
0 0 0 0 0 0 0 0 0 0 0 0 0 0 0 0 0 0 0 0 0 0 0 0 0 0 0 0 0 0 0 0
0 0 0 0 0 0 0 0 0 0 0 0 0 0 0 0 0 0 0 0 0 0 0 0 0 0 0 0 0 0 0 0
0 0 0 0 0 0 0 0 0 0 0 0 0 0 0 0 0 0 0 0 0 0 0 0 0 0 0 0 0 0 0 0
```

The z-buffer contents are

```
0 0 0 0 0 0 0 0 0 0 0 0 0 0 0 0 0 0 0 0 0 0 0 0 0 0 0 0 0 0 0 0 0 0 0 0 0 0
0 0 0 0 0 0 0 0 0 0 0 0 0 0 0 0 0 0 0 0 0 0 0 0 0 0 0 0 0 0 0 0 0 0 0 0 0 0
0 0 0 0 0 0 0 0 0 0 0 0 0 0 0 0 0 0 0 0 0 0 0 0 0 0 0 0 0 0 0 0 0 0 0 0 0 0
0 0 0 0 0 0 0 0 0 0 0 0 0 0 0 0 0 0 0 0 0 0 0 0 0 0 0 0 0 0 0 0 0 0 0 0 0 0
0 0 0 0 0 0 0 0 0 0 0 0 0 0 0 0 0 0 0 0 0 0 0 0 0 0 0 0 0 0 0 0 0 0 0 0 0 0
0 0 0 0 0 0 0 0 0 0 0 0 0 0 0 0 0 0 0 0 0 0 0 0 0 0 0 0 0 0 0 0 0 0 0 0 0 0
0 0 0 0 0 0 0 0 0 0 0 0 0 0 0 0 0 0 0 0 0 0 0 0 0 0 0 0 0 0 0 0 0 0 0 0 0 0
0 0 0 0 0 0 0 0 0 10 10 10 10 10 10 10 10 10 10 10 10 10 10 10 0 0 0 0 0 0 0 0
0 0 0 0 0 0 0 0 0 10 10 10 10 10 10 10 10 10 10 10 10 10 10 10 0 0 0 0 0 0 0 0
0 0 0 0 0 0 0 0 0 10 10 10 10 10 10 10 10 10 10 10 10 10 10 10 0 0 0 0 0 0 0 0
0 0 0 0 0 0 0 0 0 10 10 10 10 10 10 10 10 10 10 10 10 10 10 10 0 0 0 0 0 0 0 0
0 0 0 0 0 0 0 0 0 10 10 10 10 10 10 10 10 10 10 10 10 10 10 10 0 0 0 0 0 0 0 0
0 0 0 0 0 0 0 0 0 10 10 10 10 10 10 10 10 10 10 10 10 10 10 10 0 0 0 0 0 0 0 0
0 0 0 0 0 0 0 0 0 10 10 10 10 10 10 10 10 10 10 10 10 10 10 10 0 0 0 0 0 0 0 0
0 0 0 0 0 0 0 0 0 10 10 10 10 10 10 10 10 10 10 10 10 10 10 10 0 0 0 0 0 0 0 0
0 0 0 0 0 0 0 0 0 10 10 10 10 10 10 10 10 10 10 10 10 10 10 10 0 0 0 0 0 0 0 0
0 0 0 0 0 0 0 0 0 10 10 10 10 10 10 10 10 10 10 10 10 10 10 10 0 0 0 0 0 0 0 0
0 0 0 0 0 0 0 0 0 10 10 10 10 10 10 10 10 10 10 10 10 10 10 10 0 0 0 0 0 0 0 0
0 0 0 0 0 0 0 0 0 10 10 10 10 10 10 10 10 10 10 10 10 10 10 10 0 0 0 0 0 0 0 0
0 0 0 0 0 0 0 0 0 10 10 10 10 10 10 10 10 10 10 10 10 10 10 10 0 0 0 0 0 0 0 0
0 0 0 0 0 0 0 0 0 10 10 10 10 10 10 10 10 10 10 10 10 10 10 10 0 0 0 0 0 0 0 0
0 0 0 0 0 0 0 0 0 10 10 10 10 10 10 10 10 10 10 10 10 10 10 10 0 0 0 0 0 0 0 0
0 0 0 0 0 0 0 0 0 10 10 10 10 10 10 10 10 10 10 10 10 10 10 10 0 0 0 0 0 0 0 0
0 0 0 0 0 0 0 0 0 10 10 10 10 10 10 10 10 10 10 10 10 10 10 10 0 0 0 0 0 0 0 0
0 0 0 0 0 0 0 0 0 10 10 10 10 10 10 10 10 10 10 10 10 10 10 10 0 0 0 0 0 0 0 0
0 0 0 0 0 0 0 0 0 10 10 10 10 10 10 10 10 10 10 10 10 10 10 10 0 0 0 0 0 0 0 0
0 0 0 0 0 0 0 0 0 10 10 10 10 10 10 10 10 10 10 10 10 10 10 10 0 0 0 0 0 0 0 0
0 0 0 0 0 0 0 0 0 0 0 0 0 0 0 0 0 0 0 0 0 0 0 0 0 0 0 0 0 0 0 0 0 0 0 0 0 0
0 0 0 0 0 0 0 0 0 0 0 0 0 0 0 0 0 0 0 0 0 0 0 0 0 0 0 0 0 0 0 0 0 0 0 0 0 0
0 0 0 0 0 0 0 0 0 0 0 0 0 0 0 0 0 0 0 0 0 0 0 0 0 0 0 0 0 0 0 0 0 0 0 0 0 0
0 0 0 0 0 0 0 0 0 0 0 0 0 0 0 0 0 0 0 0 0 0 0 0 0 0 0 0 0 0 0 0 0 0 0 0 0 0
```

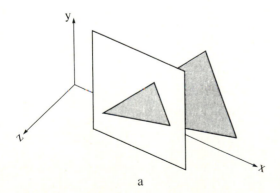

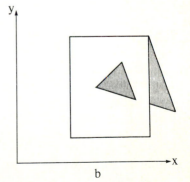

a   b

Figure 4-50 Penetrating triangle.

Recall that the lower left corner pixel is (0, 0).

Using Newell's method (see Sec. 4-3, Example 4-3), the plane equation for the triangle is

$$3x + y + 4z - 120 = 0$$

Hence, the depth of the triangle at any location is

$$z = -(3x + y - 120)/4$$

For succeeding pixels on a scan line

$$z_1 = z - 3/4$$

Calculating the intersections of the triangle edges with the scan lines, using the half scan line convention, yields the intersection pairs (24.5, 25.2), (23.5, 25.5), (22.5, 25.8), (21.5, 26.2), (20.5, 26.5), (19.5, 26.8), (18.5, 27.2), (17.5, 27.5), (16.5, 27.8), (15.5, 28.2), (16.5, 28.5), (19.5, 28.8), (22.5, 29.2), (25.5, 29.5), (28.5, 29.8) for scan lines 24 to 10. Recall that a pixel whose center is inside or on the triangle edge, i.e. for $x_1 \le x \le x_2$, is activated. Scan-converting and comparing the depth of each pixel with the z-buffer value yields the new frame buffer contents

```
0 0 0 0 0 0 0 0 0 0 0 0 0 0 0 0 0 0 0 0 0 0 0 0 0 0 0 0 0 0 0 0 0 0 0 0
0 0 0 0 0 0 0 0 0 0 0 0 0 0 0 0 0 0 0 0 0 0 0 0 0 0 0 0 0 0 0 0 0 0 0 0
0 0 0 0 0 0 0 0 0 0 0 0 0 0 0 0 0 0 0 0 0 0 0 0 0 0 0 0 0 0 0 0 0 0 0 0
0 0 0 0 0 0 0 0 0 0 0 0 0 0 0 0 0 0 0 0 0 0 0 0 0 0 0 0 0 0 0 0 0 0 0 0
0 0 0 0 0 0 0 0 0 0 0 0 0 0 0 0 0 0 0 0 0 0 0 0 0 0 0 0 0 0 0 0 0 0 0 0
0 0 0 0 0 0 0 0 0 0 0 0 0 0 0 0 0 0 0 0 0 0 0 0 0 0 0 0 0 0 0 0 0 0 0 0
0 0 0 0 0 0 0 0 0 0 0 0 0 0 0 0 0 0 0 0 0 0 0 0 0 0 0 0 0 0 0 0 0 0 0 0
0 0 0 0 0 0 0 0 0 0 0 0 0 0 0 0 0 0 0 0 0 0 0 0 0 0 0 0 0 0 0 0 0 0 0 0
0 0 0 0 0 0 0 0 0 0 0 1 1 1 1 1 1 1 1 1 1 1 1 1 1 1 0 0 0 0 0 0 0 0 0 0
0 0 0 0 0 0 0 0 0 0 0 1 1 1 1 1 1 1 1 1 1 1 1 1 1 1 2 0 0 0 0 0 0 0 0 0
0 0 0 0 0 0 0 0 0 0 0 1 1 1 1 1 1 1 1 1 1 1 1 1 1 1 2 0 0 0 0 0 0 0 0 0
0 0 0 0 0 0 0 0 0 0 0 1 1 1 1 1 1 1 1 1 1 1 1 1 1 1 2 0 0 0 0 0 0 0 0 0
0 0 0 0 0 0 0 0 0 0 0 1 1 1 1 1 1 1 1 1 1 1 1 1 1 1 2 2 0 0 0 0 0 0 0 0
0 0 0 0 0 0 0 0 0 0 0 1 1 1 1 1 1 1 1 1 2 1 1 1 1 1 2 2 0 0 0 0 0 0 0 0
0 0 0 0 0 0 0 0 0 0 0 1 1 1 1 1 1 1 1 2 2 1 1 1 1 1 2 2 0 0 0 0 0 0 0 0
0 0 0 0 0 0 0 0 0 0 0 1 1 1 1 1 1 1 2 2 2 2 1 1 1 1 2 2 2 0 0 0 0 0 0 0
0 0 0 0 0 0 0 0 0 0 0 1 1 1 1 1 1 2 2 2 2 2 1 1 1 1 2 2 2 0 0 0 0 0 0 0
0 0 0 0 0 0 0 0 0 0 0 1 1 1 1 1 1 2 2 2 2 2 2 1 1 1 2 2 2 2 0 0 0 0 0 0
0 0 0 0 0 0 0 0 0 0 0 1 1 1 1 1 1 1 2 2 2 2 2 2 1 1 1 2 2 2 2 0 0 0 0 0
0 0 0 0 0 0 0 0 0 0 0 1 1 1 1 1 1 1 1 2 2 2 2 1 1 1 2 2 2 2 0 0 0 0 0 0
0 0 0 0 0 0 0 0 0 0 0 1 1 1 1 1 1 1 1 1 2 2 2 1 1 1 2 2 2 2 0 0 0 0 0 0
0 0 0 0 0 0 0 0 0 0 0 1 1 1 1 1 1 1 1 1 1 1 1 1 1 1 2 2 2 2 0 0 0 0 0 0
0 0 0 0 0 0 0 0 0 0 0 1 1 1 1 1 1 1 1 1 1 1 1 1 1 1 2 2 2 2 2 0 0 0 0 0
0 0 0 0 0 0 0 0 0 0 0 1 1 1 1 1 1 1 1 1 1 1 1 1 1 1 0 0 0 2 2 0 0 0 0 0
0 0 0 0 0 0 0 0 0 0 0 1 1 1 1 1 1 1 1 1 1 1 1 1 1 1 0 0 0 0 0 0 0 0 0 0
0 0 0 0 0 0 0 0 0 0 0 1 1 1 1 1 1 1 1 1 1 1 1 1 1 1 0 0 0 0 0 0 0 0 0 0
0 0 0 0 0 0 0 0 0 0 0 1 1 1 1 1 1 1 1 1 1 1 1 1 1 1 0 0 0 0 0 0 0 0 0 0
0 0 0 0 0 0 0 0 0 0 0 1 1 1 1 1 1 1 1 1 1 1 1 1 1 1 0 0 0 0 0 0 0 0 0 0
0 0 0 0 0 0 0 0 0 0 0 1 1 1 1 1 1 1 1 1 1 1 1 1 1 1 0 0 0 0 0 0 0 0 0 0
0 0 0 0 0 0 0 0 0 0 0 1 1 1 1 1 1 1 1 1 1 1 1 1 1 1 0 0 0 0 0 0 0 0 0 0
0 0 0 0 0 0 0 0 0 0 0 1 1 1 1 1 1 1 1 1 1 1 1 1 1 1 0 0 0 0 0 0 0 0 0 0
0 0 0 0 0 0 0 0 0 0 0 0 0 0 0 0 0 0 0 0 0 0 0 0 0 0 0 0 0 0 0 0 0 0 0 0
0 0 0 0 0 0 0 0 0 0 0 0 0 0 0 0 0 0 0 0 0 0 0 0 0 0 0 0 0 0 0 0 0 0 0 0
0 0 0 0 0 0 0 0 0 0 0 0 0 0 0 0 0 0 0 0 0 0 0 0 0 0 0 0 0 0 0 0 0 0 0 0
0 0 0 0 0 0 0 0 0 0 0 0 0 0 0 0 0 0 0 0 0 0 0 0 0 0 0 0 0 0 0 0 0 0 0 0
0 0 0 0 0 0 0 0 0 0 0 0 0 0 0 0 0 0 0 0 0 0 0 0 0 0 0 0 0 0 0 0 0 0 0 0
```

After processing the triangle the z-buffer contents are

```
0 0 0 0 0 0 0 0 0 0 0 0 0 0 0 0 0 0 0 0 0 0 0 0 0 0 0 0 0 0 0 0 0 0
0 0 0 0 0 0 0 0 0 0 0 0 0 0 0 0 0 0 0 0 0 0 0 0 0 0 0 0 0 0 0 0 0 0
0 0 0 0 0 0 0 0 0 0 0 0 0 0 0 0 0 0 0 0 0 0 0 0 0 0 0 0 0 0 0 0 0 0
0 0 0 0 0 0 0 0 0 0 0 0 0 0 0 0 0 0 0 0 0 0 0 0 0 0 0 0 0 0 0 0 0 0
0 0 0 0 0 0 0 0 0 0 0 0 0 0 0 0 0 0 0 0 0 0 0 0 0 0 0 0 0 0 0 0 0 0
0 0 0 0 0 0 0 0 0 0 0 0 0 0 0 0 0 0 0 0 0 0 0 0 0 0 0 0 0 0 0 0 0 0
0 0 0 0 0 0 0 0 0 0 0 0 0 0 0 0 0 0 0 0 0 0 0 0 0 0 0 0 0 0 0 0 0 0
0 0 0 0 0 0 0 0 0 0 10 10 10 10 10 10 10 10 10 10 10 10 10 10 10 10 0 0 0 0 0 0 0 0
0 0 0 0 0 0 0 0 0 0 10 10 10 10 10 10 10 10 10 10 10 10 10 10 10 10 5 0 0 0 0 0 0 0
0 0 0 0 0 0 0 0 0 0 10 10 10 10 10 10 10 10 10 10 10 10 10 10 10 10 5 0 0 0 0 0 0 0
0 0 0 0 0 0 0 0 0 0 10 10 10 10 10 10 10 10 10 10 10 10 10 10 10 10 6 0 0 0 0 0 0 0
0 0 0 0 0 0 0 0 0 0 10 10 10 10 10 10 10 10 10 10 10 10 10 10 10 10 6 5 0 0 0 0 0 0
0 0 0 0 0 0 0 0 0 0 10 10 10 10 10 10 10 10 10 11 10 10 10 10 10 10 6 5 0 0 0 0 0 0
0 0 0 0 0 0 0 0 0 0 10 10 10 10 10 10 10 10 12 11 10 10 10 10 10 10 6 6 0 0 0 0 0 0
0 0 0 0 0 0 0 0 0 0 10 10 10 10 10 10 10 13 12 11 10 10 10 10 10 10 7 6 5 0 0 0 0 0
0 0 0 0 0 0 0 0 0 0 10 10 10 10 10 10 14 13 12 11 11 10 10 10 10 10 7 6 5 0 0 0 0 0
0 0 0 0 0 0 0 0 0 0 10 10 10 10 10 15 14 13 12 12 11 10 10 10 10 10 7 6 6 0 0 0 0 0
0 0 0 0 0 0 0 0 0 0 10 10 10 10 10 10 14 13 13 12 11 10 10 10 10 10 7 7 6 5 0 0 0 0
0 0 0 0 0 0 0 0 0 0 10 10 10 10 10 10 10 10 12 11 11 10 10 10 10 10 8 7 6 5 0 0 0 0
0 0 0 0 0 0 0 0 0 0 10 10 10 10 10 10 10 10 10 10 10 10 10 10 10 10 8 7 6 6 0 0 0 0
0 0 0 0 0 0 0 0 0 0 10 10 10 10 10 10 10 10 10 10 10 10 10 10 10 10 8 7 7 6 5 0 0 0
0 0 0 0 0 0 0 0 0 0 10 10 10 10 10 10 10 10 10 10 10 10 10 10 10 10 0 0 6 5 0 0 0 0
0 0 0 0 0 0 0 0 0 0 10 10 10 10 10 10 10 10 10 10 10 10 10 10 10 10 0 0 0 0 0 0 0 0
0 0 0 0 0 0 0 0 0 0 10 10 10 10 10 10 10 10 10 10 10 10 10 10 10 10 0 0 0 0 0 0 0 0
0 0 0 0 0 0 0 0 0 0 10 10 10 10 10 10 10 10 10 10 10 10 10 10 10 10 0 0 0 0 0 0 0 0
0 0 0 0 0 0 0 0 0 0 10 10 10 10 10 10 10 10 10 10 10 10 10 10 10 10 0 0 0 0 0 0 0 0
0 0 0 0 0 0 0 0 0 0 10 10 10 10 10 10 10 10 10 10 10 10 10 10 10 10 0 0 0 0 0 0 0 0
0 0 0 0 0 0 0 0 0 0 0 0 0 0 0 0 0 0 0 0 0 0 0 0 0 0 0 0 0 0 0 0 0 0
0 0 0 0 0 0 0 0 0 0 0 0 0 0 0 0 0 0 0 0 0 0 0 0 0 0 0 0 0 0 0 0 0 0
0 0 0 0 0 0 0 0 0 0 0 0 0 0 0 0 0 0 0 0 0 0 0 0 0 0 0 0 0 0 0 0 0 0
0 0 0 0 0 0 0 0 0 0 0 0 0 0 0 0 0 0 0 0 0 0 0 0 0 0 0 0 0 0 0 0 0 0
0 0 0 0 0 0 0 0 0 0 0 0 0 0 0 0 0 0 0 0 0 0 0 0 0 0 0 0 0 0 0 0 0 0
```

As a specific example, consider the pixel at (20, 15). Evaluating z at the center of the pixel yields

$$z = -[(3)(20.5) + 15.5 - 120]/4 = 43/4 = 10.75$$

Comparing it to the z-buffer value at (20, 15) after processing the rectangle shows that the triangle is in front of the rectangle. Thus, the frame buffer value at (20, 15) is changed to 2. Since for the purposes of this example the z buffer is only 4 bits deep and thus has a range of only 0 to 15, the z value is rounded to the nearest whole number. Consequently, the value 11 is placed in the z buffer at location (20, 15).

The line of intersection of the triangle and the rectangle is obtained by substituting $z = 10$ into the plane equation for the triangle. The result is

$$3x + y - 80 = 0$$

The intersection of this line with the triangle edges is at (20, 20) and (22.5, 12.5). This line of intersection where the triangle becomes visible is clearly shown by the frame buffer contents.

The z-buffer algorithm can also be used for surface sectioning. Here, the comparison is modified to

$$z(x, y) > \text{Zbuffer}(x, y) \quad \textbf{and} \quad z(x, y) \le \text{Zsection}$$

where Zsection is the desired section location. The effect is to retain only those elements at or behind Zsection.

4-8   LIST PRIORITY ALGORITHMS

The implementation of all the hidden line and hidden surface algorithms discussed above involves establishing the priority, i.e., the depth or distance from the viewpoint, of objects in a scene. The list priority algorithms attempt to capitalize on this by performing the depth or priority sort first. The objective of the sort is to obtain a definitive list of scene elements in depth priority order based on distance from the viewpoint. If the list is definitive, then no two elements overlap in depth. Starting with the scene element farthest from the viewpoint, each element is written to a frame buffer in turn. Closer elements on the list overwrite the contents of the frame buffer. Thus, the hidden surface problem is trivially solved. Transparency effects can be incorporated into the algorithm by only partially overwriting the contents of the frame buffer with the attributes of the transparent element (see Ref. 4-16 and Sec. 5-8).

For simple scene elements, e.g. polygons, the technique is sometimes called the painter's algorithm because it is analogous to that used by an artist in creating a painting. The artist first paints the background, then the elements in the intermediate distance, and finally the elements in the foreground. The artist solves the hidden surface or visibility problem by constructing the painting in reverse priority order.

For a simple scene, such as that shown in Fig. 4-51a, obtaining a definitive depth priority list is straightforward. For example, the polygons can be sorted by either their maximum or minimum z-coordinate value. However, for the scene shown in Fig. 4-51b, a definitive depth priority list cannot be obtained by simply sorting in z. If P and Q in Fig. 4-51b are sorted by the minimum z-coordinate value ($z_{\min}$), then P appears on the depth priority list before Q. If

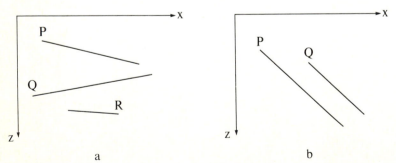

Figure 4-51 Polygonal priority.

P and Q are written to the frame buffer in this order, then Q will appear to partially hide P. However, P in fact partially hides Q. The correct order in the priority list is obtained by interchanging P and Q.

A further difficulty is illustrated by Fig. 4-52. Here, the polygons cyclically overlap each other. In Fig. 4-52a P is in front of Q which is in front of R which in turn is in front of P. For Fig. 4-52b, P is in front of Q which is in front of P. A similar cyclical overlap occurs for penetrating polygons, e.g., the triangle that penetrates the rectangle in Fig. 4-50. There, the rectangle is in front of the triangle which is in front of the rectangle. In both examples a definitive depth priority list cannot be immediately established. The solution is to cyclically split the polygons along their plane of intersection until a definitive priority list is obtained. This is shown by the dashed lines in Figs. 4-52a and b.

Newell, Newell, and Sancha (Ref. 4-16) developed a special sorting technique for resolving priority conflicts on the depth priority list. This special sorting technique is incorporated into the Newell-Newell-Sancha algorithm given below. The algorithm computes a new depth priority list dynamically before processing each frame of a scene. No restrictions are placed on the complexity of the scene environment nor on the type of polygon used to describe elements of the scene. The Newell-Newell-Sancha algorithm is designed to process polygons. Newell (Ref. 4-17) has extended the concept to three-dimensional volumes. Newell's extension is not restricted to polyhedral volumes. It also allows the processing of volumes of mixed types within the same scene.

The Newell-Newell-Sancha algorithm for polygons is

Establish a preliminary depth priority list, using z_{min} for each polygon as the sort key. The first polygon on the list is the one with the smallest value of z_{min}. This polygon, labeled P, is the farthest from a viewpoint at infinity on the positive z axis. The next polygon on the list is labeled Q.

For each polygon on the list examine the relationship of P to Q.

If the nearest vertex of P, $P_{z_{max}}$, is farther from the viewpoint then the farthest vertex of Q, $Q_{z_{min}}$, i.e. $Q_{z_{min}} \geq P_{z_{max}}$, then no part of P can hide Q. Write P to the frame buffer (see Fig. 4-51a).

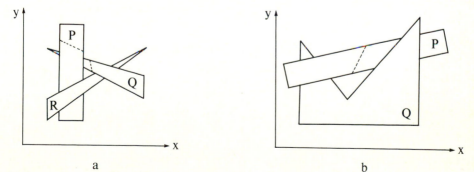

a   b

Figure 4-52 Cyclical overlapping polygons.

If $Q_{z_{min}} < P_{z_{max}}$, then P potentially obscures not only Q but also any polygon on the list for which $Q_{z_{min}} < P_{z_{max}}$. This is the set $\{Q\}$. However, P may not hide any part of any polygon in the set $\{Q\}$. If this can be determined, then P may be written to the frame buffer. A series of tests of increasing computational difficulty is used to answer this question. The tests are posed as questions. If the answer to any question is yes, then P cannot obscure $\{Q\}$. P is then immediately written to the frame buffer. The tests are

Are the bounding boxes of P and Q disjoint in x?

Are the bounding boxes of P and Q disjoint in y?

Is P wholly on the side of the plane of Q farther from the viewpoint? (See Fig. 4-53a.)

Is Q wholly on the side of the plane of P nearer the viewpoint? (See Fig. 4-53b.)

Are the projections of P and Q disjoint?

Each test is applied to each element of $\{Q\}$. If none of these tests successfully writes P to the frame buffer, then P can obscure Q.

Interchange P and Q, marking the position of Q on the list. Repeat the tests with the rearranged list. This is successful for Fig. 4-51b.

If an attempt is made to swap Q again, a cyclical overlap exists (see Fig. 4-52). In this case, P is split along the plane of Q, the original polygon removed from the list, and the two parts of P placed on the list. The tests are then repeated with the new list. This step prevents infinite looping.

Combined, the first two steps for determining whether P obscures Q are a normal bounding box test (see Secs. 2-13 and 3-1). Since many scenes are not square, it is more likely that the polygon bounding boxes will overlap in one direction than in the other. When polygons are primarily horizontal or vertical,

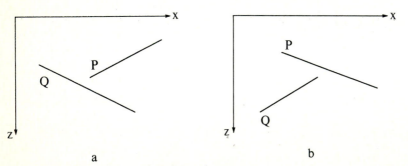

a b

Figure 4-53 Tests for overlapping polygons.

using individual tests is more efficient. As written, the algorithm assumes the scene is wider than it is high, and thus polygons are primarily horizontal. The order of the tests is interchanged if the scene is higher than it is wide. If the scene is square, or if its composition is isomorphic, then the order of the tests is immaterial.

The third and fourth tests can be implemented using any of the visibility tests previously discussed (see Sec. 3-15 and Example 3-22). Since the plane equation or the normal for each polygon is frequently available, a simple substitution test is convenient. If the relationship of the polygon Q to the polygon P is desired, then the coordinates of the vertices of Q are substituted into the plane equation of P. If the signs of the results are all the same, then Q lies wholly on one side of P. As with the other hidden surface algorithms discussed previously, a preliminary back-face cull is used if appropriate. Example 4-20 more fully illustrates this for polygons skewed in space.

Example 4-20   Relationship Test for Skewed Polygons

Consider the three polygons P, Q_1, Q_2 shown in Fig. 4-54. The polygon vertices are

P: (1, 1, 1), (4, 5, 2), (5, 2, 5)
Q_1: (2, 2, 0.5), (3, 3, 1.75), (6, 1, 0.5)
Q_2: (0.5, 2, 5.5), (2, 5, 3), (4, 4, 5)

It is desired to determine if Q_1 and Q_2 are wholly on one side of P. This is not clear from the three orthographic views in Fig. 4-54. The plane equation of P is

$$15x - 8y - 13z + 6 = 0$$

The test function is then

$$T.F. = 15x - 8y - 13z + 6$$

Substituting the vertices of Q_1 into the test function yields

$$T.F._1 = 15(2) - 8(2) - 13(0.5) + 6 = 13.5 > 0$$
$$T.F._2 = 15(3) - 8(3) - 13(1.75) + 6 = 4.25 > 0$$
$$T.F._3 = 15(6) - 8(1) - 13(0.5) + 6 = 81.5 > 0$$

Since the sign of all the test functions is positive, the polygon Q_1 lies wholly on one side of the plane of P.

Substituting the vertices of Q_2 into the test function yields

$$T.F._4 = 15(0.5) - 8(2) - 13(5.5) + 6 = -74 < 0$$
$$T.F._5 = 15(2) - 8(5) - 13(3) + 6 = -43 < 0$$
$$T.F._6 = 15(4) - 8(4) - 13(5) + 6 = -31 < 0$$

Again, all the signs of the test functions are the same; and the polygon Q_2 lies wholly on one side of the plane of P.

Figure 4-54d clearly shows that Q_1 is on the side of the plane of P away from a viewpoint at infinity on the positive z axis. Hence, it is partially obscured by P. Similarly, Fig. 4-54d clearly shows that Q_2 is on the side of the plane of P nearer a viewpoint at infinity on the positive z axis. Thus, it will partially obscure P.

From this example it is clear that

> If the signs of the test function for every vertex of a polygon are the same and positive or zero, then the polygon is on the far (hidden) side of the plane of P.

> If the signs of the test function for every vertex of a polygon are the same and negative or zero, then the polygon is on the the near (visible) side of the plane of P.

> If the test functions for every vertex of a polygon are zero, then the polygon lies in the plane of P.

The last of the series of tests is particularly expensive because it requires a full determination of whether the projections of P and Q are disjoint. These techniques have previously been discussed in the context of the Warnock algorithm (see Sec. 4-4).

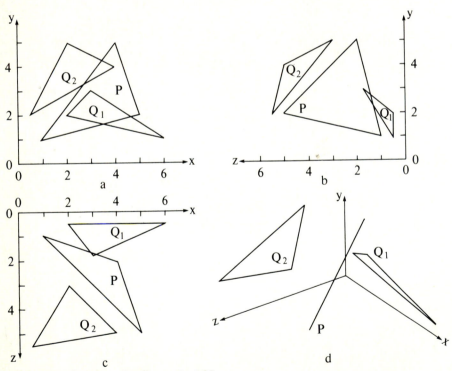

Figure 4-54 Polygons for Example 4-20.

If a cyclical overlap exists, the Sutherland-Hodgman polygon clipping algorithm (see Sec. 3-16) can be used to split the polygons along the line of the intersections of their planes. Here, the plane of Q is used as the clipping plane. Each edge of P is clipped against Q to form the two new polygons. The Cyrus-Beck clipping algorithm (see Sec. 3-11) can be used to find the intersection of each edge of P with the plane of Q.

The Newell-Newell-Sancha algorithm attempts to solve the hidden surface problem dynamically by processing all the polygons in the scene for each frame being presented. If the scene is complex and the frame rate high, as in real-time simulation systems, sufficient processing capability may not be available on a general purpose computer (see Ref. 4-18). However, for many real-time simulations, e.g. aircraft landing, the scene is static and only the viewpoint changes. Schumacker et al. (Ref. 4-19) take advantage of several more general priority characteristics to precompute, off-line, the priority list for simulations of such static environments.

The Schumacher algorithm allows only convex polygons in the scene. These polygons are grouped into clusters of polygons that are linearly separable. Clusters are linearly separable if a nonintersecting, dividing plane can be passed between them. Several two-dimensional clusters are shown in Fig. 4-55a. The separating planes are labeled α and β. They divide the scene into four regions, A, B, C, D. A viewpoint can be located in any of these four regions. The tree structure shown in Fig. 4-55b establishes the cluster priority for the scene. For any viewpoint in the two-dimensional plane the cluster priority can be precomputed. Substituting the coordinates of the viewpoint into the equations for the separating planes locates the appropriate node in the cluster priority tree. The hidden surface problem is then solved for each of the clusters in reverse priority order.

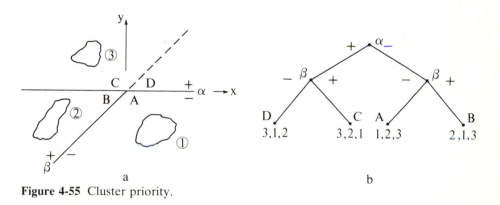

Figure 4-55 Cluster priority.

Example 4-21   Cluster Priority

Assume that the separating planes α and β shown in Fig. 4-55 intersect at the origin of the coordinate system. Further assume that α is the $y = 0$ plane and

β the plane through the line $y = x$, both perpendicular to the paper. The plane equations and appropriate test functions are then

$$\alpha: \qquad y = 0 \qquad (T.F.)_1 = y$$
$$\beta: \quad y - x = 0 \qquad (T.F.)_2 = y - x$$

A viewpoint on the line $2y - x = 0$, e.g. at (20, 10), yields

$$(T.F.)_1 = 10 > 0$$
$$(T.F.)_2 = 10 - 20 = -10 < 0$$

Thus, the viewpoint is in region D. From Fig. 4-55b, the cluster priority is 3, 1, 2.

Clusters are used to subdivide a scene. The simplest cluster is a single polygon. Clusters can be complex polygonal or nonpolygonal surfaces and volumes, each with an appropriate hidden surface technique as described by Newell (Ref. 4-17).

Within certain types of clusters, the priority of individual polygons is independent of the viewpoint (Refs. 4-19 and 4-20). This observation is one of the major contributions of the Schumacker algorithm. It allows precomputation of the entire priority list. Figure 4-56a shows a two-dimensional cluster for which the individual polygonal priorities can be precalculated. The priority of each polygon is established by considering whether a given polygon can hide any other polygon from any viewpoint. The more polygons that a given polygon can hide, the higher its priority. To establish the polygonal priority within a cluster for a given viewpoint, the self-hidden polygons are first removed. The remaining polygons are then in priority order as shown in Fig. 4-56b and c.

The list priority algorithms operate in both object and image space. In particular, the priority list calculations are carried out in object space and the result written to an image space frame buffer. The use of a frame buffer is critical to the algorithm.

Because, like the Warnock and z-buffer algorithms, the list priority algorithms process polygons in arbitrary order, applying antialiasing techniques to the resulting images is difficult. However, like the Warnock and z-buffer algorithms, the postfiltering antialiasing technique is applicable (see Sec. 2-25).

The list priority, Warnock, and z-buffer algorithms may also be implemented as hidden line algorithms. When implemented as hidden line algo-

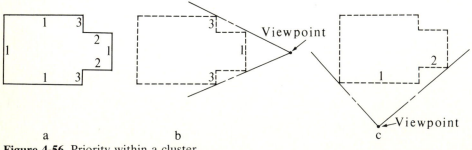

a   b   c

Figure 4-56 Priority within a cluster.

rithms, the edge of each polygon is written to the frame buffer with a unique attribute. However, the interior of each polygon is written to the frame buffer with the background attribute. In this way polygons nearer the viewpoint "obscure" polygon edges further from the viewpoint.

4-9   SCAN LINE ALGORITHMS

The Warnock, z-buffer, and list priority algorithms process scene elements or polygons in arbitrary order with respect to the display. The scan line algorithms, as originally developed by Wylie et al. (Ref. 4-21), Bouknight (Refs. 4-22 to 4-24), and Watkins (Ref. 4-25), process the scene in scan line order. Scan line algorithms operate in image space.

Scan-conversion of single polygons was discussed in Chap. 2. Scan line hidden surface and hidden line algorithms are extensions of those techniques. Scan line algorithms reduce the hidden line/hidden surface problem from three dimensions to two. A scan plane is defined by the viewpoint at infinity on the positive z axis and a scan line, as shown in Fig. 4-57. The intersection of the scan plane and the three-dimensional scene defines a one-scan-line-high window. The hidden surface problem is solved in this scan plane window. Figure 4-57b shows the intersection of the scan plane with the polygons. The figure illustrates that the hidden surface problem is reduced to deciding which line segment is visible for each point on the scan line.

At first glance it might appear that the ordered edge list algorithm discussed in Sec. 2-19 could be applied directly. However, Fig. 4-57b clearly shows that this will yield incorrect results. For example, for the scan line shown in Fig. 4-57 there are four active edges on the active edge list. The intersections of these edges with the scan line are shown by the small dots in Fig. 4-57b. The ordered edge list is shown by the numbers in Fig. 4-57b. Extracting the intersections in pairs causes the pixels between 1 and 2 and between 3 and 4 to be activated. The pixels between 2 and 3 are not activated. The result is

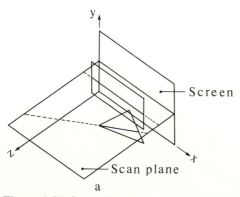

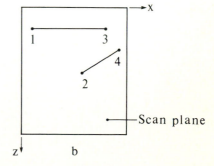

Figure 4-57 Scan plane.

incorrect. A "hole" is left on the scan line where in fact the scan line intersects two polygons. Two correct scan line algorithms are discussed in the next two sections.

4-10   SCAN LINE z-BUFFER ALGORITHM

One of the simplest scan line algorithms that solves the hidden surface problem is a special case of the z-buffer algorithm discussed in the previous section. It is called a scan line z-buffer algorithm (Ref. 4-26). In this algorithm the display window is one scan line high by the horizontal resolution of the display wide. Both the frame buffer and the z-buffer need only be 1 bit high by the horizontal resolution of the display wide by the requisite precision deep. The required depth precision depends on the range of z. For example, the frame buffer might be $1 \times 512 \times 24$ bits and the z buffer $1 \times 512 \times 20$ bits.

Conceptually, the algorithm is quite simple. For each scan line, the frame buffer is initialized to the background and the z buffer to the minimum z. The intersection of the scan line with the two-dimensional projection of each polygon in the scene, if any, is found. These intersections occur in pairs, as discussed in Sec. 2-19. As each pixel on the scan line between the intersection pairs is considered, its depth is compared to the depth recorded in the z buffer at that location. If the pixel depth is greater than that in the z buffer, then this line segment is the currently visible segment. Hence the polygon attributes for this line segment are written to the frame buffer at that pixel location; and the z buffer for that location is updated. When all the polygons in the scene have been processed, the scan line frame buffer contains the hidden surface solution for that scan line. It is copied in scan line order, i.e. left to right, to the display. Both pre- and postfiltering antialiasing techniques can be used with the scan line z-buffer algorithm.

In practice, examining each polygon for each scan line is inefficient. A variation of the ordered edge list discussed in Sec. 2-19 is adopted. In particular, a y-bucket sort, an active polygon list, and an active edge list are used to increase the efficiency of the algorithm.

Using these techniques a scan line z-buffer algorithm is

To prepare the data:

For each polygon determine the highest scan line intersected by the polygon.

Place the polygon in the y bucket corresponding to this scan line.

Store, e.g., on a linked list, at least Δy, the number of scan lines crossed by the polygon, a list of the polygon edges, the coefficients of the plane equation (a, b, c, d), and the rendering attributes for each polygon in a linked list.

To solve the hidden surface problem:

Initialize the display frame buffer.

For each scan line:

Initialize the scan line frame buffer to the background.

Initialize the scan line z buffer to z_{min}.

Examine the scan line y bucket for any new polygons. Add any new polygons to the active polygon list.

Examine the active polygon list for any new polygons. Add any new polygon edge pairs to the active edge list.

If either element of a polygon edge pair has dropped off the active edge list, determine if that polygon is still on the active polygon list. If it is, complete the edge pair for this polygon on the active edge list. If not, remove the other element of the edge pair from the active edge list.

The active edge list contains the following information for each polygon edge intersection pair.

x_l the intersection of the left element of the polygon edge pair with the current scan line.

Δx_l the increment in x_l from scan line to scan line.

Δy_l the number of scan lines crossed by the left side.

x_r the intersection of the right element of the polygon edge pair with the current scan line.

Δx_r the increment in x_r from scan line to scan line.

Δy_r the number of scan lines crossed by the right side.

z_l the depth of the polygon at the center of the pixel corresponding to the left element of a polygon edge pair.

Δz_x the increment in z along the scan line. Equal to a/c for $c \neq 0$.

Δz_y the increment in z from scan line to scan line. Equal to b/c for $c \neq 0$.

The polygon edge pairs are placed on the active edge list in arbitrary order. Within an edge pair, the intersections are sorted into left-right order. More than one edge pair may occur for a polygon.

For each polygon edge pair on the active edge list:

Extract polygon edge pairs from the active edge list.

Initialize z to z_l.

For each pixel such that $x_l \leq x + 1/2 \leq x_r$, calculate the depth $z(x + 1/2, y + 1/2)$ at the center of the pixel using the plane equation for the polygon. On a scan line, this reduces to the incremental calculation

$$z_{x+\Delta x} = z_x - \Delta z_x$$

Compare the depth $z(x + 1/2, y + 1/2)$ with the value stored in the scan line z buffer at Zbuffer(x). If $z(x + 1/2, y + 1/2) >$ Zbuffer(x), then write the polygon attributes to the scan line frame buffer and replace Zbuffer(x) with $z(x + 1/2, y + 1/2)$.

Otherwise no action is taken.

Write the scan line frame buffer to the display.

Update the active edge list:

For each polygon edge pair decrement Δy_l and Δy_r. If either Δy_l or $\Delta y_r < 0$, remove that edge from the list. Flag both its location on the list and the polygon that generated it.

Calculate the new x intercepts:

$$x_{lnew} = x_{lold} + \Delta x_l$$
$$x_{rnew} = x_{rold} + \Delta x_r$$

Calculate the polygon depth at the left edge using the plane equation for the polygon. Between scan lines this reduces to the incremental calculation

$$z_{lnew} = z_{lold} - \Delta z_x \Delta x - \Delta z_y$$

Decrement the active polygon list. If Δy for any polygon < 0, remove that polygon from the list.

Again a preliminary back-plane cull is used if appropriate. An example serves to illustrate the algorithm more fully.

Example 4-22   Scan Line z-Buffer Algorithm

Reconsider the rectangle and triangle previously discussed in Example 4-19. Recall that the rectangle had corner coordinates $P_1(10, 5, 10)$, $P_2(10, 25, 10)$, $P_3(25, 25, 10)$, $P_4(25, 5, 10)$ and the triangle vertices $P_5(15, 15, 15)$, $P_6(25, 25, 5)$, $P_7(30, 10, 5)$ as shown in Fig. 4-50. The display resolution is again $32 \times 32 \times 2$ bit planes. Again, the background is represented by 0, the rectangle by 1, and the triangle by 2. The viewpoint is at infinity on the positive z axis. Using the half scan line convention for both polygons the maximum scan line that intersects the polygons is at $y = 24$. Thus, only the $y = 24$ bucket contains any information. All others are empty.

The active polygon list at $y = 24$ for the rectangle (polygon 1) and the triangle (polygon 2) contains

rectangle: 19, 2, $P_1P_2, P_3P_4, 0, 0, 1, -10, 1$
triangle: 14, 3, $P_5P_6, P_6P_7, P_7P_5, 3, 1, 4, -120, 2$

The entries in this list correspond to Δy, the number of edges, the edge list, the coefficients of the plane equation (a, b, c, d), and the polygon number, respectively. Note that for the rectangle the list contains only two edges. Horizontal edges are ignored.

At scan line 15 (see Fig. 4-58) the active polygon list contains both polygons. For the rectangle $\Delta y = 11$. For the triangle $\Delta y = 5$. Initially the active edge list contains two pairs of intersections, the first for the rectangle, the second for the triangle:

rectangle: 10, 0, 19, 25, 0, 19, 10, 0, 0
triangle: 24 1/2, -1, 9, 25 1/6, 1/3, 14, 5 1/2, 3/4, 1/4

where the elements correspond to $x_l, \Delta x_l, \Delta y_l, x_r, \Delta x_r, \Delta y_r, z_l, \Delta z_x, \Delta z_y$. Just prior to processing scan line 15, the active edge list contains

rectangle: 10, 0, 10, 25, 0, 10, 10, 0, 0
triangle: 15 1/2, -1, 0, 28 1/6, 1/3, 5, 14 1/2, 3/4, 1/4

After first resetting the scan line frame and z buffers to 0 and then scan-converting the rectangle, the buffers contain

Scan line frame buffer

0 0 0 0 0 0 0 0 0 0 1 1 1 1 1 1 1 1 1 1 1 1 1 1 1 0 0 0 0 0 0 0 0

Scan line z buffer

0 0 0 0 0 0 0 0 0 0 10 10 10 10 10 10 10 10 10 10 10 10 10 10 10 10 0 0 0 0 0 0 0 0

Now the triangle is considered. At the left edge $z = 14.5$, which is greater than Zbuffer(15) = 10. Thus, the triangle attributes are written to the frame buffer and the scan line z buffer is updated. The results after scan-conversion is complete are shown below

Scan line frame buffer

0 0 0 0 0 0 0 0 0 0 1 1 1 1 2 2 2 2 2 2 2 2 1 1 1 1 2 2 0 0 0 0 0

Scan line z buffer

0 0 0 0 0 0 0 0 0 0 10 10 10 10 15 14 13 12 12 11 10 10 10 10 10 6 6 0 0 0 0 0

where the z-buffer values have been rounded to integers to save space. The result is the same as the corresponding scan line in Example 4-19. The frame buffer is copied, in left to right order, to the display.

At this point, the active edge list is updated. Decrementing yields $\Delta y_l = -1 < 0$. Consequently the edge P_6P_5 is deleted from the active edge list and the polygon flagged. Updating the right edge of the triangle yields

$$x_{rnew} = x_{rold} + \Delta x_r = 28\ 1/6 + 1/3 = 28\ 1/2$$
$$\Delta y_{rnew} = \Delta y_{rold} - 1 = 5 - 1 = 4$$

After updating the active edge list, the active polygon list is decremented. Since the rectangle remains on the list, the next pass through the algorithm will insert the edge P_5P_7 into the active edge list at the flagged location. At scan line 14 ($y = 14.5$) the intersection with the edge P_5P_7 yields a new $x_l = 16\ 1/2$. The triangle depth is

$$z_l = -[ax + by + d]/c = -[(3)(16.5) + (1)(14.5) - 120]/4 = 14$$

The resulting active edge list at scan line 14 is then

rectangle: 10, 0, 9, 25, 0, 9, 10, 0, 0
triangle: 16 1/2, 3, 4, 28 1/2, 4, 14, 3/4, 1/4

The complete results are shown in Example 4-19.

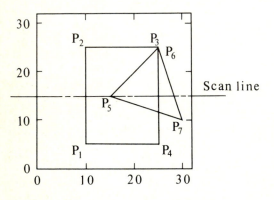

Figure 4-58 Polygons for Example 4-22.

4-11   A SPANNING SCAN LINE ALGORITHM

The scan line z-buffer algorithm calculates the polygon depth at every pixel on the scan line. The number of depth calculations can be reduced by introducing the concept of spans as in the original Watkins algorithm (Ref. 4-25). Figure 4-59a shows the intersection of two polygons with a scan plane. By dividing the scan line at each edge crossing into segments called spans (see Fig. 4-59a), the solution of the hidden surface problem is reduced to selection of the visible segment in each span. Figure 4-59a shows that only three types of spans are possible:

The span is empty, e.g. span 1 in Fig. 4-59a. The background is displayed.

The span contains only one segment, e.g. spans 2 and 4 in Fig. 4-59a. The polygon attributes for that segment are displayed for the span.

The span contains multiple segments, e.g. span 3 in Fig. 4-59a. The depth of each segment in the span is calculated. The segment with the largest z value is the visible segment. The polygon attributes for that segment are displayed for the span.

If penetrating polygons are not allowed, it is sufficient to calculate the depth of each segment in a span at one end of the span. If two segments touch but do not penetrate at the end of a span, the depth calculation is performed at the

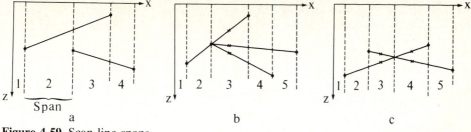

Figure 4-59 Scan line spans.

midpoint of the spans as shown in Fig. 4-59b. For span 3, a depth calculation performed at the left end of the span yields inconclusive results. Performing the depth calculation at the midpoint of the span, as shown by the x's in Fig. 4-59b, yields the correct results.

If penetrating polygons are allowed, then the scan line is divided not only at each edge crossing but also at each intersection as shown in Fig. 4-59c. Depth calculations at each span end point will yield indeterminate results. Here it is sufficient to perform the depth calculation at the midpoint of each span, as shown by the x's in Fig. 4-59c.

More sophisticated span generation techniques can reduce the number of spans and hence the computational requirements. Frequently, simple methods can also yield surprising results. For example, Watkins (Ref. 4-25) suggested a simple midpoint subdivision technique. In Fig. 4-60a, a simple comparison of the end point depths of the lines ab and cd shows that cd is always visible. However, Fig. 4-60b shows that this is not always the case. But by dividing at the midpoint of cd it is easy to show that both segments of cd are visible.

Further, it is frequently possible to avoid depth calculations altogether. Romney et al. (Ref. 4-27) showed that, if penetration is *not* allowed, and if exactly the same polygons are present, and if the order of the edge crossings is exactly the same on a given scan line as on the previous scan line, then the depth priority of the segments in each span remains unchanged. Hence, depth priority calculations for the new scan line need not be made. Hamlin and Gear (Ref. 4-28) show how, in some circumstances, the depth priority can be maintained even if the order of the edge crossings changes.

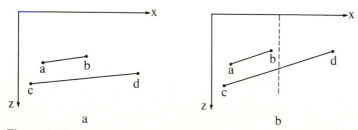

Figure 4-60 Alternate spanning technique.

The basic structure developed for the scan line z-buffer algorithm is also applicable to a Watkins-style spanning scan line algorithm. Only the inner loop, i.e., how an individual scan line is processed, and the contents of the active edge list need be changed. Here it is not necessary to maintain the polygon edge–scan line intersections in pairs. Individual edges are placed on the active edge list. The active edge list is sorted into increasing x order. A polygon identifier and a polygon active flag are used to identify left and right elements of the edge pair. The polygon active flag is initially set to *false* at the beginning of a scan line and complemented each time an edge for that polygon is processed. Encountering a left edge for a polygon will cause that polygon's flag to be set to *true*, while encountering a right edge for that polygon will return it to *false*. Example 4-23 below more fully illustrates the use of the flag.

The spans for each polygon can be determined as a scan line is processed. If penetration is not allowed, each edge intersection on the active edge list represents a span boundary. As discussed above, the number of polygons active within a span determines how a span is processed. Depth calculations are performed only if more than one polygon is active in a span. If penetration is allowed, and more than one polygon is active within a span determined by the edge intersections, then it is necessary to check for possible intersecting segments within the span (see Fig. 4-59c). A convenient method for doing this is to compare the signs of the differences in the depths of pairs of segments at the span end points. Each pair of segments in the span must be examined. For example, if two segments have depths $z_{1l}, z_{1r}, z_{2l}, z_{2r}$ at the left and right end points, then

$$\textbf{if Sign}(z_{1l} - z_{2l}) \neq \textbf{Sign}(z_{1r} - z_{2r}) \tag{4-9}$$

the segments intersect. If the segments intersect, the span is subdivided at the intersection. The process is repeated with the left hand span until the span is clear of intersections. For these spans, the depth calculation is performed at the midpoint of the span.

If either sign in the above test is zero, the segments intersect at the end of the span. Here, it is sufficient to determine the depth at the opposite end of the span rather than subdividing the span.

The structure of the spanning scan line algorithm is then

To prepare the data:

Determine for each polygon the highest scan line intersected by the polygon.

Place the polygon in the y bucket corresponding to this scan line.

Store at least Δy, the number of scan lines crossed by the polygon, a list of the polygon edges, the coefficients of the plane equation (a, b, c, d), and the rendering attributes for each polygon on a linked list.

To solve the hidden surface problem:

For each scan line:

Examine the scan line y bucket for any new polygons. Add any new polygons to the active polygon list.

Examine the active polygon list for any new polygons. Add any new polygon edges to the active edge list. The active edge list contains the following information for each polygon edge intersection:

x the intersection of the polygon edge with the current scan line

Δx the increment in x from scan line to scan line

Δy number of scan lines crossed by the edge

P a polygon identifier

$Flag$ a flag indicating whether the polygon is active on a given scan line.

Sort the active edge list into increasing x order.

Process the active edge list. The details are shown in the flowchart given in Fig. 4-61 and the modifications given in Figs. 4-62 and 4-63.

Update the active edge list:

For each edge intersection, decrement Δy. If $\Delta y < 0$, remove the edge from the active edge list.

Calculate the new x intercepts:

$$x_{new} = x_{old} + \Delta x$$

Decrement the active polygon list:

For each polygon, decrement Δy_p. If Δy_p for any polygon < 0, remove the polygon from the list.

The algorithm given above does not take advantage of depth priority coherence as suggested by Romney. If penetration is not allowed, modification of the algorithm to take advantage of depth priority coherence results in significant savings.

The simple spanning algorithm given in Fig. 4-61 assumes that polygon segments in a span do not intersect. If the segments intersect at a span end, then, as discussed above, the depth calculation is performed at the opposite end of the span for these segments. A simple modification of the calculation block for the flowchart shown in Fig. 4-61 is given in Fig. 4-62.

If the segments intersect within a span, i.e. the polygons penetrate, then either a more complex spanner must be used or the intersections must be inserted into the ordered edge list. The spanning algorithm shown in Fig. 4-61 is applicable when penetrating polygons are allowed, provided the active edge list includes the intersections, each intersection is flagged, the polygon flag complementation is modified, and the depth priority calculations are carried out at the center of the span.

Figure 4-63 illustrates a modification of the algorithm given in Fig. 4-61. The modified algorithm assumes that the active edge list does not contain the intersection points. The intersection segments must be discovered and processed on the fly. Here, each span is examined for intersecting segments. If any are found, the intersection point is calculated and the span subdivided at the intersection point. The right hand subspan is pushed onto a stack. The algorithm is recursively applied to the left hand subspan until a subspan with

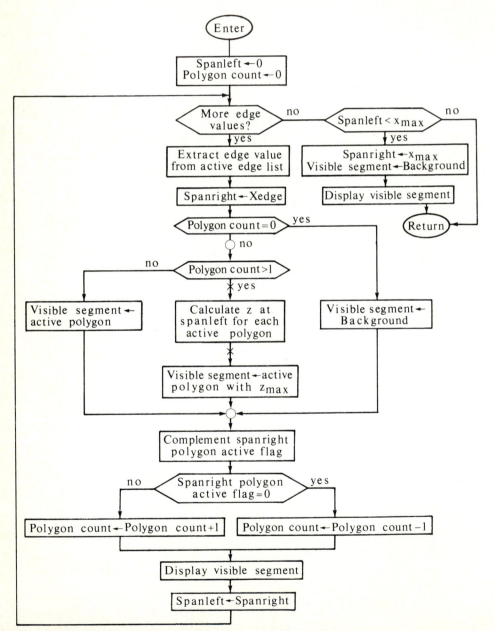

Figure 4-61 Flowchart for spanner for nonpenetrating polygons.

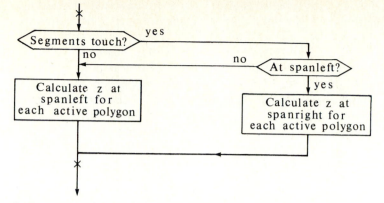

Figure 4-62 Flowchart for modified depth calculation for Fig. 4-61.

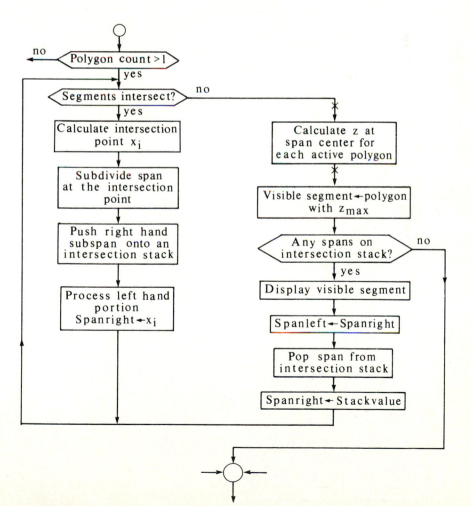

Figure 4-63 Modification of the flowchart in Fig. 4-61 for penetrating polygons.

no intersections is found. This subspan is displayed, and a new subspan popped from the stack. The process is repeated until the stack is empty. The technique is similar to that suggested by Jackson (Ref. 4-29). As a matter of interest the front and back cover photos were generated with a Watkins algorithm.

For simplicity, the modified algorithm shown in Fig. 4-63 assumes that segments intersect only if they cross. Because segments may touch at the ends of the spans, the depth calculation is carried out at the center of the span. The modified calculation block shown in Fig. 4-62 can be substituted to avoid this additional computational expense. A further modification of the algorithm performs a z-priority sort for spans with intersections to determine if the intersecting segments are visible before subdividing the span. This modification reduces the number of subspans and increases the algorithm's efficiency. If appropriate, a preliminary back-plane cull is also used to increase efficiency.

Example 4-23   Spanning Scan Line Algorithm

Again consider the rectangle and penetrating triangle previously discussed in Examples 4-19 and 4-22. Scan line 15 is to be considered. The half scan line convention is used. The intersection of the scan plane at $y = 15.5$ with the polygons is shown in Fig. 4-64. Figure 4-58 shows a projection of the polygons onto the xy plane. Just prior to processing scan line 15, the active edge list, sorted into x increasing order, contains

$$10, 0, 10, 1, 0, 15\ 1/2, -1, 0, 2, 0, 25, 0, 10, 1, 0, 28\ 1/6, 1/3, 5, 2, 0$$

where the numbers are considered in groups of five, representing x, Δx, Δy, P, *Flag* as defined in the algorithm above. Figure 4-64 shows the five spans that result from the four intersections given on the active edge list. Figure 4-64 also shows that the polygon segments intersect within the third span.

The scan line is processed from left to right in scan line order. The first span contains no polygons. It is displayed (pixels 0 to 9) with the background attributes. In the second span the rectangle becomes active. Its flag is complemented to 1:

$$Flag = -Flag + 1$$

The span contains only one polygon. Consequently it is displayed (pixels 10 to 14) with the rectangle's attributes.

The third span starts at $x = 15\ 1/2$. The triangle becomes active and its flag is complemented to 1, the polygon count is increased to 2, *Spanleft* becomes 15 1/2, and the next edge at $x = 25$ is extracted from the active edge list. *Spanright* is set equal to 25. The polygon count is greater than one. The segments are examined for possible intersection (see Fig. 4-63).

The plane equation for the triangle is (see Example 4-19)

$$3x + y + 4z - 120 = 0$$

For scan line 15, $y = 15.5$; and the triangle depth at any pixel becomes

$$z = (120 - y - 3x)/4 = (120 - 15.5 - 3x)/4 = (104.5 - 3x)/4$$

Thus using the center of the pixel, i.e. $x + 1/2$

$$z_{2l} = [104.5 - (3)(15.5)]/4 = 14.5$$
$$z_{2r} = [104.5 - (3)(25.5)]/4 = 7.0$$

Since the rectangle is of constant depth,

$$z_{1l} = 10$$
$$z_{1r} = 10$$

Recalling Eq. (4-9)

$$\mathbf{Sign}(z_{1l} - z_{2l}) = \mathbf{Sign}(10 - 14.5) < 0$$
$$\mathbf{Sign}(z_{1r} - z_{2r}) = \mathbf{Sign}(10 - 7) > 0$$

Since $\mathbf{Sign}(z_{1l} - z_{2l}) \neq \mathbf{Sign}(z_{1r} - z_{2r})$, the segments intersect. The intersection of the two segments is

$$z = (120 - 15.5 - 3x)/4 = 10$$
$$x_i = 21.5$$

The span is subdivided at $x_i = 21.5$. The value for *Spanright* is pushed onto the stack. *Spanright* is set to x_i, i.e. 21.5.

The subspan from $x = 15.5$ to $x = 21.5$ contains no intersections. The depth at the center of the subspan, i.e. at $x = 18.5$, for the triangle is

$$z_2 = (104.5 - 3x)/4 = [104.5 - (3)(18.5)]/4 = 12.25$$

which is greater than $z_1 = 10$ for the rectangle. Thus, the triangle is displayed for this subspan (pixels 15 to 20).

Spanleft is set to *Spanright* and the right hand subspan popped from the stack. *Spanright* is set to the stack value, i.e. $x = 25$. The subspan from $x = 21.5$ to $x = 25$ contains no intersections. The depth at the center of the subspan, i.e. at $x = 23.25$, for the triangle is

$$z_2 = (104.5 - 3x)/4 = [104.5 - (3)(23.25)]/4 = 8.69$$

which is less than $z_1 = 10$ for the rectangle. Thus, the rectangle is visible for this subspan (pixels 21 to 24).

The intersection stack is now empty. The routine given in Fig. 4-63 exits to that in Fig. 4-61. The span right polygon is the rectangle. The rectangle becomes inactive. Its flag is complemented to 0 which also causes the polygon count to be reduced to 1. The segment is now displayed using the rectangle's attributes. *Spanleft* is reset to *Spanright*.

The next edge extracted from the active edge list is for the triangle at $x = 28\ 1/6$. The span is from $x = 25$ to $x = 28\ 1/6$. The polygon count is 1. The active polygon in the span is the triangle. Consequently, the segment is displayed with the triangle's attributes (pixels 25 to 27). The span right polygon is the triangle. Its flag is complemented to 0, and the triangle becomes inactive. The polygon count is now 0. *Spanleft* is set to *Spanright*, i.e. $28\ 1/6$.

There are no more edges in the active edge list. Here, $x_{max} = 32$, so *Spanleft* $< x_{max}$. Thus, *Spanright* is set to x_{max} and the display segment to the background. The span (pixels 28 to 31) is displayed with the background attributes, and *Spanleft* reset to *Spanright*. Again there are no more edges, but *Spanleft* $= x_{max}$, and the processing of the scan line is complete.

The final results are identical to those shown in Example 4-19.

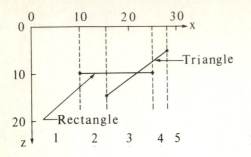

Figure 4-64 Scan plane for Example 4-23.

Scan line algorithms can also be implemented as hidden line algorithms. For example, Archuleta (Ref. 4-30) has implemented a hidden line version of the Watkins algorithm.

4-12 SCAN LINE ALGORITHMS FOR CURVED SURFACES

The Catmull subdivision algorithm for curved surfaces (see Sec. 4-6), although simple and elegant, unfortunately does not present the result in scan line order. This is inconvenient for raster scan output devices. A curved surface can of course be polygonally approximated and scan-converted using any of the scan line algorithms discussed above. However, to obtain a high degree of accuracy the number of polygons in a reasonably complex scene becomes excessive. Further, unless shading interpolation techniques are used (see Chap. 5), the result will have a faceted appearance. In any case, the silhouette edges will be piecewise linear, i.e., represented as connected, short, straight line segments.

Algorithms that display parametric bipolynomial, typically bicubic, surfaces directly from the surface description in scan line order have been developed by Blinn (Ref. 4-31), Whitted (Ref. 4-32), Lane and Carpenter (Refs. 4-33 and 4-34), and Clark (Ref. 4-35). First the Blinn and Whitted algorithms, which are similar, are discussed. Then the Lane-Carpenter and Clark algorithms, which are also similar, are considered.

Recalling that a scan line algorithm intersects the scene with a scan plane through the eyepoint and a scan line immediately shows the difference between polygonal and curved (sculptured) parametric surfaces. For a polygonal surface, all the intersections are straight lines. These straight lines are easily represented by their end points. For a curved parametric surface the intersection of the scan plane and the surface is given by the relation

$$y(u, w) = yscan = \text{constant}$$

where u and w are the parametric values for the surface. The result is a curve, called either a level curve or a contour. The curve is not necessarily single-valued. Further, there may be multiple curves at any contour level. Finally, having found the curve(s) of intersection with the scan line, it is also necessary to find each location along the scan line, i.e. each $x = x(u,w)$, and to be able to calculate the depth at that location, $z = z(u,w)$, to determine its visibility.

Mathematically, the requirement can be stated as: Given a scan line value y and a location of a point on that scan line x, obtain the inverse solution for the parameters u,w; i.e. find

$$u = u(x, y)$$
$$w = w(x, y)$$

Once the parameters u, w are known, the depth is obtained from

$$z = z(u, w)$$

Hence, the visibility of that point on the scan line may be determined. Unfortunately, there is no known closed form solution for these equations. Both Blinn and Whitted use numerical procedures to obtain a solution. Specifically, a Newton-Raphson iteration technique is used (see Ref. 4-36). The Newton-Raphson technique requires an initial estimate. Both algorithms take advantage of scan line coherence to provide this initial estimate and reduce the number of iterations per pixel. Unfortunately Newton-Raphson iteration can become unstable. Kajiya (Ref. 4-37) presents a more robust but more complex procedure based on concepts from algebraic geometry.

Briefly, in the context of the structure of a scan line algorithm, the inner loop for the Blinn and Whitted algorithms is

Given a parametric surface from the active patch list with

$$x = x(u, w)$$
$$y = y(u, w)$$
$$z = z(u, w)$$

For each scan line y:

For each pixel x on a scan line:

For each surface intersecting that scan line at x:

Solve for $u = u(x, y)$, $w = w(x, y)$.
Calculate the depth of the surface $z = z(u, w)$.

Determine the visible surface at x, y and display it.

The algorithm illustrates another fundamental difference between a polygonal surface and a curved parametric surface. The algorithm says, "For each surface intersecting that scan line." Surfaces become active at the highest intersecting scan line and inactive at the lowest intersecting scan line. These intersections occur at local maxima and minima of the surface. For polygonal surfaces, local maxima and minima always occur at a vertex. Scan line algorithms use these vertices and the surface edges that connect them to decide when a polygon should be added to or deleted from the active polygon and active edge lists.

For curved surfaces local maxima and minima do not necessarily occur at vertices. They frequently occur interior to the surface along silhouette edges.

A silhouette edge interior to a surface is identified by the vanishing of the z component of the surface normal. Several examples are shown in Fig. 4-65. For a curved surface, surfaces may be added to or deleted from the active surface list at silhouette edges, and scan line spans may start and stop at silhouette edges. Both the Blinn and Whitted algorithms solve this problem by effectively dividing the surface along the silhouette edges.

The Lane-Carpenter and Clark parametric curved surface algorithms are basically subdivision techniques. However, in contrast to the original Catmull subdivision algorithm which proceeds in arbitrary order, these algorithms proceed in scan line order. The algorithms perform a y-bucket sort of the surface patches based on the maximum y value for each patch. At each scan line, patches from an active patch list that intersect that scan line are subdivided until each subpatch either meets a flatness criterion or no longer intersects the scan line. Subpatches that no longer intersect the scan line are placed on an inactive patch list for subsequent consideration. Subpatches that meet the flatness criterion are treated as planar polygons and scan-converted using a polygonal scan line algorithm. However, each of these approximately planar polygons is a parametric subpatch. All the information available for the parametric subpatch is available for determining individual pixel attributes during polygonal scan-conversion. Using this information allows subpatches to be blended together smoothly. In fact, if the flatness criterion is less than one pixel, a smooth silhouette results. Further, back-facing or self-hidden polygons can be eliminated by simply determining the normal to the surface (see Sec. 4-3). If the normal points away from the viewpoint, the subpatch is eliminated. This saves considerable processing.

Although both the Lane-Carpenter and the Clark algorithms use the idea expressed above, the Clark algorithm preprocesses the patches before scan-converting, while the Lane-Carpenter algorithm dynamically subdivides the patches as the frame is processed. The Lane-Carpenter algorithm requires considerably less memory but performs more subdivisions than the Clark algorithm. Figure 4-66 was generated with the Lane-Carpenter algorithm.

Figure 4-65 Silhouette edges.

Figure 4-66 Teapot defined by 28 bicubic patches rendered with the Lane-Carpenter algorithm. (*Courtesy of Loren Carpenter.*)

Briefly, in the context of a scan line algorithm, the inner loop for the Lane-Carpenter algorithm is

For each scan line y:

> For each patch on the active patch list:
>
> > **if** the patch is flat **then**
> > > add the patch to the polygon list
> >
> > **else**
> > > split the patch into subpatches
> > > **if** a subpatch still intersects the scan line **then**
> > > > add it to the active patch list
> > >
> > > **else**
> > > > add it to the inactive patch list.
> > >
> > > **end if**
> >
> > **end if**
>
> Scan-convert the polygon list.

Both the Lane-Carpenter and the Clark algorithms take advantage of the characteristics of particular basis functions used to generate parametric patches to efficiently subdivide the patch. However, the algorithm is applicable for any parametric surface patch for which an efficient subdivision algorithm is available. One disadvantage of these adaptive subdivision algorithms is that tears or holes in the surface can result from mismatches between the approximate polygonal subpatches and the exact parametric surface subpatches.

Quadric surfaces are generally somewhat simpler than parametric surface patches. Quadric surfaces are defined by the general quadratic equation

$$a_1x^2 + a_2y^2 + a_3z^2 + a_4xy + a_5yz + a_6zx + a_7x + a_8y + a_9z + a_{10} = 0$$

Common examples of quadric surfaces are spheres, cones, cylinders, and ellipsoids and hyperboloids of revolution. If a_1 through a_6 are zero, then the equation reduces to that of a planar polygon.

Spheres as a subset of quadric surfaces are of particular interest in molecular modeling. Several scan line algorithms specifically for spheres have been developed. In particular, the algorithms by Porter (Refs. 4-38 and 4-39) and Staudhammer (Ref. 4-40) implement scan line z-buffer algorithms for spheres. By restricting the algorithm to orthographic views, Porter effectively uses Bresenham's circle algorithm (see Sec. 2-6) to generate the silhouette of the sphere. Further, since the intersection of the scan plane with a sphere is also a circle, Bresenham's circle algorithm can be used to incrementally calculate the depth of each sphere on the scan line. Finally, by maintaining a priority list of the spheres based on the depth of the sphere center, Bresenham's algorithm is used to antialias the silhouette edges (see Sec. 2-26). The priority sort also allows transparency effects to be added.

4-13   A VISIBLE SURFACE RAY TRACING ALGORITHM

All the hidden surface algorithms discussed in the previous sections depend upon some coherence characteristic of the scene to efficiently find the visible portions of the scene. In comparison, ray tracing is a brute force technique. The basic idea underlying the technique is that an observer views an object by means of light from a source that strikes the object and then somehow reaches the observer. The light may reach the observer by reflection from the surface or by refraction or transmission through the surface. If light rays from the source are traced, very few will reach the viewer. Consequently, the process would be computationally inefficient. Appel (Ref. 4-41) originally suggested that rays should be traced in the opposite direction, i.e., from the observer to the object as shown in Fig. 4-67. This technique was successfully implemented in a solid model display system by MAGI (Ref. 4-42). In the original MAGI implementation, rays terminated when they intersected the surface of a visible opaque object; i.e., it was used as a hidden or visible surface processor only. Subsequently Kay (Refs. 4-43 and 4-44) and Whitted (Ref. 4-45) implemented ray tracing algorithms in conjunction with global illumination models. These algorithms account for reflection of one object in the surface of another, refraction, transparency, and shadow effects. The images are also antialiased. An algorithm incorporating these effects is discussed in Sec. 5-12. The present discussion is limited to ray tracing as a hidden or visible surface technique.

Figure 4-67 illustrates the simplest ray tracing algorithm. The algorithm assumes that the scene has been transformed to image space. A perspective transformation is not applied. The viewpoint or observer is assumed to be at infinity, on the positive z axis. Hence, all the light rays are parallel to the z axis. Each ray passes from the observer through the center of a pixel on the raster into the scene. The path of each ray is traced to determine which objects in

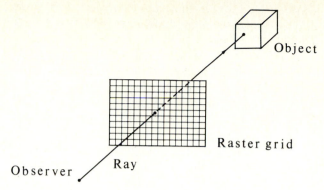

Figure 4-67 Simple ray tracing.

the scene, if any, are intersected by the ray. Every object in the scene must be examined for every ray. If a ray intersects an object, all possible intersections of the ray and the object are determined. This may yield multiple intersections for multiple objects. The intersections are sorted in depth. The intersection with the maximum z value represents the visible surface for that pixel. The attributes for this object are used to determine the pixel's characteristics.

When the viewpoint is not located at infinity, the algorithm is only slightly more complex. Here, the observer is assumed located on the positive z axis. The image plane, i.e. the raster, is perpendicular to the z axis as shown in Fig. 4-68. The effect is to perform a single-point perspective projection onto the image plane (see Ref. 1-1).

The most important element of a visible surface ray tracing algorithm is the intersection routine. Any object for which an intersection routine can be written may be included in a scene. Objects in the scene may be composed of a mixture of planar polygons, polyhedral volumes, or volumes defined or bounded by quadric or bipolynomial parametric surfaces. Since a ray tracing algorithm spends 75–95% of its effort in determining intersections, the efficiency of the intersection routine significantly affects the efficiency of the algorithm. Determining the intersections of an arbitrary line in space (a ray) with a particular object may be computationally expensive (see, for example,

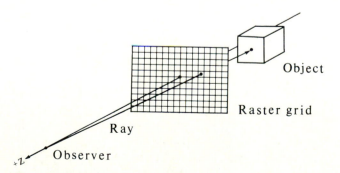

Figure 4-68 Ray tracing with perspective.

Ref. 4-37). To eliminate unnecessary intersections, the intersection of a ray with the bounding volume of an object is examined. If a ray fails to intersect the bounding volume of an object, then that object need not be considered further for that ray. Either a bounding box or a bounding sphere may be used as a bounding volume. Although, as shown in Fig. 4-69, a bounding sphere may be inefficient, determining whether a three-dimensional ray intersects a sphere is simple. In particular, if the distance from the center of the bounding sphere to the ray is more than the radius of the sphere, then the ray does not intersect the bounding sphere. Hence, it cannot intersect the object.

The bounding sphere test thus reduces to determining the distance from a point to a three-dimensional line, i.e. the ray. Using a parametric representation of the line between the points $P_1(x_1, y_1, z_1)$ and $P_2(x_2, y_2, z_2)$, i.e.

$$P(t) = P_1 + (P_2 - P_1)t$$

with components

$$x = x_1 + (x_2 - x_1)t = x_1 + at$$
$$y = y_1 + (y_2 - y_1)t = y_1 + bt$$
$$z = z_1 + (z_2 - z_1)t = z_1 + ct$$

the minimum distance d from the line to the point $P_0(x_0, y_0, z_0)$ is

$$d^2 = (x - x_0)^2 + (y - y_0)^2 + (z - z_0)^2$$

where the parameter t specifying the point on $P(t)$ for minimum distance is

$$t = -\frac{a(x_1 - x_0) + b(y_1 - y_0) + c(z_1 - z_0)}{a^2 + b^2 + c^2}$$

If $d^2 > R^2$, where R is the radius of the bounding sphere, then the ray cannot intersect the object.

Performing a bounding box test in three dimensions is computationally expensive. In general, intersection of the ray with at least three of the infinite planes forming the bounding box must be tested. Since intersections of the ray may occur outside a face of the bounding box, a containment or inside test

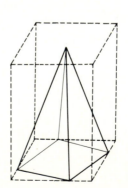

Figure 4-69 Bounding volumes.

must also be performed for each intersection. Consequently, when performed in three dimensions, the bounding box test is slower than the bounding sphere test.

A simple procedure reduces the bounding box test to sign comparison, simplifies the intersection calculation for the object, and simplifies the depth comparisons among the intersections. The procedure uses translations and rotations about the coordinate axes (see Ref. 1-1) to make the ray coincident with the z axis. The same transformations are applied to the bounding box of the object. The ray intersects the bounding box if, in the translated and rotated coordinate system, the signs of x_{min} and x_{max} *and* of y_{min} and y_{max} are opposite as shown in Fig. 4-70.

The simplification of the intersection calculation is illustrated by the general quadric surface. In any Cartesian coordinate system the general quadric surface is the locus of points given by

$$Q(x, y, z) = a_1 x^2 + a_2 y^2 + a_3 z^2 + b_1 yz + b_2 xz + b_3 xy + c_1 x + c_2 y + c_3 z + d = 0$$

After applying the combined translation and rotation transformation used to make the ray coincident with the z axis, the intersection of the ray and the surface, if any, occurs at $x = y = 0$. Thus, in general, the intersection points are given by the solution of

$$a_3' z^2 + c_3' z + d' = 0$$

i.e.

$$z = \frac{-c_3' \pm \sqrt{c_3'^2 - 4a_3' d'}}{2a_3'}$$

where the prime indicates the coefficients of the general quadric surface in the transformed orientation. If $c_3'^2 - 4a_3' d' < 0$, the solutions are complex and the ray does not intersect the surface. If an infinite quadric surface (e.g. cones and cylinders) is constrained by limit planes, then the limit planes must also be transformed and examined for intersections. If an intersection with

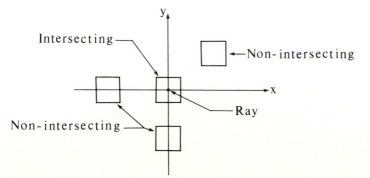

Figure 4-70 Bounding box intersections in the transformed coordinate system.
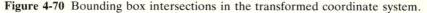

an infinite limit plane is found, an inside test must be performed. However, in the transformed coordinate system, this test can be performed on the two-dimensional projection of the intersection of the limit plane and the quadric surface. To obtain the intersections in the original orientation, the inverse transformation is applied.

Intersection calculations for bipolynomial parametric surface patches are less straightforward. Whitted (Ref. 4-45) has implemented a simple subdivision technique for bicubic surface patches. The calculations are carried out with the surface patch in its original location. If a ray initially intersects the bounding sphere for a patch, the patch is subdivided using Catmull's subdivision algorithm (see Sec. 4-6). The ray is tested against the bounding spheres of the subpatches. If there is no intersection, the ray does not intersect the patch. If the ray intersects a bounding sphere for a subpatch, the patch is further subdivided. The process is continued until no bounding spheres are intersected or the bounding spheres reach a predetermined minimum size. These minimum-sized bounding spheres represent the intersections of the ray and the patch.

By transforming the ray to be coincident with the z axis, the subdivision technique can be utilized with bounding boxes rather than bounding spheres. This reduces the number of subdivisions and increases the efficiency of the algorithm. For parametric surfaces that exhibit a convex hull property, e.g. Bezier and B-spline surfaces (see Ref. 1-1), the number of subdivisions can be further reduced, at the expense of further complexity, by using the convex hull rather than the bounding box for the subpatches.

Kajiya (Ref. 4-37) has implemented a technique for bipolynomial parametric surfaces that does not involve subdivision. The method is based on concepts from algebraic geometry. Solutions of the resulting high-degree algebraic equations are obtained numerically. A similar technique can be implemented in the transformed coordinate system. Recall that a bipolynomial parametric surface is defined by

$$Q(u, w) = 0$$

with components

$$x = f(u, w)$$
$$y = g(u, w)$$
$$z = h(u, w)$$

In the transformed coordinate system $x = y = 0$. Hence,

$$f(u, w) = 0$$
$$g(u, w) = 0$$

Simultaneous solution of this pair of equations yields the values of u and w for the intersections. Substitution into $z = h(u, w)$ yields the z component of the intersection points. Failure to find a real solution means that the ray does not intersect the surface. The degree of the system of equations for u, w is the product of the bipolynomial surface degrees, e.g., sixth degree for a bicubic surface. Consequently, numerical solution techniques are generally required. Where applicable, intersections of the ray and the convex hull can be used to obtain an initial estimate of u and w. Again, to obtain the intersections in the original orientation, the inverse transformation is applied.

For multiple intersections of the ray being traced and objects in the scene, it is necessary to determine the visible intersection. For the simple opaque visible surface algorithms discussed in this section, the intersection with the maximum z coordinate is the visible surface. For more complex algorithms with reflections and refractions, the intersections must be ordered with respect to the distance from the point of origin of the ray. The transformed coordinate system allows this to be accomplished with a simple z sort.

The procedure for a simple opaque surface ray tracing algorithm is then

Prepare the scene data:

Create an object list containing at least the following information

Complete description of the object: type, surface, characteristics, etc.
Bounding sphere description: center and radius.
Bounding box flag. If the flag is true a bounding box test will be performed, if false it will be skipped. Note, a bounding box test is not appropriate for all objects, e.g. a sphere.
Bounding box description: x_{min}, x_{max}, y_{min}, y_{max}, z_{min}, z_{max}.

For each ray to be traced:

For each object perform a three-dimensional bounding sphere test in the original location. If the ray intersects the bounding sphere, place the object on the active object list.

If the active object list is empty, display the pixel at the background intensity and continue.

Otherwise, translate and rotate the ray such that it is coincident with the z axis. Save the combined transformation.

For each object on the active object list:

If the bounding box flag is true, transform the bounding box to the same orientation as the ray using the combined transformation and perform the bounding box tests. If the ray does not intersect the bounding box, continue with the next object.

Otherwise, transform the object to the same orientation as the ray using the combined transformation and determine the ray's intersections, if any, with the object. Place any intersections on an intersection list.

If the intersection list is empty, display the pixel at the background intensity.

Otherwise, determine z_{max} for the intersection list.

Calculate the inverse for the combined transformation.

Using the inverse transformation determine the intersection point in the original orientation.

Display the pixel using the intersected object's attributes and an appropriate illumination model.

Note that for a simple opaque visible surface algorithm, it is not necessary to determine the inverse combined transformation nor is it necessary to determine the intersection point in the original orientation unless an illumination model requiring surface properties or orientation at the intersection point is incorporated into the algorithm (see Chap. 5). These steps are included here for completeness and convenience when implementing a ray tracing algorithm with global illumination (see Sec. 5-12). An example serves to more fully illustrate the discussion.

Example 4-24   Ray Tracing Algorithm

Again consider the rectangle and penetrating triangle previously discussed in Examples 4-19, 4-22, and 4-23. For simplicity, the observer is assumed to be located at infinity on the positive z axis. Hence, all the rays are parallel to the z axis. The z axis passes through the 0, 0 point on the raster. Recalling that the rectangle has corner points $P_1(10, 5, 10)$, $P_2(10, 25, 10)$, $P_3(25, 25, 10)$, $P_4(25, 5, 10)$. The center of its bounding sphere is located at $(17.5, 15, 10)$ with radius 12.5. The bounding box for the rectangle, x_{min}, x_{max}, y_{min}, y_{max}, z_{min}, z_{max} is 10, 25, 5, 25, 10, 10.

The triangle has vertices at $P_5(15, 15, 15)$, $P_6(25, 25, 5)$, $P_7(30, 10, 5)$. The center of the bounding sphere is at $(22.885, 15.962, 8.846)$ with radius 10.048. The bounding box for the triangle is 15, 30, 10, 25, 5, 15.

The object list thus contains two entries, and both bounding box flags are true.

The ray through the center of the pixel at (20, 15) is considered. Since the observer is at infinity, the ray is parallel to the z axis.

First consider the rectangle. Since the ray is parallel to the z axis, the distance from the center of the bounding sphere to the ray is a two-dimensional calculation. Specifically, using the center of the pixel, i.e. (20.5, 15.5), yields

$$d^2 = (20.5 - 17.5)^2 + (15.5 - 15)^2 = 9.25$$

Since $(d^2 = 9.25) < (R^2 = 156.25)$, the ray intersects the bounding sphere for the rectangle. The rectangle is placed on the active object list.

Similarly for the triangle

$$d^2 = (20.5 - 22.885)^2 + (15.5 - 15.962)^2$$
$$= 5.90$$

which is also less than the square of the radius of the bounding sphere; i.e., $(d^2 = 5.90) < (R^2 = 100.96)$. Thus, the ray intersects the bounding sphere for the triangle. The triangle is also placed on the active object list.

Since the active object list is not empty, the ray is transformed to be coincident with the z axis. Here the ray is translated by $-20.5, -15.5, 0$ in the x, y, z directions, respectively.

Translating the rectangle's bounding box similarly yields -10.5, $4.5, -10.5, 9.5, 10, 10$. Since the signs of both x_{min} and x_{max} *and* y_{min} and y_{max} are opposite, the ray intersects the rectangle's bounding box. The intersection of the ray and the rectangle is obtained using the plane equation. In both the transformed and untransformed coordinate systems the rectangle's plane equation is

$$z - 10 = 0$$

The intersection of the ray thus occurs at $z = 10$. The intersection is inside the rectangle. This value is placed on the intersection list.

Translating the bounding box for the triangle yields $-5.5, 9.5, -5.5, 9.5,$ $5, 15$. Again, the signs of both x_{min} and x_{max} *and* y_{min} and y_{max} are opposite, so the ray also intersects the triangle's bounding box. In the untransformed coordinate system, the plane equation for the triangle is

$$3x + y + 4z - 120 = 0$$

In the transformed coordinate system it is (see Sec. 4-2)

$$3x + y + 4z - 43 = 0$$

and the intersection is at

$$z = (43 - 3x - y)/4 = 43/4 = 10.75$$

This value is inside the triangle and is placed on the intersection list.

The intersection list is not empty. The maximum z value is $z_{max} = 10.75$, and the triangle is visible. Translating back to the original coordinate system yields the intersection point at $(20.5, 15.5, 10.75)$. The pixel at $(20, 15)$ is displayed with the triangle's attributes.

Two modifications of this simple algorithm considerably increase its efficiency. The first uses the concept of clustering groups of spatially related objects together. For example, suppose that a scene consists of a table with a bowl of fruit and a candy dish on it. The bowl of fruit contains an orange, an apple, a banana, and a pear. The candy dish contains several pieces of candy of different shapes and colors. Bounding spheres are defined for groups or clusters of related objects, e.g. the fruit bowl and all the fruit in it, the candy dish and all the candy in it, and the table including the fruit dish and fruit and the candy dish and candy. Bounding spheres that enclose more than one object are called cluster spheres. If appropriate, cluster bounding boxes may also be defined. The largest cluster sphere, called the scene sphere, containing all the objects in the scene is also defined. The bounding spheres are then processed hierarchically. If a ray does not intersect the scene sphere, then it cannot intersect any object in the scene. Hence, it is displayed at the background intensity. If the ray intersects the scene sphere, then the cluster spheres and the bounding spheres for individual objects not contained within any cluster sphere, but contained within the scene cluster, are examined for intersections with the ray. If the ray does not intersect a cluster sphere, that cluster and all objects or clusters contained within that cluster are not considered further. If a ray intersects a cluster, the process is repeated recursively until all objects have been considered. If at any point a ray intersects an individual object bounding sphere, the object is placed on the active object list. This procedure significantly reduces the number of ray bounding sphere intersections that must be calculated and hence increases the efficiency of the algorithm.

The second modification uses a priority sort to reduce the number of ray-object intersection calculations. Instead of immediately performing a ray-object intersection calculation as called for in the simple algorithm given above, the object is placed on an intersection object list. When all objects in the scene have been considered, the transformed intersection object list is sorted by depth priority (see Sec. 4-8). The centers of the bounding spheres or the maximum or minimum z value for the bounding boxes may be used to establish the priority sort. Intersections of the ray and objects on the intersection object list are determined in priority order. Unfortunately, as previously discussed in Sec. 4-8, the intersection of the ray and the first object on the prioritized intersection object list is not necessarily the visible point. Intersections with all possibly visible objects, the set $\{Q\}$ (see Sec. 4-8 for details), must be determined and placed on the intersection list. The algorithm then proceeds by sorting the intersection list as described in the simple algorithm. Fortunately the set of possible visible objects $\{Q\}$ is generally small compared to the number of objects on the intersection object list. Hence, the algorithm's efficiency is increased. These two modifications are also applicable for the general ray tracing algorithm incorporating reflection, refraction, and transparency discussed in Sec. 5-12.

The simple algorithm given here does not take advantage of eliminating self-hidden faces for polygonal volumes (see Sec. 4-2), nor does it take advantage of the coherence of the scene. For example, the order in which pixels are considered is immaterial. Considering the pixels in scan line order would allow the algorithm to take advantage of scan line coherence. Alternately, by subdividing the scene, Warnock-style area coherence would lead to fewer objects being considered for any ray and hence lead to greater efficiency. Although incorporating these techniques yields a more efficient opaque visible surface algorithm, they are not applicable for a general ray tracing algorithm incorporating reflection, refraction, and transparency. For example, when reflection is incorporated into the algorithm an object totally obscured by another object may be visible as a reflection in a third object. Since a ray tracing algorithm is a brute force technique, the opaque visible surface algorithms discussed in previous sections are more efficient and should be used.[†]

[†]Implementation of the algorithms as described in the previous sections in the same language on the same computer system for the scene described in Examples 4-19, and 4-22 to 4-24 yields performance ratios of Ray tracing:Warnock:Watkins:Scanline z buffer:z buffer as 9.2:6.2:2.1:1.9:1.

Roth (Ref. 4-46) points out that a ray tracing algorithm can also be used to generate wire frame line drawings for solid objects. The procedure assumes a scan-line-oriented generation of the rays, i.e. top to bottom and left to right. The procedure is

If the visible surface at Pixel(x,y) is the background or is different from the visible surface at Pixel($x - 1, y$) **or** at Pixel($x, y - 1$), display the pixel. Otherwise, do not display the pixel.

A ray tracing algorithm can also be used to determine the physical properties of a solid. A complete analysis is beyond the scope of this text. However, a simple example illustrates the concept. In particular, the volume of an arbitrary solid can be determined by approximating it by the sum of a set of small rectangular parallelepipeds. This is accomplished by generating a set of parallel rays at known intervals. The intersections of each ray and the volume are obtained and ordered along the ray. If the ray is translated to be coincident with the z axis as described above, the volume of each rectangular parallelepiped is then

$$V = l_x l_y [(z_1 - z_2) + (z_3 - z_4) + \cdots + (z_{n-1} - z_n)]$$

where l_x and l_y are the spacing between rays in the horizontal and vertical directions, respectively. Each ($z_{n-1} - z_n$) represents a portion of the ray inside the volume. The volume of the solid is then the sum of the volumes of all the rectangular parallelepipeds. The accuracy of the result depends on the number of rays used. The accuracy can be increased at reduced computational expense by recursively subdividing the "pixel" size if the volumes of adjacent rectangular parallelepipeds differ by more than a specified amount. This technique more accurately determines the volumes in regions of rapid change, e.g., near the edges of volumes enclosed by curved surfaces.

Because of the inherently parallel nature of ray tracing (the process for each ray is the same and independent of the results for any other ray) the algorithm could be implemented in very large-scale integrated (VLSI) hardware using parallel processing techniques.

4-14   SUMMARY

The previous sections have discussed, in some detail, a number of fundamental algorithms used to obtain solutions to the hidden line or hidden surface problem. These algorithms are by no means all those available. However, having mastered the concepts presented, the reader should be equipped to understand new algorithms as they are developed or to invent algorithms specific to a particular application.

As an example, a recent hidden line algorithm by Hedgeley (Ref. 4-47) is based on concepts illustrated by the list priority algorithm of Newell, Newell, and Sancha (Sec. 4-8), the area subdivision algorithm of Warnock (Sec. 4-4), the scan line algorithm of Watkins (Sec. 4-9), and intersection and visibility tests scattered throughout the chapter. The algorithm operates in object space, accepts convex or concave polygons as input, and exhibits linear computational growth with the number of objects.

As a further example Atherton (Ref. 4-48) has applied a modified spanning scan line algorithm (see Sec. 4-11) to the display of images from a constructive solid modeling system. The inner loop of the spanning scan line algorithm is modified to solve the one-dimensional Boolean operations required by a solid modeler using a ray tracing algorithm (see Sec. 4-13). Atherton reports that the modified scan line algorithm executes in approximately 1/60 of the time required for a straight ray tracing algorithm.

4-15 REFERENCES

4-1 Sutherland, Ivan E., Sproul, Robert F., and Schumacker, R. A., "A Characterization of Ten Hidden-Surface Algorithms," *Computing Surveys,* Vol. 6, pp. 1–55, 1974.

4-2 Williams, Hugh, "Algorithm 420, Hidden-Line Plotting Program," *CACM*, Vol. 15, pp. 100–103, 1972.

4-3 Wright, T. J, "A Two-Space Solution to the Hidden Line Problem for Plotting Functions of Two Variables," *IEEE Trans. Comput.*, Vol. C–22, pp. 28–33, 1973.

4-4 Watkins, Steven, L., "Algorithm 483, Masked Three-Dimensional Plot Program with Rotations," *CACM*, Vol. 17, pp. 520–523, 1974.

4-5 Butland, J., "Surface Drawing Made Simple," *CAD Journal*, Vol. 11, pp. 19–22, 1979.

4-6 Gottlieb, M.,"Hidden Line Subroutines for Three Dimensional Plotting," *Byte,* Vol. 3, No. 5, pp. 49–58, 1978.

4-7 Roberts, L. G., "Machine Perception of Three Dimensional Solids," MIT Lincoln Lab. Rep., TR 315, May 1963. Also in J. T. Tippet et al. (eds.), *Optical and Electro-Optical Information Processing*, MIT Press, Cambridge pp. 159–197, 1964.

4-8 Petty, J. S., and Mach, K. D., "Contouring and Hidden-line Algorithms for Vector Graphic Displays," Air Force Applied Physics Lab. Rep., AFAPL-TR-77-3, Jan. 1977, ADA 040 530.

4-9 Rogers, David, F., Meier, William, and Adlum, Linda, "Roberts Algorithm," U.S. Naval Academy, Computer Aided Design/Interactive Graphics Group Study, 1982, unpublished.

4-10 Warnock, John, E., "A Hidden Line Algorithm for Halftone Picture Representation," University of Utah Computer Science Dept. Rep., TR 4-5, May 1968, NTIS AD 761 995.

4-11 Warnock, John, E. "A Hidden-Surface Algorithm for Computer Generated Halftone Pictures," University of Utah Computer Science Dept. Rep., TR 4-15, June 1969, NTIS AD 753 671.

4-12 Weiler, K., and Atherton, P., "Hidden Surface Removal Using Polygon Area Sorting," *Computer Graphics*, Vol. 11, pp. 214–222 (Proc. SIGGRAPH 77).

4-13 Catmull, Edwin, "A Subdivision Algorithm for Computer Display of Curved Surfaces," Ph.D. Thesis, University of Utah, Dec. 1974. Also UTEC-CSc-74-133, and NTIS A004 968.

4-14 Catmull, Edwin, "Computer Display of Curved Surfaces," *Proc. IEEE Conf. Comput. Graphics Pattern Recognition Data Struct.*, May 1975, p. 11.

4-15 Cohen, Elaine, Lyche, Tom, and Riesenfeld, Richard, F., "Discrete B-splines and Subdivision Techniques in Computer-Aided Geometric Design and Computer Graphics," *Computer Graphics Image Processing*, Vol. 14, pp. 87–111, 1980. Also University of Utah, Computer Science Dept. Rep., UUCS-79-117, Oct. 1979.

4-16 Newell, M.E., Newell, R. G., and Sancha, T. L., "A New Approach to the Shaded Picture Problem," *Proc. ACM Natl. Conf.*, 1972, pp. 443–450.

4-17 Newell, M. E., "The Utilization of Procedure Models in Digital Image Synthesis," Ph.D. Thesis, University of Utah, 1974. Also UTEC-CSc-76-218 and NTIS AD/A 039 008/LL.

4-18 Schachter, Bruce J., *Computer Image Generation*, John Wiley, New York, 1982.

4-19 Schumacker, R. A., Brand, B., Gilliland, M., and Sharp, W., "Study for Applying Computer-generated Images to Visual Simulation," U.S. Air Force Human Resources Lab. Tech. Rep., AFHRL-TR-69-14, Sept. 1969, NTIS AD 700 375.

4-20 Fuchs, H., Abram, G. D., and Grant, E. D., "Near Real-Time Shaded Display of Rigid Objects," *Computer Graphics*, Vol. 17, pp. 65–72, 1983 (Proc. SIGGRAPH 83).

4-21 Wylie, C., Romney, G. W., Evans, D. C., and Erdahl, A. C., "Halftone Perspective Drawings by Computer," *FJCC 1967*, Thompson Books, Washington, D.C., pp. 49–58.

4-22 Bouknight, W. J., "An Improved Procedure for Generation of Half-tone Computer Graphics Representations," University of Illinois Coordinated Science Lab. Tech. Rep., R-432, Sept. 1969.

4-23 Bouknight, W. J., and Kelly, K. C., "An Algorithm for Producing Half-tone Computer Graphics Presentations with Shadows and Movable Light Sources," *SJCC 1970*, AFIPS Press, Montvale, N. J. pp. 1–10.

4-24 Bouknight, W. J., "A Procedure for Generation of Three-dimensional Half-toned Computer Graphics Representations," *CACM*, Vol. 13, pp. 527–536, 1970.

4-25 Watkins, G. S., "A Real-Time Visible Surface Algorithm," University of Utah Computer Science Dept. Tech. Rep., UTEC-CSC-70-101, June 1970, NTIS AD 762 004

4-26 Myers, A. J., "An Efficient Visible Surface Program", Report to the NSF, Ohio State University Computer Graphics Research Group, July 1975.

4-27 Romney, G. W., Watkins, G. S., and Evans, D. C., "Real Time Display of Computer Generated Half-tone Perspective Pictures," *IFIP 1968*, North-Holland, Amsterdam, pp. 973–978.

4-28 Hamlin, G., and Gear, C., "Raster-Scan Hidden Surface Algorithm Techniques", *Computer Graphics*, Vol. 11, pp. 206–213, 1977 (Proc. SIGGRAPH 77).

4-29 Jackson, J. H., "Dynamic Scan-converted Images with a Frame Buffer Display Device," *Computer Graphics*, Vol. 14, pp. 163–169, 1980 (Proc. SIGGRAPH 80).

4-30 Archuleta, M., "Hidden Surface Line Drawing Algorithm," University of Utah Computer Science Dept. Tech. Rep., UTEC-CSc-72-121, June 1972.

4-31 Blinn, J. F., "A Scan Line Algorithm for the Computer Display of Parametrically Defined Surfaces," *Computer Graphics*, Vol. 12, 1978 (supplement to Proc. SIGGRAPH 78); see also Ref. 4-33.

4-32 Whitted, T., "A Scan-line Algorithm for Computer Display of Curved Surfaces," *Computer Graphics*, Vol. 12, 1978 (supplement to Proc. SIGGRAPH 78); see also Ref. 4-33.

4-33 Lane, J. M., Carpenter, L. C., Whitted, T., and Blinn, J. F., "Scan Line Methods for Displaying Parametrically Defined Surfaces," *CACM*, Vol. 23, pp. 23–34, 1980.

4-34 Lane, J. M., and Carpenter, L. C., "A Generalized Scan Line Algorithm for the Computer Display of Parametrically Defined Surfaces," *Computer Graphics Image Processing*, Vol. 11, pp. 290–297, 1979.

4-35 Clark, J. H., "A Fast Scan-line Algorithm for Rendering Parametric Surfaces," *Computer Graphics*, Vol. 13, 1979 (supplement to Proc. SIGGRAPH 79).

4-36 Kunz, K. S., *Numerical Analysis*, McGraw-Hill, New York, 1957.

4-37 Kajiya, J. T., "Ray Tracing Parametric Patches," *Computer Graphics,* Vol. 16, pp. 245–254, 1982 (Proc. SIGGRAPH 82).

4-38 Porter, T., "Spherical Shading," *Computer Graphics*, Vol. 12, pp. 282–285, 1978 (Proc. SIGGRAPH 78).

4-39 Porter, T., "The Shaded Surface Display of Large Molecules," *Computer Graphics,* Vol. 13, pp. 234–236, 1979 (Proc. SIGGRAPH 79).

4-40 Staudhammer, J., "On the Display of Space Filling Atomic Models in Real Time," *Computer Graphics*, Vol. 12, pp. 167–172, 1978 (Proc. SIGGRAPH 78).

4-41 Appel, A., "Some Techniques for Shading Machine Renderings of Solids," *AFIPS 1968 Spring Joint Comput. Conf.*, pp. 37–45.

4-42 Goldstein, R. A., and Nagel, R., "3-D Visual Simulation," *Simulation*, pp. 25–31, January 1971.

4-43 Kay, Douglas S., "Transparency, Refraction and Ray Tracing for Computer Synthesized Images," Masters thesis, Program of Computer Graphics, Cornell University, Jan. 1979.

4-44 Kay, Douglas, S., and Greenberg, Donald, "Transparency for Computer Synthesized Images" *Computer Graphics*, Vol. 13, pp. 158–164, 1979 (Proc. SIGGRAPH 79).

4-45 Whitted, J. T., "An Improved Illumination Model for Shaded Display," *CACM*, Vol. 23, pp. 343–349, (Proc. SIGGRAPH 79).

4-46 Roth, Scott D., "Ray Casting for Modeling Solids," *Computer Graphics and Image Processing*, Vol. 18, pp. 109–144, 1982.

4-47 Hedgley, David R. Jr., "A General Solution to the Hidden-Line Problem," *NASA* Ref. Pub. 1085, March 1982.

4-48 Atherton, Peter R., "A Scan-line Hidden Surface Removal Procedure for Constructive Solid Geometry," *Computer Graphics*, Vol. 17, pp. 73–82, 1983 (Proc. SIGGRAPH 83).

4-49 Whitted, Turner, and Weimer, David M., "A Software Testbed for the Development of 3D Raster Graphics Systems," *ACM Transactions on Graphics*, Vol. 1, pp. 43–58, 1982.

CHAPTER FIVE

RENDERING

5-1 INTRODUCTION

Simply defined, rendering is the process of producing realistic images or pictures. Producing realistic images involves both physics and psychology. Light, i.e. electromagnetic energy, reaches the eye after interacting with the physical environment. In the eye, physical and chemical changes take place that generate electrical pulses that are interpreted, i.e. perceived, by the brain. Perception is a learned characteristic. The psychology of visual perception has been extensively studied and written about. An extensive discussion of visual perception is well beyond the scope of this book. The standard reference work on visual perception is Cornsweet (Ref. 5-1).

The human eye is a very complex system. The eye is nearly spherical and about 20 mm in diameter. The eye's flexible lens is used to focus received light onto the retina. The retina contains two different types of receptors: cones and rods. The 6–7 million cones are concentrated in the center of the rear hemisphere of the eye. Each one has an individual nerve connected to it. The cones, which are sensitive only to relatively high light levels, are used to resolve fine detail. The other type of receptor is called a rod. There are between 75 and 150 million rods distributed over the retina. Several rods are connected to a single nerve. Thus, the rods cannot resolve fine detail. The rods are sensitive to very low levels of illumination. Interestingly enough, only the cones are used in perceiving color. Because the cones are sensitive only to relatively high levels of light, objects viewed with low illumination are seen only with the rods. Hence, they are not seen in color.

There is good experimental evidence that the eye's sensitivity to brightness is logarithmic. The total range of brightness sensitivity is very large, on the order of 10^{10}. However, the eye cannot simultaneously respond to this large a brightness range. The eye responds to a much smaller relative brightness range centered around a brightness adaptation level. The relative brightness range is on the order of 100–150 (2.2 log units). The rapidity with which the eye adjusts its brightness adaptation level is different for different parts of the retina. Still, it is remarkable. The eye perceives brightness at the extremes of the relative brightness range as either white or black.

Because the eye adapts to the "average" brightness in a scene, an area of constant brightness or intensity surrounded by a dark area is perceived to be brighter or lighter than the same area surrounded by a light area. This phenomenon, illustrated in Fig. 5-1, is called simultaneous contrast. On a scale of 0–1 the brightness of the center area of Fig. 5-1a is 0.5 and that of the surrounding area 0.2. In Fig. 5-1b the brightness of the center area is again 0.5, but that of the surrounding area is 0.8. A common example is the apparent difference in brightness of a single streetlight viewed against the sky during the day and at night. For either Fig. 5-1a or a streetlight seen in daylight, the average intensity or brightness of the scene is greater than for the scene in Fig. 5-1b or the streetlight at night. Consequently, the contrast is lower and the intensity or brightness of the streetlight or the center of Fig. 5-1a is perceived as lower. A phenomenon similar to simultaneous contrast occurs for color.

Another characteristic of the eye which has implications for computer graphics is that the brightness perceived by the eye tends to overshoot at the boundaries of regions of constant intensity. This characteristic results in areas of constant intensity being perceived as having varying intensity. The phenomenon is called the Mach band effect after the Austrian physicist Ernst Mach, who first observed it. The Mach band effect occurs whenever the slope of the light intensity curve changes abruptly. At that location, the surface appears brighter or darker. If the inflection in the intensity curve is concave, the surface appears brighter; if convex it appears darker. Figure 5-2 illustrates both the concept and the results.

The Mach band effect is particularly important for shaded polygonally represented surfaces. If the direction of the normal vector for each individual

a   b

Figure 5-1 Simultaneous contrast.

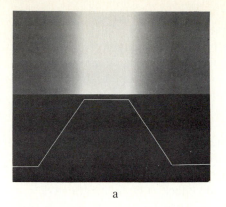 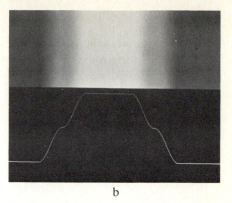

a   b

Figure 5-2 Mach band effects. (a) Piecewise linear, (b) continuous first-derivative intensity function. (*Courtesy of the University of Utah, Ref. 5-2.*)

polygon composing the surface is used to determine the displayed intensity, then the intensity will change abruptly at the polygon edges. The Mach band effect tends to destroy the ability of the eye to smoothly integrate the scene. Figure 5-3a illustrates this effect. Figure 5-3b shows that increasing the number of facets (polygons) decreases the effect but does not eliminate it.

 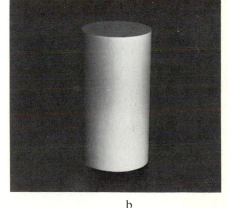

a   b

Figure 5-3 Mach band effect for plane polygonal surface representations. (a) Eight-sided model, (b) 32-sided model. (*Courtesy of the University of Utah, Ref. 5-2.*)

5-2 A SIMPLE ILLUMINATION MODEL

When light energy falls on a surface, it can be absorbed, reflected, or transmitted. Some of the light energy incident on a surface is absorbed and converted to heat. The rest is either reflected or transmitted. It is the reflected or transmitted light that makes an object visible. If all the incident light energy is absorbed, the object is invisible. The object is then called a black body.

Reflected or transmitted light energy makes an object visible. The amount of energy absorbed, reflected, or transmitted depends on the wavelength of the light. If the intensity of incident light is reduced nearly equally for all wavelengths, then an object, illuminated with white light which contains all wavelengths, appears gray. If nearly all the light is absorbed, the object appears black. If only a small fraction is absorbed, the object appears "white." If some wavelengths are selectively absorbed, the light leaving the object has a different energy distribution. The object appears "colored." The color of the object is determined by the wavelengths selectively absorbed.

The character of the light reflected from the surface of an object depends on the composition, direction, and geometry of the light source, the surface orientation, and the surface properties of the object. The light reflected from an object is also characterized by being either diffusely or specularly reflected. Diffusely reflected light can be considered as light that has penetrated below the surface of an object, been absorbed, and then reemitted. Diffusely reflected light is scattered equally in all directions. Hence, the position of the observer is unimportant. Specularly reflected light is reflected from the outer surface of the object.

Lambert's cosine law governs the reflection of light from a point source by a perfect diffuser. Lambert's law states that the intensity of light reflected from a perfect diffuser is proportional to the cosine of the angle between the light direction and the normal to the surface. Specifically

$$I = I_l k_d \cos \theta \qquad 0 \le \theta \le \pi/2$$

where I is the reflected intensity, I_l is the incident intensity from a point light source, k_d is the diffuse reflection constant ($0 \le k_d \le 1$), and θ is the angle between the light direction and the surface normal, as shown in Fig. 5-4. For angles greater than $\pi/2$, the light source is behind the object. The diffuse reflection coefficient k_d varies from material to material. It is also a function of the wavelength of the light. However, simple illumination models generally assume it to be constant.

Objects rendered with a simple Lambertian diffuse reflection illumination model or shader appear to have a dull matte surface. Because a point light source is assumed, objects that receive no light directly from the source appear

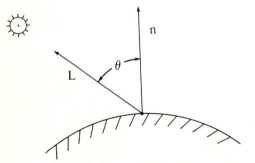

Figure 5-4 Diffuse reflection.

black. However, in a real scene objects also receive light scattered back to them from the surroundings, e.g., the walls of a room. This ambient light represents a distributed light source. Because the computational requirements for a distributed light source are very large, computer graphics illumination models treat it as a constant diffuse term and linearly combine it with the Lambertian contribution. The simple illumination model is then

$$I = I_a k_a + I_l k_d \cos \theta \qquad 0 \le \theta \le \pi/2 \qquad (5\text{-}1)$$

where I_a is the incident ambient light intensity and k_a is the ambient diffuse reflection constant ($0 \le k_a \le 1$).

If the above illumination model is used to determine the intensity of light reflected from two objects with the same orientation to the light source but at different distances, the same intensity for both objects results. If the objects overlap, then it is not possible to distinguish between them. However, it is well known that the intensity of light decreases inversely as the square of the distance from the source; i.e., objects farther away appear dimmer. Unfortunately, if the light source is assumed to be located at infinity, the distance to the object is infinite. Consequently, if the diffuse term in the above illumination model is made inversely proportional to the square of the distance from the light source, it yields no contribution. If a perspective transformation is applied to the scene, the distance from the perspective viewpoint to the object, d, can be used as the constant of proportionality for the diffuse term. However, when the perspective viewpoint is close to the object, $1/d^2$ varies rapidly. This results in objects at nearly the same distance having large unrealistic variations in intensity. Experience has shown that more realistic results can be obtained by using a linear attenuation law. The illumination model is then

$$I = I_a k_a + \frac{I_l k_d \cos \theta}{d + K} \qquad (5\text{-}2)$$

where K is an arbitrary constant. When the viewpoint is assumed to be at infinity, the distance d is determined from the location of the object closest to the viewpoint. This has the effect of illuminating the object closest to the viewpoint with the full intensity of the point light source, and all objects farther from the viewpoint at lower intensities. If the surface is colored, the illumination model is applied individually to each of the three primary colors.

The intensity of specularly reflected light depends on the angle of incidence, the wavelength of the incident light, and the material properties. The governing equation is the Fresnel equation, given in any geometric optics book. Specular reflection of light is directional. For a perfect reflecting surface (a mirror), the angle of reflection is equal to the angle of incidence. Thus, only an observer located at exactly that angle sees any specularly reflected light. This implies that the sight vector, $\mathbf{S}$ in Fig. 5-5, is coincident with the reflection vector $\mathbf{R}$; i.e., the angle α is zero. For imperfect reflecting surfaces the amount of light reaching an observer depends on the spatial distribution of the specularly reflected light.

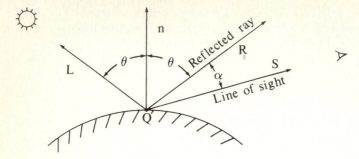

Figure 5-5 Specular reflection.

For smooth surfaces the spatial distribution is narrow or focused, while for rough surfaces it is spread out.

The highlights on a shiny object are due to specular reflection. Because specularly reflected light is focused along the reflection vector, highlights move as the observer moves. Further, because the light is reflected from the outer surface, except for metals and some solid dyes, the reflected light exhibits the characteristics of the incident light. For example, the highlights on a shiny blue painted surface illuminated with white light appear white rather than blue.

Because of the complex physical characteristics of specularly reflected light, an empirical model due to Bui-Tuong Phong (Ref. 5-2) is usually used for simple illumination models. Specifically,

$$I_s = I_l w(i, \lambda) \cos^n \alpha \tag{5-3}$$

where $w(i, \lambda)$, the reflectance curve, gives the ratio of the specularly reflected light to the incident light as a function of the incidence angle i and the wavelength λ. Here, n is a power that approximates the spatial distribution of the specularly reflected light. Figure 5-6 shows $\cos^n \alpha$ for $-\pi/2 \le \alpha \le \pi/2$ for various values of n. Large values of n yield focused spatial distributions characteristic of metals and other shiny surfaces, while small values of n yield more distributed results characteristic of nonmetallic surfaces, e.g. paper.

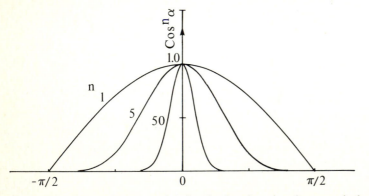

Figure 5-6 Approximate spatial distribution function for specularly reflected light.

Specular reflectance is directional; i.e., it depends on the angle of the incident light. Light that strikes a surface perpendicularly can have only a percentage of the light reflected specularly. The rest must be either absorbed or reflected diffusely. The amount depends on the material properties and the wavelength. For some nonmetallic materials the reflectance can be as little as 4%, while for metallic materials it can exceed 80%. Figure 5-7a gives examples of reflectance curves for typical materials at normal incidence as a function of wavelength, and Fig. 5-7b gives results as a function of incidence angle. Notice that at the grazing angle ($\theta = 90°$) all the incident light is reflected (reflectance $= 100\%$).

Combining the current results with those for ambient and incident diffuse reflection yields the illumination model

$$I = I_a k_a + \frac{I_l}{d + K}(k_d \cos \theta + w(i, \lambda)\cos^n \alpha) \qquad (5\text{-}4)$$

Because $w(i, \lambda)$ is such a complex function it is frequently replaced by an aesthetically or experimentally determined constant k_s. This yields

$$I = I_a k_a + \frac{I_l}{d + K}(k_d \cos \theta + k_s \cos^n \alpha) \qquad (5\text{-}5)$$

as the illumination model. In computer graphics this model is frequently called a shading function. It is used to determine the intensity or shade of each point on an object or of each displayed pixel. Again, individual shading functions are used for each of the three primary colors to yield a colored image. However, since the color of specularly reflected light depends on the color of the incident light, k_s is usually constant for all three primaries.

If multiple light sources are present, the effects are linearly added. The illumination model then becomes

$$I = I_a k_a + \sum_{j=1}^{m} \frac{I_{l_j}}{d + K}(k_d \cos \theta_j + k_s \cos_j^n \alpha_j) \qquad (5\text{-}6)$$

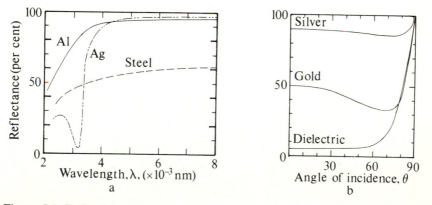

Figure 5-7 Reflection curves.

where m is the number of light sources.

Recalling the formula for the dot product of two vectors allows writing

$$\cos \theta = \frac{\mathbf{n} \cdot \mathbf{L}}{|\mathbf{n}||\mathbf{L}|} = \hat{\mathbf{n}} \cdot \hat{\mathbf{L}}$$

where $\hat{\mathbf{n}}$ and $\hat{\mathbf{L}}$ are the unit vectors in the surface normal and light source directions, respectively.

Similarly

$$\cos \alpha = \frac{\mathbf{R} \cdot \mathbf{S}}{|\mathbf{R}||\mathbf{S}|} = \hat{\mathbf{R}} \cdot \hat{\mathbf{S}}$$

where $\hat{\mathbf{R}}$ and $\hat{\mathbf{S}}$ are the unit vectors for the reflected ray and line-of-sight directions, respectively. Thus, the illumination model for a single light source is

$$I = I_a k_a + \frac{I_l}{d + K}[k_d(\hat{\mathbf{n}} \cdot \hat{\mathbf{L}}) + k_s(\hat{\mathbf{R}} \cdot \hat{\mathbf{S}})^n] \tag{5-7}$$

An example more fully illustrates this simple model.

Example 5-1   Simple Illumination Model

Recalling Fig. 5-5 assume that at point P on the surface the normal, light, and sight vectors are

$$\mathbf{n} = \mathbf{j}$$
$$\mathbf{L} = -\mathbf{i} + 2\mathbf{j} - \mathbf{k}$$
$$\mathbf{S} = \mathbf{i} + 1.5\mathbf{j} + 0.5\mathbf{k}$$

By inspection the reflection vector $\mathbf{R}$ is then

$$\mathbf{R} = \mathbf{i} + 2\mathbf{j} + \mathbf{k}$$

Assuming that there is only one object in the scene, $d = 0$ and $K = 1$. The light source is assumed to be 10 times more intense than the ambient light; i.e., $I_a = 1$ and $I_l = 10$. The surface is to have a shiny metallic appearance. Hence, most of the light will be specularly reflected. Thus, assume $k_s = 0.8$, $k_d = k_a = 0.15$ and $n = 5$. Note that $k_s + k_d = 0.95$, which implies that 5% of the energy from the light source is absorbed. Determining the various elements of the illumination model yields

$$\hat{\mathbf{n}} \cdot \hat{\mathbf{L}} = \frac{\mathbf{n} \cdot \mathbf{L}}{|\mathbf{n}||\mathbf{L}|} = \frac{\mathbf{j} \cdot (-\mathbf{i} + 2\mathbf{j} - \mathbf{k})}{\sqrt{(-1)^2 + (2)^2 + (-1)^2}} = \frac{2}{\sqrt{6}}$$

or

$$\theta = \cos^{-1}\left(2/\sqrt{6}\right) = 35.26°$$

and

$$\hat{\mathbf{R}} \cdot \hat{\mathbf{S}} = \frac{\mathbf{R} \cdot \mathbf{S}}{|\mathbf{R}||\mathbf{S}|} = \frac{(\mathbf{i} + 2\mathbf{j} + \mathbf{k}) \cdot (\mathbf{i} + 1.5\mathbf{j} + 0.5\mathbf{k})}{\sqrt{(1)^2 + (2)^2 + (1)^2}\sqrt{(1)^2 + (1.5)^2 + (0.5)^2}}$$

$$= \frac{4.5}{\sqrt{6}\sqrt{3.5}} = \frac{4.5}{\sqrt{21}}$$

or

$$\alpha = \cos^{-1}(4.5/\sqrt{21}) = 10.89°$$

Finally

$$I = (1)(0.15) + (10/1)[(0.15)(2/\sqrt{6}) + (0.8)(4.5/\sqrt{21})^5]$$

$$= 0.15 + 10(0.12 + 0.73)$$

$$= 8.65$$

Because the sight vector is almost coincident with the reflection vector, an observer would see a bright highlight at the point P. However, if the position of the observer is changed such that the sight vector is

$$\mathbf{S} = \mathbf{i} + 1.5\mathbf{j} - 0.5\mathbf{k}$$

then

$$\hat{\mathbf{R}} \cdot \hat{\mathbf{S}} = \frac{\mathbf{R} \cdot \mathbf{S}}{|\mathbf{R}||\mathbf{S}|} = \frac{3.5}{\sqrt{21}}$$

and

$$\alpha = 40.2°$$

Here

$$I = 0.15 + 10(0.12 + 0.21)$$

$$= 3.45$$

and the observed highlight at P is significantly reduced.

5-3   DETERMINING THE SURFACE NORMAL

The discussion in the previous section shows that the direction of the surface normal is representative of the local curvature of the surface and hence of the direction of specular reflection. If an analytical description of the surface is known, calculation of the surface normal is straightforward. However, for many surfaces only a polygonal approximation is known. If the plane equation for each polygonal facet is known, then the normal for each facet can be determined from the coefficients of the plane equation (see Sec. 4-3). Here the outward normal is desired.

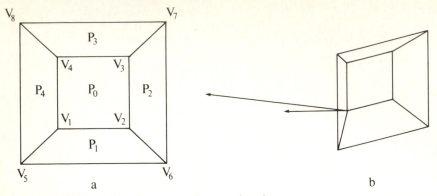

Figure 5-8 Polygonal surface normal approximations.

Many hidden line/hidden surface algorithms use only vertices or edges. In applying an illumination model in conjunction with these algorithms, an approximation to the surface normal at a vertex and along an edge is required. If the plane equations of the polygonal facets are available, then the normal at a vertex can be approximated by averaging the normals of the polygons surrounding the vertex. For example, the direction of the approximate normal at V_1 in Fig. 5-8 is given by

$$\mathbf{n}_{V_1} = (a_0 + a_1 + a_4)\mathbf{i} + (b_0 + b_1 + b_4)\mathbf{j} + (c_0 + c_1 + c_4)\mathbf{k}$$

where $a_0, a_1, a_4, b_0, b_1, b_4, c_0, c_1, c_4$ are the coefficients of the plane equations of the three polygons P_0, P_1, P_4 surrounding V_1. Note that if only the direction of the normal is required then it is not necessary to formally divide by the number of surrounding polygons.

Alternately, if the plane equations are not available, the normal at the vertex can be approximated by averaging the cross products of all the edges that terminate at the vertex. Again using the vertex V_1 of Fig. 5-8, the direction of the approximate normal is

$$n_{V_1} = V_1 V_2 \otimes V_1 V_4 + V_1 V_5 \otimes V_1 V_2 + V_1 V_4 \otimes V_1 V_5$$

Care must be taken to average only outward normals. Further, unless a unit normal is calculated, the magnitude of the approximate normal is influenced by the number and area of individual polygons or the number and length of individual edges. Larger polygons and longer edges have more influence. An example serves to more fully illustrate these techniques.

Example 5-2   Approximating Surface Normals

Consider the polygonal surface shown in Fig. 5-8a. The vertex points are $V_1(-1, -1, 1)$, $V_2(1, -1, 1)$, $V_3(1, 1, 1)$, $V_4(-1, 1, 1)$, $V_5(-2, -2, 0)$, $V_6(2, -2, 0)$, $V_7(2, 2, 0)$, $V_8(-2, 2, 0)$. The surface is a truncated pyramid. The plane equations for the faces labeled P_0, P_1, P_4 surrounding V_1 are

$$P_0: \qquad\qquad z - 1 = 0$$
$$P_1: \qquad -y + z - 2 = 0$$
$$P_4: -x \qquad + z - 2 = 0$$

Approximating the normal at V_1 by averaging the normals of the surrounding polygons yields

$$\mathbf{n}_1 = (a_0 + a_1 + a_4)\mathbf{i} + (b_0 + b_1 + b_4)\mathbf{j} + (c_0 + c_1 + c_4)\mathbf{k}$$
$$= -\mathbf{i} - \mathbf{j} + 3\mathbf{k}$$

The magnitude of $\mathbf{n}_1$ is

$$|\mathbf{n}_1| = \sqrt{(-1)^2 + (-1)^2 + (3)^2} = \sqrt{11}$$

and the unit normal is

$$\frac{\mathbf{n}_1}{|\mathbf{n}_1|} = -0.3\mathbf{i} - 0.3\mathbf{j} + 0.9\mathbf{k}$$

Incidentally, note that dividing by 3 does not yield the unit normal. The cross-products of the edges meeting at V_1 are

$$\mathbf{V}_1\mathbf{V}_2 \otimes \mathbf{V}_1\mathbf{V}_4 = 4\mathbf{k}$$
$$\mathbf{V}_1\mathbf{V}_5 \otimes \mathbf{V}_1\mathbf{V}_2 = -2\mathbf{j} + 2\mathbf{k}$$
$$\mathbf{V}_1\mathbf{V}_4 \otimes \mathbf{V}_1\mathbf{V}_5 = -2\mathbf{i} + 2\mathbf{k}$$

Approximating the normal at V_1 by averaging the cross-products yields

$$\mathbf{n}_1 = -2\mathbf{i} - 2\mathbf{j} + 8\mathbf{k}$$

The magnitude of $\mathbf{n}_1$ is now

$$|\mathbf{n}_1| = \sqrt{(-2)^2 + (-2)^2 + (8)^2} = \sqrt{72}$$

and the unit normal is

$$\frac{\mathbf{n}_1}{|\mathbf{n}_1|} = -0.24\mathbf{i} - 0.24\mathbf{j} + 0.94\mathbf{k}$$

Notice that both the direction and the magnitude of the unnormalized surface normals are different for the two approximation techniques. This is shown in Fig. 5-8b. Consequently, an illumination model will yield subtly different results depending on the technique used to approximate the surface normal.

If the surface normal is to be used to determine the intensity, and if a perspective transformation is used to display the object or scene, the normal must be determined before the perspective transformation is applied, i.e., before perspective division takes place (see Ref. 1-1). Otherwise, the direction of the normal will be distorted. Consequently, the intensity determined by the illumination model will be incorrect.

5-4   DETERMINING THE REFLECTION VECTOR

Determining the direction of the reflection vector is critical in implementing an illumination model. In Example 5-1 the direction of the reflection vector was determined by inspection. Three more general techniques are described in this section. Recall the law of reflection which states that the light vector, the surface normal, and reflected light vector lie in the same plane and that in this plane the angle of incidence is equal to the angle of reflectance (see Fig. 5-9a). Phong (Ref. 5-2) used these conditions to obtain a simple solution when the light direction is along the z axis. For an illumination model consisting of a single point light source this is often an excellent assumption. If the origin of the coordinate system is taken as the point on the surface, then the projection of the normal and reflected vector onto the xy plane lie on a straight line (see Fig. 5-9b).

Thus,

$$\frac{\hat{R}_x}{\hat{R}_y} = \frac{\hat{n}_x}{\hat{n}_y} \qquad (5\text{-}8)$$

where $\hat{R}_x, \hat{R}_y, \hat{n}_x, \hat{n}_y$ are the x and y components of the unit vectors in the reflected and normal directions, respectively.

The angle between the unit normal vector and the z axis is θ. Thus the component in the z direction is

$$\hat{n}_z = \cos\theta \qquad 0 \le \theta \le \pi/2$$

Similarly, the angle between the unit reflection vector and the z axis is 2θ. Hence,

$$\hat{R}_z = \cos 2\theta = 2\cos^2\theta - 1 = 2\hat{n}_z^2 - 1 \qquad (5\text{-}9)$$

Recalling that

$$R_x^2 + R_y^2 + R_z^2 = 1$$

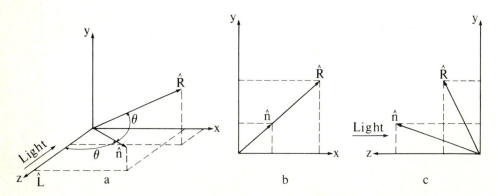

Figure 5-9 Determining the reflection direction.

then

$$\hat{R}_x^2 + \hat{R}_y^2 = 1 - \hat{R}_z^2 = 1 - \cos^2 2\theta$$

or

$$\hat{R}_y^2 \left(\frac{\hat{R}_x^2}{\hat{R}_y^2} + 1 \right) = 1 - \cos^2 2\theta$$

Using the ratio of the x and y components of the reflected and normal vectors above (Eq. 5-8) and recalling that

$$\hat{n}_x^2 + \hat{n}_y^2 + \hat{n}_z^2 = 1$$

yields

$$\frac{\hat{R}_y^2}{\hat{n}_y^2}(\hat{n}_x^2 + \hat{n}_y^2) = \frac{\hat{R}_y^2}{\hat{n}_y^2}(1 - \hat{n}_z^2) = 1 - \cos^2 2\theta$$

Rewriting the right hand side gives

$$\frac{\hat{R}_y^2}{\hat{n}_y^2}(1 - \hat{n}_z^2) = 1 - (2\cos^2 \theta - 1)^2 = 1 - (2\hat{n}_z^2 - 1)^2 = 4\hat{n}_z^2(1 - \hat{n}_z^2)$$

or

$$\hat{R}_y = 2\hat{n}_z\hat{n}_y \tag{5-10}$$

From Eq. (5-8)

$$\hat{R}_x = 2\hat{n}_z\hat{n}_x \tag{5-11}$$

If the light direction is not along the z axis, e.g., when multiple light sources are used, the above technique is not applicable. Each light source could, of course, be translated and rotated until the light direction is along the z axis. However, it is simpler to translate and rotate the normal vector until it is along the z axis with point P on the object at the origin. Here, the xy plane is now the tangent plane to the surface at P, and the x and y components of the unit light and reflection vectors are the negatives of each other. The z components of the unit light and reflection vectors are of course equal. The results in the original orientation are then obtained by applying the inverse transformations. Specifically, in the rotated-translated coordinate system

$$\hat{R}_x = -\hat{L}_x \qquad \hat{R}_y = -\hat{L}_y \qquad \hat{R}_z = \hat{L}_z$$

This technique is particularly convenient if the transformations are implemented in hardware, firmware, or microcode.

The third technique uses the cross-products of the unit normal and the unit light and reflection vectors to ensure that the three vectors lie in the same plane.

The dot products of the unit normal and the unit light and reflection vectors are used to ensure that the incident and reflection angles are equal. These conditions yield

$$\mathbf{n} \otimes \mathbf{L} = \mathbf{R} \otimes \mathbf{n}$$

or

$$(n_y L_z - n_z L_y)\mathbf{i} + (n_z L_x - L_z n_x)\mathbf{j} + (n_x L_y - L_x n_y)\mathbf{k} =$$
$$(n_z R_y - n_y R_z)\mathbf{i} + (n_x R_z - n_z R_x)\mathbf{j} + (n_y R_x - n_x R_y)\mathbf{k}$$

The directions of the cross-product vectors are the same if their *xyz* components are the same. Thus,

$$
\begin{aligned}
- n_z R_y + n_y R_z &= n_z L_y - n_y L_z \\
n_z R_x \qquad\quad - n_x R_z &= n_x L_z - n_z L_x \\
-n_y R_x + n_x R_y \qquad &= n_y L_x - n_x L_y
\end{aligned}
\qquad (5\text{-}12)
$$

At first glance the reflected vector appears to be determined. Unfortunately, for each specific case one of the three equations yields no useful information; i.e., the equations are not independent. Further, the specific equation is not known a priori.

Recalling that the incident and reflected angles are equal yields

$$\mathbf{n} \cdot \mathbf{L} = \mathbf{n} \cdot \mathbf{R}$$

or

$$n_x R_x + n_y R_y + n_z R_z = n_x L_x + n_y L_y + n_z L_z \qquad (5\text{-}13)$$

which yields the required additional condition. A matrix formulation including all four conditions for the three unknowns R_x, R_y, R_z is

$$
\begin{bmatrix}
0 & -n_z & n_y \\
n_z & 0 & -n_x \\
-n_y & n_x & 0 \\
n_x & n_y & n_z
\end{bmatrix}
\begin{bmatrix}
R_x \\ R_y \\ R_z
\end{bmatrix}
=
\begin{bmatrix}
n_z L_y - n_y L_z \\
n_x L_z - n_z L_x \\
n_y L_x - n_x L_y \\
n_x L_x + n_y L_y + n_z L_z
\end{bmatrix}
$$

or

$$[N][R] = [B]$$

Because $[N]$ is not square a trick must be used to obtain a solution.[†] In particular

$$[R] = \big[[N]^{\mathrm{T}}[N]\big]^{-1}[N]^{\mathrm{T}}[B]$$

[†]Normally this technique yields a mean solution. However, because one of the equations (Eq. 5-12) is redundant, here the solution is exact.

5-5 GOURAUD SHADING

If the illumination model is applied to a polygonal surface using a single constant normal for each polygon face, a faceted appearance results as illustrated
by the face in Fig. 5-10a. A smoother appearance is obtained using a technique
developed by Gouraud (Ref. 5-3). If a scan line algorithm is used to render
the object, a value for the intensity of each pixel along the scan line must be
determined from the illumination model. The normals to the surface are approximated at the polygonal vertices of the surface, as described in the previous
section. However, as shown in Fig. 5-11, a scan line does not necessarily pass
through the polygon vertices. Gouraud shading first determines the intensity
at each polygonal vertex. A bilinear interpolation is then used to determine
the intensity of each pixel on the scan line.

In particular, consider the segment of a polygonal surface shown in Fig. 5-11.
The intensity at P is determined by linearly interpolating the intensities of the
polygon vertices A and B to obtain the intensity of Q, the intersection of the
polygon edge with the scan line, i.e.

$$I_Q = uI_A + (1 - u)I_B \qquad 0 \le u \le 1$$

where $u = AQ/AB$. Similarly, the intensities at the polygon vertices B and C
are linearly interpolated to obtain the intensity at R on the scan line, i.e.

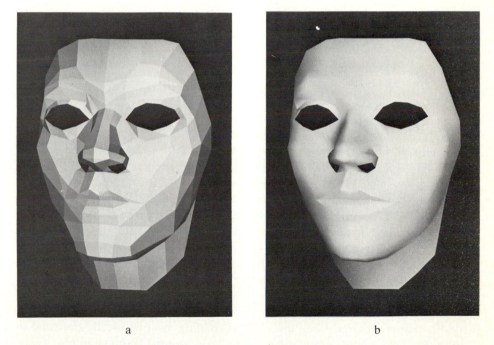

a   b

Figure 5-10 Polygonal and Gouraud shading. (*Courtesy of the University of Utah.*)

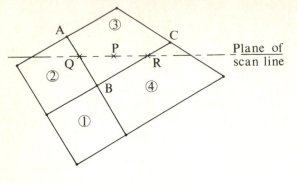

Figure 5-11 Shading interpolation.

$$I_R = wI_B + (1 - w)I_C \qquad 0 \le w \le 1$$

where $w = BR/BC$. Finally, the intensity at P on the scan line is also obtained by linearly interpolating along the scan line between Q and R, i.e.

$$I_P = tI_Q + (1 - t)I_R \qquad 0 \le t \le 1$$

where $t = QP/QR$.

The intensity calculation along the scan line can be performed incrementally. For two pixels at t_1 and t_2 on the scan line

$$I_{P_2} = t_2 I_Q + (1 - t_2)I_R$$

and

$$I_{P_1} = t_1 I_Q + (1 - t_1)I_R$$

Subtracting yields

$$I_{P_2} = I_{P_1} + (I_Q - I_R)(t_2 - t_1) = I_{P_1} + \Delta I \, \Delta t$$

along the scan line. The result of applying Gouraud shading to the polygonal approximation for the face in Fig. 5-10a is shown in Fig. 5-10b. The improvement is startling. However, close examination of Fig. 5-10b shows faint evidence of Mach banding, e.g., on the cheek bones, around the eyes, and on the chin. This is because the shading interpolation rule yields only continuity of intensity value across polygon boundaries but not continuity of change in intensity. Note also that the silhouette edges are polygonal, e.g. the eyes and nose.

An additional difficulty with Gouraud shading is illustrated in Fig. 5-12a. If the normals at the vertices B, C, D are computed using polygon averaging, then they all have the same direction and hence the same intensity. Linear interpolation then yields a constant-intensity value from B to D, which makes the surface appear flat in that area. To achieve a smooth appearance at B, C, and D it is necessary to introduce additional polygons as shown in Fig. 5-12b. If an actual crease is required, then the smooth shading must be locally defeated by "selectively" averaging the surface normals. An example is shown in Fig. 5-12c. Here $\mathbf{n}_{B_1}$ is computed only from the single face to the right of B. $\mathbf{n}_{D_1}$ and $\mathbf{n}_{D_2}$

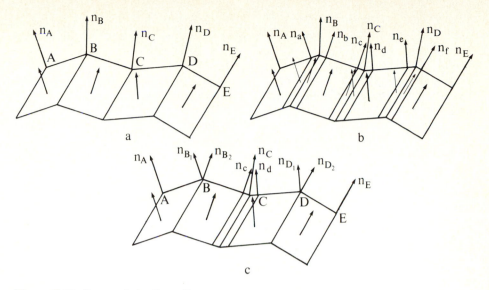

Figure 5-12 Gouraud shading effects.

are obtained similarly, while n_C is computed from the average of the faces to the left and right of C. Gouraud shading then yields a sharp edge at B and D and an apparent smooth graduation at C. The effect is shown by the lips in Fig. 5-10b.

Because of the simplicity of the shading, the shape of individual highlights from specular reflection is strongly influenced by the polygons used to represent the object or surface. Consequently a simple diffuse illumination model (see Eq. 5-1 or 5-2) yields the best results with Gouraud shading.

5-6   PHONG SHADING

Although computationally more expensive, Phong shading (Ref. 5-2) solves many of the problems of Gouraud shading. Whereas Gouraud shading inter-polates intensity values along a scan line, Phong shading interpolates the normal vector along the scan line. The illumination model is then applied at each pixel, using the interpolated normal to determine the intensity. This technique gives a better local approximation to the surface curvature and hence a better rendering of the surface. In particular, specular highlights appear more realistic.

Phong shading first approximates the surface curvature at polygonal vertices by approximating the normal at the vertex (see Sec. 5-3). A bilinear interpola-tion is then used to determine the normal at each pixel. In particular, again using Fig. 5-11, the normal at P is determined by linearly interpolating between A and B to obtain Q, between B and C to obtain R, and finally between Q and R to obtain P. Specifically

$$\mathbf{n}_Q = u\mathbf{n}_A + (1 - u)\mathbf{n}_B \qquad 0 \leq u \leq 1$$

$$\mathbf{n}_R = w\mathbf{n}_B + (1 - w)\mathbf{n}_C \qquad 0 \leq w \leq 1$$

$$\mathbf{n}_P = t\mathbf{n}_Q + (1 - t)\mathbf{n}_R \qquad 0 \leq t \leq 1$$

where again $u = AQ/AB$, $w = BR/BC$, and $t = QP/QR$. Again, the normal along a scan line can be determined incrementally, i.e.

$$\mathbf{n}_{P_2} = \mathbf{n}_{P_1} + (\mathbf{n}_Q - \mathbf{n}_R)(t_2 - t_1) = \mathbf{n}_{P_1} + \Delta\mathbf{n} * \Delta t$$

where the subscripts 1 and 2 indicate successive pixels along the scan line.

Figure 5-13 compares constant, Gouraud, and Phong shading. The left hand torus is rendered with constant normal shading, the middle torus with Gouraud shading, and the right hand torus with Phong shading. The illumination model for the left hand and middle tori is ambient plus diffuse reflection (Eq. 5-1), while that for the Phong-shaded right hand torus also includes specular reflection as shown by the highlights (Eq. 5-5 with $d = 0, K = 1$). Figure 5-14 compares the highlight obtained with specular reflection for Gouraud shading and the more realistic Phong shading.

Although Phong shading reduces most of the problems associated with Gouraud shading, it is still a linear interpolation scheme. Consequently, discontinuities in the first derivative of the intensity still give rise to Mach band effects. In general, these effects are smaller than for Gouraud shading. However, Duff (Ref. 5-4) has shown that in some cases, notably for spheres, Phong shading yields worse Mach band effects than Gouraud shading. Further, both techniques potentially render concave polygons incorrectly. For example, consider the polygon shown in Fig. 5-15. The scan line labeled 1 will use data from the vertices QRS, while that labeled 2 just below it also uses data from vertex P. This can give rise to a shading discontinuity.

Figure 5-13 Comparison of rendering techniques. (Left) constant normal, (middle) Gouraud, (right) Phong. (*Courtesy of T. Whitted.*)

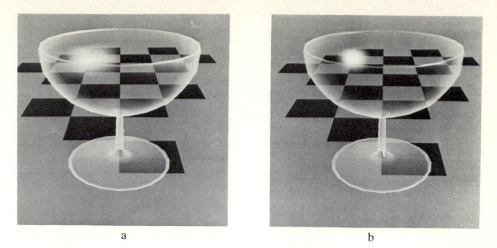

a   b

Figure 5-14 Comparison of specular reflection highlights.   (a) Gouraud shading, (b) Phong shading. (*Courtesy of the University of Utah.*)

Additional difficulties are exhibited by both Gouraud and Phong shading when used in animation sequences. In particular, the shading varies significantly from frame to frame. This effect is a result of working in image space and the fact that the shading rule is not invariant with respect to rotation. Consequently, as the orientation of an object changes from frame to frame, its shade (color) also changes. This is quite noticeable. Duff (Ref. 5-4) presents a technique for rotation independent Gouraud and Phong shading rules.

An example that computes constant, Gouraud, and Phong shading serves to illustrate the difference between the three techniques.

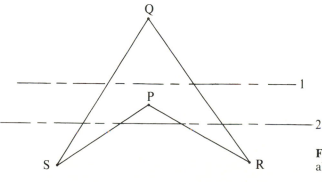

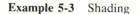

Figure 5-15 Shading anomalies for concave polygons.

Example 5-3   Shading

Consider the segment of a surface shown in Fig. 5-11. The equations of the four planes are

$$
\begin{array}{lrll}
1: & & 2z & -4 = 0 \\
2: & -x + 1.732y + 7.5z & & -17 = 0 \\
3: & -2.25x + 3.897y + 10z & -24.5 = 0 \\
4: & & 5.5z & -11 = 0
\end{array}
$$

where z is perpendicular to the plane of the paper, x is positive to the right, and y is positive upward. The point B has coordinates of $(0.366, 1.366, 2)$.

The vector to the eye is $S[1 \ \ 1 \ \ 1]$, and a single point light source is located at positive infinity on the z axis. The light vector is thus $L[0 \ \ 0 \ \ 1]$. The illumination model is given by Eq. 5-7, with $d = 0$, $K = 1$, $I_a = 1$, $I_l = 10$, $n = 2$, $k_s = 0.8$, $k_d = k_a = 0.15$. Since the light direction is along the z axis, the Phong technique can be used to determine the direction of the reflected light vector (see Sec. 5-4).

For constant shading the point P is in polygon 3. From the plane equation for polygon 3 the unit normal is

$$
\hat{n}_3 = \frac{n_3}{|n_3|} = -0.21i + 0.36j + 0.91k
$$

The angle between the normal and light vector is

$$
\hat{n} \cdot \hat{L} = (-0.21i + 0.36j + 0.91k) \cdot k = 0.91
$$

which yields an incidence angle of about $24.2°$.

From Eqs. (5-9) to (5-11)

$$
\begin{aligned}
\hat{R}_z &= 2\hat{n}_z^2 - 1 = (2)(0.91)^2 - 1 = 0.66 \\
\hat{R}_x &= 2\hat{n}_z\hat{n}_x = (2)(0.91)(-0.21) = -0.38 \\
\hat{R}_y &= 2\hat{n}_z\hat{n}_y = (2)(0.91)(0.36) = 0.66
\end{aligned}
$$

and

$$
\hat{R} = -0.38i + 0.66j + 0.66k
$$

The unit vector in the eye direction is

$$
\hat{S} = \frac{S}{|S|} = \frac{S}{\sqrt{3}} = 0.58i + 0.58j + 0.58k
$$

Using this value, the angle between the reflected light vector and the line of sight or eye is

$$
\hat{R} \cdot \hat{S} = (-0.38i + 0.66j + 0.66k) \cdot (0.58i + 0.58j + 0.58k)
$$
$$
= 0.55
$$

which yields an angle of about $57°$.

Recalling the illumination model (Eq. 5-7) yields

$$
I_P = I_a k_a + \frac{I_l}{d + K}[k_d(\hat{n} \cdot \hat{L}) + k_s(\hat{R} \cdot \hat{S})^n]
$$
$$
= (1)(0.15) + (10/1)[(0.15)(0.91) + (0.8)(0.55)^2]
$$
$$
= 0.15 + 10(0.14 + 0.24) = 0.15 + 3.8
$$
$$
= 3.95
$$

for point P.

For Gouraud shading the normal vectors for A, B, C in Fig. 5-11 are required. Approximating the normals by the average of the normals of the surrounding planes yields

$$\mathbf{n}_A = \mathbf{n}_2 + \mathbf{n}_3 = -3.25\mathbf{i} + 5.63\mathbf{j} + 17.5\mathbf{k}$$
$$\mathbf{n}_B = \mathbf{n}_1 + \mathbf{n}_2 + \mathbf{n}_3 + \mathbf{n}_4 = -3.25\mathbf{i} + 5.63\mathbf{j} + 25\mathbf{k}$$
$$\mathbf{n}_C = \mathbf{n}_3 + \mathbf{n}_4 = -2.25\mathbf{i} + 3.897\mathbf{j} + 15.5\mathbf{k}$$

where $\mathbf{n}_1$, $\mathbf{n}_2$, $\mathbf{n}_3$, $\mathbf{n}_4$ are obtained from the plane equations given above. The unit normals are

$$\hat{\mathbf{n}}_A = \frac{\mathbf{n}_A}{|\mathbf{n}_A|} = -0.17\mathbf{i} + 0.3\mathbf{j} + 0.94\mathbf{k}$$
$$\hat{\mathbf{n}}_B = \frac{\mathbf{n}_B}{|\mathbf{n}_B|} = -0.12\mathbf{i} + 0.22\mathbf{j} + 0.97\mathbf{k}$$
$$\hat{\mathbf{n}}_C = \frac{\mathbf{n}_C}{|\mathbf{n}_C|} = -0.14\mathbf{i} + 0.24\mathbf{j} + 0.96\mathbf{k}$$

The unit reflected vectors are

$$\hat{\mathbf{R}}_A = -0.33\mathbf{i} + 0.57\mathbf{j} + 0.76\mathbf{k}$$
$$\hat{\mathbf{R}}_B = -0.24\mathbf{i} + 0.42\mathbf{j} + 0.87\mathbf{k}$$
$$\hat{\mathbf{R}}_C = -0.27\mathbf{i} + 0.46\mathbf{j} + 0.84\mathbf{k}$$

The intensities at A, B, C are

$$I_A = 0.15 + 10(0.14 + 0.27) = 4.25$$
$$I_B = 0.15 + 10(0.15 + 0.30) = 4.65$$
$$I_C = 0.15 + 10(0.14 + 0.29) = 4.45$$

On a particular scan line $u = AQ/AB = 0.4$ and $w = BR/BC = 0.7$. Interpolating to find the intensities at Q and R yields

$$I_Q = uI_A + (1 - u)I_B = (0.4)(4.25) + (1 - 0.4)(4.65) = 4.49$$
$$I_R = wI_B + (1 - w)I_C = (0.7)(4.65) + (1 - 0.7)(4.45) = 4.59$$

The point P on the scan line is located at $t = QP/QR = 0.5$. Interpolating to find the intensity at P yields

$$I_P = tI_Q + (1 - t)I_R = (0.5)(4.49) + (1 - 0.5)(4.59) = 4.54$$

Phong shading interpolates the normals at A, B, C to first obtain the normal at P. The normal at P is then used to obtain the intensity at P. First, interpolating to obtain the unit normals at Q and R yields

$$\hat{\mathbf{n}}_Q = u\hat{\mathbf{n}}_A + (1 - u)\hat{\mathbf{n}}_B = (0.4)[-0.17 \quad 0.3 \quad 0.94] + (0.6)[-0.12 \quad 0.22 \quad 0.97]$$
$$= [-0.14 \quad 0.25 \quad 0.96] = -0.14\mathbf{i} + 0.25\mathbf{j} + 0.96\mathbf{k}$$
$$\hat{\mathbf{n}}_R = w\hat{\mathbf{n}}_B + (1 - w)\hat{\mathbf{n}}_C = (0.7)[-0.12 \quad 0.22 \quad 0.97] + (0.3)[0.14 \quad 0.24 \quad 0.96]$$
$$= [-0.04 \quad 0.23 \quad 0.97] = -0.04\mathbf{i} + 0.23\mathbf{j} + 0.97\mathbf{k}$$

Interpolating the normal along the scan line yields

$$\hat{\mathbf{n}}_P = t\hat{\mathbf{n}}_Q + (1 - t)\hat{\mathbf{n}}_R = (0.5)[-0.14 \quad 0.25 \quad 0.96] + (0.5)[-0.04 \quad 0.23 \quad 0.97]$$

$$= [-0.09 \quad 0.24 \quad 0.97]$$
$$= -0.09\mathbf{i} + 0.24\mathbf{j} + 0.97\mathbf{k}$$

The unit reflection vector at P is then

$$\hat{\mathbf{R}}_P = -0.17\mathbf{i} + 0.46\mathbf{j} + 0.87\mathbf{k}$$

The intensity at P is

$$I_P = 0.15 + (10)(0.15 + 0.36) = 5.25$$

Comparing the different shading models yields

Constant: $\quad I_P = 3.93$
Gouraud: $\quad I_P = 4.54$
Phong: $\quad\quad I_P = 5.25$

5-7 A SIMPLE ILLUMINATION MODEL WITH SPECIAL EFFECTS

Warn (Ref. 5-5) has extended the simple point source illumination model discussed previously in Sec. 5-2 to include special effects. The model was inspired by the lighting controls found in a professional photographer's studio.   The special effects include controls for light direction and for light concentration. Further, the area illuminated by a light source can be limited.

The Warn model allows the direction of a light source to be controlled independently of its location, as shown in Fig. 5-16a. Conceptually, the directed light can be modeled as a single point perfect specularly reflecting pseudo surface, illuminated by a point light source, as shown in Fig. 5-16b. If the point light source is located along the direction $\mathbf{L}$ normal to the reflecting pseudo sur-

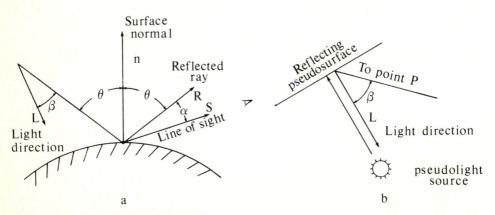

Figure 5-16 Directed lighting model.

face, then the reflection of that source illuminates the object along the direction
L. Hence, the direction of the light is controlled by rotating the pseudo surface.

With this conceptual model for the directed light source, the same illumination model can be used for both directed and point source lights in a scene. The
amount of light received at point P from the directed light source as shown in
Fig. 5-16a depends on the angle β between **L**, the light direction vector, and
the line from the location of the light to P. Using the Phong approximation
for specular reflection from a perfect surface, the intensity of the directed light
source along the line from the source to the point P is

$$I_{l_j} \cos^c \beta$$

where c is a power that determines the spatial concentration of the directed light
source (see Fig. 5-6). If c is large, the beam is narrow, simulating a spotlight.
If c is small, the beam is spread out to simulate a flood light. The contribution
of the directed light source to the overall illumination model (see Eq. 5-6) is
then

$$I_j = I_{l_j} \cos^c \beta (k_{d_j} \cos \theta_j + k_{s_j} \cos^{n_j} \alpha_j) \qquad (5\text{-}14)$$

where j designates the specific light source.

A studio photographer obtains special effects by limiting the area of concentration of lights using flaps (called barn doors by professional photographers)
mounted on the lights and with special reflectors. The Warn model simulates
these effects with flaps and cones. Flaps oriented to the coordinate planes are
implemented by limiting the maximum and minimum extent in x, y, or z of the
light, as shown in Fig. 5-17a. If a point on the object is within the range of
the flap, e.g. $y_{min} \le y_{object} \le y_{max}$, the contribution from that light is evaluated.
Otherwise, it is ignored. Implementation of arbitrarily oriented flaps is straightforward. Flaps can also be used to simulate effects that have no physical coun-
terpart. For example, a flap can be used to drop a curtain across a scene to
limit penetration of a particular light source.

A cone, as shown in Fig. 5-17b, can be used to produce a sharply delineated
spotlight. This is in contrast to the gradual decrease at the edge achieved by

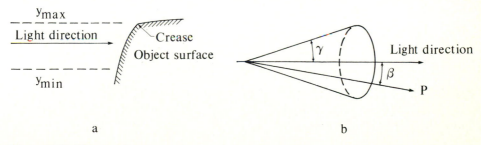

a   b

Figure 5-17 Flaps and cones.

varying c in the directed light source model. Again this simulates one effect available to the commercial photographer. Implementation of the cone effect is straightforward. If the apex of the cone is located at the light source and γ is the cone angle, then if $\beta < \gamma$, the effect of that light source on the point P can be ignored. Otherwise, it is included in the illumination model. In practice, this is accomplished by comparing $\cos \beta$ with $\cos \gamma$; i.e., $\cos \beta < \cos \gamma$.

The effects that can be achieved with this illumination model are shown by the 1983 Chevrolet Camaro in Color Plate 1. Five lights have been used. Two lights have been used on the left side of the car for back lighting. Two lights have also been used on the right side of the car. Notice in particular the use of light concentration to emphasize the crease on the right door and along the right rear fender. The fifth light, high and behind the car, is used to emphasize the taillights and the detail on the bumper. The results are exceptional.

5-8 A MORE COMPLETE ILLUMINATION MODEL

The illumination models discussed in the previous sections are relatively simple. They are based on aesthetic and experimental approximations. This is particularly true of the specular component of the reflected light. Torrance and Sparrow (Ref. 5-6) present a theoretical model for reflected light. Correlation between the Torrance-Sparrow theoretical model and experiment is excellent. Blinn (Ref. 5-7) and Cook and Torrance (Refs. 5-8 and 5-9) have used this model to generate synthetic images. Blinn assumed that the specular highlights were the same color as the incident light. Cook integrated the dependence of the specular reflectance coefficient on wavelength into the model. The results show that the color, i.e. the wavelength, of the specular highlights depends on the material properties. The color of the specular highlights approaches the color of the light source as the incidence angle approaches $\pi/2$.

To develop a more complete illumination model, first consider the solid angle subtended by a light source. The incident energy per unit time per unit area of the reflecting surface is then related to the intensity of the incident light per unit projected area per unit solid angle ω subtended by the light source by

$$E_l = I_l(\hat{\mathbf{n}} \cdot \hat{\mathbf{L}}) \, d\omega$$

For rough surfaces, the incident light is reflected over a wide range of angles. The reflected light intensity is related to the incident energy by

$$I = rE_l$$

Here, r is the ratio of the reflected intensity for a given direction to the incident energy from another direction. It is called the bidirectional reflectance. Combining the two equations yields

$$I = rI_l(\hat{\mathbf{n}} \cdot \hat{\mathbf{L}}) \, d\omega$$

The bidirectional reflectance is composed of two parts, specular and diffuse, i.e.

$$r = k_d r_d + k_s r_s \qquad \text{where } k_d + k_s = 1$$

Here k_d and k_s are properties of the materials but are not normally known. Hence, they are usually treated as arbitrary parameters.

Reflection from ambient illumination is needed to complete the model. If a surrounding hemisphere is considered the source of ambient illumination, part of that hemisphere may be blocked by other objects. With this in mind, the reflected intensity due to ambient illumination is

$$I = f k_a r_a I_a$$

where f is the unblocked fraction of the hemisphere. The ambient reflectance r_a results from integrating the bidirectional reflectance r over the hemisphere. Consequently r_a is a linear combination of r_d and r_s. The constant k_a again depends on the material properties but is normally an arbitrary parameter.

Combining the results yields the Cook-Torrance illumination model for m multiple light sources, i.e.

$$I = f k_a r_a I_a + \sum_{j+1}^{m} I_{l_j} (\hat{\mathbf{n}} \cdot \hat{\mathbf{L}}_j) \, d\omega_j (k_d r_d + k_s r_s) \qquad (5\text{-}15)$$

Notice that, in contrast to the previous illumination models, the Cook-Torrance model has the ability to account for multiple light sources of both different intensities (I_l) and different projected areas ($\hat{\mathbf{n}} \cdot \hat{\mathbf{L}} \, d\omega$). This ability can be of importance. For example, a light source with the same intensity and illumination angle as another light source but with twice the solid angle yields twice the reflected intensity; i.e., the surface appears twice as bright. Quite small solid angles can occur for large distant light sources; e.g., the solid angle for the sun is 0.000068 steradian.

The components of the model depend on the wavelength of the incident light, the material properties of the illuminated object, the roughness of the surface, and the reflection geometry. Because of their considerable influence on the realism of the resulting synthetic images, the highlights due to specular reflection are of particular interest. The Torrance-Sparrow model addresses this problem.

The Torrance-Sparrow model (Ref. 5-6) for reflection from a rough surface is based on the principles of geometric optics. It is applicable to surfaces with an average roughness large compared to the wavelength of the incident light. The model assumes that the surface is composed of randomly oriented mirrorlike microfacets. The specular reflectance component of the reflected light r_s results from single reflections from the mirrorlike microfacets. Diffuse reflection r_d is a result of multiple reflections among the microfacets and from internal scattering. Figure 5-18 shows the geometry for reflection from a rough

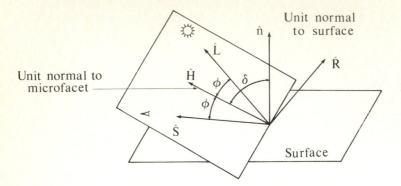

Figure 5-18 Geometry for the Torrance-Sparrow reflection model.

surface. Here, $\hat{\mathbf{n}}$ is the unit normal to the surface, $\hat{\mathbf{L}}$ is the unit vector in the direction of the light source, $\hat{\mathbf{R}}$ is the unit reflection vector for the surface, $\hat{\mathbf{H}}$ is the unit normal for a single microfacet in the surface, and $\hat{\mathbf{S}}$ is the unit reflection vector for the microfacet and also the direction of the observer. By the laws of reflection, $\hat{\mathbf{L}}$, $\hat{\mathbf{H}}$, and $\hat{\mathbf{S}}$ all lie in the same plane and the incident and reflection angles ϕ are equal. The angle between the normal to the surface $\hat{\mathbf{n}}$ and the normal to the microfacet $\hat{\mathbf{H}}$ is δ. Since $\hat{\mathbf{H}}$ is the bisector of the angle between $\hat{\mathbf{L}}$ and $\hat{\mathbf{S}}$,

$$\hat{\mathbf{H}} = \frac{\hat{\mathbf{S}} + \hat{\mathbf{L}}}{|\hat{\mathbf{S}}| + |\hat{\mathbf{L}}|} = \frac{\hat{\mathbf{S}} + \hat{\mathbf{L}}}{2}$$

and

$$\cos\phi = \hat{\mathbf{L}} \cdot \hat{\mathbf{H}} = \hat{\mathbf{S}} \cdot \hat{\mathbf{H}}$$

Only microfacets with normals in the direction $\hat{\mathbf{H}}$ contribute to the specular reflection seen by an observer in the direction $\hat{\mathbf{S}}$.

Using the Torrance-Sparrow model, Cook and Torrance give the specular reflectance r_s as

$$r_s = \frac{F}{\pi} \frac{DG}{(\hat{\mathbf{n}} \cdot \hat{\mathbf{L}})(\hat{\mathbf{n}} \cdot \hat{\mathbf{S}})}$$

where F is the Fresnel term, D is the distribution function for the microfacets on the surface, and G is a geometric attenuation factor due to shadowing and masking of one microfacet by another.

If each microfacet is considered as one side of a symmetric V-groove cavity (see Fig. 5-19), then part of a microfacet may be shadowed from incoming light (see Fig. 5-19b). Alternatively, part of the light reflected from a facet may not leave the cavity because it is masked by the opposite cavity wall. This is shown in Fig. 5-19c. The masking-and-shadowing effect is given by the ratio $\overline{m}/l$. Thus, the geometric attenuation is

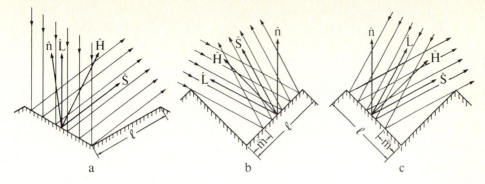

Figure 5-19 Geometric attenuation by the masking-and-shadowing effect. (a) No interference, (b) shadowing, (c) masking.

$$G = 1 - \overline{m}/l$$

From the geometry shown in Fig. 5-19 it is obvious that the geometric attenuation is a function of the angle of the incident light, the included angle between the sides of the V groove, and the length of the side of the V groove, l. When there is no interference, $\overline{m} = 0$ and $G = 1$. Both Torrance and Sparrow (Ref. 5-6) and Blinn (Ref. 5-7) have determined G for masking and shadowing effects. For masking (Fig. 5-19c),

$$G_{\overline{m}} = \frac{2(\hat{\mathbf{n}} \cdot \hat{\mathbf{H}})(\hat{\mathbf{n}} \cdot \hat{\mathbf{L}})}{\hat{\mathbf{H}} \cdot \hat{\mathbf{L}}}$$

For shadowing (Fig. 5-19b), the result is the same with $\hat{\mathbf{S}}$ and $\hat{\mathbf{L}}$ exchanged; i.e.

$$G_s = \frac{2(\hat{\mathbf{n}} \cdot \hat{\mathbf{H}})(\hat{\mathbf{n}} \cdot \hat{\mathbf{S}})}{\hat{\mathbf{H}} \cdot \hat{\mathbf{S}}} = \frac{2(\hat{\mathbf{n}} \cdot \hat{\mathbf{H}})(\hat{\mathbf{n}} \cdot \hat{\mathbf{S}})}{\hat{\mathbf{H}} \cdot \hat{\mathbf{L}}}$$

since $\hat{\mathbf{H}}$ is the bisector of $\hat{\mathbf{L}}$ and $\hat{\mathbf{S}}$. For any given situation, the geometric attenuation is the minimum of these values; i.e.

$$G = \text{Min}(1, G_m, G_s)$$

Torrance and Sparrow assume that the microfacet distribution on the surface is Gaussian. Thus,

$$D = c_1 e^{-(\delta/m)^2}$$

where c_1 is an arbitrary constant and m is the root mean square slope of the microfacets. Cook and Torrance use a more theoretically founded distribution model proposed by Beckmann (Ref. 5-10). The Beckmann distribution is

$$D = \frac{1}{m^2 \cos^4 \delta} e^{-(\tan \delta/m)^2}$$

which provides the absolute magnitude of the distribution function without arbitrary constants. Figure 5-20 compares the Beckmann distributions for $m = 0.2$ and 0.6, corresponding to shiny and matte surfaces. Each point on the surface shown represents the magnitude of the reflected intensity in the direction $\hat{\mathbf{S}}$ from the point P as the direction of $\hat{\mathbf{S}}$ varies over a hemisphere. For small values of m, the reflected intensity is concentrated along the mirror direction $\hat{\mathbf{R}}$, while for larger values of m it is more evenly distributed. Small values of m yield shiny surfaces, and large values dull mattelike surfaces. For small values of m corresponding to specular reflection, there is little difference between the Gaussian, Beckmann or Phong distribution functions. For larger values of m the differences are more significant.

If a surface has more than one roughness scale, weighted linear combinations of the distribution functions for different values of m may be used; e.g.

$$D = \sum_i w_i D(m_i)$$

where the sum of the weighting factors w_i is unity, i.e. $\Sigma \, w_i = 1$.

Ambient, diffuse, and specular reflection all depend on wavelength λ. The wavelength dependence of r_a, r_d, and F is a result of the material properties of the object. The Fresnel term in the specular reflectance r_s can be theoretically calculated from the Fresnel equation for unpolarized incident light reflected from a smooth mirrorlike surface, i.e.

$$F = \frac{1}{2}\left[\frac{\sin^2(\phi - \theta)}{\sin^2(\phi + \theta)} + \frac{\tan^2(\phi - \theta)}{\tan^2(\phi + \theta)}\right]$$

where

$$\sin\theta = \sin\phi/\eta$$
$$\eta = \text{index of refraction of the material}$$

Here, $\theta = \cos^{-1}(\mathbf{L}\cdot\mathbf{H}) = \cos^{-1}(\hat{\mathbf{S}}\cdot\hat{\mathbf{H}})$, the angle of incidence. Since the index of refraction is a function of wavelength, F is also a function of wavelength.

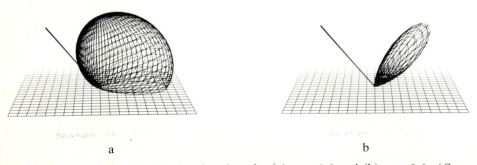

a   b

Figure 5-20 Beckmann distribution functions for (a) $m = 0.2$ and (b) $m = 0.6$. (*Courtesy of Rob Cook and the Program of Computer Graphics, Cornell University.*)

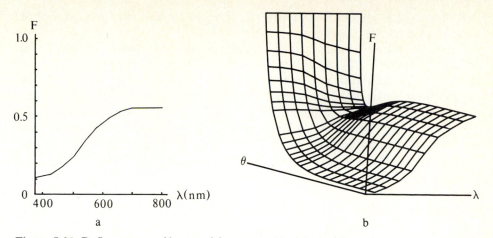

Figure 5-21 Reflectance ρ of bronze (a) at normal incidence (b) as a function of incidence angle calculated from (a) and the Fresnel equation. (*Photograph courtesy of Rob Cook and the Program of Computer Graphics, Cornell University.*)

If η is not known as a function of wavelength, F may be obtained from experimental values (see, for example, Ref. 5-11).[†] Figure 5-21a shows $F(\lambda)$ for bronze at normal incidence. Cook and Torrance suggest the following procedure for obtaining the angular dependence of $F(\lambda)$ when only the normal dependence on wavelength is known. Rewriting F as

$$F = \frac{1}{2}\frac{(g - c)^2}{(g + c)^2}\left\{1 + \frac{[c(g + c) - 1]^2}{[c(g - c) + 1]^2}\right\}$$

where

$$c = \cos\phi = \hat{\mathbf{S}}\cdot\hat{\mathbf{H}} = \hat{\mathbf{L}}\cdot\hat{\mathbf{H}}$$

$$g^2 = \eta^2 + c^2 - 1$$

and noting that at $\phi = 0$, $c = 1$, $g = \eta$, yields

$$F_0 = \left(\frac{\eta - 1}{\eta + 1}\right)^2$$

Solving for η, the index of refraction, yields

$$\eta(\lambda) = \frac{1 + \sqrt{F_0(\lambda)}}{1 - \sqrt{F_0(\lambda)}}$$

[†]Note that the reflectance spectra given in Ref. 5-11 are for polished surfaces. They must be multiplied by $1/\pi$ for rough surfaces.

This value of η is used to determine $F(\lambda)$ from the Fresnel equation. A typical result is shown in Fig. 5-21b.

The dependence of the specular reflectance on wavelength and angle of incidence implies that there is a color shift in the specular highlights as the angle of incidence approaches $\pi/2$ (see Fig. 5-21b). At near normal incidence, $\phi = 0$; the specular highlights are the color of the material. Near the grazing angle of $\phi = \pi/2$, the specular highlights are the color of the incidence light source ($F = 1$). Because calculation of the color shift is expensive, Cook and Torrance suggest a linear interpolation between the color at normal reflectance ($\phi = 0$) and the color of the light ($\phi = \pi/2$). For example, the red component is

$$Red_\theta = Red_0 + (Red_{\pi/2} - Red_0)\frac{Max(0, F_\theta - F_0)}{F_{\pi/2} - F_0}$$

The blue and green components in an RGB color space (see Sec. 5-15) are determined similarly.

Cook and Torrance take the diffuse reflectance r_d to be the normal reflectance, $\phi = 0$, from the surface. Although the diffuse reflectance does vary with angle, the effect is negligible for incidence angles less than about 70°. Hence, this is a reasonable assumption.

The two vases shown in Color Plate 2 illustrate results for the more complete illumination model. The left hand vase is bronze-colored plastic. The plastic is simulated using a colored diffuse component and white specular highlights ($F = 1$). The right hand vase is metallic bronze. For metals, reflection occurs from the surface. There is little penetration of the incident light below the surface and hence little if any diffuse reflection. Notice that here the specular reflected highlights have a bronze color. The specific details used by Cook to generate these images are given in Table 5-1.

Blinn has also used the more complex Torrance-Sparrow model with $F = 1$, i.e., without accounting for the color shift. Figure 5-22 by Blinn compares the shape of the specular highlights obtained using the Phong illumination model when the object is edge-lit. Edge-lighting occurs when the observer ($\hat{S}$) and the light source ($\hat{L}$) are approximately 90° apart. When the light and the observer are at the same location, i.e. $\hat{L} = \hat{S}$, the results for the two models are indistinguishable.

The above results are explained by Fig. 5-23 which shows a comparison of the Phong and Torrance-Sparrow distribution functions for near normal (25°) and near grazing (65°) angles for incident light. The bump represents the specular reflectance. Figures 5-23a and b show little difference between the models for near normal incidence. However, for near grazing angles the Torrance-Sparrow model exhibits a laterally narrower, vertically oriented specular reflectance bump which is not quite in the same direction as that for the Phong model. Incorporating the geometric attenuation factor G into the Phong illumination model yields results similar to those produced by the Torrance-Sparrow model for edge-lit objects.

Plate 1:

1983 Chevrolet Camaro. Rendered by D. Warn with a Watkins algorithm and the special effects illumination model of Sec. 5-7. *(Courtesy General Motors Research Laboratory.)*

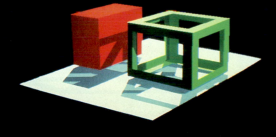

Bronze-colored Plastic

Plate 2:

Bronze vases. The vase above is bronze-colored plastic. The vase below is metallic bronze. Each vase is illuminated with two light sources and rendered using the Cook-Torrance illumination model of Sec. 5-8. *(Courtesy R. Cook and the Program of Computer Graphics, Cornell University.)*

Bronze

Plate 3:

Shadows. The Weiler-Atherton algorithm of Sec. 5-10 is used to determine the shadows from the two light sources. *(Courtesy of P. Atherton and the Program of Computer Graphics, Cornell University.)*

Plate 4:

Fractal mountains. The image above contains 16,384 fractal triangles. The image to the left contains 262,144 fractal triangles. Notice the self-shadowing from the light source at the right. *(Courtesy of J. Kajiya, Cal Tech.)*

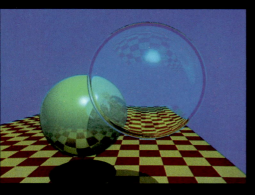

Plate 5:

Balls over a red-yellow checkerboard. Rendered with a ray tracing algorithm and a global illumination model incorporating reflections, shadows and transparency with refraction effects (see Sec. 5-12). *(Courtesy T. Whitted, Bell Laboratories, reprinted with permission from Communications of the ACM, Vol. 23, June 1980, Copyright 1980, Association for Computing Machinery.)*

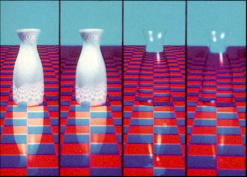

Plate 6:

Vases. Opaque and transparent vases rendered with a ray tracing algorithm. In each case the right hand image illustrates the effects of limited depth of field (see Ref. 5-32). *(Courtesy M. Potmesil and the Image Processing Laboratory, Rensselaer Polytechnic Institute.)*

Plate 7:

Spheres and cylinders with reflection and refraction, computed using the Whitted ray tracing algorithm and illumination model (see Sec. 5-12). *(Courtesy Al Barr, Raster Technologies, Inc.)*

Plate 8:

Still life. The upper image was computed with the Whitted illumination model. The lower image was computed with the Hall illumination model (see Sec. 5-13). Notice in particular the spheres. *(Courtesy R. A. Hall and the Program of Computer Graphics, Cornell University.)*

Plate 9:

Foggy chessmen. Created using a scan line algorithm and combining separate images of the chessmen, their reflections, and the chessboard. *(Courtesy of T. Whitted, Bell Laboratories, reprinted with permission from TOG, Vol. 1, January 1982, Copyright 1982, Association for Computing Machinery.)*

Plate 10:

White sands. The flowering plants were grown from a single cell using an algorithm developed by the artist Alvy Ray Smith based on mathematics by Paulien Hogeweg. The grasses were rendered by Bill Reeves using a particle system. The hidden surface software is by Loren Carpenter and the composite software by Tom Porter. *(Courtesy of Alvy Ray Smith, Lucasfilm Ltd., all rights reserved.)*

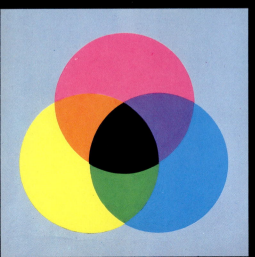

Plate 11:

The additive (above) and subtractive (below) color systems. *(Courtesy of Polaroid Corporation.)*

Table 5-1

	Plastic vase	Metallic vase
Two lights[a]	I_l = CIE standard illuminant D_{6500} $d\omega_i = 0.0001$ and 0.0002	I_l = CIE standard illuminant D_{6500} $d\omega_i = 0.0001$ and 0.0002
Specular	$k_s = 0.1$ F = reflectance of a vinyl mirror D = Beckmann function with $m = 0.15$	$k_s = 1.0$ F = reflectance of a bronze mirror D = Beckmann functions with $m_1 = 0.4$ $w_1 = 0.4$ $m_2 = 0.2$ $w_2 = 0.6$
Diffuse	$k_d = 0.9$ r_d = the bidirectional reflectance of bronze at normal incidence	$k_d = 0$ r_d = the bidirectional reflectance of bronze at normal incidence
Ambient	$I_a = 0.01I_l$ $r_a = \pi r_d$	$I_a = 0.01I_l$ $r_a = \pi r_d$

[a] See Sec. 5-15.

a

b

Figure 5-22 Comparison of edge-lit specular highlights. (a) Phong, (b) Torrance-Sparrow, magnesium oxide surface. (*Courtesy of the University of Utah.*)

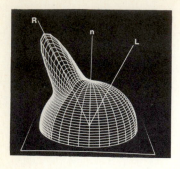

a

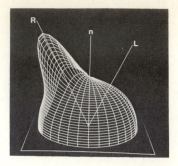

b

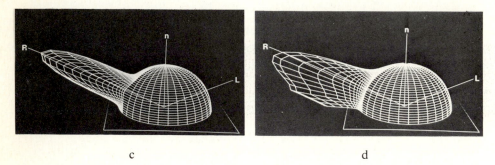

c   d

Figure 5-23 Comparison of a light distribution functions at a near normal incidence angle (25°): (a) Phong, (b) Torrance-Sparrow; and at a near grazing incidence angle (65°): (c) Phong, (d) Torrance-Sparrow.

5-9 TRANSPARENCY

Prior illumination models and hidden line/hidden surface algorithms have considered only opaque surfaces or objects. Not all objects are opaque; some transmit light, e.g., glasses, vases, automobile windows, water. When light passes from one medium to another, e.g., from air to water, the light ray is bent by refraction. The common childhood observation that a straight stick partially inserted into a pond appears bent is an example of refraction. The amount that the light ray is bent is governed by Snell's law which states that the refracted ray lies in the same plane as the incident ray and that the relationship between the incident and refracted angles is

$$\eta_1 \sin \theta = \eta_2 \sin \theta'$$

where η_1 and η_2 are the indices of refraction in the first and second mediums. Here, θ is the angle of incidence and θ' the angle of refraction, as shown in

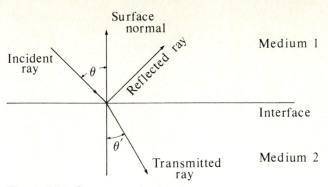

Figure 5-24 Geometry of refraction.

Fig. 5-24. No material transmits all the incident light. Some of it is reflected, as is also shown in Fig. 5-24.

By analogy with specular and diffuse reflection, light may be transmitted specularly or diffusely. Transparent materials, e.g. glass, exhibit specular transmission. Except at the silhouette edges of curved surfaces, objects viewed through transparent materials appear undistorted. If the transmitted light is scattered, then diffuse transmission occurs. Materials that diffusely transmit light appear frosted or translucent. Objects viewed through translucent materials appear dim or are distorted.

Some of the practical implications of refraction are shown in Fig. 5-25. In Fig. 5-25 the objects labeled 1 and 2 have equal indices of refraction greater than that in the surrounding medium. The objects labeled 3 and 4 are opaque. If the effects of refraction are ignored, the light ray labeled *a* would intersect object 3 as shown by the dashed line. However, because the light ray is bent by refraction, it intersects object 4. Consequently, an object that might not otherwise be seen is visible. In contrast, if refraction effects are ignored for the light ray labeled *b*, then the ray would miss object 3 and intersect object 4. However, the refracted ray intersects object 3. Thus, an object that is

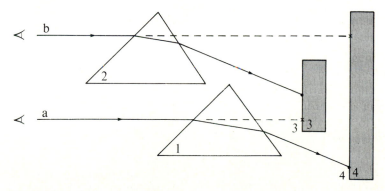

Figure 5-25 Refraction effects.

visible might not be seen. To generate realistic images these effects must be considered.

Similar effects occur when a perspective transformation is incorporated into the viewing transformation. Typically, a perspective transformation is used to obtain a distorted object that is then displayed using an axonometric projection with the eyepoint at infinity, as shown in Fig. 5-26. Figure 5-26a shows a light ray through P that intersects the undistorted object at i. The refracted ray arrives at the background at point b. Figure 5-26b shows the object after distortion by a perspective transformation. The light ray now intersects the object at the transformed point i', and the refracted ray now intersects the background at b' on the *opposite* side of the centerline from b. This effect is a result of incorrect angular relationships between the distorted object and the distorted light ray. At first glance, keeping sufficient information to generate the correct angular relations at the light ray–object boundaries might yield a correct result. However, the correct result is not obtained because the length of the light ray path in the distorted object is also different. This difference in path length has two effects. First, the exit point of the refracted ray from the distorted object is not the same as for the undistorted object. Thus, the ray still will not intersect the background at the correct point. Second, the amount of light absorbed within the object is also different. Hence, the intensity of the light ray as it exits the distorted object is changed.

These refraction effects can be eliminated either by using an object space algorithm or by appropriately transforming between object and image space. However, they are more easily incorporated into ray tracing visible surface algorithms that utilize a global illumination model (see Sec. 5-12).

The simplest implementations of transparency effects ignore refraction. When refraction is ignored, the effects illustrated in Figs. 5-25 and 5-26 do not

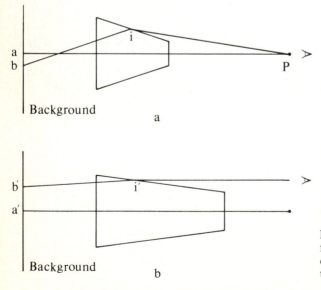

Figure 5-26 Perspective effects on refraction. (a) Undistorted, (b) with perspective distortion.

occur. These simple implementations also ignore the effect that the distance a light ray travels in a medium has on the intensity. The earliest implementation of transparency is attributed to Newell, Newell, and Sancha (Ref. 5-12) (see Sec. 4-8). Simple transparency effects can be directly incorporated into any of the hidden surface algorithms except the z-buffer algorithm. Transparent polygons or surfaces are tagged. When the visible surface is transparent, a linear combination of the two nearest surfaces is written to the frame buffer. The intensity is then

$$I = tI_1 + (1 - t)I_2 \qquad 0 \le t \le 1$$

where I_1 is the visible surface, I_2 is the surface immediately behind the visible surface, and t is the transparency factor for I_1. If $t = 0$, the surface is invisible. If $t = 1$, the surface is opaque. If I_2 is also transparent, the algorithm is applied recursively until an opaque surface or the background is found. When polygons are written to a frame buffer in depth priority order, as in the Newell-Newell-Sancha algorithm, I_2 corresponds to the value stored in the frame buffer and I_1 to the current surface.

The linear approximation does not provide an adequate model for curved surfaces. This is because at the silhouette edge of a curved surface, e.g., a vase or bottle, the thickness of the material reduces its transparency. To more adequately represent these effects Kay (Refs. 5-13 and 5-14) suggests a simple nonlinear approximation based on the z component of the surface normal. In particular, the transparency factor

$$t = t_{min} + (t_{max} - t_{min})[1 - (1 - |n_z|)^p]$$

where t_{min} and t_{max} are the maximum and minimum transparencies for the object, n_z is the z component of the unit normal to the surface, and p is a transparency power factor. Here, t is the transparency for any pixel or point on the object. Figure 5-27 compares results for the two models. Figure 5-27a

a   b

Figure 5-27 Comparison of simple transparency models. (a) Linear $t = 0.5$, (b) non-linear $p = 1$. (*Courtesy of D. S. Kay and the Program of Computer Graphics, Cornell University.*)

was rendered using the linear model, and Fig. 5-27b using the nonlinear model. Transparency effects cannot be added directly to a z-buffer algorithm (see Sec. 4-7). However, transparency effects may be included by using separate transparency, intensity, and weighting factor buffers (Ref. 5-15) with the transparent polygons tagged in the data structure. For a z-buffer algorithm the procedure is

> For each polygon:
>
> > If the polygon is transparent, save it on a list.
> > If the polygon is opaque and if $z > z_{\text{buffer}}$, write it to the opaque frame buffer and update the opaque z buffer.
>
> For each polygon on the transparent list:
>
> > If $z \geq z_{\text{buffer}}$, add its transparency factor to that in the transparency weighting buffer.
> >
> > Combine its intensity with that in the transparency intensity buffer using
> >
> > $$I_{bn} = I_{bo}t_{bo} + I_c t_c$$
> >
> > where I_{bn} is the new intensity value to be placed in the transparency intensity buffer, I_{bo} is the old value in the transparency intensity buffer, I_c is the intensity of the current polygon, t_{bo} is the old transparency factor in the transparency weighting buffer, and t_c is the transparency factor for the current polygon. This produces a weighted sum of the intensities of all the transparent polygons in front of the nearest opaque polygon.
>
> Combine the opaque and transparency intensity frame buffers. A linear combination rule is
>
> $$I_{fb} = t_{bo}I_{bo} + (1 - t_{bo})I_{fbo}$$
>
> where I_{fb} is the final intensity in the opaque frame buffer and I_{fbo} is the old intensity value in the opaque frame buffer.

Because of the memory requirements for a full z buffer, the procedure is more appropriate for use with a scan line z-buffer algorithm (see Sec. 4-10).

One interesting application of transparency is in visualization of the interior of complex objects or spaces. For this technique each polygon or surface is tagged with a transparency factor. Initially, all transparency factors are 1, i.e. opaque. Rendering produces an opaque hidden surface view of the outside of the object or space. By selectively changing the transparency factor for groups of surfaces to zero, i.e. invisible, the interior of the object or space is revealed when the scene is again rendered.

Adding refraction effects to the illumination model requires that the visible surface problem be solved for both the reflected and transmitted light rays (see Fig. 5-24) as well as for the incident light ray. This is most effectively accomplished with a global illumination model in conjunction with a ray tracing visible surface algorithm (see Sec. 5-12). Because of the large number of diffusely scattered transmitted rays generated by a translucent surface, only specularly reflected transmitted rays are usually considered. Thus, only transparent materials are simulated. The illumination model used is then a simple extension of those discussed previously (see Secs. 5-2, 5-7 and 5-8). In general the illumination model is

$$I = k_a I_a + k_d I_d + k_s I_s + k_t I_t$$

where the subscripts a, d, s, t specify ambient, diffuse, specular, and transmitted effects. Most models assume that k_t is a constant and that I_t, the intensity of the transmitted light, is determined from Snell's law.

5-10 SHADOWS

When the observer's position is coincident with the light source, no shadows are seen. As the positions of the observer and the light source separate, shadows appear. Shadows contribute considerably to the realism of the scene by increasing depth perception. Shadows are also important in simulation. For example, a specific area of interest may be invisible because it is in shadow. Further, shadows significantly influence heating, air conditioning, and solar power calculations for building and spacecraft design applications, as well as in other application areas.

Observation shows that a shadow consists of two parts, an umbra and a penumbra. The central dense, black, sharply defined shadow area is the umbra. The lighter area surrounding the umbra is called the penumbra. The point light sources generally used in computer graphics generate only umbra shadows. For distributed light sources of finite dimension both umbra and penumbra shadows result (see Ref. 5-8). While light is totally excluded from the umbra shadow, the penumbra receives light from part of the distributed light source.

Because of the computational expense, only the shadow umbra generated by a point light source is usually considered. The computational difficulty (and hence expense) of the shadow calculation also depends on the location of the light source. A light source at infinity is easiest, since an orthographic projection can be used to determine the shadows. A light source at a finite distance, but outside the field of view, is somewhat more difficult because a perspective projection is required. The most difficult case is a light source located within the field of view. Here, the space must be divided into sectors and the shadows found in each sector separately.

Fundamentally, to add shadows to a scene the hidden surface problem must be solved twice: once for the position of each light source and once for the observer's position or eyepoint. Thus, it is a two-step process. This is illustrated

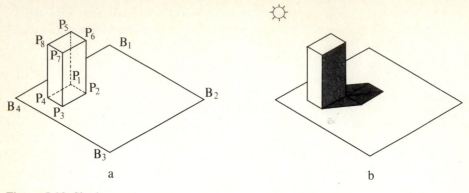

Figure 5-28 Shadows.

in Fig. 5-28 for a single light source at infinity located above, in front, and to the left of the block. The scene is viewed from in front, above, and to the right of the block. There are two types of shadows: self-shadows and projected shadows. Self-shadows result when the object itself prevents light from reaching some of its planes, e.g., the right hand plane of the block in Fig. 5-28. They are analogous to self-hidden planes and are found in the same way. Self-shadowed planes are self-hidden planes when the scene is viewed from the position of the light source.

A projected shadow results when an intervening object prevents light from reaching another object in the scene. The shadow on the base plane in Figure 5-28b is an example. Projected shadows are found by projecting all non-self-hidden planes into the scene from the position of the light source. The intersections of the projected plane and all other planes in the scene are found. These polygons are tagged as shadow polygons and added to the data structure. The number of polygons added to the data structure can be reduced by finding the silhouette of each object and projecting it instead of each individual plane.

After the shadows have been added to the data structure, the scene is processed normally from the observer's position to obtain the desired view. Note that multiple views may be obtained without recalculating the shadows. The shadows depend upon the position of the light source and not on that of the observer. An example illustrates these techniques.

Example 5-4 Shadows

As an explicit example, consider the block shown in Fig. 5-28a. The block is described by the points $P_1(1, 0, 3.5)$, $P_2(2, 0, 3.5)$, $P_3(2, 0, 5)$, $P_4(1, 0, 5)$, $P_5(1, 3, 3.5)$, $P_6(2, 3, 3.5)$, $P_7(2, 3, 5)$, $P_8(1, 3, 5)$. The block rests on a base plane given by $B_1(0, 0, 0)$, $B_2(6, 0, 0)$, $B_3(6, 0, 6)$, and $B_4(0, 0, 6)$. The light source is located at infinity along the line connecting P_2 and P_8. The block and the base plane are to be observed from infinity on the positive z axis, after first being rotated $-45°$ about the y axis followed by a $35°$ rotation about the x axis.

The self-shadowed planes are found by determining the self-hidden planes from the position of the light source. Using the formal techniques discussed in Sec. 4-3 and Examples 4-2, 4-6, and 4-7, the volume matrix for the block is

$$[V] = \begin{array}{cccccc} \textcircled{R} & \textcircled{L} & \textcircled{B} & \textcircled{T} & \textcircled{H} & \textcircled{Y} \\ \left[\begin{array}{cccccc} -1 & 1 & 0 & 0 & 0 & 0 \\ 0 & 0 & 1 & -1 & 0 & 0 \\ 0 & 0 & 0 & 0 & -1 & 1 \\ 2 & -1 & 0 & 3 & 5 & 3.5 \end{array}\right] \end{array}$$

where R, L, B, T, H, Y refer to the right, left, bottom, top, hither, yon planes, based on viewing the untransformed block from a point at infinity on the positive z axis. The vector from the light source to the block expressed in homogeneous coordinates is

$$[E] = \mathbf{P}_2 - \mathbf{P}_8 = [1 \quad -3 \quad -1.5 \quad 0]$$

Taking the dot product of the light source vector and the self-hidden planes yields

$$\begin{array}{ccccccc} & \textcircled{R} & \textcircled{L} & \textcircled{B} & \textcircled{T} & \textcircled{H} & \textcircled{Y} \\ [E] \cdot [V] = [& -1 & 1 & -3 & 3 & 1.5 & -1.5 \ ] \end{array}$$

The negative signs indicate that, viewed from the light source, the right, bottom, and yon planes are self-hidden and hence produce self-shadows.

There are several techniques for finding the projected shadows. One is to translate and rotate the block and its base plane until the vector from the light source is coincident with the z axis. Since the light source is at infinity, an orthographic projection of the visible planes of the block onto the transformed base plane yields the projected shadows. This is accomplished by substituting the x and y coordinates of the transformed vertices of the block into the plane equation for the transformed base plane to obtain z. The coordinates of the projected shadows are then transformed back to the original orientation.

The light vector from infinity through P_8P_2 can be made coincident with the x axis by

Translating P_2 to the origin

Rotating about the y axis by $33.69°$ so that P_4 is on the z axis

Rotating about the x axis by $59.04°$ so that P_8 is on the z axis.

The combined transformation is

$$[T] = \left[\begin{array}{cccc} 0.83 & 0.48 & -0.29 & 0 \\ 0 & 0.51 & 0.86 & 0 \\ 0.55 & -0.71 & 0.43 & 0 \\ -3.59 & 1.53 & -0.93 & 1 \end{array}\right]$$

Transforming the base plane and the block yields

$$
\begin{array}{c}
B_1 \\ B_2 \\ B_3 \\ B_4
\end{array}
\begin{bmatrix}
0 & 0 & 0 & 1 \\
6 & 0 & 0 & 1 \\
6 & 0 & 6 & 1 \\
0 & 0 & 6 & 1
\end{bmatrix}
\quad [T] =
\begin{bmatrix}
-3.59 & 1.53 & -0.93 & 1 \\
1.39 & 4.41 & -2.67 & 1 \\
4.69 & 0.15 & -0.09 & 1 \\
-0.29 & -2.73 & 1.65 & 1
\end{bmatrix}
\quad \text{Base plane}
$$

$$
\begin{array}{c}
P_1 \\ P_2 \\ P_3 \\ P_4 \\ P_5 \\ P_6 \\ P_7 \\ P_8
\end{array}
\begin{bmatrix}
1 & 0 & 3.5 & 1 \\
2 & 0 & 3.5 & 1 \\
2 & 0 & 5 & 1 \\
1 & 0 & 5 & 1 \\
1 & 3 & 3.5 & 1 \\
2 & 3 & 3.5 & 1 \\
2 & 3 & 5 & 1 \\
1 & 3 & 5 & 1
\end{bmatrix}
\qquad
\begin{bmatrix}
-0.84 & -0.48 & 0.29 & 1 \\
0 & 0 & 0 & 1 \\
0.82 & -1.06 & 0.64 & 1 \\
0 & -1.54 & 0.93 & 1 \\
-0.84 & 1.06 & 2.87 & 1 \\
0 & 1.54 & 2.58 & 1 \\
0.82 & 0.47 & 3.22 & 1 \\
0 & 0 & 3.51 & 1
\end{bmatrix}
\quad \text{Block}
$$

Using Newell's method (see Sec. 4-3, Example 4-3) the equation for the transformed base plane is

$$z = -0.6y$$

Substituting the x and y coordinates of the vertices of the transformed block into the plane equation to obtain z yields the projection of the shadow onto the base plane. Specifically,

$$
[P'] =
\begin{bmatrix}
-0.84 & -0.48 & 0.29 \\
0 & 0 & 0 \\
0.82 & -1.06 & 0.64 \\
0 & -1.54 & 0.93 \\
-0.84 & 1.06 & -0.64 \\
0 & 1.54 & -0.93 \\
0.82 & 0.48 & -0.29 \\
0 & 0 & 0
\end{bmatrix}
\begin{array}{c}
P_1' \\ P_2' \\ P_3' \\ P_4' \\ P_5' \\ P_6' \\ P_7' \\ P_8'
\end{array}
$$

where the prime denotes a projected shadow vertex.

Since only the front, left, and top planes are visible from the light source, only these planes yield projected shadows specifically,

Front: $P_3P_4P_8P_7$ → $P_3'P_4'P_8'P_7'$

Left: $P_1P_4P_8P_5$ → $P_1'P_4'P_8'P_5'$

Top: $P_7P_8P_5P_6$ → $P_7'P_8'P_5'P_6'$

Notice that P_2 is not contained in any visible plane. Hence, its projection P_2' is not contained in any visible projected shadow. The projected shadows are obtained in the original orientation by applying the inverse transformation, i.e $[T]^{-1}$. Specifically,

$$
[S] = [P'][T]^{-1} =
\begin{bmatrix}
1 & 0 & 3.5 & 1 \\
2 & 0 & 3.5 & 1 \\
2 & 0 & 5 & 1 \\
1 & 0 & 5 & 1 \\
2 & 0 & 2 & 1 \\
3 & 0 & 2 & 1 \\
3 & 0 & 3.5 & 1 \\
2 & 0 & 3.5 & 1
\end{bmatrix}
\begin{array}{c}
S_1 \\ S_2 \\ S_3 \\ S_4 \\ S_5 \\ S_6 \\ S_7 \\ S_8
\end{array}
$$

The projected shadow planes projected into the base plane are then $S_3S_4S_8S_7$, $S_1S_4S_8S_5$, and $S_7S_8S_5S_6$. The silhouette polygon is $S_1S_5S_6S_7S_3S_4$.

The result, rotated $-45°$ about the y axis, followed by a $35°$ rotation about the x axis, and viewed from a point at infinity on the positive z axis, is shown in Fig. 5-28b. Here, the right hand plane is visible but is self-shadowed. Hence, its intensity is shown nearly black. The projected shadow is also shown nearly black. Notice that, from this viewpoint, part of the projected shadow is hidden.

Incorporating shadows into a hidden surface algorithm was first suggested by Appel (Ref. 5-16). He suggested both a ray tracing and a scan line approach. Bouknight and Kelley (Refs. 5-17 to 5-19) improved on Appel's scan line approach. Adding shadows to a spanning scan line algorithm, e.g. the Watkins algorithm, requires two steps.

The first step is to determine the self-shadows and the projected shadows for every polygon in the scene for every light source, as discussed above in Example 5-4. Conceptually, this can be considered a binary matrix. The rows represent polygons that can cast shadows, and the columns represent polygons that are shadowed. In the binary matrix, a one indicates that a polygon can possibly cast a shadow on another, and a zero that it cannot. Along the diagonal, a one indicates that a polygon is self-shadowed.

Since for a scene containing n polygons the number of possible projected shadows is $n(n - 1)$, efficiently determining this matrix is important. Bouknight and Kelley project the scene onto a sphere centered at the light source and use bounding box tests on the projected polygons to eliminate most cases. Similarly, the technique, described in Example 5-4, of making the direction of the light source coincident with the z axis may be used. Simple three-dimensional bounding box tests can then be used to eliminate most cases. Additional possibilities can be eliminated by using more sophisticated sorting techniques, e.g., the Newell-Newell-Sancha priority sort (see Sec. 4-8). A simple example illustrates this.

Example 5-5   Shadow Matrix

For the simple scene shown in Fig. 5-28, the shadow matrix can be constructed by inspection. The result is shown in Table 5-2.

Table 5-2

Polygon being shadowed

		Right	Left	Bottom	Top	Hither	Yon	Base plane
Polygon	Right	1	0	0	0	0	0	1
casting	Left	0	0	1	0	0	1	1
the	Bottom	0	0	1	0	0	0	1
shadow	Top	1	0	0	0	0	0	1
	Hither	1	0	1	0	0	0	1
	Yon	0	0	0	0	0	1	1
	Base plane	0	0	0	0	0	0	0

In practice, the matrix is incorporated into a linked list that associates the shadows and the polygons.

The second step processes the scene from the observer's viewpoint. Two scanning processes are involved. In a spanning scan line algorithm, e.g. the Watkins algorithm, the first scanning process determines the visible segment in a span as described in Sec. 4-11. The second scanning process uses the shadow linked list to determine if any shadows fall on the polygon that generated the visible segment for that span. The second scan for the span then proceeds as follows:

If no shadow polygons are found, the visible segment is displayed.

If shadow polygons are found for the visible segment polygon but none intersect or cover the span, the visible segment is displayed.

If one or more shadow polygons completely cover the span, the intensity of the visible segment is modulated with that of the shadow polygons and the segment displayed.

If one or more shadow polygons partially cover the span, the span is subdivided at the intersection of the edges of the shadow polygons. The algorithm is then applied recursively to each subspan until the entire span is displayed.

The above algorithm states that the intensity of the visible segment is modulated with that of the shadow polygon. The simplest modulation rule assumes that the shadow is absolutely black. A few minutes experimenting with light sources and two objects will show that shadows are not always absolutely black. The intensity, i.e. the blackness, of the shadow varies with the intensity of the light source and also with the distance between the plane casting the shadow and the plane in shadow. This is because the shadow area receives light from the ambient environment, and because the light source is of finite size.

A simple modulation rule that partially simulates this effect is to make the shadow intensity proportional to the intensity of the light source. For multiple shadows the shadow intensities are additive. A computationally more expensive rule is to make the shadow intensity proportional to both the intensity of the light source and the distance between the plane casting the shadow and the plane in shadow.

The z-buffer algorithm (see Sec. 4-7) may be modified to include shadow effects (Ref. 5-20). Again, a two-step process is used. The modified algorithm is

The scene is constructed from the light source direction. The z values for this view are stored in a separate shadow z buffer. Intensity values are ignored.

The scene is then constructed from the observer's point of view. As each surface or polygon is considered, its depth at each pixel is compared with that in the observer's z buffer. If it is the visible surface, a linear transformation is used to map the x, y, z values in the observer's view into x', y', z' values in the light source view. The z' value is checked for visibility with respect to the light source by comparing its value with that in the shadow z buffer at x', y'. If it is visible to the light source, it is rendered normally in the frame buffer at x, y. If not, it is in shadow and is rendered using the appropriate shadow modulation rule. The value in the observer's z buffer is updated with z'.

The above algorithm is directly applicable to the scan line z-buffer algorithm (see Sec. 4-10). Here, the buffers are only one scan line high. Williams (Ref. 5-20) used a modified procedure to render curved shadows on curved surfaces. The complete scene is first computed from the observer's point of view. The point-by-point linear transformation to the light source direction, and consequent shadowing, are then applied as a postprocess. As pointed out by Williams, the modified procedure incorrectly renders highlights, since they are merely darkened if they lie in shadow. Highlights should, of course, not appear in shadowed areas. Williams also discusses the quantization effects that result from performing the transformation from one viewpoint to another in image space.

Atherton (Refs. 5-21 and 5-22) has extended the hidden surface algorithm (see Sec. 4-5), based on the Weiler-Atherton clipping algorithm (see Sec. 3-17), to include shadow generation. The algorithm is important because it operates in object space. Hence, the results can be used for accurate calculations as well as to produce pictures. Again, a two-step process is used.

The first step uses the hidden surface algorithm to determine the visible or illuminated polygons from the light source direction. The illuminated polygons are saved rather than the shadow polygons in order to increase the efficiency of the algorithm. If shadow polygons, i.e. invisible polygons, were saved, then it would also be necessary to save all the self-hidden polygons that are normally culled before application of the hidden surface algorithm. For convex polyhedra, this would double the number of polygons processed by the algorithm.

The illuminated polygons are tagged and transformed back to the original data orientation where they are attached to the original polygons as surface detail. This operation is accomplished by assigning a unique number to every polygon in the scene. When a polygon is passed through the hidden surface algorithm, it may be split into numerous pieces. However, each piece retains the original unique number. Thus, it is possible to associate each of the fragmented illuminated polygons with its original source polygon or any fragment of the source polygon.

In order to avoid false shadows it is necessary that the entire scene be contained within the view or clipping volume defined from the location of the light source. If not, then regions outside the clipping volume will be incorrectly assumed to be in shadow. The result, viewed from the observer's location, will then contain false shadows. This restriction also requires that the light source not be located within the extremes of the scene environment. This restriction occurs because no single perspective or axonometric transformation exists, from the location of the light source, that can contain the entire scene.

The second step processes the combined polygon data from the observer's point of view. If an area is not illuminated, the appropriate shadow modulation rule is applied. The general procedure is shown in Fig. 5-29.

For multiple light sources, multiple sets of illuminated polygons are added to the data base. The color image shown in Color Plate 3 illustrates a result with two light sources.

The visible surface ray tracing algorithm previously discussed in Sec. 4-13 can also be extended to include shadows (Ref. 5-16). Again, a two-step process

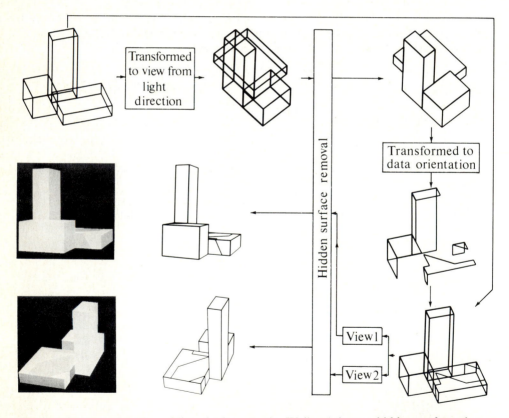

Figure 5-29 Procedure for adding shadows to the Weiler-Atherton hidden surface algorithm. (*Photographs courtesy of P. Atherton and the Program of Computer Graphics, Cornell University.*)

is used. The first step traces the ray from the observer or eyepoint through the plane of projection to determine the visible point, if any, in the scene, as in the previously discussed algorithm.

The second step traces the vector (ray) from the visible point to the light source. If any object in the scene lies between the visible point and the light source, then light from that source cannot reach that point. Hence, the point is in shadow. The technique is illustrated in Fig. 5-30. The techniques previously discussed in Sec. 4-13 can be used to make the search along the local light direction vector more efficient.

Although, as mentioned above, shadow penumbras are not usually included, Cook (Ref. 5-8) suggests a relatively simple technique for including them. Since the Cook-Torrance illumination model assumes a finite area light source subtending a solid angle $d\omega$ (see Sec. 5-8), blocking a fraction of the area of the light source reduces the effective solid angle and hence the incident intensity from the source. The reflected intensity is then also reduced proportionally.

Figure 5-31 illustrates the effect for a simple straight edge and a spherical light source. The midshadow line is calculated by considering a point light source at the center of the spherical source. From Fig. 5-31, using similar triangles, the projection of the penumbra half width r in the direction $\mathbf{L}$ is

$$\frac{r(\mathbf{n} \cdot \mathbf{L})}{d} = \frac{R}{D}$$

where d is the distance from the shadow casting point to the corresponding point on the midshadow line, D is the distance from the shadow casting point to the center of the spherical light source, and R is the radius of the spherical light source.

Viewed from the polygon casting the shadow, the solid angle of the light source $d\omega$ is

$$d\omega = \pi \left(\frac{R}{D}\right)^2$$

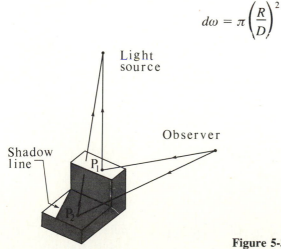

Figure labels: Light source, Observer, Shadow line, P_1, P_2

Figure 5-30 Ray tracing with shadows.

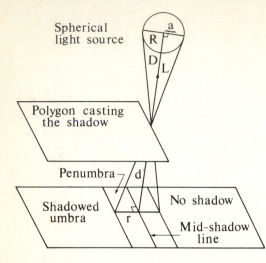

Figure 5-31 Penumbra shadows.

Thus, the penumbra half width is

$$r = \frac{d}{\hat{\mathbf{n}} \cdot \hat{\mathbf{L}}} \frac{R}{D} = \frac{d}{\hat{\mathbf{n}} \cdot \hat{\mathbf{L}}} \sqrt{\frac{d\omega}{\pi}}$$

The result shows that the shadow is sharper (i.e., r is smaller) for light resources that subtend smaller solid angles $d\omega$. For a point light source, $d\omega = 0$, which yields $r = 0$. Hence, no penumbra is generated. Further, as the polygon casting the shadow approaches the surface, d and r both decrease. This also makes the shadow sharper.

Within the penumbra the intensity of each point is determined by the fraction of the light source that is visible. For a spherical light source only partially visible from $-R$ to a this fraction is

$$A_{frac} = \frac{1}{\pi R^2} \int_{-R}^{a} 2\sqrt{R^2 - x^2} \, dx = \frac{1}{2} + \frac{1}{\pi} \left[\frac{a}{R}\sqrt{1 - \left(\frac{a}{R}\right)^2} + \sin^{-1}\left(\frac{a}{R}\right) \right]$$

The results show that a shadow penumba is sharper at one edge. Cook recommends storing the results of this calculation in a look-up table. However, the linear approximation

$$A_{frac} = \frac{1}{2}\left(1 + \frac{a}{R}\right)$$

yields a less than 7% error and is computationally less expensive.

5-11 TEXTURE

In computer graphics, the surface detail in an object is called texture. Two aspects of texture are generally considered. The first is the addition of a separately specified pattern to a smooth surface. After the pattern is added, the surface still appears smooth. Adding a pattern to a smooth surface is basically a mapping function. The second is adding the appearance of roughness to the surface. Adding the appearance of roughness to a surface is basically a perturbation function.

Adding a texture pattern to a smooth surface was first suggested by Catmull (Ref. 5-23) as a consequence of his subdivision algorithm for curved surfaces (see Sec. 4-6). This basic idea was extended by Blinn and Newell (Ref. 5-24) to include reflection and highlights on curved surfaces.

Since the basis of adding texture patterns to smooth surfaces is mapping, the texture problem reduces to transformation from one coordinate system to another. If the texture pattern is defined in an orthogonal coordinate system (u, w) in texture space, and the surface in a second orthogonal coordinate system (θ, ϕ), then adding the texture pattern to the surface involves determining or specifying a mapping function between the two spaces, i.e.

$$\theta = f(u, w) \qquad \phi = g(u, w)$$

or alternately

$$u = r(\theta, \phi) \qquad w = s(u, w)$$

Although not necessary, the mapping function is generally assumed to be linear, i.e.

$$\theta = Au + B \qquad \theta = Cw + D$$

where the constants A, B, C, D are obtained from the relationship between known points in the two coordinate systems. A simple example serves to illustrate the technique.

Example 5-6 Mapping

The pattern shown in Fig. 5-32a is to be mapped onto the surface patch defined by the octant of the sphere shown in Fig. 5-32b. The pattern is a simple two-dimensional grid of intersecting lines. The parametric representation of the octant of the sphere is given by

$$
\begin{aligned}
x &= \sin\theta \sin\phi \\
y &= \cos\phi \\
z &= \cos\theta \sin\phi
\end{aligned}
\qquad
\begin{aligned}
0 &\le \theta \le \pi/2 \\
\pi/4 &\le \phi \le \pi/2
\end{aligned}
$$

Assuming a linear mapping function

$$\theta = Au + B \qquad \phi = Cw + D$$

and assuming that the corners of the quadrilateral pattern map into the corners of the quadrilateral surface patch, i.e.

$$
\begin{aligned}
u &= 0, \; w = 0 \text{ at } \theta = 0 & \phi &= \pi/2 \\
u &= 1, \; w = 0 \text{ at } \theta = \pi/2, \; \phi &= \pi/2 \\
u &= 0, \; w = 1 \text{ at } \theta = 0, & \phi &= \pi/4 \\
u &= 1, \; w = 1 \text{ at } \theta = \pi/2, \; \phi &= \pi/4
\end{aligned}
$$

yields

$$A = \pi/2 \qquad B = 0 \qquad C = -\pi/4 \qquad D = \pi/2$$

Thus, the linear mapping function from uw space to $\theta\phi$ space is

$$\theta = \frac{\pi}{2}u \qquad \phi = \frac{\pi}{2} - \frac{\pi}{4}w$$

The inverse mapping from $\theta\phi$ space to uw space is

$$u = \frac{\theta}{\pi/2} \qquad w = \frac{\pi/2 - \phi}{\pi/4}$$

The results of mapping a single line in uw space into $\theta\phi$ space and thence into xyz Cartesian coordinates is shown in Table 5-3. The complete results are shown in Fig. 5-32c.

Table 5-3

u	w	θ	ϕ	x	y	z
1/4	0	$\pi/2$	$\pi/2$	0.38	0	0.92
	1/4		$7/16\pi$	0.38	0.20	0.91
	1/2		$3/8\pi$	0.35	0.38	0.85
	3/4		$5/16\pi$	0.32	0.56	0.77
	1		$\pi/4$	0.27	0.71	0.65

The texture pattern shown in Fig. 5-32a is a simple mathematical definition. Other sources of texture might be hand-drawn artwork or scanned-in (digitized) photographs or other patterns. Displaying a texture pattern on a surface involves a mapping from object space to image space, as well as the previously discussed transformation from texture space to object space. Any viewing transformation must also be applied. Assuming that image space implies a raster device, there are two slightly different techniques.

The first technique is based on Catmull's subdivision algorithm (see Sec. 4-6). Catmull's algorithm subdivides a surface patch until a subpatch covers a

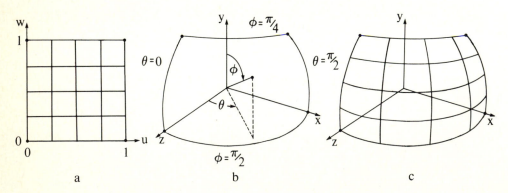

Figure 5-32 Mapping.

single pixel center. The parametric values of the center of the subpatch or the pixel center could then be mapped into texture space and the texture pattern at that point used to determine the intensity of the pixel. However, as Catmull points out, this point sampling technique leads to severe aliasing effects. For example, large portions or perhaps all of the simple mathematically defined texture pattern shown in Fig. 5-32a might be missed if all the sample points occurred in the "white" areas of the texture. To alleviate this effect, Catmull subdivides the texture pattern along with the surface patch. When a subpatch is found that covers only a single pixel center, the average intensity in the associated texture subpatch is used to determine the pixel intensity.

In general the texture subpatch will not be rectangular. If the texture pattern is rasterized, then the intensity of the texture subpatch is taken as the weighted average of the intensities for the texture pixels in the subpatch. The weighting function is the ratio of the area of the texture pixels inside the subpatch to its total area. Blinn and Newell used this technique with a better 2×2 pyramidal antialiasing filter suggested by Crow (see Sec. 2-25). Results, obtained by Barsky, by texture mapping a simple checkerboard pattern onto a β-spline patch used to construct a bottle are shown in Fig. 5-33.

Conceptually, the Catmull subdivision algorithm starts with the surface patch in object space and transforms in two directions: one into image space, and one into texture space. An example serves to further illustrate the technique.

Figure 5-33 Texture pattern mapped onto a β-spline patch defined bottle. (*Courtesy of B. Barsky.*)

Example 5-7 Texture Subdivision Algorithm

Again consider the surface patch formed from the octant of the unit sphere, as shown in Fig. 5-32b, and the simple grid texture pattern shown in Fig. 5-31a. The surface patch is to be rotated about the y axis by $-45°$ and then about the x axis by $35°$ and displayed on a 32×32 raster using an orthographic projection (see Fig. 5-34a). The simple grid texture pattern is rasterized at a resolution of 64×64, with each line assumed to be one pixel wide as shown in Fig. 5-34b.

First the patch is subdivided. It is then transformed into image space with the object space origin corresponding to the center of the 32×32 raster. Figure 5-34a shows that four subdivisions are required before a subpatch covers only a single pixel center. This subpatch is rectangular in image space and was generated with parameters $0 \le \theta \le \pi/32$, $31\pi/64 \le \phi \le \pi/2$ in object space.

Recalling the inverse mapping functions from $\theta\phi$ object space to u,w texture space from Example 5-5, i.e.

$$u = \frac{\theta}{\pi/2} \qquad w = \frac{\pi/2 - \phi}{\pi/4}$$

yields the corners of the subpatch in texture space. Specifically, in texture space the vertices of the subpatch are

$\theta = 0,\ \phi = \pi/2$	$\rightarrow$	$u = 0,\ w = 0$
$\theta = 0,\ \phi = 59\pi/64$	$\rightarrow$	$u = 0,\ w = 1/16$
$\theta = \pi/32,\ \phi = 59\pi/64$	$\rightarrow$	$u = 1/16,\ w = 1/16$
$\theta = \pi/32,\ \phi = \pi/2$	$\rightarrow$	$u = 1/16,\ w = 0$

As shown in Fig. 5-34b, this is a square in texture space. On a 0 to 64 raster, 1/16 corresponds to 4 raster units as shown in Fig. 5-34b. The other subdivisions are also shown in Fig. 5-34b.

The intensity of the pixel in image space is obtained by averaging the intensities of the pixels in the subdivided texture space. The diffuse reflection component is scaled by this factor. From Fig. 5-34b there are seven black pixels in the 4 × 4 subdivision. Thus, the intensity of the displayed pixel in image space (Fig. 5-34a) is 7/16 on a scale of 0 to 1.

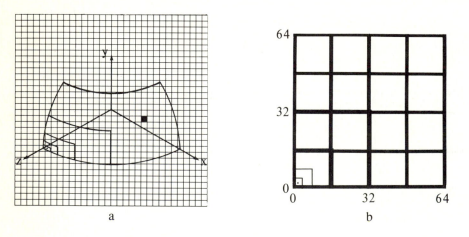

Figure 5-34 Texture mapping by patch subdivision.

One of the advantages of the Catmull subdivision algorithm is that it does not require knowledge of the inverse transformation from image space to object space or the depth (z value) of the subpatch in image space. However, one of the disadvantages is that the subpatch may not precisely cover a single pixel in image space (see Fig. 5-34a). Frequently, the depth (z value) is available from the visible surface algorithm. The inverse transformation can be determined by saving the three-dimensional viewing and object-to-image space transformations prior to projection onto the image plane. Consequently, the precise area covered by a pixel in image space can be transformed to texture space. The procedure is to transform the pixel area from image space to the surface in object space and then to texture space. The intensity of the pixel in image space is determined by averaging the intensity of the pixels covered by that area in texture space. The diffuse component in the illumination model is then scaled by this factor. Other more sophisticated antialiasing rules may, of course, be used. A simple example serves to illustrate the technique.

Example 5-8   Texture by Inverse Pixel Mapping

Again consider the surface patch formed from the octant of a unit sphere as shown in Fig. 5-32b and the simple grid texture problem rasterized at a 64 × 64 pixel resolution (see Fig. 5-34b). Again the surface patch is to be rotated about the y axis by $-45°$ and about the x axis by $35°$ and displayed on a 32 × 32 raster using an orthographic projection (see Fig. 5-34a).

Consider the intensity of the pixel at $P_x = 21$, $P_y = 15$ shown in Fig. 5-34a. Pixels are specified by their lower left hand corners. The pixel area is then specified by $21 \le P_x \le 22$ and $15 \le P_y \le 16$. Assuming that the object space window that corresponds to the 32 × 32 raster in image space is $-1 \le x' \le 1$, $-1 \le y' \le 1$ yields

$$x' = \frac{P_x}{16} - 1 \qquad y' = \frac{P_y}{16} - 1$$

Recalling the equation for a unit sphere gives

$$z' = \sqrt{1 - (x'^2 + y'^2)}$$

where x', y', z' represent object space coordinates after application of the viewing transformation. The object space coordinates of the corners of the pixel on the surface of the patch are then

P_x	P_y	x'	y'	z'
21	15	0.3125	−0.0625	0.948
22	15	0.3750	−0.0625	0.925
22	16	0.3750	0	0.927
21	16	0.3125	0	0.950

The viewing transformation before projection onto the image plane and its inverse are

$$[T] = \begin{bmatrix} 0.707 & -0.406 & 0.579 & 0 \\ 0 & 0.819 & 0.574 & 0 \\ -0.707 & -0.406 & 0.579 & 0 \\ 0 & 0 & 0 & 1 \end{bmatrix} \qquad [T]^{-1} = \begin{bmatrix} 0.707 & 0 & -0.707 & 0 \\ -0.406 & 0.819 & -0.406 & 0 \\ 0.579 & 0.574 & 0.579 & 0 \\ 0 & 0 & 0 & 1 \end{bmatrix}$$

Using the inverse of the viewing transformation yields the corners of the pixel on the surface patch in the original orientation. Specifically

$$[x \ y \ z \ 1] = [x' \ y' \ z' \ 1][T]^{-1}$$

and

P_x	P_y	x	y	z
21	15	0.795	0.493	0.341
22	15	0.826	0.479	0.296
22	16	0.802	0.532	0.272
21	16	0.771	0.545	0.329

Recalling that the parametric representation of the unit sphere is

$$x = \sin \theta \sin \phi$$
$$y = \cos \phi$$
$$z = \cos \theta \sin \phi$$

yields

$$\phi = \cos^{-1} y \qquad \phi = \sin^{-1} \left(\frac{x}{\sin \phi} \right)$$

in parametric space. Recalling the mapping transformation from parametric space to texture space given in Example 5-6, i.e.

$$u = \frac{\theta}{\pi/2} \qquad w = \frac{\pi/2 - \phi}{\pi/4}$$

yields for the corners of the pixel area in texture space

P_x	P_y	ϕ	θ	u	w
21	15	60.50°	66.04°	0.734	0.656
22	15	61.34°	70.30°	0.781	0.636
22	16	57.88°	71.28°	0.792	0.714
21	16	56.99°	66.88°	0.743	0.734

The results are shown in Fig. 5-35, where the curved area is approximated by a quadrilateral.

The rasterized grid pattern passes through the left hand edge of the pixel area. Again, several techniques can be used to determine the intensity of the display pixel (see Sec. 2-25). One simple technique is to use a weighted average of the intensities of the texture pixels whose centers are inside the display pixel boundaries. Here, the ratio of the "black" texture pixels representing the grid to the total texture pixels with centers inside the display pixel is 5/18. The intensity of the diffuse component of the illumination model is scaled by this factor.

The above techniques add texture patterns to smooth surfaces. The resulting surfaces also appear smooth. To add the appearance of roughness to a surface a photograph of a rough-textured pattern could be digitized and mapped to the surface. Unfortunately, the results are unsatisfactory because they look like rough-textured patterns painted on a smooth surface. The reason is that true rough-textured surfaces have a small random component in the surface normal

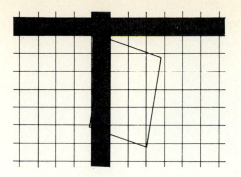

Figure 5-35 Display pixel in texture space.

and hence in the light reflection direction. Blinn (Ref. 5-25) recognized this and developed a method for perturbing the surface normal. The results give a visual impression of rough-textured surfaces.

At any point on a surface $Q(u, w)$ the partial derivatives in the parameter directions u, w, i.e. Q_u and Q_w, lie in the plane tangent to the surface at that point. The cross-product of Q_u and Q_w defines the surface normal n at that point, i.e.

$$\mathbf{n} = \mathbf{Q}_u \otimes \mathbf{Q}_w$$

Blinn defined a new surface giving the visual appearance of having a rough texture by adding a perturbation function $P(u, w)$ to the surface in the direction of the normal to the original surface. Thus, for any point on the new surface $Q(u, w)$ the position vector is

$$\mathbf{Q}'(u, w) = \mathbf{Q}(u, w) + P(u, w)\frac{\mathbf{n}}{|\mathbf{n}|}$$

The normal vector to the perturbed surface is then

$$\mathbf{n}' = \mathbf{Q}'_u \otimes \mathbf{Q}'_w$$

The partial derivatives Q'_u and Q'_w are

$$\mathbf{Q}'_u = \mathbf{Q}_u + P_u\frac{\mathbf{n}}{|\mathbf{n}|} + P\left(\frac{\mathbf{n}}{|\mathbf{n}|}\right)_u$$

$$\mathbf{Q}'_w = \mathbf{Q}_w + P_w\frac{\mathbf{n}}{|\mathbf{n}|} + P\left(\frac{\mathbf{n}}{|\mathbf{n}|}\right)_w$$

Since P is very small, i.e. a perturbation function, the last term may be neglected. Hence,

$$\mathbf{Q}'_u \doteq \mathbf{Q}_u + P_u\frac{\mathbf{n}'}{|\mathbf{n}|}$$

$$\mathbf{Q}'_w \doteq \mathbf{Q}_w + P_w\frac{\mathbf{n}}{|\mathbf{n}|}$$

The perturbed normal is then

$$\mathbf{n}' = \mathbf{Q}_u \otimes \mathbf{Q}_w + \frac{P_u(\mathbf{n} \otimes \mathbf{Q}_w)}{|\mathbf{n}|} + \frac{P_w(\mathbf{Q}_u \otimes \mathbf{n})}{|\mathbf{n}|} + \frac{P_uP_w(\mathbf{n} \otimes \mathbf{n})}{|\mathbf{n}|^2}$$

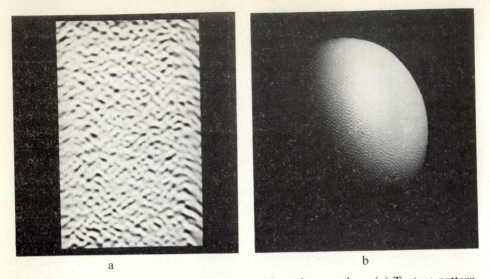

a   b

Figure 5-36 Texture pattern mapped onto bicubic surface patches. (a) Texture pattern, (b) result. (*Courtesy of T. Van Hook, Adage, Inc.*)

The first term is the normal to the unperturbed surface $\mathbf{n}$ and the last term is zero, so

$$\mathbf{n}' = \mathbf{n} + \frac{P_u(\mathbf{n} \otimes \mathbf{Q}_w)}{|\mathbf{n}|} + \frac{P_w(\mathbf{Q}_u \otimes \mathbf{n})}{|\mathbf{n}|}$$

where the last two terms represent the effect of the perturbation on the surface normal and hence on the illumination model after scaling to unit length.

Almost any function for which the derivatives can be defined may be used as the texture perturbation function P. Blinn used a simple mathematically defined grid pattern, character bit maps, z-buffer patterns, and random hand-drawn patterns. An example, rendered by T. Van Hook, is shown in Fig. 5-36, where a texture pattern has been added to bicubic surface patches. For non-mathematically defined patterns, the perturbation function is represented in a two-dimensional look-up table indexed by the parameters u, w. Intermediate values are obtained using bilinear interpolation of the values in the look-up table, and the derivatives P_u and P_w are determined using finite differences.

The rough texture effect is not invariant with scale changes of the object. In particular, if the object size is scaled by a factor of 2, then the magnitude of the normal vector will be scaled by a factor of 4, while the perturbation to the normal vector will be scaled by only a factor of 2. This results in smoothing the texture effect as the object size increases. However, scale changes due to object movement toward or away from the viewer in perspective space do not affect the texture scale.

The results of perturbation texture mapping can also exhibit aliasing effects. However, if texture area averaging, as described above, or prefiltering antialiasing techniques are used, the result is to smooth out or reduce the texture effect.

As pointed out by Blinn (Ref. 5-25), the proper antialiasing technique is to compute the image at a higher-than-display resolution and postfilter or average the results to obtain the lower resolution display images (see Sec. 2-25).

A recent rough texture technique uses fractal surfaces. A fractal surface is composed of stochastically defined polygonal or bipolynomial defined surfaces. The technique was originally applied to texture generation in computer graphics by Carpenter (Ref. 5-26) and Fournier and Fussell (Ref. 5-27). Fractal surfaces have been used to render a number of natural textures, e.g., stones, trees, terrain, and clouds. The fractal technique is based on original work done by Mandelbrot (Ref. 5-28).

A polygonal fractal surface is obtained by recursively subdividing an original polygon as shown in Fig. 5-37. One technique is to define the midpoints of each of the sides of the polygon and then to perturb the location of these points using a random function for each individual point. The center of the polygon is also similarly perturbed. Figure 5-37 illustrates the result. Notice that neither the original polygon nor any derivative polygon need be planar.

One advantage of fractal surfaces is that they may be "infinitely" subdivided. Consequently any arbitrary level of detail may be obtained. Further, the level of detail may be made dependent on the location of the observer; the closer the observer, the greater the detail. When the observer is far away, considerable processing can be saved. Any appropriate hidden surface algorithm and illumination model can be used to render the fractal surface. However, the number of subsurfaces increases at a greater than linear rate. Hence, the number of subdivisions and the level of detail must be a compromise, or excessive computational requirements result.

A typical result, rendered by Kajiya (Ref. 5-29) using an opaque visible surface ray tracing algorithm, is shown in Color Plate 4. The scene in Color Plate 4a contains 16,384 fractal triangles, and that in Color Plate 4b contains 262,144 fractal triangles. Notice the self-shadowing in the images.

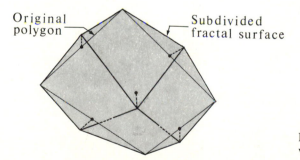

Original polygon

Subdivided fractal surface

Figure 5-37 Fractal surface subdivision.

5-12 A GLOBAL ILLUMINATION MODEL USING RAY TRACING

An illumination model is designed to determine the intensity of light reflected to an observer's eye at each point (pixel) in an image. The illumination model can be invoked either locally or globally. Invoked locally, only light incident from a light source(s) and the surface orientation is considered by the illumination model in determining the intensity of the light reflected to the observer's eye. Invoked globally, the light that reaches a point by reflection from, or transmission through, other objects in the scene, as well as light incident from any light sources, is also considered in determining the intensity of the light reflected from a point to the observer. Using a global illumination model has significant implications. Figure 5-38 illustrates some of the effects.

The sphere and the triangular and rectangular blocks shown in Fig. 5-38 are assumed to be opaque and to have surfaces capable of a high degree of specular reflection. An observer located at O looking at the point labeled 1 on the sphere will see not only the sphere but also the triangular block at point 2. The triangular block, which is otherwise obscured by the rectangular block, is thus visible because it is reflected in the sphere. Point 5 on the triangular block is visible at point 3 on the sphere even more indirectly. Here, the image of the triangle at point 5 is reflected from the *back* of the rectangular block at point 4 onto the surface of the sphere at point 3 and then to the observer. Point 5 on the triangle is also visible to the observer at point 1' with only one reflection from the surface of the sphere. Hence, multiple images of the triangular block are observed reflected in the sphere. Since only one reflection is involved, the image centered around point 1 is reversed. In contrast, the image centered around point 3 is not reversed, since two reflections occur. This second image is also less intense. Finally, the back of the rectangular block is visible as a reflected image in the sphere even though it does not receive any light directly from the source. It is illuminated by ambient light and by light reflected from the other objects in the scene.

From this discussion it should be clear that the normal backface culling operation commonly used by hidden surface algorithms cannot be used with a global illumination model. Further, an initial priority sort to determine visible faces also cannot be used. These two considerations eliminate all the hidden surface algorithms discussed in Chap. 4 *except* ray tracing. Consequently,

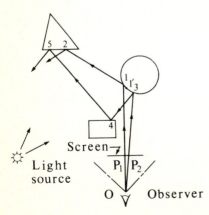

Figure 5-38 Global illumination.

global illumination models are implemented as part of ray tracing visible surface algorithms.

Whitted (Ref. 5-30) and Kay (Refs. 5-13 and 5-14) originally implemented ray tracing algorithms that utilized global illumination models. Whitted's algorithm, which is more general, has been extensively used and extended. Synthetic images generated by Whitted (Ref. 5-30), Potmesil (Refs. 5-31 and 5-32), and Barr (Ref. 5-33) with the Whitted algorithm or extensions of the algorithm are shown in Color Plates 5, 6, and 7. These images illustrate reflection, transparency, refraction, shadows, and texture effects.

The Potmesil extension replaces the traditional pinhole camera used in computer graphics with a more realistic model that approximates the lens and aperture characteristics of a real camera. The model considers the effects of depth of field, focus, lens distortion, and filtering. In animation sequences it provides a fade-in, fade-out capability. The technique is a two-step process.

The first step uses a traditional pinhole camera ray tracing algorithm to produce a point sampled image. In addition to the usual RGB intensities at each pixel, z depth and visible surface information are also retained. The second step, acting as a postprocessor, invokes the finite aperture camera model. Each sample point is converted to a circle of confusion using the laws of geometric optics. The size and intensity distribution for the circle of confusion are determined by the z value at the sample point, the characteristics of the lens, and the lens aperture. The intensity at a given pixel is determined by summing the intensities of all the circles of confusion overlapping that pixel. Typical results are shown in Color Plate 6.

The illumination model used by Whitted retains the ambient, Lambertian diffuse, and Phong specular reflection terms of the local illumination model given in Eq. 5-7. The global specular reflection and the transmission terms are based on the model shown in Fig. 5-39. Here, the incoming ray being traced, $\mathbf{v}$, reaches the surface at the point Q. At Q the ray is both reflected in the direction $\mathbf{r}$ and, if the surface is transparent, refracted in the direction $\mathbf{p}$. I_t is the intensity incoming to the surface at Q along the $\mathbf{p}$ direction that is refracted through the surface and reaches an observer located in the direction $-\mathbf{v}$.

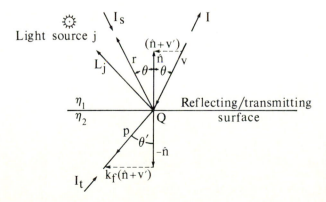

Figure 5-39 Specular reflection and transmission effects for the Whitted global illumination model.

Similarly, I_s is the intensity of the specularly reflected light incoming along the direction $-\mathbf{r}$ that is reflected at Q and that also reaches the observer located in the direction $-\mathbf{v}$. $\mathbf{n}$ is the surface normal at Q, $\mathbf{L}_j$ is the direction of the jth light source, $\mathbf{S}$ and $\mathbf{R}$ are the local sight and reflection vectors, and η is the index of refraction of the media. Here, n is the Phong spatial distribution value for specularly reflected light (see Sec. 5-2). The intensity reaching the observer I is then

$$I = k_a I_a + k_d \sum_j I_{lj}(\hat{\mathbf{n}} \cdot \hat{\mathbf{L}}_j) + k_s \sum_j I_{lj}(\hat{\mathbf{S}} \cdot \hat{\mathbf{R}}_j)^n + k_s I_s + k_t I_t \qquad (5\text{-}16)$$

where k_a, k_d, k_s, and k_t are the ambient, diffuse, and specular reflection coefficients and k_t is the transmission coefficient. Whitted holds these reflection coefficients constant. However, any of the previously discussed illumination models may be used to determine their variation with incidence angle and wavelength. The first and second summation terms in Eq. 5-16 represent the diffuse and specular reflection from light sources.

In contrast to the previous opaque surface ray tracing algorithm discussed in Sec. 4-13, the visibility calculations for the global illumination model do not end at the first intersection. Here, the incoming ray $\mathbf{v}$ is assumed to be reflected from the surface in the direction $\mathbf{r}$ and transmitted through the surface in the direction $\mathbf{p}$ as shown in Fig. 5-39 at point Q. Thus, two additional rays are generated at the point Q. These two rays are traced to determine their intersections with objects in the scene. The process is repeated until none of the rays intersects any object in the scene. The process, illustrated in Fig. 5-40a for single surface ray intersections, is easily represented using the tree structure shown in Fig. 5-40b. Each node of the tree represents a ray surface intersection. At each node of the tree two subbranches are generated. The right hand branch is due to refraction, and the left due to reflection of the ray at the surface. Notice that a branch terminates when the ray leaves the scene.

At each surface ray intersection, the directions of the reflected and transmitted rays are obtained using the laws of geometric optics. In particular, the

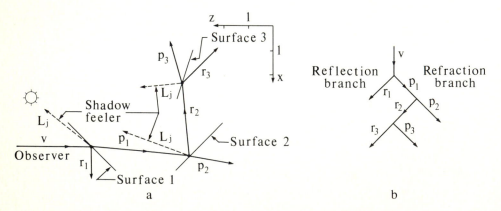

Figure 5-40 Ray tracing surface reflections and refractions.

reflected ray **r** and the incident ray **v** lie in the same plane and make equal angles with the surface normal **n** (see Sec. 5-3). The transmitted ray obeys Snell's law of refraction (see Sec. 5-9). In the context of the present model and notation, the directions of **r** and **p** are given by

$$\mathbf{r} = \mathbf{v}' + 2\hat{\mathbf{n}}$$

$$\mathbf{p} = k_f(\hat{\mathbf{n}} + \mathbf{v}') - \hat{\mathbf{n}}$$

where

$$\mathbf{v}' = \frac{\mathbf{v}}{|\mathbf{v} \cdot \hat{\mathbf{n}}|}$$

$$k_f = (k_\eta^2 |\mathbf{v}'|^2 - |\mathbf{v}' + \hat{\mathbf{n}}|^2)^{-1/2}$$

$$k_\eta = \frac{\eta_2}{\eta_1}$$

where k_η is the ratio of refractive indices and $\hat{\mathbf{n}}$ is the unit normal vector in the direction of the incoming ray. If the denominator of k_f is imaginary, then total internal reflection occurs and I_t is assumed zero.

Determining the intensity at each ray-surface intersection requires traversing the ray tracing tree in the reverse direction. The illumination model is applied recursively at each node of the tree. The intensity at each node of the tree is attenuated by the distance between the surface intersection points before being used as input for the next node up the tree. When the tree has been completely traversed, the resulting intensity is displayed for that pixel.

Theoretically, the ray tracing tree is infinitely deep. In addition to being terminated when all rays leave the scene, the tree may be terminated when the intensity at a node falls below a specified value or when the allocated storage is exceeded.

Figure 5-41 shows the effect of internal reflection for a closed transparent object. The rays specularly reflected from the inside surfaces of the object are trapped within the object and are eventually absorbed. Hence, they cannot contribute to the light intensity perceived by the observer. However, at each

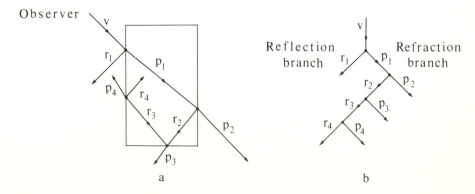

Figure 5-41 Internal reflection for transparent objects.

ray-surface intersection a transmitted ray **p** is generated. These rays escape the object and may directly or indirectly reach the observer. Thus, they must be traced.

If shadows are also included in the algorithm, then at each ray-surface intersection shadow feelers in the direction of each light source L_j are generated. If a shadow feeler intersects an object before reaching the light source, then that ray-surface intersection lies in shadow with respect to that light source. The contribution of that light source to the local diffuse and specular reflection at the point is then attenuated (see Sec. 5-10). If the intervening surface is opaque, no light reaches the surface. If the intervening surface is transparent, the illumination characteristics of the surface are used to attenuate the light. Shadow feelers are shown in Fig. 5-40.

Example 5-9   Global Illumination and Ray Tracing

Consider the simple two-dimensional single plane scene in Fig. 5-40a. The planes are normal to the plane of the paper which is assumed to be the xz plane. The observer is located at infinity on the positive z axis at $x = 5$. A single point light source is located at $x = 3$, $z = 10$. The surfaces are defined using the plane equations, i.e.

Surface 1: $x + z - 12.5 = 0$ $4 \leq x \leq 6$

Surface 2: $x - z - 2 = 0$ $4 \leq x \leq 6$

Surface 3: $x - 3z + 9 = 0$ $1 \leq x \leq 3$

The illumination characteristics for each surface are

Surface 1: $k_{a_1} = 0.15$, $k_{d_1} = 0.15$, $k_{s_1} = 0.8$, $k_{t_1} = 0.5$, $k_{\eta_1} = 1/1.1$

Surface 2: $k_{a_2} = 0.15$, $k_{d_2} = 0.15$, $k_{s_2} = 0.8$, $k_{t_2} = 0.5$, $k_{\eta_2} = 1.1$

Surface 3: $k_{a_3} = 0.15$, $k_{d_3} = 0.15$, $k_{s_3} = 0.8$, $k_{t_3} = 0$, $k_{\eta_3} = 1.1$

The intensity of the ambient light is $I_a = 1.0$, and the intensity of the light source is $I_l = 10$. The Phong spatial distribution value for specularly reflected light is $n = 50$ for each surface.

A ray is fired from the observer toward the scene. The resulting ray tree is shown in Fig. 5-40b. The ray first intersects surface 1. Noting that the equation of the ray before it intersects the surface is $x = 5$ and substituting into the surface equation yields

$$x + z - 12.5 = 5 + z - 12.5 = 0 \qquad \rightarrow \qquad z = 7.5$$

Thus, the intersection of the ray and the surface, which represents the first node on the ray tree, occurs at $x_1 = 5$, $z_1 = 5$ At that point the unit normal to the surface is

$$\hat{\mathbf{n}}_1 = \frac{\mathbf{i}}{\sqrt{2}} + \frac{\mathbf{k}}{\sqrt{2}}$$

Determining the refracted and reflected rays yields

$$\mathbf{v}_1 = -\mathbf{k}$$

and

$$\mathbf{v}_1' = \frac{\mathbf{v}_1}{|\mathbf{v}_1 \cdot \hat{\mathbf{n}}_1|} = \frac{-\mathbf{k}}{\left| (-\mathbf{k}) \cdot \left(\frac{\mathbf{i}}{\sqrt{2}} + \frac{\mathbf{k}}{\sqrt{2}} \right) \right|} = -\sqrt{2}\mathbf{k}$$

The direction of the reflected ray is

$$\mathbf{r}_1 = \mathbf{v}_1' + 2\hat{\mathbf{n}}_1 = -\sqrt{2}\mathbf{k} + 2\left(\frac{\mathbf{i}}{\sqrt{2}} + \frac{\mathbf{k}}{\sqrt{2}} \right) = \sqrt{2}\mathbf{i}$$

Noting that

$$\mathbf{v}_1' + \hat{\mathbf{n}}_1 = -\sqrt{2}\mathbf{k} + \frac{\mathbf{i}}{\sqrt{2}} + \frac{\mathbf{k}}{\sqrt{2}} = \frac{\mathbf{i}}{\sqrt{2}} - \frac{\mathbf{k}}{\sqrt{2}}$$

then

$$k_{f_1} = \left[k_{\eta_1}^2 |\mathbf{v}_1'|^2 - |\mathbf{v}_1' + \hat{\mathbf{n}}_1|^2 \right]^{-1/2} = \left[\left(\frac{1}{1.1} \right)^2 (2) - 1 \right]^{-1/2} = 1.238$$

which yields the refracted ray

$$\mathbf{p}_1 = k_{f_1}(\hat{\mathbf{n}}_1 + \mathbf{v}_1') - \hat{\mathbf{n}}_1 = 1.238 \left(\frac{\mathbf{i}}{\sqrt{2}} - \frac{\mathbf{k}}{\sqrt{2}} \right) - \left(\frac{\mathbf{i}}{\sqrt{2}} + \frac{\mathbf{k}}{\sqrt{2}} \right)$$

$$= 0.168\mathbf{i} - 1.582\mathbf{k}$$

At this point the reflected ray leaves the scene and is not considered further. The intersection of the transmitted refracted ray with the second surface yields the second node in the ray tree. Writing the refracted ray $\mathbf{p}_1$ in parametric form yields

$$x = 5 + 0.168t$$
$$z = 7.5 - 1.582t$$

Substituting into the surface equation yields

$$x - z - 2 = 5 + 0.168t - 7.5 + 1.582t - 2 = 1.75t - 4.5 = 0$$

Consequently $t = 2.571$ and the intersection point is

$$x_2 = 5 + (0.168)(2.571) = 5.432$$
$$z_2 = 7.5 - (1.582)(2.571) = 3.433$$

The distance between the two intersection points is

$$d_{12} = \sqrt{(x_2 - x_1)^2 + (z_2 - z_1)^2} = \sqrt{(5.432 - 5)^2 + (3.433 - 7.5)^2} = 4.09$$

The reflected and refracted rays at this intersection point are obtained by using $\mathbf{p}_1$ as the incoming ray, i.e.

$$\mathbf{v}_2 = \mathbf{p}_1 = 0.168\mathbf{i} - 1.582\mathbf{k}$$

The unit surface normal is

$$\hat{\mathbf{n}}_2 = \frac{-\mathbf{i}}{\sqrt{2}} + \frac{\mathbf{k}}{\sqrt{2}}$$

The results are

$$\mathbf{p}_2 = 0.215\mathbf{i} - 1.199\mathbf{k}$$
$$\mathbf{r}_2 = -1.278\mathbf{i} + 0.136\mathbf{k}$$

Here the transmitted refracted ray leaves the scene without intersecting additional objects. Thus, this ray tree branch terminates. The intersection of the reflected ray and the third surface yields the third node in the ray tree. Here, the intersection of $\mathbf{r}_2$ and the third surface is required. Using the parametric form of $\mathbf{r}_2$ and the plane equation for the surface yields

$$x = 5.432 - 1.278t$$
$$y = 3.433 + 0.136t$$

for the ray. Substituting into the plane equation yields

$$x - 3z + 9 = 5.432 - 1.278t - 3(3.433 + 0.136t) + 9 = -1.686t + 4.133 = 0$$

Consequently, $t = 2.451$ and the intersection point is

$$x_3 = 5.432 - (1.278)(2.451) = 2.299$$
$$z_3 = 3.433 + (0.136)(2.451) = 3.766$$

The distance between the two intersection points is

$$d_{23} = \sqrt{(x_3 - x_2)^2 + (z_3 - z_2)^2}$$
$$= \sqrt{(2.299 - 5.432)^2 + (3.766 - 3.433)^2} = 3.151$$

The reflected and refracted rays at this intersection point are obtained using $\mathbf{r}_2$ as the incoming ray, i.e.

$$\mathbf{v}_3 = \mathbf{r}_2 = -1.278\mathbf{i} + 0.136\mathbf{k}$$

The unit surface normal on the incoming ray side of the surface is

$$\hat{\mathbf{n}}_3 = \frac{\mathbf{i}}{\sqrt{10}} - \frac{3\mathbf{k}}{\sqrt{10}}$$

The results are

$$\mathbf{p}_3 = -1.713\mathbf{i} + 0.483\mathbf{k}$$
$$\mathbf{r}_3 = -1.765\mathbf{i} - 1.643\mathbf{k}$$

Here, both the reflected and refracted rays leave the scene. The ray tree terminates at this point. In fact, examination of the illumination characteristics for the surfaces shows that $k_{t_3} = 0$. Hence, the surface is opaque and no transmitted ray is generated.

The intensity calculations begin at the bottom of the ray tree at the third node. Since surface 3 is opaque, there is no light transmitted through the surface. A shadow feeler shows that the surface itself is between the incident ray and the light source. Consequently, the point of intersection of the ray and the surface is in shadow. Thus, the point receives only ambient light. The intensity is

$$I_3 = k_{a_3}I_a = (0.15)(1) = 0.15$$

This intensity is transmitted along the reflection vector $\mathbf{r}_2$ to the second surface. When it reaches the second surface, it is attenuated by the distance between the intersection points d_{23}. Thus,

$$I_{s_2} = \frac{I_3}{d_{23}} = \frac{0.15}{3.151} = 0.0476$$

At the second node in the tree representing the intersection of the ray and the second surface, the shadow feeler does not intersect any object. Hence, the point receives light from the source. The vector from the point to the light source is

$$\mathbf{L}_2 = (x_l - x_2)\mathbf{i} + (z_l - z_2)\mathbf{k} = (3 - 5.432)\mathbf{i} + (10 - 3.433)\mathbf{k}$$
$$= -2.432\mathbf{i} + 6.567\mathbf{k}$$

and

$$\hat{\mathbf{L}} = -0.347\mathbf{i} + 0.938\mathbf{k}$$

Consequently

$$\hat{\mathbf{n}}_2 \cdot \hat{\mathbf{L}}_2 = \left(\frac{-\mathbf{i}}{\sqrt{2}} + \frac{\mathbf{k}}{\sqrt{2}}\right) \cdot (-0.347\mathbf{i} + 0.938\mathbf{k}) = 0.909$$

The reflected direction for the ray from the light source is

$$\hat{\mathbf{R}}_2 = -0.938\mathbf{i} + 0.347\mathbf{k}$$

Here the unit sight vector is $-\hat{\mathbf{p}}_1$ and

$$-\hat{\mathbf{p}}_1 \cdot \hat{\mathbf{R}}_2 = (-0.168\mathbf{i} + 1.582\mathbf{k}) \cdot (-0.938\mathbf{i} + 0.347\mathbf{k}) = 0.707$$

Thus,

$$I_2 = k_{a_2}I_a + I_l k_{d_2}(\hat{\mathbf{n}}_2 \cdot \hat{\mathbf{L}}_2) + I_l k_{s_2}(-\hat{\mathbf{p}}_1 \cdot \hat{\mathbf{R}}_2)^n + k_{s_2}I_{s_2} + k_{t_2}I_{t_2}$$
$$= (0.15)(1) + (10)(0.15)(0.909) + (10)(0.8)(0) + (0.8)(.0476) + (0.5)(0)$$
$$= 1.552$$

This intensity is transmitted along the refraction vector $\mathbf{p}_1$ to the first surface where, attenuated by the distance between the surfaces d_{12}, it becomes

$$I_{t_1} = \frac{I_2}{d_{12}} = \frac{1.552}{4.09} = 0.379$$

Here, the shadow feeler also does not intersect any object. Hence, the point on the first surface receives light from the source. The vector from the point to the light source is

$$\mathbf{L}_1 = (x_l - x_1)\mathbf{i} + (z_l - z_1)\mathbf{k} = (3 - 5)\mathbf{i} + (10 - 7.5)\mathbf{k}$$
$$= -2\mathbf{i} + 2.5\mathbf{k}$$

and

$$\hat{\mathbf{L}}_1 = -0.625\mathbf{i} + 0.781\mathbf{k}$$

Consequently

$$\hat{\mathbf{n}}_1 \cdot \hat{\mathbf{L}}_1 = \left(\frac{\mathbf{i}}{\sqrt{2}} + \frac{\mathbf{k}}{\sqrt{2}} \right) \cdot (-0.625\mathbf{i} + 0.781\mathbf{k}) = 0.110$$

The reflected direction for the ray from the light source is

$$\hat{\mathbf{R}}_1 = 0.781\mathbf{i} - 0.625\mathbf{k}$$

Here, the unit sight vector is $-\hat{\mathbf{v}}_1$ and

$$-\hat{\mathbf{v}}_1 \cdot \hat{\mathbf{R}}_1 = (\mathbf{k}) \cdot (0.781\mathbf{i} - 0.625\mathbf{k}) = -0.625$$

Thus,

$$I_1 = k_{a_1}I_a + I_l k_{d_1}(\hat{\mathbf{n}}_1 \cdot \hat{\mathbf{L}}) + I_l k_{s_1}(-\hat{\mathbf{v}}_1 \cdot \hat{\mathbf{R}}_1)^n + k_{s_1}I_{s_1} + k_{t_1}I_{t_1}$$
$$= (0.15)(1) + (10)(0.15)(0.11) + (10)(0.8)(0) + (0.8)(0) + (0.5)(0.379)$$
$$= 0.505$$

This is the intensity transmitted to the observer. Because the resulting intensity is low, the point is only dimly seen. The low intensity results because the surface is almost edge-on to the light source. Further, the results show that more than a third of the intensity is transmitted through the first surface from surface 2. Finally because of the large value of n local specular highlights are not seen.

   If color is used, then the above calculation is performed three times, once for each of the red, green, and blue components. Further, separate illumination characteristics for each component are required.

   Figure 5-42 shows a flowchart for a ray tracing algorithm with global illumination. The algorithm is implemented using a pushdown ray stack. The stack serves to communicate reflected and transmitted illumination information among the elements of the ray tree. Since the stack holds only part of the ray tree at any one time, it need only be long enough to contain the longest anticipated branch. A particular branch of the ray tree is terminated when both the reflected and refracted rays at an object intersection leave the scene or when the available stack length is exceeded. When both rays leave the scene, their contribution to the illumination at the source ray is zero. When the available stack length is exceeded, the algorithm calculates the illumination at the source ray using only the ambient, diffuse, and specular reflection components at the source ray intersection. The algorithm can be extended one additional depth in the tree without exceeding the maximum stack depth. The flowchart for this modification is shown in Fig. 5-43.

   The efficiency of the algorithm can be increased by reducing the average size of the ray tree or stack and hence the number of required intersection calculations. The average size of the ray stack can be reduced by placing on it only rays that significantly contribute to the intensity at the observer's eye. The maximum relative contribution of a particular node of the ray tree to the intensity at the observer's eye can be approximated using the following technique. The approximate intensity at the first ray-surface intersection, including any shadow effects, is determined using only a local illumination model, e.g., the ambient, Lambertian diffuse, and Phong specular reflection terms from Eq. 5-16. This value is saved. At each succeeding ray-surface intersection the maximum intensity contribution is approximated by the same local illumination model but without considering shadow effects. The resulting intensity is attenuated by the cumulative effects of refraction and reflection and by the cumulative distance traveled by the ray from the first ray-surface intersection to that under consideration. For example, the approximate intensity at surface 3 in Fig. 5-40 would be attenuated by $k_{s_2}k_{t_1}/d_{23}d_{12}$ (see Example 5-9). If the resulting intensity exceeds a fixed percentage of the approximate intensity at the first ray-surface intersection, then refracted and reflected rays, as appropriate, are placed on the ray stack. If not, then the ray branch is terminated at that point. Hall (Refs. 5-34 and 5-35), using a similar technique, found that the average tree size and the computational expense was reduced by a factor of more than 8. Unfortunately, the technique is not completely correct. Specifically, if a major contribution to the intensity at the observer's eye due to global illumination effects occurs after the ray tree has been terminated, the resulting image will be incomplete. However, the probability of this occurring for most general scenes is small. Thus, the significant savings that result justify use of the technique.

The algorithm assumes an object description list similar to that discussed in Sec. 4-13 for the opaque visible surface ray tracing algorithm. The ray stack contains the following information for each ray.

Ray number	uniquely assigned for each ray
Ray type	v, a pixel ray from the eye; r, a reflected ray; or p, a refracted ray
Ray source number	the number of the ray that generated this ray
Ray source type	v, r, or p as above
Intersection flag	one if an intersection for this ray has been found, otherwise zero
Object pointer	gives the location of the intersected object in the object description list
Intersection values	x, y, z, coordinates of the intersection that generated this ray
Direction cosines	specify the direction of the ray
d	distance between this ray intersection and the intersection of the source ray
I_t	intensity of transmitted light along this ray
I_s	intensity of specularly reflected light along this ray

When a ray is initially pushed onto the stack, the values of I_s, I_t, d, and the intersection flag are set to zero. Subsequent passes through the algorithm update these values as required.

The Whitted illumination model as shown in Fig. 5-39 is used with the algorithm. The flowchart shown in Fig. 5-44 corresponds to the block labeled "Calculate intensity" I, in Fig. 5-42. If color is incorporated into the model,

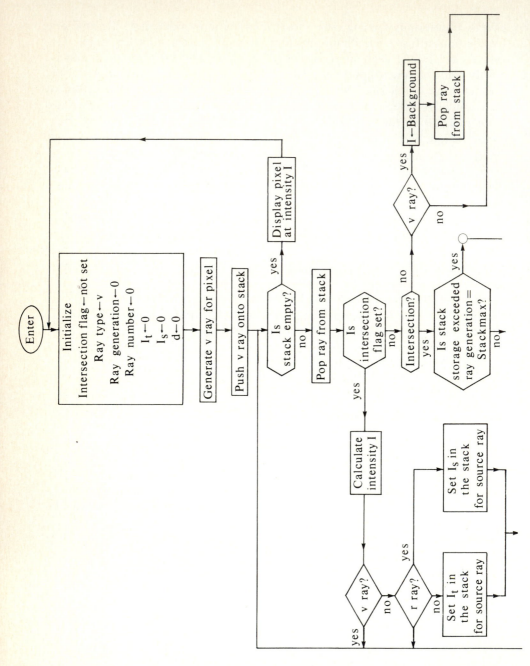

Figure 5-42 Flowchart for a ray tracing algorithm with global illumination.

374

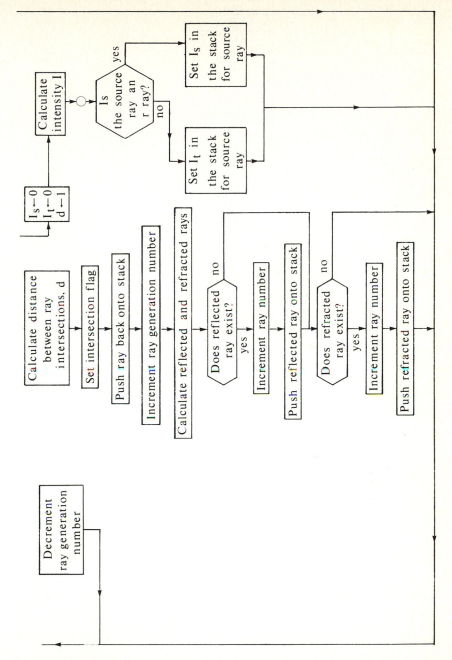

Figure 5-42 (Continued.)

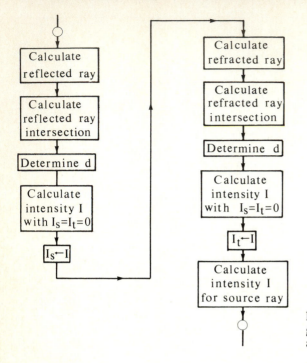

Figure 5-43 Modification of the global illumination ray tracing algorithm.

the "Calculate intensity" block is executed three times; once for each color component. Here, the path of the vectors (shadow feelers) from the surface intersection point to the various light sources is checked for intersection with other objects in the scene. If an intersection occurs with an opaque object, that light source does not contribute to the local diffuse or specular reflection at that point. If all the intersections along the path are transparent, the intensity of the light source I_{l_j} is attenuated appropriately. In particular, the attenuation factor is based on the transmission coefficients of the occluding surfaces. Thus, opaque occluding objects produce sharp black shadows, while transparent occluding objects yield faint shadows. Refraction of incident light from the source through transparent objects to the surface is not accounted for. The transmitted and specularly reflected light incident at a point is attenuated by the distance between ray intersections. The algorithm assumes that the surface normal is available from the object description. Other more complex illumination models can be incorporated into the model by modifying this routine (see Secs. 5-7, 5-8 and 5-13).

The intersection processor was previously described in Sec. 4-13 in the context of an opaque visible surface ray tracing algorithm. The only modification required here is to specifically translate the ray-surface intersection point for each ray to the origin of the coordinate system before rotating to make the ray coincident with the z axis. The ray points in the direction of $-z$. The same procedure is used to determine the intersections of the shadow feelers with objects.

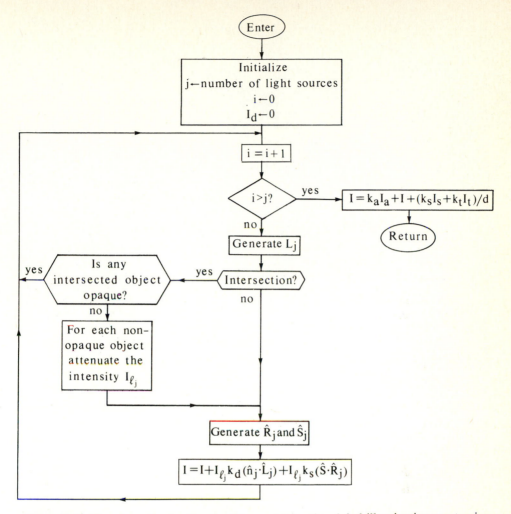

Figure 5-44 Flowchart for the illumination model for the global illumination ray tracing algorithm.

In operation, the algorithm described in Fig. 5-42 first generates the ray tree along the right hand "refraction" branch from the root node until the branch terminates, as shown in Fig. 5-45 by the dashed line with arrows. The branch is then traversed upward, calculating the intensities at each node until the root node is reached. The left hand "reflection" branch from the root node is then generated and traversed in the reverse direction. At any intermediate node the process may be repeated. The downward pointing arrows in Fig. 5-45 indicate ray generation (pushed onto the stack), and the upward pointing arrows indicate intensity generation (popped from the stack). After the intensity contribution for a ray at a particular node has been determined, the ray is

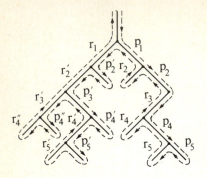

Figure 5-45 Ray tracing tree.

discarded. When only the root node remains, the pixel intensity is determined and sent to the display.

Whitted (Ref. 5-30) incorporates antialiasing into the ray tracing algorithm. Aliasing effects are most apparent for regions with high-intensity gradients, e.g., at object edges, at silhouette edges, within texture patterns, and for objects smaller than the interval between sample points. To reduce computational requirements, the antialiasing technique used is a dynamically invoked Warnock-style recursive subdivision. Instead of tracing rays through each pixel center, Whitted traces rays through sample points at each corner of the pixel square, as shown in Fig. 5-46a. For an $n \times m$ raster this requires $(n + 1) \times (m + 1)$ sample points, which is only a modest increase. If the intensities at the four corner sample points are nearly equal, and if no small object lies between them, then the intensity values are averaged and displayed for that pixel. If the four intensity values are not nearly equal (see Fig. 5-46b), the pixel square is subdivided into four subsquares and the process repeated. Recursive subdivision continues until the corner values are nearly equal, the allotted storage is exceeded, or the resolution of the computer is exceeded. The intensity contribution of each subpixel is weighted by its area, and the results summed to obtain the pixel intensity. Although still a point sampling technique, in the limit, the technique is equivalent to area antialiasing (see Sec. 2-26).

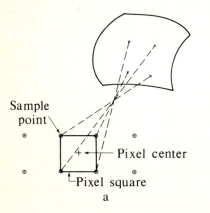

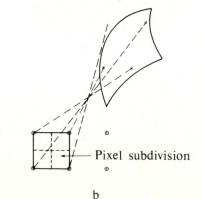

Figure 5-46 Antialiasing for ray tracing.

Implementation of this scheme requires that either a row or column of sample point intensity values, which ever is smaller, be saved on a rolling basis as the image is generated. Saving the sample point intensity values makes it unnecessary to backtrack or regenerate previously determined intensity values. When a pixel square is subdivided, a stack is used to save intermediate intensity values as the subdivision progresses. (See the Warnock algorithm in Sec. 4-4.)

Whitted prevents small objects from being lost by using a minimum size bounding sphere that is larger than the spacing between sample points. When the algorithm encounters a minimum radius bounding sphere and no ray-object intersection is found, the four pixel squares that share the ray through that sample point are recursively subdivided until the object is found. This technique is adequate for directly viewed objects or for objects viewed indirectly via planar surfaces. However, objects viewed indirectly via curved surfaces may be lost. These objects are lost because closely spaced rays reflected or refracted from highly curved surfaces may diverge sufficiently to miss the object. This effect is shown in Fig. 5-47 for reflection from a sphere. Continued subdivision may exceed machine resolution before an intersecting ray is found. Color Plate 5 was generated using these techniques.

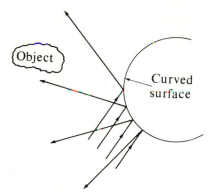

Figure 5-47 Reflection from a curved surface.

5-13 A MORE COMPLETE GLOBAL ILLUMINATION MODEL USING RAY TRACING

Hall (Ref. 5-34) and Hall and Greenberg (Ref. 5-35) have used a more complete global illumination model than that described in the previous section. The Hall global illumination model includes the scattering of light directly from light sources along the refracted or transmitted ray in addition to along the reflected ray. The scattering model is an adaptation of the Phong model. The model also uses the Fresnel relationships for the wavelength and angle of incidence dependence of refracted and reflected light, and uses the filter properties of specific materials to attenuate light passing through transparent media. Specifically the Hall global illumination model for j light sources is

$$I = k_d \sum_j I_{l_j} R_d(\hat{\mathbf{n}} \cdot \hat{\mathbf{L}}_j) + k_s \sum_j I_{l_j} R_f(\hat{\mathbf{n}} \cdot \hat{\mathbf{H}})^n$$

$$+ k_t \sum_j I_{l_j} F_t(\hat{\mathbf{n}} \cdot \hat{\mathbf{H}}')^{n'} + k_a R_d + k_s R_f I_s T_r^{dr} \qquad (5\text{-}17)$$

$$+ k_t F_t I_t T_t^{dt}$$

Here, the ambient globally diffuse term ($k_a R_d I_a$) and the Lambertian diffuse reflection for light scattered directly from light sources include $R_d(\lambda)$ the material- and wavelength-dependent diffuse reflection curve. Similarly the specular reflection term for light scattered directly from light sources and the global specular reflection term contain $R_f(\lambda)$, the material- and wavelength-dependent Fresnel reflectance curve (see Sec. 5-8). The third term in Eq. 5-17, which represents the specular transmission of light directly from light sources along the refracted ray, and the global transmission term include F_t, the material- and wavelength-dependent Fresnel transmissivity curve. From conservation-of-energy considerations $F_t = 1 - R_f$. The approximate technique suggested by Cook and described in Sec. 5-8 is used to determine $R_f(\lambda)$ and $F_t(\lambda)$. The global specular reflection and specular refraction terms also include T_r and T_t the transmissivity per unit length for the reflected and transmitted (refracted) rays. The distances traveled by the reflected and transmitted (refracted) rays from the last intersection are given by d_r and d_t, respectively. Following Kay (see Sec. 5-9), T_r and T_t are raised to a power to represent the effects of passage through a material. Here, the distances, d_r and d_t are used as the powers.

The specular reflection term for light received directly from light sources is adapted from the Torrance-Sparrow model discussed in Sec. 5-8. Here, the angle between the surface normal $\hat{\mathbf{n}}$ and the bisector of the angle between the light source direction and the observer's direction $\hat{\mathbf{H}}$, i.e., $\hat{\mathbf{n}} \cdot \hat{\mathbf{H}}$ raised to a power n, is used to represent scattering of specularly reflected light. Similarly, the angle between the surface normal and a vector $\mathbf{H}'$ raised to a power n' is used to represent scattering of specularly transmitted light. The vector $\mathbf{H}'$ represents the normal direction for Torrance-Sparrow (see Sec. 5-8) surface microfacets that refract light received directly from a light source in the direction $\mathbf{p}$ (see Fig. 5-39).

The direction of the $\mathbf{H}'$ vector can be calculated using Snell's laws (see Sec. 5-9). Referring to Fig. 5-48, using the similar triangles afd and bed, and Snell's law yields

$$\mathbf{ad} = \frac{\eta_2}{\eta_1} \mathbf{bd}$$

Now

$$\mathbf{ab} = \mathbf{v} - \mathbf{p}$$

and

$$\mathbf{ad} = \mathbf{ab} + \mathbf{bd}$$

Thus,

$$\mathbf{bd} = \frac{\mathbf{v} - \mathbf{p}}{\eta_2/\eta_1 - 1}$$

Since

$$\mathbf{H'} = \mathbf{bd} - \mathbf{p}$$

combining these results yields

$$\mathbf{H'} = \frac{\mathbf{v} - (\eta_2/\eta_1)\mathbf{p}}{\eta_2/\eta_1 - 1}$$

Color Plate 8 compares results for the Whitted and Hall global illumination models. Both images are of the same scene and were created using a ray tracing algorithm. Color Plate 8a was rendered using the Whitted global illumination model described in Eq. 5-16. Color Plate 8b was rendered with the Hall global illumination model described in Eq. 5-17. Compare the appearance of the metallic spheres in both scenes. Notice the color of the blue placemat edge reflected in the metallic sphere. Compare the color of the transparent spheres. Notice the slight bluish-green color of the sphere and its shadow in Color Plate 8b. This color results from including the material filter properties in the Hall model. Although, as shown by Color Plate 8, the Hall global illumination model is empirically derived and hence, as pointed out by Hall (Ref. 5-34), fundamentally incorrect, the images are some of the most realistic produced to date.

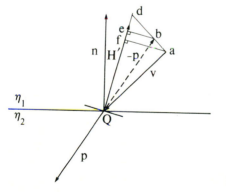

Figure 5-48 Determining the $\mathbf{H'}$ vector.

5-14 RECENT ADVANCES IN RENDERING

Although the techniques discussed in previous sections provide powerful tools for rendering synthetic images, they fall short of realism in a number of areas. Chief among these are the rendering of natural objects, providing motion without aliasing, and modeling distributed light sources. Because these are areas of on-going research, detailed discussions are beyond the scope of this book. However, an attempt will be made to *direct* the reader to *some* of the current research.

The typical point light source used in the illumination models discussed above intrinsically depends on the particle character of light. Thus, each ray must be traced individually. Accomplishing this for the hundreds of rays generated by a diffuse light source and/or by diffuse reflection from a surface is prohibitively expensive. Moravec (Ref. 5-36) suggests a solution based on the wave characteristics of light. Preliminary results are interesting, but again prohibitively expensive.

Aliasing in computer-generated animation falls into two broad categories. The first is typified by the common aliasing problems of small objects appearing and disappearing from frame to frame and by the phenomenon of "crawling" along silhouette edges. These effects can be mostly eliminated using standard spacial antialiasing techniques on each individual static image.

The second category is referred to as temporal antialiasing or motion blur. When an object moves rapidly through space, it is perceived as slightly blurred. Three recent papers address this problem. Korein and Badler (Ref. 5-37) present a technique for generating temporally and spacially synchronized multiple images of a moving object within a single frame. Potmesil and Chakravarty (Ref. 5-38) have extended their camera model (Ref. 5-31) to include motion blur. The effect is obtained by defocusing individual objects and by generating multiple images (exposures) within a single frame. Reeves (Ref. 5-39) incorporates motion blur within a stochastic particle system by generating special particle shapes.

Rendering naturally occurring objects is difficult because they are complex, rough, dirty, cracked, and otherwise irregular. Examples are fire, smoke, clouds, fog, grass, and trees. Considerable work has been done in this area. Selected recent references are Blinn (Ref. 5-40), Dungan (Ref. 5-41), Marshal, Wilson, and Carlson (Ref. 5-42) and Csuri (Ref. 5-43).

Of particular interest is a particle system presented by Reeves (Ref. 5-39). Because many natural phenomena are difficult to model with polygons or curved surfaces, Reeves and his co-workers, as well as a number of previous investigators, have turned to individual particles as a modeling mechanism. These particles are "fuzzy"; i.e., they do not have smooth, well-defined surfaces but rather, irregular, complex surfaces of nonconstant shape. The particles change form and characteristics with time under the action of physical or stochastic models. Over time, particles are generated or born into the system, move within the system, and die or leave the system. With these particle systems the following procedure is used to generate a single frame

New particles are generated, assigned individual attributes, and introduced into the system.

Old particles in the system that have died are extinguished.

The remaining particles are moved using an appropriate motion model.

An image of the remaining particles is rendered.

Some of the most realistic synthetic images to date have been generated using this technique. An example is shown in Color Plate 10.

5-15 COLOR

Color has been casually mentioned throughout this text. It now remains to consider it in some detail. Color is both a psychophysiological phenomenon and a psychophysical phenomenon. The perception of color depends upon the physics of light considered as electromagnetic energy and its interaction with physical materials, and on the interpretation of the resulting phenomena by the human eye-brain visual system. As such, it is a vast, complex, fascinating subject, the details of which are well beyond the scope of this text. Additional information can be obtained by consulting Refs. 5-44 to 5-47. The approach taken here is to develop a basic color vocabulary, a basic understanding of the physical phenomena involved, and a basic understanding of color specification systems and the transformations between them.

The human visual system interprets electromagnetic energy with wavelengths between approximately 400 and 700 nanometers as visible light. A nanometer (nm) is 10^{-9} meter or a billionth of a meter. Light is perceived either directly from a source of illumination, e.g. a light bulb, or indirectly by reflection from the surface of an object or refraction through an object.

When perceived light contains all the visible wavelengths with approximately equal weights, the light source or object is achromatic. An achromatic light source appears white. When the reflected or transmitted light from an object is achromatic, it appears white, black, or an intermediate level or shade of gray. Objects that achromatically reflect more than about 80% of the incident light from a white light source appear white. Those that achromatically reflect less than about 3% of the incident light appear black. Intermediate achromatic reflectance levels yield various shades of gray. It is convenient to consider the intensity of the reflected light in a range between 0 and 1, with 0 equated to black and 1 to white. Intermediate values are gray.

Although it is difficult to distinguish between the concepts of lightness and brightness, lightness is most conveniently considered a perceived property of a non-self-luminous or reflecting object (white-black), and brightness a characteristic of the perceived amount of illumination (high-low) present from a self-luminous or emitting object. The perceived lightness or brightness of an object is dependent on the relative sensitivity of the eye to various wavelengths. Figure 5-49 shows that for daylight the eye is most sensitive to light at a wavelength of approximately 550 nm. The eye's sensitivity decreases rapidly at the ends of the visible light range or spectrum. The curve in Fig. 5-49 is called a luminous efficiency function. It provides a measure of the light energy or intensity corrected for the sensitivity of the eye.

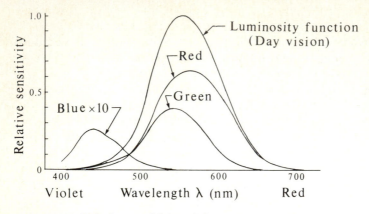

Figure 5-49 Relative sensitivity of the eye.

When perceived light contains wavelengths in arbitrary unequal amounts, the color of the light is said to be chromatic.[†] If a single concentration of wavelengths is near the upper end of the visible spectrum, the color of the light is interpreted as red or "reddish"; i.e., the dominant wavelength is in the red portion of the visible spectrum. If near the lower end of the visible spectrum, the color is interpreted as blue or "bluish"; i.e., the dominant wavelength is in the blue portion of the visible spectrum. However, note that electromagnetic energy of a particular wavelength has no color. It is the eye-brain combination that interprets the physical phenomena as the sensation of color. The color of an object depends on both the distribution of wavelengths of the light source and the physical characteristics of the object. If an object reflects or transmits light in only a narrow band of wavelengths, absorbing all others, then the object is perceived as colored. The wavelengths of the reflected or transmitted light determine the color. Interaction of the color of incident and reflected or transmitted light can yield startling results. For example, the reflected light from a green light incident on a normally white object will also appear green; i.e., the object is perceived as green. However, a red object illuminated with green light appears black since no light is reflected.

A chromatic color is psychophysiologically defined by its hue, saturation, and brightness. Hue is the "color" of the color. It is the name by which the color is designated. Saturation is a measure of the degree to which the pure color is diluted by white. A pure color is 100% saturated. As white is added, the degree of saturation decreases. Achromatic light is 0% saturated. Brightness is the intensity of the achromatic light.

The psychophysical equivalents of hue, saturation, and brightness are dominant wavelength, purity, and luminance. A perceived color generated by electromagnetic energy of a single wavelength in the visible spectrum is monochromatic. Figure 5-50a shows the energy distribution for such a monochromatic

[†]The operative words here are "perceived" and "arbitrary." As shown later discrete chromatic lights can be combined in specific ways to generate achromatic perceptions.

light with a wavelength of 525 nm. Figure 5-50b shows the energy distribution for a low level of "white" light with energy E_2 and a single dominant wavelength of 525 nm with energy E_1. In Fig. 5-50b, the color of the light is determined by the dominant wavelength, and the purity of the color by the relative magnitudes of E_1 and E_2. E_2 represents the amount by which the pure color of wavelength 525 nm is diluted by white light. As the magnitude of E_2 approaches zero, the purity of the color approaches 100%. As the magnitude of E_2 approaches that of E_1, the color of the light approaches white and the purity approaches zero. Luminance is proportional to the energy of the light and is usually considered as intensity per unit area.

Pure monochromatic light is seldom found in practice. Perceived colors are a mixture. The tristimulus theory of color mixing is based on the assumption that three types of color-sensing cones exist in the central portion of the eye. One type of cone senses wavelengths near the middle of the visible light range, which the eye-brain visual system converts into the sensation called green. The other two types sense long and short wavelengths near the upper and lower ends of the visible light range, which are interpreted as the sensations red and blue, respectively. Figure 5-49, which shows the relative sensitivity of the eye, indicates that the eye is most sensitive to green and least sensitive to blue. If all three sets of cones sense equal radiance levels (energy per unit time), the result is interpreted as white light. Natural white light, of course, contains radiance levels for all wavelengths in the visible spectrum. However, because physiologically the eye contains three different types of cones, the sensation of white light can be produced by a properly blended combination of any three colors, provided that a mixture of any two of the colors cannot produce the third. These three colors are called primary colors.

There are two primary color mixing systems of importance in computer graphics: the red, green, bluc (RGB) additive color system and the cyan, magenta, yellow (CMY) subtractive color system. The two systems are shown in Fig. 5-51 and in Color Plate 11. The colors in the two systems are complements of each other. Cyan is the complement of red, magneta the complement of green, and yellow the complement of blue. A complement is white minus the color. Thus, cyan is white minus red, magenta is white minus green, and

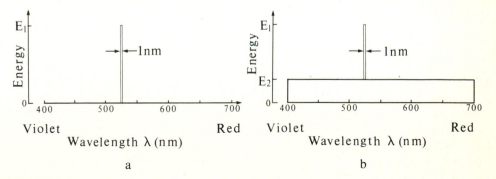

Figure 5-50 Wavelength characteristics of light.

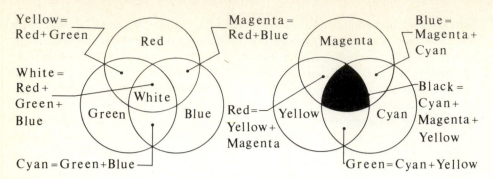

Figure 5-51 The additive (a) and subtractive (b) color mixing systems.

yellow is white minus blue. Although, technically, red can also be considered the complement of cyan, traditionally red, green, and blue are considered the primary colors, and cyan, magneta, and yellow their complements. It is interesting to note that magenta does not appear in the spectrum of colors created by a rainbow or prism. Hence, it is only a creation of the eye-brain visual system.

For reflective sources, e.g., printing inks and film and non-light-emitting displays, the CMY subtractive system is used. In the subtractive color system, the wavelengths representing the complement of the color are subtracted from the white light spectrum. For example, when light is reflected from or transmitted through a magenta colored object, the green portion of the spectrum is absorbed or subtracted. If the resulting light is then reflected from or transmitted through a yellow object, the blue portion of the spectrum is subtracted. The result is red. Finally, if the remaining light is reflected from or transmitted through a cyan object, the result is black because the entire visible spectrum has been eliminated (see Color Plate 11). Photographic filters work this way.

For light-emitting sources, e.g., a color CRT display or colored lights, the RGB additive color system is used. A simple experiment illustrates that three monochromatic colors is the minimum number required to match or produce almost all colors in the visible spectrum. The experiment involves a single, arbitrary, monochromatic test light incident on a background. An observer attempts to perceptually match (hue, saturation, and brightness) the test light by shining a monochromatic light or lights onto the background adjacent to the test light. The intensity of the matching light or lights is variable. If only a single matching light is used, then it must have the same wavelength as the test light in order to match the test light. Thus, only one color can be matched by a single monochromatic matching light. However, if the observer discounts the hue and saturation of the test light, then, for any intensity of the test light, its brightness can be matched. This procedure is called photometry. It leads to gray scale monochromatic reproduction of colored images.

If the observer now uses two superposed monochromatic light sources, more test lights can be matched. However, there are still a large number that cannot be matched. Adding a third matching light allows almost all test lights to be matched, provided that the three matching lights are widely spaced in the visible spectrum and provided no two of the matching lights can be combined to yield the third; i.e., the colors represented by the lights are primary colors. A good choice of lights is one from the high-wavelength end of the visible spectrum (red), one from the medium wavelengths (green), and one from the low wavelengths (blue). Adding these three lights together to match the perceived color of the monochromatic test light mathematically corresponds to

$$C = rR + gG + bB$$

where C is the color of the test light to be matched, R, G, and B correspond to the red, green, and blue matching lights, and r, g, and b correspond to the relative amounts of the R, G, and B lights used, with values in the range 0 to 1.

However, most of the test lights still cannot be matched by adding the three matching lights together. For example, if the test light is blue-green, the observer adds the blue and the green matching lights together, but the result is too light. Adding red in an attempt to darken the result only makes it lighter because the energies of the lights add. This effect gives the observer an idea: Add the red matching light to the test light to lighten it. It works! The test patches generated by the lights match. Mathematically, adding the red matching light to the test light corresponds to *subtracting* it from the other two matching lights. This is, of course, a physical impossibility, since a negative light intensity is impossible. Mathematically the result corresponds to

$$C + rR = gG + bB$$

or

$$C = -rR + gG + bB$$

Figure 5-52 shows the color-matching functions r, g, b for monochromatic lights at wavelengths of 436, 546, and 700 nm required to match all wavelengths in the visible spectrum. Notice that, except for wavelengths near 700 nm, one of these functions is always negative. This corresponds to "adding" the matching light to the test light. The study of these matching functions is part of colorimetry.

The observer also discovers that, when the intensity of a test light is doubled, then the intensities of each of the matching lights are also doubled, i.e.

$$2C = 2rR + 2gG + 2bB$$

Finally, the observer discovers that, when the same test light is matched in two different sessions, the values of r, g, and b are not necessarily the same. The matching colors for the two different sets of values of r, g, and b are called metamers of each other. Technically, this means that the test light can be matched by two different composite light sources, each of different spectral

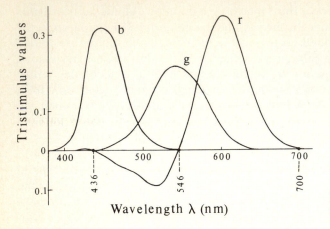

Figure 5-52 Color matching functions.

energy distribution. In fact, the test light source can be matched by composite light sources with an infinite number of different spectral energy distributions. Figure 5-53 shows two very diverse spectral reflectance distributions that both yield a medium gray.

The results of this experiment are embodied in Grassman's laws (see Ref. 5-44). Simply stated, Grassman's laws are:

> The eye distinguishes three different stimuli. This establishes the three-dimensional nature of color. The stimuli may, for example, be dominant wavelength (hue), purity (saturation), and luminance (brightness), or red, green, and blue.

> Four colors are always linearly related; i.e., $cC = rR + gG + bB$, where $c, r, g, b \neq 0$. Consequently, if two colors $(cC)_1$ and $(cC)_2$ are mixed, then $(cC)_1 + (cC)_2 = (rR)_1 + (rR)_2 + (gG)_1 + (gG)_2 + (bB)_1 + (bB)_2$. If color $C_1 =$ color C and color $C_2 =$ color C, then color $C_1 =$ color C_2 regardless of the spectral energy compositions of $C, C_1,$ and C_2.

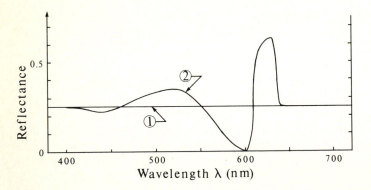

Figure 5-53 Metamers.

If in a three-color mixture, one color is continuously changed with the others kept constant, the color of the mixture will change continuously. This means that three-dimensional color space is continuous.

Based on experiments similar to those described above, it is known that the visual system is capable of distinguishing approximately 350,000 colors. When the colors differ only in hue, the visual system can distinguish between colors with dominant wavelengths differing by about 1 nm in the blue-yellow part of the spectrum. However, near the spectrum extremes approximately a 10 nm separation is required. About 128 distinct hues are distinguishable. If only differences in saturation are present, the visual system's ability to distinguish colors is more limited. Approximately 16 different saturations of yellow and about 23 different saturations of red-violet are distinguishable.

The three-dimensional nature of color suggests plotting the value of each tristimulus component along orthogonal axes as shown in Fig. 5-54a. The result is called tristimulus space. Any color C is represented by the vector from the origin with components rR, gG, and bB. Meyer (Ref. 5-48) gives a detailed discussion of three-dimensional color space. The intersection of the vector C with the unit plane gives the relative weights of the R, G, B colors required to generate C. The relative weights are called the chromaticity values or coordinates. They are given by

$$\bar{r} = \frac{r}{r + g + b} \qquad \bar{g} = \frac{g}{r + g + b} \qquad \bar{b} = \frac{b}{r + g + b}$$

Consequently, $\bar{r} + \bar{g} + \bar{b} = 1.0$. Projection of the unit plane as shown in Fig. 5-54b yields a chromaticity diagram. The chromaticity diagram directly provides a functional relationship between two colors and indirectly with the third, since, for example, $\bar{b} = 1 - \bar{r} - \bar{g}$. If the color matching functions shown in Fig. 5-52 are plotted in three space, the result does not entirely lie in the positive octant. Projection onto a two-dimensional plane would also yield negative values. These negative values are a mathematical nuisance.

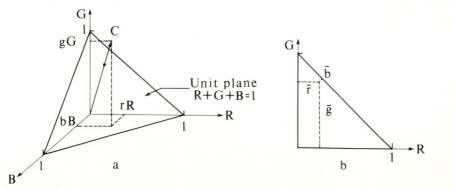

Figure 5-54 Three-dimensional color space.

The Commission Internationale de L'Eclairage (CIE), at a meeting on international color definition and measurement standards held in England in 1931, adopted a universal two-dimensional chromaticity diagram and a set of standard tristimulus observer functions that not only eliminate the negative values but also exhibit a number of other advantages. The result is known as the 1931 CIE chromaticity diagram. The CIE tristimulus values or primaries are derived from the standard observer functions shown in Fig. 5-55 and tabulated in Ref. 5-44. The three CIE hypothetical primaries are X, Y, and Z. The CIE XYZ primaries are hypothetical because eliminating the negative values makes it impossible for the primaries to correspond to physically real lights. The triangle formed by X, Y, and Z was selected to contain the entire spectrum of visible light. The CIE chromaticity values xyz are

$$x = \frac{X}{X + Y + Z} \qquad y = \frac{Y}{X + Y + Z} \qquad z = \frac{Z}{X + Y + Z} \qquad (5\text{-}18)$$

and $x + y + z = 1$. When the XYZ triangle is projected onto a two-dimensional plane to form the CIE chromaticity diagram, the chromaticity coordinates are selected as x and y. The chromaticity coordinates represent the relative amounts of the three primary XYZ colors required to obtain any color. However, they do not indicate the luminance (intensity) of the resulting color. Luminance is incorporated into the Y value. The X and Z values are then scaled to the Y value. With this convention, both the chromaticity and the luminance are given by (x, y, Y) coordinates. The inverse transformation from chromaticity values to XYZ tristimulus values is

$$X = x\frac{Y}{y} \qquad Y = Y \qquad Z = (1 - x - y)\frac{Y}{y} \qquad (5\text{-}19)$$

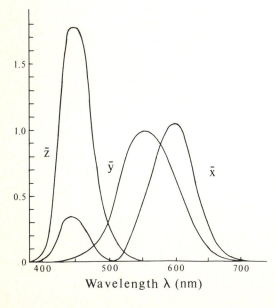

Wavelength λ (nm)

Figure 5-55 1931 CIE standard observer.

The final decision of the commission was to align the *XYZ* triangle so that equal values of the three hypotetical *XYZ* primaries produce white.

The 1931 CIE chromaticity diagram is shown in Fig. 5-56. The wing-shaped outline represents the locus of all visible wavelengths, i.e., the locus of the visible spectrum. The numbers along the line indicate the wavelength of visible light at that location. Red is at the lower right corner, green at the point, and blue in the lower left corner of the diagram. The straight line connecting the ends of the spectrum locus is called the purple line. The curved line labeled the blackbody locus represents the color of a theoretical blackbody as it is heated from approximately 1000° K to infinity. The dashed lines indicate the temperature along the blackbody locus and also the direction along which color changes are least discernible to the human eye. The equal energy alignment white is shown as point $E(x = 0.333, y = 0.333)$. The locations of CIE illuminants $A(0.448, 0.408)$, $B(0.349, 0.352)$, $C(0.310, 0.316)$, D_{6500} $(0.313, 0.329)$ are also shown. Illuminant A approximates the warm color of a gas-filled tungsten lamp at 2856° K. It is much "redder" than the others. Illuminant B approximates noon sunlight, and illuminant C the light from an overcast sky at midday. Illuminant C is used by the National Television Standards Committee (NTSC) as the alignment white. Illuminant D_{6500}, which corresponds to a blackbody radiating at 6504° K, is a somewhat "greener" white used as the alignment white for many television monitors.

As Fig. 5-57 illustrates, the chromaticity diagram is quite useful. The complement of a spectrum color is obtained by extending a line from the color through the alignment white to the opposite spectrum locus. For example, the complement of the reddish-orange color $C_4(\lambda = 610\,\text{nm})$ is the blue-green color $C_5(\lambda \doteq 491\,\text{nm})$. A color and its complement added together in the proper

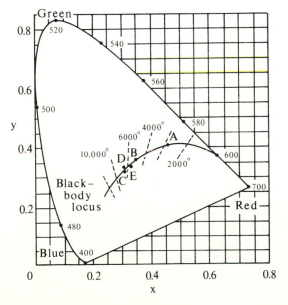

Figure 5-56 CIE diagram showing the blackbody locus, illuminants A B, C, D_{6500} (D), and equal-energy white (E).

proportions yield white. The dominant wavelength for a color is obtained by extending a line from the alignment white through the color to the spectrum locus. For example, in Fig. 5-57 the dominant wavelength for color C_6 is 570 nm, a yellow-green. If the extended line intersects the "purple line," then the color will have no dominant wavelength in the visible spectrum. In this case, the dominant wavelength is specified by the complementary spectrum value for the color with a c suffix. The value is obtained by extending a line "backward" through the alignment white to the spectrum boundary. For example, the dominant wavelength for color C_7 in Fig. 5-57 is 500c nm.

The pure or fully saturated colors lie on the spectrum locus and are 100% pure. The alignment white is "fully diluted" with a purity of 0%. The purity of intermediate colors is given by dividing the distance from the alignment white to the color by the distance from the alignment white to the spectrum locus or the purple line. For example, the purity of color C_6 in Fig. 5-57 is $a/(a + b)$ and that of C_7, $c/(c + d)$ expressed as a percentage.

The CIE chromaticity coordinates of a mixture of two colors is obtained, using Grassman's laws, by adding their primary values. For colors $C_1(x_1, y_1, Y_1)$ and $C_2(x_2, y_2, Y_2)$ the mixture of C_1 and C_2 is

$$C_{12} = (X_1 + X_2) + (Y_1 + Y_2) + (Z_1 + Z_2)$$

Recalling Eqs. (5-18) and (5-19) and defining

$$T_1 = \frac{Y_1}{y_1} \qquad T_2 = \frac{Y_2}{y_2}$$

the chromaticity coordinates of the mixture are

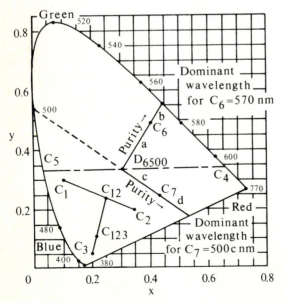

Figure 5-57 Uses of the chromaticity diagram.

$$x_{12} = \frac{x_1 T_1 + x_2 T_2}{T_1 + T_2} \qquad y_{12} = \frac{y_1 T_1 + y_2 T_2}{T_1 + T_2} \qquad Y_{12} = Y_1 + Y_2$$

These results are applicable to mixtures of more than two colors when applied successively to the mixture and each additional color. An example illustrates the technique.

Example 5-10   Color Mixing

Determine the CIE chromaticity coordinates of the mixture of the colors C_1 (0.1, 0.3, 10), C_2(0.35, 0.2, 10), and C_3(0.2, 0.05, 10) shown in Fig. 5-57. Applying the above results successively, the mixture of C_1 and C_2 is first determined. From the specifications

$$T_1 = \frac{Y_1}{y_1} = \frac{10}{0.3} = 33.33 \qquad T_2 = \frac{Y_2}{y_2} = \frac{10}{0.2} = 50$$

and

$$x_{12} = \frac{x_1 T_1 + x_2 T_2}{T_1 + T_2} = \frac{(0.1)(33.33) + (0.35)(50)}{33.33 + 50} = 0.25$$

$$y_{12} = \frac{y_1 T_1 + y_2 T_2}{T_1 + T_2} = \frac{(0.3)(33.33) + (0.2)(50)}{33.33 + 50} = 0.24$$

$$Y_{12} = Y_1 + Y_2 = 10 + 10 = 20$$

Thus, the mixture of C_1 and C_2 is C_{12}(0.25, 0.24, 20). Note that the coordinates for the mixture lie on the line between C_1 and C_2 in the chromaticity diagram. Continuing, the mixture of C_1, C_2, and C_3 is given by the mixture of C_{12} and C_3. Hence,

$$T_{12} = \frac{Y_{12}}{y_{12}} = \frac{20}{0.24} = 83.33 \qquad T_3 = \frac{Y_3}{y_3} = \frac{10}{0.05} = 200$$

$$x_{123} = \frac{x_{12} T_{12} + x_3 T_3}{T_{12} + T_3} = \frac{(0.25)(83.33) + (0.2)(200)}{83.33 + 200} = 0.215$$

$$y_{123} = \frac{y_{12} T_{12} + y_3 T_3}{T_{12} + T_3} = \frac{(0.24)(83.33) + (0.05)(200)}{83.33 + 200} = 0.106$$

$$Y_{123} = Y_{12} + Y_3 = 20 + 10 = 30$$

The mixture of C_1, C_2, and C_3 is C_{123}(0.215, 0.106, 30) and lies on the line between C_{12} and C_3 in the chromaticity diagram.

Figure 5-58 shows the correspondence between the CIE diagram and common perceptual color names (see Ref. 5-49). In the abbreviations used in Fig. 5-58 for the color names, a lowercase letter takes an -ish suffix; e.g., yG is yellow*ish*-green. For each color area, saturation or purity ranges from nearly zero, i.e. a very pastel color, near the illuminant area, to a fully saturated, i.e. a vivid, color near the spectrum boundary. Notice that most of the upper area of the diagram is occupied by greenish hues, with the reds and blues

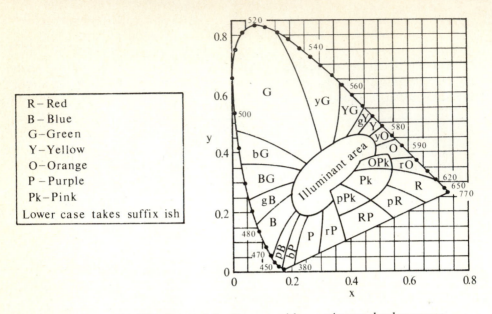

Figure 5-58 The 1931 CIE chromaticity diagram with superimposed color names.

crowded into the lower region near the purple line. Consequently, equal areas or distances on the diagram do not represent equal perceptual differences. A number of transformations of the diagram have been proposed to correct this deficiency. These uniform color spaces are discussed in Refs. 5-44 to 5-47.

Color television monitors, color film, printing inks, etc., cannot produce the full range or gamut of colors in the visible spectrum. For additive color systems, the reproducible gamut appears as a triangle on the CIE chromaticity diagram. The vertices of the triangle are the chromaticity coordinates of the RGB primaries. Any color within the triangle can be reproduced by the primaries. Figure 5-59 and Table 5-4 show the gamut of reproducible colors for the RGB primaries of a typical color CRT monitor and for the NTSC standard RGB primaries. For comparison, the subtractive CMY color system (converted to CIE coordinates) used in a color film reproduction process is also shown. Note that this gamut is not triangular. Note also that the gamut for this color film is larger than the one for the color monitor. Consequently some film colors cannot be reproduced by the monitor. The CIE *XYZ* primary spectrum colors are also shown. These values lie on the spectrum boundary and correspond to red at 700 nm, green at 543.1 nm, and blue at 435.8 nm. These primary spectrum colors are used to produce the matching functions in Fig. 5-52.

The CIE chromaticity coordinates or tristimulus values provide a precise standard specification of a color. However, each industry that uses color employs a unique set of primaries or conventions to specify color. Transferring color information from one industry to another is facilitated by using the CIE chromaticity coordinates. Thus, transformation from CIE values to another set of primary colors, and vice versa, is of interest. For computer graphics,

Table 5-4

CIE chromaticity coefficients for RGB primaries

		x	y
CIE *XYZ* primaries	Red	0.735	0.265
	Green	0.274	0.717
	Blue	0.167	0.009
NTSC standard	Red	0.670	0.330
	Green	0.210	0.710
	Blue	0.140	0.080
Color CRT monitor	Red	0.628	0.346
	Green	0.268	0.588
	Blue	0.150	0.070

the most common requirement is to transform between CIE *XYZ* values and the RGB primary system used for television monitors. Consequently, the discussion concentrates on these transformations. More general discussions are given in Refs. 5-44 to 5-46 and 5-48.

The transformation between two additive color systems is governed by Grassman's laws. The transformation from RGB color space to CIE *XYZ* color space is given by

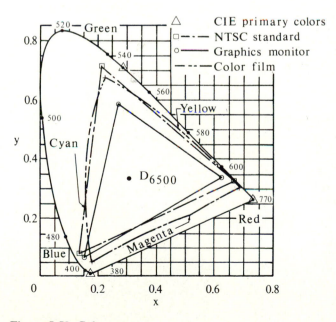

Figure 5-59 Color gamuts.

$$\begin{bmatrix} X \\ Y \\ Z \end{bmatrix} = \begin{bmatrix} X_r & X_g & X_b \\ Y_r & Y_g & Y_b \\ Z_r & Z_g & Z_b \end{bmatrix} \begin{bmatrix} R \\ G \\ B \end{bmatrix} \tag{5-20}$$

where X_r, Y_r, Z_r represent the tristimulus values required to produce a unit amount of the R primary, and similarly for X_g, Y_g, Z_g and X_b, Y_b, Z_b. For example, if $R = 1$, $G = 0$, $B = 0$, then from the equations $X = X_r$, $Y = Y_r$, $Z = Z_r$. If the CIE chromaticity values (x,y) of the RGB primaries are known,

$$x_r = \frac{X_r}{X_r + Y_r + Z_r} = \frac{X_r}{C_r}$$

$$y_r = \frac{Y_r}{X_r + Y_r + Z_r} = \frac{Y_r}{C_r} \tag{5-21}$$

$$z_r = 1 - x_r - y_r = \frac{Z_r}{X_r + Y_r + Z_r} = \frac{Z_r}{C_r}$$

and similarly for x_g, y_g, z_g and x_b, y_b, z_b. With $C_g = X_g + Y_g + Z_g$ and $C_b = X_b + Y_b + Z_b$, Eq. 5-20 then becomes

$$\begin{bmatrix} X \\ Y \\ Z \end{bmatrix} = \begin{bmatrix} x_r C_r & x_g C_g & x_b C_b \\ y_r C_r & y_g C_g & y_b C_b \\ (1 - x_r - y_r)C_r & (1 - x_g - y_g)C_g & (1 - x_b - y_b)C_b \end{bmatrix} \begin{bmatrix} R \\ G \\ B \end{bmatrix} \tag{5-22}$$

or in more compact notation

$$[\mathbf{X'}] = [\mathbf{C'}][\mathbf{R'}]$$

C_r, C_g, and C_b are required to completely specify the transformations between primary systems. If the luminance Y_r, Y_g, and Y_b of the unit amounts of the RGB primaries is known, then

$$C_r = \frac{Y_r}{y_r} \qquad C_g = \frac{Y_g}{y_g} \qquad C_b = \frac{Y_b}{y_b}$$

If the tristimulus values for the alignment white (X_w, Y_w, Z_w) are known, then solution of Eq. (5-22) with $[\mathbf{R'}] = [C_r \; C_g \; C_b]^T$ and $[\mathbf{X'}] = [X_w \; Y_w \; Z_w]^T$ yields the required values. If the chromaticity coordinates and the luminance (x_w, y_w, Y_w) are known instead of the tristimulus values, then (Ref. 5-48)

$$C_r = (Y_w/y_w)[x_w(y_g - y_b) - y_w(x_g - x_b) + x_g y_b - x_b y_g]/D$$

$$C_g = (Y_w/y_w)[x_w(y_b - y_r) - y_w(x_b - x_r) - x_r y_b + x_b y_r]/D \tag{5-23}$$

$$C_b = (Y_w/y_w)[x_w(y_r - y_g) - y_w(x_r - x_g) + x_r y_g - x_g y_r]/D$$

and

$$D = x_r(y_g - y_b) + x_g(y_b - y_r) + x_b(y_r - y_g) \tag{5-24}$$

The inverse transformation from CIE XYZ color space to RGB color space is then given by

$$[\mathbf{R'}] = [\mathbf{C'}]^{-1}[\mathbf{X'}] = [\mathbf{C''}][\mathbf{X'}] \tag{5-25}$$

where $[\mathbf{C}''] = [\mathbf{C}']^{-1}$ has components

$$C_{11}'' = [(y_g - y_b) - x_b y_g + y_b x_g] / C_r D$$

$$C_{12}'' = [(x_b - x_g) - x_b y_g + x_g y_b] / C_r D$$

$$C_{13}'' = [x_g y_b - x_b y_g] / C_r D$$

$$C_{21}'' = [(y_b - y_r) - y_b x_r + y_r x_b] / C_g D$$

$$C_{22}'' = [(x_r - x_b) - x_r y_b + x_b y_r] / C_g D$$

$$C_{23}'' = [x_b y_r - x_r y_b] / C_g D$$

$$C_{31}'' = [(y_r - y_g) - y_r x_g + y_g x_r] / C_b D$$

$$C_{32}'' = [(x_g - x_r) - x_g y_r + x_r y_g] / C_b D$$

$$C_{33}'' = [x_r y_g - x_g y_r] / C_b D$$

An example further illustrates the technique.

Example 5-11   CIE to RGB Color Primary Transformations

It is desired to transform a color with CIE chromaticity coordinates $x = 0.25$, $y = 0.2$, and luminance $Y = 10.0$ for display on a color monitor with RGB primary chromaticities given in Table 5-4. The monitor is aligned to D_{6500} white. Consequently, the monitor primary components are

$$x_r = 0.628 \qquad x_g = 0.268 \qquad x_b = 0.150$$
$$y_r = 0.346 \qquad y_g = 0.588 \qquad y_b = 0.070$$

The alignment white components are

$$x_w = 0.313 \qquad y_w = 0.329 \qquad Y_w = 1.0$$

First, calculating D yields

$$D = x_r(y_g - y_b) + x_g(y_b - y_r) + x_b(y_r - y_g)$$
$$= 0.628(0.588 - 0.07) + 0.268(0.07 - 0.346) + 0.15(0.346 - 0.588)$$
$$= 0.215$$

Now

$$DC_r / (Y_w / y_w) = x_w(y_g - y_b) - y_w(x_g - x_b) + x_g y_b - x_b y_g$$
$$= 0.313(0.588 - 0.07) - 0.329(0.268 - 0.15) + 0.268(0.07)$$
$$- 0.15(0.588)$$
$$= 0.0539$$

and

$$C_r = \frac{0.0539}{D} \left(\frac{Y_w}{y_w} \right) = \frac{0.0539}{0.215} \left(\frac{1}{0.329} \right) = 0.762$$

Similarly

$$C_g = 1.114 \qquad C_b = 1.164$$

Calculating the XYZ tristimulus values from the chromaticity coordinates yields

$$X = x\frac{Y}{y} = 0.25\frac{10}{0.2} = 12.5$$

$$Z = (1 - x - y)\frac{Y}{y} = (1 - 0.25 - 0.2)\frac{10}{0.2} = 27.5$$

The transformation is then given by Eq. (5-22)

$$[\mathbf{R}'] = [\mathbf{C}''][\mathbf{X}']$$

$$\begin{bmatrix} R \\ G \\ B \end{bmatrix} = \begin{bmatrix} 2.739 & -1.145 & -0.424 \\ -1.119 & 2.029 & 0.033 \\ 0.138 & -0.333 & 1.105 \end{bmatrix} \begin{bmatrix} 12.5 \\ 10.0 \\ 27.5 \end{bmatrix} = \begin{bmatrix} 11.133 \\ 7.209 \\ 28.772 \end{bmatrix}$$

The transformation of RGB coordinates to CIE chromaticity coordinates is accomplished in a similar manner.

Example 5-12   RBG to CIE Color Primary Transformations

Transform the color with RGB components $(255, 0, 0)$, i.e., the maximum red intensity on the monitor, to CIE chromaticity coordinates. The monitor primaries and alignment white are the same as in Example 5-11. Consequently, D, C_r, C_g, C_b are also the same. Using Eq. (5-21) yields

$$\begin{bmatrix} X \\ Y \\ Z \end{bmatrix} = \begin{bmatrix} 0.478 & 0.299 & 0.175 \\ 0.263 & 0.655 & 0.081 \\ 0.020 & 0.160 & 0.908 \end{bmatrix} \begin{bmatrix} 255 \\ 0 \\ 0 \end{bmatrix} = \begin{bmatrix} 121.94 \\ 67.19 \\ 5.05 \end{bmatrix}$$

The chromaticity values are

$$x = \frac{X}{X + Y + Z} = \frac{121.94}{121.94 + 67.19 + 5.05} = \frac{121.94}{194.18} = 0.628$$

$$y = \frac{Y}{X + Y + Z} = \frac{67.19}{194.18} = 0.346$$

$$Y = 67.19$$

which, of course, are the chromaticity coordinates for the red monitor primary (see Table 5-4).

The RGB color primary system used for standard color television broadcasting is dictated by the requirement to confine the broadcast signal to a 0–6 MHz bandwidth and by the requirement for compatibility with the standard for black-and-white television. In 1953 the NTSC adopted a standard called the YIQ color primary system. The YIQ color primary system is based on concepts from the CIE XYZ system. Because of bandwidth restrictions, one value, Y, was chosen to contain the luminance or brightness information. The signal for Y occupies the major portion of the available broadcast bandwidth (0–4 MHz). The proportions of the NTSC red, green, and blue primaries in the Y signal were chosen to yield the standard luminosity curve. Since Y contains the brightness information, only its value or signal is used by a black-and-white monitor. The NTSC alignment white was originally CIE illuminant C, but CIE illuminant D_{6500} is generally used at the present time (Ref. 5-50). The differences are small.

Certain characteristics of the visual system are used to reduce the bandwidth required for the color, i.e. hue and saturation, information transmitted. Specifically, the ability of the eye to sense color decreases with decreasing apparent object size. Below a certain apparent object size, objects are perceived by a two-color vision process. Objects below a certain minimum size produce no perceived color sensation.

The YIQ system uses linear combinations of the differences between the red, green, and blue values and the Y value to contain the hue and saturation "color" information. The I color value (or in phase signal) contains orange-cyan color hue information, while Q (the quadrature signal) contains green-magenta hue information. The I value contains hue information that provides the all-important flesh tones while the Q value contains the remainder. Consequently, a bandwidth of about 1.5 MHz is used for I, but only about 0.6 MHz is used for Q. The transformation from RGB to YIQ values is given by

$$\begin{bmatrix} Y \\ I \\ Q \end{bmatrix} = \begin{bmatrix} 0.299 & 0.587 & 0.114 \\ 0.596 & -0.274 & -0.322 \\ 0.211 & -0.522 & 0.311 \end{bmatrix} \begin{bmatrix} R \\ G \\ B \end{bmatrix}$$

and from YIQ to RGB as

$$\begin{bmatrix} R \\ G \\ B \end{bmatrix} = \begin{bmatrix} 1 & 0.956 & 0.623 \\ 1 & -0.272 & -0.648 \\ 1 & -1.105 & 0.705 \end{bmatrix} \begin{bmatrix} Y \\ I \\ Q \end{bmatrix}$$

Transformation from CIE XYZ tristimulus values to YIQ, or vice versa, is accomplished by combining these equations with Eqs. (5-22) and (5-25).

As with the CIE XYZ tristimulus values, the RGB and CMY color spaces are three-dimensional. Both the RGB and CMY spaces are conveniently represented by three-dimensional color cubes or solids as shown in Fig. 5-60.

The RGB color cube uses black as the origin, while the CMY color cube uses white. For both models the achromatic colors, i.e. the grays, lie along the diagonal from black to white. Also, the complementary colors lie on opposite corners. The transformation between RGB and CMY color spaces is

$$[R \ G \ B] = [1 \ 1 \ 1] - [C \ M \ Y]$$

Unfortunately, it is difficult for users to specify subjective color concepts in the systems discussed above. For example, what is the CIE, RGB, or CMY specification for a pastel reddish-orange (see Fig. 5-58)? Artists specify colors

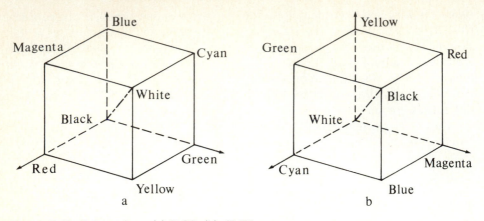

Figure 5-60 Color cubes. (a) RGB (b) CMY.

in terms of tints, shades, and tones. Given a pure pigment, an artist adds white to obtain a tint, black to obtain a shade, and both to obtain a tone of the color. These ideas can be combined into a useful triangular representation, as shown in Fig. 5-61. The triangular representation shown in Fig. 5-61 is for a single color. By arranging triangles for each pure color around a central black-white axis, a useful subjective three-dimensional representation of color is obtained. This basic idea is central to the Ostwald (Ref. 5-51) color system.

A useful implementation of a basic subjective color model is the HSV (hue, saturation, value) color solid proposed by Smith (Ref. 5-52). If the RGB color cube shown in Fig. 5-60a is projected onto a plane along the diagonal looking from white to black, a hexagon is formed, with the pure RGB primaries and their complements at each vertex. Decreasing the saturation or purity of the primary colors decreases the size of the RGB color cube and the gamut of possible colors. Projection then yields a smaller hexagon. If the projections of the RGB color cube and its subcubes are stacked along the main diagonal representing the value or lightness of the color from black = 0 to white = 1, a three-dimensional hexcone is formed. This is the HSV model shown in

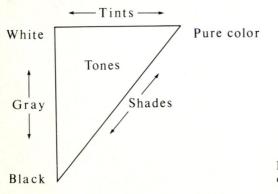

Figure 5-61 Tints, shades, and tones of a pure color.

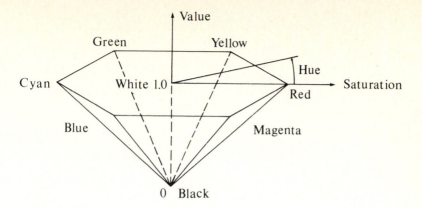

Figure 5-62 HSV hexcone color solid.

Fig. 5-62. Value increases along the axis of the hexcone from 0 at the apex to 1 at the top surface, where the maximum value colors occur. Saturation is given by the distance from the axis, and hue by the angular distance (0 – 360°) measured from red. Here, the projection of the RGB color cube has been rotated counterclockwise 120° to place red at 0°. The value of saturation ranges from 0 at the axis to 1 along the outer rim. Notice that saturation is specified relative to the possible gamut of colors, i.e. relative to the distance from the axis to the outer rim for any value of V. The fully saturated primary colors or their complements occur for $S = 1$. A mixture of three nonzero primaries cannot be fully saturated. If $S = 0$, the hue H is undefined and the color is achromatic, i.e., some shade of gray. The shades of gray occur along the central axis.

The HSV model corresponds to the way artists form colors. The pure pigments are given for $V = 1$, $S = 1$. Tints are formed by adding white, i.e. decreasing S. Shades are formed by decreasing V, i.e. adding black, and tones by decreasing both V and S.

Conversion from HSV to RGB color space using geometrical relations between the hexcone and the color cube is straightforward. The following pseudocode algorithm adapted from Smith (Ref. 5-52) accomplishes this.

HSV to RGB conversion algorithm

H *is the hue (0–360°) red at 0°*
S *is the saturation (0–1)*
V *is the value (0–1)*
RGB *are the red, green, blue primary colors (0–1)*
Floor *is the floor function*

    check for the achromatic case
   if S = 0 **then**
      if H = Undefined **then**

```
                    R = V
                    G = V
                    B = V
            else
                    if H has a value an error has been made
            end if
    else
            chromatic case
            if H = 360 then
                    H = 0
            else
                    H = H/60
                    I = Floor(H)
                    F = H − I
                    M = V*(1 − S)
                    N = V*(1 − S * F)
                    K = V*(1−S*(1−F))
                    (R, G, B) = (V, K, M) means R = V, G = K, B = M etc.
                    if I = 0 then (R, G, B) = (V, K, M)
                    if I = 1 then (R, G, B) = (N, V, M)
                    if I = 2 then (R, G, B) = (M, V, K)
                    if I = 3 then (R, G, B) = (M, N, V)
                    if I = 4 then (R, G, B) = (K, M, V)
                    if I = 5 then (R, G, B) = (V, M, N)
            end if
    end if
    finish
```

Conversion from RGB to HSV color space is given by the following pseudocode algorithm, also adapted from Smith.

RGB to HSV conversion algorithm

RGB *are the red, green, blue primary colors (0–1)*
H *is the hue (0–360°) red at 0°*
S *is the saturation (0–1)*
V *is the value (0–1)*
Max *is the maximum function*
Min *is the minimum function*

```
    determine the value
    V = Max(R, G, B)
    determine saturation
    Temp = Min(R, G, B)
    if V = 0 then
            S = 0
```

else

   $S = (V - \text{Temp})/V$

end if

determine the hue

if $S = 0$ **then**

   $H = \text{Undefined}$

else

   $Cr = (V - R)/(V - \text{Temp})$
   $Cg = (V - G)/(V - \text{Temp})$
   $Cb = (V - B)/(V - \text{Temp})$

   the color is between yellow and magenta
   if $R = V$ **then** $H = Cb - Cg$
   the color is between cyan and yellow
   if $G = V$ **then** $H = 2 + Cr - Cb$
   the color is between magenta and cyan
   if $B = V$ **then** $H = 4 + Cg - Cr$
   convert to degrees
   $H = 60*H$
   prevent negative value
   if $H < 0$ **then** $H = H + 360$

end if

finish

Joblove and Greeenberg (Ref. 5-53) discuss an alternate formulation of an HSV color space based on a cylindrical rather than a hexcone representation.

An extension of the hexcone model is the HLS (hue, lightness, saturation) double-hexcone model. Since the HLS model applys to self-luminous sources, lightness as used here corresponds to brightness as defined at the beginning of this section. In the HLS model the RGB color cube is projected to yield a double hexcone as shown in Fig. 5-63, with lightness (value) along the axis from black = 0 at one apex to white = 1 at the other. Again, as in the HSV model, saturation is given by the radial distance from the central axis. Here the fully saturated primary colors and their complements occur at $S = 1$. Again, H is undefined when $S = 0$.

Conversion from HLS to RGB is given below by a pseudocode algorithm adapted from Refs. 5-54 and 5-55.

HLS to RGB conversion algorithm

H *is the hue (0–360°) red at 0°*
L *is the lightness (0–1)*
S *is the saturation (0–1)*
RGB *are the red, green, blue primary colors (0–1)*
Max *is the maximum function*
Min *is the minimum function*

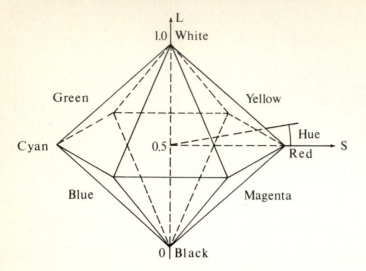

Figure 5-63 HLS double-hexcone color model.

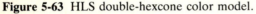

if L ≤ 0.5 **then**
    M1 = L*(1−S)
else
      M1 = L + S − L*S
end if
M2 = 2*L − M1
check for zero saturation
if S = 0 **then**
    if H = Undefined
        R = 1
        G = 1
        B = 1
    else
        Error because incorrect data has been provided
    end if
else
    determine RGB *values*
    call RGB(H, M1, M2; Value)
    R = Value + 120
    call RGB(H, M1, M2; Value)
    G = Value
    call RGB(H, M1, M2; Value)
    B = Value − 120
end if
finish

subroutine to determine the RGB values

subroutine RGB(H, M1, M2; Value)

H *is the hue (0–360°) red at 0°*

    adjust the hue to the correct range
    if H < 0 **then** H = H + 360
    if H > 360 **then** H = H − 360
    determine the value
    if H < 60 **then** Value = M1 + (M2 − M1)*H/60
    if H ≥ 60 **and** H < 180 **then** Value = M2
    if H ≥ 180 **and** H < 240 **then** Value = M1 + (M2 − M1)*(240 − H)/60
    if H ≥ 240 **and** H ≤ 360 **then** Value = M1
    return

Conversion from RGB to HLS is given by the following pseudocode algorithm.

RGB to HLS conversion alogorithm

RGB *are the red, green, blue primary color(0–1)*
H *is the hue (0–360°) red at 0°*
L *is the lightness (0–1)*
S *is the saturation (0–1)*
Max *is the maximum function*
Min *is the minimum function*

    determine the lightness
    M1 = **Max**(R, G, B)
    M2 = **Min**(R, G, B)
    L = (M1 + M2)/2
    determine the saturation
    achromatic case
    if M1 = M2 **then**
        S = 0
        H = Undefined
    else
        chromatic case
        if L ≤ 0.5 **then**
            S = (M1 − M2)/(M1 + M2)
        else
            S = (M1 − M2)/(2 − M1 + M2)
        end if
        determine the hue
        Cr = (M1 − R)/(M1 − M2)
        Cg = (M1 − G)/(M1 − M2)
        Cb = (M1 − B)/(M1 − M2)
        if R = M1 **then** H = Cb − Cg

```
        if G = M1 then H = 2+Cr-Cb
        if B = M1 then H = 4+Cg-Cr
        H = 60*H
        if H < 0 then H = H + 360
    end if
    finish
```

A cylindrical representation is also used in the Munsell color-order system (Ref. 5-56). The Munsell system is based on a collection of color samples. Hence, it is a reflective standard. In the Munsell system, a color is designated by its Munsell hue, Munsell chroma (purity or saturation), and Munsell value (lightness). The central axis of the cylinder represents values between black at the bottom and white at the top. Increasing radial distance from the central axis represents increasing chroma or purity for the color. The color hues are represented by angular positions around the central axis as shown in Fig. 5-64. One major advantage of the Munsell system that has resulted in wide industrial acceptance is that equal increments in chroma, hue, and value result in equal perceptual changes. Because of this characteristic, the entire volume of the cylinder is not filled. Transformation of the subjective Munsell color representation into CIE tristimulus values is available (see, for example, Ref. 5-57). Meyer and Greenberg (Ref. 5-58) have successfully displayed Munsell colors on a color monitor. They used CIE *XYZ* tristimulus values as an intermediate standard color space. First, Munsell color values were transformed to CIE *XYZ* tristimulus values, and then these values were transformed to the RGB values required for the color monitor. Using this technique, Meyer and Greenberg were able to display some Munsell colors previously known only by extrapolation from existing samples.

The work by Meyer and Greenberg illustrates the practical value of the standard CIE *XYZ* color space. The use of CIE *XYZ* tristimulus values to specify colors is particularly important when computer graphics is used to either simulate existing commercially available colorants, e.g. paints or dyestuffs, or to design colors for reproduction using commercially available colorants. As an example consider selection or simulation of the paint color for the Chevrolet

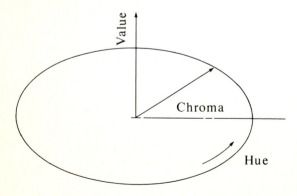

Figure 5-64 Conceptual representation of the Munsell color-ordering system.

Camaro shown in Color Plate 1. If the paint color is selected from that shown on the monitor, then it is necessary to provide color specifications to the paint manufacturer. Transforming from the display RGB value to CIE *XYZ* values and supplying these to the manufacturer accomplishes this. The paint manufacturer converts these values to those used to design the paint, e.g. Munsell hue, chroma, and value. Alternately, if the appearance of the Camaro with an existing commercially available paint is to be evaluated, then the paint specifications are converted to CIE *XYZ* tristimulus values and then to RGB values for display on the monitor. Other applications are apparent.

If a linear relation between the values obtained from the above color models and the voltage applied to the electron guns of a television monitor is assumed, the resulting display will not look right because a color monitor requires calibration.

The intensity displayed on the monitor is proportional to the voltage supplied to the electron gun. Specifically,

$$I = \text{constant}(V)^{\gamma}$$

Then for any desired intensity value I_k, the voltage supplied to the monitor must be

$$V_k = \left(\frac{I_k}{\text{constant}} \right)^{1/\gamma}$$

Catmull (Ref. 5-59) discusses a detailed procedure for determining both the constant and γ. Experience shows that $1 \le \gamma \le 4$ with typical values of 2.3 –2.8 for a color monitor. The results of the calibration are used as values in a look-up table.

The above procedure, called gamma correction, calibrates only the intensity of the display. Calibrating the color of the display involves determining the CIE chromaticities of the red, green, and blue phosphors used in the display as well. Cowan (Ref. 5-60) discusses a detailed calibration procedure for color monitors for both gamma correction and determination of the phospher chromaticities.

Applying either Gouraud or Phong shading (see Secs. 5-5 and 5-6) for color images can yield startling results. The results depend on the color model used to specify the interpolated shading and the model used to display the results. If the transformation between the two color models is affine, i.e., a straight line transforms into a straight line, then the results will be as expected. If not, then visual discontinuities may appear. As shown above, transformations among CIE, RGB, CMY, and YIQ color models are affine. However, transformations between these models and either the HSV or HSL color model are not affine. A similar effect occurs when blending colored transparent effects, e.g., in a hidden surface algorithm.

Finally, there is the question of color harmony, i.e., how colors are selected for pleasing effects. The literature is vast on this topic alone. A good starting place is Marcus (Ref. 5-61) or Judd and Wyszecki (Ref. 5-45). One of the basic principles is to select colors using an orderly plan. An acceptable plan might select the colors from an orderly path in a color model or confine the colors to a single plane in the color model. It is generally considered best to select colors that differ by equal perceptual distances. Examples of harmonious colors are frequently taken from nature, e.g., a sequence of greens. Another technique is to select colors of constant saturation or hue, i.e., colors that are more or less alike.

5-16   REFERENCES

5-1 Cornsweet, T.N., *Visual Perception*, Academic Press, New York, 1970.

5-2 Bui-Tuong, Phong, "Illumination for Computer Generated Images," doctoral thesis, University of Utah, 1973. Also as Comp. Sci. Dept. Rep. UTEC-CSc-73-129, NTIS ADA 008 786. A condensed version is given in *CACM*, Vol. 18, pp. 311–317, 1975.

5-3 Gouraud, H., "Computer Display of Curved Surfaces," doctoral thesis, University of Utah, 1971. Also as Comp. Sci. Dept. Rep. UTEC-CSc-71-113 and NTIS AD 762 018. A condensed version is given in *IEEE Trans. C-20*, pp. 623–628, 1971.

5-4 Duff, T., "Smooth Shaded Renderings of Polyhedral Objects on Raster Displays," *Computer Graphics*, Vol. 13, pp. 270–275, 1979 (*Proc. SIGGRAPH* 79).

5-5 Warn, David R., "Lighting Controls for Synthetic Images," *Computer Graphics*, Vol. 17, pp. 13–21, 1983 (*Proc. SIGGRAPH* 83).

5-6 Torrance, K.E., and Sparrow, E.M., "Theory for Off-Specular Reflection from Roughened Surfaces," *Journal of the Optical Society of America,* Vol. 57, pp. 1105–1114, 1967.

5-7 Blinn, James F., "Models of Light Reflection for Computer Synthesized Pictures," *Computer Graphics*, Vol. 11, pp. 192–198, 1977 (*Proc. SIGGRAPH* 77).

5-8 Cook, Robert L., "A Reflection Model for Realistic Image Synthesis," master's thesis, Cornell University, 1982.

5-9 Cook, Robert L., and Torrance, K.E., "A Reflectance Model for Computer Graphics," *ACM Trans. on Graphics*, Vol. 1, pp. 7–24, 1982.

5-10 Beckmann, P., and Spizzichino, A., *Scattering of Electromagnetic Waves from Rough Surfaces*, MacMillan, New York, 1963, pp. 1–33, 70–98.

5-11 Purdue University, *Thermophysical Properties of Matter*, Vol. 7: *Thermal Radiative Properties of Metals*, Vol. 8: *Thermal Radiative Properties of Nonmetallic Solids*, Vol. 9: *Thermal Radiative Properties of Coatings*, Plenum, New York, 1970.

5-12 Newell, M.E., Newell, R.G., and Sancha, T.L., "A Solution to the Hidden Surface Problem," Proc. ACM Annual Conf., Boston, August 1972, pp. 443–450.

5-13 Kay, Douglas Scott, "Transparency, Refraction and Ray Tracing for Computer Synthesized Images," master's thesis, Cornell University, 1979.

5-14 Kay, Douglas Scott, and Greenberg, Donald, "Transparency for Computer Synthe- sized Images," *Computer Graphics*, Vol. 13, pp. 158–164, 1979 (*Proc. SIGGRAPH* 79).

5-15 Myers, Allen J., "An Efficient Visible Surface Program," Rep. to NSF, Div. of Math. and Comp. Sci., Computer Graphics Res. Group, Ohio State University, July 1975.

5-16 Appel, Arthur, "Some Techniques for Shading Machine Rendering of Solids," *SJCC 1968,* Thompson Books, Washington, D.C., pp. 37–45.

5-17 Bouknight, Jack, "A Procedure for Generation of Three-dimensional Half-toned Computer Graphics Presentations," *CACM*, Vol. 13, pp. 527–536, 1970.

5-18 Kelley, Karl C., "A Computer Graphics Program for the Generation of Half-tone Images with Shadows," master's thesis, University of Illinois, 1970.

5-19 Bouknight, Jack, and Kelley, Karl C., "An Algorithm for Producing Half-tone Computer Graphics Presentations with Shadows and Movable Light Sources," *SJCC 1970,* AFIPS Press, Montvale, N.J. pp. 1–10.

5-20 Williams, Lance, "Casting Curved Shadows on Curved Surfaces," *Computer Graphics*, Vol. 12, pp. 270–274, 1978 (*Proc. SIGGRAPH* 78).

5-21 Atherton, Peter R., "Polygon Shadow Generation with Application to Solar Rights," master's thesis, Cornell University, 1978.

5-22 Atherton, Peter, R., Weiler, Kevin, and Greenberg, Donald, "Polygon Shadow Generation," *Computer Graphics*, Vol. 12, pp. 275–281, 1978 (*Proc. SIGGRAPH* 78).

5-23 Catmull, Edwin, "A Subdivision Algorithm for Computer Display of Curved Surfaces," doctoral thesis, University of Utah, 1974. Also as UTEC-CSc-74-133, NTIS A004968.

5-24 Blinn, James F., and Newell, Martin, E., "Texture and Reflection in Computer Generated Images," *CACM*, Vol. 19, pp. 542–547, 1976.

5-25 Blinn, James F., "Simulation of Wrinkled Surfaces," *Computer Graphics*, Vol. 12, pp. 286–292, 1978 (*Proc. SIGGRAPH* 78).

5-26 Carpenter, Loren C., "Computer Rendering of Fractal Curves and Surfaces," pp. 1–8, suppl. to *Proc. SIGGRAPH* 80, August 1980.

5-27 Fournier, Alain, and Fussell, Don, "Stochastic Modeling in Computer Graphics," pp. 9–15, suppl. to *Proc. SIGGRAPH* 80, August 1980.

5-28 Mandelbrot, B., *Fractals: Form, Chance, and Dimension*, W. H. Freeman, San Francisco, 1977.

5-29 Kajiya, James T., "New Technique for Ray Tracing Procedurally Defined Objects," *Computer Graphics*, Vol. 17, pp. 91–102, 1983 (*Proc. SIGGRAPH* 83). Also in *ACM Trans. on Graphics*, Vol. 2, pp. 161–181, 1983.

5-30 Whitted, Turner, "An Improved Illumination Model for Shaded Display," *CACM*, Vol. 23, pp. 343–349, 1980.

5-31 Potmesil, M., and Chakravarty, I., "A Lens and Aperture Camera Model for Synthetic Image Generation," *Computer Graphics*, Vol. 15, pp. 297–305, 1981 (*Proc. SIGGRAPH* 81).

5-32 Potmesil, M., and Chakravarty, I., "Synthetic Image Generation with a Lens and Aperture Camera Model," *ACM Trans. on Graphics*, Vol. 1, pp. 85–108, 1982.

5-33 Barr, Alan H., private communication.

5-34 Hall, Roy A., "A Methodology for Realistic Image Synthesis," master's thesis, Cornell University, 1983.

5-35 Hall, Roy A., and Greenberg, Donald, "A Testbed for Realistic Image Synthesis," *IEEE Computer Graphics and Applications*, Vol. 3, pp. 10–20, 1983.

5-36 Moravec, Hans P., "3D Graphics and the Wave Theory," *Computer Graphics*, Vol. 15, pp. 289–296, 1981 (*Proc. SIGGRAPH* 81).

5-37 Korein, J., and Badler, V.R., "Temporal Anti-Aliasing in Computer Generated Animation," *Computer Graphics*, Vol. 17, pp. 377–388, 1983 (*Proc. SIGGRAPH* 83).

5-38 Potmesil, M., and Chakravarty, I., "Modeling Motion Blur in Computer-Generated Images," *Computer Graphics*, Vol. 17, pp. 389–399, 1983 (*Proc. SIGGRAPH* 83).

5-39 Reeves, William T., "Particle Systems—A Technique for Modeling a Class of

Fuzzy Objects," *Computer Graphics*, Vol. 17, pp. 359–376, 1983 (*Proc. SIGGRAPH* 83), and *ACM Trans. on Graphics*, Vol. 2, pp. 91–108, 1983.

5-40 Blinn, James F., "Light Reflection Functions for Simulation of Clouds and Dusty Surfaces," *Computer Graphics*, Vol. 16, pp. 21–29, 1982 (*Proc. SIGGRAPH* 82).

5-41 Dungan, W. "A Terrain and Cloud Computer Image Generation Model," *Computer Graphics*, Vol. 13, pp. 143–150, 1979 (*Proc. SIGGRAPH* 79).

5-42 Marshall, R., Wilson, R., and Carlson, Wayne, "Procedural Models for Generating Three-dimensional Terrain," *Computer Graphics*, Vol. 14, pp. 154–162, 1980 (*Proc. SIGGRAPH* 80).

5-43 Csuri, C.A., "Panel: The Simulation of Natural Phenomena," *Computer Graphics*, Vol. 17, pp. 137–139, 1983 (*Proc. SIGGRAPH* 83).

5-44 Wyszecki, G., and Stiles, W.S., *Color Science*, Wiley, New York, 1967.

5-45 Judd, D.B., and Wyszecki, G., *Color in Business, Science and Industry*, Wiley, New York, 1975.

5-46 Hunt, R.W.G., *The Reproduction of Color*, 3d ed., Wiley, New York, 1975.

5-47 Hunter, Richard S., *The Measurement of Appearance*, Wiley, New York, 1975.

5-48 Meyer, Gary W., "Colorimetry and Computer Graphics," Program of Computer Graphics, Report Number 83-1, Cornell University, April 1983.

5-49 Judd, Deane B., "Colorimetry," National Bureau of Standards Circular 478, 1950. Updated in Nimerof, I., "Colorimetry," NBS monograph 104, 1968.

5-50 Pritchard, D.H. "US Color Television Fundamentals—A Review," *IEEE Trans. on Consumer Electronics*, Vol. CE-23, pp. 467–478, 1977.

5-51 Ostwald, N., *Colour Science*, Vols. I and 11, Wimsor & Winsor, London, 1931.

5-52 Smith, Alvey Ray, "Color Gamut Transformation Pairs," *Computer Graphics*, Vol. 12, pp. 12–19, 1978 (*Proc. SIGGRAPH* 78).

5-53 Joblove, George H., and Greenberg, Donald, "Color Spaces for Computer Graphics," *Computer Graphics*, Vol. 12, pp. 20–25, 1978 (*Proc. SIGGRAPH* 78).

5-54 "Status Report of the Graphics Standards Committee," *Computer Graphics*, Vol. 13, August 1979.

5-55 *Raster Graphics Handbook*, Conrac Division, Conrac Corporation, 600 N. Rimsdale Ave., Covina, California 91722.

5-56 Munsell, A.H., *A Color Notation*, 9th ed., Munsell Color Company, Baltimore, 1941. The latest *Book of Color* is available from Munsell Color Company, 2441 North Calvert Street, Baltimore, Maryland 21218.

5-57 Keegan, H.J., Rheinboldt, W.C., Schleter, J.C., Menard, J.P., and Judd, D.B., "Digital Reduction of Spectrophotometric Data to Munsell Renotations," *Journal of the Optical Society of America*, Vol. 48, p. 863, 1958.

5-58 Meyer, Gary W., and Greenberg, Donald, "Perceptual Color Spaces for Computer Graphics," *Computer Graphics*, Vol. 14, pp. 254–261, 1980 (*Proc. SIGGRAPH* 80).

5-59 Catmull, Edwin, "Tutorial on Compensation Tables," *Computer Graphics*, Vol. 13, pp. 1–7, 1979 (*Proc. SIGGRAPH* 79).

5-60 Cowan, William B., "An Inexpensive Scheme for Calibration of a Colour Monitor in Terms of CIE Standard Coordinates", *Computer Graphics*, Vol. 17, pp. 315–321, 1983 (*Proc. SIGGRAPH* 83).

5-61 Marcus, Aaron, "Color—A Tool for Computer Graphics Communication," *Close-up*, Vol. 13, pp. 1–9, August 1982.

PSEUDOCODE

The pseudocode described is intended as an aid in understanding and implementing the algorithms presented in the text. It is not intended as a precise syntactically correct complete language. The elements of the pseudocode are drawn from several common computer programming languages: BASIC, FORTRAN, PASCAL, etc. The pseudocode contains structured constructs, specifically **if-then-else** and **while**. The common unconditional **go to** statement is included for convenience. The **for-next** loop statement is taken from BASIC. Subroutine modules are included. Functions, and special routines, e.g. **Min**, **Max**, **Push**, **Pop** are individually defined within the algorithms. **Draw** and **Plot** are self-explanatory.

The general conventions used in presenting the algorithms are briefly given here. All key words are set in bold face, lower case characters. All statements within the body of an **if-then-else**, **while**, or **for-next** loop are indented. All comments are set in italics and indented along with the statements to which they refer. Variable names longer than one character have the first character capitalized. Subsequent characters are lower case. Single character variables may be either lower case or upper case. Functions are set bold face with the first character capitalized. Detailed descriptions of these conventions follow.

A-1 COMMENTS

Comment statements are set in italic. They are indented along with the statements to which they refer. Sufficient comments are given at the beginning of an algorithm to briefly describe its purpose and to define the variables used.

A-2 CONSTANTS

All constants are decimal numbers unless specified otherwise in comments. For example, $9, -3, 6.732, 1. \times 10^{-9}, -5.83$ are all constants.

A-3 VARIABLES

A variable is a name used to store a value. This value may change. The first character of a long variable name is capitalized. The remaining characters are lower case unless the use of a capitalized character aids in understanding by comparison with the notation used in the body of the text. Single character variables may be either lower case or upper case. Subscripted characters may be used for understanding. Typical examples are Flag, P_2', x, y.

A-4 ARRAY VARIABLES

An array variable is the name for an indexed collection of values. Naming conventions are the same as those for variables. An entire array is referenced by its variable name alone. Individual elements of the array are referenced by the variable name followed by a subscript in parentheses. Examples are Window, Window(1, 3).

A-5 ASSIGNMENT STATEMENT

The equal sign is used to assign the value of the expression on the right hand side to the variable on the left hand side.

A-6 ARITHMETIC EXPRESSIONS

The common arithmetic operators: multiplication, division, addition, and subtraction are indicated by $*, /, +, -$.

A-7 LOGICAL AND RELATIONAL OPERATORS

The logical operators **and** and **or** are set in boldface lower case as shown. The relational operators equal, not equal, less than, greater than, less than or equal, greater than or equal are indicated by $=, \neq, <, >, \leq, \geq$ respectively. These operators are used for testing purposes. The result of the test is either true or false.

A-8 THE *finish* STATEMENT

The **finish** statement is used to show termination of the algorithm.

A-9   THE *while* AND *end while* STATEMENTS

The statements within the **while-end while** block are executed repeatedly while some condition is true. The condition is tested at the beginning of the block. When the condition is no longer true, execution continues with the statement following the **end while**. The **end while** statement is used to indicate the end of a block. All statements within a **while-end while** block are indented. The general form is

> **while** (condition)
>   [*statements to be executed*]
> **end while**

As an example

> i = 0
> **while** (i < 5)
>   x = x + 5
>   i = i + 1
> **end while**
> **finish**

A-10   THE *if-then* STATEMENT

The **if-then** statement is used to select an alternate execution path or to assign an alternate value to a variable depending on whether a condition is true or false.

If the argument of the **then** is a statement number, and if the condition is true, execution continues with that statement. If not, execution continues with the next sequential statement. Statement numbers are labels.

If the argument of the **then** is an assignment statement, and if the condition is true, then the assignment statement is executed. If not, the assignment statement is not executed and execution continues with the next sequential statement. The general forms are

> **if** (condition) **then** (statement number)
> **if** (condition) **then** (assignment statement)

Examples are

> **if** (i < 10) **then** 3
> **if** (i < 10) **then** x = x + 1

A-11 THE *if-then-else* and *end if* STATEMENTS

The **if-then-else** statement is used to select alternate blocks of statements for execution depending on whether a condition is true or false. The **end if** statement is used to indicate the end of the **if-then-else** block. The **if-then-else** statement does not imply repetition. Only one of the alternate statement blocks is executed. Execution then continues with the next sequential statement after the **end if** statement. All statements within the **if-then-else** block are indented. The general form is

> **if** (condition) **then**
>   [*statements to be executed if the condition is true*]
> **else**
>   [*statements to be executed if the condition is false*]
> **end if**

An example is

> **if** (i ≥ 0) **then**
>   x = x + 1
> **else**
>   x = x − 1
> **end if**

If an **if-then-else** statement is written on a single line the **end if** statement is omitted. Note also that if the **else** and the second group of statements is omitted, a block **if-then** statement results.

A-12 THE *for-next* STATEMENT

Loop control is achieved with a **for-next** statement as well as the **while** statement. Execution of the statements within the body of the **for-next** loop occurs repeatedly while the index value is within the specified range. All statements within the body of the loop are indented. The general form is

> **for** (index variable) = (initial value) **to** (final value) **step** (increment in index value)
>   [*statements to be executed*]
> **next** (index variable)

If **step** is absent the increment is assumed to be one. Negative **step** values are allowed. The initial, final, and increment values may be variables. An example is

> **for** x = 1 **to** n **step** a
>   y = y + x
> **next** x

A-13 THE *go to* STATEMENT

The **go to** statement causes an unconditional branch to the statement identified by its argument. The general form is

go to (statement number)

Statement numbers are labels. They are positioned at the extreme left edge of the statement.

A-14 SUBROUTINE MODULES

A subroutine is a separate program module. It is invoked by means of the **call** statement. The beginning of a subroutine is defined by the **subroutine** statement. Exit from a subroutine module is indicated by the **return** statement. Upon exit from the subroutine module, control returns to the next sequential statement after the **call** statement in the calling program. The **subroutine** statement contains a list of input and a list of output variables. Communication between the calling program and the subroutine module occurs only through these variables. All other variables within a subroutine module are local to the module. The general form of the **call**, **subroutine**, and **return** statements is

call name(input variables; output variables)
subroutine name(input variables; output variables)
return

The input and output variable lists for the **call** and **subroutine** statements are separated by a ;. The lists must match. The first character of a subroutine name is capitalized. The remaining characters are lower case. An example of a subroutine module is

```
subroutine Check(x, y; Flag)
if x < y then
    Flag = 0
else
    Flag = 1
end if
return
```

A-15 FUNCTIONS

Various functions are defined within specific algorithms throughout the text. The function names are set in boldface type with the first letter capitalized An example is

Max(x_1, x_2)

which returns the larger of the values of x_1 and x_2.

PROJECTS

Since computer graphics is very much a learn by doing discipline, a number of programming projects are given. To reduce computational requirements and also to illustrate effects by exaggeration, a 32 × 32 raster grid is recommended where a raster device is assumed. If a raster device with greater resolution is available, this can be accomplished by addressing a group of pixels as a unit. If a single pixel is not square, then the group of pixels should be adjusted to be as nearly square as possible. If a vector display is available a 32 × 32 grid is drawn on the screen as shown in Fig. 4-43c. Pixel activation is indicated by placing a number in the pixel or by cross-hatching. Suggested projects are grouped by chapter.

CHAPTER 2

2-1 Using both a simple DDA (Sec. 2-2) and Bresenham's algorithm (Sec. 2-5), write a program to draw lines from any point to any other point on a pseudo 32 × 32 raster grid. Use a pseudo frame buffer represented by a single vector array to first store the image and then write from this pseudo frame buffer to the display. Demonstrate the program using a test pattern consisting of at least 16 lines from the center of a circle to points equally spaced around its circumferences. Allow for arbitrary location of the center of the circle. Compare the results visually. List the activated pixels for the line from $(0,0)$ to $(-8,-3)$ for both algorithms. How does initialization affect the results? Compare the computational efficiency of the two algorithms by timing the rasterization of 100 random lines for each algorithm.

2-2 A rasterized circle can be generated using the Bresenham circle generation algorithm described in Sec. 2-6. It can also be generated by rasterizing the edges of an inscribed polygon using Bresenham's line rasterization algorithm. Write a program using both techniques to rasterize a circle of radius $R = 15$ on a 32 × 32 grid. Compare the results for inscribed polygons of $4, 8, 16, 32, 64$, and 128 sides and the Bresenham circle generation algorithm. Use a pseudo frame buffer represented by a single vector array to first store the image and then write from the pseudo frame buffer to the display. Provide a list of rasterized points using a row-column format for each algorithm assuming that the origin $(0, 0)$ of the pseudo raster is in the lower left corner. Compare the results both visually and computationally.

2-3 For the polygon with an exterior described by the points $(4, 4)$, $(4, 26)$, $(20, 26)$, $(28, 18)$, $(28, 4)$, $(21, 4)$, $(21, 8)$, $(10, 8)$ and $(10, 4)$ and an interior hole described by $(10, 12)$, $(10, 20)$, $(17, 20)$, $(21, 16)$ and $(21, 12)$ on a 32×32 raster, write a program using the simple ordered edge list algorithm described in Sec. 2-18 to scan convert and display the solid area interior to the polygon. List the filled pixels in scan line order from top to bottom and left to right using a row-column format assuming that $(0, 0)$ is in the lower left hand corner of the raster.

2-4 For the polygon of Project 2-3, write a program using the more efficient ordered edge list algorithm described in Sec. 2-19 to scan convert and display the solid area interior to the polygon. Use an active edge list. Use a linked list to implement the y-bucket sort. List the contents of the active edge list for scan line 18 of the 32×32 raster. List the displayed pixels in scan line order and the contents of the linked list.

2-5 Write programs using the edge fill and fence fill algorithms described in Sec. 2-20 to scan convert the solid area interior to the *exterior only* of the polygon described in Project 2-3. Use a pseudo frame buffer represented by a two diminsional array to store the image and then write from the pseudo frame buffer after scan converting each edge. Compare the results. Compare the computational and input/output efficiencies of the two algorithms. Is it possible to correctly scan convert the entire polygon, including the interior hole, with these algorithms?

2-6 Write a program using the edge flag algorithm described in Sec. 2-21 to scan convert the solid area interior to the *exterior only* of the polygon described in Project 2-3. Use a pseudo frame buffer represented by a two dimensional array to store the image and then write from the pseudo frame buffer to the display. Display the frame buffer contents after determining the contour and after completing the scan conversion. Compare the results with those of Project 2-5. Is it possible to correctly scan convert the entire polygon, including the interior hole, with this algorithm? If it is, then, if required, modify the program to accomplish this. If not, why not?

2-7 Write a program using the simple boundary defined seed fill algorithm described in Sec. 2-23 to fill the interior of the polygon given in Project 2-3. Provide a list of the boundary pixels. Generate and provide a filled pixel list as the algorithm progresses for a seed pixel of $(14, 20)$. Be able to show the stack contents at any point. What is the maximum stack depth?

2-8 Perform Project 2-7 using the scan line seed fill algorithm described in Sec. 2-24. Compare the results.

2-9 Using the 2×2 bilevel pattern cells shown in Fig. 2-62 develop a program to show eight "gray" levels from left to right across a 32×32 raster. Repeat with 64×64 and 128×128 rasters and compare the results. Add ordered dither to the 128×128 raster and compare the results.

CHAPTER 3

3-1 For a two-dimensional rectangular clipping window implement the line clipping algorithm described in Sec. 3-1, the Sutherland-Cohen line clipping algorithm described in Sec. 3-2, and the mid-point subdivision line clipping algorithm described in Sec. 3-3 and compare their efficiencies. The algorithms should immediately identify and draw totally visible lines and immediately identify and reject totally invisible lines.

3-2 Write a program to implement the two-dimensional Cyrus-Beck line clipping algorithm for both interior and exterior clipping to an arbitrary convex polygonal clipping window. The algorithm should identify and reject concave clipping windows. For the special case of a rectangular clipping window, compare the results with those of Project 3-1. Vary the number of sides of the polygonal clipping window and plot the execution time versus number of sides. What is the relationship?

3-3 Extend Project 3-2 to arbitrary three-dimensional convex polyhedral volumes (see Sec. 3-11).

3-4 Write a program implementing the Sutherland-Hodgman polygon clipping algorithm described in Sec. 3-16 for arbitrary polygons clipped to rectangular windows. Show the resulting polygon after each clipping stage. In particular, clip the polygon described by vertices $(-4, 2)$, $(8, 14)$, $(8, 2)$, $(12, 6)$, $(12, -2)$, $(4, -2)$, $(4, 6)$, $(0, 2)$ to the window $(0, 10, 0, 10)$.

3-5 Extend Project 3-4 to arbitrary convex windows.

3-6 Using the Sutherland-Hodgman polygon clipping algorithm with the Cyrus-Beck line clipping algorithm to determine the line end point visibilities and the line surface intersections, clip the planar polygon defined by the points $P_1(-0.4, 0.4, 0)$, $P_2(0.1, 0.1, 0)$, $P_3(0.3, 0.3, 0)$, $P_4(0.2, 0, 0)$, $P_5(0.3, -0.2, 0)$, $P_6(0.1, -0.1, 0)$, $P_7(-0.4, -0.4, 0)$, $P_8(-0.2, 0, 0)$ rotated by $+45$ degrees about the x axis to the cylinder with axis along the z coordinate direction, a radius of 0.3 and a length along the z axis of ± 0.3. Do not forget that the cylinder has ends. The cylinder is to be represented by an inscribed polygonal volume with 32 sides. Display the cylinder and the clipped polygon using an appropriate viewing transformation. Provide a list of the polygon points after clipping.

3-7 Using the data from Project 3-6, modify the Sutherland-Hodgman algorithm to clip the polygon to the exterior of the cylinder. Display the cylinder and the clipped polygon using an appropriate viewing transformation. Provide a list of the polygon points after clipping.

3-8 Modify the algorithms developed in Projects 3-6 and 3-7 to clip one cylinder to another with the capability to perform the classical boolean operations of union and intersection. This project has implications for solids modeling.

3-9 Write a program implementing the Weiler-Atherton concave polygon clipping algorithm described in Sec. 3-17. Show the entering and leaving intersection lists. Show the resulting subject and clip polygon lists. In particular, clip the subject polygon with exterior boundary $(0, 0)$, $(20, 0)$, $(20, -20)$, $(0, -20)$ and interior hole $(7, -13)$, $(13, -13)$, $(13, -7)$, $(7, -7)$ to the clip polygon with exterior boundary $(-10, -10)$,

$(-10, 10)$, $(10, 10)$, $(10, -10)$, and interior hole $(-5, -5)$, $(5, 2\ 5)$, $(5, 5)$, $(2\ 5, 5)$. See Fig. 3-34c. Show the original clip and subject polygons and the final clipped polygon.

CHAPTER 4

4-1 Develop a computer program using the floating horizon technique described in Sec. 4-2 that will remove the hidden lines for the surface function

$$F(x,z) = 8 \cos (1.2R)/(R + 1) \qquad R = \sqrt{x^2 + z^2} \qquad 2\pi \leq x, z \leq 2\pi$$

viewed from a point at infinity on the positive z axis after having been rotated $25°$ about the x axis followed by a $15°$ rotation about the y axis.

4-2 Using Roberts' technique, by hand, eliminate the hidden lines from the scene defined below. The scene is viewed using a dimetric transformation with the observer at infinity on the positive z axis. A dimetric transformation without projection onto the $z = 0$ plane is given in Ref. 1-1 by the 4×4 homogeneous coordinate transformation

$$[T] = \begin{bmatrix} 0.92582 & 0.13363 & -0.35355 & 0 \\ 0 & 0.92541 & 0.35355 & 0 \\ 0.37796 & -0.32732 & 0.86603 & 0 \\ 0 & 0 & 0 & 1 \end{bmatrix}$$

The inverse of the transformation matrix is its transpose. The scene consists of a cube and a rectangular parallelepiped given by

cube

$$\begin{bmatrix} 3 & 1 & 11 \\ 6 & 1 & 11 \\ 6 & 4 & 11 \\ 3 & 4 & 11 \\ 3 & 1 & 8 \\ 6 & 1 & 8 \\ 6 & 4 & 8 \\ 3 & 4 & 8 \end{bmatrix}$$

parallelepiped

$$\begin{bmatrix} 1 & 2 & 7 \\ 10 & 2 & 7 \\ 10 & 3 & 7 \\ 1 & 3 & 7 \\ 1 & 2 & 1 \\ 10 & 2 & 1 \\ 10 & 3 & 1 \\ 1 & 3 & 1 \end{bmatrix}$$

4-3 Write a program to implement Roberts algorithm. Use the scene from Project 4-2 as a test case.

Projects 4-4 to 4-11 use the basic test scene described in Example 4-19 and a modification. The basic test scene consists of a triangle penetrating a rectangle from behind. A 32×32 raster grid is used. If required, use a two-dimensional array to simulate a frame buffer. The corner coordinates of the rectangle are $P_1(10, 5, 10)$, $P_2(10, 25, 10)$, $P_3(25, 25, 10)$, $P_4(25, 5, 10)$ and the triangular vertices are $P_5(15, 15, 15)$, $P_6(30, 10, 5)$. $P_7(25, 25, 5)$, The modified scene consists of the rectangle and a non-penetrating triangle with P_5 changed to $P_5(15, 15, 5)$.

4-4 Write a program to implement the basic Warnock algorithm described in Sec. 4-4. Display the results for both test scenes described above. Display each window or subwindow as the algorithm processes the scene.

4-5 Increase the efficiency of the algorithm of Project 4-4 by implementing a more sophisticated outsider test. Also add the ability to recognize single surrounder, single contained, and single intersector polygons. Add a depth priority sort to the algorithm. Add a list structure to take advantage of prior level information. Add antialiasing to the algorithm (Sec. 2-26). Use more sophisticated scenes to test and compare the algorithms.

4-6 Write a program to implement the Weiler-Atherton algorithm (see Sec. 4-5) for the test scenes described above.

4-7 Implement a z buffer algorithm (see Sec. 4-7). Use the two scenes described above to test it. Display the contents of the frame and the z buffer after each polygon is processed. What is the effect of truncating the z value to correspond to $32, 16, 8, 4$ bits of precision for the z buffer?

4-8 Write a program to implement the Newell-Newell-Sandra list priority algorithm described in Sec. 4-8. Add a diamond with vertices $P_8(15, 20, 20), P_9(20, 25, 20)$, $P_{10}(25, 20, 20)$, $P_{11}(20, 15, 20)$, to the test scenes described above. Display the contents of the frame buffer after each polygon is processed.

4-9 Implement the scan line z buffer algorithm described in Sec. 4-10. Use the two scenes described above to test it. Display the result scan line by scan line. Be able to display the active polygon and edge lists for each scan line.

4-10 Implement the spanning scan line algorithm (Watkins) described in Sec. 4-11. Use the two scenes described above to test it. Display the result scan line by scan line. Be able to display the active edge list and intersection stack at any scan line.

4-11 Implement the opaque visible surface ray tracing algorithm described in Sec. 4-13. Use the two scenes described above to test it. Assume the observer is at infinity on the positive z axis. Display the result pixel by pixel as it is generated. Be able to display the active object list as each pixel is processed. Improve the efficiency of the algorithm by defining a bounding box for the entire scene and projecting it onto the image plane. Any pixel outside the projected area need not be traced. Compare the results with and without this addition.

CHAPTER 5

The following projects are most conveniently implemented with a raster display having at least 16 intensity levels or colors. More intensity levels or colors will yield more aesthetically pleasing results. The academic requirements of the projects can be satisfied on a vector display by converting the binary representation in an n bit plane frame buffer to a decimal number and displaying the number in the appropriate raster location.

5-1 Consider an n sided polygonal representation of an opaque cylinder of radius R with its axis normal to the view direction. For $n = 8, 16, 32$, a simple Lambertian plus ambient illumination model (see Eq. 5-1), and a suitable hidden surface algorithm write a program to display a cylinder of radius $R = 15$. See Fig. 5-3. Assume that a single point light source is located at infinity on the positive z axis as is the observer. Rotate the cylinder 90° about the z axis and compare the results.

5-2 Add Gouraud shading (see Sec. 5-5) to the cylinder of Project 5-1 using the simple illumination model. Compare the results. Add specular reflection to the illumination model (see Eq. 5-7). Vary the parameter n.

5-3 Add Phong shading (see Sec. 5-6) to the cylinder of Project 5-1 using the simple illumination model. Compare the results to those of Projects 5-1 and 5-2. Add specular reflection to the illumination model (see Eq. 5-7). Compare the results, in particular the shape of the specular reflection, to those for Gouraud shading.

5-4 Using the rectangle plus triangle test scene described above for Projects 4-4 to 4-11, write a program to display a transparent triangle (see Sec. 5-9) and an opaque rectangle using the Newell-Newell-Sancha (see Sec. 4-8) or the spanning scan line hidden surface algorithm (see Sec. 4-11). Ignore refraction effects. Use a linear combination of the intensity of the visible transparent surface and the opaque surface immediately behind it to represent the intensity of the combined surface. Vary the transparency factor and observe the effects. Make the rectangle transparent and the triangle opaque and compare the results.

5-5 Add shadows to the spanning scan line algorithm implemented in Project 4-10. Assume both the triangle and the rectangle are opaque. The observer is located at infinity on the positive z axis. The single point light source is located at $x = 30$, $z = 40$. How would you handle the shadow from a transparent triangle?

5-6 Add shadows to the opaque visible surface ray tracing algorithm implemented in Project 4-11. Assume the triangle and the rectangle are opaque, the observer is at positive infinity on the z axis, and the single point light source is at $x = 30$, $z = 40$. How would you handle the shadow from a transparent triangle?

5-7 Write a program to add the texture pattern shown in Fig. 5-34 to the octant of the sphere as also shown in Fig. 5-34 using the patch subdivision technique (see Sec. 5-11). Use an appropriate hidden surface algorithm to display the results on a 32 × 32 raster grid. Use a 64 × 64 raster grid and compare the results.

5-8 Implement the global illumination model with the ray tracing algorithm described in Sec. 5-12 and Figs. 5-42 to 5-44. Use the simple test scene described in Example 5-9 to test the program.

5-9 Write a program to draw simple variable-sized colored squares on a color monitor. Modify the program to allow the color of the current square to be added to, subtracted from, or to replace the color of the previous square. Use the program to verify the additive color system (see Sec. 5-15) e.g. Red + Blue = Magenta. Experiment with the effects of simultaneous contrast by drawing a small purple square inside both a bright red and a bright blue square.

achromatic, 383
active edge list, 52-54, 53 (Fig. 2-16), 54 (Fig. 2-17), 79, 279, 280, 417
   floating pointers, 52
   ordered edge list algorithm, 76
   (*see also* hidden surface, Watkins algorithm)
aliasing, 10, 93 (Fig. 2-50), 382
   animation, 93, 93 (Fig. 2-52)
   jagged edges, 93
   small objects, 93, 93 (Fig. 2-51)
   temporal, 382
   texture, 93
   thin objects, 93
   (*see also* antialiasing)
alignment white, 391
ambient light (*see* reflection, diffuse)
antialiasing, 10, 92, 93
   area, 95, 96, 96 (Fig. 2-56)
   Bresenham's algorithm, 96-98, 96 (Fig. 2-57)
   clipping, 101, 101 (Fig. 2-61)
   prefiltered, 101
   prefiltered (*see also* convolution integral)
   temporal, 382
   uniform averaging, 93, 94, 94 (Fig. 2-53), 94 (Fig. 2-54)
   weighted averaging, 94, 94 (Fig. 2-53), 95 (Fig. 2-55)
   (*see also* aliasing)
   (*see also* convolution integral)
Appel, A., 296, 349
area coherence, 240, 241
Atherton, P. R., 179, 259, 306, 351
averaging, uniform, 93

back face culling, 282, 364
   hidden surface, Watkins algorithm, 290

back face culling (*cont.*):
   (*see also* Roberts algorithm, self-hidden planes)
Badler, V. R., 382
bandwidth, communication, 8
Barr, A. H., 365
Barsky, B., 155, 162, 179, 357
Beckmann distribution function, 335
Beckmann, P. 335
bit plane, 10
black body, 311
black body locus, 391
Blinn, J. F., 162, 292, 293, 332, 335, 338, 355, 357, 361-363, 382
Bouknight, W. J., 279, 349
bounding box, 67, 67 (Fig. 2-30), 69, 70 (Fig. 2-33)
   algorithm, 67
   pseudocode, 67
box function (*see* convolution kernal)
Bresenham's algorithm:
   circle generation, 42-48, 296, 417
      algorithm, 48
      derivation, 43, 43 (Fig. 2-10)
      Example 2-5, 50
      flowchart, 49
      pixel selection, 44 (Fig. 2-12)
      pseudocode algorithm, 48
      results, 51 (Fig. 2-15)
   line drawing, 34-42, 417
      antialiasing, 96-98, 98 (Fig. 2-57)
         flowchart, 98
         pseudocode, 97
      basis, 35 (Fig. 2-4)
      error term, 35 (Fig. 2-5), 36
      Example 2-3, 37
      first octant algorithm, 36
         results, 39 (Fig. 2-7)
      flowchart, 37 (Fig. 2-6)
      generalized algorithm, 40

Bresenham's algorithm, line drawing,
    generalized algorithm (*cont.*):
        Example 2-4, 40
           pseudocode, 40, 41
           results, 42 (Fig. 2-9)
        integer algorithm, 38, 39
           pseudocode, 39
        pseudocode algorithm, 36, 37
brightness, 383, 384, 403
brightness adaptation, 310
bump mapping (*see* texture, rough)

Carlson, W. 382
Carpenter, L. C., 292, 363
cathode ray tube, 15, 15 (Fig. 1-16), 16
    calligraphic, 3
    color, 16, 17 (Fig. 1-18)
    pitch, 16
    raster scan, 3
    shadow mask 16, 16 (Fig. 1-17), 17 (Fig.
        1-18)
    storage tube, 3
Catmull, E., 265, 355-358, 407
cell encoding, 60, 60 (Fig. 2-22), 61, 61 (Fig.
    2-23), 61 (Fig. 2-24)
    characters, 60
    color, 62
    interaction, 61
    line drawings, 61
Chakravarty, I., 382
character display, 67
character mask (*see* mask)
chroma, Munsell, 406
chromaticity coordinates, 389
    CIE, 390
    CIE XYZ primaries, 394, 395, 395 (Fig.
        5-59)
    color monitor primaries, 394, 395, 395
        (Fig. 5-59)
    film, 394, 395, 395 (Fig. 5-59)
    NTSC standard primaries, 394, 395, 395
        (Fig. 5-59)
chromaticity diagram, 389
    CIE, 390, 391, 391 (Fig. 5-56)
    use of, 392, 392 (Fig. 5-57)
chromaticity values, CIE, 390
circle generation (*see* Bresenham's algorithm)
Clark, J. H., 292
clipping, 140 (Fig. 3-13)
    character 185, 186, 186 (Figs. 3-36 to 3-
        38)
    concave windows, 146 (Fig 3-17), 179-
        185

clipping (*cont.*):
    Cyrus-Beck algorithm, 131, 135-145, 139
        (Fig. 3-12), 157-162, 419
    Example 3-9, 137
    Example 3-10, 139
    Example 3-11, 140
    Example 3-12, 141
    Example 3-13, 145
    exterior clipping, 144 (Fig. 3-15)
    flowchart, 143 (Fig. 3-14)
    homogeneous coordinates, 163, 164
        Example 3-20, 163, 164
    irregular window, Example 3-13, 145
    nontrivially invisible lines, Example
        3-12, 141
    partially visible line, Example 3-9, 137,
        138
    three dimensional, 157, 159 (Fig. 3-
        22), 161 (Fig. 3-23)
        Example 3-17, 158, 159
        Example 3-18, 160, 161
        Example 3-19, 161, 162
        Example 3-20, 163, 164
    totally visible lines, 139
    trivially invisible lines, Example 3-11,
        140
    end point codes, 121
        perspective volume, 153-155
        three dimensional, 153
        two dimensional, 113, 114, 114 (Fig.
        3-2)
    explicit algorithm, 117, 120, 121
        flowchart, 118, 119 (Fig. 3-4)
        Example 3-1, 115
        pseudocode 117, 120, 121
    exterior, 146, 419
    generalized two dimensional, 131
    homogeneous coordinates, 162-164
        Example 3-20, 163, 164
    interior, 419
    intersection calculation, 115, 125
        parametric lines, 116 (Fig. 3-3)
    irregular windows, 131 (Fig. 3-7)
    midpoint subdivision, 125-131, 125 (Fig.
        3-5)
        algorithm, 126, 128-131, 419
        flowchart, 128, 129 (Fig. 3-6)
        Example 3-3, 126, 127
        three dimensional, 155
            algorithm, 156
            Example 3-16, 156, 157
            pseudocode algorithm, 128-131
    multiwindow, 146 (Fig. 3-16)
    normal vectors, 135, 136 (Fig. 3-10)

clipping, normal vectors (*cont.*):
    Example 3-8, 136
    parametric lines, 132, 134
        Example 3-4, 132
        Example 3-5, 134
        Example 3-6, 134
        Example 3-7, 134
        trivially invisible, 134, 135 (Fig. 3-9)
        trivially visible, 134, 135 (Fig. 3-9)
    plane, relation of point to, 170, 171, 171 (Fig. 3-29)
        Example 3-23, 172
    polygon, 168-185, 169 (Fig. 3-26), 169 (Fig. 3-27)
    polygon, concave, 179
        Weiler-Atherton algorithm, 179-185, 180 (Fig. 3-34), 181, 185 (Fig. 3-35), 419
            Example 3-26, 182, 183
            Example 3-27, 183, 184
            Example 3-28, 184, 185
    polygon, Sutherland-Hodgman algorithm, 169-179, 170 (Fig. 3-28)
        Example 3-25, 178
        flowchart, 174 (Fig. 3-32)
        pseudocode algorithm, 175-177, 419
    regular window, 111
    simple visibility algorithm, 112
    Sutherland-Cohen, 121-124
        algorithm, 122, 419
        Example 3-2, 122
        pseudocode algorithm, 122-124
    three dimensional, 152, 153 (Fig. 3-20), 419
        perspective, 154
    trivially invisible, 112, 114, 115, 153
    trivially visible, 112, 113, 115, 153
    visibility test, pseudocode 112, 113
    volume, 152
    window, 112 (Fig. 3-1)
Cohen, E., 265
Cohen-Sutherland (*see* end point codes)
coherence, 190
    area, 240, 241
    scan line, 70
    spacial, 70
color, 383-408
    achromatic, 383
    brightness, 384
    chromatic, 384
    complements, 385, 386
        from chromaticity diagram, 391
    cube:
        CMY, 399, 400 (Fig. 5-60)

color, cube (*cont.*):
        RGB, 399, 400 (Fig. 5-60), 401, 403
    dominant wavelength, from chromaticity diagram, 392
    gamut, 394, 395 (Fig. 5-59)
    harmony, 407
    hue, 384
    mixtures, 389, 392
        Example 5-10, 393
    perceptual names, 393, 394, 394 (Fig. 5-58)
    primaries, 385, 387
    saturation, 384
color-matching functions, 387, 388 (Fig. 5-52)
color space, 389, 389 (Fig. 5-54)
    NTSC (*see* color space, YIQ)
    YIQ, 398
color system:
    additive, 385, 386 (Fig. 5-51)
    HSL (hue, saturation, lightness), 403, 404 (Fig. 5-63)
    HSV (hue, saturation, value), 400, 401 (Fig. 5-62)
    Munsell, 406 (Fig. 5-64)
    Ostwald, 400
    subtractive, 385, 386 (Fig. 5-51)
    transformation from:
        CIE-Munsell, 406
        CIE-RGB, 396, 397
            Example 5-11, 397, 398
        CIE-YIQ, 399
        CMY-RGB, 399
        HLS-RGB pseudocode algorithm, 403, 404
        HSV-RGB pseudocode algorithm, 401, 402
        Munsell-CIE, 406
        RGB-CIE, 395, 396
            Example 5-12, 398
        RGB-CMY, 399
        RGB-HLS pseudocode algorithm, 405, 406
        RGB-HSV pseudocode algorithm, 402, 403
        RGB-YIQ, 399
        YIQ-CIE, 399
        YIQ-RGB, 399
colors, distinguishable, 389
complimentary spectrum value, 392
concave polygons, splitting, 151, 152
    Example 3-15, 152
concave volumes:
    Roberts algorithm, 206

concave volumes (*cont.*):
    splitting, 166, 167
        Example 3-22, 167, 168
cones, 309
contained polygon (*see* hidden surface, War-
    nock algorithm)
contour filling, 69
convex polygon, identifying, 147, 149-151, 150
    (Fig. 3-19)
    Example 3-14, 148, 149
convex volume, identifying, 164, 165 (Fig. 3-
    24)
    Example 3-21, 165, 166
    Roberts algorithm, 206
convolution integral, 98, 99 (Fig. 2-59)
    graphical explanation, 99
    limits, 100
convolution kernal, 98-100
    box, 101
    conical, 101
    Gaussian, 101
    pyramidal, 101
    triangular, 101
    two-dimensional, 101
Cook, R. L., 332, 337, 338, 353, 380
coordinates:
    screen, 5
    user, 7
    world, 6, 7
Cowan, W. B., 407
cross-hatching, 69, 69 (Fig. 2-32)
Crow, F., 94, 357
Csuri, C. A., 382
Cyrus-Beck (*see* clipping)

depth priority, 190
digital differential analyzer, 30-34, 34 (Fig. 2-
    3), 417
    algorithm, 31
    Example 2-1, 32
    Example 2-2, 33
    pseudocode, 31
disjoint polygon (*see* hidden surface, Warnock
    algorithm)
display:
    buffer, 5, 6
        segmentation, 6, 7, 7 (Figs. 1-5 and
        1-6)
            dynamic, 8
    controller, 5, 6
    processor, raster, 52
    random scan, 4, 5
    refresh, 16

display (*cont.*):
    storage tube, 4 (Fig. 1-2), 16
distribution function, 334
    Beckmann, 335, 336, 336 (Fig. 5-20)
dither (*see* ordered dither)
dominant wavelength, 384
double buffering, 6
Duff. T., 326
Dungan, W., 382
dynamic display:
    linked list, 55
    y-bucket sort, 55
dynamic motion, 4, 6, 7 (Fig. 1-4)
    raster display, 52

edge fill algorithm, 79
edge fill algorithm (*see also* scan conversion)
end point codes:
    three dimensional, 152
    two dimensional, 113
eye, 309
    brightness adaptation, 310
    cones, 309
    rods, 309
    sensitivity, 309, 383

facsimile, 59
fence fill algorithm (*see* scan conversion)
filtering (*see* antialiasing)
flicker, 17
    rate, 5
    storage tube, 4
floating horizon algorithm, 191-205, 420
    complete algorithm, 196
    cross hatching, 203, 205, 205 (Fig. 4-12)
    edge filling, 195, 196
    Example 4-1, 201-203
    intersection techniques, 194, 195
    linear interpolation, 193
    lower horizon, 192, 193
    narrow regions, 196, 197
    pseudocode algorithm, 197-201
    upper horizon, 192
flood fill algorithm, 84
Floyd-Steinberg, 104, 106 (Fig. 2-68)
    pseudocode algorithm, 106
Fournier, A., 363
fractal surface, 363, 363 (Fig. 5-37)
frame buffer, 10, 10 (Fig. 1-9), 62, 63 (Fig.
    2-25), 80, 280, 343
    architecture, 63 (Fig. 2-27)

frame buffer (*cont.*):
    color, 11-14, 12 (Fig. 1-12), 13 (Fig. 1-13), 14 (Fig. 1-14)
    conceptual configuration, 62
    gray level, 10, 11 (Figs. 1-10 and 1-11)
    memory, 62, 63
    shift register, 63
frame rate, video, 18, 19
Fresnel equation, 334, 336, 337 (Fig. 5-21), 379
    angular dependence, 338
    wavelength dependence, 338
    (*see also* reflection, specular)
frustum of vision, 152, 162, 163
Fussell, D., 363

gamma correction, 407
gamut, 394, 395 (Fig. 5-59)
Gear, C., 285
geometric attenuation, 334, 335 (Fig. 5-19)
global illumination model (*see* illumination model, global)
Gouraud, H., 323
Gouraud shading, 323-325, 323 (Fig. 5-10), 325 (Fig. 5-12), 326 (Fig. 3-26, 422
    Example 5-3, 327-330
    Mach band effect, 324
    specular highlights, 327 (Fig. 5-14)
graphics devices, 3
Grassman's laws, 388, 389, 392, 395, 396
gray level, 10
Greenberg, D. 379, 403, 406

half scan line convention, 80-82
halftoning, 102-108 (*see also* image processing)
Hall, R. A., 373, 379
Hamlin, G., 285
Hedgeley, D. R., 305
hexcone color solid (*see also* color system, HSV and HSL)
hidden line:
    floating horizon algorithm, 191-205, 420
    (*see also* floating horizon algorithm)
    image space algorithm, 190, 191
    list priority algorithm, 278, 279
    object space algorithm, 190, 191
    ray tracing algorithm, 305
    Roberts algorithm, 205-240, 420
    (*see also* Roberts algorithm)

hidden line (*cont.*):
    Warnock algorithm, 241, 242
hidden lines, sorting, 190
hidden surface:
    curved surfaces:
        Blinn-Whitted algorithm, 293, 294
        Catmull subdivision algorithm, 264, 265, 265 (Fig. 4-49), 292, 294
        Clark algorithm, 294
        Lane-Carpenter algorithm, 294, 295
        scan line algorithm, 292-296
    image space algorithm, 190, 191
    list priority algorithm, 190, 272-280
        antialiasing, 278
        cyclical overlap, 273 (Fig. 4-52)
        depth priority sort, 272
        Newell-Newell-Sancha algorithm, 273-277, 421
            cyclical overlap, 277
            special sort, 273, 274
        Schumacker algorithm, 277
        transparency, 272
    object space algorithm, 190, 191
    ray tracing algorithm, 296-305, 421
        calculation of physical properties, 305
        cluster priority, 303, 304
        Example 4-24, 302, 303
        global illumination, 363-381, 422
        intersections, 297, 298, 302
            bounding box test, 298, 299, 299 (Fig. 4-20)
            bounding sphere, 298
            parametric surfaces, 300, 301
            quadric surfaces, 299, 300
        shadows, 352, 353, 353 (Fig. 5-30), 422
        (*see also* ray tracing)
    Roberts algorithm, 205-240, 420
    scan line algorithm, 279-296
        Watkins algorithm, shadows, 350
    scan line z-buffer algorithm, 280-284, 421
        antialiasing, 280
        Example 4-22, 282-284
        shadows, 351
    sorting, 190
    spanning scan line algorithm, 421
    Warnock algorithm, 241-260, 421
        antialiasing, 241
        bounding box test, 245, 246, 246 (Fig. 4-36)
        contained polygon, 245, 246

hidden surface, Warnock algorithm, contained polygon (*cont.*):
  Example 4-14, 247
  depth priority sort, 253, 254
  disjoint polygon, 245, 246
    angle counting test, 250 (Fig. 4-40)
    Example 4-14, 247
    infinite line test, 249
  Example 4-17, 259, 260
  flowchart, 255 (Fig. 4-42)
  intersecting polygon, 245, 246, 249 (Fig. 4-37)
    Example 4-15, 247, 248
  polygon types, 245, 245 (Fig. 4-35)
  pseudocode algorithm, 254-259
  surrounding polygon, 245, 246
    angle counting test, 250, 250 (Fig. 4-40), 251
      Example 4-16, 251
    depth calculation, 252, 253, 253 (Fig. 4-41)
    infinite line test, 249, 249 (Fig. 4-38)
  window subdivision, 241, 242 (Fig. 4-32), 244 (Fig. 4-34), 244-246
  window tests, hierarchical application, 252
  window tree structure, 243 (Fig. 4-33), 244
Watkins algorithm, 284-292, 421
  active edge list, 286-288
  depth calculation, 287, 290
    flowchart, 289 (Fig. 4-62)
  Example 4-23, 290, 291
  flowchart, 288 (Fig. 4-61)
  penetrating polygons, 284, 286, 287
    flowchart, 289 (Fig. 4-63)
  polygon active flag, 286
  spans, 284, 285, 285 (Fig. 4-59), 285 (Fig. 4-60)
    depth calculations, 285, 286
Weiler-Atherton algorithm, 259-264, 421
  cyclical overlap, 264, 264 (Fig. 4-48)
  Example 4-18, 263, 264
  priority (depth) sort, 261, 262 (Fig. 4-46)
  recursive subdivision, 262, 263 (Fig. 4-47)
  shadows, 351, 352
z-buffer algorithm, 265-272, 421
  antialiasing, 266, 267
  depth calculation, 267

hidden surface, z-buffer algorithm (*cont.*):
  Example 4-19, 268-271
  segmentation, 266
  shadows, 350
  surface sectioning, 272
  translucency, 266
  transparency, 266
hue, 384
  Munsell, 406

illuminants, CIE, 391
illumination model:
  Cook-Torrance, 332-335
  distance attenuation, 367
  global, 296, 345, 364, 365, 422
    camera effects, 364, 364 (Fig. 5-38), 365, 365 (Fig. 5-39), Color Plate 6
    Hall model, 379-381, Color Plate 8
    Whitted model, 365, 366, 373, 381
  local, 364
  Phong, 339 (Fig. 5-22), 340 (Fig. 5-23)
  simple, 311-317, 422
    Example 5-1, 316-317
  special effects, 330-332
    barn doors, 331
    cone, 331, 331 (Fig. 5-17), 332
    flaps, 331, 331 (Fig. 5-17)
    flood light, 331
    spot light, 331
  Torrance-Sparrow, 332, 333, 334 (Fig. 5-18), 335, 339 (Fig. 5-22), 340 (Fig. 5-23), 380
  Warn, 330-332
image processing (*see* ordered dither, patterning, thresholding)
image space, 190, 191
  algorithm, 265
  Warnock algorithm, 241
infinite line test (*see* hidden surface, Warnock algorithm)
interactive device:
  logical:
    button, 20
    keyboard, 20
    locator, 20
    pick, 20, 24, 27
    simulation, 26
    valuator, 20, 22-24, 27
  physical:
    control dial, 20, 22, 24, 24 (Fig. 1-26)

interactive device, physical (*cont.*):
 function switch (button), 20, 24, 25
  (Fig. 1-27)
 joystick, 20, 22, 23, 23 (Fig. 1-24)
 keyboard, 20, 20 (Fig. 1-21)
 light pen, 20, 24, 25, 25 (Fig. 1-28),
  26, 26 (Fig. 1-29), 27
 mouse, 20, 22, 23, 23 (Fig. 1-25), 24
 tablet, 20, 21, 21 (Fig. 1-22), 22, 22
  (Fig. 1-23), 24, 27, 27 (Fig. 1-
  30)
 touch panel, 22
 track ball, 22, 23
interlacing, 17, 18
intersecting polygon, substitution test, 247
 (*see also* hidden surface, Warnock
 algorithm)

Jackson, J. H., 290
jaggies (*see* aliasing)
Joblove, G. H., 403
Judd, D. B., 407

Kajiya, J., 293, 300, 363
Kay, D. S., 296, 343, 365, 380
Kelley, K. C., 349
Korein, J., 382

Lambert's cosine law (*see* reflection, diffuse)
Lane, J. M., 292
Liang, 155, 162, 179
light emitting sources, color system, 386
light, wave characteristics, 382
lightness, 383, 403, 406
line drawing:
 algorithms, 29
 Bresenham's algorithm, 34-42
 digital differential analyzer, 30-34
 incremental methods, 30
 requirements, 29
 (*see also* Bresenham's algorithm)
 (*see also* digital differential analyzer)
line intersection, 173 (Fig. 3-31)
 parametric, Example 3-24, 173
linked list (*see* list, linked)
list:
 linked, 55, 56 (Fig. 2-19), 77 (Fig. 2-
  39), 79, 417
  hidden surface, Watkins algorithm,
  286

list, linked (*cont*):
  ordered edge list algorithm, 76
  scan line *z*-buffer algorithm, 280
 sequential indexed, 53-55
look-up table, 11, 11 (Fig. 1-11), 14 (Fig. 1-
 14)
 color, 12
luminance, 384, 385
 CIE, 390
Lyche, T., 265

Mach band effect, 310, 311, 311 (Fig. 5-2),
 311 (Fig. 5-3)
 Gouraud shading, 324
 Phong shading, 326
Mach, E., 310
Mandelbrot, B., 363
Marcus, A., 407
Marshal, R., 382
mask:
 character, 67
  insertion in frame buffer, 68
  transformation, 68
metamer, 387, 388 (Fig. 5-53)
Meyer, G. W., 389, 406
minimax test (*see* bounding box)
monochromatic, 384
Moravec, H. P., 382
motion blur (*see* antialiasing, temporal)
Munsell chroma, 406
Munsell hue, 406
Munsell value, 406

National Television Standards Committee
 (NTSC), 391
natural objects, rendering, 382
Newell, M. E., 273, 278, 343, 355, 357
Newell-Newell-Sancha algorithm (*see* hidden
 surface, list priority algorithm)
Newell-Newell-Sancha priority sort, 273, 274,
 349
normal, surface determination, 317-319
 Example 5-2, 318, 319
 using rotations and translations, 321
normal vector, clipping, 135
 determination, 147, 148, 164, 165 (Fig.
  3-24)
  Example 3-21, 165, 166
NTSC (National Television Standards Committee), 391

object space, 190, 191, 205
ordered dither, 105 (Fig. 2-67), 106, 418
    algorithm, 107, 108
    patterns, 107
ordered edge list algorithm (*see* scan conversion)
Ostwald, N., 400

painters algorithm (*see* hidden surface, list priority algorithm)
particle system, 382
patterning, 102-103, 418
    2 × 2 cells, 102 (Fig. 2-62)
    3 × 2 cells, 103 (Fig. 2-64)
    3 × 3 cells, 103 (Fig. 2-63)
    multiple bits per pixel, 103
    multiple dot sizes, 103, 104 (Fig. 2-65)
Phong, B. T., 325
Phong shading, 325-330, 326 (Fig. 5-13), 422
    Example 5-3, 327-330
    Mach band effects, 326
    specular highlights, 327 (Fig. 5-14)
photometry, 386
picture representation:
    edges, 2
    points, 1, 2
    polygons, 2
pixel, 9
    averaging (*see* antialiasing)
    coordinate addressing, 32, 71
    half scan line convention, 71
plane equation, 207, 208
    Example 4-3, 209, 210
    Newell's method, 209
        Example 4-3, 209
        Example 4-4, 211
    non-planar polygons, 208
        Example 4-4, 211
points, representation, 2
polygon filling, scan conversion, 69
    simple technique, 69
polygons:
    clusters, 277, 278
    cluster priority, 277
        Example 4-21, 277, 278
    concave, 179
        splitting, 151, 152
    contained 245, 246
    convex, identifying 147, 149-151, 150
        (Fig. 3-19)
    disjoint, 245, 246
    intersecting, 245-247, 249 (Fig. 4-37)

polygons (*cont.*):
    linearly separable, 277
    non-planar, 208
    penetrating, 284, 286, 287
    picture, representation with, 2
    relationship between, 275, 276
        Example 4-20, 275, 276
    surrounding, 245, 246
    types, 245, 245 (Fig. 4-35)
    (*see also* scan conversion)
    (*see also* hidden surfaces, Warnock algorithm)
Porter, T., 296
post filtering (*see* antialiasing)
Potmesil, M., 365, 382
prefiltering (*see* antialiasing)
primary colors, 387
    CMY (cyan, magenta, yellow), 385
    RGB (red, green blue), 385
priority sort, 364
pseudocode definitions, 411-415
purity, 384, 406
purple line, 391, 392

quadric surfaces, 295

raster, 9
    addressing, 64, 65
        Example 2-6, 65
        Example 2-7, 66
    coordinate system, 64
    display, real time, 12, 13
    line display, 66
    selective erase, 66 (Fig. 2-29)
rasterization, 29, 29 (Fig. 2-1), 30
ray tracing;
    illumination model, global, 422
        antialiasing, 378, 378 (Fig. 5-46)
        Example 5-9, 368-372
        flowchart, 374, 375 (Fig. 5-42), 377 (Fig. 5-44)
        object description, 373
        shadows, 368
    intersections, 366, 376
    recursive subdivision, 378
    reflected ray direction, 367
    reflections, 366, 366 (Fig. 5-40)
    refracted ray direction, 367
    refractions, 366, 366 (Fig. 5-40)
    shadows, 376
    stack contents, 373

ray tracing (*cont.*):
    tree structure, 366, 368 (Fig. 5-40)
    tree termination, 367, 372
    (*see also* hidden surface)
Reeves, W. T., 382
reflectance:
    bidirectional, 333
    diffuse, angular dependence, 338
    specular:
        angular dependence, 338
        wavelength dependence, 338
reflection, 190, 296
    ambient, 313, 366, 373
        wavelength dependence, 336
    diffuse, 312, 312 (Fig. 5-4), 333, 366
        distance effect, 313
        Lambertian, 365, 373, 380
        Lambert's cosine law, 312
        wavelength dependence, 336
    global illumination model, 365
    internal, 367, 367 (Fig. 5-41)
    light energy, 332
    light intensity, 332
    specular, 312-315, 314 (Fig. 5-5), 333, 380
        angular dependence, 338, 340 (Fig. 5-23)
        Fresnel equation, 313
        Phong model, 314, 314 (Fig. 5-6), 365, 366, 373
        wavelength dependence, 336
reflection direction, determination, 320-322, 320 (Fig. 5-9)
    Phong's method, 320, 321
    using cross products, 321, 322
reflection law, 320
reflective sources, color system, 386
refraction, 190, 296
refraction effect, 341, 341 (Fig. 5-25), 342, 342 (Fig. 5-26)
    global illumination model, 365
    Snell's law, 340, 341 (Fig. 5-24), 367, 380
    specular, 380
refresh:
    cycle, 6
    display, 3
        calligraphic, 3, 5, 6 (Fig. 1-3), 9 (Fig. 1-7)
        random scan, 5
        raster, 3, 8, 9, 62
    rate, 5, 6, 17
    storage tube, 4

region:
    4-connected, 84, 84 (Fig. 2-45), 85 (Fig. 2-46), 87, 92
    8-connected, 84, 84 (Fig. 2-45), 85 (Fig. 2-46)
    boundary defined, 83-85, 84 (Fig. 2-44), 85 (Fig. 2-46), 87, 88, 91
    clipping, 135, 137, 141
    interior defined, 83, 84, 84 (Fig. 2-43), 84 (Fig. 2-45)
Reisenfeld, R., 265
Roberts algorithm:
    algorithm for tminmax, tmaxmin, 225, 226
    bounding box test, 217
    complete example, Example 4-13, 232-240
    efficient algorithm, 228-231
    flowchart, (Fig. 4-26), 226
    lines hidden by volumes, 217, 218 (Fig. 4-18), 281
        conditions for, 220
        Example 4-10, 222, 223
        Example 4-11, 224
        Example 4-19, 221, 222
        Example 4-8, 218, 219
        solution technique, 220, 220 (Fig. 4-19), 220 (Fig. 4-20)
    penetrating (juncture) lines, 254 (Fig. 4-24)
        Example 4-11, 224
    priority sort, 217
    self-hidden lines, 216, 217
    self-hidden planes, 214, 217 (Fig. 4-17)
        Example 4-6, 215
        Example 4-7, 215, 216
    totally invisible lines, 228
    totally visible lines, 227, 227 (Fig. 4-27)
        Example 4-12, 226, 227
    volume matrix, 206
    (*see also* hidden line)
rods, 309
Romney, G. W., 285, 287
Roth, S. D., 305
run length encoding, 56, 58, 58 (Fig. 2-20), 60 (Fig. 2-21)
    color, 59
    data compression, 58, 59
    disadvantage, 59
    solid figures, 59

sampling (*see* aliasing)
Sancha, T. L., 273, 343

saturation, 384 , 406

scan conversion, 17, 29
  active edge list, 53
  display generation, 51
  half scan line convention, 80-82
  horizontal lines, 55 (Fig. 2-18), 72
  polygons, 70
    edge fill algorithm, 80, 418
    edge flag algorithm, 81-83, 418
      Example 2-11, 82
    fence fill algorithm, 80, 81, 81 (Fig. 2-41), 418
    filling, 69
    ordered edge list algorithm, 73, 74, 76, 279, 418
      Example 2-8, 73
      Example 2-9, 75
      Example 2-10, 76
    vertex intersections, 72, 72 (Fig. 2-36)
  real time, 52
  solid area, 69, 70 (Fig. 2-34), 74 (Fig. 2-37)
  y-bucket sort, 55
  (*see also* seed fill algorithm)
scan line algorithm, Watkins algorithm, 349
scan line, coordinate system, 71 (Fig. 2-35)
  half interval, 76
scan plane, 279, 279 (Fig. 4-57)
  curve surfaces, 292
Schumacker, R. A., 277
screen coordinates, 5
(*see also* coordinates)
seed fill, 69
seed fill algorithm, 83, 85, 418
  Example 2-12, 87
  scan line, 88-91, 89 (Fig. 2-49), 418
    Example 2-14, 91
    pseudocode, 90, 91
  simple, 85-88, 86 (Fig. 2-47), 87 (Fig. 2-48)
    Example 2-13, 87, 88
    pseudocode, 86
  stack, 86
segmentation, display buffer, 6, 7
shade, color, 400, 400 (Fig. 5-61)
shading function (*see* illumination model)
shading:
  Gouraud, 323-325, 407, 422
  Phong, 325-330, 407, 422
  simple, 215, 316
  (*see also* illumination model)
shadow matrix, Example 5-5, 349

shadows, 189, 296, 345-354, 346 (Fig. 5-28)
  Atherton-Weiler algorithm, 351, 352, 352 (Fig. 5-29)
  Example 5-4, 346-349
  global illumination model, 365
  modulation rules, 350
  penumbra, 345
    calculation technique, 353, 354, 354 (Fig. 5-32)
  projected, 346-348
  ray tracing algorithm, 352, 353, 353 (Fig. 5-30), 422
  scan line (Watkins) algorithm, 350, 422
  scan line z-buffer algorithm, 351
  self, 346, 347
  umbra, 345
  z-buffer algorithm, 350, 351
silhouette edge, 292-294, 294 (Fig. 4-65), 378
  transparency, 341, 343
simultaneous contrast, 310
Smith, A. R., 400-402
Snell's law, 367
Snell's law (*see also* refraction)
solid figure, 15, 15 (Fig. 1-15)
span, 88
span (*see also* hidden surface, Watkins algorithm)
span buffer, 79
Sparrow, E. M., 332, 335
spectrum locus, 391, 392, 394
specular highlights (*see* reflection, specular)
stack, 86, 88, 91, 92
  FIFO (first in first out), 62
  FILO (first in last out), 85
  push down, 85, 87
  shift register, 62
standard observer functions, 390, 390 (Fig. 5-55)
Staudhammer, J., 296
storage tube display, 3
  interactivity, 5
surface normal, simple hidden surface algorithm, 214, 215
surrounding polygon (*see* hidden surface, Warnock algorithm)
Sutherland-Hodgman algorithm (*see* clipping)

texture, 190, 354-363
  antialiasing, 363
  bump mapping (*see* texture, rough)
  fractals, 363
  global illumination model, 365

texture (*cont.*):
    inverse pixel mapping, 359
        Example 5-8, 359, 360
    mapping, 355, 356 (Fig. 5-32)
        Example 5-6, 355, 356
    perturbation mapping (*see* texture, rough)
    rough, 360, 361, 362 (Fig. 5-36)
    subdivision, 356-358, 422
        Example 5-7, 357, 358
thresholding:
    Floyd-Steinberg, 104
        pseudocode algorithm, 106
    simple, 103-105, 105 (Fig. 2-67)
tint, 400, 400 (Fig. 5-61)
tone, 400, 400 (Fig. 5-61)
Torrance, K. E., 332, 335, 337, 338
translucent, 341
transmission, 296
    diffuse, 341
    global illumination model, 365
    specular, 341
transmission of light, 366
transmissivity, 380
transparency, 190, 296, 340-345, 422
    models, 343 (Fig. 5-27)
    z-buffer algorithm, 344
transparent materials, 379
tree structure, ray tracing, 366
tristimulus space, 389
tristimulus theory, 385
tristimulus values (XYZ), 390

update:
    dynamic, 8
    intelligent, 8
    rate, 6, 17

value, Munsell, 406
Van Hook, T., 362

video:
    525 line standard, 19
    blanking, 19
    field, 18
    frame rate, 18, 19
    horizontal retrace, 18, 18 (Fig. 1-19), 19
    interlaced, 18
    monitor, (*see* cathode ray tube)
    noninterlaced, 19
    scanning pattern, 18, 18 (Fig. 1-19)
    standard, 17
    vertical retrace, 18, 18 (Fig. 1-19)
visibility of a point, 171, 172 (Fig. 3-30)
    Example 3-23, 172
visibility test:
    application order, 113
    pseudocode algorithm, 112, 113
visible light, 383
visible spectrum, 385
visual perception, 309
volume matrix, 206
    Example 4-2, 206, 207
    transformation, 211, 212
    transformation, Example 4-5, 212, 213

Warn, D. R., 330
Warnock, J., 241
Watkins, G. S., 279, 284, 285
Weiler, K., 179, 259
Whitted, T., 292, 293, 296, 300, 365, 378, 379
Williams, L., 351
Wilson, R., 382
wire photos, 59
write-through mode, 4
Wylie, C., 279
Wyszecki, G., 407

y bucket sort, 54 (Fig. 2-17), 56 (Fig. 2-19),
    74, 75, 75 (Fig. 2-38), 76, 79, 280
    hidden surface, Watkins algorithm, 287